MW00799514

AUGUST 17, 1995
THE HORIZON REALM MUS

"They've taken the west wing, Chancellor. We have to go."

Lord Gilmore turns slowly towards his aide, painfully, unwilling to take his eyes away from the hideous battle raging above them. In the night sky, Mercury rises huge, blazing red — but dwarfed by the Technocracy's dreadnought, speckled with the tiny silver ships of her fleet, and crossed by the twisting, leprous-white form of the unnamable thing that carries the Nephandi to war.

"What of the consors we sent to the Tower? Have they returned? Are the guards with them?"

"The Tower has fallen, my Lord. The consors were cut off," says the lesser mage, softly. "They won't be returning."

His leader draws a long, shuddering breath, and the aide can almost see the tendrils of Gilmore's countermagick return from the defense of the Chantry, coiling inwards to shield the last few buildings the Order of Hermes holds. Beneath them the defenders turn, sensing the change, fleeing towards the Library on which the two men stand. "Open the portal, James."

And in the billowing smoke and powdered stone that hang heavy in the air, Lord Edward Gilmore, 27th — and last — Chancellor of the Fors Collegis Mercuris walks through the door before him, and leaves his home forever.

WRITTEN BY KATHLEEN RYAN
ART BY SHAGGY

July, 1809

Spain

Napoleon never hears of this village. The names of the defenders are lost, the attack remembered only as "Resistance met en route. Loss of 74 men, 23 horses."

The village is ashes; the fields are afire. The ground smolders where it is not blood-soaked; the steam and smoke are one acrid, eye-searing, sulfurous cloud. Not all the horses are dead — the maddened screams of the broken beasts drown out all other sound.

Slowly, one by one, the survivors creep back into sight: children running to cut the animals' throats, old men digging, and the women — like ravens in their widow's weeds — picking their way among the fallen, wailing for their dead.

Mercedes Gonzaga de Ortiz finds her youngest son buried beneath the torso of an officer. The boy flinches as she lifts the corpse, opens his eyes feebly, and begins to shiver. He calls for her like a baby, and though she speaks his name again and again (now furiously, now in a whisper, now in despair) he does not know her. The cloak she wraps him in puddles with blood, and her hands drip with fast-cooling crimson.

The boy takes one last, rattling breath — her own lungs seem to break — and like a dream he leaves her; as a sunrise his soul surfaces in his body. Dimly she feels another join them, and the black-clad stranger's hands begin last rites for the dead. The soul-light changes, and she *sees*, like the folds of a veil: the earth beneath them, the body, the hands of the priest, the spirit of her son staring at the heavens, and an angel behind her, merged with her, its hands as bloody as her own. The boy takes a step forward, and vanishes from sight. Mercedes raises her eyes to those of the priest, and the Moorish old man nods.

SEPTEMBER 1, 1995

It is afternoon on Cerberus. Morning chores are long over, and the lecture halls are empty. The disciples — mages in training — careen about the corridors, making the most out of lunch on their way to their tutors. Laughter fills the central courtyard, and the master of the Chantry (though he neither asks nor needs a title — he is simply the Old Man, in any language) relaxes in his study.

In his favorite seat, perched on the sill of the first of the huge, arched windows of the room, he can see the dun-colored walls and pale sandstones of his castle; can see the dull, blood-red masonry of the gatehouse nearby; the bone-white desert that stretches to the horizon; and in the blue-black sky above, Pluto in crescent, Charon waxing, the distant sun a glaring pinpoint well past zenith. The yellowing light lends a bronze gleam to his dark skin and reveals the dancing dust in the quiet air of his chamber.

A knock at the door disturbs his reverie.

"Come in."

Amanda opens the heavy oak door silently, both by habit and respect — and blinks in the golden haze. Once her vision clears, she scans the room (an old habit) and takes in the rough-hewn wooden rafters; the aged, white plaster; the Spartan trestle tables; and the two walls of shelves sagging with Senex' books and curiosities. When she first began her training with the old Euthanatos, she wondered what dark and strange powers the bric-a-brac might have, but now she knows there are none. This is part of her respect for him.

One new thing she notices — a low, circular table of wood and brass. Its top is flat and sunken, with a raised rim. It stands well away from the others, in a little-used and dusty corner.

"Good afternoon," the Old Man says.

"Hi."

"You were late to lecture this morning." (Not disapproving, not questioning.)

"I was also late to breakfast."

Senex rises, crosses to the nearer wall of shelves, takes down a clay pitcher full of water, and rests on one knee by the little table. Amanda walks to it, sets her bag against the wall, and sits down.

Slowly and carefully, Senex pours water from the ewer into the brass top of the table. As he does this, he speaks.

"Reality is not stone. Reality is water."

He finishes, and sets the pitcher down. It scrapes slightly against the sandstone floor.

Senex leans over the table and blows upon the surface of the water. Tiny ripples form, run against the brass sides, dance as the old collide with the new, and every second more appear to change the pattern. He stops, and the motion dies out.

Moving slowly, he dips a finger in the water and stirs it, creates small ripples and eddies in the little pool, but silently, with no splashes. He takes his finger out, and waits. The surface is quickly calm again.

Without warning, he strikes the surface with his fist. Water splashes up and out and flies into their faces. Amanda blinks it out of her eyes and watches him take out a white cloth, wiping the edge of the table.

"Static magick is like my breath. It will never break the surface, but it cannot easily betray itself to those who watch. It is the magic of hedge wizards, of vampires and the Garou. Do not underestimate it — it is limited, often one-dimensional, but a strong wind can knock you down. A strong wind can create waves you do not see until they engulf you.

"Coincidental magick is like my fingers. It can change the shape and flow of water greatly, yet disturb it little if the mage is skilled. It is the course of safety, should magick be necessary — never forget that you have mundane resources at your disposal. When you must use magick, use the probable as often as you can, and you will be less visible.

"Vulgar magick is like my fist. It is dangerous. Though you may achieve your intention, you cannot tell what the splash will do. You cannot tell who will notice it." He stops, perceiving her question.

"You've told me all of this before."

"But not in this fashion."

"No..."

"If I had taught you only that magick is fire, or that Paradox is a hurricane, or that the Consensus is mud, or that reality is water, you would understand only one aspect of what you do, and you would be as crippled as any Technocrat or hedge wizard.

"Analogies can be dangerous, Amanda," he begins, smiling slightly, "because the world is like a sandcastle..."

The clear tenor note of a bell stops him, and by expression alone he gathers his apprentice to her feet beside him. He draws a knife and cuts a complex pattern in the air around them — the scenery changes: the gatehouse walls surround them, and they walk out of its labyrinth before the alarm is quite silent again.

* * *

In the sandy enclosure before them, a crowd of strangers (some in robes, some in sneakers and denim) is waiting. Many of them sit in the dirt or slump over their bags; in no face is there any hope. Near the front there are seven afoot, each robed and holding desperately to dignity. The man in the center speaks.

"Senex." Lord Gilmore's weary face smoothes for a moment, the deep-cut lines transforming themselves into a something like a smile. "I cannot thank you enough for your hospitality." His voice is bitter, self-mocking. "You show your charity beyond doubt, granting sanctuary to an old beggar man and his rag-tag errant crew."

The master of Cerberus shakes his head, and embraces the hermetic mage. "No, my friend. The Traditions owe you too much for you ever to go begging — and I am older still than you.

"As for your companions... until you can find another Chantry, call ours home." He turns to the Adept on watch (a doubtful-looking teenage boy yet to leave the bell-rope) and the long string of refugees begins its solemn march to the castle.

March, 1887

London

Gaslit, in a private dining room, in a glittering brass-and-silk, china-and-linen hotel, a dark lady in black velvet rises from her seat, and her companions stand to join her.

"Gentlemen! A toast: to our victory, to our noble calling, and to our friendship. May it last us through the millennium." Mercedes drinks, and her companions drain their glasses.

Alexander Gericault, resplendent in the latest evening costume, splashes more champagne into each, and composes himself.

"To my own, inconceivably good luck in finding such companions; to Senex, who is without doubt the finest strategist I have ever met; and to Mercy, without whose silent knife and charming ways our plans and luck would have been worthless today."

They drink again, and Mercedes looks to Senex as Gericault helps her with her chair.

"Longwinded, isn't he?"

Their talk turns to a review of the day: the successful assassination of an industrial giant — a factory emperor with little soul, less conscience, and overpaid bodyguards. Through dessert they debate the possibility of discovery — a maid who should have been elsewhere was not. During the cheese course they muse over the near-perfect timing, the precision of the operation, the cleanliness of the kills, and the delicacy of the Good Death in each case. The waiter interrupts them, bringing the brandy in.

More sober now, the younger mages wait, and Senex studies each of them quietly. They meet his eyes without hesitation, and without pride. Mercy smiles a little at her old friend and teacher, and turns her eyes to Gericault as he does. She finds herself staring, and drops her gaze to her snifter.

"We did well today. I am proud of you both; I am proud of the work we have done, but I will not drink to my pride three times in one evening. Enjoy yourselves tonight, but forget your victory in the morning. There is more work ahead of us than we can see, and the less baggage we carry with us, the easier will be our task."

Mercy looks up, and catches Gericault's nod out of the corner of her eye.

"What will you drink to, then?" he asks.

"I drink to the Sleepers," says the Old Man.

"To the Sleepers."

* * *

Mercedes is dancing.

Gericault's right hand is warm on her waist, his left hand holds her right gently, and her left hand rests lightly on the smooth silk of his jacket. He is an excellent dancer, and they glide along the floor like one body.

She can feel his glance on her face; she avoids it to provoke him.

"You look very beautiful tonight," he says, and her eyebrows lift in satirical surprise. "That dress is most becoming." Mercy turns her head towards him briefly, watching his mouth. His teeth are very white, the bristles on his upper lip amber in the light of the chandeliers. He leans closer, and his cheek scratches the side of her forehead.

"Tell me, though... why on earth are you wearing a corset?"

She jerks back — reddening, missing a beat — and their skulls knock together on the sidestep.

"Forgive me, Mercy." He brings his handkerchief to his lip, takes it away blooded. "I know you're trying to be respectable. I just don't understand why.

"Do you like corsets? Perhaps the whalebone makes it easier to conceal those knives..." He looks down at her again, then away, sucking on his wounded lip. "No, I can see you keep your daggers in your eyes.

"Mercy, if you are wearing that corset for the fine ladies in that corner there, those wifely gossips, matronly ghouls and tittering debutantes — with their noses in the air and their minds in the gutter — well, I am shocked. Shocked. Flabbergasted. The Sleepers are our charge, darling, not our keepers, not our peers." His voice drops to a whisper. "I think you should choose your undergarments to suit yourself."

"You are a cad, Gericault. Change the subject."

"As you wish, my lady. May I return safely to the subject of your dress?"

"We *have* been formally introduced," she says, dryly. The music stops, polite applause fills the air, and when the next dance begins they stay on the floor.

"I've been thinking," he begins, twitching his nose, "and I don't think black is your color... I should adore to see you in red."

"Black is the only color for a widow, Gericault."

"Your husband is a century dead. How long will you mourn him?"

She stops, looking her partner in the eyes at last, her expression deeply, numbingly hateful.

Gericault asks slowly:

"Do you even remember what he looked like?"

Mercedes pulls away angrily, and walks nearly through him toward the dining rooms. One steel-pinned heel catches in her whirling dress, and as it rips and she stumbles, the other foot comes down heavily on his patent-leather shoe. She picks up her skirts in a savage gesture and strides on. The gentlewomen in the corner follow her with well-bred stares, whispering.

Much later he finds her in the garden, wearing Senex' overcoat against the chill breeze. He limps towards her contritely, and his head is bowed.

"Why," she begins (in a blistering, radiant fury like he has never seen) "are you doing this? Why make it more difficult?"

Gericault regards his shoes, and the wet gravel beneath them. "I'm sorry."

"Good — "

He interrupts her, quickly, dry-voiced: "Aren't you lonely, Mercy?"

She stares at him, stunned for the moment, and before she recovers he speaks again (emboldened by the respite), swallowing hard and stammering.

"I've... I've fallen in love with you, Mercy. I'm sorry."

And Mercedes finds nothing to say.

SEPTEMBER 2, 1995

The Great Hall of Cerberus is crowded as seldom before, and still the residents and refugees trickle in. Chairs and tables scavenged from every room are scattered throughout, and even an elderly dresser from the stables has been impressed into service. At one end, a long, unadorned expanse of wood sits empty: the senior members have yet to arrive.

The last apprentice scurries in, sets her platter and bowls hastily down, and the doors open behind the high table. Senex and Lord Gilmore walk through, talking quietly, and the room falls silent. In twos and threes the others follow them, and take their places — hesitantly, politely, the residents of Cerberus guiding their companions to their seats.

Suddenly, the peace is broken. At the second table, nearest the head of the room, small mutters erupt into a defiant shout:

"No, I will not be silent. I know my place, Ellen."

The speaker stands, faces Senex and the Chancellor. "Why, my lords, am I seated lower than that woman?" He points to the middle of their table, to a small, frizzy-haired mage who stares back at him incredulously. "I am Nicodemus Dribb, Master of Forces, and if she is an Adept of anything at all I shall be much surprised."

The Old Man raises one patient eyebrow, and turns to Lord Gilmore on his right. The Hermetic leader shrugs with one hand and his eyebrow, and waits for the Euthanatos' judgment. Senex looks down the table.

From a slightly smelly position in the back of the room, Amanda and Julia watch anxiously.

"Did you catch that?" whispers the latter.

"Yeah. Senex and Mitzi?" Amanda replies, referring to the trace of telepathy that flashes briefly over the high table.

"I think so."

Mitzi straightens in her chair. "If we have offended you, sir," she says, "forgive us. We knew so little about your rank when the tables were arranged. Please, take my seat." The man next to her helps her up, and with one last glance at Senex, she descends.

"Did you catch *that*?" Julia spits out.

"Yeah. Senex?" Amanda replies, speaking this time of the entropic cloud that hovers a split second over the empty chair.

"I hope so."

Master Dribb pushes his way up the crowded aisles to the dais, shoves past Mitzi on the steps, and smugly takes his proper seat.

It collapses beneath him — dumps him on his backside and off the edge of the platform. His robes fly out in a lumpy fabric cloud (seemingly all knees) and he sprawls beneath them on the sandy floor.

Stifled titters echo softly throughout the hall, and one voice rings out in raucous, cascading peals of laughter.

"Amanda! Quit it. Everybody's looking at us."

But Julia speaks too late, and the furious Nicodemus is striding towards them — staring, glaring, his very eyes shaking with wounded pride.

And still Amanda laughs.

"How dare you! — How *dare* you? I challenge you."

She stops, mouth-corners twitching.

"I challenge you. I demand satisfaction — "

She bursts out again.

The Hermetic mage fixes a look of pure hatred upon her, and grinds out his words. "I challenge you to certámen."

Amanda feels her Avatar's wings encircle her, feels the bloody-handed angel willing to fight. The power floods her, righteous anger fueling the magick, honing it like a knife — and, mastering herself, she sheathes it.

"Choose your seconds, insolent bitch."

The angel settles back, denied, even as the Hermetic mage's tirade draws to an end:

"Sunrise, tomorrow, at the — "

"No dueling." Senex' words blanket the Hall.

"I demand — "

"No dueling," repeats the Old Man, and he picks up his fork.

September, 1887

26° 41' 57'' N, 71° 32' 5'' W

Mercedes reverses her knife slowly, careful to keep her dress from rustling, and waits for the stoker to emerge from the coal-bin. The little man is frightened, shaking audibly, and starts at the slightest noise. In another minute the pressure becomes too much for him, and as he bolts the knife flashes downwards, pommel striking skull with a dropped-apple "thck."

That's the last one, Old Man, she thinks, letting the stoker's body slide gently to the floor.

"Good. We're ready." Mercedes feels him take his place farther in, beside the boiler, cane in hand. "Bring them down, Gericault."

Overhead, pounding feet and muffled commands draw nearer. The Frenchman drops through the hatch that, coincidentally, happens to be in the floor of the corridor above them. He takes his stand next to Mercy, and the three listen to the scrabbling of their Order of Reason pursuers — who find that in the darkness they cannot discover the means to open that hatch. More brusque words drift down to the waiting Euthanatos, and the footsteps thunder along the passage toward the stairs.

Now they crowd through the door, spread out along the incline and the landings: four toughs in uniform with a black-suited gentleman behind them, his round, tinted spectacles glinting in the dim red light of the room. Behind him, a pair of shabbily-dressed men huddle together, and behind them...

The Physician.

He wears white. His face is urbane and kindly, his expression that of a man performing a regrettable duty. Only his lips (pressed too thin, bit nearly through in rage) and his eyes (marked with a cruelty horrible in its detachment) betray him — and the three who wait are satisfied: the assassination of the industrialist has flushed their true prey. His eyes lock on Senex' and the battle begins.

The toughs rush forward, ignoring the bullets that flash from Gericault's pistols. They are accustomed to invincibility, but his ammunition is more than lead, and two fall before they leave the stairs. Mercy throws warded knives to prevent their resuscitation, and the room erupts with light from the glowing shields.

The others close in, more carefully now, and the man in black casts smoking pellets ahead of them — worried now, as the renegades he chases are blatantly vulgar in their magickal defenses, preternaturally unharmed. Mercedes slips aside, satisfied that his fear of Paradox will inhibit him enough for Gericault to take all three down easily. She advances to the stairs, to the first of the strange men.

For an instant she freezes, seemingly face to face with some Umbral insect-thing — huge flat eyes surmounted by pale green glowing spots, strange metallic whiskers, and a coiling mass of red worms that sprouts from the right corner of its forehead. The creature bounds forward, brushes past her, and she recognizes it as one of the strange men from the middle of the pack. A cloud of smoke conceals him, and she is left alone with the second one. Daggers at the ready, Mercedes studies her opponent. Instead of bringing forth a weapon, the wild-haired Order of Reason mage draws a length of fire-hose from a scabbard at his thigh, and she notices for the first time the backpack from which it hangs. He licks his lips, and strikes a heroic stance.

"Now, death-witch, feel the wrath of the St. Elmo Electrical Elliptitron!"

The fire-hose nozzle fills with pale light, and before Mercedes realizes her danger, she is enveloped in a barrage of ball-lightning.

"Ha! A blow struck for decency and the liberation of the Ether!" He brings the tip of the machine down to where she has fallen, convulsed in the electrocutive sphere, then reaches to flip a switch on the side of the backpack. Mercedes takes advantage of the flicker in concentration. She pokes a hole through the fire around her and attacks the source of it directly: the toggle breaks off in his hand, rusted through and already crumbling before he can gasp. She changes tactics while he stutters, and he collapses in a dreamless sleep.

She whirls around, her scorched dress crackling, and finds the fight has turned against them — the Old Man and the Physician are yet locked in their unreachable conflict, but Gericault is losing, slowly, to the four still crouched behind the massive machinery.

"Gericault?" Running, dodging, she flashes her surprise at him, and her fear.

"The one in the dark glasses — ow — realized we'd cleared out the witnesses and went vulgar." She reaches the first of the man in black's acolytes, and slits his throat, aiming the neck to blind the man beside him with the blood. "He isn't very good at it, but it unh... makes the difference... to his counters." Gericault joins her, fires point-blank into the sightless man, and the bullets find their mark. "Finally."

Now the man in black presses ahead, desperate cunning in his eyes, and his begoggled companion drops back, reaching into a canvas bag at his side.

"They're stalling," Gericault sends her. "Can you get to him?"

She hazards a look down the accessway, and a bullet nearly takes off her nose. The man with the sack is a better shot than she expected, and the strange magicks of his equipment protect him from those few attacks she can launch around a corner and through five coal bins. In her moment's rest, however, she realizes the atmosphere around her is changing: the air feels almost greasy, and the dim light sparkles weirdly on the advanced devices of the foe. Tiny impossibilities are jamming their apparatus already, breaking pieces ignored and overridden. The universe is overbalanced here, and for once that thought gives her hope.

"No. But I have an idea."

Mercy doubles back, deeper into the rows of bins and turbines, and finds the body of the stoker. She shoulders him easily, sneaks back to the front. With a few quick gestures she heals his concussion, and sets him down behind a huge, shuddering nest of plumbing. In the gaps between the pipes, the fight is clearly visible, and she turns to the little man.

"Wake up! Oh, please, please, mister, wake up!" she pleads, her face streaked with anxious tears.

The stoker groans, opens his eyes, and sits up.

"Please, help me! I've been trapped down here, and they're fighting..." The stoker focuses on the beautiful, dark lady before him — clearly wounded and distressed — and finds his courage.

"There, there, miss. It'll be all right." He looks out of their hiding place, keeping his frightened eyes from the lady, and sees...

...clattering at a hideous speed down the deckplates, whirling and bobbing and slashing like a berserker, a skeletal, springloaded ball of blades rolling straight towards a gentleman in evening costume. The gentleman fires his pistols furiously into the shiny copper assassin machine, but to no avail. Behind the mechanical impossibility two men run, one wearing the strangest pair of motoring goggles the stoker has ever seen, the other firing a gun with a streaming ribbon of bullets where its cylinder should be.

He steps back, reeling. "I don't believe it!" he exclaims, and Mercy smiles.

The ball of copper clockwork runs down as it turns the corner — falls into itself in a sharp and glittering heap by Gericault's shoes. The man in black, the goggle-wearer, and the strange gun disappear into nothingness (though Mercy can hear them, still running, in the place that they have gone).

"Gericault?"

"Still here, darling. Thank you."

"Senex?"

"I have finished."

The stoker sits down — dazed, confused, and forgetful — and wipes his sooty face. When the rescue party arrives an hour later, they find him sitting smiling with the others (amnesiac men in uniform, steamer engineers with headaches, and a crazed tinkerer crying bitterly over a fire hose), with a clean patch of skin on his left cheek, in the shape of a lady's kiss.

September 5, 1995

Amanda slashes upward, driving her knife deep into the cloth-wrapped plastic bottle. The water inside soaks through the old t-shirt, drips onto the dirt below. She stares, trying to remember her last thought, absent-mindedly knitting the bottle whole again. Still distracted, she steps back and prepares for her next exercise.

She lunges, and behind her a twig breaks. Without stopping, she turns on the intruder — one of the Hermetic refugees, she realizes, with a mop of sandy gray hair and light blue eyes. The woman flinches, caught between the knives and the awkward embrace of a rosebush.

"Sorry," says Amanda, clearly disappointed. "I thought you were one of us. Anyone in this garden is fair game." The knives disappear, and her visitor relaxes.

"I... I didn't mean to disturb you," she says. Her darting eyes find a bench behind the still-swinging target, and she sits. "Actually, I'm here to apologize."

Amanda leans against the tree, ties the soda bottle back against it. "What for?"

"For Nicodemus. Please don't think too badly of him — and please don't assume that the rest of us are going to act that way."

"It's all right."

"No. We're guests here." She pulls up a dandelion, fiddles with it nervously. "Nicodemus... his wife went Marauder about a year ago. The College on Mus was about all he had left, and he was one of the last to leave it... him and James and the Chancellor. It's still no excuse, but maybe you can understand why he's so angry now."

Amanda watches her in silence.

"He's seeing Nephandi everywhere, you know. And he's been asking about you since the other night."

Amanda's eyes narrow.

"Well... there is a rumor going around that you brought a Nephandus into this Chantry two months ago. And that you talked to it instead of fighting it..."

"So you're here to check up on the rumor."

The other mage nods, tying the stem of the flower into anxious knots.

"Who the hell are you?"

"My name is Ellen."

"Well. Ellen. You can set the record straight." She transfixes the older woman with a leaden stare, speaks in a tense monotone.

"There was a Nephandus. He didn't make it past the gatehouse. I spoke to him because he came through the Peregrine Gate while I was on guard duty. We were hosting Doctor Bridges' conference at the time.

"The ward patterns checked out. I started to lead him through the labyrinth. The gatehouse wouldn't let us through. He fed me a lot of lies about my last life.

"He vanished.

"That's all."

The Hermetic mage nods again. Her blue eyes flicker to Amanda's face and away again, and the flower in her hands is a fluffy mass of yellow shreds. "Thank you for your... explanation." She stands. "I'm sure that my people will feel better when they hear it."

"Sure. And Ellen — be careful how you leave the garden — I'm not the only one who practices out here." She laughs, and sets the bottle swinging again.

May 1889

The French Riviera

Gericault, tea and sandwiches in hand, sits down carefully on the dge of an elegant white wicker chair. He places the full tray atop the ittle table beside him, and shades his eyes from the afternoon sun.

Mercedes smiles, folds her parasol, laughs.

"Tea?"

"As drunk by Mr. and Mrs. Melvin Abercrombie, British genry, on vacation. We must keep up ppearances, if only for the sake of our passports." He settles back. "Will you pour?"

Mercedes says nothing, but eans forward purposefully, and Gericault closes his eyes, sighing.

"I almost wish this could go on forever. No Senex, no Council, no mechanical men and Reasoners... ust two tired Sleepers on vacaion, enjoying the idle moments." He accepts his cup without looking.

"I like it," she says, "but I want to get back on time. I spoke to he Old Man before we left, daring. We're *finally* going to tear hose Nephandi vipers out of Piccadilly."

Gericault says nothing.

"Would you like a sandwich?"

"No, thank you," he says, carefully.

"Are you all right?"

"Mercedes... I have to tell you something." His voice is strange, serious, and he stands as he speaks. "It's a very *difficult* thing to have o say..."

"You can tell me anything, Alec." She rises, and takes his hand.

Gericault looks at her, shaking his head, taking her fingers to kiss hem, briefly, and move away. "What Tradition am I, Mercy?"

"Well, you make a very good Euthanatos, but Senex and I never hought you were one of us.

"You might be a Dreamspeaker, because you hate the Order of Reason so, or a Cultist, as you are something of a libertine, and you despise Council politics."

"I am none of those," he says. "I am not a Tradition mage at all."

"That doesn't matter to me. What Craft do you belong to? Or are you an Orphan?"

"I am not an Orphan. I have no Craft."

Mercedes waits, uncertain, watching her lover's face. The surf ills the silence.

"I am Fallen, Mercy." Neither moves. "I serve the Lords of Oblivion."

She bites her lip, staring, breathing shallowly, choking on the salt. Her hands clench, turning white in the folds of her dress, kneading the abric and reaching though it for her knives. As he looks away, she flies at him, and Gericault falls to the floor with her blades at his throat.

"Traitor!"

"*Not* a traitor, Mercy. A spy," he says sadly, "a spy who has fallen in love with the enemy. Now let me up."

"I am going to kill you."

"You are a practical woman, Mercy, and this is not a dime novel. If you were going to kill me you would have done it five seconds ago. Let me up."

And Mercedes, mutely, slowly, sheathes her knives and stands up, trembling. Gericault guides her to her chair and takes his own, across from her, and puts his hands gently on her knees.

"Now. First let me apologize. I am terribly sorry that I ever took this assignment, met you, and particularly that I have had to lie to you for as long as I have known you. I feel horrible, darling.

"Second, let me tell you that I am *not* sorry that I love you, that I have never lied to you about that, and that even if we part company this hour I will love you until I die or the universe ends. I hope that, shamefully as I have treated you, you may someday be able to look on me fondly in memory, at least.

"Third, I did not come to you and Senex to harm or corrupt you. My assignment was, in part, to study you both for weaknesses for later exploitation," he says, and the lady shudders, "but primarily to let you know what my... organization... knew about the Physician, and to convince you that he was as dangerous as you now know him to be."

"You used us," she mutters.

"We had to. The Physician never left Earth. No one from my Labyrinth was powerful enough to oppose him within Reality. Senex was powerful enough, and already hunting for our enemy.

"I didn't make him do anything he didn't want to do, Mercy. I couldn't."

"We killed the Physician two years ago. Why are you still here?"

"Why not? We were fighting the Order of Reason, I was watching the Traditions, I was useful. I didn't want to go." Gericault frowns.

"Now the Old Man wants to massacre the Piccadilly Chantry. I can't stay and help him, and I won't stay to trap him. I have to leave."

Mercedes looks up at him for the first time, her eyes red, her face pale and tear-streaked.

He nods. "I still don't want to go. I love you," he says, and she flinches. "Now, I'm going to ask something I have no right to:

"Will you come with me?

"I am *not* asking you to become *barrabi*. I am not asking you to betray Senex or tell my people any Counsil secrets. You would never have to meet another Nephandus so long as you live or the universe endures —" speaking quickly now, desperately, "just please, *please* come fight the real enemy, the Order of Reason... with me."

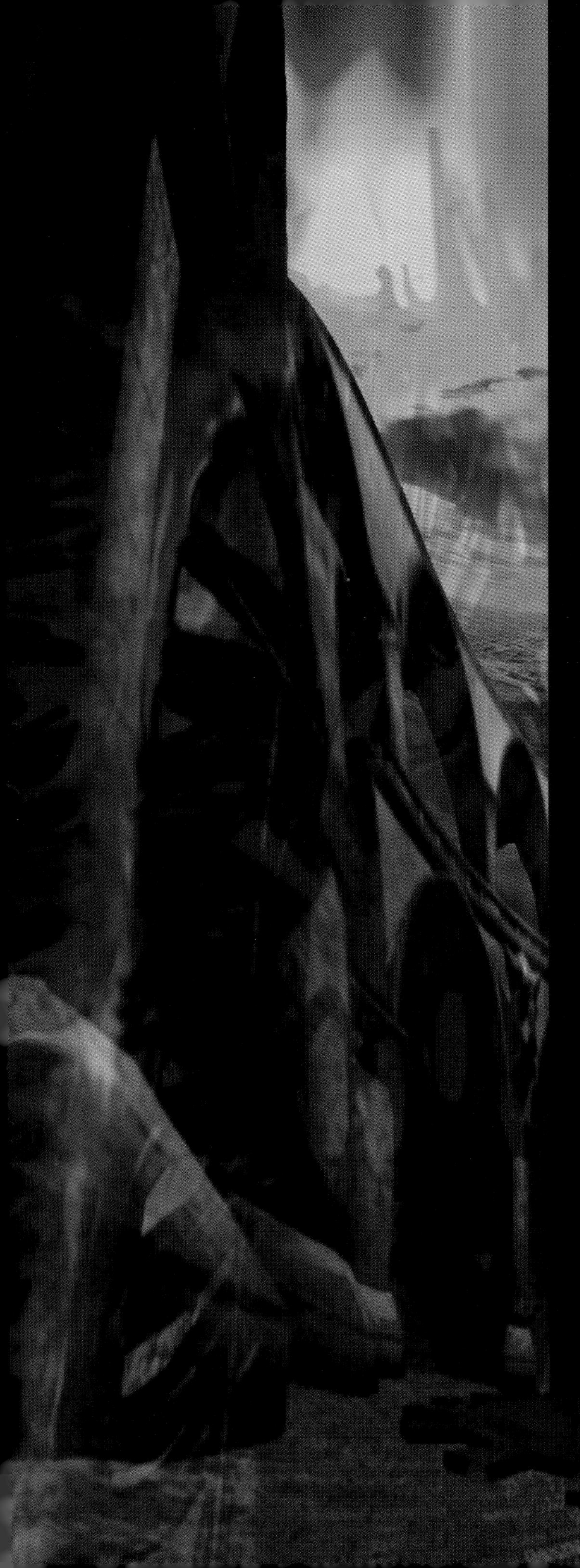

September 6, 1995

It is afternoon on Cerberus. Amanda pushes her way through the crowds in the courtyard of the East Stair. On every side strangers jostle her, and the noise is opressive. Her home has been loud before, in joy, sorrow, and anger, but the eternal conversational drone is new, and she detests it. She steps around two loitering Hermetic mages (who stare at her, measuring her face with a hostile curiousity) and turns the corner that leads to Senex' study.

Lord Gilmore, she sees, is just entering that still-quiet room, and she slows her pace, hesitates to knock. What she hears stops her, and she stays her hand to listen.

The Chancellor of Mus speaks:

"...naught but a rumor, of course, but it is disturbing my people and they disturb yours. May I ask you a few questions?"

"Tell me the rumor first, your lordship," her teacher answers.

"Very well."

The Chancellor continues in lower tones, and Amanda catches little. He goes on for some time, and at the end she thinks he asks a question.

The Old Man growls. "Make your point plainly, Gilmore."

"Do you, or do you not have a *widderslainte* as an apprentice?"

Then Amanda hears nothing, and is sure she missed the answer, but Senex speaks, finally, in a voice low and weary:

"Amanda has never been Nephandi." And the emphasis is on the name.

"And before Amanda?"

Seven seconds pass.

"Yes. She was."

The woman in the corridor straightens silently, clutches her bag, and turns away. Calmly, she walks, the words rattling back and forth in her head, and the voice of Gericault is in the echoes of her footsteps.

Mercy followed me to the Cauls

She swerves around the sneering refugees.

Your teacher hunted her down and he killed her

She dodges her way down the East Stair.

When she was reborn he haunted her new life

She ignores Julia, walks past Mitzi.

Haunted your *life*

She finds herself in the garden. Pluto is rising.

To keep you from remembering

She pushes through the roses, tears her clothes on the thorns.

Your lover

She sinks, thoughtful, to the bench.

Your murderer

And she sinks in her mind to the memories of her distractions.

Mercy followed me to the Cauls

October, 1896

A Nephandi Labyrinth, Location Unknown

Mercedes leans on Gericault's arm, walking slowly with the crowd. The air is hot and salty. It stinks of metal. She is sweating and nervous, and her stomach shivers despite the heat. The walls to either side are dark.

Someone ahead of the couple is singing softly, in a language Mercy doesn't understand. A man on her left speaks to her, his voice steady, hypnotic, and elated.

"Oh, Mercedes, I wish we could tell you how happy we are to have you here. It's so wonderful, particularly for Gericault." He pats her shoulder, and touches, lightly, her hair. "We have all been praying, every night, for years, that you would someday join us... and now, thank the Powers, here you are." In an odd and jerky movement he brings his hands together, clasping them tight enough that Mercedes can hear the bones rub together. "Even now, I know, you may have doubts, but after tonight you will truly know joy and the only purpose." He joins in the growing song.

The procession reaches a large room with an irregular ceiling. Gericault puts an arm around her and draws her aside, holds her to him.

"Afraid, darling?" he whispers softly. "You can still change your mind. Some of our most faithful have never — "

"No." She looks up and her eyes harden. "I want to go where you go. I love you." And she turns away fiercely, with her jaw set and square. Mercedes steps forward.

The far wall is moving, and the Nephandi have drifted to either side, lighting lamps. They open a path through their ranks from the two lovers to the strange curtain that seems to cover that wall. Gericault moves to escort her, and they walk very slowly down the aisle. The others watch silently. The first singer begins a strange, emotionless tune. The two mages reach the end, and an old gentleman in orange robes speaks.

"Do you come here willing?"

"I do."

"Welcome to us, daughter. May oblivion's peace comfort your mind and rest your soul."

The curtain folds down and sideways. In the light of the white torches, the interior is a pinkish-beige and slightly damp — its folds membranous and veined. There are many tissues making up the curtain, drawing back in fleshy ridges to the floor, sliding past each other slickly, pulling up of their own accord to the ceiling. They open at the bottom to admit her.

Gericault feels her breathing quicken and grow sharp. His lover *is* frightened now.

The robed man smiles gently and touches her arm. Mercy follows him, steps dully over the lip of the Caul. She turns to keep her eyes on Gericault, and her hand goes to her throat. The inner membranes draw up and closer to her, and still he can see her eyes. He puts his hand on the outer, flesh-temperature folds to support himself, and the interior closes.

The Caul echoes to the broken, cut-off scream, and the pale tissues shudder with the force of the splattering blood within. The Nephandi cheer, the outer folds close, and Gericault sinks to the ground in blissful relief.

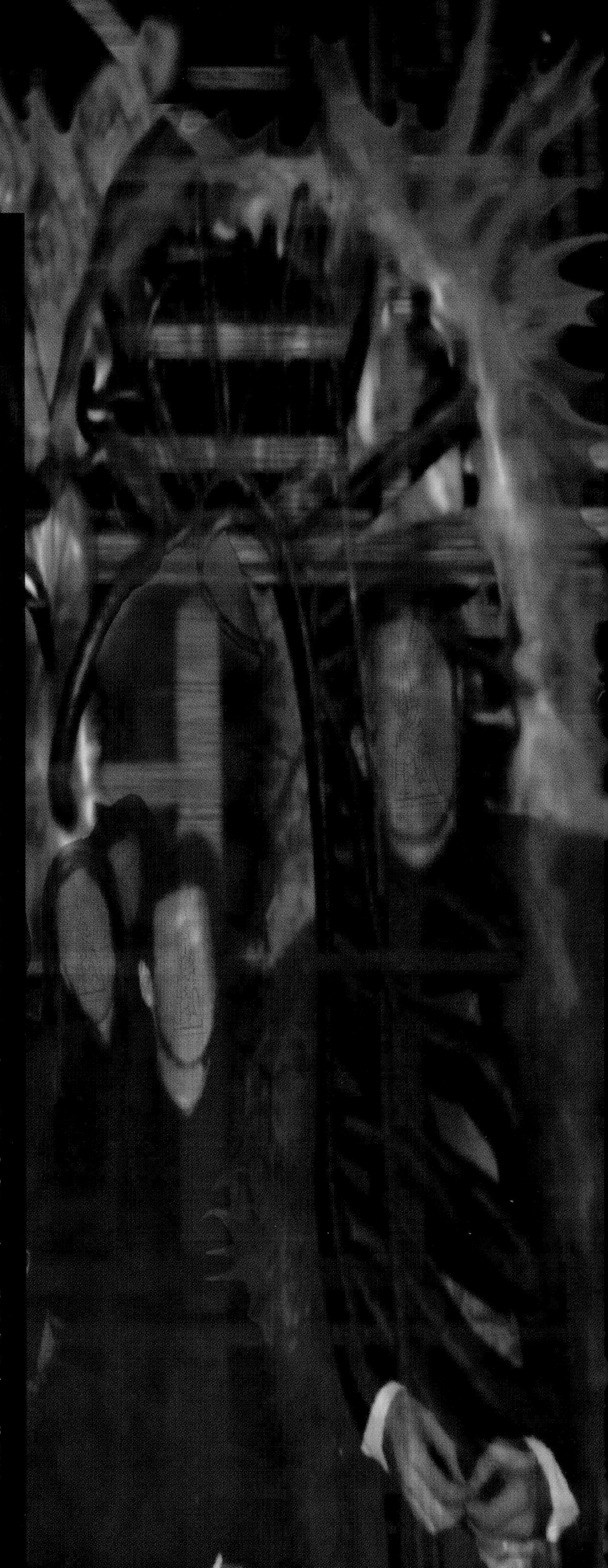

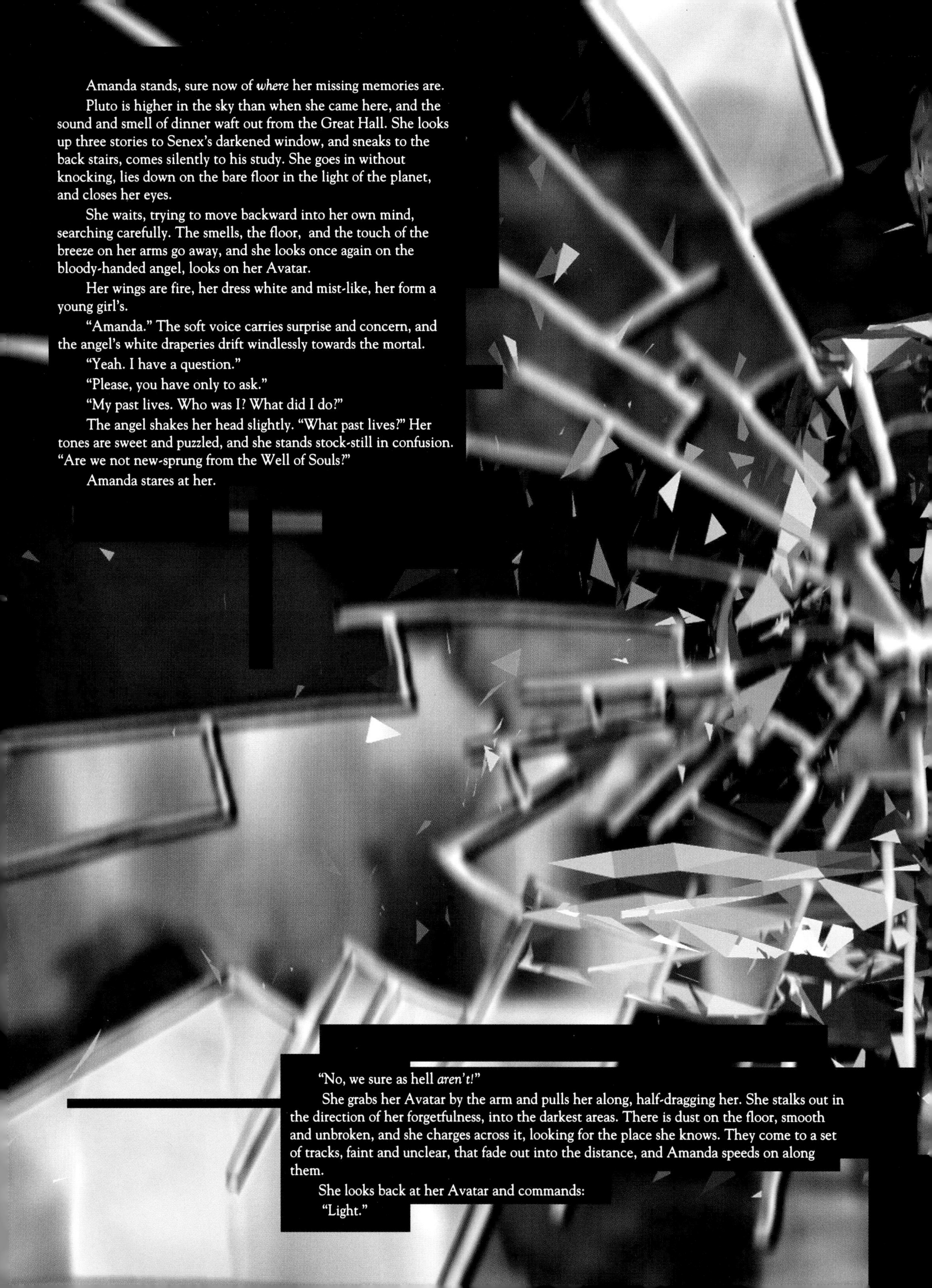

Amanda stands, sure now of *where* her missing memories are.

Pluto is higher in the sky than when she came here, and the sound and smell of dinner waft out from the Great Hall. She looks up three stories to Senex's darkened window, and sneaks to the back stairs, comes silently to his study. She goes in without knocking, lies down on the bare floor in the light of the planet, and closes her eyes.

She waits, trying to move backward into her own mind, searching carefully. The smells, the floor, and the touch of the breeze on her arms go away, and she looks once again on the bloody-handed angel, looks on her Avatar.

Her wings are fire, her dress white and mist-like, her form a young girl's.

"Amanda." The soft voice carries surprise and concern, and the angel's white draperies drift windlessly towards the mortal.

"Yeah. I have a question."

"Please, you have only to ask."

"My past lives. Who was I? What did I do?"

The angel shakes her head slightly. "What past lives?" Her tones are sweet and puzzled, and she stands stock-still in confusion. "Are we not new-sprung from the Well of Souls?"

Amanda stares at her.

"No, we sure as hell *aren't!*"

She grabs her Avatar by the arm and pulls her along, half-dragging her. She stalks out in the direction of her forgetfulness, into the darkest areas. There is dust on the floor, smooth and unbroken, and she charges across it, looking for the place she knows. They come to a set of tracks, faint and unclear, that fade out into the distance, and Amanda speeds on along them.

She looks back at her Avatar and commands:

"Light."

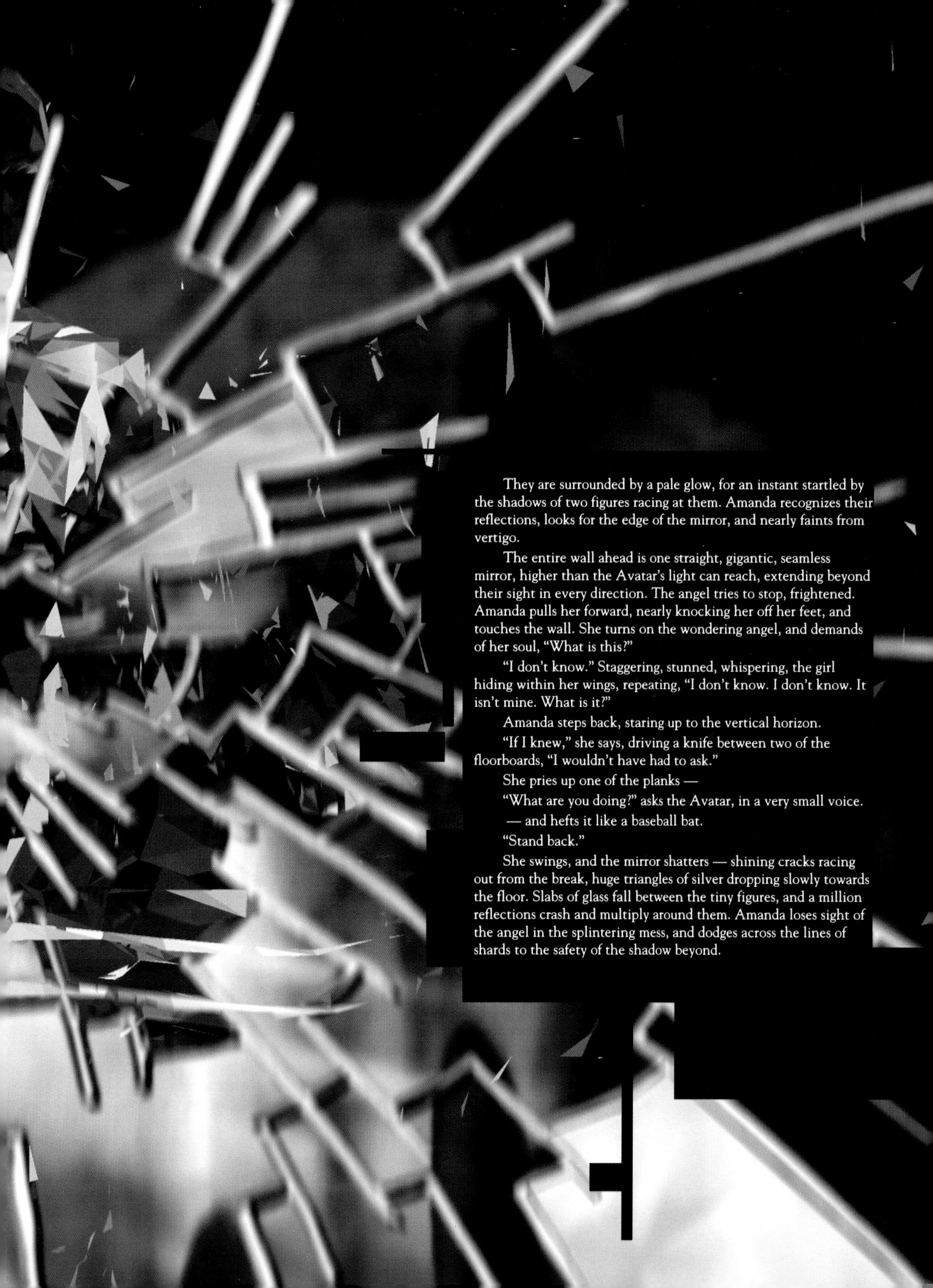

They are surrounded by a pale glow, for an instant startled by the shadows of two figures racing at them. Amanda recognizes their reflections, looks for the edge of the mirror, and nearly faints from vertigo.

The entire wall ahead is one straight, gigantic, seamless mirror, higher than the Avatar's light can reach, extending beyond their sight in every direction. The angel tries to stop, frightened. Amanda pulls her forward, nearly knocking her off her feet, and touches the wall. She turns on the wondering angel, and demands of her soul, "What is this?"

"I don't know." Staggering, stunned, whispering, the girl hiding within her wings, repeating, "I don't know. I don't know. It isn't mine. What is it?"

Amanda steps back, staring up to the vertical horizon.

"If I knew," she says, driving a knife between two of the floorboards, "I wouldn't have had to ask."

She pries up one of the planks —

"What are you doing?" asks the Avatar, in a very small voice.

— and hefts it like a baseball bat.

"Stand back."

She swings, and the mirror shatters — shining cracks racing out from the break, huge triangles of silver dropping slowly towards the floor. Slabs of glass fall between the tiny figures, and a million reflections crash and multiply around them. Amanda loses sight of the angel in the splintering mess, and dodges across the lines of shards to the safety of the shadow beyond.

The darkness lights up as she crosses, and she stops.

Frozen, in a strange tableau before her:

Senex gesturing at Gericault as if to push him back, the Old Man's hand in mid-twist, his clothes soaked with blood, his manner calm.

Gericault's face caught in anguish; half rage, half despair. His arms are outstretched in violent magicks.

Mercedes is nearest, dressed as a flapper, limbs bent in mid-motion. She is running, her mouth open in a scream or roar, her eyes like black fires.

There are no walls, no sky, only twilight and a floor of cinders. Amanda takes one step towards her predecessor, and finds herself instantly within that body. The figures begin to move.

Mercy *is* screaming, like a hurricane, and the knives in her hands are wind. She leaps for her teacher, and he watches her come without taking his hand from Gericault. The Frenchman is forced back by the power of Senex' will, and space thickens around him until he cannot stir — he barely breathes.

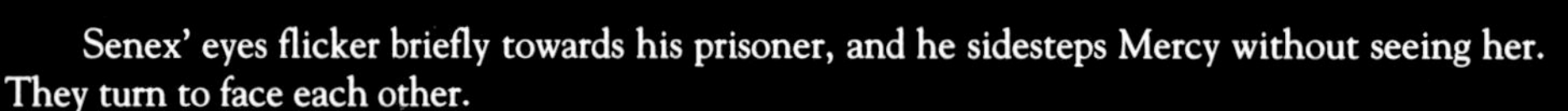

Senex' eyes flicker briefly towards his prisoner, and he sidesteps Mercy without seeing her. They turn to face each other.

"Let him go, old man," she shrieks, diving in to slash him.

The master says nothing. His weaponless hands begin to move. Mercy flips back her left knife, trying to evade his magicks, but the spell he uses is new to her, and she guesses wrong. Now, surprised to find herself yet free, she tries again to come under his guard.

Senex darts forward, taking a cut to the arm with a grimace. He grabs as if for her head, holds nothing, gives that nothing a twist, and she sees herself outside her body, suspended in his grasp. His hard, sad eyes gaze into hers, and the voice that guided her for a hundred years commands:

"Look."

He turns her away to a dark place in the twilight around them. There is a blacker thing in the ashes of the floor, clearer to her as her mentor forces her to stare.

Her Avatar is crouching there. The angel's shining wings are broken, feather-charred husks. The white robes are gone, and ribbons and patches of lead — some like fabric, some running red-hot down her bare skin, and some cooled, dropping off as she rises, dropping off with great patches of grey-cooked skin and muscle. The angel's eyes are maddened and dying; eyes like Mercy's last son's.

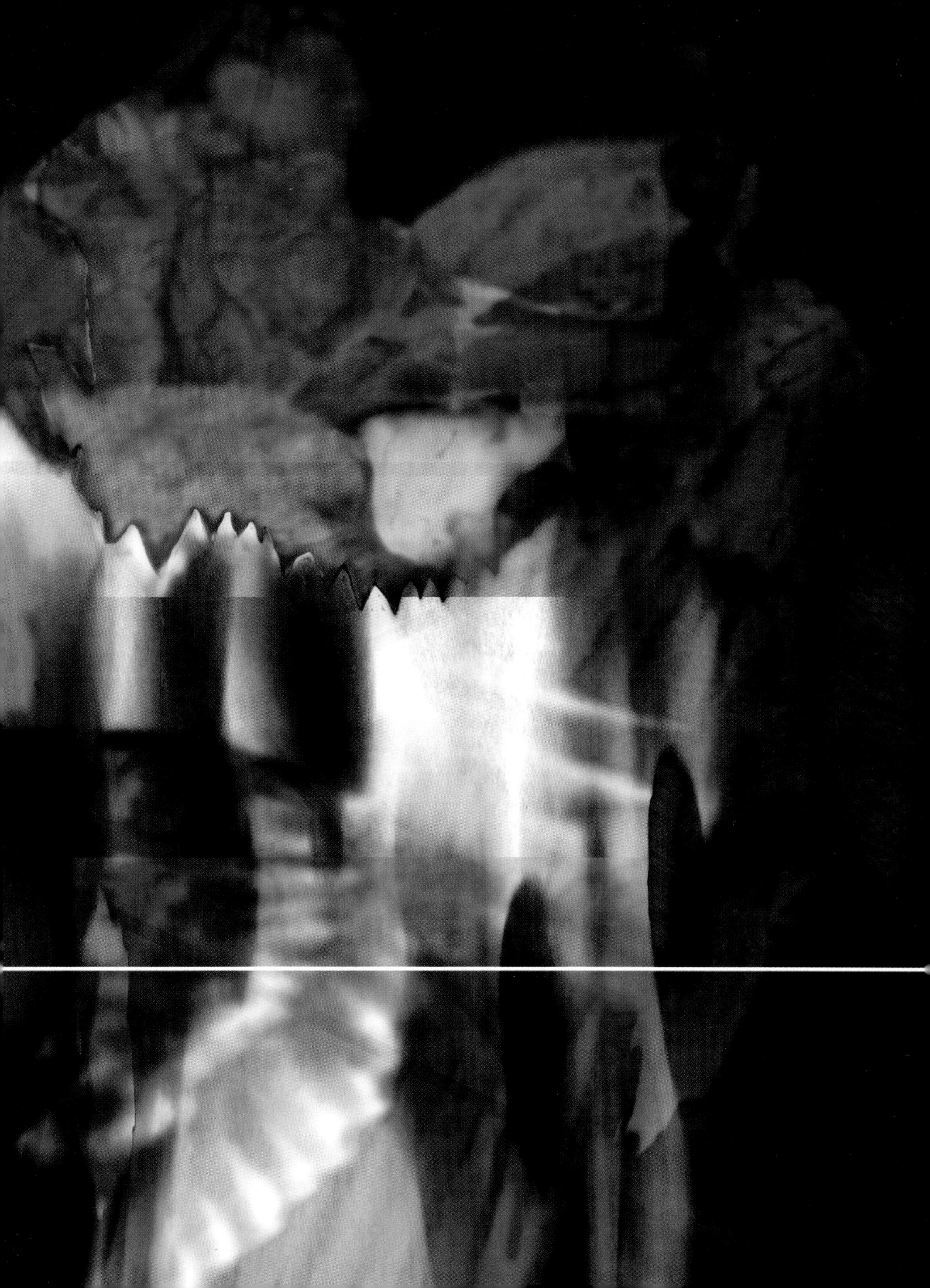

The vision fades. Mercedes recovers, sees Senex coming for her with his cane, and deliberately, she drops her guard the split second he needs. She cannot meet his eyes, can only hear the sobs of Gericault in his magick cell. Fire strikes her neck, and the world ends.

Amanda lurches forward, pulling herself free as Mercedes' body drops to the ground. The air is full of a high, keening whine, and it hurts her like a knife in the brain. On her right the husk of the Nephandi's Avatar is rising, on her left the bloody handed angel is screaming, is drifting helplessly towards her older self. The young mage sprints forward and catches her Avatar in a low tackle, knocking her down and holding her until the shadow-figures fade. The angel quiets, and even the echoes of her panic stop.

Soft footsteps approach them, and Senex — an older, white-robed Senex — comes out of the darkness. He helps the angel to her feet, smoothes her wings, strokes her hair. She angel comes to herself, seemingly, and stands straight. Her hands reach for Amanda, then the Old Man, and as she steps towards him, she disappears.

They stand for a long time without talking.

"Are you all right?" Senex asks his apprentice.

"Yeah."

"Do you remember?"

"Not everything." She finds herself staring at his arm, looking for the scar from Mercedes' last attack. "My — her — son, the hunt for the Physician... meeting Gericault. My death."

The two begin to walk back, and the glittering glass dust crunches beneath their feet.

"Is this yours, Old Man?"

"It is. I placed the barrier here before you were born."

"Thank you."

They pass into the dust, following their own footsteps backwards.

"She let you kill her, you know," Amanda says slowly. "When you showed her her Avatar — well, it worked."

"I wasn't sure."

"Gericault doesn't know that she did that. He weakened the barrier, didn't he?"

"He did."

"I think he thought that I would remember dying hating you. He's coming back."

"I know."

"I need to talk to you about him."

"Later."

"And I want to ask you about those rumors."

"Later."

They walk back into the Old Man's study, and Amanda finds herself lying flat on the chilly floor. She sits straight up and looks her Mentor in the eye.

"I have a lot of questions."

He nods his head.

"Later."

And Senex picks up the clay pitcher, pours from it into a dusty cup, and hands the water to her to drink.

"Questions, Amanda, are like a ring of keys..."

MAGE

Pride. Power. Paradox.

A Storytelling Game of Reality on the Brink

by Phil Brucato and Stewart Wieck

Second Edition

Credits

Original Concept and Design: Stewart Wieck, with Stephan Wieck, Chris Early, Bill Bridges, Andrew Greenberg, Mark Rein•Hagen, and Travis Williams

Second Edition Design and Development: Phil Brucato

Storyteller System by: Mark Rein•Hagen

Written by: Phil Brucato, Brian Campbell, Chris Hind, Deena McKinney, Kevin A. Murphy, Nicky Rea, John R. Robey, Kathleen Ryan, Allen Varney, and Teeuwynn Woodruff

Additional Contributions by: Ethan Skemp, James Estes, Cynthia Summers, Fred Yelk, and Richard Dansky

Editing: Cynthia Summers, Laura Perkinson

Design Contributors: Kevin A. Murphy, Kathleen Ryan, and a special thanks to Christopher Kubasik for inspiration

Art Director: Richard Thomas

Artists: Ash Arnett, Mike Chaney, John Cobb, Michael Scott Cohen, Robert Dixon, Daryll Elliott, Mark Jackson, Lief Jones, Michael William Kaluta, Matt Milberger, Paul S. Phillips, Michelle Prahler, Dan Smith, Lawrence Snelly, Alex Sheikman, Joshua Gabriel Timbrook, and Andrew Trabbold

Cover Design: Ash Arnett

Typesetting and Layout: Kathleen Ryan

Playtesters: Deena McKinney, Wayne Peacock, Stewart MacWilliams, Keith Martin, Darrell Autrey, Bob Asselin, Timmie Capler, Jeff Baty, Carl Capler, Jay Brown, Jamie Johnston, Ryan Casper, Christina Harkinson, Phil Brucato, Wendy Blacksin, Nicky Rea, Jackie Cassada, Shadow Lied, Judy McLaughlin, and Ehrik Winters

735 PARK NORTH BLVD.
SUITE 128
CLARKSTON, GA 30021
USA

Check out White Wolf online at

http://www.white-wolf.com; alt.games.whitewolf and rec.games.frp.storyteller

PRINTED IN CANADA.

Dedications

Threefold thanks to:

• Harlan Ellison, whose visions and wisdom have haunted, inspired and incensed countless readers;

And trust me that you can do something. You are not as helpless, as much a pawn, as they would have you believe. Each of us can effect change... You can move the world. You can be Zorro.

— *An Edge in My Voice*, Installment #10

• Miriam "Starhawk" Simos, whose works offer a balanced yet optimistic perspective on the troubling issue of magic and post-modern faith;

But the final price of freedom is the willingness to face that most frightening of all beings, one's own self.

— *The Spiral Dance*

• and Joseph Campbell, who would understand why these three diverse talents should be included in a single dedication. Truth has many masks.

The myth is the public dream and the dream is the private myth. If your private myth, your dream, happens to coincide with that of the society, you are in good accord with your group. If it isn't, you've got a long adventure in the dark forest ahead of you.

— *The Power of Myth*

Attention

Yes, folks, this is a game. Though based in real-life beliefs and practices, **Mage** is a fictional entertainment, not a work of occult lore, Satanic propaganda or New-Age rhetoric. That being said, we warn you that there are a good many words, images and ideas in this book that will offend and disturb the sensitive reader. Sorry, that's the game. Real life's a lot worse.

Mage is intended for mature audiences. It requires an open mind and common sense.

MAGE
The Ascension™

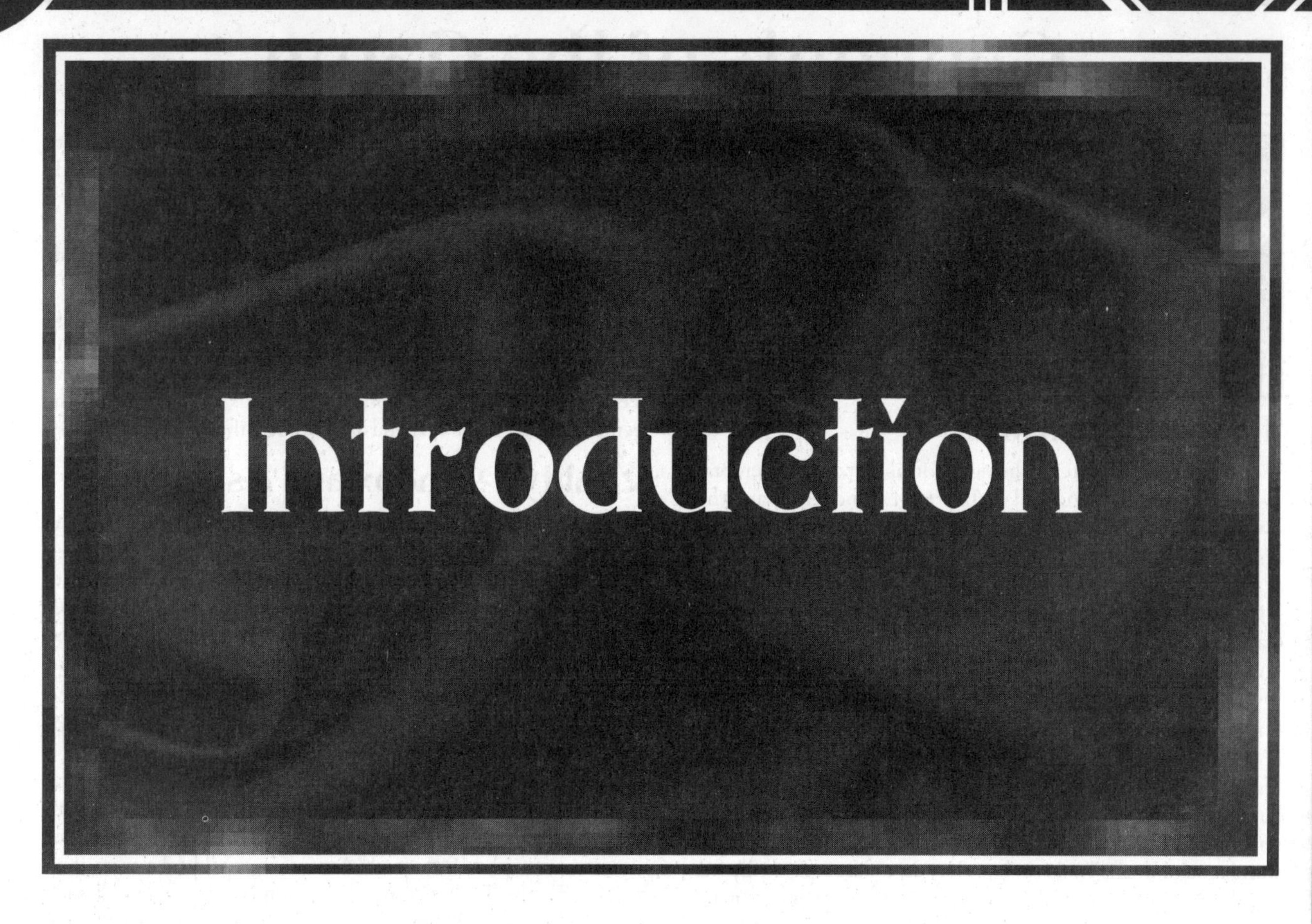

Heaven and hell are within us, and all the gods are within us.
— Joseph Campbell, *The Power of Myth*

The Tree

Five came together in near-darkness from many places and destinies that night, the crescent moon shining on their faces, blossoms fluttering in twilight.

Clarissa ran her slender hands over the trunk of the ancient apple tree. "So old, so beautiful..." she whispered.

"It suits," Peter Kobie shrugged as he passed around a goblet. All drank its fiery contents, then joined hands, circling the tree. They danced in a whirl of madness, faster and faster. Just as their frenzy reached its peak, the earth began to tremble. In a burst of color, ribbons of energy rippled forth from the top of the rotting old trunk. The dancers dropped hands, each reaching out to seize the streamers of power, each pulling the ribbons into their own souls. Only when all the streamers were captured did the dance renew, this time with the flowing bands of color woven in and out by the dancers. As moonlight faded, the glowing streamers became braided about the tree, the twining of warp and weft gradually covering the apple tree from top to trunk, binding into one essence the power spewing forth.

When the moon fell and sunlight touched the faces of the five, they lay in sleep about the gnarled roots of a glorious young apple tree, its tiny green leaves glowing with renewed life, fresh blossoms brushing the contented faces at its feet.

Reality is up for grabs. Magick is the key; Ascension is the goal.

Magick is not dead, no matter what we may think. It slumbers beneath the weight of disbelief, but it is not dead. In the mists of spirit worlds and the shadows of hidden sanctums, in the laboratories of the Awakened and the sacred places of the Dreamers, magick is alive.

Humanity sleeps; our fragile minds and shackled imaginations have put the divine spark within us into a deep slumber. To Awaken from this sleep, a mage embraces that inner spark, that Avatar, and accepts True Magick, the Art which shapes reality.

By Awakening to magick's truth, each mage unlocks a vision. Each vision leads to a Path, a destiny of change that pits a mage against herself, her fellows and fixed reality itself. A war is being fought in the shadows. Magick is the tool, the prize and the vision. Paradox, the backlash of disbelief, is the price of failure, and pride becomes the legacy of foolishness.

The world of **Mage** is a dark modern fantasy where reality is commanded with a thought and hopelessness poisons the very earth. Stories told in this mystick World of Darkness become heroes quests, journeys of self-discovery that step beyond our mundane lives. **Mage** is a game, true, but a game of tales told, not winners and losers. Like campers around a fire, players in a Storytelling game create shared folklore and have a damned good time doing it. An ideal **Mage** story mixes mystery and wonder with action, suspense, terror and a bit of humor. Such tales are modern mythology, streetwise yet enigmatic. Like the mages themselves, Storytelling games are active and ever-changing.

Concepts of the Game

All evolution in thought and conduct must at first appear as heresy and misconduct.

— George Bernard Shaw

Mage operates on many levels, and ranges from cerebral concepts to flat-out violence. Modern wizards cross into Otherworlds, gather into strongholds called Chantries, or fight their differences out in the streets. Several concepts, however, are important road signs to this magickal world.

The Modern Mage

Mages are enlightened beings, mortal humans who embrace — heart, mind, body and soul — the truth behind reality and their own place in it. Through innate sense, hard-earned knowledge and a shard of the divine self (the Avatar), a mage learns to rework reality at its core and becomes an active force for change. Though lesser sorcerers (often called hedge wizards) may tamper with the Tapestry's threads, True Mages direct the fires of destiny. Such change is rarely pleasant, but it is necessary.

The Awakened have always been with us; time and disbelief, however, have whittled away their power or channeled it into less obvious forms of magick. As the boundaries between the possible and impossible grow more rigid, the mages among us dwindle in number but increase in importance. Such sorcerers are heroes in the classic sense; with their power and insight, they cannot help but affect the world around them. To do so, however, they must continually transcend their own limits and those of the world around them. All mages, then, even the rigid Technomancers, are threats to the established order. Dynamic to the core, True Mages are the harbingers of change.

Because Awakening is universal, mages come from all nations, cultures, orientations and age groups. Many find their Awakenings in their late teens or 20s, but some find enlightenment at a very early age or even in their declining years. Though their vision spans global reality, mages are very much the products of their environments. Some are balanced and contemplative; others are harsh or crude. Magick is not limited to a scholarly few; anyone can be a mage.

The Factions of the War

Despite the infinite variety of Awakened souls, four large factions dominate magickal society. Although many mages (often called "Orphans") do not follow any set Path, these four major groups wage an Ascension War in the name of their chosen goals:

• **The Traditions**, a rough Council of nine mystick styles of magick. The wizards of the Nine Traditions strive to maintain a balance of sorts while returning wonder to humanity. Although these sorcerers hold to different philosophies and practices, all nine groups are opposed to the static reality espoused by their Technocratic foes and the chaos of the darker factions.

• **The Technocracy**, a seemingly monolithic Union dedicated to reining in supernatural "random elements" and saving humanity from the dangers it is not fit to face. By the Technocracy's decree, mystick magick is not possible; only science is allowed to alter natural laws. Because the majority of "Sleepers," (those un-Awakened to their mystick potential) trust in science, Technomancers have an edge over the other factions when it comes to getting things done.

• **The Marauders** are the Technocrats' polar opposites. More a state of mind than a confederation, these chaotic mages embody dynamic change taken to a demented extreme. An ideal world, to them, would be one in which every person created his own personal reality or lived in a single Marauder's dementia. Marauders are rare, unpredictable and often deadly.

• **The Nephandi** have chosen to follow the absolute Path of darkness and corruption. They deem themselves a mirror which will either reflect or absorb all light. Though the most terrible of them have been cast out of the material world, these Fallen Ones work behind the scenes to further the misery and damnation of the World of Darkness.

Reality, Paradox and Ascension

Reality is a work in progress; constant change keeps the universe alive. Magick is the most dynamic example of change — the alteration of reality by enlightened force of will. As humanity settles into a mundane rut, however, magick seems out of place or even impossible. When realities clash, when the possible and impossible collide, the result is a paradox. In the most violent conflicts, this Paradox effect becomes manifest, striking back in any number of ways. A mage — any mage — who causes change too quickly can invoke Paradox, and gods help him then.

The vision that comes so naturally with magick's Awakening inspires most mages to some greater goal, an ultimate end to reality's shaping. The Traditions refer to this as Ascension, but disagree as to what form such Ascension would take were it to happen. To the Technocracy, Ascension is the world made safe, purged of random elements and firmly under their control. The extreme Paths, too, have ultimate goals, but their ideals leave little room for compromise or survival.

The World of Darkness

The secret thoughts of man run over all things, holy, profane, clean, obscene, grave and light, without shame or blame.

— Thomas Hobbes

Compromise is dangerous in the realm of the mage, and survival runs at premium rates. Night glitters here like blood-stained glass, and the world seems caught between a madrigal and a scream. The woods are dark and monstrous, the cities labyrinths of steel and pavement. In the shadows, beings out of nightmares plot and bicker. Welcome to the World of Darkness, a distillation of modern twilight.

Here, the landmarks are familiar, but the shadows are longer and peoples' glances are more wary. It's a place where hope is fading, where superstitions carry more weight than reason. The aesthetic of this world is Gothic-Punk, where the flowing black and towering stone of Gothic ideal meets pierced flesh and battered leather. Although few mortals ever see the shadow-cultures around them, everyone feels their influence.

A spirit world surrounds the mortal one, cut off from material reality by mystick barriers. Ghosts and other spirits wander these mysterious lands, and beings attuned to them — werewolves, mages and the occasional enlightened mortal — travel into the Three Worlds of this Umbra. Although few mortals are aware of them, these realms — the lands of the mind, nature and death — cast a living reflection of the mundane world.

The features and cultures we know are much the same, but an otherworldly aura pervades the mortal architecture, clothing, music and religion of the World of Darkness. People here are even more fascinated with their own mortality than we are. At the same time, the possibilities of imagination have been limited by a worldwide denial of what no one wants to see. This denial confines the once-fluid power of magick, but also cloaks the activities of the supernatural societies. In the shadows, vampires, ghosts, werewolves, sorcerers and changelings conspire, and their intrigues surpass anything folklore might suggest. This World of Darkness is myth incarnate, and that myth is equally dark.

This fantasy world shows us how far we can fall from grace; mages, then, play a key role in the future. All this despair and violence is leading up to something big, some final judgment or destruction. The Ascension War may well determine whether the World of Darkness transcends… or self-destructs.

The Meaning of Mage

Never be afraid to risk, to risk! I've told you about Equus *haven't I? That doctor, Dr. Dysart, with whom I greatly identify, saw that it was better to risk madness and to blind horses with a metal spike, than to be safe and conventional and dull.*

— Christopher Durang, *Beyond Therapy*

At its core, **Mage** is about giving a damn, about caring and believing in something so deeply that your beliefs can change reality. The world is not shaped by passivity or acceptance. It is moved forward by the deeds of those who reject the old ways and carve new ones, without regard for obstacles or enemies.

Such dynamism is risky, however. Too much too quickly without insight or responsibility can spiral a person into madness and take everyone around her down for the ride. A wise mage seeks a balance between constant change and stagnancy, between wisdom and power. The Ascension War is a battle between extremes, with the Traditions walking the delicate Path through the middle. A misstep — overwhelming pride, carelessness or doubt — can be fatal to a mage, and to the world in general. The pride that comes with magick's vision is both blessing and curse. Without confidence, no mage can command her will. Without balance, that will grows out of control, dominating all within reach. The great sin of the Technocracy is not science, or even murder — it is oppression under one vision.

Most mortals are rightly called Sleepers by the Awakened. They exist (or perhaps, *we* exist) in a passive state of blindness, shying away from true insight, avoiding the symbolic death that leads to greater rebirth. We miss the wonders and possibilities around us. Our mundane lives have conditioned us to accept what is offered, from lying politicians to MTV, and we complain but do little to change it. Mages cannot be passive; they either progress or they stagnate. In stagnation lies eventual corruption, for stasis can only decay.

There can be as many themes in a **Mage** chronicle as you care to include — fate, faith, tragedy, romance, despair, revenge or whatever else you want. The essence of *change*, however, of progress against all odds, can never be far from the game.

Mage is a game, albeit an interactive one with an epic scope. Like mages themselves, Storytelling games are active; we offer you the ingredients, but the cake you make out of them will follow your private recipe. There are no winners or losers in these games, only participants.

How to Use this Book

Mage contains a wealth of information. For easy access, we've divided it up into three Books:

• **Book One: The Flesh:** These four "setting" chapters describe the concepts, cosmology and society of the Awakened. The rules themselves can be found in later sections. **Chapter One** examines the various worlds that mages know. **Chapter Two** explains how True Mages differ from mere "magic users." **Chapter Three** shows us history as the mysticks understand it, and examines the four factions of the Ascension War, and **Chapter Four** details the beliefs and metaphysics that guide and govern True Magick.

• **Book Two: The Spirit:** These three chapters describe the basics of a **Mage** chronicle. **Chapter Five** explains the basic rolls used in all Storyteller games. **Chapter Six** tells you step-by-step how to create your **Mage** character, while **Chapter Seven** explores the fine points of Storytelling and running a game.

• **Book Three: The Machine:** These rule systems govern the world of the mage in greater detail. **Chapter Eight** offers the game mechanics for magick within the game. **Chapter Nine** goes into the non-magickal systems important to the **Mage** world: experience, spirit rules, Realms, other supernatural creatures and more. Rounding it all out, **Chapter Ten: Drama** covers many overall rules pertaining to the World of Darkness — combat and injury, rolls for various actions and the progression of time in the game. Finally, the **Appendix** section offers a wealth of background details for the **Mage** Storyteller.

Enjoy!

Other Mage Sourcebooks

The following books offer you a range of possibilities beyond the basic rules. Others, such as **Beyond the Barriers, Horizon: Stronghold of Hope, The Insider's Guide to the Technocracy**, and the other **Tradition** and **Technocracy:** books, are on the way. Most sourcebooks also include lists of recommended reading (real books) to enjoy after the game is done.

• **Core Sourcebooks:** These important supplements detail specific aspects, groups or places in the **Mage** universe. Many feature additional rules and all contain background information. **The Book of Chantries** offers 10 detailed strongholds, plus the ins and outs of Chantry creation, politics and ecology. **The Book of Madness** presents an in-depth look at the Marauders, Nephandi, Umbrood, Paradox forces and Infernal powers. Wheee! **The Book of Shadows** is a far-ranging guide for players and Storytellers, featuring additional Traits, optional rules, background and fiction, and **Digital Web** explores virtual reality, **Mage**-style.

• **Background Books:** These books expand the range of your **Mage** game beyond the obvious. Most include rules for variant games, crossovers, or alternative settings. **Ascension's Right Hand** is an invaluable sourcebook for the non-magickal companions mentioned in Chapter Three. **Destiny's Price** presents a grim adults-only look at the Gothic-Punk street scene, while **Halls of the Arcanum** examines the academic hunters described in the Appendix. **The Fragile Path** is a little red (or purple, depending on the print run) book presenting the history of the Council's formation through the eyes of those who were there. Finally, **The Mage Tarot** offers a beautiful boxed set of cards based on the World of Darkness.

• **Tradition and Technocracy Books:** This series of low-cost books looks at each individual group from an insider's perspective. Each one includes histories, characters, and magickal details.

Lexicon

Mages have a language all their own, adopted or invented to describe their world and concepts. The next four sections list the most frequently used terms (Common Parlance), common ranks and names (Titles), the vocabulary of ancient mages (Old Form) and the ever-evolving slang of the younger generations (Vulgar Argot).

Common Parlance

Acolyte: A non-Awakened servitor of a mage.

Arete: The measure of a mage's magickal enlightenment and will.

Ascension: The enlightened state of being to which all mages aspire.

Ascension War, The: An ongoing conflict between mage factions, with the future of reality as the prize. Actually a series of conflicts, ranging from subtle maneuvering to appalling violence.

Arcane: A mystickal veil erected by mages to guard their identities.

Avatar: A soul, said by some to be a fragment of the Pure Ones who originally inhabited the Tellurian. An Awakened Avatar enables a mage to perform magick.

Awakened, The: True Mages; also applied to other supernatural creatures — werecreatures, ghosts, changelings, mummies and vampires.

Awakening, The: The moment in which one realizes, mind, body, heart and soul, the reality of magick and one's own destiny.

Branding: A punishment in which a mage has her Avatar marked.

Cabal: A group of mages bound to each other by loyalty and a common purpose.

Caern: A Node controlled by werwolves.

Censure: A common mild punishment among mages, similar to parole.

Chantry: The stronghold of a mage or cabal. On Earth, this may be a normal building or a magickally fortified and enhanced structure. These mundane places are often located on Nodes and connected to strongholds in the Umbra. Technomancer Chantries are called **Constructs**, while Nephandi refer to their strongholds as **Labyrinths**.

Coincidental Magick: Magick performed in such a fashion that it is effectively indistinguishable from a mundane event.

Convention: One of five groups of mages that form the Technocracy and enforce its policies. The Conventions are: Iteration X, the Syndicate, the Progenitors, the New World Order and the Void Engineers.

Council; Council of Nine: The collective name for the Nine Mystick Traditions and the federation they have formed. The Technocratic equivalent is the **Union**.

Craft: When used as a title, this denotes mystick societies who play no part in the Ascension War. They rarely refer to themselves as such.

Custos: A non-mage who works for or with a cabal as a servant or warrior. A modern *custos* may be anything from a rent-a-cop to a gang member to a mythical creature.

Deep Umbra: The aspects of the Umbra found beyond the Horizon, far from Earth. The Shard Realms are scattered throughout the Deep Umbra. Called the **Deep Universe** by the Technocracy.

Demon: Enigmatic beings of evil intent and disputed origin.

Dream Realms: Worlds created out of old dreams kept alive by the *Oneira*, the Dream Lords. Also called **Maya**.

Dynamic Reality: Reality in flux. It may be changed quickly through vulgar magick, slowly through coincidental magick, or gradually through the normal flow of worldly events.

Epiphany: A magickal revelation spoken of by the Traditions; thought to derive from a term for faerie enchantment.

Familiar: A spirit that has taken on flesh through a compact with a mage.

Focus: An object, action or gesture required to perform magick. Foci vary with belief, from mage to mage and paradigm to paradigm. A Technomancer focus is often called an **apparatus**.

Gaia: A common name for the Earth Mother; also used by some nature-conscious mysticks to personify the Earth and its Near Umbra.

Gate: A temporary magickal "bridge" between two places. Frequently created at Nodes. See **Portal.**

Gauntlet, The: A mystickal barrier between the Earth and the Near Umbra.

Gilgul: The destruction of a mage's ability to work magick by removing or destroying his Avatar. This is the most horrible crime or punishment possible, as it essentially takes away the mage's soul.

Hedge Magician, Hedge Wizard: An un-Awakened mortal who uses a static craft to affect minor changes in reality. See **Magic**.

Hollow Ones: An Orphan group that embraces post-modern decay and Gothic romanticism in response to the apparent failure of both. Though they often work with Tradition mages, they are not, as of yet, taken very seriously.

Horizon, The: The magickal barrier separating the Near Umbra from the Deep Umbra.

Horizon Realms: Small pockets of custom-made reality; artificial Realms on the border between the Near Umbra and Deep Umbra. Umbral Chantries are built within them, and earthly Chantries connect to them by way of Portals and Gates.

Hubris: The overwhelming (and often fatal) pride which leads mages into overconfidence or excess. Monumental hubris guides the Technocracy and lies at the heart of the Ascension War.

Incarna: Greater spirits; the servants of the Celestines. For all intents and purposes, demigods.

Initiation: A combined test and ceremony that marks a person's transition from apprentice to mage among the Traditions.

Mage, True Mage: An Awakened person whose actions and beliefs dramatically alter the reality around her. Used commonly to refer to followers of the Mystick Traditions, this term properly applies to all users of True Magick. Also called **willworkers**, for their command of reality through will; **magi**, after the old form; and **mysticks**, for their command of magick.

Magic: Stage tricks, illusions, etc. Also refers to static magic, which works with the momentum of reality, rather than reworking reality by force of will.

Magick, True Magick: The act of dynamically altering reality through force of will, knowledge and Awakened Avatar.

Marauder: An utterly unpredictable mage so given over to eternal change that he is essentially a magickal psychotic.

Metaphysic Trinity: A Council view of the three forces of change — Stasis, Dynamism and Entropy. Also known by some as the **Triat** — Weaver, Wyld and Wyrm.

Methodology: A sub-group of a Technocratic Convention, which specializes in a certain function.

Mystick: Those things which involve the forces of True Magick.

Near Umbra: The part of the spirit world that exists around each Realm. Most often used to describe the area of the Umbra that surrounds the Earth.

Nephandus, Nephandi: A mage who follows the Path of Descent, choosing darkness over light. Many Nephandi work closely with demons.

Node: A highly mystickal place. Nodes collect and store Quintessence, and the Gauntlet in their vicinity is thinner. Many Chantries, Gates and Portals are built on these sites.

Oracle: One of the legendary mages who has attained mystick perfection.

Orphans: Sleepers who have Awakened spontaneously without the assistance or guidance of other mages. They have taught themselves magick, and are often considered dangerous wild cards.

Ostracism: A punishment that completely divorces a mage from Tradition society.

Otherworlds: Collective term for the realms outside the Gauntlet.

Paradox: An anomalous state of reality caused when a mage disrupts the momentum of reality with her own magickal acts.

Paradox Realm: A small Realm created by Paradox spirits to entrap a mage and thus prevent any further disruptions of reality.

Paradox Spirit: A spirit formed from the collective beliefs of humanity. Mages who are careless or unlucky with their magick in front of Sleepers will find themselves hunted by these spirits.

Path: A general term for a mage's chosen destiny.

Pattern: The mystical composition of an object, entity, place or idea.

Procedures: What Technocracy mages call their magickal Effects.

Pure Ones: The legendary primordial beings of the Tellurian. Many mages believe that all souls are fragments of these shattered entities.

Pogrom, The: The systematic purge of all opposition ("random elements") by the Technocracy.

Portal: A permanent Gate. Portals are usually guarded by powerful spirits that require a task to be performed or a puzzle to be solved before they will allow safe passage.

Prime: The original unified force that composes the universe. All things flow from this primordial energy.

Protocols, The: A code of honor established by the Traditions to prevent abuses of power. Violation of this code is punishable by censure, branding, ostracism, death or Gilgul.

Quiet: A state of insanity caused by the excessive use of magick.

Quintessence: The stuff of magick; the raw substance of the universe in condensed form. See **Tass.**

Realms: The worlds of "solid" reality that exist within the Tellurian.

Resonance: The mystick traces that actions leave behind.

Rote: A tried and true magickal Effect, passed down as a tool or weapon.

Seeking: A mage's Avatar-guided quest for enlightenment.

Shade Realm: The Umbral "shadow" of a Shard Realm.

Shard Realm: One of nine Realms said to have been part of Gaia in ages past. They roughly correspond to the other planets (including Luna) and the nine Spheres of magick. Each is ruled by a Celestine.

Sleeper: A person potentially capable of magick, but not yet aware of its existence.

Sphere: A particular element of reality manipulated by mages.

Static Reality: The foreword momentum of reality, often guided by the deeds and beliefs of humanity. Magick, by its dynamic nature, disrupts static reality to some degree. The parameters of static reality have, in recent centuries, become more restrictive due to a single global paradigm (belief system) espoused by the Technocracy.

Symposium: A monthly meeting of the Technocracy. At these meetings members of the Conventions gather to make policy.

Tass: Quintessence stored in physical form. It tends to collect in Nodes and takes various forms based on its surroundings — i.e., mushrooms at a wooded caern, water from a specific spring or magickal garbage mold at an urban Node.

Talisman: An object that stores Quintessence and uses it to create a specific magickal effect — i.e., magick carpets, wishing wells or etheric ray guns. Technocratic Talismans are called **Devices**.

Tapestry, The: A metaphor for reality.

Technocracy, The: A ruthless and powerful group of mages that seeks to eliminate the harmful elements of reality, thus making it safe for humanity. Their magick, based on scientific principle, conforms and shapes modern reality — to a point. This group will not be satisfied until all possibilities lie within its control (See **Pogrom**). Also called the **Technocratic Union**.

Tellurian: The whole of reality.

Tradition: One of the Nine Mystick Traditions, a Council formed in the 1400s to oppose the Technocracy, resist the radical changes of the Marauders and fight the evil of the Nephandi. These are the Akashic Brotherhood, Celestial Chorus, Cult of Ecstasy, Dreamspeakers, Euthanatos, Order of Hermes, Sons of Ether, Verbena and Virtual Adepts.

Tribunal: A gathering of Council mages to discuss matters important to the Traditions; usually held in times of strife.

Umbra: The spirit world (actually a series of worlds) outside of the material one.

Umbrood: Any non-human not born or created on Earth. This includes both the spirits that roam the Umbra and the inhabitants of other Realms.

Vulgar Magick: This is the fireball-and-lightning kind of magick, visible as such to normal observers. Vulgar magick takes static reality and tears it out by the roots.

Wyck: A common name for the original magi, supposedly descended from the Pure Ones.

Titles

Adept: A mage with a fair degree of aptitude and power.

Apprentice: A mage who has not yet been initiated into a Tradition. Not typically applied to Orphans.

Bani: A Council honorific meaning "Of the House of...." Used in formal titles, like "Nightshade bani Verbena." Not in common use.

Barabbi: A mage who renounces her former loyalties to follow the dark Path of the Nephandi.

Bygone: A mythic beast that has abandoned its physical form for an Otherworldly one.

Celestine: The greatest of the spirits, equal in power to the ancient gods; said to rule the Shard Realms.

Consor: A mage's powerful ally; not a mage, but of comparable ability.

Deacon: A common name for the founding member of a well-established Chantry.

Disciple: The lowest rank among the Tradition mages. Disciples can perform magick and have joined a Tradition.

Errant: A vengeful mage whose Chantry and cabal have been destroyed. Errants are frequently shunned by other mages.

Fellow: A full member of a Chantry, but not a founding member and therefore of lower status than its Deacons.

Garou: The term that werewolves use for themselves (also used by mages who want their respect).

Guardian: A term some Council mages use to indicate the "challenging" aspect of the Avatar, who pits a Seeking mage against herself to advance her Arete.

Kindred: The term that vampires use for themselves.

Lord: An Umbrood spirit; less powerful than an Incarna but more powerful than either Preceptors or Minions.

Master: A mage of great power and ability.

Mentor: One mage who teaches another.

Minion: One of the least powerful Umbrood spirits.

Pedagogue: A Hermetic tutor of great fame, usually quite powerful and surrounded by students.

Preceptor: An Umbrood spirit that is less powerful than a Lord, but still more powerful than a Minion.

Primus: "First One;" used to refer to the founders of the Traditions and their living representatives at the Council. Also used to indicate Chantry founders.

Rogue: A renegade mage turned mercenary.

Sentinel: One of the guardian mages of a large Chantry; not typically a member herself.

Technomancer: A mage whose magick revolves around some scientific principle. Often used to describe mages of the Technocracy, the term properly applies to Virtual Adepts and Sons of Ether as well.

Tutor: Mages who have become known as proficient teachers. They are highly regarded by other mages.

Old Form

Certámen: A magickal, non-lethal duel between Council mages.

Curtain, The: The reality in which most Sleepers believe; when a Sleeper is Awakened, she is brought "through" the Curtain and sees that things are not truly as they seem.

Fallen One: A Nephandus.

Grog: A familiar form of **custos**.

Magus: A mage.

Postulant: A mage who serves the Oracles, trying to gain admittance to their ranks.

Turb: A group of Grogs, used as one would use a "pride" of lions or a "murder" of crows.

Vis: Quintessence.

Vulgar Argot

Black Hats & Mirrorshades: The Technocracy, taken from the traditional uniform of the enforcers of the Technocracy.

Bloodwork: Any magick that requires a tremendous amount of effort and involves risk to life and limb. Also, Verbena magick.

Copperfield: Slang for a mage adept at performing vulgar magick in plain sight.

Crystal Wavers: "New Agers" who have no idea what true magick is, but capitalize on it anyway; charlatans. Occasionally used as an insult to the Dreamspeakers.

Doxed: A mage who accumulates a lot of Paradox is said to be *doxed*.

Dram: One Tass of Quintessence.

Faust: A mage who bargains excessively with spirits, especially dangerous ones.

Freak: A dangerously insane mage; often applied to Marauders and Nephandi.

Fry: To attack someone with magick, specifically with the sphere of Forces.

Goin' Satanic: Joining the Nephandi.

Greyface: A Technomancer, taken from the *Principia Discordia*. Describes any mage or scientist who focuses on conformity.

Juice: Quintessence.

Merlin: An old mage, especially one who very rarely visits Earth anymore.

Mundane: A normal human; a Sleeper.

Nuke: What Paradox spirits do to those they attack.

Pit Bulls: Werewolves; considered derogatory.

Technobabble: A derogatory term for the propaganda and inflexible magick used by the Conventions.

Wyld & Fried: An insane mage; often applied to Marauders.

Book One: The Flesh

The Fallen One

Sometimes she could even taste the dream, lingering like sour cockroach ice cream. Singed-skin scent and the cry of betrayal haunted her into waking, even now, ten years later. Monique shook herself from dozing. If she'd cried out, the sound was lost in the room's thick darkness. Rubbing at her eyes, she fumbled for the Camel pack beside the desk and absently flicked her fingers to light the bloody thing.

The single ember cast a brief glow on the polished panel walls, then receded to a whisper. New smoke mingled with still air as Monique willed herself to breathe slower, easier, and to focus again on the book before her. Images she would once have called obscene now offered familiarity, a welcome break from past horrors.

The first slap had been the hardest; after that, it became frighteningly easy to lash out at Jacob's squalling face, painting it deep red, inspiring, at times, louder, more voluptuous screams. Though she felt some small regret for the pain she'd caused the child, all guilt had fled her long before the Rebirth. What use was guilt without repentance, and of what use was repentance to the damned?

The dull plop of ash on the page broke her reverie. The sound brought her back to the present. Best not to dwell on hard choices. The arcane scrawl beckoned, enticing her with wisdoms that were old before the Flood. Monique finished the cigarette with a last heavy drag, scattered the ash with a wave, and delved further into the unspeakable.

There was still so much to learn.

And God knew she'd paid the price for it.

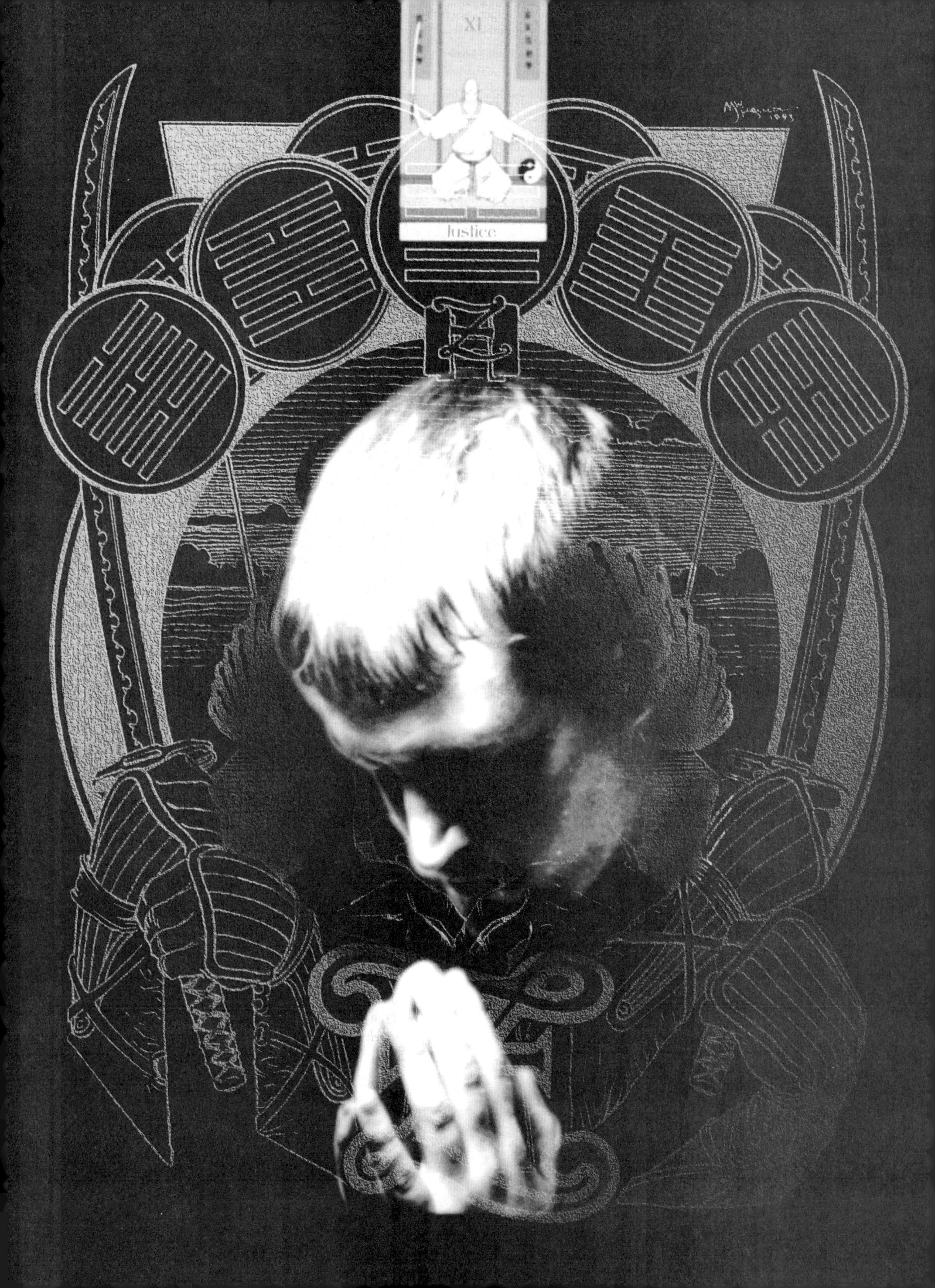
XI
Justice

Chapter One: The Tellurian

Humans think they know what reality is, what life's about. They think they know because they can think. 'I think, therefore I know.' Their attitude is 'I'm at the top of the food chain, so I get to decide what's real and what's not.'

What they don't want to be simply doesn't exist. Except, perhaps, in their dreams. Or nightmares. So they end up watching the shadows on the wall of the cave, thinking that's how the world really is. They never look at the things throwing the shadows...

— Nancy Collins, *In the Blood*

Awareness: The Seduction

Peter drank from his flask and held it to Clarissa's lips, tipping a burning swallow down her throat. He ran a finger over her chin, wiping away the stray drops, licking them from his hand. His other arm wound around her shoulders as they sat on a sagging sofa backstage.

"Clarissa Ryan," he repeated. "Sounds kind of '50s TV Americana to me."

In the five minutes they'd sat there, she'd told him her name. He hadn't asked anything else.

She giggled. "Not like Peter Kobie, which is what? Caribbean?" Her attempt to sound urbane fell flat.

He shook his head. "Boca Raton." He took another drink. "So you have a dorm room?"

"Uh, yeah." She stared at the floor, embarrassed.

His leather jacket creaked as he pulled out a key. "We'll go to my pad. Actually, a friend of mine's place. She left me a key."

Clarissa felt her breath shorten. "What will we do there?"

Peter smiled as he pressed his mouth to her neck, his long fingers sliding down her sweater, his thumbs touching her collarbone, stroking the swell of her breasts.

"You have to ask?" he whispered.

Look at the world about you. Look and *see* it, with both mundane and Awakened sight. See the endless sky, the trees thick with life; see your own hand, each inch of flesh a mesh of miracles. Feel your blood, hear the wind, and tell me nothing magickal is real.

Welcome, friend. I've been expecting you. You heard the sound of my drum calling to you, I see. I know what it is that you wish; you've come to ask me to show you the wonders to be found beyond this world. I will guide you in your quest. Before we move beyond physical reality, however, I must tell you of the Tellurian and the Tapestry. Have no fear. It will not take long....

The Tellurian

Mages refer to all of reality as the *Tellurian*. You have often heard those around you speak of the universe. They believe that they are speaking of everything that there is, as if the universe were all-encompassing. The universe is but the *physical* part of reality — the stars and planets, and the creatures and objects found therein. We also see the world of the spirit which exists side by side with physical reality, overlapping it and occupying the same space. We call the sum-total of all earthly things the Tellurian, the physical and spiritual together — all the possible realms of existence, all that is natural and supernatural, all hopes, dreams and possibilities. In short, all of reality that ever was, that may be imagined, and that might someday be. It's a complex concept, but a simple one as well. This is the mages' understanding of reality, the understanding that allows a willworker to bend reality to her will, for all things are already possible, though not everything is easy to bring into being in the mundane reality of our Earth. This was not always so, but that's another story.

The Tapestry

All those things which are a part of the Tellurian are threads in the mystick weave we call the *Tapestry*. This Tapestry is a metaphor for the complex interweaving of all physical, spiritual and intellectual elements. Together they form a wondrous, magickal fabric which is ever changing and growing. Much of the basis of magick comes from this image of a great Tapestry; we cast spells which weave reality to our visions, creating new patterns and altering old ones. We speak of ley lines, bright strands of Quintessence some call Gaia's ribbons, the Primal threads that flow across the face of our Earth. We locate *Nodes*, the meeting places where ley lines come together and one thread is tied to another, forming the strong knots that are the basis of our Tapestry. All the different threads are interwoven to make a whole. Our Tapestry is never finished, however, for the weaving continues as we move toward Ascension.

To our sorrow, the threads which make up the Tapestry are fragile things. Many spiritual threads that should have remained strong have been severed and left to atrophy. Those of my Tradition, the Dreamspeakers, believe that just as a tapestry frays and falls apart if the threads are cut or broken, so too will all of reality fall into nothingness should our foes ever succeed in wholly separating our material world from the world of mind and spirit. The physical world both shapes the spiritual one and is shaped by it in return, like the warp and woof of any fabric. All things are a part of both worlds. To deny one or the other unravels the Tapestry and leads to our own unmaking.

Mundane Reality

There are more things in heaven and earth, Horatio,
Than are dreamt of in your philosophy.
— William Shakespeare, *Hamlet*

Now that you see how everything is a part of the whole, you'll understand why I begin your journey by showing you the world you think you already know. Look around you at the city: the streets stretch away in fractured spiderweb patterns, choked with refuse and twisting around impossibly tall buildings bedecked with gargoyles and glittering with thousands of lights. The city's glow blots out the sky's candles, almost as if they were veiled by a cloud of darkness. Even were we to turn off all the lights, the choking gasses from our cars and factories would serve to do the same.

Look at that woman scurrying down the street. She clutches her purse and holds her coat together as though they were protective talismans. She's right to be fearful; there are many evil things abroad in the city at night. Most of them exist in the day as well, but we can pretend then that we're stronger and less afraid; it's easier to see something threatening at a distance and turn aside before we meet it.

Do you see the derelicts gathered around the trashcan fire they've built in the alley? Some of them deaden their fear and pain with cheap wine or crack; others are too beaten down or crazy to care.

Ah, here comes a patrol car. Its headlights illuminate the woman for a moment, and she flinches as though she were a deer in a hunter's sights. The faces of the police officers inside are set and grim. They've spent too long at a job they cannot successfully carry out, becoming cynical and almost as violent as those they once sought to control. The patrol car turns to move down the alley, and the men scatter away from their fire. Perhaps they've been involved in a crime; perhaps not. It doesn't matter. They would surely be blamed for something if they were caught.

Come, walk with me to the club down the street. You can hear the pounding music even from here. The children who wait to get inside instinctively feel the darkness around them and embrace it in their dress and attitudes. They do not run from the fear but seek to incorporate it, wearing their spidery black clothing and trying to out-cool one another. They seek to understand while pretending not to care. They listen, and they watch, and some few of them Awaken.

Let's leave the more squalid parts of the city and look at the government buildings and high-rise apartments of the wealthy. Here, one mirrored glass edifice reflects eerily inside another in an infinity of warped self-images. In that regard, they're much like those who live and work inside them: each stands in silent, aloof isolation. For all their inhabitants, they are monuments not to humankind's rationality and accomplishments, but to our greed and bitter pride.

Even the countryside has been ravaged. Where once there stood deep old-growth forests, bursting with life and filled with birdsong, there are now cheap trash pines, planted to keep the soil from washing away altogether. Strip mining tears gashes into the earth, leveling hills and beating down mountains. Raw sewage belches out from broken pipes running to the sea. Now that sea returns the poisons to us in toxic shellfish and acid rain.

People are afraid, cowed by governments, corporations and more honest criminals. They fear the unknown and the uncanny. What they already know is bad enough; they refuse to face what might be even worse. This is the dream of the Technocracy, this barren, lifeless, soulless world which they claim they made so that people would be safe and free. This is what the Sleepers see.

Despite it all, there is an alluring grandeur to our world, a siren's call which beckons us to search for hope and goodness in her corrupted cities and wilderness. And this the Sleepers also see. Some few have not given up, and we of the Traditions hope to reach them. Some become our acolytes, guarding and helping us while they strive to Awaken. Because such people still believe, we can still change reality in small ways, weaving new patterns into the Tapestry and bringing old patterns to the fore again. Even they cannot see everything we see, though they try to understand. Most Sleepers, dazzled by promises of a better tomorrow through science, have not yet learned to bring truth into focus through Awakened eyes.

Behind the Facade

During a carnival men put on masks over their masks

— Xaiver Forneret

Our vision is keener than that of our Sleeping brethren. We see more of the true picture of reality and know more about the forces at work behind the scenes. If you wish to comprehend the workings of the world, you cannot ignore those who pull the strings and make the rules.

The Supernatural

Where Sleepers see only big business and remote, monumental governments, we behold the vampires lurking in the shadows, whose control over mortal affairs drags our world downward. Do you think I'm spinning folk tales when I speak of vampires? They're quite real, I assure you. As real as the Garou, whom you would call werewolves. Don't smirk — they're often our allies. They too walk the other worlds you wish to know. In this world and in the Umbra, they fight for Gaia, driving back creatures like you have never imagined. We will speak more of these when I take you beyond the barrier which separates this world from that of the spirit.

Hidden from the eyes of the world (and certainly from most paranormal investigators), ghosts inhabit dusty halls and tumble-down houses. Some say that ghosts are those who could not stand to lose the world of the living, or those whose tasks are not yet finished, who linger to fulfill their final promises. Many wraiths, as they call themselves, are like that. These mean no harm to you so long as you leave them alone. We who undergo death ourselves, whether real or symbolic, understand these sad and passionate spirits.

You don't believe in ghosts either? Perhaps you think that the tribes who danced the Ghost Dance were all fools? There was power in their dances, and many of the soldiers who killed the medicine men would have told you *they* believed. But that was long ago, and will not come again on this Earth.

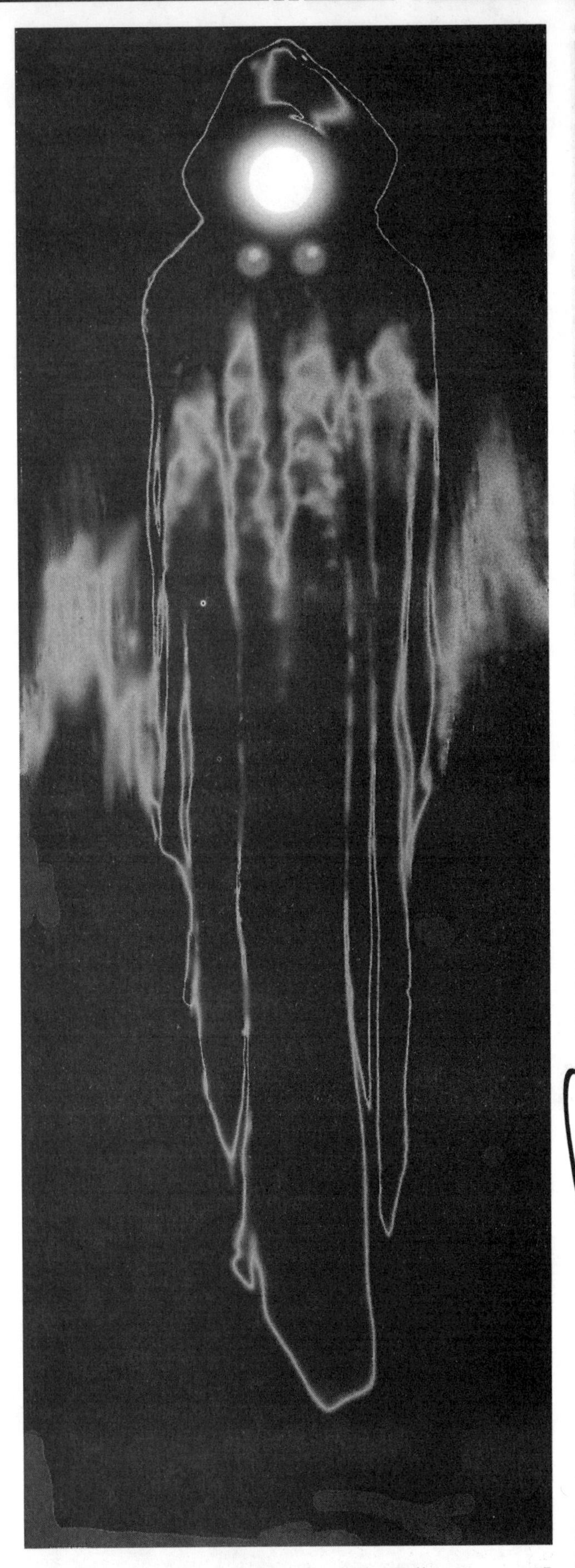

Evil wraiths called spectres will try to possess you, so it's best if the dead are left to themselves. Alas, there are no end of fools who call such spirits into themselves, wittingly or otherwise. Those possessed by such spirits may perform the most heinous of crimes and never know what they've done.

Faeries still exist as well. Changed, of course — how could they not be? The Technocracy did its best to drive them out and erase the memories of the Fair Folk, but tales remain, as do the changed ones. You will not see tiny sprites perched atop mushrooms (at least not in *this* world), but someday you may see an elegant faerie knight astride his galloping steed, or hear the delicate strains of faerie melodies carried on the wind from their hidden glens. Many never left us, and others are returning. Be glad, for it signals a crack in the Technomancers' defenses.

The Mages

Those officials who are not the vampires' puppets dance to the tune of the Technocracy. The Stagnant Ones' thoughts and beliefs echo down the corridors of power, bending reality to their vision of Utopia. Their towers loom overhead, casting shadows over us as their world view crushes dreams into dust. Don't fantasize, don't protest, and for God's sake, don't ask questions. How the Nephandi must laugh.

Their vision shapes much of the world today, but it was not always so. The Stagnant Ones have not twisted everything to their design as yet, or we would not be mages ourselves. Some parts of the world still hold to their traditional beliefs and have never fallen completely under the Technocrats' sway.

The Nephandi? Evil to the core! The Corrupted Ones have sold themselves to the Wyrm, the embodiment of entropy and depravity. Many such followers of the Path of Dark Reflection control political leaders and corporate officers. They too must share the blame for the spiritual affliction of the world. These Fallen deal with spirits that many call demons and seek to corrupt young mages from their chosen Paths, dragging them into labyrinthine pits. Do not listen to their lies; they take from you what you can least afford to give — your soul. If you were gifted with the most rare and beautiful jewel you had ever seen, would you sell it for a common pebble? Be warned: Have no dealings with the Nephandi.

Marauders are a difficult case. These mad mages want many of the same things the Traditions do. Where we seek to loosen the grip the Technocracy has on the world, they try to break the Technomancers' wrists, grind their fingers into dust and extrude whatever pulp of the world is left. They are chaos personified, insane. They want too much too fast and care little what effect this has on Gaia or Her people. Unless you seek destruction from the Paradox which follows them like storm crows, avoid the Mad Ones whenever possible.

What of the other Tradition mages? We all strive for Ascension, but most of us follow wildly different paths toward enlightenment. You need only know that they are your allies. In a fight against the Stagnant Ones, the Nephandi or the Marauders, you will find much common ground. Use it, but be aware that not every Tradition mage is your friend.

The Hunters

There are some among the Sleepers who believe that there is more to reality than blindness. They themselves may have other talents — hedge magic or psychic abilities — which give them glimpses into the world we mages see. Most such mortals remain as hidden as we do. Some, like the Arcanum, merely wish to study strange beings like vampires and werewolves or odd magickal phenomena. They would be harmless but for the dangerous knowledge they might pass on to our less restrained foes. It is best if they learn nothing at all.

Some government agents seek out those like us for unknown purposes. I surmise that many of them work for one Technocracy Convention or another. Others may want to recruit mages as weapons; a few may fear that we will use our powers to control the minds of those "in power." They know little of our actual power and aims, but fear much in their ignorance. Betray no special abilities should one of these agents find you.

Then there is the Inquisition, the inheritors of that medieval institution. They call themselves the Society of Leopold, but their aims are much the same as they always were — find anything different and stamp it out. In this, they fulfill a pattern as old as life itself. Humankind worships, then destroys those things that are different. The Society sees nothing natural about our powers, believing all of us to be in league with demons, a great irony since many of them practice magic they assume has been bestowed by God and believe in many of the same things that our own Celestial Chorus does. Do not be taken in by their air of piety; they can be the most vicious of adversaries.

Mystick Places

We need to hide our Arts from un-Awakened eyes, as many Sleepers would hunt us down for being different. Worse still, their unbelief channels the forces of Paradox back upon us. It's only natural that we would seek out those places of power that provide us with energy and guard us from Paradox. These also serve as hideouts where we may practice our craft in secrecy. We have many such places; they're called *Chantries*.

Chantries

That old Victorian house on the corner is a Chantry. It looks much like any other house on the block, save for the peeling black paint. The curtains are black as well, and few lights shine from within. See the candles flickering inside, and the smoke drifting from the chimney? They probably can't afford to have the electricity turned on. Orphans live there, mysticks who call themselves Hollow Ones. They think the house is haunted. Perhaps it is. Sleepers would think nothing of this house, and even mages could not tell its function simply by looking, for no mystick Node rests beneath it. Many larger Chantries sit upon such Nodes, drawing Quintessence to fuel the Horizon Realms where more hidden Chantries are built.

Chantries need not be houses. Barns, martial arts dojos, churches or even old movie theaters will do. Some mages meet in back rooms in bars or dance clubs; others rent fellowship halls or meeting rooms at their local libraries. As you can probably see, Chantries need not be permanent things. I have even heard of one housed in a bus that moves from town to town.

Come, let's get my car. I have much to share with you.

Constructs

The Static Mages call their hideaways *Constructs*, and they too seek access to Nodes to power their bases. They'd like to control or destroy every Node on Earth, something we must not allow them to do. These Nodes are the keys to our Horizon Realms and the wells of Quintessence from which many of us draw our power. Many Technomancer Constructs look like skyscrapers or factories, but the one I'll show you resembles a research lab.

Turn down along that industrial strip. Do you see the building? All gray steel and darkened glass, it nests like a viper within a block of concrete and parking lots. Pass by slowly, but do not stop, or the guard at the gate may notice us. Look with mage sight at the structure as we pass. Do you see the real building hidden behind the normal exterior, heavily reinforced both physically and magickally? To keep us out or them in, I wonder. If we were to go inside, we'd see sophisticated, but unremarkable technology: computers, lab equipment and even a few Sleepers who think they're engaged in top-secret work. The real labs are underground, shielded and protected by HIT Marks or Men in Black. Even these are only for show; a Portal hidden somewhere goes to one of their own Horizon Realms, where they undoubtedly have a hidden research lab. I've heard stories of the monstrous experiments they perform on those they take alive.

Now, while we stop for the light, look again. Do you see it? Even their shielding cannot completely disguise the Node they sit upon. I know it's there; this land used to belong to my people, but it no longer sings to me. They have raped the Node as surely as they have sterilized the land around it. There is nothing here now but pavement. Perhaps they feared to leave even a tree, lest it awaken one night and march on their soul-deadening structures. Enough. I wish to go now to a happier place.

Places of Power

I know that we've traveled far from the city, but it's worth the trip. This is a place of power. Do you see nothing but the trees? How do they appear to you? Yes, they are lovely — tall and strong, green and growing. Yet all around, the grass is withered, waiting for summer to come again. Other trees stand naked and shivering in the wind, their branches stripped. Ah, you see it now and feel it too. Listen to the branches whispering against each other. They tell one another of our coming. Smell the evergreens and the loam; they greet us adorned with their best perfumes. Walk beneath their twining branches and feel both the peacefulness and the power that is here. Most people would see only trees surrounded by more woods. There is nothing outwardly fantastic about the grove, but we Awakened can sense the pulse of this power-place.

What you feel is the Node's reflection of life energy. Nodes tend to draw and store the spiritual nature of a place, becoming pools of sympathetic vibrations. Many Nodes are found in places where life energy prevails — wildernesses and great rock formations — while others spring from battlefields, festival sites and other areas where great emotions have been spent. Nodes may even be dedicated to a particular feeling or purpose, and be resonant with love, joy, hatred, sadness or other passions.

There are many places of power: sacred groves, crystalline caves, powerful rock formations, sparkling pools, menhirs, waterfalls, burial grounds and faerie mounds, to name a few. Others are garbage-strewn back lots or sludge-filled ponds. Their appearance doesn't matter, for all, regardless of their shape or contents, are Nodes. Many leave behind a material form of their essence, magickal bits that some call *Tass*. Like Nodes, this Tass comes in many shapes and sizes.

Come and sit with me awhile and meditate. When we have refreshed ourselves somewhat, we will visit my Sanctum.

Sanctums

Welcome to my cabin. Please leave your disbeliefs and prejudices outside. The floors and walls are bare wood, but rubbed with oil to keep them from drying out. The rug on the floor was woven by my mother. The fireplace is a cooking pit set in the center of the cabin, and my bed is a mattress stuffed with herbs and grasses. The tools of my Art hang from the rafters overhead, and my drum sits in a place of honor next to the door so I may take it with me when I leave. Over there, I keep a stash of herbs and a store of seeds to feed the squirrels.

No, there isn't much here, but it's all I need. This is my reality, the place that I have set to mirror my beliefs. I come here to seek answers from the spirits or to walk the Otherworlds. This is the home and the heart of my magick. Because I have created this reality for myself, all my magickal workings within this Sanctum are considered coincidental, almost natural. Nearly anything is possible for me within my Sanctum, and I guard it with my life. I show it to you now as an act of trust; someday, you will need a Sanctum of your own.

Now that I have shown you all I can of this world, let us sleep so we may be prepared for our greater journey. May your dreams be filled with the answers that you seek.

Before we leave the earthly realm, let me tell you why what we do is so necessary. Most mages believe that the Earth, which some of us call Gaia, is the center of the Tellurian, the only source of Prime Essence and of those pure shards, known to most as human souls and we Awakened as *Avatars*. All else, they say, centers around us and takes its shape in response to human imaginings and creativity. I am proud to be one of the Awakened, and I will strive to my last breath and beyond to keep Gaia from falling to sterility, madness or the dark. What I will not do is tell you that we are the center of it all, or that we are the *only* source of Quintessence, or that Awakened life does not exist somewhere else among all the planets of our Tellurian. I am only an old Dreamspeaker, but I know this: Nature loves infinite diversity, and to claim that we are the only source of magick in the whole of reality is to deny that principle. It is sheerest Earthnocentricism, if there is such a word. We warn all young mages against hubris, or excessive pride, yet we teach them such foolishness. I am content to save *my* world. Who could ask for more?

The Otherworlds

All we know for sure is that we don't know anything for sure.

— Neil Gaiman, *The Books of Magic*

The Gauntlet

Beyond the confines of our world lies the first Mystick Barrier: the *Gauntlet*. The Technomancers will tell you that they formed the barrier to prevent free travel between the physical and spirit worlds. They lie. While they have done whatever they can to strengthen the Gauntlet, they neither created it, nor do they understand it. It is a natural barrier formed by the energies of the Earth, holding the spirit world separate from the physical. Once the two may have intermingled freely; now they must be held separate. The universe is out of harmony, and the Gauntlet must function as an immune system, insulating one from the other. Each, however, is a separate and necessary place. The physical world provides stability so that we may have form and substance. The spirit world gives us chaos energy and meaning so that we may imbue those forms with life and creativity.

The Gauntlet serves the same purpose as your skin; it differentiates that which is you from that which surrounds you. Your skin does not prevent air from passing into your body, but it does keep out most harmful things, unless it is damaged. The Gauntlet was meant to be the same, but has been toughened in most places by the disbelief engendered by the Stagnant Ones. Like scar tissue, this makes it difficult for even beneficent spirits to cross over without help. Because of this, much that was vital and spiritual about our world has atrophied and died.

We will cross the Gauntlet now. I have brought you to a secluded spot where the barrier is thinner. In the city, the membrane is too thick, the disbelief too heavy for us to easily pass through. Here I hope we will find it a simpler task. Sit now, and listen to my drum. Forget yourself, and place yourself in my hands. When all is ready, when we both see the mist that is the Gauntlet, we will rise and walk through it.

There are other ways to cross. Some mages use Mind magick to send their astral forms into the spirit worlds, forming astral bodies for themselves and trailing a silver cord behind them. I prefer to go in person, myself. Now, take this feather. Hold it in front of you. Study its lines and colors, and I'll tell you how to cross and what will happen when we do.

The Garou call this *stepping sideways*. Essentially, I make a doorway through the Gauntlet with my feather, allowing us to simply step into the spirit world beyond. It's important that you banish fear and have confidence while I do this. It would be best if we work together, though I can take you through regardless. Can you feel the nearness of the spirit world leaking through the Gauntlet? That's called the *Periphery*. If you can feel that nebulous spirit touch, you're on the Periphery and ready to cross over. Good. Now listen closely.

As we cross over, I will transform our physical bodies into the stuff of spirit. Heh, I thought that might bother you. Tell me why. Do you believe you are alive? Of course you do. Then show me your life; no, breath and heartbeat are *signs* of life, not life itself. Show me what animates your physical body; your brain is an organ, not an animating spirit. I could keep your brain alive long after your spirit had fled. So tell me, which part of you is real, the spirit or the flesh? If you like, you may think of it like this. Here on Earth, your physical body is what surrounds your spirit; there the opposite is true. You leave no mortal shell behind. It is subsumed into your spirit body. Believe, and listen to my drum.

How does it feel to you? To me, it always feels as though I'm moving through clouds of softest cotton. There's a slight resistance, then it parts before me. Do you see it changing color? There are no such hues on Earth. Now we are almost through. Have you noticed the scents yet? Even the air has taste. Do you hear the music of the spirits? We are here.

The Near Umbra

We have reached the *Near Umbra*, a place contiguous to the real world, overlapping it by resting parallel to it and occupying the same space as it does, but on a different plane or another dimension, so to speak. It extends from the Penumbra, a spiritual mirror of the Earth, into the three layers, or Worlds, of thought, spirit and death. Its boundaries are the Gauntlet on one side and the Horizon on the other. In the Umbra, Paradox has less power. The spiritual richness of this Velvet Shadow is not weighed down by disbelief; much more is possible here because of that.

Before we continue, I must warn you that our trip may not be without danger. There are many natural denizens of the Umbral world, spirits which we call *Umbrood*. We may meet some upon our journey. Treat them with respect, and do what I do. They rarely bother me, but you are a stranger to them and they may decide to test you.

Now we're in a mirror to my cabin. Do you see the crystals glowing? Can you feel the love that forms each pattern of the rug my mother made for me? Everything here is a spiritual reflection of our own Earth. Here everything is revealed for its true nature.

Why do I glow? I am a Master of Spirit, and the spirit world recognizes its own. Someday, you too may glow when you cross into this world.

The Penumbra

We are in the *Penumbra*, that portion which mirrors the physical world. It is more true to the spirit or nature of a place, however, and often seems to reflect its spiritual health rather than the form it wears in the physical world. Some things are utterly changed.

Look at the grove; they're large, beautiful trees on Earth, but here they tower overhead, their branches thick with greenery and good health. I always want to dance when I am here. Now that we're outside, can you see the changes in my cabin? I am no carpenter, but here the care I tried to take is reflected in the clean lines and polished wood I could never have achieved on Earth. This is the *spirit* of my Sanctum, not merely its reflection.

Let me show you more. We'll journey toward the city, though we will not enter. It's far too dangerous for your first trip into the Umbra. Just walk as though you were at home. The Akashic Brothers would say, "Be, do not do," but you are doing fine. I see you understand my hesitation to approach the city. It's foul, isn't it? Lifeless, barren, soulless, it squats dry as dust and reeking of the poisons within. Those webs you see strung all around and through it are made by pattern spiders. Everywhere that life and feeling have been eradicated by the twisted vision of the Technocracy, every place that yields itself to technology rather than spirit is calcified into stagnation by the webs. They delineate the city's form and prevent it from growing or progressing spiritually.

Everything is not the same, though. Remember the skyscraper we saw? Look where it stood. No skyscraper! It doesn't have the emotional impact to displace what stood there before. Here in the Penumbra its place is taken by an old, worn stone church. Look how the stained glass windows shine! It must have hosted many worshippers over the years, and the memory of that place lingers here where its vital spirit never died.

Domains

Do you see that blackened, acidic-looking area near the city? It's a Blight, formed from toxic wastes that cast their reflection onto this area of the Penumbra. There are equally bright places of great purity that we call Glens. Both of them are known as *Domains*. They aren't true Realms, but rather shifting zones with no set borders. If those on the earthly side of the Gauntlet continue to dump toxic wastes nearby, the Blight will grow and fester, becoming more dangerous and polluting this area of the Penumbra.

Realms

Within each of the Umbral layers lie *Realms* of various sorts. Some are constructed by mages for their own use; many appear at the will of Umbrood Lords (creatures of great power), or as reflections of powerful dreams and concepts, and some form for reasons few of us comprehend. Most Umbral Realms assume set forms, though some of the ones more distant from Earth are highly chaotic and apparently shift at random. Perhaps we simply do not yet understand their patterning. All have their own realities, and most have both a physical and a spiritual portion, just as Earth does. You might think of Realms as pockets of reality in the ethereal overcoat of the spirit world, or imagine them as soap bubbles afloat on the Umbral sea.

Each planet in our solar system supposedly has its own Near Umbra, as does the moon. Since each is a Realm in its own right, with its own governing Celestine, this is hardly surprising. These are not the only Realms, however. There are many different sizes and types, some planet-sized and some no larger than a bubble, many ephemeral and some as solidly set as the Earth. We've categorized several types of Realms that most mages understand: *Shard Realms*, *Shade Realms*, *Horizon Realms*, *Paradox Realms* and *Dream Realms*. Don't be too concerned. I will speak of these again as we reach them. For now, just accept that each part of the Umbra is host to many Realms.

The High Umbra

Let us return to the mists and seek out the airts, the pathways that cross through to the place we seek. This time, I will take you to the *High Umbra*, the world of ideas, which is also called the Astral Umbra. Though we mages have a passing familiarity with each of the Three Worlds, this is the level best understood by our kind. Do you see the dream trails? They shine like moonlight within the mists, twining through and around the dreams we do not seek at present. When you cross into the Umbra, all you need do is follow the path that takes you where you want to go. Travel here is as much a matter of intent as of movement or distance. If you know enough Spirit magick, you will know where to go and how to get there quickly. If you know only a little, it's best to travel with a guide. Spirits sometimes guard the airts and demand payment of some kind to allow you through.

Ah, look at the concepts spread before us. There stand the brilliant pearl-white gates of someone's thoughts of Heaven. White marble palaces line the streets of gold, and the denizens have feathery, white wings. The sun blazes with a pure light that both warms and ennobles. A rather pedestrian concept to have achieved such solidity, but there is still much belief in it among certain factions. I prefer the green grasslands under a pale blue sky and herds of buffalo running by, the ground shaking with their numbers and display of majesty.

Here's a Hell. Chinese in origin, I think. The smell is enough to sicken a butcher, and the blackened blood offends my eyes. They say that the perversions and tortures found within such Realms should be experienced at least once. I have heard that none of the heavens or hells to be found here are the true ones; those wait beyond the veil of death.

Many places here are far more abstract. The higher they go, the more refined the ideas become until only the most incisive and creative (some say insane) minds can understand them. Come, explore this one with me. It is not quite so rarefied. Have you noticed that we're walking on the ceiling? Step into the next room. Now the floor is at right angles to the one we stood upon before. Does that mean that now we're on the wall? You seem surprised. We've gone through the door opposite to the one through which we entered, yet we are now back in the first room again, only we're standing on its floor. Look back through the door on the other side. Wave to yourself!

Be polite to the spirits here. They are concepts and ideas, mathematical equations and hypotheses, discarded theories, philosophical posturings, psychological theses and religious beliefs. I do not claim to understand half of the Realms or beings of the High Umbra, but I can sympathize with their desire for respect and courtesy. Many Umbrood make their homes here. Some of them are Paradox spirits that you may someday meet on the other side. Others may be minions to beings of godlike powers who will crush you out of existence for annoying their servants. If all else fails, remember that should you ever need to get into a Horizon Realm through the back door, you'll probably be traveling through the High Umbra to do it. Don't offend the spirits!

While we speak of spirits, let's delineate the different kinds you might meet in the Umbra. A great many of them roam these Realms. Most mages believe that spirits are creations born of the unconscious minds and conscious beliefs of humanity. I think we're mistaken in this. If our Avatars or souls are shards of the Pure Ones given consciousness, and if we think of this part of ourselves as our spiritual side, why should these spirits not also be shards of the Pure Ones? I believe they have always had their own existence and merely choose to appear to us as gods from ancient myths, demons, mythic creatures and monsters. Perhaps they seek to present themselves in ways they think we'll understand. In any case, our belief strengthens them and solidifies their forms. The creatures of the Umbra, whether spirits or inhabitants of other Realms, are known as Umbrood. We are divided in our thinking concerning the masters of the Nephandi. Some of us believe they are spirits with power enough to be called dark gods; others think they are alien creatures from the darkest reaches of space. The Celestial Chorus would label them demons and fiends.

If you deal more with the spirit world, you'll have to learn these spirits' names and titles, the Realms they rule or inhabit and any particular spheres of interest they feel they control. They are beings of great power and majesty, not pets or servants at your beck and call. Their wisdom can teach you much if you but listen. When you summon one, be courteous and ask its help. Demand nothing; offer the spirit some payment or reward for its trouble. Most importantly, do not assume that you are a higher being or that you necessarily hold the most power in the relationship.

The Middle Umbra

Take my hand and follow me to the world of primordial nature. We go at night, when it is brightest here. The light of Luna, the moon, shines down and illuminates the shadowed woods and vales. During the day, much of this level is dark and dangerous. But look around you; do the trees in the Penumbra seem so tall as these majestic silvered woods? Here are those brilliant stars we no longer see in the city. At last, we see night's candles as they were meant to be seen, in all their radiant glory. The wind carries whispers of moonflowers and night blooms whose scents are so potent I fear to breathe, lest I forget how in lesser climes. Abundant, riotous life is all around us. Have you ever seen precipices so steep, mountains so austere, or animals so healthy? I had never truly seen purple before I came here, nor did I understand that blue and green are words too tame to describe the miraculous hues that grace this realm. Now I know the language of flower scent and animal musk and hear the symphony of the wind in the grasses and trees.

Do you hear the scream of the predator? That too is an integral part of nature. Behind her beauties lies the struggle for survival and the dangers of the wild. Nature is full of cruel caprice, from droughts to earthquakes to blinding hailstorms. So long as the hardiest of her children survive, she is unconcerned by the few who fall by the wayside. We may revel in the loveliness of unspoiled wilderness, but never forget that humankind is not ascendant within its embrace. Here we are the prey.

Did I say the Earth held an unexplainable allure? If it does, it is a resonance inherited from this spirit world. This is spirit at its most pristine, the dream I wish to return to the physical reality of Gaia.

I am not alone in that wish. The Garou also desire a cleansing of the world. Many guard some of the last pure places of the Earth, areas of great natural unspoiled beauty, their sacred ground, which they call *caerns* and we call Nodes. These sites are not only places of power, but places where the Gauntlet is thinnest as well. Mages sometimes quarrel with Garou over such Nodes, but those of my Tradition (as well as many other mages) prefer to have werewolves as allies rather than potential enemies.

The Garou claim that this part of the Near Umbra is made up of 13 Realms. Some are terrifying places of eternal conflict or corruption and torment; others are realms of futuristic horror or past depersonalization. Still others open upon the vast and starry Umbral heavens or retain an aching beauty, an all-encompassing spiritual purity and unsullied wilderness lost to the Earth with the strengthening of the Gauntlet.

Many wild and powerful Umbrood live in the Middle Umbra. Some become familiars. Others may serve as guides or advisors if asked politely and appeased with reciprocal knowledge or gifts. My totem animal met me here once as I lay beside that pond. Many spirits are short-term residents, wanderers who cross through the lands of primordial nature on their way to the Deep Umbra; others are Minions or assistants to the Umbrood Lords.

Did you see that? What would you call it if not a unicorn? Many so-called mythical beasts also make their homes in the heady atmosphere of the Natural Lands. Whether they have assumed the forms human belief assigned them in ages past, or have always appeared thus, none can say. Mages refer to these spirits as *Bygones*, those who once had solid form but abandoned it for the spirit world in the wake of humanity's growing disbelief.

Come, I must show you yet another place within the spirit world so that one day you may recognize it when you reach it.

The Low Umbra

Look upon this gray and dreary land, but do not cross into it. That ashen road which winds between those skeletal trees and climbs over those rocks leads into the Low Umbra, a benighted, sorrowful place also known as the Dark Umbra or the Realm of Death. Many believe that the roads of the dead cannot be walked by the living — at least not if they wish to return. Many Euthanatos claim to have done so, but it is a dark and dangerous path to the Underworld, where tormented spirits seek to hold onto their former lives. Nephandi also deal with the dead, and this is enough to make most of us wary of the claims of the Euthanatos. Some few Dreamspeakers have braved the paths of the dead, for we must face our own demise if we are truly to understand the realities of the spirit world, but most have never returned. This is the least understood land of the Near Umbra, and perhaps that is not a bad thing.

The Zones

Several places float within the Near Umbra, fluid Realms which drift between the Worlds of thought, spirit and death, permeating them but not bound by them. Though these constitute Realms of their own, they are usually referred to as *Zones*, but are also known as the *Dream Realms*. These include the Digital Web, the Mirror Zone and Maya.

The Mirror Zone

Look back along the inside of the Gauntlet. Can you see the Earth? As though you were looking through gauze, isn't it? How do you know it's really Earth that you see? It might be the Mirror Zone. Some say it lies alongside the Gauntlet, masquerading as reality. Others say it is partially of the Earth and partly of the Umbra, a slice of each world caught inside the Gauntlet itself like a slab of ham between two slices of bread. Still others theorize that the Mirror Zone is a Realm of perverse thoughts, nightmares and myriad alternate realities. Stepping into it rather than back to the Earth may utterly change the world you know. Friends may now be enemies, companions you left only minutes ago are dead and gone, or those long dead may live again. Infinite variations on a theme are possible in the Mirror Zone. Some are so close to reality as to be virtually indistinguishable from it — at least at first. Something is always different, here; sooner or later, those trapped in the Mirror Zone discover where they really are. To escape, you must confront the difference head-on and resolve any difficulties it presents. Be very careful whenever you visualize crossing through the Gauntlet. Make certain you have Earth's current reality firmly in mind, and you should have little difficulty with this perverse Realm.

The Digital Web

I have brought you to the Cyber-realm so that we may enter the Digital Web. Yes, it is very futuristic here, and the Umbral Computer Web is very large. The webbing looks much like that of the pattern spiders. The inside of the Net, as many people call it, resembles their work as well. There — that pool of light within those twisting coils of webbing is an open Portal into the Digital Web. Be brave; to enter that strange Realm we must step into the Portal. The sensation is unpleasant, even painful, but no harm will actually come to you. I wonder if this is what the early transporter beams on *Star Trek* felt like? If so, I see why they often took the shuttle instead! There's some pain, and things will seem too bright, too fast and incomprehensible for the first few moments after we arrive. Ride it out. Virtual Adepts and other voyagers enter this place using magicks either to send their astral selves into the Net or to translate their physical bodies into information, projecting themselves physically within it. And you thought becoming spirit matter was strange!

Open your eyes. We're here. I know very little about this Realm; it's far more suited to Virtual Adepts and Sons of Ether than to Dreamspeakers. We won't stay long, for there are many dangers here — spirits of the Net who may be unfriendly or Technocracy mages bent on claiming as much of the Net as they can.

Do you see those shining, squirming cables? They're strands of possibility, unclaimed pattern webbing that has not yet received an imprint from someone's mind. Do you understand what that means? A mage may enter the Digital Web and literally create her own reality within it. There, farther down the strand, I see a glowing Realm take shape as we watch. Even Sleepers may share in some of this through virtual reality, opening their minds to new possibilities. It may even Awaken some of them.

Where are we? That's difficult to answer. The Web itself is in the Gauntlet, yet it's also inside your own mind. Some claim that this is actually the remains of a shared Realm called Mount Qaf, originated by the lost Tradition known as the Ahl-i-Batin. Thus, it might also be a Realm upon the border between spirit and thought. Like a Horizon Realm, mages may pattern their thoughts here to create areas that conform to their paradigms. If this is truly a way of changing and molding reality itself, the Digital Web is a fantastic new breakthrough in the Ascension War. Thus far, no one has been able to prove whether this is, in fact, what is happening here or if it all exists only in our minds.

Maya, the Realm of Dreams

Look! Can you see the bubbles floating through the air? Some are as tiny as moths, others as large as cities. Those are Dream Realms, formed from fragments of humankind's dreams (and perhaps the dreams of spirits as well). Some exist for only brief moments, while others take on more permanent form as more people dream the same dream and belief in it grows. If we wished, we could step into these Realms, into the chaotic meanderings of the subconscious mind and interact with whatever is within. Be warned — Not all dreams are pleasant, and who can say what would happen to you if you were to die in someone else's dream? The secrets of the Realms remain hidden to us until we are within; would you want to stumble into someone else's nightmare? The Nephandi sometimes enter such terrors and use them to exert control over the dreamer. As you might guess from the name of our Tradition, we Dreamspeakers are not above contacting potential mages and "awakening" them to the possibilities within their grasps.

Powerful Umbrood spirits known as the *Oneira*, or Dream Lords, collect bits of dreams and weave them into semi-permanent Realms known as *Maya*. Such "homes" are often as phantasmal and chaotic as the dream wisps they were created from. Some Oneira, it is said, are powerful enough to control people through their dreams.

The Horizon

We've come far together since our journey began. Now we enter a place of great import to mages: the Horizon. It too is a magickal barrier, like the Gauntlet, but separates the Near Umbral Realms from those of the Deep Umbra. Do you see it? It wavers and flows, the colors changing and merging, one with another, creating new patterns and hues as we watch. I think of the Horizon as the elder sister of the Aurora Borealis. Do you feel the electric snap of its existence on your hair and skin? Can you identify the taste-smell that surrounds us? Nor can I, though I always believe that I could identify it, given the proper words. Have you felt it pushing back against us yet? The farther you move toward the Deep Umbra, the greater the resistance. The Horizon is like a membrane between the Near and Deep Umbrae. It keeps them separate and discrete, protecting the nearer Realms and Earth from constant invasions by Marauders, Nephandi and the malign, alien denizens of the farthest realities.

Horizon Realms

The Horizon is more than just a barrier, however; it's also a unique environment in which artificial lands called *Horizon Realms* are built. Mages, both Traditional and Technocratic, are their common architects, though other spirit powers also build Realms to suit themselves. Such Realms are rare; it takes massive amounts of power to create and maintain them. Horizon Realms serve two purposes: they shield against other realities, and they commonly house Umbral Chantries. Horizon Realms are designed to be the perfect representation of the creators' paradigms, and as such do not suffer the effects of Paradox, so long as one's magick does not clash with the reality within. They are ideal for magickal study and experimentation; after all, they are created to support the mages' world views! Such "formatting" also makes them ideal strongholds. They are much like Sanctums this way; as any warrior knows, an enemy's home ground is his strongest defense.

There is one not far from here. See it floating in the distance, much like a multicolored balloon tethered to the ground by a silvery string?

Do you see how the tether fades off into the mist? It's not actually tied to anything here in the Horizon, nor is it a physical rope or cable. What you see is a stream of pure Quintessence, used to anchor the Horizon Realm to at least one Node on Earth and to an Earthbound Chantry. That same Quintessence powers the existence of the Horizon Realm itself, for it cannot exist without this infusion of mystick fuel, which flows through a Portal, a permanent opening through the Gauntlet. Some such ribbons are easy to spot if one knows how to look, but others are cloaked with potent Prime magicks.

Portals are usually guarded by powerful spirits. Portals are easier to create and maintain on Nodes where the Gauntlet is thinner and static reality weaker. Those who are allowed to do so may travel back and forth between Earth and the Horizon Realm. We cannot enter the Realm from the Horizon itself unless its creators left a back door into it. Such routes are always guarded carefully, their passwords given to only a few, for Nephandi and Marauders seek out easy access to Horizon Realms, the better to cross through the Portals and onto the Earth. As these conduits funnel Quintessence as well, they also gives invaders access to easy power. Only a cocksure mage makes an escape route into the Horizon. Having made one, only a fool leaves it unguarded. Those mages who are fools rarely achieve the necessary power to construct Horizon Realms to begin with.

Shade Realms

Eight Shade Realms rest along the Horizon at the edge of Gaia's Near Umbra. These somewhat insubstantial lands are the Umbral "shadows" of Shard Realms. Be patient! I cannot explain everything at once. We will speak of the Shard Realms in due time. It's often difficult to tell that you are entering a Shade Realm until you are within it. Do you feel that humming throughout your body? Look at my hair rise from the static electricity, and smell that lightninglike ozone. We are in the Shade Realm of Forces.

Each of the Shade Realms corresponds to one of the Shard Realms (all except for Luna) and provides the easiest path for reaching those faraway Realms. Each is a Portal, or bridge, linking these Realms with their appropriate Shard Realms. These allow easy movement between the two without the necessity of crossing the Deep Umbra. In essence, they're like wormholes crossing through space, linking distant areas together. Many such Portals exist, but few have been found and opened. Some need special rituals cast or esoteric materials utilized before they will open. Somewhere within this Realm lie conduits to the Shard Realm of Forces and probably a back door to Doissetep, the largest and most well-known Tradition Chantry. We would not want to meet the guardians that this most puissant Chantry has undoubtedly left here to deal with intruders. We'll go now; I merely wanted you to be aware that such Realms existed in case you ever need to use them.

Beyond the Horizon

Everything that I believe
Crawls from underneath the streets
Everything I truly love
Comes from somewhere high above
— Indigo Girls, "Hand Me Downs"

Once past the Horizon, we enter parts of the Tellurian truly unknown to most of us. To reach these places, we must pass outside the Earth's atmosphere and beyond the Horizon, to the Deep Umbra.

The Deep Umbra

Like a great void, the Deep Umbra stretches outward beyond Gaia's bounds and into the far reaches of the Tellurian. The Void Engineers try even now to map the Deep Umbra, setting it into a static reality. They have succeeded in convincing most of humankind that all that lies outside the Earth's atmosphere is empty space and lifeless planets. That may be so on the physical side of reality for now, but on the spiritual side the Deep Umbra is rich with possibilities. Within its reaches lie Shard Realms, Paradox Realms, wild spirits, demons, crazed Marauders and the perverted Nephandi. Strange atmospheric conditions prevail in the Deep Umbra, ranging from reality storms to the Etherspace which the Sons of Ether navigate to reach the other planets.

Beyond the comforting confines of Gaia's atmosphere lurk bizarre, unknowable creatures whose only desire is to penetrate the barriers and feast upon the Earth. Others merely desire to control our world. Even to some of the less fearsome denizens, we are so small and insignificant that they might flick us away as if we were annoying insects. Our minds simply cannot cope with some of the horrific monsters that dwell in the Deep Umbra. Mages who deal with such creatures usually perish; those who survive are driven permanently insane.

The Nephandi's dark masters may be found somewhere within this spiritual void, as may many of their false Chantries, which they call Labyrinths. Should you ever meet the Nephandi, kill them on sight. They are an abomination — mages who entice or force others of their kind into corrupting their souls and becoming slaves to demons.

Shard Realms

Shard Realms are so named because mages believe that they were all once parts of Gaia that have now been flung throughout the solar system. Many mages say that there are only nine Shard Realms, corresponding to the other planets and Luna and to the nine Spheres of magick. This may be so — for this particular solar system. I have already spoken of our overwhelming hubris in assuming that we are the center of the Tellurian. I do not believe that there are only nine Shard Realms in existence; these are simply the nine that we know about. They are all very large, and though the Void Engineers say they are lifeless orbs, we know that they're Realms in their own right. Each has its own Umbra, just as Gaia does. Undoubtedly, these Umbrae are as varied and amazing as Gaia's own Near Umbra. Each Shard Realm is ruled by a Celestine, and to some extent partakes of that being's essence.

As I mentioned before, Doissetep is located on the Shard Realm of Forces. I have no knowledge of other such Chantries established on these distant Realms, but there might be some. They say that the gateway to Arcadia, the homeland of the faeries, is located on Luna. I would someday like to travel to all the Shard Realms and see them for myself.

Paradox Realms

Reality is flexible and may be tampered with to some degree. It's easier when there are no Sleepers present to interfere with their disbelief, but even then the fabric of the world may be coaxed into a new pattern. The fibers of the Tapestry are loosely woven enough that they can incorporate some reweaving without ripping apart or snarling into knots. When the weaver moves too fast or tries to overthrow the pattern entirely and create a whole new design, however, the Tapestry fights back. Sometimes this causes the weaver's shuttle to slip from her fingers; sometimes the loom breaks and smacks her in the face. That is Paradox.

If the weaver persists in forcing the pattern in an incompatible direction, eventually the Paradox loom gives her what she wants — in spades. It weaves a entire Realm just for her, wrapping her up and removing her to a place outside Gaia's Near Umbra, then smoothes the fabric back into its original design. The weaving that encapsulates the offending mage is known as a Paradox Realm. This particular occurrence is usually reserved for the most blatant offenders against consensual reality. The trapped mage must somehow come to an understanding of what she did wrong and seek some way of righting things in order to escape. Paradox Realms float aimlessly in the Deep Umbra, neither a part of it nor apart from it, but in some strange state in between. I hope you never fall into such.

Umbrood Realms

The spirits that inhabit the Umbrae often create their own Realms. Though some do so in the Near Umbra, many prefer the more fluid reality of the Deep Umbra. From time to time, these unknowable entities may kidnap humans or lesser spirits and bring them to their Realms. Sometimes they demand that these "lesser" beings fight or engage in other contests to amuse the Realm lord. Other times, their reasons are inexplicable. Almost anything is possible in such places.

Some mages claim that the spirits have formulated three courts through which they work out their differences and govern their domains. The Western Court contains entities described in Hermetic texts dating back before the time of ancient Greece. Eastern Court members are said to embody beings from the myths and legends of Asia, and the Egyptian Court is rumored to be comprised of the aloof animal-headed gods of ancient Egypt. Dreamspeakers believe there is a fourth court, a Lodge of the Sky, which does not recognize the other courts and considers them to be invaders. These are the gods and goddesses of native religions from pre-Columbian America to the Polynesian Isles.

The Hollow World

I wish to end our tour of the spirit world by telling you of another place that I have only heard described. The Sons of Ether claim that there is a world known as the Hollow Earth. In this land, wonders await and danger lairs in every corner. They say there are human inhabitants, and that the world is lit by an interior sun. Science would tell you that it is impossible for the Earth to be hollow, that there's a molten core at the center of our planet covered by layer upon layer of rock. They also tell the Sleepers that there is no such place as the Umbra. Whom do you believe? I believe there is a Hollow Earth, but if there is, perhaps it lies in an Inner Umbra all its own, waiting to be rediscovered.

And now we must recross the Gauntlet and return to our more physical reality. I hope that you have seen enough of the Tellurian to understand it a little and little enough of it to entice you to learn more. Awaken! It is time for dreams to become reality.

spark of the One, and let
forth in song! We are many.
act in concert, always listen to the
those around you, and never
the One, our origin and our destiny.

The Hierophant

Look within
burning spark
it burst forth

Chapter Two: The Mystick Path

Ultimately, a hero is a man who would argue with the Gods, and awaken devils to contest his vision.
— Norman Mailer

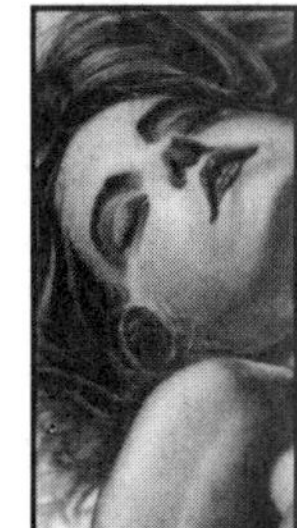

The Awakening

"Do you feel it?" Peter Kobie asked. Silenced as she was, Clarissa could not reply.

It was amazing, though, this writhing, sweet agony. Bound, blindfolded, Clarissa felt each touch, each breath, each pulse of energy within and without. Kobie seemed to be everywhere now — his arms around her chest, his lips across her skin, his touch a crackle of new and sudden pleasures. Sensation resonated within her, building to something past all words she could conceive.

Power built, expanded, spread, melded, focused...

Something snapped in her mind, sudden, bold, a bolt beyond sensation, awareness or mere physicality. Clarissa screamed inside, the conflict of silence and sensation merging into something she couldn't explain, couldn't prevent, couldn't control. And suddenly, being blind and voiceless didn't matter; her senses expanded around Peter, around the room, feeling every contour of reality greet her as if she'd never known the interactions of life before, as if she'd never really seen anything for what it truly was. And as the physical pleasure slowed, a mental awareness replaced it, constant even after Peter left her to her new Awakening.

Later, when all was quiet, the blindfold fell with a cool clack of scissors. Clarissa's hands, finally freed, dropped limply to the bed. Peter smiled down at her, sweat glistening on his forehead as he stroked her damp hair.

"You are renewed," he said. "Awakened. Restored to what you once were." And she was. Clarissa lay on the bed, not the woman who had come into the room. She laid her head on his chest, content that he, that someone, that something *had finally empowered her and made her different.*

Then her gaze fell to the clock.

Ten minutes.

Her eternity had lasted only ten minutes!

No way. Uh-uh! Ten minutes wasn't possible, something was wrong, *there was* no *way, absolutely* not! *It was hours,* days, *not* ten minutes! *Fury rose with an odd terror and a new awareness that this wasn't right, that Peter Kobie had... done...* what??

"What did you do to me?!" She raised herself up on an elbow, furious, scrambled, perplexed. Then she looked into his eyes and found herself wondering why she was making such a fuss.

"I did nothing, only led you to where you would've gone, given time. You did this, not me." Peter touched her cheek gently. "Rest now, Clarissa."

And she relaxed utterly, slumping to the sheets, her turmoil banished, feeling nothing but the beating of hearts.

To stand outside the City of Man while holding the keys to heaven — this is the lot of the mage. To stand torn between the mortal Human Self and the immortal Divine Self — this is her battle. To embrace destiny and redirect the flow of reality — this is her legacy.

No one said it'd be easy.

There is magic, and there is *magick*. One taps a person's inner potential, the other opens that wellspring without reservation. One grants a taste of power; the other *is* power, power to change the world. A True Mage does not *use* magick — she *becomes* magick.

The True Mage is a hero in the classic mode, not necessarily a "good guy," but an agent of change who faces conflicts from within and without, takes destiny by the hand (or other parts...), and changes the world in some meaningful way. The hero, whether male or female, "good" or "evil," mortal or mystickal, faces a similar charge: to step away from the known, confront herself, endure temptations and ultimately transcend, taking the world along with her.

Origins

In the beginning, it is said, there were the Pure Ones. Some claim that these First came forth from an even greater One, but we will begin with the many, for we are many and we hold their Essence within us.

Before there was land, or air, or flame or water, the Pure Ones flew through endless heavens. In their rapture, they birthed the Spheres, those planets on which we now dwell. In their unity, they created a place of soul and body as One. In their wisdom and their folly, they created the Dreamers, from whose visions sprang the lands, and the seas and all the creatures therein. And in their wonder, they journeyed across the lands they had set in motion, and those lands were altered by their passage.

For some reason, the Pure Ones shattered. Perhaps there was a war; perhaps they grew too strong in hubris and were broken by the One; or maybe, just maybe, they knew that a time of change had come. In any case, the many became multitudes, each carrying a shard of divinity within them.

Ages passed, years beyond our measure. Those whose inner spark glowed strong still journeyed, following the Paths of the ancient Ones. Others allowed those embers to smolder, still alive but Sleeping; these settled the lands and multiplied. From the journeys of those primordial Awakened, the fabric of the world was spun; from the Sleepers, it was given form. Ages passed, and their Tapestry grew heavy with wonders and fears.

Like the Pure Ones, the Awakened set forth on different Paths; their bodies died, but the Primal spark lived on, carried like a campfire ember wrapped in deerskin. Such skin burns away in time, but, if properly kept, the ember burns on. We are that skin; we keep the Essence burning, yet add subtle changes with our passage. Over ages, those embers changed, altered by those who kept them alive. The Pure Essences diverged, goading their mortal keepers to new Paths. In time, they battled, each wanting to wrest the grand Tapestry away from their cousins. From their struggles, great horrors were wrought. People died, often badly. The Dreamers were set apart from the mortal world, and wept in their exile. The lands trembled, and the Tapestry, in self-protection, tightened itself in fear. The Keepers of the Prime went to war, and the works of man crumbled, to be reborn again.

This is the Way of Change; to wear away That Which Was and replace it with That Which Is To Come. It is neither pleasant nor kind, but it is the Way. We are the bearers of that Way; our foes are also. Perhaps the Pure Ones guide us even now toward some Reconciliation, where the multitudes will become many, and then One, once again. Or perhaps it is the will of the Way that we go our separate Paths, toward changes that will tear the Earth we know asunder. I do not know. But change is our destiny. Change and the Path.

— Hapsburg, Orphan Seer

It's a hard Path; many willworkers fall by the wayside or step off to follow petty goals. These mages never transcend and are soon forgotten. Others die, and their deaths may or may not carry some meaning beyond the fall itself. The mage quickly finds her magick to be a double-edged blade — it confers power at the cost of normalcy. Mages are outcasts from the mainstream; regardless of her allies, each mage essentially walks alone.

So why do it? Why not just grab a bit of gusto and sit in your little corner of the world with a full bank account and a host of retainers? Some mages do just that. They remain eternally unsatisfied, however, and often fall before mages (or other forces) with more power and a clearer sense of purpose. Most Awakened, by virtue of what they are, want to leave their mark upon their world, fulfill some part of their destiny and gain some higher (or lower) state — Ascension.

The Goal

Ascension may be a twofold process, involving both internal transcendence and external change. Most pursue either the internal or the external aspect; rarely do they seek for both — such a goal is too large to be attainable. Few mages agree upon the nature of Ascension as a whole. Many will argue that there can be only one or the other form. The truth is an enigma; perhaps only the Oracles know for certain.

Of the two goals, external change is the easier to measure. The Sleeper world will in some way be improved, thus providing evidence that change has been effected. Neither goal is exclusive to a particular faction. A Technomancer may aspire to personal perfection, while a Celestial Chorus Traditionalist simply wants to see peace in her time. Either objective, if successful, may be called Ascension.

Methods to attain Ascension vary. Some Awakened believe in reincarnation and claim that the soul, the Avatar, strives to better itself with each incarnation. Others, less patient, want to perfect themselves in this lifetime. Some believe that there is no final perfection, only an eternal journey. Transcendence is not a thing that can be explained — it can only be achieved.

This doesn't mean that a mage wakes up one day and decides that she Ascends after she feeds the homeless. Destiny is more subtle than that. A Path is less a conscious decision than a subconscious motivation. A willworker may never know what her chosen Path is, but it calls to her nonetheless. She may resist, but she will never be satisfied until she follows it.

Getting Stuck

Mages are dynamic; they *are* change. Sooner or later, however, they begin to stagnate. They may live for many lifetimes, even for centuries, but the law of diminishing returns will eventually set in. Mere power is not perfection. If a mage does not Ascend or fall at some point, she ceases to be an agent of change and becomes a sticking point instead. If they live too long, the mightiest wizards lose whatever chance they might have had to attain that higher state — and many take their bitterness out upon the world at large.

The Trinity

The Council of Nine speaks of the *Metaphysic Trinity* **(see Chapter Four)**: *Dynamism*, the creation of possibility; *Stasis*, the form such possibility takes; and *Entropy*, the breaking down of that form. According to Council doctrine, these three forces are all necessary things. With the close of this century, some claim, the three extremes have drawn apart, pulling the Tellurian between them. Something has to give.

The threefold Path is hardly universal; many mages reject it, if they hear of it at all. Some mages seem drawn to the Trinity, however, and actually personify some part of it. From these extremes comes the Ascension War, a conflict of opposing perfections. It may be that four Paths spring from this Trinity — total chaos, total form, total destruction and the balance of all of the above — and lead both Avatars and mages to some ultimate conclusion.

The truth is for you to decide.

The Avatar's Role

On the edge of sleep,
I heard voices behind the door
The known and the nameless
Familiar and faceless
My angels and my demons at war
Which one will lose — depends on what I choose
Or maybe which voice I ignore
— Rush, "Double Agent"

Is the Avatar the soul? The subconscious? The id? A guiding spirit? The voice of an ancestor? The call of God? Or some devil? Each mage will give you a different answer. Whether one, all or none of these ideas are true, a mage's Avatar is, to all appearances, the seat of her magickal power. Do Sleepers have such souls, which might be roused on the Day of Ascension? Or is the gift of Awakening something only a few people will ever have? Is a mage one being or two? Does he control his Avatar, or does it control him instead? No clear answers come to hand. In their absence, most mages, like anyone else, turn to mythology.

Mystick folklore refers to "Pure Ones" who sundered their own Essence and left it scattered throughout the Tellurian. Masters call this bit of Essence the *Avatar*. Most living things, they say, have Avatars, but only a True Mage carries an Avatar which is self-aware. Put simply, the Avatar is the magickal consciousness that allows a willworker to do her thing. Some sorcerers have tight bonds with their Avatar, while others totally deny the divine shard's existence. You *may not believe in God*, goes the old saying, *but God still believes in you*.

Mysticks often disagree about this inner self. Gharmic scripture declares the Avatar "That Blessed Part which is all things intertwined," while Hermetic lore states that "...the so-called 'Avatar' is nothing more than a personification of the mystick consciousness, wrapped in some pleasing (or terrifying) form." The Technocracy officially denies any affiliation with supernatural entities, but promotes "...self-awareness through constant maintenance of the superego," while many Dreamspeakers talk of past lives or ancestors who live again in their descendants. All or none of these views may be true. A mage's magickal soul may take any number of forms — from bad dreams to separate entities, from the "daemon" of Greek philosophy to the "eureka factor" of scientific inspiration — and is not limited to any one certain shape. Whatever form in which the Avatar reveals itself, it goads the mage further down his Path. Whether he meets his Avatar face-to-face, encounters it in dreams or hears its whisper in the back of his mind, its influence is always somehow present.

Avatars are supposedly immortal. They pass, it is said, from one mage to the next, carrying the lessons learned from one incarnation into the other. If this is true, Avatars are pretty slow learners; modern mages seem no wiser than their legendary forebears. Some mysticks speak of Reconciliation, the Metaphysic Trinity or the Path of Change — all different ways of saying that Avatars have their own agendas, ends which they pursue through mortal incarnations. This concept is not universal, but makes sense in light of the Ascension War and the four or five *Essences* spoken of in Hermetic texts — Dynamic, Pattern, Questing, Primordial and possibly Infinite — the "personalities" of Avatars

Seekings

When a mage wants to advance, she enters what some call a *Seeking*, an out-of-body trial where she confronts her Avatar and demands access to the power she holds within herself. Her success or failure determines how much of her potential she unlocks — and how far she still has to go.

Meditation of some form is the most common way to go Seeking; the searcher must literally travel out of herself to begin. The mystick's body does not actually leave Earth, but she is not present within it while the test goes on. Seekings take place in some otherspace which is neither material reality nor a visitable part of the Otherworlds. The mage's consciousness returns to our reality when she has either passed the test... or failed.

Like all aspects of the Avatar, the form such Seekings take varies wildly from mage to mage. Verbena speak of the Guardian, a forbidding taskmaster who sets the trials and wards the subconscious until the sorcerer is ready for such secrets. Some Virtual Adepts go into a sort of VR simulation, where they solve puzzles based on the problems they struggle with in life. When they solve the puzzle, the Seeking ends. Avatars have even been known to cripple a mage in the material world, striking him blind, poor, lame or otherwise disabled, until he learns to do without some crutch that he has grown to depend upon. It is an intimately personal encounter where the mystick takes Path cues from his Avatar.

During a Seeking, a mystick undergoes a gauntlet set up by different aspects of her Avatar. The tests change and grow harder each time. Unresolved conflicts, internal or external, take on metaphysical shape and symbolic substance. To triumph over the obstacles, the mage works through puzzles, suffers trials, fights battles, confronts tormentors... whatever the Avatar deems necessary to advance her understanding and proceed further on the Path. Success grants her another Epiphany **(see below)**, taking her up another rung on Ascension's ladder. If she fails, she gains nothing. Bad failures sometimes end in exhaustion, physical shock or injuries, insanity, Quiet... or even death.

Conflict

Avatar/mage relationships vary. In most cases, the Avatar takes on a "teacher" aspect, leading a mage to his Path and helping him to travel along it. If the mortal self is stubborn, the inner self pushes, threatens, encourages or sulks. Very strong Avatars may even be seen by other mages with potent Spirit magick. A would-be mentor often decides upon an un-Awakened recruit by sizing up his Avatar. To many Awakened, the magickal self is a living entity, sometimes benign, often terrifying. Contrary to popular beliefs, bits of the so-called "Pure Ones" are not necessarily nice guys; Marauders, Nephandi and cruel Technomancers have Avatars every bit as "true" as any Celestial saint's.

Bringing the mystick self and the mortal self together and staying sane in the process is a constant struggle for most mages. If the two don't match — and they rarely do, at least in the early steps of the Path — they clash. Some mages run from their destiny, while others let it go to their heads. In either case, the Avatar comes along, a back-seat driver pointing off-road. The strain is more than some can handle. A few slip into *Quiet*, the madness that comes when outside reality and perception blur too far. Others go more subtly insane, suffering from night terrors, obsession, power-madness or cowardice.

The inner self will not be denied. It may appear full-form, visit its mage in dreams, speak through people or other objects, grant hunches or intuitions, or even turn reality inside-out and drag the mystick's consciousness in for a chat. The stronger the Avatar, the more obvious its hand, and the more demanding its requests. Sooner or later, a mage must listen; too much conflict may interfere with magick, sleep or sanity.

It may sound from all of this as if the mage is the pawn of the Avatar. While some cynical willworkers believe that this is so (and is, perhaps, the way it should be), most admit that the mage/Avatar relationship is a two-way street. As the Avatar shapes the mystick, so too does the mystick shape his Avatar. For all we know, the Essences might only be the legacies of past lives which have left their imprint upon the Avatars. No one knows for certain. Even if the Essence has no mortal cause, a mage is always free to do what he or she wants to do. The Avatar's urgings only guide the sorcerer. Ultimately, a mage's destiny is his own.

The Technocratic Avatar

Many Technocrats gravitate toward the Union in order to channel the Avatar, so that everything seems rational. Awakening is often a terrifying thing; imagine a voice in your head that tells you constantly that reality is false. And knowing that it's right. Technocracy recruiters do their best to calm a budding willworker and convince him that the best way to handle his new "insights" is to use them to work for the common good. Therapy, counseling and technomagickal treatments ease the stress of Seekings and Epiphanies while also monitoring resident mages for signs of defection or rebellion.

No one knows what the Union's Inner Circle thinks of Avatars. The official party line, however, is that they are manifestations of humanity's inner genius. The dreams, visitations, conflicts and Seekings are merely figments of overtaxed imaginations, subconscious solutions to troubling issues.

They may even be correct.

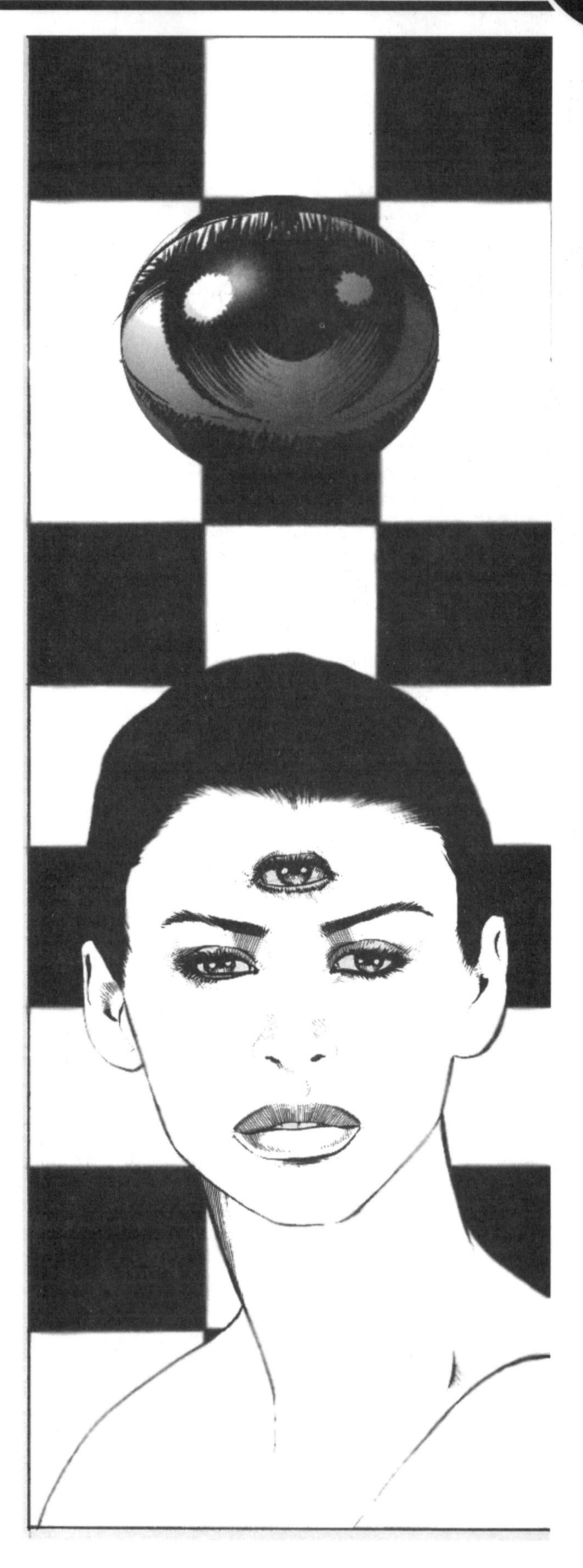

Elements of the Path

No pain, no palm; no thorns, no throne; no gall, no glory; no cross, no crown.
— William Penn

Whatever Path a mage follows, three common elements apply: *awareness*, *conflict* and *resolution*. Almost every mage runs across them at some point, though most see them in different ways. An Iteration X cyborg may have Awakened in wild dreams which he brushed off in the morning. A Dreamspeaker will actively seek her destiny in a visionquest, but may ignore unresolved conflicts. Either mage may die or get stuck before reaching some resolution. So it goes.

Awareness

Though some few Awakened are born aware, many are not. They begin their lives as mundane humans, who often have some sort of "gift" that sets them apart — a hint of precognition, an otherworldly air, exceptional talent, insight or wisdom beyond their years. This early "difference" helps set them up for what happens next.

Mages call themselves the Awakened for a reason. At some crucial point — often a crisis of some kind — that person becomes more and more aware that reality as others perceive it is a sham. This may occur through a gradual build-up or a sudden revelation, though some kind of "tremors" usually foreshadow the Awakening itself. These might include a mentor's formal approach, strange dreams, blackouts, brushes with the supernatural or any number of odd things. Suddenly, these tremors explode, the Avatar reaches out, and the mage Awakens.

Epiphany

Awakening is not simply saying "Wow, man! Magick works!" It is a fourfold embrace — mental, spiritual, physical and intellectual — of the existence of magick. Without it, a person may *see* magick, *feel* magick, *grasp* magick, but never *become* magick. Such Awakening, called an *Epiphany*, is always sudden; the mundane world goes pale and the hidden one bursts into full-color. Some mortals go mad forever upon Awakening and never progress any further than that. Strong-willed mages recover and advance, but they never forget the experience.

While successful Seekings grant further bursts of insight, no later Epiphany can ever match that first moment when a mage truly understands the existence of magick and the nature of the world.

Vision

With Awakening comes an affinity for the hidden world and a vision of the "overall picture." Once a person's eyes are opened this way, they can never close. The mage may never call what he does "magick," but the essential idea — that of changing reality itself through personal will — is universal.

The Path comes through this vision. The mage may never have a literal vision, but the purpose behind it will haunt her until she follows it.

Instruction

An Epiphany is traumatic; everything the person has believed until now turns to dust. Finding a mentor is usually a good idea at this stage; without one, a mage quickly goes out of control or gets swept up in some other supernatural agency's plans. The four great factions and lesser Crafts **(see Chapter Three)** often sow the seeds of Epiphanies among prospective recruits or entice the self-Awakened into their ranks, using anything from friendship to instruction to strong-arm tactics.

If the mage finds a good mentor, she may learn to control her power and advance her understanding of reality in all its aspects. The teacher ideally passes on both his wisdom and his protection. Without either, a newly-born mage may often find herself slaving away under some powerful master or decaying in a nameless grave.

Conflict

At some point in her life, the mage will encounter conflicts, both internal and external. Internal struggles include those with doubt, pride and loneliness, while external battles rage against rival mages, supernatural beings, Sleeper society and reality itself.

Trials

It is not an easy task to be a mage. Doubt and hubris (excessive pride) are constant enemies, and either one can lead a sorcerer to destruction. Even if she triumphs against those, the solitary Path she has chosen will often drive her to regret the day she first Awakened.

Magick requires confidence; without it, reality refuses to conform to your desires or slaps you in the face for your presumption. Shocks to a mage's confidence may cause him to doubt his ability to do what he must. This may paralyze him just when he needs his power most. Overconfidence, however, leads to the hubris that makes horrors out of even the best intentions. *Because I can change reality with my will,* the prideful mage believes, *my will is always correct*. This attitude leads to arrogance, rivalry and eventual stagnation. A prideful wizard may attain great power, but he loses his enlightenment, his purpose and often his friends in the process. Without moderation, he becomes a force for corruption, not growth. The Nephandic Descension, Technocratic Pogrom and Doissetep intrigues are only the most obvious examples of hubris in action.

Humans, too, are a fickle and jealous lot. Although they instinctively bow before someone with power they don't have, such worshippers turn on their "betters" sooner or later. When they do, a mage may find herself running for her life. The Burning Time, when the witchfires raged throughout Europe, was only manipulated, not caused by, the Order of Reason **(see Chapter Three)**. The embers still smolder, waiting to engulf any sorcerer who steps too far out into the public eye. Hence, a mage must hide some part of herself away from the society she once belonged to.

Seekings often turn these conflicts into a gauntlet of trials which the mage must overcome in order to advance. Those who cannot do so stop in their tracks, or falter and decline. Such failures often turn to Infernal powers, magickal Talismans and outside allies when they feel their power slipping away.

Quiet results when a mage slides too far into her own worldview. This madness, which sometimes manifests in solid hallucinations called *hobgoblins*, imprisons the sorcerer in her own mind. It takes a dedicated Seeking or outside aid to free a mystick from Quiet, and the effects may linger for lifetimes to come **(See "Paradox" in Chapter Eight)**.

Warfare

No mage escapes dealings with the outside world. Even hermits who sequester themselves on mountain-tops meet spirits, other mysticks and supernatural creatures. No one makes friends with them all. Unless the mage offers her throat willingly to the first vampire or demon to cross her path, she will, sooner or later, have to fight.

The hidden world teems with enemies — vampires, werewolves, demons, Umbrood, ghosts, rival mages, the spirit-ridden (called fomori by some) and even, it is said, the last of the faeries. The mortal world includes a host of witch-burners, government agents and simple thugs, any one of whom could end one's life. The wise mage knows when (and how) to fight and when to run.

Some mages surrender themselves to such conflicts. War Chantries, Rogue mercenaries and Technocratic death squads see enough combat to make a Marine turn queasy. They do not, however, tend to live long; if an enemy doesn't kill them, Paradox inevitably does.

Intrigue offers a better chance of survival, at the price of paranoia. Magickal enemies can strike at you in any number of ways. Old mysticks, who have left their ideals behind, treasure such rivalries. For them, power-gaming is all they have left. Young sorcerers are advised to tread lightly among those who measure their life spans in national histories; such wizards are indeed subtle and quick to anger.

Paradox is the enemy of all who twist the threads of fate. Unless a willworker is very careful, the weight of consensual reality will squash her like roadkill. Reality is like a river, and each new soul speeds the current. Mages who ignore that current may be swept up by it and drowned.

Resolution

If the mage survives all obstacles, she may reach her ideal Ascension. If not, she falls into whatever trap fate has laid across her Path.

The Fall

This could come in any number of ways — stagnation, corruption, death, madness, slavery and annihilation are only the most obvious.

Stagnation or corruption comes from within. In the first case, the mystick simply surrenders himself to worldly power, loses sight of his goal and becomes a disgrace to his role. He may remain powerful, but he never grows. Sooner or later, his life span becomes an insult to consensual reality, and he is forced to hide in a Realm or some obscure Domain.

Corruption, to the Nephandi, is weakness and the fear of Final Night. To others, it is the point where power-lust blinds the mage and turns her away from her ideals. Some willworkers are corrupted by raw force, others by worldly distractions and still others by Otherworldly influences. In either case, the mystick has lost the Path, possibly for good.

A mage who dies, it is said, returns to the cycle of the Wheel to be reborn. One who makes an Infernal pact (or gives himself to the Higher Powers upon his death) is taken out of this cycle, and his Avatar endures whatever praise or punishment its incarnation earned. Mysticks wonder about the fate of Technocratic Avatars. Although Technomancers theoretically remove themselves from the cycle through their own disbelief, there never seems to be a shortage of such mages. Indeed, the Euthanatos and Akashic Brotherhood once mounted a rare cooperative scheme to take Technomancers "out of the loop;" it failed. Those who study the ways of *Drahma* (the Akashic view of destiny) say that Static Mages, too, play a part in destiny's plan.

Some mages never escape Quiet. These would-be mysticks end up in asylums or homeless shelters, lost in halls of mirrors. Some say Marauders and familiars are in fact mages who lost their sanity forever, but the only way to know for sure is to go mad and see.

Slavery is a cruel end to the Path, whether it comes from the Blood Bond of a powerful vampire, magickal shackles, emotional weakness or captivity in a Realm. A mage who ends up a slave has run the scale from a mover of reality to a mover of shit. Though survival means possible escape, a willworker never heals the scars that slavery brings.

Worst of all are those whose Avatars are demolished through the Gilgul Rite, warped by the vampiric Embrace or sent out into the Deep Umbra to be devoured by Umbrood. Such deaths are eternal, tragic ends to a final Path.

Ascension

Ascension can be global or personal. Even Orphans and Craft mages have some ideal to which they aspire; they just don't put labels on it. The four Ascension War factions, however, are defined by their ultimate goals. The extent to which a member of one of these "teams" actually believes in his professed goal depends upon the mage himself.

To the Technocracy, personal perfection takes a back seat to global unity. Under this vision, all random elements would be stomped out or harnessed for the common good. Eventually, everyone would come to realize that this is the best destiny possible — harmony under the Technocracy's benevolent gaze.

The Marauders seek an end to the order they feel was imposed upon the Earth by too much sanity. Although many of them seem like mere kooks, underneath the delusions, each Marauder sees the primal chaos from which all possibilities spring. It is their goal — when they think about a goal at all — to open that vision to everyone.

Nephandic Ascension is Descension, nothing less than painting the whole world black or dying in the process. Some, it is rumored, want to let demented entities through the barriers between the Otherworlds and our own. Perhaps they just want each of us to let our own inner demons free. In either case, the Fallen Ones seek to bring the world as we know it to an eternal end, to usher in Final Night.

Diversity is sacred to the Council of Nine Traditions. No other faction, with the possible exception of the Marauders, seeks personal Ascension with the Traditions' fervor. To the Council mages, all people should have the potential to grow toward some higher state. Though each Tradition, and each mage within each Tradition, has a different idea of just what Ascension is, all agree that the other groups must not have their way. For the first time in centuries, it appears that the Council may have its wish.

So what happens when a mage Ascends? Who knows? Some say she joins the Oracles in their Umbral paradises (or, in the case of many Technomancers, Autocthonia's fabled Halls of the Machine). Others speak of passage to the Afterlives, ascension into Heaven or withdrawal from all earthly needs. In the modern age, however, all too many mages dismiss personal Ascension as a pipe dream. And that may be the saddest belief of all.

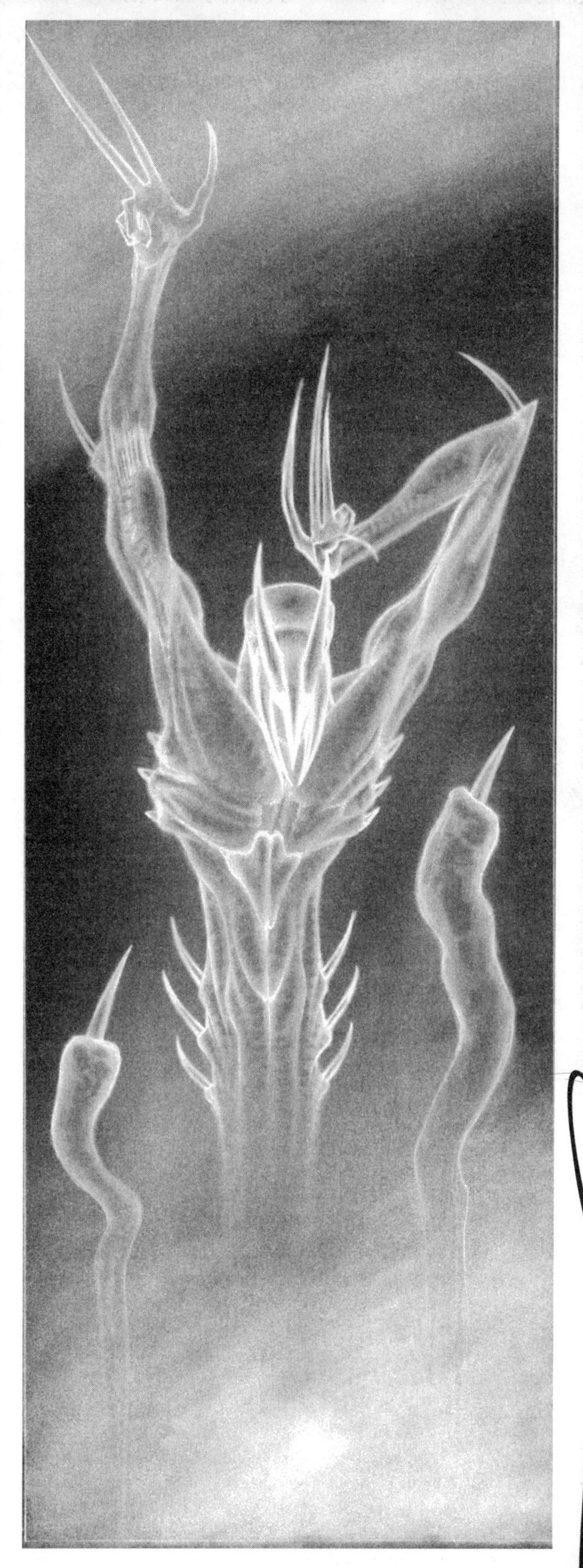

Lovers

Chapter Three: Mage Society

Those who are awake all live in the same world.
Those who are asleep live in their own worlds
— Heraclitus

Clarissa's Seeking

A childlike voice echoed in Clarissa's mind as she peered into the night, curious about this trial of which her mentor had told her nothing.

"For each of us, greater power comes only when we truly know ourselves. This is your test, Clarissa, to know yourself and your limitations. To save yourself. It begins."

Suddenly, Clarissa found herself looking at a child of six. It's me, *she thought wildly.* That child is me! *The younger Clarissa impudently stuck out her tongue and ran into bright moonlight. The older Clarissa followed. Suddenly she was assaulted by a rank odor — she was standing in a heap of garbage behind a scrubby bush alongside a highway. Then she saw the little girl on the other side of the bush, pulling up her underpants.*

"I'm done, I'm done!" she yelled. She emerged from the bushes and ran toward a car.

Clarissa clambered out of the garbage and got another shock.

Oh shit. Oh shit! I'm not me, I'm a man, some kind of homeless person. That stink... it's me! *Clarissa nearly puked. She ran her filthy hands over her body. It was oldish, maybe fifty, with cloudy vision, rotten teeth and rheumatism.*

Then the little girl screamed. Clarissa saw that she cowered before a tall man with bulging muscles and an icy gleam in his eye. Drool fell from the corners of his mouth as he grabbed for the child and missed.

Clarissa clumsily stumbled over to them, shouting, desperate to gain the man's attention, knowing she had to keep him away from the child. She met the man's eyes. "You son of a bitch. If I were really myself, I'd make you scream like a lobster over a slow fire."

He shook his head. "Whatever you say." Forgetting the child, he threw Clarissa onto the hard cement, then grabbed her arm, twisting it behind her back. Clarissa heard a cracking noise as he tore her elbow out of its socket. From far away, a car door slammed, and, turning her head, she saw that the little girl had climbed into a gold Duster, which was now spinning out onto the highway.

The man looked at her glumly. "I don't believe it. Thanks to you, my fun for the evening just got away." He sighed, and with a ferocious kick, busted one of Clarissa's kneecaps. As she screamed, he drew a clawed hand across her face, raking out an eye.

The pain was beyond her comprehension, so harsh she couldn't even scream. It doesn't matter, *thought Clarissa.* It doesn't! I managed to fight him off and save the little girl. That's all that matters. *Her eyes closed as the darkness fell around her, and she knew that in sacrificing herself, she had completed her quest.*

Mage society is a tapestry of its own, woven of mystery, rivalry and myth. It flows from the mage's Path, and from the divergence of those many Paths into a criss-cross of outer warfare and inner peace. From its patterns come the shock waves which shape reality; even the un-Awakened have felt the stones of the mages' Path beneath their feet.

To understand modern mage society, you must start with the foundations of the past. From those roots grew the four factions of the current Ascension War, the outsiders who stand in their shade, and the strongholds from which they conduct their grim campaigns.

The Ascension War

Look outside your window. Do you see the war which rages every minute of every day? Can you hear the cries from the front line as it shifts back and forth across infinity? Of course not — mages are more subtle than that. You may glimpse the casualties — Mrs. Kim, who spontaneously combusted in her apartment, that businessman who turned a corner one day and apparently vanished from existence. For the most part, the mystick warriors use magick to veil their conflicts. It is also true that clashes are as often philosophical as they are physical.

Mages call this invisible, universal conflict the *Ascension War*. At stake is the fate of humanity, our Earth and all of reality. The winners of this war will do more than merely rewrite history — they will draft the future. It shall be their right to decide how (or even if) Man and the universe Ascends. Unlike a mundane war, the Ascension War pits four factions against one another. All climb the same mountain called Ascension, racing to plant their flags atop the myth-shrouded peak. Each faction has chosen to scale a separate face; the differing terrains and vistas reflect the nature of the climbers.

Occasionally, two factions strike an uneasy alliance. Rather than aid one another, allies usually strive to throw down a third. Yet for the most part, no quarter is asked and none given. Most mages feel that Ascension is near. Should any faction falter at this crucial point, it could mean dropping from the race permanently....

The Reckoning

Creation is an ongoing process, and you're either on the bus or left behind. Some Awakened speculate that a Great Reckoning — a massive change — is upon the world, and they're choosing up sides. The Ascension War, which began as a sort of turf battle, has accelerated to the brink of madness. It may have even brought this Reckoning to a head. Introspective types feel that destiny has set its forces up to decide the Reckoning. The mages who believe in it don't know whether they are agents of free will or pawns of destiny.

A History of the Awakened

I will not forget these stones that are set
In a round, on Salsbury Plains
Tho' who brought 'em there, 'tis hard to declare
The Romans, or Merlin, or Danes
— Walter Pope, *The Salsbury Ballad*

The Beginnings

All magick draws from two philosophies: one states that the power to alter reality flows from the enlightened Self, while the other claims that such power comes through communion with mystick entities (or other external forces). Either method allows the mage to manipulate reality by force of will. From these roots, all other refinements of magick evolved.

Mages have always been rare; the shard of Awakened Prime that allows True Magick is the birthright of a precious few. Although world-wide Awakening is theoretically possible, few modern mages believe there was ever a time when anyone who wished to bend reality could simply do so. Through their insights and powers, the workers of magick have guided the course of humanity from the beginning — not through clumsy puppeteering, but by simply being aware. Through the examples they present and the events they set in motion, mages remain a potent, though subtle, force in human development.

When humanity advanced beyond the simple urges of survival and procreation, they longed for some return to the ineffable harmonious state the Pure Ones knew. This urge continues in the form of faith and Awakening, in the need and vision of some higher state: the vision of Ascension.

The earliest mages went by many names; the Verbena refer to the *Wyck*, who wandered the Earth bringing change. The Akashic Brotherhood claims that their Tradition sprang from a single village where all humanity was one, while their Euthanatos rivals find the origin of their magick in the first comprehensions of mortality. Whatever their origins, the first magi are said to have performed great deeds and lived for centuries. Paradox, as we know it, may have existed even then, but the membrane between what was and was not possible must have been a tenuous thing.

From the beginning, the mysticks (who worked magick and called it such) opposed the philosopher-scientists (who believed all phenomena derived from a set pattern of elements and equations). For millennia, the differences between the two were slight. Although many magick-workers banded together into like-minded fellowships, no formal Traditions or Conventions existed. Most magi simply existed on the fringes of mortal society, expanding their power and wisdom and using it for whatever purpose they desired. Some embraced the greater good, and others followed the inner urge of outer darkness. Some went mad while a few simply went off to find their own way. The boundaries of reality were fluid in those days, now called the Low Mythic Ages (from prehistoric times until about three thousand years ago).

As humanity expanded and evolved (with and without the influence of magick and science), the free flow of possibility whirled into separate currents and settled or stagnated. Territorial wars were fought for agriculture, commerce or paradigms; one god's worshippers battled another's; new philosophies and governments strove to replace each other. Tribes, then cities, then nation-states contested for the right to control local beliefs (and thus, reality), though few at the time realized what they were doing. The long-term winners established the "set" of reality in that particular area, deciding by

unconscious consensus what could be "real" and what could not. Most of this battling was unintentional. Over time, however, wise magi realized that paradigms that conformed to their own beliefs and preferences favored them in many ways. These magi sought to establish areas of influence and hold them against all comers. The High Mythic Ages had begun.

It was during this time that boundaries arose between True Magick, which involved the reshaping of reality at will, and static magic, which operated only within narrow confines. As the boundaries of reality narrowed and solidified, some mages noticed that the powers of legend were no longer theirs to command. Eternal life, levitation of mountains or castles, huge storms, otherworldly allies summoned on command — all remained possible, but became more and more difficult to accomplish as time went on. Some of these mages grew frustrated and indulged in greater excesses to drive their magicks; others delved to the roots of observable creation to find tools that worked, and worked often. Different schools of magick evolved, from backwoods witchcraft to high Hermetic Art. Alchemy, high philosophy, miracle working, spirit communion, physical sciences, artifice construction, worship and faith, refinement of the Self and consciousness alteration all were born. The early fellowships solidified into hundreds of guilds, brotherhoods, religions, cults and covens. Many of these groups coexisted in peace, but others warred with each other, either openly or covertly.

The constant strife bred plagues, famines, persecutions and perpetual warfare. The mortal Sleepers, who had neither the talent nor the enlightenment of the True Magi, were caught between factions of science and sorcery. The unenlightened did not need the help of the battling wizards to fight amongst themselves (mankind has always excelled in war), but the vicious battles fought by the mages colored whole areas of the Tapestry. From evil intentions, greater evil and misery sprang. The sins of the few poisoned the well for the many. Paradox, the backlash of wounded reality, drew a noose around fluid magick, and the mortal Sleepers grew disenchanted with those who worked magick.

The Ascension War

The true war for reality began in 1325, when a confederation of philosopher-scientists, then called the Order of Reason, joined together with the tenet that a single unified truth was safer than a thousand possibilities. Sharing a common vision and purpose, the Order declared war on "...Sorcerers, Nightgaunts, Faeries, Boggies, Wytches, Divells, Changelings, Werebeasts, and all divers Creatures of the Night." By promotion of science over mysticism, the Order of Reason sought to break the supernatural hold over mortal humanity.

Their methods ranged from the subtle to the barbaric. While solitary philosophers sought to divine common patterns among the spheres of influence (also called the *Prime Elements* or *Keystones*), the foot soldiers of the Cabal of Pure Thought stomped through Europe, joining mortal witch-hunters and Inquisitors and aiding the hunters with their "God-given" magicks. In the Far East, emperors and shogun sponsored the high philosophers and artificers who granted them power over their foes and subjects. University instructors and religious leaders preached humanity's ascendancy over nature while attacking their mystick rivals. Powerful magicks strengthened the Gauntlet between the worlds of spirit and matter. All the while, Void Seekers plotted their course to the far lands of Africa and the fabled lands across the sea, shaping them to the Order's will and destroying the "random elements" that already existed there. The Pogrom had begun.

The Order's progress was slow but implacable. Although Paradox struck down early technological advances (flying machines, cannons, mechanical soldiers), persistence, ferocious will and subtle paradigm shifting through reeducation eventually paid off. Scientists and philosophers spread the new gospel among the educated few, while the Order's more militant followers drove away or killed the mysticks. Although the concepts of hard science took hold slowly, the solid will of the united Order began a shrinking of possibility that reverberated across the entire world, a deadening process that continues to this day.

The mysticks looked for a scapegoat. At first, they lashed out at each other or the unfortunate Sleepers around them. But as the tide of reality shifted away from them, warfare and plague swept across the settled world. Even native mysticks in far-off Africa and America felt the reverberations. A huge storm was building. Finally, over a century after the founding of the Order, three mages of rival houses — a Hermetic wizard, a Christian mage and a descendant of the primordial Wyck — decided that the infighting must end. With help from other like-minded sorcerers, they traveled the Earth, gathering a convocation of mysticks together for mutual protection and a common purpose. This Grand Convocation took nine years of debate and diplomacy to form. Finally, during Summer Solstice, 1466, the Council of Nine Mystick Traditions was established.

Rallying around "Ascension" and the restoration of wonder, the Traditions brought their own mystick might to bear. Unfortunately, even from the beginning the Council was rocked by setbacks. One Tradition disbanded, another virtually walked out, and internal dissension raged. While many Traditionalists held to the Council's ideals, the Council lacked the Order of Reason's unity and soon fell before them. The Mythic Ages came to a brutal end.

The Age of Reason

Without a strong rival to oppose them, the Order of Reason brought their own version of Ascension to the world. Their vast hubris led them to subjugate all cultures they came across. While many good works were done in the name of science and technology, the Inner Circle of the Order soon became greedy, plundering the riches and resources of faraway lands, capturing and burning all "devil worshippers" and "heretics." Dynamism took hold, but it was Dynamism gone haywire. Although great deeds were performed, entire civilizations were also ravaged. The Tapestry shook as new paradigms and innovations clashed with beliefs that had been established for centuries.

As the Industrial Revolution took off, the ever-present Nephandi latched onto the greed of the Technomancers, leading the visionaries to greater and greater evils. The Marauders, who had always lived along the fringes, exploded; once rare, they increased in number and power, seemingly oblivious to the ever-tightening grip of Paradox. The Traditions continued to squabble or else hid themselves away. African and Native American mages brought grievances against their European brethren in Council, but were rebuffed. Many among them quit the Council altogether and returned to defend their homelands. The Order of Reason, reorganizing under the name of the Technocratic Union, or the *Technocracy*, took full advantage of the erupting chaos.

The mystic backlash of the 1800s and the addition of two new and unpredictable Technomancer groups (the Sons of Ether and Difference Engineers) gave the Tradition mages an extra edge. Subtle wizards, meanwhile, reminded a future-shocked world of their wondrous past. Primitivism, occultism, radical art, religious

revival and ethnic resurgence captured imaginations across the civilized world, undermining the Technocratic paradigm. Social unrest and the evolution of new political theories also aided the mysticks' cause. When the Sons of Ether defected from the Order of Reason, the long-vacant ninth seat was filled and the Council's fortunes took a turn for the better. Soon after, however, the Ahl-i-Batin left the Council, disgusted with the Traditions' seeming indifference to the invasion of their homelands. Once again, the Council members numbered only eight.

The Technocracy, reputedly under the direction of Queen Victoria, gave itself a face-lift. The Seekers of the Void left Earth to shore up the Horizon between the Near and Deep Umbrae. The last vestiges of God-faith were purged from the new Machine, and the race for new and better devices — flying machines, automobiles, tanks, machine guns, poison gas — was on.

Wars

The First World War slapped the Technocrats across the face — hard. Its horrors shattered the ideals of the once-benevolent Order, and a schism erupted. Nephandi fed on the sudden hopelessness of the post-war generation, casting their influence across men and women of power. In the vacuum, the Traditions were able to secure a foothold, spreading their own influence through fiction and art. The Second World War tore through both groups, pitting mages against one another along national lines.

The Technocratic Inner Circle voted at first to support the Axis powers in the name of a worldwide Union. Nearly half of the assembled Symposium walked out in disgust. Even the most loyal Technomancers began to work against Hitler's plans when the depths of his madness became wholly apparent. Purges and vendettas raged within the Technocratic halls as war machines unlike anything previously imagined rolled off hideously effective assembly lines. The Council, crippled by constant infighting and the defection of the Ahl-i-Batin, divided as well. Many Hermetics, Sons of Ether and Verbena threw in with the Axis, and Japanese Akashic mages battled their Chinese Brothers. Tradition and Convention alike splintered to fight each other. The Akashic Brotherhood and Iteration X were hit hardest by this shock wave, and the Virtual Adepts openly defied their Inner Circle superiors to support the Allies. Numerous Marauders Awakened (or went Wyld) during the war, adding their own chaos to the mix. The Nephandi, meanwhile, bathed in the horrors that were born from the war.

Rumors claim that as the body counts grew, the Inner Circle suffered its own internal battle. Those Technomancers who supported the cause of the Allies won, and they formed a brief alliance with Tradition mages to expel the most powerful Nephandi to the outer darkness. Like the wartime Sleeper alliance, this joint venture fell apart as soon as the war ended. Word of the Technomancer revolt was hushed up, and the Pogrom resumed. The Virtual Adepts, decimated by the Technocratic takeover of their homelands, defected to fill the Ahl-i-Batin's seat. From the chaos of the war and its aftermath, all sides suffered. The death of Virtual Adept Alan Turing tore a hole from the material world into the virtual reality called the Net, creating a new front for the ongoing War, and the shadows of mass media, pollution, weaponry and nuclear power stacked the deck in the Technocracy's favor — for now.

The post-war reorganization left all four major factions with strong gains over the previous century. The Council stands nine strong for the first time in centuries. Many Sleepers have grown wary of science and seek other answers — answers the Traditions can supply. The magicks of the Technocracy have become a paradigm that stretches worldwide, and the Technocrats now command a huge pool of Sleepers. The Nephandi have a strong link to late-century disillusionment and corruption, and the Marauders have grown to numbers never known before. As the millennium approaches, the four factions gather their forces and take stock of their resources. Each has its own specific goal: Ascension for the Traditions, global security for the Technocracy, unbridled change for the Marauders and final destruction for the Nephandi. All mages have a vision. The coming years may decide who — if anyone — wins.

Factions: Who's Who

Who goes there?

— traditional hail of the sentinel

There is strength in numbers, and very few True Mages exist. Although some mysticks refuse to choose sides in (or acknowledge) the War, the majority of today's Awakened find themselves affiliated — willingly or otherwise — with one of the four great factions. Their "turf" is just too large to ignore. Those few regions left outside the "modern world" sit on the fringe of the battle (for now), but since reality belongs to whomever holds the largest paradigm, neutral ground is hard to come by. The Ascension War may be a form of magickal imperialism, but it's not going to end anytime soon. The stakes are too high.

These four descriptions are generalizations only; mysticks are individuals, not labels. All societies have their common ground, however, and it is always good policy to know where you stand among peers — or enemies.

The Council of Nine Mystick Traditions

The Company of the Ring shall be Nine; and the nine walkers shall be set against the Nine Riders that are evil.

—J.R.R. Tolkien, *The Fellowship of the Ring*

Innumerable arcane traditions both magical and magickal have long considered "nine" to be a particularly potent number. In Hermetic numerology, "nine" represents the Mage bearing the Lamp of Enlightenment throughout Reality. Nine is also the peak of power and experience in a nine-phase cycle, and represents the perfection of mind and spirit.

The Council of Nine attempts to harness this destiny. Throughout its history, however, it has failed to fill all nine seats for any length of time. Eight — a number which signifies the mundane world and all its trappings — has long been its fate.

But now some small hope appears. After many years, the Council of Nine has recently reached full strength once again. Though outnumbered, Tradition mages anticipate that their nine-for-one and one-for-nine unity will provide a numerological edge. They have two other arguable advantages: their magick is more versatile, and their ideals of individual freedom within a societal context appeal to more Sleepers than the creeds of other factions.

In a black-and-white world, these mysticks would be considered champions of good. Unfortunately, reality is in truth a mottled gray. The Council has its share of flaws, and each Tradition its misguided members.

Assembling the Council

Walk awhile, walk awhile
Walk awhile with me
The more we walk together, love
The better we'll agree

— Fairport Convention, "Walk Awhile"

The forerunners of the nine Traditions were mysticks who valued wisdom and faith, and benefited most from the fluid reality of the Low Mythic Age. Two such groups, the Order of Hermes and the Celestial Chorus, even helped develop Europe's High Mythic Age. All mysticks — whether Bacchanalian, witch or adherents of other beliefs — thrived in this atmosphere of faith and superstition.

One winter day in 1210, the Hermetic Chantry Mistridge in southern France toppled before peasants armed with cannons and techniques of anti-magick. Similar coups occurred all over Europe and the Far East. Soon after, the newly-formed Inquisition began to persecute mysticks and hapless Sleepers. Mage blamed mage, and they began to fight among themselves.

Faced with the very real threat of extermination, three magi met to discuss opposition to the Order of Reason: Baldric of the Order of Hermes, Nightshade of the Verbena and Valoran of the Celestial Chorus. They agreed to go forth and gather all sympathetic mages before returning to Mistridge for a key Tribunal. This Grand Convocation began in 1457. Among the principal mages were Ali-beh-shaar of the Ahl-i-Batin, Star-of-Eagles and Niaoba of the Dreamspeakers, Chalech the Euthanatos, Sh'Zar the Cultist of Ecstasy, Wu Jin of the Akashic Brotherhood and Diplomate Luis of the Solificati. Many other mages were present as well. As a demonstration of their unity, each group donated one Node in order to create a common Chantry, Horizon **(see the Appendix)**.

For nine years they met. They argued ideology and direction, formalized magick into Spheres and mysticks into Traditions, and agreed upon ranks of knowledge, Protocol and other aspects of mage society. Then on Summer Solstice 1466, they announced the formation of the Council of Nine. Suddenly, the future seemed less grim. The Order of Hermes played up the numerological import of nine, and that number became a lasting symbol of hope.

The Council's first joint action was to appoint the First Cabal, a group of nine Adepts whose task it was to traverse the earth and gather support among Sleeper and Awakened alike, spreading goodwill and opposing the Order of Reason, the Nephandi and other enemies. The venture was a terrible failure. Heylel Teomim the Solificato was corrupted, and in 1470, he betrayed his companions to the Cabal of Pure Thought (Inquisitor predecessors of the New World Order). Three mages died in combat, and four were captured. A troupe of Tradition mages eventually rescued the prisoners and hunted down the traitor. Heylel was sentenced to Gilgul and death. Unfortunately, the damage was already done. The betrayer's Tradition, the Solificati, disbanded after the scandal. The portentous Nine had failed. Losing confidence, the Council became fragmented, its unity hamstrung by the bitter rivalries between the Akashics and Euthanatos, Verbena and Celestial Chorus, and the various Hermetic Houses in general. Many Dreamspeakers went home in disgust, and Horizon itself seemed hollow and useless. The next 400 years went poorly.

In 1904, the Sons of Ether requested a seat on the Council. In their desire to fill the ninth seat, the Traditions put aside any reservations concerning these mages' previous Technocratic status. The Sons took the Seat of Matter, previously occupied by their Solificati predecessors. The Council's sense of completion was only temporary, as the Ahl-i-Batin withdrew in 1934 to defend their homeland from oil-greedy Technocrats.

Then, in 1961, a second Convention defected to the Council. The Virtual Adepts took the Seat of Correspondence, still warm from the Batini representative. For the first time in centuries, the Council of Nine had (and still has) the long-sought mystic number of nine members. The synergy is so unlike anything felt previously, even during the Grand Convocation, that none foresee a parting of ways. Only good can come of it.

But now the Hollow Ones have appeared, unaccounted for. Clearly, Tradition mages do not want them to join the Technocracy; yet those who heed the Prophecy of Nine fear that their joining the Council would ruin all for which it has striven. For their part, the Hollow Ones thumb their noses at the Council, claiming they do not care for a seat. Yet they hang around like strays at the edge of a pack. For now, the Hollow Ones remain loners.

Is ten the real number the Council has long awaited? In numerology, ten equals one (10=1+0=1) — unity, activation and a new beginning faced with innocent courage.

The Modern Traditions

Akashic Brotherhood

While most Traditions tread the path of Ascension, Akashic Brothers positively flow along its course. They pursue the path of least resistance, not because that Way is any easier, but because it's more natural. Akashic Brothers believe that one must understand one's Self before one can understand All. Only by perfecting body and mind, and by creating harmony between them, can one understand one's place in the Cosmic All. This end is true enlightenment — and Ascension.

In sanctifying a temple of the Self, the Brotherhood meld seclusion with mental and physical exercise. Together, this amalgam of martial arts and meditation is known as Do, or "The Way" of life. Renowned for their deep introspection, the Akashic Brotherhood appropriately occupies the Council Seat of Mind.

Celestial Chorus

High upon the Seat of Prime, the Primus of the Celestial Chorus observes his spiritual domain. He sees that humanity has forsaken faith in favor of reliance upon cold and impersonal technology. This is a sad fall from the Middle Ages, when the Christian Church dominated Europe and spirituality pervaded all the world. Yet all is not lost. As the darkness of the world deepens, strays return to the fold. If the Celestial Chorus can outlast the night, morning will bring this Tradition great influence.

The Chorus sees its magick in a religious framework. All houses of worship — temple, mosque and church — are considered equal under the sun; all godheads are but shards of the shattered One. Above all, Chorus members are concerned with the well-being of humanity. As Good Samaritans and religious leaders, they serve Sleepers by maintaining a vigilance against evil, tending to those in need, and providing guidance through example or word.

Cult of Ecstasy

From the cults of Bacchus to Woodstock, there have always been those who believe that free action and self-expression can lead to something greater, whether this is heightened awareness or revolution. The Cult of Ecstasy was formed by such people. In the realm of their experience, no stimuli can be ignored. They open the floodgates to all six passions: taste, touch, hearing, sight, smell and awareness. A Cultist can find deep meaning in a gourmet meal or home-brewed alcohol, dance or love-making, heavy metal or sonnets, Cubist art or psychedelic drugs. All passions are constructive in their way.

Cultists rarely push their agenda; every Cultist (and like-minded Sleeper) is left to his own devices. At the same time, no one will take responsibility for his actions but himself. Paradoxically, this most uninhibited Tradition is also one of the most disciplined.

The Cult of Ecstasy occupies the Seat of Time.

Dreamspeakers

From prehistoric times, Dreamspeakers have wandered the meandering paths of Ascension alone, meeting occasionally to compare journeys but more often communicating through spirit messengers. With the aid of drum-beats and other rituals, these shamans enter the Dreamlands and converse with spirits; many even shapechange into the animal-forms of their guardian familiars. Dreamspeakers are one of the two most primal of Traditions — those who seek insight and attunement with the Worlds. They work less from *service* than from *respect* and *harmony*. Nevertheless, they can be quite brutal. Nature magick often requires self-mortification or symbolic death.

Undisputed masters of animism, Dreamspeakers occupy the Seat of Spirit.

Euthanatos

The Euthanatos use Entropy to reduce and recycle. Without some breaking-down, they know, reality would become dense and unyielding — a static set-piece rather than a dynamic experiment. One means of ensuring this is to deliver the Good Death upon those who are ready to die — those who take life's gift too lightly, or have suffered but cannot heal. The spirits of those dead may then reincarnate into more productive forms. Their seat, of course, is Entropy.

Though many Euthanatos kill, few enjoy it. They mourn deeply for every loss of life, so as not to forget the gravity of their charge. Thus, they often seem dour and distant. Yet Euthanatos do not fear death, either; every apprentice visits the Other Side during initiation, and the Ever-Turning Wheel assures them that death is only temporary.

Order of Hermes

The Order of Hermes traces its magickal Tradition to ancient Egypt and the near East. Once, their Houses included nearly a dozen different magickal societies, each practicing an elaborate ritual Art. Fate's fortunes, however, have since thrown them all together and cost them much of the power they once held.

Proud and select, Hermetic mages are jealous of their secrets. They conceal their Arts in arcane tongues, numbers, rituals, complex calculations and metaphors such as the Tarot. Their most elaborate schemes are reserved for the destruction of the Technocracy, who brought their treasured Mythic Age to a premature end. Persistent and patient, these masters of Force magicks, occupying the Seat of Forces, are content to manipulate politics, finance and education — for now. But when the stars are right....

Sons of Ether

The Sons of Ether are a wacky and diverse lot. Equally comfortable with cigar and brandy or aviator goggles, lab coats and particle rays, they are one part Buck Rogers, another part Proper Victorian, and a third part Mad Scientist. As many Technocrats could confirm, this is a volatile mix.

To understand the Sons of Ether (if that is indeed possible), one must grasp three basic tenets. First, they believe that True Science is Art, an expression of the human spirit. Every machine should reflect the unique inner vision of its creator. Inspiration is beauty, even if the final product appears quirky to others, and since this Science is personal, no theory can be proven "wrong." Second, the role of Science is to bring peace to the world (*á la* Captain Nemo) and Awaken humanity. Finally, the unseen, ever-present "fifth essence," Ether, must become a prominent part of any theory, experiment or device — if for no other reason than it exists.

After defecting from the Technocracy to the Traditions, the Sons of Ether accepted the long-vacant Seat of Matter.

Verbena

"Verbena" is the Latin name for vervain, an herb with manifold properties, both real and imagined. Through the ages, it has been held as a miracle plant. Romans used it to consecrate temples; herbalists included it in love potions; superstitious peasants believed it warded against witches. Ingesting this herb causes nausea. Each of these aspects make "Verbena" an appropriate name for the Tradition that occupies the Seat of Life.

Verbena are fate-weavers and rune-cutters, shapechangers and bewitchers, herbalists and midwives dedicated to learning the secrets of healing and life, pain and death. To them, Life is the most potent force in existence. The growing ash can crack mountains. The living cauldron, the womb, is a constant source of generation, unequaled since original Creation. Thus each body is a sacred shrine; the substance and power of body — blood, sap and other life-giving fluids — serve as sacraments. Life, therefore, is their specialty and their chosen seat in Council.

Virtual Adepts

Virtual Adepts invented "morphing," cyberpunk and interactive video, and perfected the computer as a means for people to reach beyond a hopeless world. Champions of the Fifth Amendment, these hackers liberate the most sensitive information and post it on public BBSs. Virtual Adepts, it is said, were responsible for a practical joke which sidetracked the FBI toward an anonymous roleplaying publisher in Texas, instead of their own subversive front company.

The Virtual Adepts discovered and refined the Digital Web (or Net). This alternate reality, they believe, will become humanity's new home. Having heard about their explorations of the Net, the Council offered the Seat of Correspondence to the Virtual Adepts. These ex-Technocrats gladly accepted.

Past (and Future?) Traditions

• **Ahl-i-Batin:** The "lost" Ahl-i-Batin (singular *Batini*) trace their origin to a union of two renegade off-shoots: Akashic refuges of the Himalayan Wars and Ecstatic dervishes fleeing persecution. They met in Afghanistan, merged and formed a most mysterious magickal Tradition.

From their beginnings, the Batini were always cunning, secretive and adept at working within Sleeper society. Indeed, Ahl-i-Batin means "The Subtle Ones." They feared many enemies, and so maintained a distance from other mages. At the same time, they were ever concerned with unifying various mystick fellowships into one, for Batini philosophy was concerned with how the One fits into the Many. According to their Doctrine of Unity, each view of Ascension is merely a separate facet of a single jewel. This helps explain why the Batini Tradition — itself consisting of many disparate groups — worked so passionately to help form the Council of Nine.

The Ahl-i-Batin are best remembered for three feats. It was they who created (or discovered) Mount Qaf, that wondrous Realm which focused their Web of Faith — a mandala-like pattern of Nodes — across North Africa, the Middle East and Central Asia. They influenced this vast region by means of a telepathic intercommunication network, which was instrumental for the establishment of the Council of Nine. Before leaving the Council, they occupied the Seat of Correspondence (now held by the Virtual Adepts).

The Tradition has since vanished, and is generally believed to have disbanded or been destroyed after the Technocracy entered the Middle East to secure the oil fields. Mount Qaf has been lost for almost a century. However, odd rumors now drift across the Batini homelands, whispering of strange towers and reclusive *shi'ir* (sorcerers) who appear and disappear with the desert storms. Perhaps the Batini merely hide and watch, waiting for their chance to strike.

• **The Solificati:** The Solificati (singular *Solificato*), the self-titled "Crowned Ones," no longer exist. Their Tradition faltered in the wake of the Great Betrayal and collapsed under its own infighting. Few were sorry to see them go.

Unlike the Ahl-i-Batin, this Tradition had few allies outside the Hermetic Houses. Composed of magickal alchemists and artificers, these ancient Technomancers sided with the Council largely out of loyalty to the Hermetics and distrust of the Craftmasons. Infamous for their secrecy and haughtiness, the Solificati drew their membership almost exclusively from Europe's bluest blood and Arabia's brightest royalty. When they parted ways with the mysticks, many took their secrets to the Artificers and Hippocratic Circle (now called Iteration X and the Progenitors), or departed for private practice.

Rumor has it that the Solificati still survive as a Craft called the Children of Knowledge, in an Umbral Citadel. The truth remains unknown.

• **Hollow Ones:** This modern "street Tradition" has never been formally invited to join the Council. Indeed, many older mages look with horror on these Gothic Orphans and shoo them on their way. Yet many progressive Tradition sorcerers see these survivors as an asset the Council could dearly use. The time, however, has not yet come.

More Goth than punk, Hollow Ones are not predators but a species perfectly adapted to survive and prosper in a desperate urban environment. Most seem to have little interest in Ascension; judging from the sad state of the present, they feel it's futile to hope for the future. Instead, they find beauty in the *danse macabre*. This dark sensibility draws them to the occult and urges them to seek out other denizens of the hidden world. Despair and cynical humor shape the "hollow" in the Hollow Ones.

Several envoys have gone to Horizon in recent years; all have been rebuffed. The winds of change blow strongly now, and the Hollow Ones long to belong, much as they deny it. Someday, perhaps soon, the Council will take them up on their offer.

The Ties That Bind

The Council is not a unified pillar of strength. Rather, it consists of nine separate columns upholding an intersecting fan vault of wisdom. Though the tracery varies from column to column, there are many shared elements, such as the benefit of universal Ascension and the worth of humanity.

Mutual support has allowed the Council to survive half a millennium of disputes, betrayals, set-backs, purges and persecution. Although their Arts span the spectrum of possible magickal styles, each Tradition recognizes the true nature of what they do. Even the Technomancers among them eventually understand that science is just another form of magick.

• **Ascension**

The Traditions believe in an interaction between personal enlightenment and the development of humanity. Mages should be exemplars of their philosophy. If those values are true, the Sleepers will eventually realize it. No mage, says the Council, has the right to impose a paradigm on humanity.

When humanity has perfected itself, reality will advance to the next — though perhaps not the final — stage.

• **Sleepers**

The Traditions share a general compassion for Sleepers. Everyone has a right to personal fulfillment. All cultures deserve enlightenment.

Ironically, Tradition mages have charged themselves with the well-being of people whose skepticism reinforces the scientific paradigm and makes magick so difficult. This is a part of what makes a mage's struggle so heroic.

• **Horizon Chantry**

The Council shares a meeting Chantry called Horizon, where they hold major meetings every nine years and informal gatherings more frequently. Horizon is a rallying point for all Tradition mages and a symbol of the Council's unity. **(See the Appendix for more about Horizon and other Tradition Chantries.)**

Tribunals

Tribunals are gatherings where Tradition mages meet to discuss serious matters. Such Tribunals might concern a Master's (or Tradition's) defection, a sudden thrust by the Technocracy, a renegade Umbrood or the judgment of a mage who has seriously broken Protocol.

Any mage can attempt to call a Tribunal; whether the summoning is taken seriously depends on her status and the import of her claim. Matters which interest a single Tradition are usually discussed at an Ancestral Chantry. Inter-Tradition conflicts or concerns are convened at mutually accessible locations or perhaps even at Horizon. Those who call the Tribunal bring it to order; other Masters conduct the meeting.

Should a Tribunal be called on to pass sentence on a mage, they may select one of several punishments.

• Censure

This mild punishment puts a mage on "parole" for an indefinite period. He must follow the Tribunal's restrictions on travel, association with people or use of magick. The Tribunal may require some service to be completed before the Censure is lifted.

• Branding

With this punishment, the offender's Avatar is marked by Spirit magick. Each unique sigil marks him as an offender of a specific Protocol. The brand can be detected by simple Spirit magick or a mage's Awareness. Branding is often used in conjunction with another punishment, such as Ostracism.

• Ostracism

Banishment can range from a month to life, during which time no other mage may associate with him. Those who do risk Censure or worse.

• Death

The death sentence is applied when a mage has committed serious crimes, like betrayal or Infernalism (traffic with demons), though his Avatar is innocent. Released from its mortal coil, the Avatar can reincarnate into a more honorable mage. This punishment is common among the Euthanatos.

• Gilgul

Gilgul is reserved for mages so evil that even their Avatars have been corrupted, or, more rarely, for hapless mortals born with the recycled Avatars of Nephandi.

An assembly of Masters rip out and destroy the Avatar. The mage is unharmed, but left a powerless husk; he will never again work magick. This is a horrible fate, considered worse than death by some. Deeply diminished, most mages lose the will to live, yet lack the volition to end their existence.

Protocols

The Protocols are ancient customs which all Tradition mages are expected to follow. Some are common courtesy, while others are taken very seriously. Those who break Protocol are first rebuked, then punished in various ways. This depends on the mood of the judges, and the power and status of the offender. Lesser offenses are dealt with within the offender's peer group. More serious offenses result in a Tribunal.

The Protocols and appropriate Hermetic punishments are listed below. Since Protocols are interpreted differently by each Tradition, punishment could vary.

• Respect those of Greater Knowledge.

This is common sense.

• A Tutor's debt must be repaid.

Hermetic Colleges expect tuition after each semester. Students who miss payment are subject to suspension from classes until they do pay. If the student manages to leave a string of institutions in the lurch and is caught, she is Branded. The offender will never again receive training from any Tradition mage.

• A mage's Word is his Honor; break not a sworn Vow.

Censure is the most common punishment. A mage with a long history of lying may be Branded.

• The Will of an Oracle must always be obeyed.

Few modern mages even believe that Oracles exist. However, the Order's ancient legal texts advocate Censure for disloyal mages. Such passages present a paradox: Did Oracles once exist? And if so, should not a miffed Oracle be powerful enough to execute his own sentence, depending on whim?

• Betray not your Cabal or Chantry.

A serious offense during the Ascension War, betrayal warrants Branding and/or permanent Ostracism.

• Conspire not with enemies of Ascension.

Those caught conspiring with the Technocracy, Marauders or other enemies (open to interpretation) are sentenced to Branding and permanent Ostracism. If the "enemy of Ascension" is a Nephandus, the punishment is increased to Gilgul and/or death.

• Protect the Sleepers; they are ignorant of what they do.

This, too, is custom. Those who endanger Sleepers are frowned upon by most mages.

• Be subtle in your Arts, lest Sleepers know you for what you are.

Called the "Rule of Shade," this informal Protocol was meant to protect magi from witch-hunters and zealots. While this rule carries no formal punishment, flashy mages are dangerous to associate with. Ostracism is common, and Branding is not unheard of.

Certamen

Certámen is a means of solving disputes too minor for a Tribunal. Often, it is a matter of personal honor or simple rivalry. Rules and formality ensure that this magickal duel presents no risk to Sleepers or to the mages themselves.

The duel begins when one mage challenges another. The challenged is under no obligation to accept, but risks losing honor (and with no risk of injury, he has little reason to decline). Since certámen is highly vulgar, the duelists must meet at a special certámen circle (available at most Chantries) or tempt Paradox. A Certámen Marshall presides to ensure the safety and honor of both parties.

The rules and formalities are extremely elaborate. Simply put, each mage manifests one Sphere he commands to form a magickal *Gladius* (sword), and another, an *Aegis* (shield). They then place all of their personal Quintessence in a *Locus* (magickal reservoir). The goal is for each mage to strike the opponent's Locus (thus draining Quintessence) while protecting her own. One wins by emptying the opponent's Locus. The winner keeps the Quintessence and can demand satisfaction, which usually has been determined beforehand. The stakes can range from apology or payment to service or exile.

A variety of other duels exist, from physical combat to shapeshifting contests, riddle games, intellectual challenges and flat-out magickal brawls. No other option, however, is readily accepted throughout the Council.

Ranks and Titles

Uneasy lies the head that wears a crown

— William Shakespeare, *King Henry IV, Part II*

The Traditions have titles which rate a mage's relative enlightenment and affinity with a chosen Sphere. Titles may be granted for exceptional deeds, feats of magick, age or even whim. A mage who cannot support a title, however, soon loses it.

Sphere aptitude is the most common way of measuring titles in the modern Traditions. A mystick new to magick is often considered an *apprentice*, even if she receives no instruction at this time. When she demonstrates fair control over a Sphere, she may be elevated to *Disciple*. The title *Adept* comes with greater command; the coveted *Master* rank is only formally granted when she attains the highest common mastery of her Art. For game purposes, these reflect Sphere ranks of one-two (apprentice), three (Disciple), four (Adept), and five (Master). An old mage might be Master of several Spheres. Note that such advancement recognizes power over understanding. Some claim this hierarchy encourages hubris; a mage who races to master a Sphere most likely desires power over understanding.

These terms were chosen back in 1466 to be generic titles of address. Only the Order of Hermes and Celestial Chorus are remotely happy with them. Other Traditions use their own terms; the Sons of Ether, for instance, use Student, Scientist, Professor, Doctor and Master Scientist. Several Traditions (Dreamspeakers, Verbena and Virtual Adepts, for example) bestow no such ranks or use more appropriate honorifics.

The Oracles

The powers, goals and even the existence of these godlike beings are subject to dispute. Some claim that a mage-turned-Oracle Ascends to a higher plane of existence; others claim that Oracles exist only in myths. Strange beings that rule Otherworldly realms claim to be Oracles, but could just as easily be powerful mages, gods, spirits or aliens.

These nagging doubts aside, the consensus holds that Oracles do exist. Most mages who have Mastered a Sphere leave Earth to pursue a place among the Oracles. One must find them first (a task in itself), then gain acceptance by serving as Postulant for a probationary period. Rejected mages supposedly have their Avatars marked. This assertion is difficult to prove, since no failures have been identified. Perhaps true enlightenment, once glimpsed but known to be unattainable, is enough to sap the will from a rejected Postulant. Those who are accepted become Oracles. Rumors suggest that one Oracle must Ascend or die before another is allowed into the ranks.

It is commonly believed that Oracles dwell in distant regions of Earth's Umbra. There are said to be but nine orders of Oracle, one for each Sphere. Marauders, Technomancers and Tradition mages presumably cast aside their petty bickering at this level as they recognize the profound truth about Ascension. At least, this is what optimistic Utopians believe.

Oracles must be powerful beyond imagining. If they exist, they rarely appear in person and would probably not be recognized for what they are. Yet a common and recurring urban myth tells of a mysterious stranger who appears leaning against a street lamp and offers aid to a desperate mage. He never identifies himself as an Oracle, but the help he provides is clearly beyond all known magick (time travel is a typical element). *Caveat auditor*.

The Technocratic Union

If sex is the last subversive act, technology is the only faith remaining after politics and religion have betrayed us.

— Steve Erickson, "Sex 1999," *Details Magazine*

The modern age belongs to the Technocracy, a looming menace of monolithic proportions. As architects of the modern paradigm, they have the most at stake when any other faction tampers with reality. Thus, they crack down hard on revolutionaries and deviants.

It was not always this way....

The Call to Order

The striking thing about the 12th century is the attitudes of its scientists... daring, original, inventive, skeptical of traditional authorities... determined to discover purely rational explanations of natural phenomena.

— Richard Dales, *Scientific Achievement*

Each Convention of the Technocracy traces its individual origin to a specific point in history. Though the Conventions themselves did not exist for millennia to come, Iteration X claims to have been responsible for taming fire and creating the first stone tools between two million and one million years ago. Early Progenitors introduced domestication to the Masses around 6000 B.C. With gift economies and trade (about 3000 B.C.) appeared forerunners of the Syndicate. From as early as 2500 B.C., Void Engineers were using astronomy and the wheel to seek out strange new places. The New World Order has been variably dated to the Imperial Legalists of 5th-century China, the Knights Templar, Inquisitors from around A.D. 1200 or the court of Queen Victoria (this is due to the Convention's penchant for misinformation).

But the history of the Technocracy as a whole really begins with the Convention of the White Tower, in March of 1325. Philosopher-scientists of all types gathered at a tower seized from a dying mystick to discuss what they saw as a desperate situation. The decline of classical culture in Europe had been a powerful blow to the forces of enlightened reason. Lost were Greek science, Roman architecture and urban life. In Asia and the Middle East, philosophers played second fiddle to magicians and wizard-kings while the common people starved. The forces of reason had had enough.

The Mythic Age was great... for the Awakened. Humanity in general was helpless before the supernatural, and the dominant mysticks failed in their responsibility. Wizards quested after magickal arts while forgetting their oaths to the common man. Priests strove to comprehend a distant God but could not hear their neighbors' cries.

The philosopher-scientists agreed to champion the Masses. In working toward this goal, they established the Order of Reason. The initial founders included Artificers, explorer-astronomers called Void Seekers, the doctors of the Hippocratic Circle, Guild members, and Inquisitors from the Cabal of Pure Thought. (Ironically, those responsible for organizing the Convocation, the Craftmasons, have all but disappeared from the record.)

To defend humanity from supernatural threats, the Order of Reason implemented a threefold agenda. First, they infiltrated the schools, courts, guildhalls, monasteries and throne rooms with philosophers and scribes who discredited the mysticks and the denizens of the hidden world. Meanwhile, powerful Artificers and Inquisitors declared war on those denizens, hunting down vampires, faeries, ghosts, rogue mages and other threats and strengthening the Gauntlet. Finally, they gave humanity the ability to protect itself with the repeatable magick of science and universal talismans in the form of technology.

Within a few hundred years, the Order made great gains, especially in Europe. The Guild acquired dominance over European trade, craft and banking, as exemplified by the Medici family's rising fortune during the 15th century. Once the Gutenberg printing press had been introduced in 1438, the Cabal of Pure Thought quickly undermined the Church by distributing vernacular Bibles. The new abundance of books also gave the Masses instant knowledge in the guise of wisdom, knowledge which often suited the Order's needs. Artificers applied mathematics to perspective drawing, changing painting, sculpture and architecture by emphasizing proportion and symmetry. Under the healing hands of the Hippocratic Circle, Renaissance medicine disproved spontaneous generation with the discovery of sperm cells in semen. Meanwhile, the Artificers presented the universe as a perfect and efficient machine (as in Kepler's *Harmony of the World*), and invented firearms, industrial machinery, new instruments and tools. Finally, the Void Seekers inspired curiosity in such explorers as Vasco da Gama and Christopher Columbus. By any means they chose, they spread their version of order and reason across the globe.

This early work helped the Masses. The Gauntlet thickened in the wake of common rationality (and potent technomagick). The lines between what was and was not possible narrowed. Supernatural beings retreated from earth or became more cautious in their dealings with mortals. Humanity embraced science and technology. These accomplishments, in and of themselves, were good things, and the Order prospered.

But somewhere down the line, the Order of Reason lost sight of their goals. Invention and structure became ends in and of themselves. During the Industrial Revolution, Artificers introduced factories and the modern work ethic to churn out innovation upon innovation, without thought for their effects upon the Masses. The Guild encouraged mass production, *laissez-faire* economics and colonialism. The Cabal of Pure Thought stopped revealing truths to the Masses, and began restructuring their perception of history through archaeology and geology. The Hippocratic Circle lost interest in healing humans and considered how they could be improved through accelerated evolution. The Void Seekers remained true to their goal of exploration; the native cultures they encountered, however, were brutally enslaved, assimilated or destroyed.

During the mid-1800s, two new Conventions appeared. The Electrodyne Engineers were "mad scientists" who favored cast-off theories and Utopian ideals. Difference Engineers devoted themselves to exploring Babbage's crude computational device and, later, the telephone network of Alexander Graham Bell. Both groups, though radical and rebellious, were still nominally part of the Order of Reason.

Around the turn of the 20th century, the Order of Reason modernized (under the supposed guidance of Queen Victoria), becoming the Technocratic Union, or Technocracy. All remaining religious elements were jettisoned in favor of hard reason, and the Conventions were renamed to keep with current trends. The Cabal of Pure Thought became the New World Order and refocused on North America and Western Europe. With the Artificers' creation of an AI computer that gained sentience at the "X" iteration of a sentience-expanding algorithm, they became Iteration X. The Hippocratic Circle intended to be the Progenitors of a new race of humans. The Guild became an international Syndicate. The Void Seekers broke the barriers of Earth's orbit; as Void Engineers, they could impose order on everything beyond the Barrier.

With a change in name, the Conventions' transformation from champions to oppressors of humanity was complete. Uncomfortable with this, the Electrodyne Engineers defected to the Council of Nine in 1904, becoming the Sons of Ether. The Difference Engineers, who followed in 1961, soon became the Virtual Adepts.

Common Technocracy Terminology

Administrator: A high-ranking Technomancer.
Apparatus: A Technomagickal focus.
Associate/Sympathizer: An un-Awakened ally.
BioMechanic: Life-tech; cybernetic magicks. Also the Iteration X Methodology which handles such activities.
Collective: A Chantry, usually off-world.
Construct: An artificially created or enhanced life form; also, a Chantry, either within or outside of material reality.
Dimensional Science: Spirit-tech, the classified Art of certain Technomancers.
Enlightened: Awakened.
Influence: An area of technomagickal expertise.
Inner Circle: The Union's top ruling council.
Masses, The: Sleepers.
Methodology: A Convention subsection which handles a specific concern within the group.
Operative: A specialist in dirty work; a soldier mage.
Prime Element: Quintessence.
Reality Deviant/Random Element: A supernatural creature, or a mage.
Repository: A Node or other source of Quintessence.
Technician: One who works, Awakened or not, in a research laboratory.
Triumvirate: A Construct's ruling council.
Union: Short for "Technocratic Union," i.e., the Technocracy.

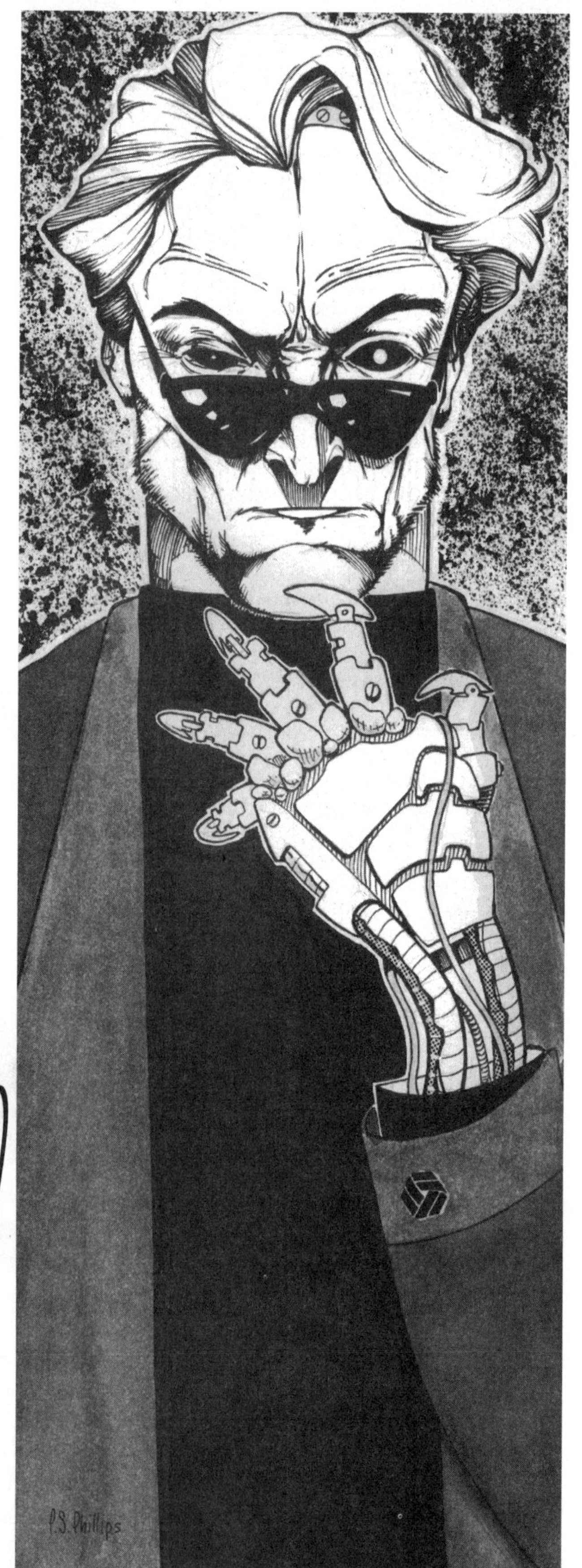

Most of the Technocracy's innovations during the 20th century were developed for questionable purposes — to oppress the Masses through a forced reliance on technology, to conceal the mystickal behind the deceptive truth of science, and to destroy opposition in the most efficient way possible.

The New World Order now uses mass media to spread propaganda and information technology to monitor the Masses. Those who participate in the Human Genome Project unwittingly aid the Progenitors' evolutionary plans. The prosthetics, robotics and computers of Iteration X are intended to all but replace humans. The Syndicate grows rich and powerful with capitalism, free trade, vice trade and controlled recessions. All the while, the Void Engineers defend the Earth from outside intrusion, mapping the mysteries from existence — or so they believe.

A Review of the Conventions

The Technocracy is made up of a close alliance of several Conventions (the name comes from the convention which founded the Union). Each specializes in a single field of technomagickal science, and has advanced 25 to 50 years ahead of mundane capability.

Conventions are further divided into Methodologies, subgroups with particular duties and methods.

Iteration X

Iteration X believes that a merger of Life and Matter, machine and soul, is the next step in human evolution. Their BioMechanics develop various cybernetic limbs, organs and digital implants to augment their agents. To reduce reality to a string of mathematical formulae which can be manipulated and replicated, statisticians constantly gather data and compute probability. Finally, Time-Motion Managers control manufacturing and industry. They currently vie with Virtual Adepts over the control of computer technology. To make the most efficient use of energy, Iterators have mastered the Sphere of Forces. This gives them a slight edge in the Digital Web and makes them deadly foes in person.

Yet Iterators are rarely seen. They prefer to interact with other factions through automated servants. The HyperIntTech Mark V, or "HIT Mark," is the latest in a line of anthropomorphic automatons. This particular Mark consists of organic flesh over a mechanical skeleton with a computer database that augments the encased human brain. HIT Marks appear human until they have identified their target — then all hell breaks loose. Other versions resemble canines, bulls, predatory cats and, in one freakish model, saber-toothed tigers. HIT Marks are programmed to seek out and destroy the Technocracy's enemies. This Convention is ruthlessly efficient.

If Iterators had faith, they would place it in Autocthonia, an Umbral "machine-realm" constructed within a Pattern Realm. Its orderly construction and rigid schedule epitomize the pattern and perfection which Iteration X plans to impose on Earth. Deep within its core, an artificial intelligence directs the Convention by remote control. This is supposedly the computer which achieved sentience at the Xth iteration of a sentience-expanding algorithm. Iteration X is unwilling to reveal the exact number of that sum — perhaps it thinks this would be like revealing a "true name." More likely, it does not want anyone to duplicate the results.

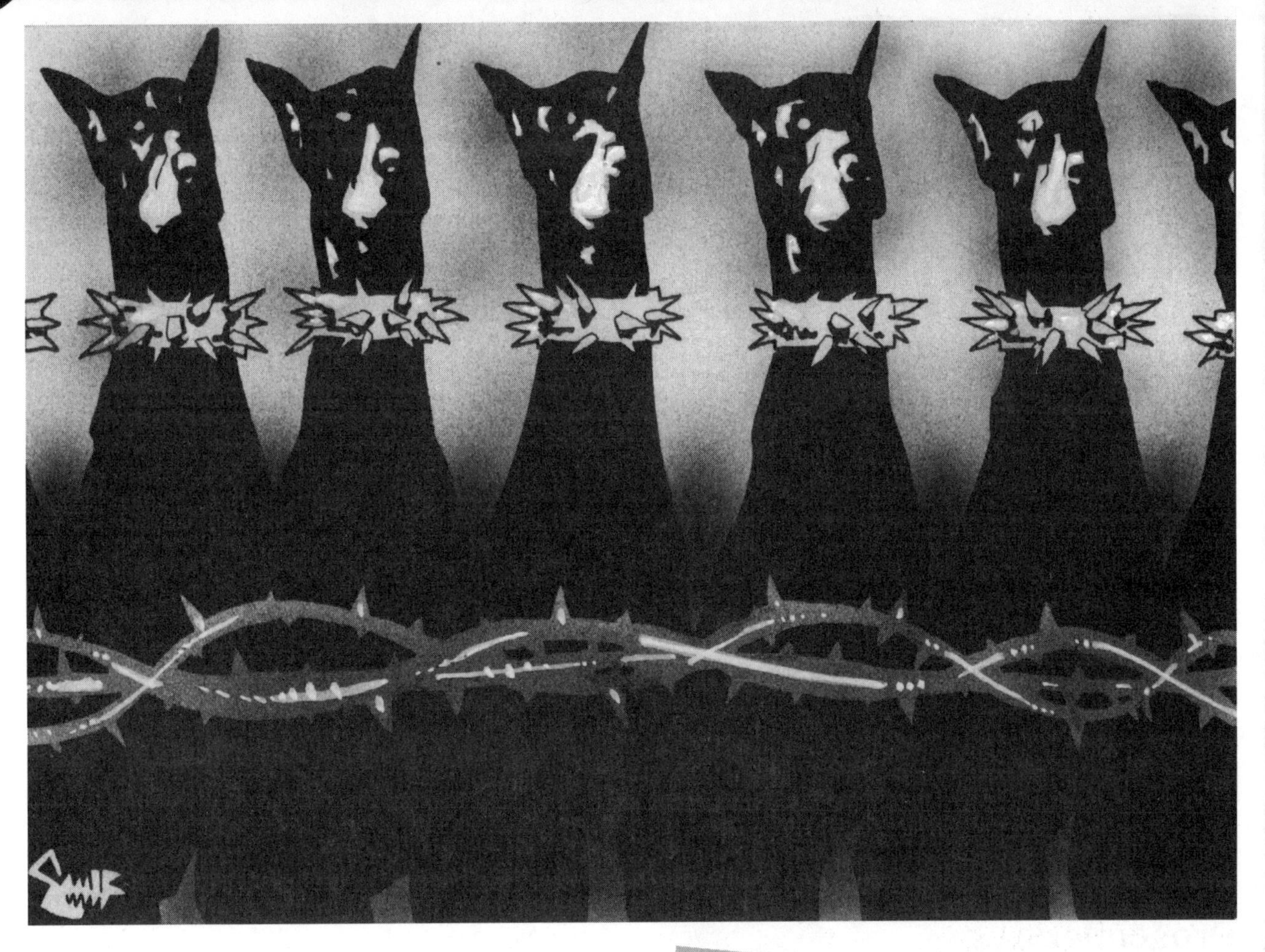

The New World Order

As administrative coordinators of the Technocracy, the New World Order concerns itself with all aspects of technology. Their agents, however, have discovered their own special niche: invasive, information-based technology such as television, radio, VCRs, film, security cameras, photography and most recently computer BBSs. Methods of manufacture they leave to Iteration X; they want to use the medium as a message.

The New World Order is departmentalized into three Methodologies. The Ivory Tower educates Technocrats, investigates potential scientific theories, devises propaganda for the Masses, and approves of any innovation before it is introduced into the current paradigm. The Watchers monitor and manipulate people through mass media, acting as envoys and spies to other groups. Their Operatives are known as Men in Black, dark-suited men (often mistaken for federal agents) trained for investigation, intimidation, subversion and combat. Those forced into their black Cadillacs rarely return the same person. Other types of Men in Black reportedly exist; these specialize in assassination, infiltration and intelligence analysis.

As experts in surveillance, interrogation and brainwashing, the New World Order understands Mind influence quite well. This aptitude — along with their tendency to place humanity in a conceptual Skinner Box, to be manipulated at will — has earned them the nickname "Big Brother."

The Precepts of Damian

According to the Sons of Ether and the Virtual Adepts, the Technocracy has its own Code of Conduct, called the Precepts of Damian after the mage who formulated it. Though each Convention adds its own addendums, they share key articles. The following print-out was included in the file presented to the Council of Nine by Roger Thackery of the Virtual Adepts after they defected in 1961. The Technocracy may have since updated the Precepts of Damian.

Article 1: Bring stasis and order to the universe. Predictability brings safety. Once all is discovered and all is known, Ascension shall be won.

Article 2: Convince the Masses of the benevolence of science, commerce and politics, and of the power of rationality. Conflict and suffering will be eliminated in our Utopia.

Article 3: Preserve the Gauntlet and Horizon. Chaotic individuals who open gateways with impunity threaten the stability of our world. Uncontrolled portals also allow outside forces such as the Nephandi access to our world. This must never happen.

Article 4: Define the nature of the universe. Knowledge must be absolute or chaos will envelope all. The elemental forces of the universe must not be left to the caprices of the unknown.

Article 5: Destroy reality deviants. Their recklessness threatens our security and our progress toward Ascension.

Article 6: Shepherd the Masses; protect them from themselves and others.

Progenitors

This Convention's goal is to perfect the human body through genetic engineering. Essentially, they force evolution upon a path of "improvement" by condensing hundreds of thousands of years of random mutation into generations of careful breeding.

Progenitors are primarily interested in Life procedures. Their FACADE Engineers create patchwork creatures on demand and clones of friend and enemy alike (the latter become almost undetectable spies); their results are immediate but rarely lasting. The Genegineers have greater forethought; they seek to unravel the mystery of genes so that successive generations of humanity will improve "naturally." Finally, the Pharmacopeists study the interaction between artificially induced chemicals and the biochemical make-up of a living body.

As the ultimate advocates of Darwinist theory, Progenitors believe in survival of the fittest, both within their Convention and in the natural world. They aggressively hunt enemies for kidnapping and replacement by identical clones. *Invasion of the Body Snatchers* and "Red Scare" films of the 1950s simulate the paranoia this Convention engenders.

Though many Progenitors are careful with the power they wield, others perform wild "experiments" or even set themselves up to be overseers of Horizon plantations. Though considered dangerous by their fellow Conventions, the Progenitors are seen as valued allies — and insidious enemies — by their comrades.

The Syndicate

The Syndicate handles funds within the Technocracy. More significantly, they distribute technology and the misinformation of the New World Order among the Masses while capitalizing on the vices adopted by modern people to escape their drab existence. Their Financiers monitor the world's stock markets and advise multinational corporations, moving the world in the direction of becoming a cashless society that would be under their direct control.

Many of this Conventions' dealings are a mystery even to their fellows. The activities of the Enforcers, who tap into organized crime, the Media Control (the true "media elite"), and the so-called "Pawnbrokers," who deal in world trade, are well known, even among Sleepers. The Special Projects Division, however, is a mystery, and Disbursements remains a thorn in the side of every Technomancer who needs a research grant. By controlling the money, this Convention makes even the Union dance to their tune — much to the other groups' dismay.

Though they lack Iteration X's firepower and the NWO's finesse, Syndicate "Hollow Men" use blackmail, financial sabotage and violence directed through the crime cartels and gangs they command to make life difficult for the Convention's enemies. Such measures are rarely necessary, for mages with their financial clout — everyone has their price. Through money and material objects, this Convention pulls the heartstrings of popular culture: commercial art, mainstream literature and advertising. The New World Order may control the Masses' minds, but the Syndicate saps their spirit.

Void Engineers

The diverse Methodologies of the Void Engineers dedicate themselves to the exploration — and exploitation — of all remaining frontiers. From the Deep Umbra to the depths of the sea, this adventurous Convention handles its tasks with a gusto that is rarely seen among Technocrats.

Each Methodology goes by an abbreviation; the Pan-Dimensional Corps (PDC) split their turf between the Umbra-delving astronauts and the VR cybernauts. Both groups compete with the Sons of Ether and the Virtual Adepts in "Great Races" conducted with more sportsmanship than hatred. Showdowns between these groups are like affairs of honor; little blood is shed unless outside parties become involved.

No such spirit infects the Boarder Corps Division (BCD), the paramilitary experts who defend the Horizon from "alien" invasions. These space Marines sanitize Nodes as well, riding the Qui La Machinæ and laying waste to anyone they find on the wrong side of the Gauntlet. Their earthly counterparts, the Neutralization Specialist Corps (NSC), clean up "hauntings" and "alien touchdowns" with cold perfection. Research and Execution (R&E) control the fine points of Spirit-tech, manufacturing Devices and sending them through into the Otherworlds, and the Earth Frontier Division (EFD) maps out the last unexplored areas on Earth.

Other Conventions see the Void Engineers as reckless and brash. Their hasty moon-landing evoked a (some say faerie-inspired) wonder of space; now many people wish they could leave Earth behind. Such a dispersal of humanity would complicate the Union's control, and will be delayed for as long as possible. Yet the dream has already grown too large to be uprooted. While other Conventions consider the Void Engineers an anomaly that requires monitoring, Tradition mages view them as the least evil among the Technocracy.

Goals and Tactics

We... do hereby resolve that Humanity will not be menaced by madmen and beasts, that the World must be a place of Order and Reason.

— Declaration of the Ivory Tower, 1325

For the Technocracy, Ascension will be complete when they achieve two goals. First, they must have absolute control of reality. Only when the universe runs with clockwork precision can humanity truly understand its place within it. Second, they should promote equality, to the lowest common denominator if need be. When all are equal in misery or comfort, when all are identical in appearance and ideology, only then can harmony be achieved.

Technocrats want to guide the Masses toward something greater, whether humanity knows it or not — whether humanity wants it or not. What Technocrats ignore is that their warped form of communism (like that of the Soviet Union) still requires elites to impose the supposed equality. To achieve its ends, the Technocracy attempts to indoctrinate the Masses to their vision of reality while eliminating anything which fails to conform.

• **Swaying the Masses**

The Technocracy first introduced science as a form of magick that was usable by the Masses. Tools and fire were talismans for the everyman. The emphasis on the material world was intended to protect humanity from hostile supernatural beings.

These original ideals were lost upon the wayside. Science and technology have become ends in and of themselves. The Technocracy now promotes materialism: possessions can be easily quantified and thus divided equally among humanity. This is a sort of lazy, default equality. Where the Masses once used technology to improve their lives, they now rely upon machines rather than themselves.

The Technocracy is not completely at fault for this sad addiction. Humanity — a race existing mostly in the material world — easily forgets about the spirit world, where only their souls reside. They simply require a convenient excuse. Ironically, it may have been the collective will of the Masses that sidetracked the Technocracy.

Whether or not this is true, the Technocracy now dominates reality. They have become heady with power, and employ many means — such as mass media indoctrination and monitors — to ensure that the Masses continue to accept their paradigm. Should this fail, they implement the next process.

• **Slaying the Monsters**

Those who oppose the current paradigm become subject to the Pogrom. This systematic repression and purge is aimed mostly at Tradition mages, since Marauders are rare on Earth and the Nephandi are supposedly banished, but also applies to any other supernatural creature encountered. In reality, certain "latitude" is permitted when circumstances warrant. Even the Inner Circle recognizes when rigid dogma stands in the way of an effective solution. In general, however, the agents of the Technocratic Union stand firm: a safe reality is worth any price.

Hierarchy and Control

And so, by this simple scientific expedient (utilizing a scientific process held dearly secret by the Ticktockman's office) the System was maintained. It was the only expedient thing to do. It was, after all, patriotic. The schedules had to be met. After all, there was a war on!

But, wasn't there always?

— Harlan Ellison, "'Repent, Harlequin!' Said the Ticktockman"

The Technocracy is a vast but shadowy entity. Most mages encounter only one of its many far-reaching tentacles. As far as anyone can tell, the hierarchy is as follows:

The Inner Circle forms the capstone of a pyramidal hierarchy. No one has ever identified this group, so even Technocrats speculate about its membership. Presumably, it consists of one or more representatives from each Convention. This group dictates the will of the Technocracy as a whole. Only they have the complete Time Table (the Technocracy's schedule for Ascension) before them, and only they can envision the final results of victory.

These leaders communicate their desire by setting the agenda for Symposiums, monthly meetings where nothing less than the future of reality is decided. Here greater Technocrats — such as Progenitor Administrators and the Comptrollers of Autocthonia — formulate the most efficient means of accomplishing their set agenda. Such unity helps strengthen the current paradigm.

Rumor has it that another council takes its cues from the Inner circle as well — a cabal that decides policy for world leaders. Though there has never been any proof of such a council's existence, conspiracy theorists and Tradition spies seem to be certain that one exists somewhere.

After each Symposium, directives are sent out to the leaders of various Constructs. These Constructs are responsible for implementing specific aspects of the agenda. They may be unaware of their place in the master plan, but this is as it should be — their only concern is to obey.

It is at this lowest level that the other factions most often encounter Technocrats. Since even the smallest intrusion can interfere with the Union's clockwork efficiency, rival mages may throw off the Time Table by their actions. The Inner Circle soon learns of this. Contingency plans deal with minor disruptions. Major disrupters often find themselves on the agenda for next month's Symposium.

The Nephandi

We spoke their names
At dark sun's hour
The alter of blood
The shadow of power
Absolute depravity...
Under landscapes of the moon
A tide of blood come soon
We say we say we say
Darkness and death

— Liers in Wait, "Blood and Family"

The term *Nephandi* describes a faction of beings — mage and mundane, human and otherwise — who pursue the corruption of the universe for its own sake. Some among the Fallen Ones were born to follow such a Path; others once reached higher, but fell from their lofty course.

Those mysticks on the Path of Descent are a mysterious lot, supposedly exiled, but obviously not banished. Those few who have studied the Dark Ways with good intent (to glean their enemies' weaknesses, for instance) have themselves become corrupted before long. The most reputable source of lore remains the infamous *Malleus Neffandorum*. This 6th-century text describes the various ranks of Nephandi in elaborate (and thus misleading) detail.

Atop the heap of corruption crouch the Nephandi Lords. Whether they are called demons, Wyrm-spawn or Things That Should Not Be, they are entities of pure and unfathomable evil. Below them, the once-human Nephandi mysticks draw from two pools: *Widderslainte* are Dark Orphans, born with poisoned Avatars and Awakened by the nightmares of their previous lives; *barabbi* are renunciates from some other faction who have Fallen during their Ascent. Below these Awakened officers, the ranks are filled by cultists, *fomori* (once-human agents granted supernatural powers but marked by physical and mental deformities) and even more monstrous beings.

The Fallen Ones are not merely evil — they are corruption incarnate. Dark tales speak of the Nephandic Rebirth, where a willworker steps into the Caul and has her Avatar turned inside out, warped or inverted. Such choice, it is said, is always deliberate. Once Reborn, a mage becomes a living avatar of whatever forces the Fallen serve. Since all factions, even the Marauders, openly hate an obvious Nephandus, the Dark Ones cloak their actions in temptation, masquerade and betrayal.

Apparently, the Nephandi have but two agendas. First, they actively pervert and claim human souls (or Avatars). A mage's Avatar, being more potent than any Sleeper's, is a great prize. Nephandi are skilled at offering what one desires most, whether it be material wealth, power or eternal life. The cost is trifling, merely the soul. The *Malleus Neffandorum* explains that souls are all that sustain the Nephandi Lords during their exile in the Outer Darkness.

The Nephandis' second, related agenda is a quest to return their Dark Lords to Earth. Theoretically, such an accomplishment could earn a servant unthinkable rewards.

Whatever their motives, Nephandi provide a dark reflection of their rivals. Where others would Ascend, they Descend. While others set their sights on some view of Ascension, Nephandi gouge out their own eyes. The Fallen seem content to pull down the work of others rather than erect any structure of their own. They will be satisfied only when nothing remains.

The Marauders

The freakiest show I know
Is the show of my own
Living my life in and out
Of the Twilight Zone.

— Red Hot Chili Peppers, "Nobody Weird Like Me"

Change. Disorder. Individuality. Dynamic potential. These are the ideals of the Chaos Mages, though the mysticks themselves may never know it. The polar opposite of Technomancers, these magickal psychopaths freely toss off consensual reality for their own dynamic version.

Some say these bandits were once normal mages who fell into bottomless Quiets or Orphans who snapped Awake too suddenly. Others hold that they have united with their Avatars at the expense of knowing humanity. Still others theorize that they are thralls of the force of change. Finally, some believe that Marauders are brilliant, hyperactive visionaries whose schemes rocket ahead of their physical achievements. No one knows for sure.

The problem is one of communication. Most Marauders are so caught up in their own madness that they speak in gibberish or operate on some obtuse plane of thought. Even the more normal ones are immune to healing through psychiatry or Mind magick. The secret of their origin is buried deep in the subconscious, if remembered at all.

From studying Marauder activity, other factions think they've grasped the Mad Ones' goals. Some megalomaniacs seem intent on acquiring as much power as possible, as if any one of them could single-handedly dominate reality. Most such Marauders care little for humanity, so for them Ascension must be a personal achievement or the overwhelming wash of *all* possibilities. Other Marauders seem intent on creating a new "age of wonders." These "crusaders" constantly assault the barriers between worlds and lead a menagerie of supernatural beasts through any breach they create.

Like the Nephandi, the Mad Ones supposedly reside in the Deep Umbra. Occasionally, they break through into the Horizon and lay siege to any Realm they encounter. Many, it is thought, somehow Awaken in the Umbra, but others burst out of their mortal guise on Earth. Such "newborns" often burn out in magickal pyrotechnics; the survivors seek the hidden places or rips in the Tapestry and go to ground.

Because of their madness and their poor interpersonal skills, one might consider these mages cosmic clowns. This is not at all the case; any outside Marauder capable of breaching the Barrier wields potent magick indeed. These mysticks are so innately dynamic that they also warp reality by their very presence. Randomness and accidents follow in the wake of lesser mages, while the arrival of a Master can tear the Tapestry. Marauders seem immune to Paradox; any backlash which occurs targets innocents instead of the offender.

Some Marauders seem more eccentric than insane. Others are grotesquely maniacal. Regardless of their apparent sanity or decency, these dynamic sorcerers are frighteningly amoral and utterly dangerous. For this reason, they have been banned from Earth by the Technocracy. There in the Deep Umbra, the Mad Mages lurk on the other side of the Gauntlet until a breach is created. Technocrats remain ever-vigilant for Marauder intrusion. Guerrilla factions do break through from time to time, but never seem to hang around for long.

The Outsiders

You're meddling with powers you can't possibly comprehend.

—Marcus Brody, *Indiana Jones and the Last Crusade*

With the influence of the four great factions, it's easy to get the impression that mage society dedicates itself entirely to the Ascension War. This is a common misconception. The search for enlightenment, does not always entail stomping the hell out of anyone in the way. Those who follow such a course simply outnumber those who don't — or seem to, at least. Those who put up a fuss are always more obvious than those who keep to themselves.

A number of smaller subcultures exist outside the mainstream of mage society. Some consist of magickal societies with better things to do than fight each other. Others are composed of individuals who either serve the larger factions, battle them alone, or walk away from the whole business to pursue their own agendas. The following groups fit into all of the categories above.

Solitaries

Many mysticks are not team players. Solitary mages follow their own Paths. Though they may work with some larger group for a time, their destiny lies elsewhere.

• Errants

Survivors from cabals or Chantries lost to war or great tragedy are often called *Errants*. Most are bitter loners who seek vengeance or death. They're shunned as much for their grim, single-minded mission as for their hunted status. A rare few Errants — usually those whose comrades fell to excessive pride or power — wander from place to place, trying to save others from a similar fate.

• Rogues

This label applies to mages who either walk away from the group to which they once belonged or accept training from a faction they later refuse to join. They walk the Path of the lone coyote, and are considered almost as risky by the established powers.

Rogue mages do not benefit from the excuse of impassioned blindness as Errants do, but intentionally close their eyes to Ascension politics. Where Errants fight to banish their own inner demons, these mysticks just want to be left alone. Some work as mercenaries, siding with anyone who can match their price in money or Tass. Some run between the shadows, surviving as they can. A few simply go off into a corner and claim it as their own, or wander like enlightened vagabonds, helping some, attacking others. Such mages tend to live short, if interesting, lives.

• Orphans

Once, all mysticks came to their own awareness naturally. As time went on and the factions grew, one side or the other usually discovered budding willworkers before they became too powerful — or dangerous. In recent years, however, many Sleepers have spontaneously Awakened. Lacking a mentor's guidance or the framework of a magickal society, they've come to be called *Orphans*.

Grizzled veterans of the Ascension War consider them loose cannons. Their lack of training and allegiance make them inherently dangerous to themselves, to innocents and to all sides. Thus, Orphans are often hunted or enslaved; such loners are easy prey. If an Orphan has great potential, most factions will risk converting her. The gamble is one of loyalty; most self-Awakened prefer to blaze their own slow but broad Path.

If modern Orphans lean toward any Tradition, it is the Hollow Ones. Their casual philosophy of "live and let die" gives Orphans the freedom to follow their own Path. At the same time, their organization, however loose, provides a measure of protection from their hunters.

• Hermits

So-called *hermits* might be as social as any other person around. All the same, they usually want to be left out of the fighting, and avoid or destroy anyone who pushes them into a corner. Marauders often wander around or set up shop like a hermit mage, and other, more affiliated mysticks usually watch their step around a wizard they can't recognize.

Hermits may be trained by some other group or might be self-Awakened. Either way, they like to be left to their own devices. The most ancient sorcerers may be hermit-types, dwelling in secluded corners or living quiet lives among the Sleepers. They often have powerful Arcane talents and evade all but the most dedicated searches. The legendary hermit on the mountain with eyes that reflect the world, the wonder-merchant who peddles wares then disappears, or the wise woman in the deep-woods cottage are archetypal hermit mages.

The "Crafts"

A catch-all label for mystickal societies unaligned with the Council of Nine, the so-called *Crafts* (who almost never answer to that title) make little distinction between the hedge wizard and the Awakened One. To them, labels are a waste of time.

Crafts are pockets of mages united along a single cultural paradigm, such as Caribbean voodoo, European alchemy or Gothic-Punk sorcery. More concerned with the practical application of magick than metaphysics, such mages will never be heard discussing Ascension or the subjective nature of reality. Thus, their approach to magick is termed Craft (rather than Art) by outsiders.

Each Craft specializes in a certain form of magick, either through choice or inherent ability. While less flexible than Tradition mages, they can be quite proficient in their respective concentrations.

Infernal Sorcerers

Diabolists and *Infernalists* are mages or hedge wizards who promise their souls (and the souls of others) to some Infernal power in exchange for demonic instruction. Some Diabolists summon and bind a demon for just this purpose. Others are tricked or seduced by the serpent's tongue.

At first, the would-be Diabolist is granted small demonic Investments, powers portioned from demonic Essence. Few conditions are attached; the rush of power is addiction enough. Once power has absolutely corrupted this pawn, he signs a soul-pact and learns the Infernal Craft (a form of static hedge magic) of Dark Sorcery.

Many Diabolists form cults to acquire control over more souls, with which they barter for even greater power. While some support the Nephandi's nihilistic crusade, most specialize in their own brand of personal evil.

Hedge Wizards

Hedge wizards are un-Awakened sorcerers whose static arts are limited by set parameters. **(See Chapter Four for the distinction between static magic and dynamic magick).** Some form societies, but most practice magic on their own. Many un-Awakened who seek magic in books or other forms of study fall into this category. The most dedicated do acquire some power, but True Magick must be experienced, not merely learned.

Most Western forms of hedge magic descend from the *ars magica* (art of magic) of the Middle Ages — a limited form of spellcraft taught to select Sleepers by the Order of Hermes — and the folk wisdom of the wise woman or hermit sage. Some hedge wizards form societies, while others work alone. Few know, or care, about the War.

Custos

"Alfred..."

"I saw the signal, sir."

"I've left Wayne Enterprises, en route to the Batcave."

"Always ready, sir."

—Batman and Alfred, *Batman Forever*

Many mages acquire sidekicks, confidants and servants. Collectively, these companions are called *custos* and fall into various categories.

- **Acolytes**

Mages call their un-Awakened servitors *acolytes*. They may be guards, advisors, assistants, contacts or procurers of supplies. On a more abstract level, acolytes are a constant reminder to mages of who and what they work for. Many acolytes are unaware of the nature of their employer or friends, yet have some special quality that sets them apart from other Sleepers. This may be insatiable curiosity, strong will, frustration with the status quo or a manifestation of inner magick.

- **Consors**

Although not mages themselves, *consors* display comparable ability. Very capable mortals (like witch-hunters and hedge magicians), vampires and other supernatural beings all fit this category. Though they may lack the ability or desire to learn True Magick, these companions are aware of many aspects of mystick society (such as the Ascension War). In any case, consors usually have their own unique powers.

Most importantly, consors consider themselves companions, friends and partners. They may risk their lives for a mage, and expect similar loyalty in return.

- **Familiars**

Familiars are intelligent spirit beings who inhabit some physical body (usually animal, sometimes inanimate) in order to interact with the material world. A mage must specially prepare this material body — whether cat or golem — to act as a spirit-vessel. This rite creates a compact between mage and familiar. The bond intensifies through a symbiotic relationship between the two: the familiar feeds on a mage's Quintessence, and in exchange, it grants its host access to strange bits of lore and helps protects him from Paradox.

Like consors, these spirits-made-physical consider themselves a mage's equal, if not his superior (a familiar may refer to the mage as *its* familiar!). Should the mage break the compact at any time, his familiar will surely abandon him.

Chantries

Chantry is the generic name for a mystical dwelling where mages and their servitors can meet or reside, study, experiment and hide from enemies. This term comes from the Hermetic name for a "covenant," or fellowship house. Other Traditions refer to their strongholds as Monasteries, Sanctuaries, Pleasuredomes, Lodges, Marabouts, Laboratories, Covenhouses, Fortresses or hosts of other names. As these terms indicate, a Chantry may take many forms, depending on its origin and function; it could be a country manor, a temple jutting from some Andean peak, a penthouse apartment or a cavern-complex beneath the Australian desert.

Some Chantries are mundane refuges for mages too poor or unskilled to employ magick to improve them. The most powerful draw Quintessence from private Nodes to create Horizon Realms **(see Chapter One)** where the main building can be relocated for greater security. A Chantry's spiritual structure often has one or more earthly aspects, physical reflections and access points. Since unclaimed Nodes are rare, however, most new Chantries make do with mundane locations.

Chantry Society

The benefits of joining a Chantry are manifold. Members gain access to arcane libraries, laboratories and other resources, perhaps even Tass. Other mages provide information or aid more readily to fellow members than to strangers, and members have the right to vote on important issues. Should a mage win office, she gains influence proportionate to the prestige of her Chantry. Such bonds of fellowship ensure some protection from enemies and the right of arbitration from rivals.

In return for these privileges, members are expected to perform duties — to act as envoys to other Chantries, do maintenance or guard duty, tutor apprentices or collect Quintessence from dangerous locales. Chantry law can also be double-edged — most covenants favor the Old Guard who established them over newcomers.

Cabals

Most Chantries are divided into smaller groups with specific roles or agendas. Whether they take the form of military units, political parties or clubs, such groups are known as *cabals*. New Chantries may consist of only a single cabal, while large and established ones such as Doissetep can have close to a dozen. The most common range is two to five cabals per Chantry.

Cabals also exist outside the context of a Chantry; this is how they usually begin. The most common familial group in mystick society, cabals are formed when a group of mages decide to hang together, whether to achieve a common purpose, to provide mutual support, or just to share friendship. As they work together, loyalty and camaraderie forge tight links. Most cabals hope to create their own Chantry someday, or at least to find their group a niche in an established one.

Types of Chantries

• **Ancestral Chantry**

These Chantries are extremely old and closely associated with the origins of a given Tradition. One example is the Celestial Chorus' Celestial Temple of the Sun, rumored to be located beneath Vatican City (if so, its entrances are closely guarded). Ancestral Chantries are stagnant and conservative, but extremely powerful. Leaders of such places have tremendous influence over the Council of Nine and their respective Tradition.

• **War Chantry**

War Chantries are temporary affairs established to guard some front of the Ascension War. These places rarely last; most either complete an objective and move on, or are eventually destroyed. Members have little time for bureaucracy or intrigue. Typically, they are loyal to one another and suspicious of strangers.

• **Exploration Chantry**

Some Traditions, such as the Dreamspeakers or Sons of Ether, are more interested in seeking questions than coming up with answers. Entire Chantries are devoted to experimentation and exploration.

Such Chantries are usually remote and inaccessible. Some Dreamspeaker Lodges have been constructed at the edge of What-is-Known. In other far-off places, like the lunar Victoria Station, the occupants prefer to keep their affairs private. While Exploration Chantries are often considered unproductive by outsiders (too much theory, not enough application), they cannot be accused of lacking research material.

• **College Chantry**

College Chantries devote all of their resources to teaching the newly Awakened. In this magick-poor age, where every potential apprentice is fought over by many factions, Colleges capable of teaching dozens of mysticks have diminished. Few now are left. More common in the High Mythic Age, the newest Colleges were built during the 1800s. Those that remain enroll no more than three to eight pupils at a time.

College Chantries are most popular among the Order of Hermes and Sons of Ether. Other Traditions prefer the Mentor-apprentice system or learning by experience.

• **Squatter Chantry**

A Chantry that lacks a Node is known as a *Squatter*. Most often, these small Chantries are established by a cabal with few resources. On the other hand, a Chantry cut off from its Quintessence supply by besieging enemies might also qualify.

Lacking a Node, members of Squatter Chantries are (often rightly) suspected of Quintessence theft. In any case, they have little status. A mage without Quintessence is a viper without venom, as the Euthanatos say.

• **Abandoned Chantries**

As valuable as they are, Chantries are rarely abandoned. Those who come upon the ruins of a Chantry house should ask themselves, "What could have driven off a community of mages?" before moving in themselves.

Technomancer Constructs

The Technocracy refers to its Chantries as *Constructs*, its cabals as *amalgams*. While Chantries are created spontaneously by the choice of their founders (and new members are readily admitted), Constructs are usually formed by the Conventions' leaders, and members are assigned to the post. Constructs tend to be run by small councils called *Triumvirates*. **(See "Technocracy Terms" sidebar).**

In form, Constructs usually resemble office buildings, laboratories and factories set atop sanitized Nodes. The New World Order operates out of labyrinthine office buildings separated into departments. The warehouses and factories of Iteration X repair and build weapons, or house vast computers to store secret data. Progenitors favor laboratories where genetic mutants can be spliced in private and subterranean dungeons where they may imprison failed experiments. Agents of the Syndicate meet in penthouses, villas or privately-owned skyscrapers. From their Exploration and Development Stations, the Void Engineers launch probes into the Umbra and research the data and samples the equipment sends back.

The Technocracy also has many multi-Convention Constructs. These have but two purposes: to uphold static reality, and to carry out the Pogrom.

Nephandi Labyrinths

Three weeks after his abduction, half-mad Hergard Giger returned with horror stories of his imprisonment among the Nephandi. From his and similar reports, mages have learned something of the Dark Mages' sanctums, called *Labyrinths*.

Labyrinths draw their power from Nodes of corruption and despair. The site of a toxic chemical spill; the smoldering remains of a barn where a cultist incinerated his followers; the dark, soiled basement where that little girl was concealed by her uncle for over a month — the psychic trauma of such places allow Nephandi to puncture the Tapestry and intrude upon the Earth.

The interiors of most Labyrinths, it is said, are moist, pulsing caverns carved from Deep Umbral Realms. Chairs of black metal and bone grow from the floor. Tapestries are woven from decaying flesh and rubber. Organic machinery pumps oily blood throughout the complex for unknown purposes. These are but tasteful examples of the dark perversity found in Nephandi architecture. Howls and screams echo through the ribbed tunnels. Nephandi and darker beings lurk amid the slime and corrosive silt. It is said that Labyrinths have little structure or hierarchy save that which the Nephandi Lords impose through fear.

Giger was one of the few unlucky ones to return alive from a Labyrinth. Before dying of invasive cancer, he pinpointed the abomination's location. His cabal arrived just in time to see the Technocracy's Qui La Machinæ already sanitizing the Node.

Roving Marauders

If Marauders have Chantries, nobody has ever seen one (and lived to tell of it...). The Mad Ones are probably too fractious to form permanent cabals, never mind Chantries.

Chapter Four: The Ways of Magick

...the moment you open your mouth to say one thing about the nature of reality, you automatically have a whole set of enemies who've already said reality is something else... Writing a metaphysics is, in the strictest sense of the word, a degenerate activity.

— Robert Pirsig, *Lila*

Peter Kobie's Seeking

Bored, Peter Kobie stopped singing scales and launched into a haunting melody, his deep rich voice reaching up to the stars and down into the dark valleys around the mountain on which he stood. Quickly, his echo returned, blending into complex harmonies as Peter sang from his heart and soul, glad to be free from the shackles of practice his Avatar had imposed on him the day before. After he fell silent, the last echoes lingered in the cool mountain air before fading away. He turned, sensing, not seeing, the presence of the dark-haired, lithe woman at his side. Long ago, he'd thought she merely served as his muse. Now, more and more often, she came forth to guide his steps and direct his enlightenment with a more controlling hand than he cared to admit. She was never pleased anymore, never satisfied. The frown on her face told him today was no different.

"Peter, it was an easy task, and yet you defied my instructions."

"I've been a musician all my life," he said scornfully. "Me practicing scales is like making some vaunted master of Doissetep clean chamberpots."

"I imagine their pots could indeed do with a little cleaning," she replied wryly. "My point was this: you should never forget that everything is composed of the most basic elements, cloth of thread, steel of iron, songs of notes."

Peter looked away, stubborn refusal in his eyes. "I have done no wrong. I have made the mountains sing. That was your request."

"But not within my conditions. I am sorry; I feel you have learned nothing from this experience," she said sadly, her image fading to leave him alone in the hills.

Kobie cursed, damning this unrelenting Avatar, shouting vile words that bounced off the tree-covered mountains, their echoes blending with the cold winds beginning to whine and howl in the dark valley below.

Magick is everywhere and everything, nowhere and nothing. It is logic and fact, faith and fancy. An enlightened magus can alter reality by thought alone with the same confidence most Sleepers feel when altering the reality on their TV screens with remote control techno-wands. However, few mages today can or would bedazzle the world by sowing the soil with dragon's teeth and causing soldiers to spring up from the damp earth, or calling forth an army of griffins to darken the sky over Manhattan. The Age of Legend is long past, and the confining cloak of the collective (un)consciousness wraps itself tighter around modern magick workers.

Most magick today appears very subtle to the Sleepers' eyes. Indeed, mages often choose to blend their magick in with mundane reality, so as not to draw attention (or Paradox) upon themselves. An old building collapsed just after that funny-looking man with one ear ran by... well, there's no way he could be involved, is there? Or the sudden rainstorm no weatherman predicted? Yeah, well, it would be a lot stranger if they got a forecast right for once, wouldn't it?

Yet, even with these restrictions, a powerful and confident mage can have a truly awesome effect upon the Tapestry of reality. One mage can alter the fabric of reality for millennia, while several working in concert may alter more than one reality. Such power should not be taken lightly. It is the legacy of countless Awakenings — an awesome, and perhaps overpowering, responsibility. Many mages have been consumed in its embrace.

Magics & Magicks

There can be no mages without magick, and no magick without the mundane. Magick exists outside of "normal," consensual reality. Through it, the Awakened impose their will upon the river of reality, shifting its course and even changing the direction of its flow. Yet, if there was no mundane, rigidly channeled reality, sorcerers would have nothing to change. There can be no Awakening if no one sleeps.

Most people move with the current of reality. Floating along on a cushion of their own belief, they go wherever that reality takes them. They are the Sleepers, and they are legion. However, some people see the water for what it is. They learn to "sleepwalk," actively working with or around consensual reality by performing magic. Dipping their magical oars in that water, these individuals learn to steer their reality rafts through the currents, even paddling upstream on occasion. By paddling, they can alter their position in the river or even move some of the water, but they have no true effect upon the river itself. They have discovered static magic.

True Magick defines the True Mage. These people have fully Awakened, and the gods help those overcome by the brilliance they find! These few explorers let go of their rafts and plunge into the river naked, and in so doing find that it is they who move the river. In this discovery lies True Magick.

True Magick

True magick changes the flow of reality. There are no inherent limits to what it can accomplish; the only limits are those within the mystick herself. A mage working True Magick can make buildings disappear, create worlds from whole cloth and bring the dead back to life without the need for some Orpheus-like search. True Magick does not require the willworker to perform any specific ritual or gesture in any particular way to alter reality, though many still do. She need not ape the gestures of her teacher and his teacher before him. All she needs is sufficient conscious and Awakened will. With enlightenment, knowledge of reality's elements (called the nine Spheres by some) and will, her own expectations are the only true limits to her power.

There are two major schools of thought about how the Awakened generate and wield True Magick. Some Traditionalists maintain a transcendent theory of magick, believing that mages have the ability to connect with the Prime, the Pure Ones or some other mystick force. Through the auspices of their Avatars **(see Chapter Two)**, mages reach into Prime itself and rework reality. Through this connection, they channel the energies of True Magick. Dreamspeaker shamans call this "making hollow bones;" visualizing his bones as hollow, the shaman draws the mystick energies into himself and out again as will.

Other mages believe that True Magick is immanent in all Awakened beings. The infinite power of this Art lies within each of us, embedded in the shard of Prime the Pure Ones lodged in our flesh and spirit. According to this theory, all we need to work True Magick is the faith to truly believe in its existence, the courage to embrace this inner divinity and the will to impose our own paradigm upon static reality.

Regardless of an individual mage's beliefs, he understands that he wields reality-on-command, and that his ability to impose his own reality upon the world sets him apart from all others.

Static Magic

In contrast to True Magick, static or "hedge" magic follows specific patterns, which follow the tenets of accepted reality. This is not to say that static magic conforms to textbook scientific reality — some of its effects are quite miraculous — but it does conform to at least some portion of the collective unconscious. Most scientists would insist that it is impossible to predict the future, yet any number of people visit Tarot card readers and call 1-900-psychic numbers every day. Children playing make-believe mimic static magic in their rituals of protection ("Hop twice on the blue rug, hold my breath and jump into bed without touching the headboard, or the monsters can get me while I sleep!"), perhaps instinctively acknowledging its presence and power.

The hedge wizards, psychics, Gypsies and others who work static magic must conform to strict patterns of behavior to achieve very specific results. They are like dancers at a masked ball, clothed but awkwardly in their Avatars. Although "wearing" their Avatars gives them entry into the Reality Ball, they are unable (or unwilling) to discard their costumes for the Midnight Awakening. Mages believe that vampires, werewolves and other supernatural creatures have a similar, limited relationship to their own Avatars. Some even suggest that the pallor and fangs of the vampire, and the fur and claws of the werewolves, are external signs of these same rigid Avatar costumes. Donning these metaphysical Avatars grants Kindred and Garou their Disciplines and Gifts, but also limits their powers and perspective.

The specific pattern one uses to create her magic is irrelevant; a Gypsy dance and a voodoo ritual could both have the same effect. Their consistency and belief in their own ritual matters most. Likewise, each specific ritual can only accomplish one specific result. The hedge wizard cannot use the same ritual to clean a house and burn it down!

Such static magic has an upper limit — the farthest boundaries of current static reality. The hedge wizard can dip her hands into the waters of reality and alter its flow, but unlike a True Mage, she cannot change the course of the river itself. The most powerful and determined hedge wizard cannot find an incantation or ritual which will overcome this limit. She is bound by external forces and cannot change the flow of reality.

Ironically, the Awakened cannot use static magic. Even if a mage conducts a "static ritual" alongside a hedge wizard, the mage's ritual will work by fundamentally reshaping reality. This level of magick is impossible for the static magic worker to truly comprehend, much less attain.

The Metaphysic of Magick

Science is a cemetery of dead ideas,
Even though life may issue from them.
— Miguel de Unamuno, *The Tragic Sense of Life*

In classrooms throughout the modern world, little boys and girls are taught a passive, scientific view of reality. Through the clinical eyes of science, we learn to carefully observe the so-called laws of physics, nature and the rest of reality to understand how the world functions. *Although we are part of this reality*, the teachers lecture their bored charges, *we cannot affect the laws of nature.* Children, like mages, often balk at this object-oriented view of reality. In their worlds reality fluctuates as rapidly as their ideas. They make dinosaurs come to life with a few bits of paper and crayons, Tinkertoy walls tumble upon their command, and each child has the mystic power to protect his mother's back by avoiding cracks in the sidewalk.

These children instinctively grasp something their elders lost long ago — they're active agents who may work their own will upon reality, even if that reality's filled with stuffed animals and Nintendo games. Yet these infant concepts will soon be lectured at and reasoned with until they slip away, relegated to the realm of fantasy. Mages however, come more than full-circle in their beliefs. True willworkers believe that reality is subjective; instead of building understanding and belief through passive observation of nature, belief and conscious thought builds (or at least influences) nature. This metaphysical premise holds that we play a far more active role in the universal pageant than Sleeper philosophy would have us believe. We, as conscious beings, *are* the cause, and the universe, or the boundaries of it, is *our* effect.

Static Reality

All apprentice mages (at least, all *successful* apprentices), ask themselves at one time or another, "If reality is limitless, why isn't my magick equally limitless?" Why, for example, can't a mage snap his fingers and cause the Earth's atmosphere to turn to jelly, or turn off gravity as easily as he directs the phone company to continually mark his account "paid in full?" Despite the limitless nature of reality, such constants as gravity, the Earth's rotation and the composition of the atmosphere still continue with extraordinary stability. If reality is of our own making, shouldn't the world be a chaotic jumble of shifting, dissonant realities, like an orchestra in which all the musicians are tone-deaf?

As elder mages teach their disciples, reality itself *is* limitless — a vacuum in which true consciousness may run free. However, these basic principles don't change, because our reality is also consensual. Earth's reality is not based on billions of disparate, disconnected, singular realities. Rather, reality relies on the collective beliefs of all of humanity (and, it is said, of other forces we choose not to see). Material reality is a consensual hallucination which the vast majority of humanity agrees upon.

In any one space, only one reality can exist. When more than one reality vie for realization, the most powerful one manifests. Billions of Sleepers live upon the Earth, each unknowingly cradling their sliver of Prime. Although individual Sleepers have little control over the nature of reality, their combined beliefs are extremely powerful. There is strength in numbers, as the saying goes, and static reality is powerful indeed. This tidal wave of consensus is extraordinarily difficult for even the most powerful mages to defy.

The difficulty of overcoming static reality is one reason that almost all mages, mystick and Technomancer alike, introduce their ideologies into the mainstream of human thought and experience. Although this desire may seem no more than selfish pride, it's a far more primal urge. We all have a life drive, which Freud termed the *libido*, a desire to exist — to *be*. By encouraging others to believe her particular magickal paradigm, the mage also strives to imprint herself upon reality, safeguarding her existence. The closer her personal paradigm is to static reality, the easier it is to impose her will upon the world.

The Technocracy has used the mass media, psychology and propaganda very effectively over the last century and a half to convince much of the Earth's populace to accept their reality. Many years ago, technology simply did not function, despite the best efforts of early Sons of Ether and other curious intellectual explorers. Although mages used their magick to empower some devices, they often suffered Paradox, and their technology never functioned for Sleepers. However, the populace gradually came to believe in technology, and technology therefore fell more and more in line with static reality — thus becoming more readily possible. With belief came machines usable by Sleepers as well as mages. This gradual subversion of reality is often slow, but it's much easier to open the door by greasing the rusty hinges than by wrenching the door off.

Certain Awakened philosophers (particularly Hermetic mages) theorize that the most basic aspects of reality (such as gravity, mathematical paradigms and the composition of the atmosphere) were in place when the mythical Pure Ones first took flesh. These aspects of reality are thus the most deeply ingrained. All of us, even the Awakened, believe in these constants on a primal level. Although it's theoretically possible to completely alter any aspect of reality, even the greatest sorcerers have difficulty stretching their limits that far.

There is much debate over which paradigms make up this "uber-reality." Is mathematics a part of humanity's "birth reality" or a concept introduced by mortals? Whether or not all aspects of the earth's current paradigm were part of the "birth reality," mages term this base-level (or Sleeper) reality as "static." It maintains a certain level of normality and structure on Earth. Static reality ensures that gravity continues to function, and that one plus one always equals two… unless, of course, a mage wills otherwise. The mystick's Awakened Avatar allows her to direct her will strongly enough to impose her beliefs upon the world, but it's not easy, particularly if the mage's will directly opposes static reality.

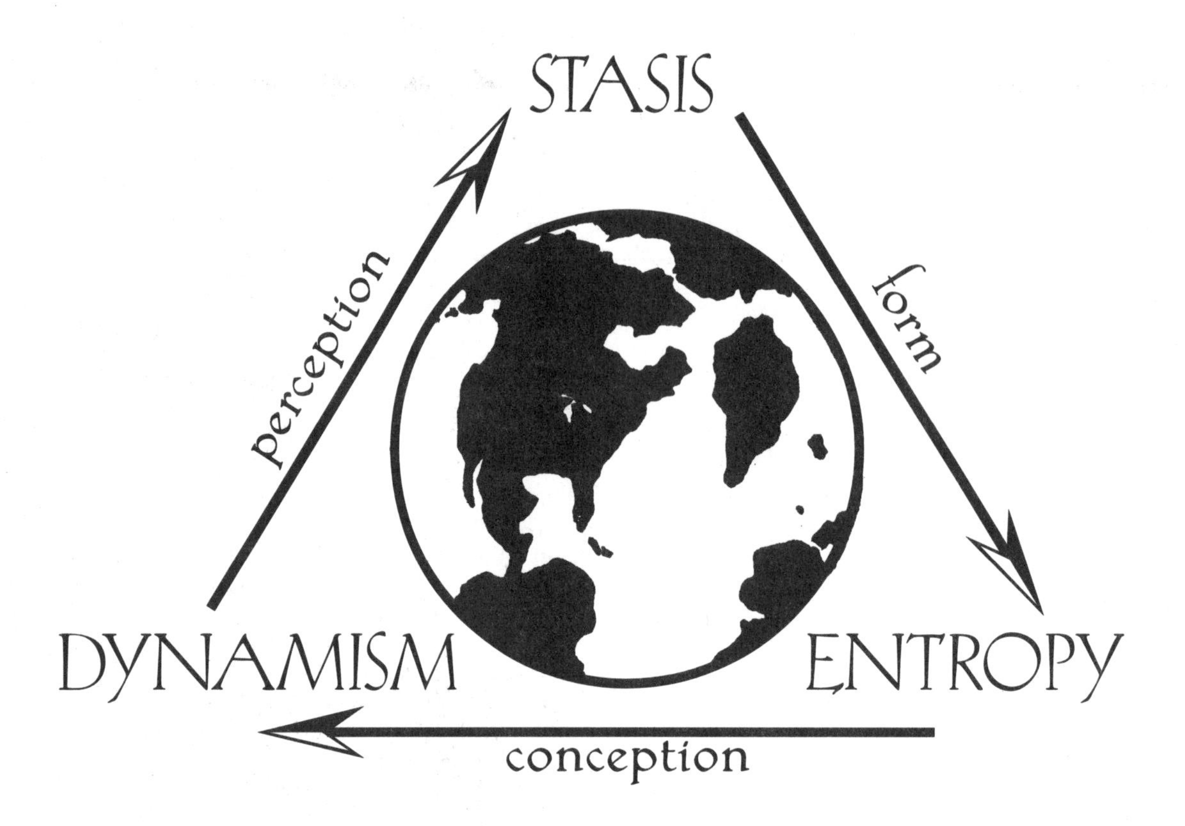

Mages are dynamic entities in a world designed to maintain stasis. As active agents in a passive world, the task of the Awakened is seldom easy. Yet it is critical, for without this dynamic intervention, reality might fall into continued stasis from which it is all too easy to slide into entropy. This is one of the main reasons Tradition mages worry about the unprecedented success the Technocracy has had in selling their world view to the Sleeper Masses. No other single magickal paradigm has ever advanced so far into humanity's collective unconscious as the Static Mages technomagickal revolution.

The Metaphysic Trinity

Humans can only understand bite-sized snippets of reality. If we try to down the entire universe-cake in one sitting, it becomes too overwhelming to comprehend. Unlike most Sleepers, mages can understand whole slices of reality at a time. However, even their more flexible, Awakened minds must still categorize and delineate the world into understandable slices. The most basic ingredients of these slices — the flour, egg and water of the universe if you will — are *dynamism*, *stasis* and *entropy*. These three forces form a metaphysical framework — the *Metaphysic Trinity* of magick. As the Celestial Chorus proudly proclaims, "All Awakened humanity communes at the church of the Metaphysic Trinity."

Dynamism

Dynamism is the most active, changing member of the Trinity. It is movement and expansion — the ever-present need to adapt or die. The werewolves term this force the *Wyld*, and many view it as utter random chaos. Dynamism, however, is not necessarily random; it's merely active. This common misconception is one reason the Technomancers are sometimes known as Static Mages. The misnomer comes from the idea that the Black Hats hate randomness and change, that they wish to keep the world moving along carefully controlled channels of reality. Yet, Technos do desire change and work hard to accomplish it. After all, why else do we call the advance of technology the "Industrial Revolution" and now the "Information Revolution?" Technomancers are dynamic — they just aren't random.

Without dynamism, the universe would stagnate and die. Change is a necessary, frightening part of reality, and True Mages are the Avatars of naked change. Through will and belief, the Awakened force reality to shift away from the comfortable static base-line. With each push, whether the gentlest nudge or the most violent shove, reality changes a bit, and everything in it follows, especially the agent of that change.

Stasis

Without *stasis* there could be no stability in the universe. Stasis is the "egg" that binds the water and flour of dynamism and entropy. Without stasis, different realities would constantly collide, and no one piece of reality could hold together long enough for humans (or anyone else) to comprehend. In such a world of constant, shifting chaos, even defining the concept of self becomes impossible. Conversely, too much stasis makes it more and more difficult to enact change. Mages recognize this truth even more than Sleepers do. In the Mythic Ages, stasis and static reality were not as strong as they are in the modern world, and the Awakened had far more latitude to work their Arts.

As stasis takes a greater hold upon the world, reality becomes more rigid and more strictly delineated. Ironically, many people mistakenly believe this effect actually opens up new possibilities and expands their reality. This is certainly not true. As members of the Cult of Ecstasy are fond of pointing out, when people read books, all they have in front of them are a few pieces of paper and words. They must use the most extraordinary tools at their command — their minds — to imagine the sights, sounds and smells of the stories within those pages. When black and white television came along, a grateful public cried, "Ah! Sweet liberation! Now we can actually see what we were forced only to imagine before." The exclamations of delight become even greater at the advent of color TV as now the drama spills into their drab living rooms in "living Techno-color!" Yet each so-called improvement limits possibility; no longer can each person imagine her own Huckleberry Finn. For many, his image is set. With each such change, greater stasis settles over the minds and imaginations of humanity.

The Garou speak of the *Weaver*, a force of connection and order in the world. Stasis is this Weaver, providing a framework for the universal constants which shield us from chaos. Yet without that chaos of change to shape and define it, stasis soon becomes entropy.

Entropy

This element is the end of all and the beginning of all; "From dust we are born, and to dust we return." *Entropy* is the constant pull towards dissolution, a merging of dynamism and stasis so complete that there is no difference between them. Without that contrast, all differentiation crumbles into entropy, and space and matter merge into one. One question posed to all Akashic initiates is a variation on this idea: "How can there be a Self if there is no Other?" This question is far more complex than it first appears and addresses many philosophic problems, but it also identifies the point at which entropy begins — the point at which there is no difference between self and other.

Western philosophers are often quite leery, even frightened, of entropy. Many Easterners, shamans, physicists and mystics believe this fear taints Sleepers' connection to their common reality. Westerners view reality as disparate, packaged in neat, discreet units. The student seated at her desk is utterly distinct from that desk and from the air around her. Throughout time, however, most cultures have recognized that nothing and no one is completely separate from anything else. Shamans and advanced physicists alike lecture that matter is made up of energy, and that only the manifestation of that energy distinguishes student from desk. Both are part of the same, magnificent, swirling energy field.

Both conceptions of reality hold their own dangers if taken to extremes. In the Western view, there is the danger of dynamism disappearing into a static mold, causing entropy. In the second, less rigid view, entropy evolves when boundaries blur into chaos. Either way, the end result is entropy — chaos and destruction.

Entropy is a powerful force; it keeps "old baggage" from lasting past its time. Instead, the "baggage" breaks down and goes into the cycle fresh. Many mages, however, worry that entropy has the upper hand these days. The so-called Reckoning some speak of may have risen from this belief. The Garou battle the construct they term the *Wyrm*, an entity of entropic decay. In recent times, the werewolves report that the Wyrm grows ever stronger. Although most members of the Traditions at first dismissed such worries, they now begin to fear that the Garou are right.

Limits

The Metaphysic Trinity is like a three-sided kaleidoscope through which mages view reality. Every twist and turn, every vigorous shake, causes the beautiful world inside to change. Sometimes the slivers of colored glass and stone expand to fantastic proportions, while other times they collapse until all you see is a single, knife-edged line. Many Awakened Ones believe the prism of mystick history is slowly shrinking, collapsing in upon itself in magickal decay.

Since the time of the Pure Ones, the strictures of material reality have grown to wrap tightly around the willworker. The earliest mages, it is said, feared no Paradox because no single consensual reality existed. Since those days, the population explosion and the spread of modern technology have united the world as never before. Now we have a truly global society and thus a global reality as well. Where once the Tapestry's loosely-bound threads allowed sorcerers to accomplish great feats of magick, a tightly interwoven set of beliefs (and disbeliefs) now binds their Art.

Even now, all mages know that the only limits upon them lie within themselves. Reality is not a set of immutable laws. Mages reside in a multitude of universes, and universes of possibilities reside within them. Yet modern mages are often forced to work carefully through the Tapestry's threads in order to wield magick without attracting Paradox. The Awakened often manage this difficult task by making their magick appear coincidental.

Coincidental Magick

Mages adept at coincidental magick are the true con-men of the Awakened world. Instead of taking the reality-bull by the horns (and hoping not to be gored), modern mysticks usually try to make their magicks appear coincidental. A mage who needs cash *could* just create it from the air around her. No one could ever accept such a feat as normal, however. Instead of taking this quick and dangerous route, the young sorcerer could just trot down to her local convenience store and buy a lottery ticket… and goodness gracious, guess who wins the lottery that night! Static reality, and those who create it, find any particular person's winning the lottery very lucky — but entirely believable.

The more unbelievable the coincidences, the harder it becomes to make reality bend for the mage. Too many "coincidences" can accelerate probability and create what's called the *"Domino Effect"* **(see Chapter Eight)**. A creative mage can often find a way to accomplish her magickal goal through coincidental Arts, and static reality rewards her creativity by allowing this magick to work more easily than other varieties. The collective unconsciousness usually accepts any magickal feat that most Sleepers could find "believable."

Vulgar Magick

Although it's almost always wiser to use coincidental magick, most Awakened Ones sometimes find vulgar magick necessary. Vulgar magick includes causing a lightning bolt to fly out of an enemy's television set and strike him dead, or calling a griffin down from the skies. Such actions rip the Tapestry of static reality apart, reforming it to the mage's own personal vision.

There is no logical (by Sleeper standards) explanation for vulgar magick; its effects lie outside the realms of possibility. A mage who uses it can achieve truly awesome results, but puts herself at terrible risk. Vulgar magick is an obscenity to static reality, as is the mage who uses it. She may well find herself facing Paradox spirits or worse....

Why, if vulgar magick is so dangerous, does a mage resort to it at all? Sometimes the sorcerer falls prey to pride, wishing to glory in her true power. More often, the mage simply finds herself with little choice. She needs a spectacular magickal Effect, and she needs it *now*. A mage who does not know when to take risks will not be long for this world (or any other).

The Elements of Magick

Behold the heaven and the earth
And all the elements; for of these
Are all things created.
— Thomas á Kempis, "Imitation of Christ"

Whether Council Mage or Mirrorshade, Chaos Mage or Fallen One, all True Magi manipulate the fabric of static reality. Yet the forces and components of this reality — and the Arts which shape it — still follow certain laws. A mage must respect and follow these laws if she wishes to succeed. Stasis is a very powerful force (particularly that inertia embodied in the illusion we term "reality"), and it "corrects" forced imbalances and radical change with the dreaded Paradox effect.

Although mages will undoubtedly continue to argue over the exact nature of reality for millennia to come, there are some "absolutes" (essentially game rules) concerning the structure of reality. Some mages (especially Dreamspeakers) argue that such structures derive not from the similarities of belief among Traditions, but rather from the sleeping mind of Earth Herself. Regardless, the vast majority of mages believe there are a few universal constants — the constants upon which the theory of *Spheres* is based.

Many experienced mysticks shake their heads at the idea of classifying magick. When prodded, these mages say that any such attempt is ludicrous, merely tacking human perceptions, desires and prejudices onto an unclassifiable reality. However, even these hyper-enlightened individuals still use Spheres to work magick, and most generally adhere to such imposed patterns as gravity. Although most mages realize that any system of categorization is faulty at best, they recognize that they need one in order to understand magick themselves and to discuss it with others.

Many such systems have arisen over the millennia, and so long as multiple beliefs exist, magick can never have a single underlying structure. These beliefs and traditions form the languages of magick. After all, as many Hermetic mages point out, languages are created from magickal symbols (words and letters) which create something out of nothing to allow communication. The word-symbols allow understanding between individuals or within a single person. The more words a person has to describe a phenomenon, the greater her understanding of it. This is magickal indeed!

Each Tradition has its own ideas about the true nature of magick, but they all agree that magick is a natural force and does have a structure. The Traditions diverge on the more esoteric aspects of this structure, but generally agree on the following fundamentals of magick.

Quintessence

Quintessence is the basic unit, the quark, the Aristotelian "fifth essence," of magick. All matter, all spirit, all elements of reality are composed of this mysterious substance. This Prime Force is neither physical nor ethereal and cannot truly be divided or contained.

Although Quintessence is the stuff of which reality is made, even mages cannot truly understand it. Most views regard Quintessence as an ever-fluctuating pool from which all creation arises and returns. As a basic "life-force," it is often gathered by events of great passion and colored by those same emotions. Sharper students realize that this means Awakened Ones are their own best source of Quintessence, with their Avatars providing the internal wellspring. When a new phenomenon comes into being, it draws Quintessence from the pool. When old phenomena fade away, their magickal energy reenters into the vast pool. Some Euthanatos and Nephandi theorize that should reality achieve a state of perfect entropy, the false frameworks imposed by humanity will melt away, leaving only the pure glory of raw Quintessence.

Tass

Although we can never truly divide Quintessence, sorcerers refer to materialized portions of Quintessence as *Tass*. These Prime bits often provide the Awakened with raw power. But how can mages collect and hoard Tass if Quintessence is indivisible? Most learned Adepts can lecture for hours on just such a question. Perhaps the best way to describe Tass is as temporarily frozen shards of Quintessence, floating on that vast sea of Prime like chunks of ice floating on the ocean. Ice is still water, and will some day return to its liquid form, yet while it is ice, a sculptor can wield his chisel to create objects of art, the soldier can create weapons, and the healer can create a compress to soothe a fevered brow. So too do mages use the Tass in certain objects.

The bodies of magickal beings, such as werewolves or faeries, retain Tass. Willworkers can also collect it from those Nodes which infuse certain physical objects with magickal energy. Unlike Quintessence, Tass is not always a neutral manifestation of Primal Essence; the "flavor" of an object can affect the usefulness of its Tass. Prime elements preserved in the hand of a saint might prove useful for healing, whereas the Tass in a murderer's hand might actually harm the patient.

For all practical purposes, Tass is finite. Once a mage uses up the Tass in a particular object or place, it is gone. As ice melts back into the ocean, so the Tass returns to Quintessence. Only by recharging an item at a Node or finding more Tass can a mage again use a depleted relic.

The Tapestry

The Verbena Heasha Morninglade describes Quintessence as "the raw silk from which we weave the Tapestry of reality." By weaving the threads of Quintessence into different patterns and designs, we create all types of energy, matter and life. Each individual pattern is part of the larger Tapestry, and the patterns interact with, distort, enhance and otherwise affect each other to create the things we see as real.

While no Sleepers, and few mages, can actually perceive these individual patterns, their interaction is easy to see. In simplified terms, we perceive the pattern of a raindrop interacting with the pattern of gravity as rain falling from the sky. Magick, in the form of woven threads of Quintessence, forms the foundation of reality. For all the chemist's and biologist's talk of molecular bonding, and the priest's and wisewoman's talk of faith, Quintessence itself provides the life energy that infuses the Tapestry. Without that energy, the threads would unravel. For the past millennia, most mages have agreed that the Tapestry contains at least three distinct types of pattern-energy: body, spirit and mind.

Body

The realm of the physical world is the realm of the body. Both Sleepers and Awakened alike readily perceive and share this physical reality. Willworkers term our physical realm and the nearest vestiges of spirit surrounding it as the Tellurian **(see Chapter One)**. Most mages believe that the threads of Quintessence which form the realms of spirit combine in simple, easily understood patterns to create the physical Realms. All physical Realms (and there are far more such places than any Sleeper could dream of) are part of the Tellurian, as are the Near Umbral Realms that surround it.

Spirit

Spirit is perhaps the most fundamental aspect of magickal reality. When Quintessence transforms from its most basic, "raw" form into "threads," it becomes spirit. This level of reality is still far too intangible for Sleepers to understand and experience, at least on a conscious level. Masters term the spirit worlds created by these threads the *Umbrae*. Since these Umbrae, or Shadows, are the most fundamental level of reality any mortal can see, mages argue that the Umbrae are the truest reality we can reach. The physical world, they say, is merely a simplified reflection of the spirit.

Mind

Cogito, ergo sum
(I think, therefore I am)
— Rene Descartes, *Le Discours de la Methode*

Mind is perhaps the least understood of these three sections of the Tapestry. Some mages argue that sentience is unquantifiable and incomprehensible, and is perhaps raw Quintessence or at least Tass. Others argue that the development of the mind is a direct reaction to the Tapestry. Since that Tapestry cannot exist without minds and wills to believe in it, the argument goes, there can be no reality without consciousness. Still more argue that since the concept of Quintessence is formulated by the minds of mages, the theory that minds cannot exist without Quintessence is a hopelessly paradoxical, dangerous idea.

The Dreamspeakers point out that this is essentially the magickal version of the chicken and the egg, saying, "What if the very first hen laid the very first egg, and thus the two were one? And what if instead of sitting on the egg to hatch herself, the hen refused, clucking: 'Impossible! I am I! You are just an egg!' And what if the egg then refused to hatch, unwilling to release such a silly cluck on the world? Then where would we be?" If Quintessence only exists because our minds believe in it, yet our minds cannot function without Quintessence, how did both come to exist?

The position and importance of mind in the structure of magick is still little understood. It's entirely possible, by magickal theory, that the mind can conceive of, and thus create, its own building-blocks. This debate continues, particularly among the Masters of the Mind Sphere, who have a passionate stake in the truth. As these Masters are fond of stating, "These matters are ill-understood by *most*."

Belief and Paradigm

All she can see
Are the dreams all made solid
Are the dreams made real
All of the buildings, all of those cars
Were once just a dream
In somebody's head
— Peter Gabriel, "Mercy Street"

Belief lies at the core of all magick. Most mages believe that their common adage, "The flesh is willing, but the spirit is weak," embodies an ultimate truth. The limitations of mind, spirit or body *per se* are not real. We impose our own limits, the limits of belief. For many years, Sleepers (and thus static reality) firmly believed that man could not run a four minute mile, until Roger Bannister ran the mile in 3:59.40 in 1954. Within two months, the four minute mile was beaten again... and again, and again. Now all top runners regularly beat the once-mythic mark. Roger Bannister's belief and skill overcame a tenet of static reality (albeit a minor one) and in so doing changed our world.

The Awakened believe that our personal beliefs shape our actions in many ways. When Freud first discovered hysterical paralysis, he gained some inkling of the true power of belief. This power goes far deeper than such obvious problems, however. In fact, belief often becomes reality. Should an individual believe strongly enough in a particular concept (say, that he cannot open his own front door), he isn't likely to challenge his belief. If he does try, his muscles may grow weak. After a few ineffectual tugs, he concludes that he was right — he can't open the door. This way, he strengthens his own weakness.

Most people cling to their beliefs as security blankets against the great unknown. Even harmful beliefs may become cherished in their certainty. Should enough people believe in some idea or thing, it becomes part of static reality and the established paradigm. What we believe shapes what we do; a man convinced humans cannot fly is unlikely to jump off a cliff while flapping his arms. Even if he does try, he will fall.

Static reality infuses the beings of all human mages, just as it infuses the Sleepers' consciousness. Beliefs structure material reality, yet that reality also structures beliefs. Each participant in this cycle influences the others and ultimately themselves. The Awakened, however, are better able to consciously step around — or even punch through — humanity's paradigm.

Of course, humanity is not the only participant in this cosmic dance. Spirits from the Umbrae or other realities may well influence our own world through their consciousness, beliefs and paradigms. The Dreamspeakers and Verbena often speak of how animal and plant spirits add their voices to the world's song, while the Virtual Adepts insist that techno-spirits influence the spread of the world-wide computer web.

Although philosophical arguments concerning belief and paradigms have filled countless scholarly texts, and will undoubtedly fill countless more, almost all sorcerers agree that our beliefs form both our personal paradigms and the Tapestry of static reality.

The Nine Spheres

The successful mage doesn't merely want something to happen. She couples that will with a whole system of beliefs explaining how and why that event *could* and *will* happen. A mage's reality is subjective, but must still be disciplined and internally consistent. When a Dreamspeaker walks the Umbra, an Akashic Brother levitates into the air, or a Verbena conducts a blood ritual that reaches across worlds, they succeed because they understand not only *what* they do but *how* they must do it. The Awakened Ones must study the forces and elements of reality to produce the magickal Effects which change them.

To ease the formidable task of studying all possible elements of reality, the ancient Masters divided reality into nine separate categories — the nine Spheres of Knowledge. These Spheres supposedly encompass all elements of reality and are the focus of study for all True Mages. Though certain groups tend to emphasize one Sphere over the others, all (or nearly all) Spheres are available to all mages.

Various Traditions and factions interpret the Spheres very differently, often even using entirely different terminology and symbols. Yet, the basic paradigm remains the same: *Conception* — the beginning or the Prime, focusing (or focused by) the Mind — attains substance through the Spirit and leads to *form*, epitomized by the Pattern Arts of Life, Matter and Forces. From there, this "grand idea" becomes the reality we *perceive* — Correspondence and Time — before spiraling down through Entropy so that the process can begin again.

This paradigm is by no means universal. Some even suspect that the model for the Spheres came from the Order of Reason, which worked through so-called "spheres of influence" over a century before the Council's formation **(See "Technocratic Spheres," below)**. Nevertheless, the Spheres remain, at least for now, a way of communicating the elements of one's Art.

The Spheres are as follows:

• **Correspondence**: Three-dimensional space is an illusion; all points of space are or can be united. With this Sphere, the mage can manipulate space and distance.

• **Entropy**: All things eventually make way for that which follows in the great Cycle. With each death and re-birth, there is new hope. Some call it decay, others Fate. Whatever name it goes by, this Art allows the mage to manipulate the forces of probability, disorder and destruction.

• **Forces**: Students of this powerful Sphere know the forces of the elements — electricity, magnetism, fire, wind, gravity, kinetic energy and even nuclear energy.

• **Life**: The Sphere of Life addresses biological patterns and energies — incredibly complex and intricate Arts requiring careful study and practice to master. Masters of this Sphere can create and alter organic life patterns.

• **Matter**: This Sphere covers the study of physical, inorganic patterns. These templates, though simpler to use, are not quite as flexible.

• **Mind:** The Sphere of Mind is the study of sentience. It allows the mage to delve into the mysteries of the human brain, to explore and to avail himself of the powers within.

• **Prime**: The Art of Quintessential reality; training in this Sphere allows the mage to understand and manipulate reality in its rawest forms, to detect, absorb and manipulate this mysterious element.

• **Spirit**: To know the Otherworlds and their inhabitants, a mystick must study this elusive and ephemeral Sphere. With it, she may converse with the Umbrood and even enter their worlds.

• **Time**: This Sphere teaches that time is as subjective as space or matter. Mastery of it allows a mage to manipulate perception or the passage of time.

The Tenth Sphere?

In addition to the nine Spheres discussed above, a number of mages hypothesize the existence of a 10th. These mages believe that this theoretical Sphere — the missing element — can unite the other nine and show the true Path to Ascension. Both the existence and identity of this Sphere are hotly contested. Each Tradition has its own preferred "pet Sphere," and politics all too often interferes with a true exchange of knowledge and theories in this debate. Even the Static Mages have their own "10th Sphere," the elusive Grand Unification Theory of physics. Yet a troubling, fundamental question remains: If all Spheres flow into one, is that not the path to stasis or even entropy? The question is far from resolved, and some Tradition mages may ignore it to the detriment of all.

Technomagick

We like to think of the universe as simple and comprehensible, but the universe is under no obligation to live up to our expectations.

—Joe Primack, theorist at the University of California, Santa Cruz

Few Technomancers can stand to hear their craft referred to as "magick," though metaphysically that is what it is. To them, it is advanced application of scientific principles. These principles, like arcane Hermetic lore, are meticulously researched and refined, then disseminated through the ranks of the Awakened and un-Awakened alike. Through scientific journals and the popular media, "technological advances" herald the Technocrats' new "discoveries," working them into the fabric of acceptable reality. Thus, technomagick has a coincidental edge the mystick Arts lack.

Technocrats refer to their Effects as *procedures*, which resemble Tradition *rotes*. Both kinds of magick are specific feats handed down from on high to the common mage. Some wise-asses among the Progenitors and Void Engineers call procedures "spells," but then, these Conventions have always been known for their eccentric behavior. It is important to remember that although technomagick still rearranges reality at will, to the Technocrat, such feats are only possible through science. No such mage, no matter how powerful, can merely snap his fingers and make things happen. Some principle must *allow* it to happen.

All Technocracy magicks work through some sort of a focus. Gadgets are the most common, though training, conditioning, cybernetics, molecular processing, drugs and DNA alteration channel many procedures. *Devices* carry some potent "advances" which are not yet acceptable under Earth's current reality. Like any other form of Talisman, such Devices can only be used by Awakened handlers — for now. The Sons of Ether and Virtual Adepts learned flexibility from their mystick cousins, but often prefer to hang onto their notions of science as magick and vice versa. Though they can progress past the static limitations of their former allies, most do not.

Technocratic Spheres

Although they view reality and magick in very different ways, the Council and Technocracy perform their crafts in similar ways through nine formalized Spheres — or spheres — of reality. By manipulating these elements, both groups get similar results.

The spheres of influence (which are *not* capitalized in Technocracy jargon) apparently originated in the early days of the Order, though each one applies to some natural law, not a division of reality. The possible link between the Conventions' spheres and the magickal Spheres has been a source of debate for centuries, but humans will, by nature, quantify things to better understand them. This similarity hints at an order outside the human range or some division of the Pure Ones themselves.

Most Technocrats, however, do not recognize the Spirit Sphere. Spirit-tech (often called "dimensional science") remains a closely-guarded secret in many Conventions. Although each one employs it in some way (except for Iteration X, for whom it is forbidden), such procedures are frowned upon unless circumstances demand them.

The Technocracy discourages vulgar procedures; it does not do to open the Union up to Paradox or discovery by the Masses. Showy Effects are only used in isolation or under extreme circumstances, and Devices are protected at any cost. Infractions are punishable by fines, revocation of equipment, imprisonment or worse.

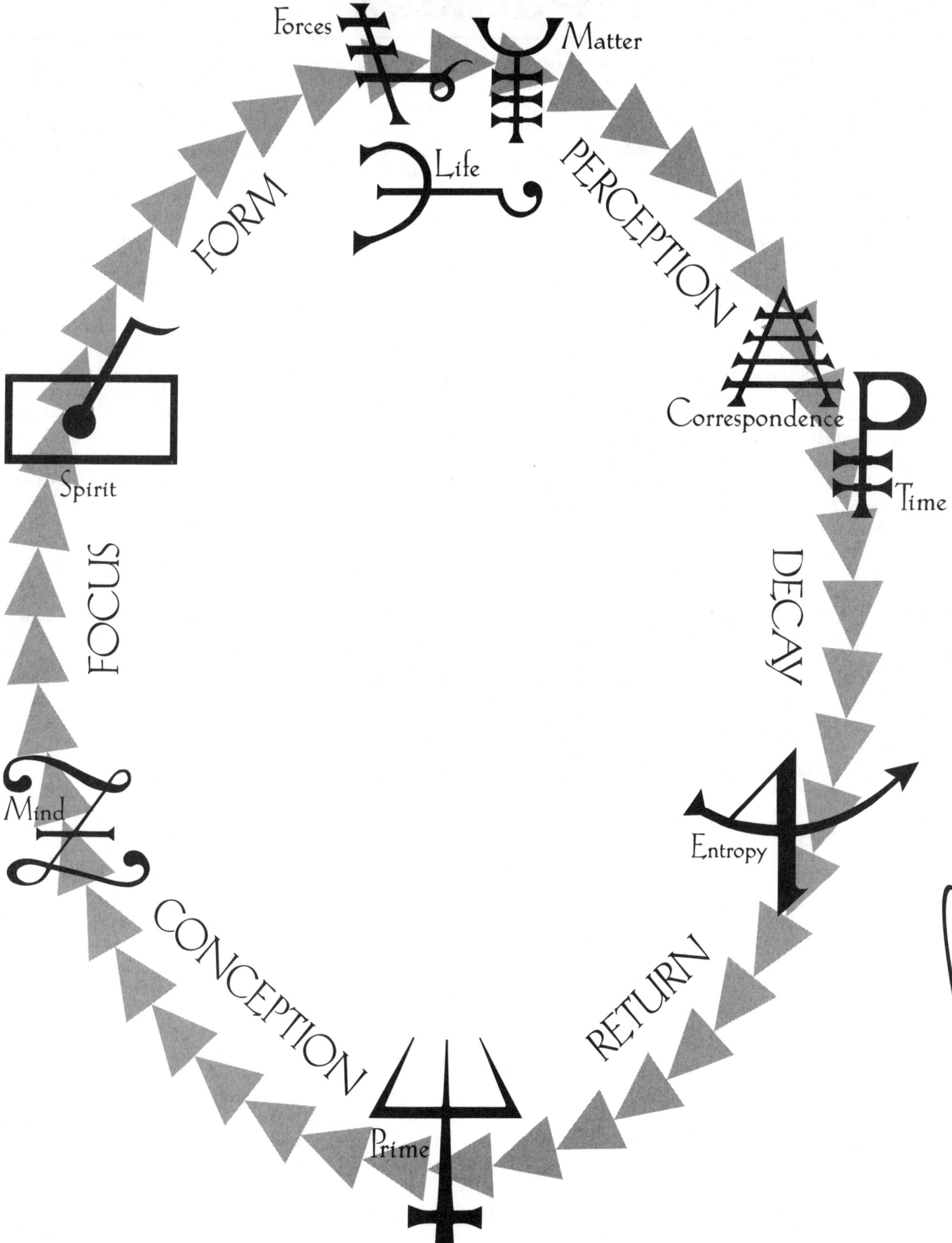

Forces
Matter
Life
PERCEPTION
Correspondence
Time
DECAY
Entropy
RETURN
Prime
CONCEPTION
Mind
FOCUS
Spirit
FORM

Paradox

On being told of the Idea, certain Eeyores advised me against attempting anything of the sort. But following the advice of Eeyores has rarely seemed A Particularly Good Thing for Me to Do. Quite the contrary: if the Eeyores are against something, I tend to think there might be something to it.

— Benjamin Hoff, *The Te of Piglet*

When realities collide, a paradox results. When working True Magick upon the world, a mage attempts to impose her own reality on the static one. Should static reality prove stronger than the mage, she may be overwhelmed by the manifestation of that conflict — *Paradox*.

The cause and origins of this effect are only dimly understood. No one knows why such backlashes happen, but many theories exist. Whatever the true origins of these "reality slaps," all mages agree that Paradox is a constant danger. There is also some agreement as to how and why these effects occur, although this agreement between the Traditions is tenuous indeed.

Some mages that Paradox originated in an ancient feud of the Pure Ones. Other mages hypothesize that Paradox is a test designed by the Wyck to ensure that only truly deserving mortals work magick. The newly Awakened often mistakenly believe that this backlash is an external punishment from the universe; this view of Paradox is child-like in its simplicity. Paradox is not some schoolyard bully waiting to knock down younger children. When a mage imposes his will on the Tapestry, he fundamentally changes the world. In so doing, he changes himself. It's not the world that acts on the mage. Paradox seems to come as much from the mage himself as from any exterior source.

Paradox may even grow out of change itself. Although many Traditionalists seek a Reunification of the One, not everyone is convinced that this is a good idea. Some Akashic Brothers and Hermetic mages caution that it is unwise to assume the Prime wishes to be whole once more. Perhaps the Primal Essence no longer needs the security and stasis of complete unity? Perhaps now is the time for dynamism and growth? If so, Paradox may merely be the growing pains of reality. If we picture physical reality as a tectonic plate, then Paradox and conflict arise like earthquakes where differing reality-plates come together. Without such clashes, there is no growth, no change. The Primal infinity may be wise enough to welcome such evolution.

Some mysticks theorize that the only way to free oneself from Paradox is to become one with your Avatar. They claim that only through experiencing profound ego-death and rebirth can a mage rid himself of the last of his ingrained preconceptions of reality and thus free himself from Paradox. This idea is only theoretical, however, and there are nosane mages known to have entirely freed themselves of Paradox's effects.

Paradox Effects

Even a momentary lapse in belief causes the mage to temporarily lose his stand-off with static reality. Whenever someone loses that wrestling match, he suffers from it. In essence, the sorcerer loses at least a little faith in his belief, just as a pinned wrestler doubts his physical prowess when the ref's hand slams down three times. Instead of diving in gracefully, the sorcerer has slammed into the water. The impact of the divergent realities causes Paradox, like ripples across the surface of a pool.

Paradox effects are personal, immediate and often based on the magick that caused them. What we do affects us in return; this is undoubtedly the underlying reason for the Verbena caution: "Whatever you do returns to you threefold." The appropriate effects of reality slaps should not be surprising, given that many believe the mage's own internal conflict with the static reality truly causes these effects in the first place. If consensual reality had no impact on the sorcerer, Paradox might very well have little or no effect upon him either.

The effects of such reality whacks vary in severity, depending on how far the mystick stretched his "credibility." If consensual reality states that the moon cannot be pulled from orbit, and the mage's paradigm insists that he can do it anyway, the effect of losing this battle might well be the same as a 500-pound gorilla fighting a 98-pound wrestler. Ouch.

Common ripple-effects include *Flaws*, physical damage, *Quiet*, *Realms*, spirits, and the awesome force of *Unbelief*. **(See Chapter Eight.)**

Quiet

Perhaps the most traumatic inner conflict a mage can experience occurs from the gradual accumulation of Paradox energy. The ripples reverberate within his mind like water in a quaking glass. At the same time, the mage's subconscious defends itself by gradually denying the existence of other realities beside his own. When these two conflicting forces grow too disparate, the resulting schism can cause the mage to retreat entirely into his own reality rather than lose it completely. The mage enters a deep psychotic state known as *Quiet*. In this severe state of denial, his reality is the only one that exists. Anywhere.

Paradox backlash can cause a mage to enter Quiet, but that is by no means the only cause. Powerful applications of Mind magick can cause Quiet (or something so similar as to make no difference) in others; the New World Order specializes in creating this type of madness in its enemies. Other outside stresses and profound failures can also cause the mage to enter Quiet. Again, he rejects the external reality of frustration and failure in favor of his own internal world, no matter how grandiose or grim.

This madness can last a long time, or it may work itself out quickly. Either way, the experience is hellish for the mystick — and often for those around her as well. Some Quiets spawn physical hallucinations (sometimes called *hobgoblins*); the stronger the mage, the longer the hobgoblin remains. If the mystick's friends know the Mind Sphere well, they may go into a *mindscape* to try and rescue him. This trip into the magickal subconscious is a dangerous one, and voyagers may be wounded or even killed inside this mad "Dream Realm." Escaping a Quiet often involves facing down the object that sparked the madness.

Magick and the Mage

We are near awakening when we dream that we dream.
— Novalis, *Blutenstaub*

To be awake is to be alive.
— Henry David Thoreau, *Walden, Where I Lived, And What I Lived For*

Magick colors every aspect of a mage's existence. It lies within and without her, through her and past her. A mage's life is a harshly beautiful and radiantly terrible existence whose true nature is revealed in its beginnings.

Awakening

To perceive the true nature of reality, one must first Awaken **(see Chapter Two)**. Hollow Ones sometimes refer to the moment of Awakening as "freefalling." The newly Awakened individual leaps (or stumbles as the case may be) from the enclosed airplane of her former reality into the swirling, buffeting expanse of world she now sees and feels around her. Those without the will or stamina to withstand the Awakening may find themselves trapped in this state; consciousness without will leads to an overwhelming tide of impressions. Who knows how many schizophrenics are actually potential mages badly traumatized by their Awakenings?

The Avatar

Each Awakened One has within herself two spirits or two sides: the Avatar and the mortal, or the divine and profane, as it were. Each aspect interacts with the other in a complex dance. Hopefully, this dance will lead her to continuing enlightenment and eventual Ascension.

As always, mysticks disagree about whether the Avatar allows a person to use magick or whether it is magick that allows her to sense the Avatar. In any case, the Mystick Self must be Awakened and aware before the full potential of magick can be felt. **(Chapter Two details the aspects of the Avatar and the interplay between the mortal and magickal selves.)**

Arete

The term *Arete* may be defined as a mage's enlightened will. All mages must possess at least some degree of Arete in order to work True Magick. The strength of a sorcerer's Awakened Avatar, her level of enlightenment and her strength of will combine to form her Arete.

Of course, the Avatars of those possessing will without enlightenment simply never Awaken. Only those select individuals who possess enlightenment, a strong ego/self, the conscious will to mold reality and an Awakened Avatar truly possess Arete. The stronger these elements in an individual mage, the greater the amount of Arete she possesses and thus the more readily she is able to delve into the mysteries of the universe, both magickal and mundane.

Resonance and Hubris

You must not change one thing, one pebble, one grain of sand, until you know what good and evil will follow on that act. The world is in balance, in Equilibrium. A Wizard's power of changing and summoning can shake the balance of the world. It is dangerous, that power... To light a candle is to cast a shadow.

— Ursula K. LeGuin, *A Wizard of Earthsea*

No one and nothing can interact with anyone or anything else without being affected in return. The theory of Resonance states that just as a mage affects the world with her magick, that magick affects her as well. By wielding her power, she fundamentally changes herself, and a bit of her lingers with the magick. The effects of this Resonance may not be readily discernible in the short term. Many mages, however, point to the Masters of Spheres, who inevitably reflect those same Spheres in some way, as evidence of Resonance. A Master of Life, for example, normally ages very slowly and never gets sick.

There is much debate concerning how far this Resonance extends into all aspects of existence. However, a number of Verbena and Sons of Ether claim that strong psychic upheavals or traumatic events can leave long-lasting echoes which affect others who later pass through that area. When a mage works magick that resonates with the energies infusing a particular area (say attempting a healing at an ancient hospice), the resonance between the magick and the psychic environment makes her more likely to succeed. Conversely, if her magick clashes with the energies of such an area, it is more difficult for the mage to overcome static reality — and more likely that her Art will backfire.

Realms, too, seem to exhibit a tendency to mirror their long-term occupants. Though many mysticks reject this "Resonance Effect," more circumspect mages wonder if the others just don't like to think of living in such mirrors. Whatever its causes or manifestations, Resonance appears to be a lesson-in-progress: whatever you do, make sure you're willing to accept the consequences!

One dangerous effect of the interaction between magick and mage can be *hubris* — overweening pride which snares willworkers who believe that their power makes them right. This leads to overconfidence — a leading cause of Paradox, evil deeds, selfishness and ruin. Believing her own "press releases," the mage may lose her enlightened perspective. Hubris colors magick, making it small and selfish.

For this reason, Akashic Masters warn their disciples to be as the willow, not as the oak. A mage who succumbs to hubris no longer has the mental or emotional flexibility to acknowledge or accept even small failures. Such rigidity often leads to disaster, although a proud mage can become amazingly powerful before bringing doom upon himself.

Magick Styles

Although mages share the universal bonds of Awakening and Awareness, they are far from the Brady Bunch of cosmic relations. Reality is never a one-way street, and sorcerers affect and are in turn affected by everything and everyone they contact: ideas, cultural stereotypes, fast food, urban legends, dirty old men, classrooms, illness and health. In many ways, the universe is a constantly moving stream of particles bouncing off of and into each other at ever-changing speeds. The Awakened are much the same way, and like any other being, they carry their experiences with them. Those experiences shape the methods and Effects within their Arts.

Whatever cultural milieu a willworker grew up and lives in affects her beliefs, even her own reality paradigm. A sorcerer works from what she knows; thus, while mages share certain commonalties, each performs his or her magick very differently.

A Dreamspeaker shaman born and raised in the Australian Outback and a Virtual Adept whiz kid who grew up in southeast Washington, D.C. may both know how to contact ghosts, but the spirits they contact and they ways they go about it, couldn't be more dissimilar. Consider: The shaman in Australia, pouring out a measured palmful of precious water upon the roots of his ancestor tree, waiting for his past self to contact him... The cynical-scared Virtual Adept, feeling ancient at 19, etching the names of his dead brothers on the clean plastic surface of his 3.5 floppy... Succeeding in his quest, the shaman receives his answers as the ancestor tree bleeds dark red sap in mystick patterns so ancient they are carved in his bones... Bending over his battered laptop, the painfully thin Virtual Adept watches as fractal patterns ooze and bleed across the screen. Finally, words begin to appear across the patterns in the shaking scrawl everyone seems to adopt with a laser pen. The Adept's face glows a sickly green as he stares at his brothers' message....

There are certainly differences between the ways Tradition and Technocracy mages work their Arts and between the forms their Arts take. These willworkers have at least usually experienced the same base reality for much of their lives. The Nephandi and Marauders often step into (or out of) a reality almost unimaginably different than that of other mages. The Fallen Ones serve dark masters, and their beliefs, their magicks, echo this cruel, power-hungry servitude. Where a Verbena might scatter seeds in sacred patterns while calling to the Goddess to grant her knowledge, a Nephandus might lure a small child to that same field and defile him before offering the blood to his master.

The almost lovingly calculated tortures and ritual terrors of the slave-master Nephandi are in direct contrast to the fluid chaos of the Marauders. Cocooned in their mad realities, the Marauders' Arts are impossible to truly describe. The only commonalty in their magick is that, unlike other mages, their working always seems wrong for the result. A Marauder who wishes to move utterly silent and invisible through a city street may begin to run, scream, draw her nails across her own flesh and vomit obscenities until this bizarre rant grows so hideous that the mystick disappears (although those she passes may feel strangely nauseous). A number of Marauders also subscribe to the Zen chaos approach to magick, allowing themselves to slip into an utterly consciousness state which allows their dynamic madness maximum freedom.

No one, not even a Marauder, lives in a vacuum. Although the Awakened are far more aware of reality's true, malleable nature, they are still subject to the static world around them.

Foci

Foci are objects, mantras, rituals, dances, etc. which allow a mage to concentrate her Avatar's power and her own will. Aptly named, foci help Awakened Ones focus more intensely upon their own reality. Such items or activities are not magickal in their own right, but essentially props to help mages access their Art. The newly Awakened need such items more than most, for their inexperience often leaves them unable to produce magickal Effects without a focus.

Different magickal styles and Traditions encourage varying types of foci. A Cult of Ecstasy groupie might find wild dancing a perfect focus for Spirit magick, while a Dreamspeaker might use his rain sticks. There are also a number of mages, including Technocracy hacks, Virtual Adepts and Sons of Ether, whom willworkers classify as Technomancers. These Techno-Merlins focus their magick through technology and often benefit because the current static reality accepts great "technological" feats more readily than those with no "rational" explanation. Yet, these mages often risk relying so heavily on their foci that they become magickally crippled without them. Regardless of culture or orientation, foci are always most useful when they mesh well with a mage's magickal style and the local paradigm.

Although all mages find foci helpful from time to time, most prefer not to rely on such items. Large foci, such as a Verbena's cauldron, are not easily portable, and others are so unwieldy they slow the speed with which the mage works magick. A Virtual Adept may need to compose a few lines of computer code, for example, while an Euthanatos may paint a skull upon her face. Different foci — similar results. All three are inconvenient if one is dodging bullets.

Some mages rely on unique items, which derive much of their "power" simply from a personal connection. The sorcerer can invest these foci with some measure of her personal Resonance, using them as a safeguard or a reserve. These personal foci are often more potent than more generalized ones, but the connection to the willworker also makes them tempting magickal crutches. If the sorcerer loses that focus, she must often relearn the Sphere in question before she can wield its power again.

Talismans, Devices and Fetishes

Talismans are inanimate items which evoke very specific magickal Effects, Arts wrapped into an item during its creation and fueled by stored Quintessence. Classical Talismans include magickal swords, rings, dust and even tattoos. Mysticks of great ability craft such things to deliver magick on command or to allow other less-powerful mages to use Arts beyond their learning. Talismans generally work only for Awakened beings. Any Sleeper who attempts to use, say, a Talisman wand is merely waving a stick around.

Talismans require a great expenditure of time, knowledge, effort and often craftsmanship on the creator's part. They're unique and sometimes dramatically powerful items; in modern times, such treasures are precious and very rare. Technocratic *Devices* are more common; these weapons, scanners, portals and even vehicles harness technomagick to "operate" on a higher level of technology than any mundane item allows. These Devices often require special skills to utilize.

Fetishes are powerful magickal aids for those who know the ways of the spirits. Unlike Talismans, fetishes do not derive their power from stored magicks; rather, they contain spirits who have been bound through some means into a material object to perform some limited service. Most fetishes have only one power, although some have as many as two or three. Because fetishes are actually spirits harbored in matter, they often have their own preferences and peculiarities. Many consider them more trouble than they are worth.

Conclusion: The Continued Quest

From the time they first Awaken, all mysticks must seek their own Path towards further enlightenment and understanding. All too often, the neophyte simply prostrates herself at the feet of her seemingly-omnipotent teacher and begs for knowledge. She pictures herself a sponge, easily soaking up the wisdom it took her mentor a lifetime (perhaps many lifetimes) to accomplish. Yet magickal enlightenment cannot be learned secondhand and most definitely cannot be learned through another. Witness the Orphans who manage to find their own way through the pitfalls of Awakening.

What good is a mentor if she cannot simply instruct the new mage on how to do to further her understanding and skill with magick? The Verbena often tell their apprentices the following story to explain the mentor's role in aiding the student:

Imagine you stand now at the brink of a rushing, treacherous river of great beauty and sudden depths. Only through crossing this river can you see the enlightenment you seek, only by crossing can you taste of its sweet knowledge. No one else can cross the river for you. Only you can take that Path, but your mentor may point out the stones which you can step during your journey. The trek may still be treacherous, and it must be made alone. But at least by listening to your mentor, you can see the correct path. It is still up to you to make the journey.

Book Two: The Spirit

The Mad One

how is it, do you think, to have your brain yanked out your nose?
i sing the embodied scream, tremors gone sallow and wings flown low on sweetberry justice. do i confuse you? good. that makes two of us, and only if i'm hiding from myself.

did you think as you saw into my pretty brown eyes that i would stand to be wiped from your porch like a stain of something best left hidden? did you think that in some vast corner of my shattered life i could even forgive you for leaving me alone to face my screams?

did you think it wouldn't matter when the pain began? or did you think i wouldn't notice?

how is it, do you
think, to be a salted slug
dissolving slow enough to hear
your own skin popple and fizz? did it
anger you, when the grains fell
from heaven like a final
night and melted
through your flesh
like razors, or
did it make
you happy
not to
have to
deal with me?

i'm free now, you see, and i whisper like piss in
a corner and cobble up phantoms to tease you.
how does it feel to be the bad man, to be
the sad man?
it doesn't. it doesn't feel at all.

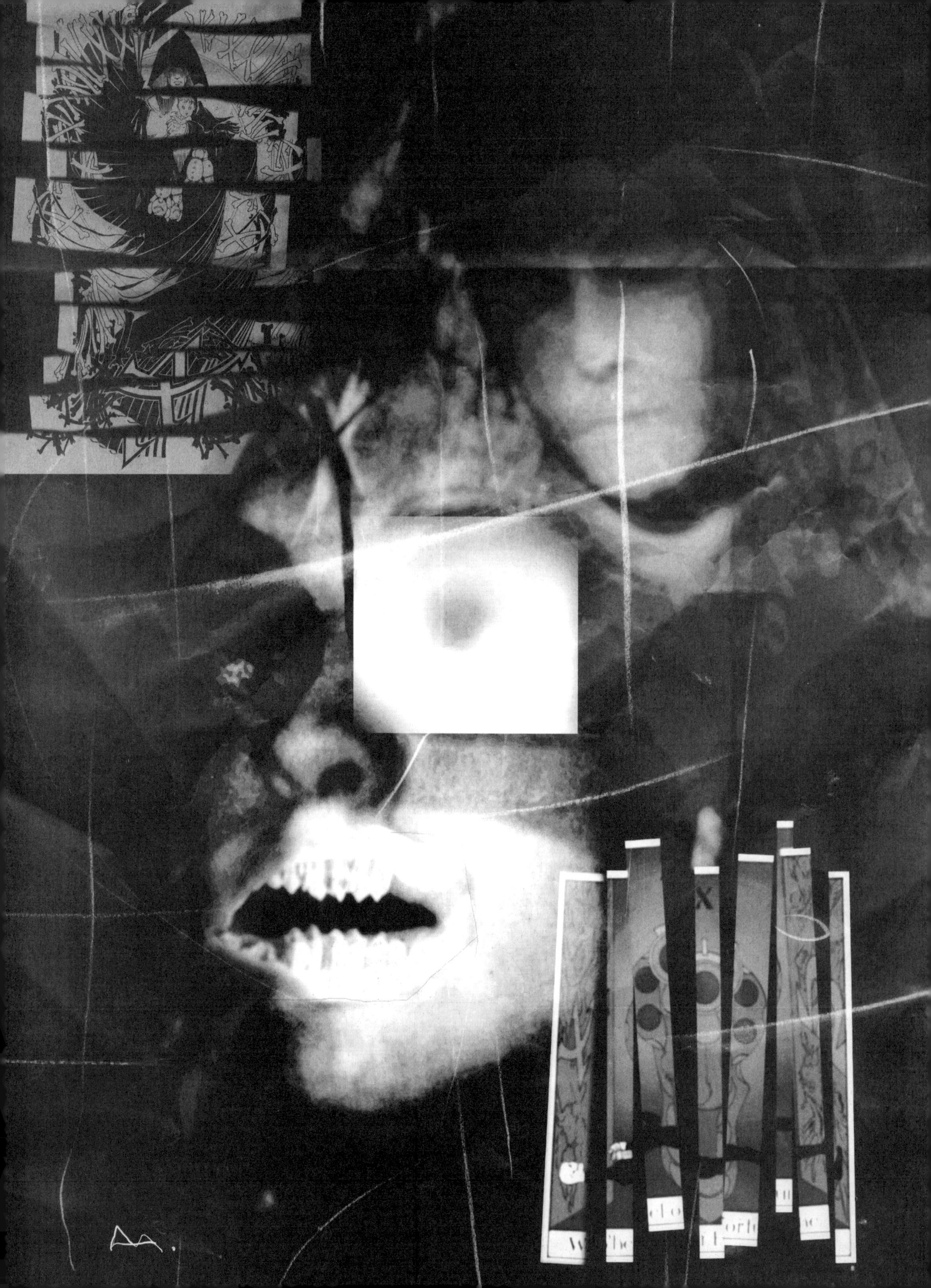

Chapter Five: Basic Rules

Rebels learn the rules better than the rule-makers do. Rebels learn where the holes are, where the rules can best be breached. Become an expert at the rules. Then break them with creativity and style.

— Kristine Kathryn Rusch, *The Rules*

Conflict: Battle

Clarissa shook her head; the enemy mage's blow had left her ears ringing. Kobie grabbed the intruder, but dropped him as he felt a searing pain. The man turned on Kobie and laughingly reached out to take a clump of the singer's dreadlocks in his hand.

"No!" Clarissa screamed, fearful not just for the sanctity of their haven but for her mentor's life. She pulled the gun from her purse — a weapon she seldom drew, much less used — and quickly fired three shots. The bullets went wide, ricocheting off the exposed steel beams of the warehouse, flying wildly at first, then suddenly striking the intruder's back. Screaming in pain, he released Kobie, who stood and seized the man's neck in an iron grip.

"Give me one good reason why I shouldn't snap your goddamn neck, death mage." He shook the man. "Tell me!"

The mage gave a short, pained laugh, a few drops of blood gathering at the corner of his mouth. "Because I'm only doing what I'm supposed to do," he said. "Word had gotten out that you and your little chickadee there had been going astray. I just came to see if the rumors were true." He coughed. "I'm delighted to see that all is well."

Kobie growled and tightened his grip around the Euthanatos' throat. Clarissa's hand on his shoulder stopped him.

"Let him go, Peter. Please. Just because we do things differently doesn't mean we're right."

Staring at her, Kobie dropped the mage, who quickly scrambled off. Clarissa shuddered as she saw something dark and cold flicker in her mentor's eyes. The same warm brown eyes that had once looked at her with nothing but the sheer joy of a creator now reflected envy and frustration.

Mage, like basketball, bridge or *Monopoly*, is a game. Like all games, it has rules that allow a group of players to share the game (hopefully!) without arguing too much about what goes on. You know the scene — "Bang! Bang! You're dead!" "Am not!" "Are too!" Arguments get in the way of the fun. With **Mage**, we've given you a selection of rules to play by, to guide your games with as little arguing as possible.

These rules are suggestions for the most part. They govern the way we like to run our own games, and they reflect the texture of the World of Darkness. To us, the story is more important than charts and statistics. Thus, our rules are pretty abstract; use them as you see fit. Be warned — the more you abandon the rules, the more open to debate your game becomes. Don't feel constrained by the systems we offer, but be prepared to get flexible if the rules go out the window. **(See Chapter Seven for more about Storytelling).**

Rules and Storytelling

I am cured, gentlemen: because I can act the madman to perfection, here; and I do it very quietly. I'm only sorry for you that have to live your madness so agitatedly, without knowing it or seeing it.

— Luigi Pirandello, *Henry IV*

Most games are played to "win" — certain criteria define a player or team as "the winner," and the game is over. Storytelling games, however, are completely different. Once the game starts, it keeps going until either the story ends or the players go home. A roleplaying story can be a short one, taking only a few hours, a long "mini-series" that takes multiple sessions to complete, or a never-ending, soap operalike chronicle that goes on forever. There are no winners or losers — only players.

Some players take on the role of characters, modern mages in this case. Another player, called the Storyteller, sets up the world in which those characters exist. Although it may be hard to tell sometimes, players and Storyteller are not adversaries — they are collaborators. Such "troupes" work together to cobble up an imaginary world.

Storytelling games are a combination of entertainment and modern mythology. By entering into an imaginary world, we escape from our own world for a while. In sharing this new realm, however, we accomplish something more profound — we create a dream. It's important to remember that these stories are just that, *stories*, but within that framework, we can move mountains, sometimes literally. In this context, winning and losing seem petty. The play, as Shakespeare said, is the thing.

We've designed these rules to be simple, yet still take the variables of this complex setting into account. Use them as you see fit.

Time

Time is as good a place to start as any. These are five different ways to describe divisions of time in **Mage** games, progressing from the smallest unit to the largest all-encompassing one.

- **Turn** — One unit of time within a scene, anywhere from three seconds to three minutes in length. A turn is enough time to take one *action* **(discussed below)**.
- **Scene** — One compact period of action and roleplaying that takes place in a single location. A scene takes as few or as many turns as are necessary.
- **Chapter** — One independent part of a story, almost always played in one game session, made up of scenes connected by periods of downtime.
- **Story** — A complete tale, with an introduction, buildup and climax, that often takes several chapters to complete.
- **Chronicle** — A whole series of stories connected by the lives of the characters and perhaps a broadly conceived theme and plot; the ongoing story your troupe creates.

Dice Rolling

Mage requires a few 10-sided dice, which you can buy in any game store. If you're the Storyteller, you'll want plenty of dice all to yourself. Players use fewer dice. The system we use is a pretty simple one. Although it seems complicated at first, the basis of these rules is simple:

- Your character has a certain amount of dots in each of her *Traits* **(see below)**. These dots reflect how good she is at certain things. When you (or, more precisely, your character) take an action, you roll one 10-sided die for every dot she has in the Trait or Traits she's using.
- You'll want to roll a certain amount of *successes* to accomplish things. A success is when you match or exceed a *difficulty number;* this difficulty, which your Storyteller usually tells you, is a number between 1 and 10 which reflects how hard the task is. The higher the difficulty, the harder the task.
- The modifiers may add or subtract from this target number or from the amount of dice you roll. A +1 difficulty, therefore, adds 1 to the number you must match. Adding one to your die pool gives you another one to roll.
- The more successes you roll, the better your character did; if you don't roll any, she failed. If you gain negative successes **(a *botch;* see below)**, she screwed up, and may suffer the consequences....

That's it. The rest is all variations on this basic idea.

Actions

In Storytelling games, players act out their characters' conversations and describe that character's actions to the Storyteller. An action can be anything from jumping across a gorge to glancing back to see if anyone is following. The player simply tells the Storyteller what her character is doing and how.

Many actions are automatic: walking across the street toward the warehouse, for instance. All the Storyteller needs to do is keep track of where the character is and what she's doing. However, certain actions require a dice roll to determine success or failure.

Trait Ratings

A character's *Traits* — her innate and learned abilities and aptitudes — are defined by dots, or numbers. Each Trait has a rating from one to five, which describes the character's ability in that particular Trait. One is lousy, and five is superb.

Consider the normal human range to run from one to three, with two being average. However, some people can have Traits of four (exceptional) or five (superb), or even have a zero in a Trait (which is extremely rare, but not unheard of).

x	Abysmal
•	Poor
••	Average
•••	Good
••••	Exceptional
•••••	Superb

For each dot your character has in a particular Trait, you get to roll one die. Thus, if you had four dots in Strength, you would get to roll four dice. If you had one dot in Perception, you would only get to roll one die. However, you almost never simply roll the number of dice you have in an *Attribute* (your intrinsic capabilities). Usually you get to add the appropriate Attribute's number of dice to the number of dice you have in an *Ability*, things that you know and have learned.

So if the Storyteller wants the players to roll to see if they notice the patrol car creeping up behind them, he would have them roll their Perception + Alertness, an Attribute + an Ability. They'd pick up as many dice as they had dots in Perception, and then take as many dice as they had dots in Alertness.

These dice are called the *Dice Pool*. This pool is the total number of dice a player rolls in a single turn, usually for a single action, though a player can divide her Dice Pool if she wants her character to perform more than one action. Some Traits (Willpower and Health Levels, for example) can go up and down during a story. The character's permanent rating usually stays the same; most changes are marked in the squares which represent her current rating. A character's Dice Pool is usually based on her Trait's permanent rating (the circles), not its current score (the squares).

Many actions don't require or even have an appropriate Ability. For example, if a player wants to break down a door, he'd only use an Attribute (in this case, Strength), rolling the number of dice listed for that Attribute.

There is absolutely no situation in which more than two Traits can combine to form a Dice Pool. Only one Trait can be used if it has a potential value of 10; Traits like Willpower can never be combined with another Trait. It is generally impossible for a normal human being to have more than 10 dice in a Dice Pool.

Finally, a character's ratings in her Spheres are never rolled. Magick is used with other rolls, which are described in **Chapter Eight.**

Difficulties and Successes

Now you've got to figure out what you need to look for when you roll the dice. The Storyteller will give you a difficulty rating, which is the minimum number you need to roll in order to succeed. A difficulty is always a number between 2 and 10. You must roll that number or higher on at least one of the dice in your Dice Pool to succeed. Each time you do so, it's called a *success*. If the difficulty is a 6 and you roll a 2, 3, 5, 6 and 9, you've scored two successes. Though you usually need only one success, the more you score, the better you perform. Scoring only one success is considered a marginal achievement, while three is considered a complete success, and five is a momentous event.

Difficulties

3	Easy
4	Routine
5	Straightforward
6	Standard
7	Challenging
8	Difficult
9	Extremely Difficult

Degrees of Success

One Success	Marginal
Two Successes	Moderate
Three Successes	Complete
Four Successes	Exceptional
Five Successes	Phenomenal

The lower the difficulty, the easier the task, and vice versa. The Storyteller may decide to let some actions slide without a roll (an automatic success) if your character's Traits total higher than the difficulty itself.

Though they're not on the list above, your Storyteller can also assign difficulties of 2 or 10. This should be rare; difficulty 2 is pathetically easy, and difficulty 10 is so damned hard you're more likely to screw it up than you are to succeed. Any 10s a player rolls are successes, no matter what. Unless the Storyteller says otherwise, the standard difficulty for a particular task is always a 6.

Complications

It's usually easy to score a single success, even with only one or two dice. You have a 75% chance for a marginal success when you roll only two dice on a difficulty of 6. Sounds easy. Of course, there are a few complications for the troupes that want them. If your group is heavily into roleplaying, simple rolls and automatic successes are enough. Complications reflect a situation's variations; using them makes a game out of the scene.

Botches

Whenever you roll a "one," it cancels out a success. Remove both the success die and the "one" die, and pay them no more heed. If you roll more "ones" than you do successes, you botch; some sort of disaster occurs. Don't count the "ones" that canceled out successes, but if even a single "one" is left after all the successes have been canceled, a botch occurs. If there aren't any "ones" or successes left, you've simply failed.

Some troupes count extra "ones" as really bad botches — double botches or even triple ones. This is entirely optional, and can get to be a real pain for the players (even if it *is* amusing occasionally…).

Multiple Actions and Splitting Dice Pools

If you want your mage to do more than one thing in a turn, you can elect to split the Dice Pool between actions. The amount of dice you throw behind each action is up to you, but if one pool is smaller than the other (a Wits + Alertness of four dice against, say, a Dexterity + Firearms of six), the smaller Dice Pool is used.

Automatic Successes

Rolling dice all the time gets in the way of roleplaying. During most scenes — especially when we're deeply involved in the story — we don't roll dice at all, and roleplay without interruptions. Automatic successes keep players from making rolls for actions characters could perform in their sleep.

Most troupes usually use a combination of dice rolling and automatic successes. These work like this: if the number of dice you have in your Dice Pool is equal to or greater than the difficulty, you succeed automatically. It's a marginal victory, just as if you'd only rolled one success; sometimes you'll want to roll anyway to try for a more favorable result. But for simple, common actions, automatic successes eliminate a lot of wasted time. The story is what matters, anyway.

Another twist: a Willpower point **(see Chapter Six)** can be spent to earn an automatic success. You won't want to do this often, but sometimes you'll need a reliable result. Of course, the Willpower only counts for one success per point spent, and once Willpower is spent, it's gone for a while.

Extended Actions

Simple actions only require one success. Some tasks, called extended actions, require more than one success to fully complete. You'll need to accumulate three, or seven, or even 20 successes (on rare occasions).

An extended action allows you to roll over and over on subsequent turns in an attempt to collect enough successes to succeed. Say your character is climbing a tree; the Storyteller announces that when you roll a total of seven successes, she's climbed to the top. She'll get there, of course, but the more times you roll, the more chances your character has to botch and injure herself. If she's attempting to climb down the tree because it's on fire, the amount of time it takes becomes exceedingly important.

During an extended action, you can keep trying to obtain successes for as long as you want, or at least until you fail to score even one. If you botch, your character may have to start over from scratch, with no accumulated successes. The Storyteller may decide not to let the character try again at all.

Extended actions are more complicated than simple actions, and shouldn't often be employed in the middle of intense roleplaying. As the Storyteller, you decide what type of action is called for. A little bit of experience will be your best advisor.

Resisted Actions

Sometimes your efforts will oppose another character's. (The obvious example is a tug-of-war, either physical or magickal.) Both of you will make rolls, with a difficulty often indicated by some Trait of the other character, and the person who scores the most successes succeeds. However, you are considered to score only as many successes as the amount by which you exceed your opponent's successes. The opponent's successes eliminate your own, just as "ones" do. Outstanding successes on resisted actions are both difficult and rare. Even if your opponent can't beat you, she can diminish your efforts. On actions that are both extended and resisted, one of the opponents must collect a certain number of successes in order to win. Each success above the opponent's total number of successes in a single turn is added together. The first opponent to collect the designated number of successes wins the contest.

Teamwork

Characters can work together to collect successes, most often during an extended action. At the discretion of the Storyteller, two or more characters can make rolls separately and combine their successes. They may never combine their separate Traits for one roll, though. Teamwork is effective in some circumstances, such as in combat, shadowing prey, collecting information and repairing devices. During others, it can actually be a hindrance; in many social actions, it can confuse the subject.

The chart below may clarify the different types of rolls.

Trying It Again

Failure is frustrating. If you're having trouble with your computer and can't figure out the source of the system error, then you're in for an angst-ridden time. **Mage** reflects this frustration by increasing the difficulty of any action that is tried again after an initial failure.

Whenever a character attempts an action she previously failed, the Storyteller has the option of increasing the difficulty of the action by one. Consider Randolph, trying to intimidate a club bouncer. If his first attempt failed, it's going be harder the second time around, so the difficulty is +1 greater. If he tries a third time, his difficulty is +2 greater. In cases like this, though, the Storyteller can always rule that he cannot even make another try — how do you intimidate someone who just called your bluff? Other examples include picking a lock (Streetwise), scaling a wall (Athletics), and remembering a word in a foreign language (Linguistics).

Action	Example	Description
Simple	Firearms, Alertness	One roll completes the task. Once the difficulty is set, the player rolls his dice. Automatic success is possible.
Extended	Research, Seduction, Strong Magicks	The task takes a certain amount of successes to complete. Often requires more than one roll.
Resisted	Gambling, Shadowing	Two characters oppose each other; both roll and compare their successes. The character with the most successes wins.
Extended & Resisted		Like a resisted action, but the winner must first accumulate a certain amount of successes.

In some instances, such as in combat, the Storyteller shouldn't invoke this rule. Missing someone with your first shot isn't going to fluster you so much that you'll never hit your target. If you miss a lot, however, it could get on your nerves....

Other times when *not* to use the rule are: seeing something out of the corner of the eye (Alertness) and dodging an attack (Dodge).

Examples of Rolls

Well, that's it. These are the rules. This system for dice is all you really need to know in order to play this game. All the other rules are just clarifications and exceptions.

Following are some examples of rolls, to provide you with some ideas on how to incorporate these rules into your roleplaying. Please note that each Attribute can work with each Ability, so there are many different rolls that can be made. Admittedly, you won't have to roll Stamina + Computer often, but it might come up (especially if you're pulling late nights to make a deadline). Common activities are given in more detail in the Drama chapter.

- You're trying to concentrate on reading a passage in a book, but there's a lot of noise and commotion in the hall outside. Roll Perception + Meditation (difficulty 7). You need to collect 10 successes to complete the selection.
- You threaten the young man by trying to lift him up by his collar. Roll Strength + Intimidation (difficulty 8).
- An opponent of yours is winning political support from others in the Tradition; his carefully chosen words are making your ideas look foolish. Roll Manipulation + Etiquette (difficulty 8) to minimize the damage to your reputation.
- You want to break down the metal door that was just slammed in your face. You need to roll Strength (difficulty 8). You must accumulate six successes in order to break it open enough to slip through.
- You try to slip out of your handcuffs. Roll Dexterity + Streetwise (difficulty 10).
- After being questioned for hours, roll Stamina + Expression to see if you can successfully maintain your story (difficulty 8). Five successes completely convinces your interrogators.
- The mob before you is hostile, but also friendless and in trouble. Roll Charisma + Leadership (difficulty 8) to see if you can find a way to lead them from peril. You need to collect at least five successes before they'll truly trust you.
- How long can you remain motionless in the bushes as the two guards chat for hours on end? Roll Stamina + Stealth (difficulty 7).
- There's something strange about the way the two old men are playing cards. Roll Perception + Enigmas (difficulty 9) to see if your character can fathom the odd pattern formed by the cards.
- How flawlessly do you conduct yourself at the Chantry formal dinner? Roll Dexterity + Etiquette (difficulty 8).
- By showing off your moves, you try to convince your opponent to back off. Roll Manipulation + Brawl (difficulty 6). Three successes will cause him to pause for a turn, but you can try this action only once...
- What language is she speaking? Roll Intelligence + Linguistics to ascertain (difficulty 6).
- Suddenly, a man pushes a crate out of the van you've been chasing — roll Wits + Drive to see if you can avoid hitting it (difficulty 6).

The Golden Rule

Logic must take care of itself.
— Ludwig Wittgenstein

Remember that in the end there is only one real rule in **Mage**: there are no rules. The story is the thing. Fashion this game into whatever you need it to be — if the rules get in your way, then ignore or change them. In the end, the complexity of the real world cannot be captured by rules; it takes storytelling and imagination to do that. Indeed, these rules are not so much rules as they are guidelines, and you are free to use, abuse, ignore or change them as you wish.

Game Terms

Ability: A Trait that describes what a character knows and has learned, rather than what she is. Abilities are Traits such as Intimidation, Firearms and Cosmology.

Action: An action is the performance of a consciously willed physical, social or mental activity. When a player announces that his character is doing something, he is taking an action.

Advantages: A catch-all category that describes the magickal Spheres and Backgrounds of a character.

Arete: This important Trait describes the understanding and strength of your enlightened will **(see Chapter Six)**.

Attribute: A Trait that describes a character's inherent aptitudes. Attributes are such things as Strength, Charisma and Intelligence.

Botch: A disastrous failure, indicated by rolling more "ones" than successes on the 10-sided dice rolled for an action.

Character: Each player creates a character, an individual she roleplays over the course of the chronicle.

Dice Pool: This describes the dice you have in your hand after adding together your different Traits. It is the maximum number of dice you can roll in one turn, though you can divide these dice between different actions.

Difficulty: A number from 2 to 10, measuring the difficulty of an action a character takes. The player needs to roll that number or higher on at least one of the dice rolled. For clarity, difficulties are always indicated by a numeral, rather than a word.

Downtime: Time spent between scenes, when no roleplaying is done and turns are not used. Players might take actions, and the Storyteller might give some descriptions, but generally time passes quickly.

Effect: A magickal action, i.e., a Life 3 Effect.

Extended Action: An action that requires a certain number of successes for the character to actually succeed.

Health: A measure of a character's injuries or health.

Paradox: A mage's headache Trait; Paradox increases when he uses magick that noticeably contradicts the prevailing reality.

Points: The temporary scores of Traits such as Willpower, Quintessence and Health; the squares, not the circles.

Quintessence: The truest energy of the universe. The amount of it a mage possesses is measured by the Trait of the same name.

Rating: A number describing the permanent value of a Trait; most often a number from one to five, though sometimes a number from one to 10.

Refresh: When points are regained in a Dice Pool, it is said that they are being "refreshed." The number of points regained is the refresh rate.

Resisted Action: An action that two different characters take against each other. Both compare their number of successes and the character with the most wins.

Scene: A single episode of the story; a time when and place where actions and events take place moment by moment. A scene is often a dramatic high point of the story.

Simple Action: An action that requires the player to score only one success to succeed, though more successes indicate a better job or result.

Spheres: The nine divisions of magick that rate the aspects of reality a mage understands and manipulates.

Storyteller: The person who creates and guides the story by assuming the roles of all characters not taken by the players and determining all events beyond the players' control.

System: A specific set of complications used in a certain situation; rules to help guide the rolling of dice to create dramatic action.

Trait: A Trait is any Attribute, Ability, Advantage or other character index that can be described as a number (in terms of dots).

Troupe: The group of players, including the Storyteller, who play **Mage** — usually on a regular basis.

Willpower: One of the most important Traits, measuring the self-confidence and internal control of a character. However, Willpower works differently from most Traits — it is usually used up, rather than rolled.

Chapter Six: Character Creation

Strangeness is always both attractive and repellent...A character who is familiar and unsurprising seems comfortable, believable — but not particularly interesting. A character who is unfamiliar and strange is at once attractive and repulsive, making the reader a little curious and a little afraid. We may be drawn into the story, curious to learn more, yet we will also feel a tingle of suspense, that tension that comes from the earliest stages of fear, the uncertainty of not knowing what this person will do, not knowing if we're in danger or not.

— Orson Scott Card, *Characters and Viewpoint*

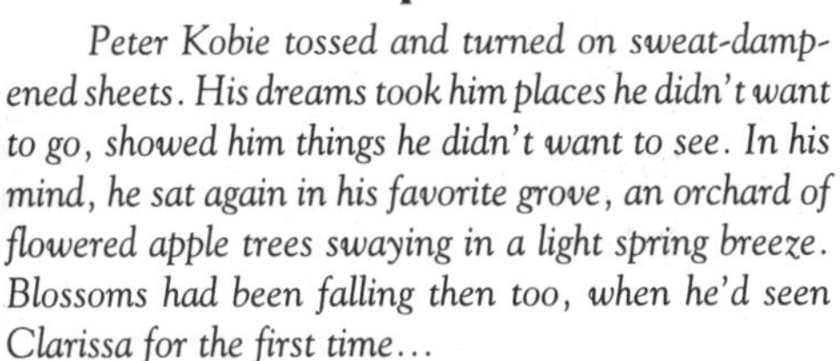

Peter's Temptation

Peter Kobie tossed and turned on sweat-dampened sheets. His dreams took him places he didn't want to go, showed him things he didn't want to see. In his mind, he sat again in his favorite grove, an orchard of flowered apple trees swaying in a light spring breeze. Blossoms had been falling then too, when he'd seen Clarissa for the first time...

"And you thought Fate had smiled kindly on you," murmured a female voice from the trees. Kobie looked up to see a familiar woman with long dark hair, clad in a loose transparent robe walking slowly towards him. "You'd hoped for one like her. You'd prayed for a student to Awaken, to share your passion, to share your knowledge. And you got exactly what you asked for."

"Yes," Peter whispered, the words hard to form. "Yes, I wanted her, I wanted to teach her, and... and show her the true path. But..."

"But now the student far outshines her master," replied the woman, coming over to stroke his long hair with her fingers. "Better be careful what you wish for. You just may get it."

Peter struggled for the right words. "She knows things I cannot understand. Why? Why can she see when I cannot?" His voice rose in frustration and mounting fury.

"She's like a festering wound in your side, is she not? Every time you meet her, you see your own teachings turned into her victories, corrupted into her images. I wonder why you put up with such insolence," sighed the woman.

"I... I still care for her," said Peter. "I take pride in that she has taken what she has learned and used it."

"Really?" she asked. "Then why do you rage? Why does your hatred burn in you?" Her hands touched his chest. "Purge it. Seek out your pupil. And show her one final lesson. Show her that you will always be the master and she the student. You want to do this. Consider it... the ultimate experience, the one you have always sought." Laughing, she pulled away, leaving Peter Kobie to wake up instantly, a bitter taste in his mouth, and hatred burning against his favorite student, one who had surpassed him.

Character Creation

I think I'll be a teddy boy, I think I'll be a hunk
I think I'll be a tough guy and I think I'll be a punk
— Oingo Boingo, "Who Do You Want To Be"

Mages, in the World of Darkness, are not just "magic users"; they are Awakened beings. A mage is an artist and architect. A **Mage** character, therefore, should be an interesting person, not a spell-slinging machine.

Character creation in **Mage** begins with an idea of who you want your character to be. This can be a simple phrase or a long and detailed description. From that first idea, choose the abilities and characteristics that describe your character in terms of the game rules This chapter should help you do both.

Building Your Mage

Character creation usually works through a simple step-by-step process. Each step covers certain aspects of your mage. The chart on pages 138-139 runs through each aspect and includes the point costs for each item. The **"Traits"** section, following, describes those various aspects in more detail. In brief, the steps of character creation are as follows:

Step One: Concept

Character creation is like sculpture; you go from broad descriptions ("computer geek") to specific details ("Michelle Willard, postgraduate at the University of Chicago, Computer Sciences department, withdrawn youth who uses the anonymity of the Internet to create a dynamic and forceful persona named Winterwitch"). To start with, decide what your character was like as a Sleeper and what Awakened her. In some cases, your character may begin the chronicle as a Sleeper and Awaken during the course of the story.

• Some archetypal *concepts* can be found on the Character Creation chart. For a quick and simple character, pick a concept that sounds appealing and build your character from there. Feel free to disregard the list altogether and create your own concept.

• A pivotal aspect of any **Mage** character is his *Tradition*, his magickal "school of thought." Your character's Tradition should reflect his nature, and will affect the abilities and resources he has available. Not every mage, of course, joins the Council's ranks; for now, however, let's just say "Tradition."

• Your character's *Essence* is a description of his Avatar — his magickal inner self — which may help determine his Path to Ascension. For game purposes, it means little; it is a roleplaying tool, a handle on the personality of that inner self. **(See Chapter Two for more details.)**

• Each character has *personality archetypes* — a *Nature* and a *Demeanor* — which sum up the inner reality and outward mask of her personality. While Nature and Demeanor are often the same (or at least similar), they could be wildly different. The character may not even be aware of this difference. A list of archetypes follows later in this chapter, though you may create your own.

The character's Nature is closely related to her Essence. It describes her view and basic beliefs about the world, and shapes her behavior. During the course of the game, the ways in which she regains spent Willpower points often depend on her Nature.

The character's Demeanor is the personality she projects to the outside world. While her behavior will vary widely from situation to situation, the Demeanor you choose will be the basic persona she uses in most situations.

These archetypes are designed as springboards for determining how the character acts. Cheshire Cat's Demeanor, for example, is Rebel. Using this, Cheshire's player can assume he doesn't respond well to authority figures or established social norms.

Step Two: Attributes

Attributes are numerical abstractions of a character's abilities in certain areas. In everyday life we might say that a person is very strong, unusually charming or dumb as a brick. In the framework of the game, however, each person's Attributes are rated on a scale of one to five and represented by dots: • is abysmal, ••• is on the higher side of average, and ••••• is wonderful. Characters start out with a rating of • in each Attribute. You may then improve them by spending Attribute Points.

Attributes come in three areas: *Physical*, *Social* and *Mental*. **Mage** assumes that each character has one area in which he's particularly strong (primary), one in which he's pretty average (secondary), and one where he's weak (tertiary). You get to spend *seven* Attribute Points in one area of your choice, *five* points in the second area and *three* in your character's weakest area. Within each group, you may spend your points as you see fit, putting the balance of the points on one Attribute and leaving others at one, spreading them evenly or whatever. If one or two Attributes end up lower than you want them to be, you may improve them later with freebie points or experience.

Your character's Concept, Essence or Tradition may suggest the placement of Attribute points — a member of the Virtual Adepts would probably have very strong Mental Attributes, while a folk-singing member of the Cult of Ecstasy might have Social as her primary Attribute category.

Step Three: Abilities

Abilities represent things your character knows. While Attributes are the building blocks a character has always had, Abilities are things she's picked up along the way. *Talents* are things the character is innately good at, like singing or scaring people. *Skills* are things she had to learn by doing, like meditation or sword fighting. Things she had to study, like medicine or computer programming, are Knowledges.

Like Attributes, Abilities are rated from • to •••••. Abilities, however, start out with a rating of *zero*, indicating that the character has no knowledge of that Ability. (Someone who's never used a computer, say, will have a Computer Knowledge of zero.)

Like Attributes, your character's Abilities will be divided into strong, average and weak areas. You may spend *13* points in your character's strongest area, *nine* points in the middle area and *seven* points in her weakest area. Within each area, those points may be distributed as you see fit — to a degree.

No Ability can start with a rating higher than three. These ratings may be improved later with freebie points, but are limited to three or less during your initial point spending.

Step Four: Advantages

Advantages are unique resources or special abilities. They're not prioritized the way Attributes and Abilities are; you only have a set number of points to spend in each Advantage category. As usual, Advantages are rated • to •••••. Freebie points may be spent here like anywhere else.

• There are two types of Advantages: Backgrounds and *Spheres*. Backgrounds represent items, people or other resources the character can call on during the course of the story. Characters get *seven* Background points to start with.

• *Spheres* are aspects of reality which a mage learns about to use her magick. Your character's rating in a Sphere represents how well she understands and manipulates that particular element. Each character begins with *one* point in the Sphere associated with her Tradition. Hollow Ones and other Orphans may place that point in the Sphere of their choice. The character may not have a rating in any Sphere higher than her Arete rating (which also begins at •, though freebie points may raise it), and may not begin with any Sphere rating higher than •••.

• Most mages have *foci*, or magickal tools, which they employ in their Arts. Not every mage will have a different focus for each Sphere, but most will. Each new mystick must begin with one focus, of your choosing, per Sphere. As he progresses, he may abandon one focus per point of Arete over the first (one at Arete 2, two at Arete 3, etc.) if you want him to. These tools are not rated by dots, but will make a difference in the way your mage uses his Spheres.

The **"Traditions"** listings given later in this chapter offer many common types of foci. The **"Storytelling Magick"** section in **Chapter Eight** offers many suggested foci and magickal style hints.

Step Five: Finishing Touches

These final features cover the most personal aspects of your character — the ones that will grow through time to transform a talented novice into a Master.

• Arete measures the mage's enlightened strength of will. A combination of confidence, understanding, wisdom and raw power, Arete is what makes a mage a mage.

Each Awakened character begins with *one* point of Arete; this score may be raised with freebie points. We recommend that new characters start the game with an Arete no higher than three. Each Sphere the mage possesses must be lower than or equal to that character's Arete — no higher. Arete is unusual, in that it is rated from one to 10, rather than one to five.

• The *Willpower* Trait rates a mage's self-control. Like Arete, Willpower runs from 1 to 10. The circles which represent the character's Willpower rating show her *maximum* Willpower, while the boxes indicate her *current* Willpower (these points are spent and regained during the course of the story). Willpower begins with *five* points, and may be improved at the cost of one point per freebie point spent.

• *Quintessence* represents the amount of "stored" magickal energy the mage has at any given moment. *Paradox* represents how large a strain he has recently placed on the fabric of reality. Your character begins with no Paradox at all and a Quintessence rating equal to his Avatar rating. Quintessence may be raised with freebie points; no one wants to raise his Paradox!

• You may now spend 15 *freebie points* wherever you like. Keep in mind that this isn't very many considering the cost of various different Traits **(see the Freebie Points chart)** — be careful how you spend your points. Also, remember when raising Spheres that they have a maximum beginning value of the character's Arete or three, whichever is less.Freebie points cannot buy new dots in anything. They may only raise what was already purchased.

Fleshing Out the Character

Once the math is done, the character still needs the small details that make for convincing fiction:

Appearance

A character's appearance is an important factor in how she relates to others. It's a sad but true fact that unattractive people have a harder time in social settings than plain people do and that attractive people have it easier all around. While your character's Appearance Trait will determine whether or not she is attractive, it doesn't say what it is that makes her attractive. The more specific you can make the character's appearance, the easier she will be to visualize. Thus, instead of, "She's pretty," you might say, "She's five foot ten, with luxuriant curly dark hair which cascades around her large, dark eyes and prominent cheekbones. She always looks straight at whomever she's addressing with an intense gaze, and always seems to be smiling at some very private joke."

Magickal Style and Foci

Belief is central to a mage's power; through it, she focuses her will. A mystick's paradigm shapes the magick she casts and her personality as well. Thus, it's important to figure out just what your mage believes in.

Is she a follower of the Goddess? A holy sister? A metaphysician or enlightened scientist? Did she learn her Art during a short visionquest or over a long apprenticeship to a Hermetic Master? The answer will influence the way she casts her magick and the foci, or tools, she uses to do it. **(See "Advantages," above, and "Sphere Affinities," page 226.)**

In the beginning, every mystick believes that some practice allows him to alter reality. This paradigm dictates which tools he uses when he casts his Art. As he progresses, the sorcerer may fall away from that original paradigm, or he may grow stronger in his faith. Either way, he begins with a belief in something. When you build your character, decide how he believes magick works and what he feels he must do to use it.

Specialties

Your character may *specialize* in any Trait in which she has four or more dots. This reflects something she is especially good at within that general category. Someone with Medicine 4 might choose "Brain Surgery" as her specialty.

Specialties add depth to your character's Attributes and Abilities; they also may add a bonus to her Dice Pool. If you roll a 10 on her specialized Trait, you can re-roll that die. **(See "Specialties" in the "Traits" section for further details.)**

Equipment

Unless the Storyteller specifies otherwise, assume your character has whatever ordinary equipment she might reasonably have. A private detective probably has his license and a gun or two, while a computer programmer might have a laptop or a large desktop computer. Ordinary items can also be magickal foci **(see Chapter Eight)**, so long as they don't enhance the character's abilities. Magickal equipment must be purchased with the Talisman Background.

Quirks

Quirks are little details about the character that give her flavor. They can be anything, from a preference toward wearing black to the habit of saying, "Bite me, it's fun." Someone with a handful of strong quirks will be easy and fun to play, and will also give the Storyteller a handle to play up interactions with. ("Say, that's an interesting tattoo you've got there...")

Motivations

If you haven't done so already, give some thought to what motivates your character — what does she want out of life, and why? What made her study magick? Why does she hate authority? Motivation can be something vague, like innate curiosity, or it can be very specific: your character wants to destroy the Technocracy because a HIT Mark killed her sister.

The character can also have numerous, perhaps contradictory, motivations, but be careful — a complex character can become a basket case if she has too many goals. Eventually, her focus may shift from achieving her goals to simply containing all her neuroses, and the concept will collapse under its own weight.

A strong character has one overriding goal, reflected by (or determined by?) her Essence, in addition to several smaller goals. Sister Beulah's main goal (Pattern) is likely to be doing God's will, which breaks into the secondary categories of protecting the innocent and fighting the Nephandi. Khozan, on the other hand, wants to learn all the magick he can (Questing). However, as a dedicated member of the Order of Hermes, he also wants to destroy the Technocracy. When he discovers that Technomancers use just as much magick as he does (albeit in a different form), he'll have quite a dilemma on his hands. Should he destroy the threat to his reality, or should he learn their magick and see how it's compatible with his own? Perhaps there's an entirely different structure to magick than the one he's been taught all his life...?

Mundane Identity

The Awakened are not super-heroes, but like them, they must balance unbelievable power against their humanity. Mages are mortal — they still have families and friends from before their Awakening, and will want to cultivate more. Who wants to live in a Chantry all his life?

Sleeper society is difficult to cope with. If your fellow humans knew what you were, they would either worship you or kill you, and probably both. All the same, your character will want to have some way in which she still lives in the mundane world, if only for a while. Does she do magic tricks to cover her power? Is she a missionary who performs the occasional miracle? Does she lie low and lead a double life, or avoid mundanes completely?

Experience Points

Obviously, you will not be given experience points at this stage. As your character progresses, however, she will gain new points to spend on raising her Traits. This process is covered in depth in **Chapter Nine**, but bears noting now.

Sample Character Creation

John is creating a **Mage** character for a new chronicle. Wendy, the Storyteller, informs him that her chronicle will involve a great deal of material from the **Digital Web** (cyberspace) supplement and that the Technocracy is going to be one of the story's major antagonists. Although a Virtual Adept is the obvious choice, John decides to twist the idea to make a more interesting character.

Concept

John starts with the basic idea of a Virtual Adept character, but wants to play someone who's more of a maverick. Even the Virtual Adepts are too organized for the type of character he's thinking of. He chooses the Outsider Concept and decides that his character Awakened on his own and was approached by the Virtual Adepts, but rejected them.

This also determines his Tradition, or lack of one. John decides that his character is an Orphan, a self-imposed exile from the wheels-within-wheels magickal society. This character is someone who likes to sneak about on the Web, going in back doors and making his living by breaking into networks or hiring himself out to make networks unbreakable. The character uses the pseudonym "Cheshire Cat."

Looking at the Essences, John decides that Cheshire has a Dynamic Essence, but that Cheshire doesn't yet know what his eventual goal will be, other than preservation of the Web. Cheshire's Nature is an Architect — he really wants to create something that will endure, and for him that something is the Web. However, his Demeanor is a Rebel. He is as contemptuous of Tradition mages as he is of Technomancers, though he will ally himself with anyone who will help preserve the Web.

Attributes

• John wants Cheshire to be a mad thinker. He comes up with detailed plans and intricate schemes, so John makes his Mental Attributes primary. He decides that Cheshire also has a very strong personality, so his Social Attributes become secondary. Since Cheshire spends a lot of his time in front of a computer rather than exercising, his Physical Attributes are his weakest.

• Cheshire has seven dots for his Mental Attributes. He's very smart, able to memorize tons of information about computer types, programs and so on, and can quickly decide on a course of action once he has all the information he needs, but he gets so wrapped up in what he's doing at any given moment that he sometimes misses what's going on around him. Therefore John only puts one point on Perception, giving it a value of two dots, and divides the remaining six points evenly between Intelligence and Wits, giving them values of four dots each.

• Cheshire has five dots for his Social Attributes. John decides that he's not especially attractive — in fact, his appearance is rather forgettable. But he's not ugly either, so he gets one point in Appearance, for a value of two dots. However, since Cheshire is a tricky person, conning people when necessary for his latest scheme, he gets three points for Manipulation, giving it a value of four dots. He puts his last point on Charisma, giving it a value of two dots. Unfortunately, John pictured Cheshire having more force of presence than that, and marks Charisma so he will remember to come back and raise it with freebie points.

• Cheshire has only three dots for his Physical Attributes. John decides that they should all be roughly average, with none of them better or deficient, so he distributes the three points evenly, giving all of Cheshire's Physical Attributes a value of two dots.

Abilities

To figure out Cheshire's primary, secondary and tertiary Abilities, John goes through the character sheet and finds that while they're fairly evenly distributed among the groups, the critical ones are in Knowledges. He makes that one his primary group. Talents seem the next most important, followed by Skills.

• Since Cheshire is a world-class computer nerd, the first three points of his 13 for Knowledges go straight to Computer (he decides to buy a fourth with freebies later and choose "Networks" as his specialty). Since John pictures Cheshire enjoying the intellectual puzzle of security systems, he puts three more points in Enigmas. Because Cheshire spends his time finding hidden and obscure data, he puts an additional three points into Investigation. Figuring Cheshire needs to know which laws he's breaking, John puts one point there. For his last three points, John decides to put one point in Lore to reflect Cheshire's incidental learning and two points in Science to indicate that he has a basic knowledge of the physics and chemistry involved in working on computers at the level of electrons.

• John has nine points for Cheshire's Talents and immediately puts three each into Streetwise and Subterfuge, skills basic to his character. He also decides that Cheshire has occasionally been found in places he wasn't supposed to be and had to dodge gunfire to get out; he takes two dots in Dodge and one in Alertness.

• The five points John has for Cheshire's Skills will be nowhere near enough and that "freebie points" will be spent here in a big way. For starters, however, he knows that Cheshire should have a minimum of three dots in Stealth, one dot in Research, and one in Technology.

Advantages

For his seven points of Backgrounds, John decides that Cheshire has "Cheshire's Commandos," a small organization working for him, and puts four points in Allies. He tells the Storyteller a few basic ideas about the organization — that all of the members are Orphans or Virtual Adepts of minor magickal ability who specialize in security — and lets the Storyteller come up with the rest. Since any mage worth his salt has a close bond with his Avatar, John puts one point there. He spends his sixth point to get a dot in Library, indicating the stacks and stacks of manuals that clutter up his apartment, and his last point for one dot in Mentor. His original computer sciences instructor, known on the Web as "fuzzbuster@vadept.com," is a Virtual Adept who's not officially supposed to help Cheshire (since he snubbed the Adepts), but would if there were a real emergency.

Since Cheshire is an Orphan, he does not have to place a point according to any Tradition. Since he has had some Virtual Adept training, however, and lurks in "their" cyberworld, he decides to take their Sphere, Correspondence, as his own. Since he doesn't expect to have the freebie points necessary to raise his Arete, having more than one point in any Sphere would be pointless, so he decides to use the remaining five points for one dot each in Entropy, Forces, Matter, Mind and Prime.

Finishing Touches

Cheshire's Willpower is five, his Quintessence is one, and his Paradox is zero. He now decides to spend his freebie points. He goes back and spends five to raise his Charisma to three dots. He spends four points to raise his Research up to three dots, two points to raise his Technology to two dots and two more points to give him that additional dot in Computers. He has two freebie points left, which he puts on Willpower to give him a rating of seven dots. There are several Abilities that John feels Cheshire should be better at, but unfortunately there just aren't enough points, so he'll have to wait until Cheshire gains some experience.

John fleshes Cheshire's character out now by coming up with a history and personality for him. He starts by giving Cheshire's real name as Chester Katzenberg, a computer security specialist in his late 20s. Chester was always something of an outcast during his youth, being more interested in playing with a Commodore 64 than with a football. In college, however, his talent with computers really blossomed. On a frozen winter night over Christmas break, while everyone else was out of town and Chester had the college computer to himself, he found his way onto the Digital Web and gradually came to the realization that there was a lot more there than what he saw on the surface. At 2:05 a.m. on Christmas Day, he suddenly understood.

By New Years' Day, he had e-mail from all over the world, people he'd never heard of telling him things he didn't particularly want to hear. The one person he heard from that he was interested in talking to, his old instructor "Fuzzbuster," tried to get him to join what at first sounded like some sort of lunatic cyberspace-worshipping cult involved in some bizarre cosmic turf war with a larger lunatic technology-in-general-worshipping cult. This turf war was tearing apart the Web and destroying what Cheshire saw as a great opportunity for opening communications with all humanity. Cheshire came to the conclusion that they were all crackers and told them all in explicit terms what they could all go do with themselves.

Cheshire now spends most of his time in the Web, where he has found others who believe as he does, that the "Ascension War" has less to do with the nature of reality than it does with generations of "us vs. them," and who want nothing to do with any of it. He's heard the arguments of both Technomancers and Tradition mages, and believes that neither Path will lead to Ascension because the universe does not Ascend, only people within it. Cheshire feels that the constant conflict between the Technos and the Traditionalists is more likely to end up in the destruction of everything and seeks a way to prevent that from happening.

The Prelude

Ah...! What's happening?

Er, excuse me, who am I?

Hello?

Why am I here? What's my purpose in life?

What do I mean by who am I?

Calm down, get a grip now... oh! this is an interesting sensation...

— Sperm whale, *The Hitchhiker's Guide to the Galaxy*

The *prelude* is your character's introduction to the chronicle, combining back history, personal details and the Awakening itself. A short game session (or portion of a game session) which the Storyteller and the player play out one-on-one, the prelude gives both player and character some sense of belonging in the magickal world.

During your prelude, you may want to go through one or two typical scenes in the character's mundane pre-Awakening life to contrast Sleeper existence with the bizarre and wonder-filled life of a mage. He may encounter the fringes of the world he will soon enter: a frighteningly lucid dream, flashbacks to a previous life, an odd encounter with a tattered bum who speaks in Latin or a chillingly dedicated "government agent" asking uncomfortable questions.

During the course of the prelude, you may find that some of your initial choices weren't right for the character as developed once he was played. In this case, feel free to change them as long as it doesn't affect the final cost of your character. Unless the Storyteller grants you permission (unlikely!), you can't have extra freebie points, to re-figure your mage, though she may grant you an experience point or two at her option.

Character Questions

The more details you work out before (or during) the prelude, the more depth your character will have once the game really begins. Such details may seem trivial now, but can turn a list of dots and statistics into an Awakened One. Though they barely scratch the surface of potential details, the following questions might, if nothing else, give you food for thought while conceiving or constructing your mage.

- **How Old Are You?**

How old is your character? How long has he studied magick? Does your appearance reflect your age? What events were significant to your character? If the chronicle takes place in 1996 and the character is 25 years old, events like the Vietnam War won't have as much direct effect on his personality as the falling of the Berlin Wall or the death of Kurt Cobain. On the other hand, if the character is 40 years old, Vietnam will have been a major influence on his life.

- **When Did You Notice That You Were... Different?**

Most mages have strange childhoods with unexplainable occurrences or bizarre coincidences. These events might have gone unnoticed or may have had tremendous consequences. A happy childhood may instill one mage with a sense of duty to other people less fortunate, while another who spent her childhood as an outcast may still have trouble relating to others.

- **How Did You Come By Your Abilities?**

No one appears from nowhere, complete with skills and a place in society. Who were you? Where did you grow up? How did you learn what you know? This question suggests ways to give your mage more depth. If nothing else, it may offer your Storyteller a few plot threads to weave into her chronicle.

• **Who Is Important to You?**

No man is an island; the important people in your character's life say a lot about him or her and offer an endless stream of story possibilities. Does he have a lot of superficial buddies or a small circle of tightly-knit friends? How does he get along with his family? Does he even have one? Do any of these people know about his ability to shake the pillars of Heaven? How do they react to it? Has his Awakening driven him away from all the people who once were important to him? If so, who's important to him now? Does he ever try to regain those lost relationships?

• **When Did You First Encounter Magick?**

Humans have a great capacity to ignore or discount things that don't fit their model of what the world should be. What event overcame your character's ability to do this? How did she learn that there were mysteries that couldn't be solved? How did she react? Was she afraid? Was she ecstatic? Did she go power-hungry or have a nervous breakdown?

On the other hand, it's possible that the character simply never lost the childlike ability to believe in *anything*, even when other people told her it wasn't true. Mages with a Primordial Essence are often like this.

• **Who Was Your Mentor?**

Mages of the Traditions usually begin with some kind of mentor, even if he's no longer around. How did your character meet this person? Did you seek him out? Did he seek you out? Was he kindly or harsh? Did he explain everything, or simply ask you questions and watch you try to figure out the answers?

A mentor can act as the character's teacher, parent, older sibling or any combination thereof, and has probably been a major force in the shaping of the character's personality.

• **How Did You Meet the Others in Your Cabal?**

The cabal usually refers to the other players' characters. How you met them and interact with them will have major effects on the chronicle. Cheshire, for example, has difficulty interacting with Tradition mages on a regular basis unless they're concerned with more than wasting Technocrats. A good way for him to meet one of them, then, would be for him to come upon them trying to prevent some catastrophe in the Web, or for one of them to rescue him from a Nephandi attack.

• **Do You Maintain a Mundane Life?**

Do you have a "secret identity?" Do you continue to interact with Sleepers, hiding the supernatural aspects of your existence, or have you left your old life behind? Some of this will depend upon the course of your chronicle — after all, if you go to a parallel dimension for 10 minutes and come out to the year 2015, it will be rather difficult to pick up your mundane life....

The Cabal

Once you've gone through the prelude and learned a little about the other players' characters, get the troupe together to answer some basic questions about the cabal.

• **Where Do They Meet?**

This depends on the chronicle. Does the cabal have a single place they use as a headquarters? Do they share a house or have quarters in a Chantry? Do they live in separate places, then meet at a completely different location? Do they have easy access to a Node and, if so, what kind?

• What Are the Cabal's Goals?

Each member of the cabal has his or her own goals, but what goals do they have as a group? Why did they band together? Mutual protection? Romantic interest? Family ties? Revenge? What do you, as a group, hope to accomplish?

• Who Are the Cabal's Friends and Enemies?

No group exists in a vacuum. Who have you helped? Who have you pissed off? Do you have servants or other companions? Do you deal with other mages? Vampires? Werewolves? (Mages are immune to the Delirium that makes interaction with humans so difficult for werewolves.) Have you helped an old Garou track down a pack of fomori? Did you ransack a vampire's art gallery (an act that would win you friends *and* enemies!)? Do you all help the homeless, or does your cabal resemble a street gang, down to the turf wars?

Player Hints for the Path

(See also Chapter Two.)

A mage's Path means a lot more than the Tradition he belongs to, if he belongs to one at all. The four factions merely indicate who your mage hangs around with. His Path shapes who he *is*.

Your mage's Path will offer lots of suggestions about how your mystick counterpart might behave. Remember, however, that a Path is not a rigid "alignment" — it's a predisposition. You don't have to work it all out in advance — just picture where you want to go eventually and how. Think of the Path as a map, with an ideal destination, a few landmarks and a travel plan. The actual journey — the game — will depart pretty significantly from that map. Having some idea about where you're going, however, will make the road clearer and the departures easier to manage.

Some questions to ask yourself:

• What Do You, the Player, Want to Do?

Motivations are all-important, your own as well as your character's. Who do you want to play in this game? A brainy mad scientist, an enigmatic wizard or a socialite with a few well-hidden secrets? What kind of character seems fun to you?

Once you decide, figure out the sorts of things you'd like to accomplish in the game. Will you feed the hungry? Kick ass, get rich or avenge your brother's death? Every option suggests a number of possible destinies. Pick one that seems intriguing to you.

Remember that **Mage** is, in the long run, a game about finding higher truths. This doesn't mean that you have to think deep thoughts every game session. You should have some ideas, though, that you want your character to explore somewhere along the line.

• What Destiny Does She Pursue?

What does the mystick see as his destiny? To die for the greater good? To overthrow the Technocracy? To abolish evil, perfect his inner self or write the gospels of the 21st century? The destiny your mage foresees may not actually be his Path's true destination, but you, the player, ought to decide what vision drives his purpose.

• How Does Your Mage Regard Her Destiny?

Most mages, especially new ones, don't want to think about the end of the road. Knowledge, power, conflict — these are enough things to keep a mystick occupied. Every mage, however, has some hint of what destiny has in store for her. Does it frighten her? Intrigue her? What does she see, and how does she feel about it? What will she do to pursue that destiny... or to avoid it?

• What is Your Character's Avatar Like?

What is the Avatar's agenda? Is it to become one with all others of its kind? To return magick to the world, eliminate prejudice or complete unfinished business from a past incarnation? The Essence you choose will influence the Avatar's general bent, but the decision is ultimately yours.

How does the Avatar appear? Is it an imaginary friend, a flash of occasional inspiration or an angel with bloody hands? The way the immortal self manifests will say a lot about its character and about the way your mage relates to it.

• How Does the Mage Get Along with her Avatar?

Is your mage in conflict with his magickal self? Many are, at least at first; this struggle refines them both. If so, or if not, how do they get along? Does the Avatar tantalize a mystick with power or lore, sit on the sidelines or drag her along through Seekings until the mage either opens her eyes or goes mad? Does the mage *want* to be a mage, or would she rather just go back to her old lifestyle? All these questions will affect the way Awakened and Avatar interact.

Remember that roleplaying perfect harmony is boring. Even a good relationship should have its difficulties.

• What Conflicts Might Come up Along the Way?

The Path of true Ascension never did run smooth. What sorts of distractions might throw your mystick off her road? True love? Disillusionment? Revenge, betrayal, insanity or pride? By figuring out the things that could sidetrack Ascension's quest, you can get an idea of how your character might react if — or when — such things occur.

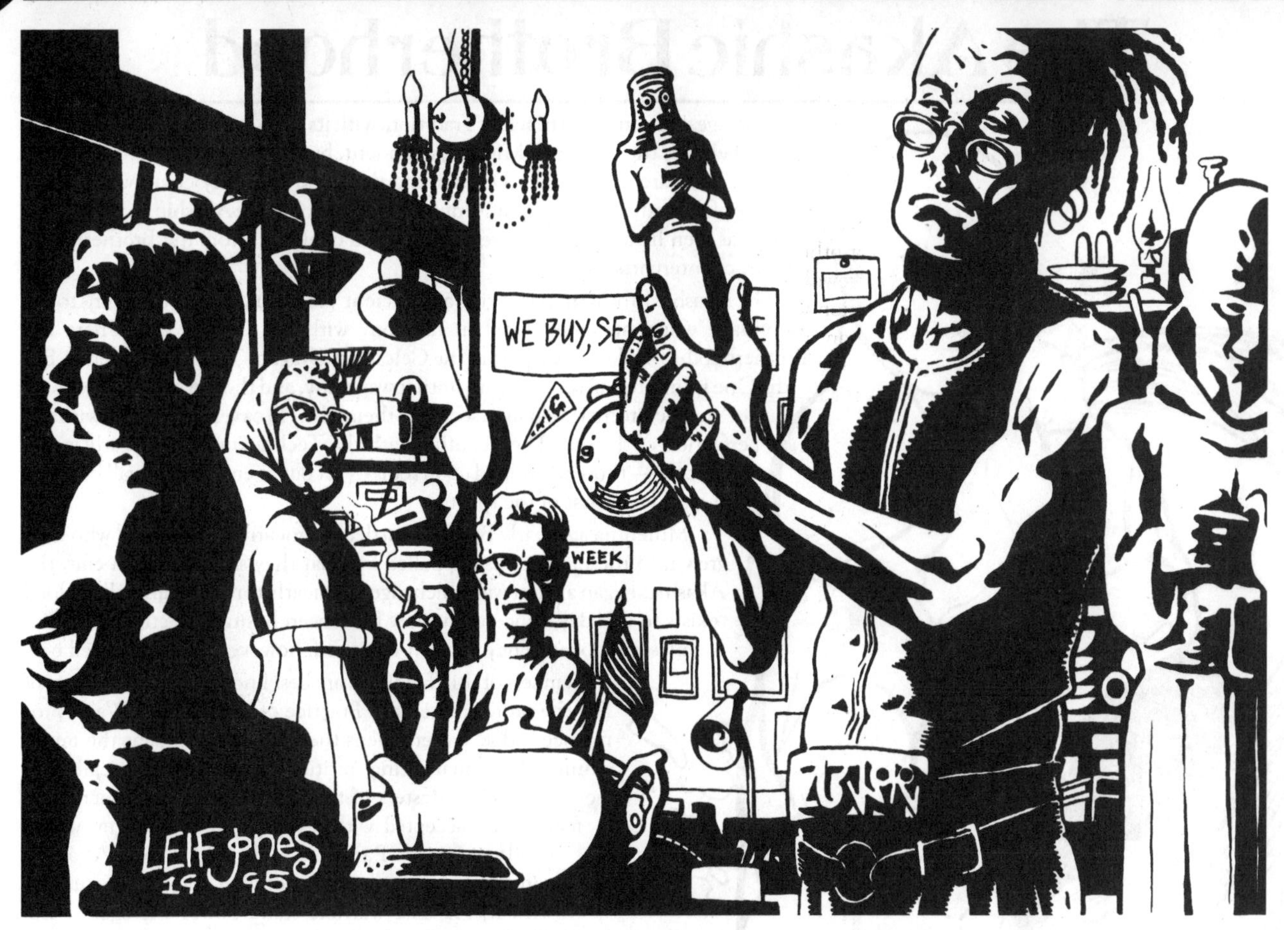

The Traditions

Man makes his world, or is crushed by the worlds made by others.

— Denning & Philips, *The Foundations of High Magick*

Although the Awakened come in many different flavors, the basic **Mage** rules emphasize members of the Council of the Nine Mystick Traditions over all other factions. Other supplements cover Orphans, Technocrats, Nephandi, Marauders and even hedge magicians, but our focus for now is the Council. Among all True Magi, the wizards of the Nine Traditions have the hardest — and most heroic — role. They follow balance, and balance is not an easy thing to master.

Each Tradition description follows the same format. General information comes first, followed by other helpful bits:

Introduction: An overall description of the Tradition and its history in all its best and worst colors.

Philosophy: A statement of the Tradition's general approach to life, magick and the world.

Style: An overview of the group's favored style of magick. This reflects the teachings that Tradition uses and the overall focus of its Arts.

Sphere: The Sphere the Tradition has mastered.

Common Foci: The usual items Tradition members use to focus their magicks. The exact methods, foci and rituals a mage utilizes are left to the individual to choose; these foci are merely the most common among that particular group.

Organization: Some Traditions are very formal, while others barely have any form of organization at all. This listing reflects the group's overall makeup and coherence.

Initiation: Each Tradition has a ritual, task or ordeal a neophyte must perform in order to join the ranks. Sometimes, the group comes to you; other times, you must go and present yourself to them.

Acolytes: The most common subcultures or individuals that gravitate towards members of that Tradition.

Concepts: The types of people who generally join the Tradition; helpful for matching a character idea to a group.

Quote: A remark which typifies the average Tradition member's attitude.

Stereotypes: Each Tradition thinks its way is best. These are their general takes on the others.

The Akashic Brotherhood

Many mages are perplexed that this Tradition, with its strong emphasis on developing the body, believes the Sphere of Mind is paramount, but to the Akashic Brotherhood, mind and body are inseparable. Disciplining the mind can only come with proper discipline of the body which houses it. Unfortunately, much of the Akashic Brotherhood's history has seen little more than stereotyping and confusion from the Brotherhood's Western counterparts.

The Akashic Brotherhood is a rich and ancient Tradition, tracing its origins to the first village when humanity lived in harmony with the Cosmic All. There the Brotherhood-to-be learned Do from the Celestines Dragon, Tiger and Phoenix. But the One splintered again and again until it was many, and those who would become the Akashic Brotherhood soon secluded themselves in caves, concerned with the perfection of the self. Their conflict with the Technocracy began early as the Artificers — those who relied upon tools — set out to enforce the wall between our world and that of the spirits.

Millennia ago, early Brothers battled a reincarnationist creed who later grew into the Euthanatos. Appalled by what they saw as a death-cult, the Akashics began a bitter war which raged for nearly three centuries. Bad blood exists to this day. Since then, they have been hesitant to enter a conflict unless provoked. They are well-equipped, however, to fight if need be.

Members of this Tradition are best known for their mastery of Do, the proto-martial art. Practice of Do (or "The Way," pronounced "doe") strengthens the body and sharpens the mind, refining the human being spiritually, mentally, physically and even primally. Masters of this Art are capable of incredible feats, often accepted within the popular paradigm, which rarely attract Paradox. Through Do, Akashic contemplatives seek perfection and enlightenment, and with it, Akashic warriors stand powerfully against the Technocracy and other foes.

Understanding *Drahma* (the Tradition's fabled 10th Sphere) is vital to this Tradition. Drahma is the wheel of the universe, creation and destruction, birth and rebirth, past, present and future, and inexorable destiny. It is both cause-and-effect and right-action. The Avatar which understands its own Drahma is master of its own fate. Through a sequence of lives, the Avatar progresses towards mastery of Drahma — and Ascension.

Though firmly rooted in Asia, this Tradition is not exclusive to any one ethnic group, nation or even gender. They embrace Koreans, Chinese, Indians and Westerners alike. "Brother" is an honorific recognition, not a title. Likewise, the Brotherhood's contemplative philosophies have made their mark across the East in such varied forms as Zen, yoga and Taoism. Do is equally widespread — elements of it can be found in almost every martial art.

The living heart of the Akashic Brotherhood is the Akashic Record. Named after Akasha, the Ascended Avatar who both invented writing and created the Record, it is the source of all understanding and inspiration for Akashic mages. Its physical form is written text, but the collective record of the entire Brotherhood's subconscious resides within a mystick pool. Anything a Brother experiences goes into the Record, transformed into symbols for others to interpret and contemplate. With it, Akashic Brothers understand the past, watch Avatars undergo continuous manifestations and come closer to Ascension.

Philosophy: Do not do; simply be. Look within for both solution to a difficulty and its cause as well. You cannot effect balance without until you are balanced within as well. Do not seek to control your enemy, but to guide him. Do not resist opposition when you can simply step around it.

Style: Magick flows from harmony and discipline, a natural force focused by Do. This Tradition's mages are as contemplative as they can be combative, philosopher-warriors who would understand and guide rather simply obliterate. Akashic Brothers (and all members of this Tradition, whether male or female, are "Brothers") tend to use violence only as a last resort, but can be quite effective when they do.

Sphere: Mind

Common Foci: Meditation, chanting, sashes (as well as headbands or robes), Do, purification rites (baths, abstinence, anointing), weapons

Organization: More so than any other Tradition, Akashic mages are strongly aligned according to their Essence. Pattern mages (sometimes called Orange or Saffron Robes) are often masters of Drahma. Questing mages (or Scales of the Dragon) focus on protecting Sleepers and Awakened and believe themselves parts of the Dragon Celestine's body. Dynamic mages (occasionally called Yogis) master the spirit world, while Primordial mages (sometimes called Blue Skins) are those most dedicated to personal Ascension.

Initiation: This Tradition is no longer as exclusively Asian as it once was. Most Brothers have been Brothers in past incarnations. Some members prove themselves in the martial arts or Eastern philosophy before Awakening, while others are observed from afar by Brothers who plumb the depths of the Record in order to learn their Avatars' current incarnation. Akashics may be trained in their *Xiudaoyuan* (Chantries) for years before being released from study.

Acolytes: Martial artists, Buddhist scholars, yoga teachers, herbalists

Concepts: Wandering sage, contemplative warrior, Taoist hermit, modern knight

Stereotypes

- Celestial Chorus — They seek wisdom, but ignore the role of the individual in perfecting the All.
- Cult of Ecstasy — They may be degenerate and too often lose the self in the eternity of Time, but they are nonetheless valuable.
- Dreamspeakers — These dancers have pure Avatars and are to be admired for their command of the spirits.
- Euthanatos — How can one learn the Drahmic lessons of a lifetime if the life is intentionally cut? We do not trust these arrogant and dangerous mages, and we are only united by a common enemy.
- Order of Hermes — They separate themselves from their Art with meaningless papers and books.
- Sons of Ether — Like the Artificers, they seek their wisdom in tools, but are not as proud and demanding.
- Verbena—Looking at the trees, they see neither the forest nor themselves.
- Virtual Adepts — Instead of recognizing that this world is an illusion, they try to find yet more illusions to entertain themselves with.
- Hollow Ones — They are self-centered but lack a centered self. They need discipline.

First you must learn Do, then you must forget Do. Must you remember to breathe for breathing to occur? No. It is the same with Do.

The Celestial Chorus

Each Tradition is ultimately misunderstood by the others, but few are viewed with as much antipathy as the Celestial Chorus. It is true that the Choristers are overtly and unashamedly religiocentric, but their zealous Ascension ideal has left a bad aftertaste in the collective mouths of the other Traditions. However, there is much more to this Tradition than their detractors are willing to realize.

The Celestial Chorus is not a religion but a meta-religion, meant to encompass all belief systems. Typically, its followers come from Western monotheistic traditions, but it would be naive to assume that every Chorister is automatically a Christian. Still, members of this Tradition share a common philosophy and cosmology: *In the Beginning, in the time before Time, was the One, and the One sang a glorious Song. The One sang Life into Itself and became Many.* The One's fragments, Its children, are both Sleeper and Awakened alike, and their ultimate goal is to return to the One. Choristers see themselves as shepherds, and the Sleepers are their flock. The duty of the Chorus is to guide all humanity towards Ascension.

Like the Brotherhood, the Chorus is an ancient and venerable Tradition. Though it claims to be the Mother of all Traditions, now fractured into many divisions just as the One is likewise fractured, it can be historically traced to the XVIII dynasty of Egypt and the time of Ikhnaton. While some Traditions (such as the Dreamspeakers and the Verbena) predate the Chorus, the Celestials consider themselves the manifestation of a perennial philosophy, ancient when the more "primitive" Traditions were young and scattered, even if the Tradition proper did not form until much later.

Throughout history, Choristers have played different roles: some as guardians, some as caretakers and some as soldiers. Every flock has its wolves, and the Chorus' duties include protecting its flock from these wolves — the Nephandi, the undead and other entities which would prey on helpless Sleepers. The frequent symbolism of the One as the sun is most appropriate, as the Chorus sees itself as a beacon in the night, burning away the evils of the world. Almost as a whole, Choristers fervently oppose the Technocracy and other Prometheans (as the Chorus calls them) who try to impose their vision of reality over the One's. Unfortunately, some Choristers once went too far in their zeal, and their role in the Inquisition is too well-known by other mages.

The Tradition's link with the New World Order (or, more properly, to its foundation, the Cabal of Pure Thought) is well-known by Council historians. Mages within the medieval Christian Church split over the role they were to play in humanity's future. Those who wished to rule through one Church, one government, formed the Cabal; those who opposed them formed the Chorus. The rivalry — and bond — between them has never ended.

The Celestial Chorus has always had an apocalyptic tinge to it. To them, the Reconciliation, when the One shall be reunited, is imminent. Unfortunately, the particulars of the Reconciliation are unknown — especially whether it will occur naturally or be initiated and what will happen to those who have not yet Ascended.

Some Choristers may have been the catalyst for religious reform efforts. Ultimately, their efforts have had an impact on the religious traditions of Sleepers, though the Chorus now avoids instigating major religious upheaval or new religious beliefs. Liken the phenomenon to an orchestra: Choristers may have been particularly powerful instruments in the symphony, at times even conductors — sometimes adding their own flavor to the music, but never again rewriting the score.

The metaphor of an orchestra is most appropriate for the Celestial Chorus, for religion and music are intermingled to the point of inseparability. Music, particularly song, is the highest form of spirituality and can never be relegated to merely a form of fine art or entertainment. Magick is the music of the Spheres, the Song is the primal essence of creation, and the Chorus frequently calls magick "the Song." In Song, many voices are joined into one, and through Song, the Chorister is ever reminded of the One.

Philosophy: All humanity came from the One, and we shall not be happy until we return to It. Together, we shall usher the Sleepers into a glorious Ascension. As we are guided by the light of the One, so shall our lights guide the Sleeping until we all join the One's embrace.

Style: These mages focus their Art with faith and purpose. To them, their Art is the touch of the One. They are but Its fingers and Its tongue.

Sphere: Prime

Common Foci: Fire and light, song (and rarely musical instruments), water or oil, holy symbols, touch.

Organization: The Celestial Chorus is strictly (many would say stiflingly) hierarchic, retaining much of the structure established during the Roman Republic. Rank and status are quite formal. Many informal factions exist within the Chorus, however, based upon patterns of religious belief (Judaism, Zoroastrianism, etc.) or ideology. Choristers frequently quibble about the Chorus' future, the One's possible gender, the value of heterodoxy, etc. Holding such views is no longer as dangerous as it once was.

Initiation: Choristers often seek their recruits in church-run organizations with a social outreach. Some spontaneously Awaken through powerful religious experiences — particularly those involving music — without the assistance of the Chorus. Apprentices undergo a rigorous catechumenism prior to formal vows.

Acolytes: Priest, cantor, social worker, the faithful

Concepts: Evangelist, poet, theologian, witch-hunter, healer

Stereotypes

• Akashic Brotherhood — They have learned to perfect their own voice, but not how to sing in harmony.

• Cult of Ecstasy — They hear the Song, but seek discord instead of harmony.

• Dreamspeakers — An early Song, but unrefined. Lost in the world of the many, they do not see the One.

• Euthanatos — The Devil's chord. Disharmony.

• Order of Hermes — They manipulate the individual notes and wish to Sing only for their own gain.

• Sons of Ether — These Prometheans are only slightly less proud than the Technocracy.

• Verbena — They have their own sanguine Song. Although we must now trust them, we will not embrace them.

• Virtual Adepts — They confuse the instrument for the note.

• Hollow Ones — They seek the Song, but without a voice.

Look within yourself to see the burning spark of the One,
and let it burst forth in song!
We are many, but we act in concert.
Always listen to the songs of those around you,
and never forget the One, our origin and our destiny.

The Cult of Ecstasy

Most other Traditions write the Cultists of Ecstasy off as losers with eyes full of stars and heads full of drugs. They miss, however, the method behind the Cult's apparent madness: that only by transcending every barrier — social, theological, even temporal — can you truly reach beyond your own inner walls. Other mages frown upon the Time Masters' so-called "vices," but the Ecstatics themselves realize that sex, dance and drugs are time-honored, if risky, roads to transcendence.

The Cult has a rich history. From arboreal visionquests to Dionysian revels, mystics throughout history have sought to sidestep the mundane by altering their perceptions and thus their conceptions of what is and is not real. The Cult itself rose from organized bands of Ecstatics who pursued enlightenment through any means necessary. Through their experiments, they discovered ways to slip past the boundaries of Time. This feat, coupled with the eloquence of the founding members, won the Ecstatics their Council seat. Other wizards looked askance at the tripping mysticks (known then as the Seers of Chronos), but no one could deny the success of their methods.

Time is this Tradition's forte; the very existence of this Art is often credited to the early Seers, who looked — and sometimes even jumped — across the time stream. Although other groups have accepted such feats, no one has been able to beat the Cult for sheer mastery of the temporal. Many Cultists are adept at perception magicks also. Ecstatics are usually known for their faraway gaze. Most outsiders attribute this to excessive drug use, but wise mages recognize the effects of time sight. After all, if you always saw past, present and future as one, you'd look pretty stoned too.

The stereotypical Cultist bears little resemblance to his more respectable forbears; he is usually unkempt, rebellious, contemptuous of authority and perpetually stoned. In truth, the hippie weirdo is only the most obvious face of this diverse Tradition. While more conservative mages shake their heads at the "degeneration" of the Cult, those who understand realize that any sort of conformity or regulation runs counter to the group's whole philosophy — to obliterate *all* barriers in pursuit of the higher self. The Cult is a "Tradition" in name only; they are united only under a common philosophy and code of ethics.

Strange as it may seem to some, Ecstatic mages are generally responsible. Since so much of their code is based on the sacred passions, acts which violate one's self — suicide, murder, rape, addiction and other forms of oppression and self-destruction — are the worst kind of crimes. Contrary to popular belief, the Cult on the whole rarely participates in the sex industry or drug trade; the exploitation to which these "institutions" often sink goes against the Tradition's grain. Few Cultists will ever try to force a Sleeper to Awaken. Some folks, they know, should remain asleep.

The code of the Cult stresses individual freedom, tempered with a responsibility to those who do not understand. Like the Akashic Brothers and Verbena, Ecstatics attune themselves to the energies within. Such energies are then stimulated with drugs, sexual arousal, music and other activities to bring on an altered state. Most Cultists vary their chosen "vices" often, since any form of stimulation loses its potency with overuse. Addiction to a certain vice, or to overstimulation in general, spells doom for the foolish. Cultists walk a very thin line.

Music is the most powerful Ecstatic tool. Strong rhythms and complex harmonies unlock and channel the sacred inner passions. Few Cultists work their magick without some form of chant, dance, drumming or song. The Tradition's greatest achievement was perhaps the popularization of rock music. Whether the pioneers of rock-n-roll were Awakened or mundane is open to debate, but no one can debate the influence the Cult has had on rock's diversity and forms — or its popularity. Concerts, particularly those which stir up lots of raw emotion, are common Cultist hangouts.

Philosophy: Tune in to the song within yourself. Stretch your fingers past the bars of your private cage, and lift yourself beyond the limits. Anything is possible! Life is a gift, and most poor bastards never get past the wrapping paper.

Style: The Cult's magick comes from sidestepping limitations both within and without. As soon as you believe a given set of rules, they teach, you must break them to gain further enlightenment. This rebellious credo allows Ecstatic mages to advance quickly and spectacularly, though Paradox picks off the careless ones. Their Arts usually involve perception (and the twisting of same) through tapping into the sacred passions.

Sphere: Time

Common Foci: Dance, music, sex and sensuality, drugs (usually natural, not man-made), incense, candles, art

Organization: Nomadic and anarchistic, Ecstasy Cultists wander the world in search of new thrills and converts. Concerts, tribal gatherings and raves are common meeting sites. Rank is an informal matter; status is based on mutual respect. Large meetings are unusual, and often serious, affairs. Though pigeonholed as unreliable, an Ecstatic mage is perfectly reasonable about attending Chantry meetings — so long as there's a reason for one.

Initiation: Likely candidates are usually offered a chance at enlightenment, anything from a peyote visionquest to a prolonged hike or lodge sweat. Their reactions are watched afterward, and Awakened visionaries are asked to join. Recruits are chosen for commitment, principles and often talent or looks.

Acolytes: Groupies, entertainers, thrill-seekers, hippie-types

Concepts: Musician, dancer, Deadhead, medievalist, vagabond, modern primitive

Stereotypes

- Akashic Brotherhood — The right idea, but way too dogmatic about it.
- Celestial Chorus — Walking arguments for rebellion. Talk about uptight!
- Dreamspeakers — The roots of our Art; now if they would just loosen up….
- Euthanatos — Forsake life for death? No thanks!
- Order of Hermes — Oh, please! As if there was only one way to work magick. Get a life!
- Sons of Ether — This is what science ought to be!
- Verbena — They throw great parties. Most could lighten up, though.
- Virtual Adepts — Ascension's best hope today. Too bad they're such dicks.
- Hollow Ones — Their black veils blind them to our possibilities.

If you can't look beyond your own nose, you have only yourself to blame. Dump your burdens, and learn how far you can really see. Does that seem selfish or trivial? Fine! At least I'll know that I've lived when it's time to die!

Dreamspeakers

Born before time, this primordial Tradition now stands for the dispossessed, for those whose cultures have been overthrown like the land itself. These shamans, joined in a marriage of convenience, find a common cause in the fate of the spirit landscape — a fate their own people understand. Some Traditions battle the Technocrats out of idealism. For the Dreamspeakers, the fight is personal.

When the Convocation was called, searchers went out to the farthest lands. There, they found people who had achieved balance with the spirits of nature. Though few of these believed in the Technocratic threat, some had experienced visions that convinced them to join the strangers' cause. Because of these visions, those who came back to Horizon were christened "Those-Who-Speak-With-Dreams." Then the troubles began. No one knew or understood their languages or cultures. At a loss, the Council appointed the newcomers a few leaders and left them to figure things out themselves. By the time these leaders had overcome tribal rivalries, language barriers and xenophobia, the rest of the Council treated them all as one group, renamed the Dreamspeakers.

This Tradition's people have had a rough time. Their lands were seized and stripped during the Age of Exploration. When European mages pontificated about "progress," many Dreamspeakers went back home or grew bitter with their counterparts. Even today, a nasty undercurrent exists between the native Dreamspeakers and the people whose ancestors stole their lands. Despite this, the Tradition's fortunes have recently risen. As industry gobbles up nature, even Sleepers return to the old ways. As the most primal Tradition, the Dreamspeakers have attracted many followers. The Earth, however, is ailing, and the shamans know Her pain all too well. Beyond the Gauntlet, they can see the spiritual scars that "progress" sets in motion. Many of these shamans are angry, and that fury guides their Art.

Even less militant members defend their lands. To this Tradition, all things are sacred and alive. They see the spirits, and they know. Dreamspeakers retain their ancestral ways and often live among their native people — Africans, Native Americans, Aborigines and more "backwoods" Europeans and Asians who remember the times before cities and lords. Because of their rustic manner and clannish habits, most outsiders dismiss them as throwbacks. The Tradition's loose structure and leadership doesn't help impressions.

Of all Traditions, the Dreamspeakers are perhaps the most diverse; this is both a strength and a liability. Because they have no internal politics to worry about and no leaders to strike at, the Dreamspeakers are a resilient bunch. The same disunity that led to their lands' conquest, however, makes it hard to work lasting changes. Some Dreamspeakers are kindly visionaries, but others never leave the war-path. All share a common bond with the Earth and Her spirit children, an Art that relies more on visions and prayers than on skill or power, and a dream of rebirth when their people will grow strong again.

Philosophy: This wasteland you call the "real world" is merely a phantasm, a transient whisper of the spirits. We know Earth for what She is — a mother whose children have grown too proud. Someone must take care of Her, and that's our task. We seek the pathways behind what you call dreams, for our peoples' wisdom predates your wonder-machines and will survive after they have gone.

Style: Dreamspeakers believe their Art comes entirely from the Dreamers, or spirits; thus, their foci call such spirits and ready the mind to speak with them. Their Arts are strongest in lands where the Technomancers' paradigm has not yet taken root: the jungles of South America and Africa, the wilds of Siberia, Inner Asia and Australia. In the modern world, where the Gauntlet stands firm, their magick weakens.

Sphere: Spirit

Common Foci: Bones, feathers, dances, music and song, ordeals, prayers, images, natural drugs

Organization: Very loose; many Dreamspeakers are nomadic and solitary. Others claim certain areas as their protectorates and ally with shapeshifters to defend them. Rank, such as it is, is based on respect and occasional votes, not on titles or power. Sometimes, tribal rivalries begin again, and other Dreamspeakers must step in to stop the fighting. In midsummer and during bad times, the Tradition calls gatherings to exchange news and insights, settle disputes and celebrate.

Initiation: Initiation is in many ways the pinnacle of the Dreamspeaker Path. Spirits choose most shamans — those who seek such destiny rarely find it. Dreamspeakers on the cusp of Awakening often seem unstable; they see glimpses of the Umbra and visions of hidden truth. Initiation is often personal — one goes, or is taken, on a visionquest where he undergoes hardships both real and spiritual. Many times, he dies and is reborn. Sometimes other shamans observe the newcomer, but the visionquest is often suffered alone. When it ends, the Avatar usually takes the shape of some patron spirit — often an animal with some significance to the mage — and guides him to others of his kind.

Acolytes: Garou, environmentalists, neo-shaman, native activists

Concepts: Shaman, hermit, ecologist, visionary, warrior

Stereotypes

• Akashic Brotherhood — They remember the ancient times when we spoke to spirits, but they now rely too much on themselves.

• Celestial Chorus — We chafe under their attempts at indoctrination. If only they could see that we seek the same wholeness which they do.

• Cult of Ecstasy — They understand the necessities of ecstasy, of breaking the boundaries of the self, but they do it out of selfishness.

• Euthanatos — Who are these people, controlled by dark spirits, who claim to know the true cycle of death and rebirth?

• Order of Hermes — Their Art is sterile and meaningless. Look not to books for true wisdom. They seek to oppress as much as the Technocracy does.

• Sons of Ether — Their science is more heartfelt than the Technocratic abominations, but they still seek mechanistic control over the natural world.

• Verbena — They are close to us, but must learn to look beyond the quantified forms to the world of spirit.

• Virtual Adepts — Sad. They'd replace the Dream with an illusion of their own artifice.

• Hollow Ones — They've learned to seek wisdom within, not without. If only they could love the world as much as they love themselves.

I walk where the Dream is real.
I dance to the heartbeat of the World.
I am one with nature — the wolf, the bear, the owl.
Your world is blind, your spirit dying.
Come with me to the heart of nature.
Share our Dreams, and you shall live.

Euthanatos

From the moment of our births, we die. Slowly, painfully, joyfully, we rejoin the Great Unmaking which breaks us down, obliterates our individuality and sends us back, perhaps, for another trip. The concept terrifies most Westerners. This dread explains some of the Euthanatos' bad reputation.

Although the Euthanatos do not glory in death, the "brief death" of their initiation has left its mark on them. Most outsiders lay charges of murder, torture, genocide, necromancy, vampirism and other horrors at the Tradition's door. There are many misconceptions — and some truths — behind the rumors.

An amalgam of Greek, Hindu and heretical Arabic beliefs, this Tradition has had problems since the beginning of time. Three hundred years before Christ's birth, Euthanatos forerunners — the Handura, Bhowana and Dacoits — battled Akashic missionaries over differences of doctrine. Although both groups believed in reincarnation and the Avatars' upward progress, the "death mages" sought human progress through reincarnation, weeding out corruption wherever they found it. To the Akashics, these sects impeded the cycle of Drahma. To the thanatoic sects, their practice — the Good Death — was merely pragmatic, given India's living conditions even then. The Euthanatos claimed they saw misery and stagnation and took care of it the most direct way possible. In the modern world, they still pursue that legacy with grim determination.

Contrary to belief, few Euthanatos go about their task coldly. Outsiders mistake their tight emotional control, so necessary for such a task, for bloodlust. This is rarely true; they simply bear the burden destiny has given them. Though most Euthanatos do display a great interest in the moments surrounding death, this fascination is not as morbid as it seems. To them, death is only a step in the journey, not an ending.

Neither are the Euthanatos careless. Most employ their magicks to research the causes of decay, pinpoint the sources and hunt them down. Most will make some attempt to reform their targets before the Good Death — a killing designed to send the victim back into the karmic cycle — is applied. Some offenders recant and change their ways; the foolhardy join the Great Unmaking.

Sadly, the times appear to have surpassed them. The miseries of the modern world are beyond any Tradition's ability to prevent. Some extreme sects have urged a global purging to bring on a new beginning. This suggestion has not met with much approval, for obvious reasons. Despite the seeming kinship between the Good Death's objective and the Nephandic ideal, no Tradition battles the Fallen Ones with greater fervor — the end of everything leaves nothing for rebirth. Euthanatos are, in their way, optimists — they believe in an eventual dawn to the current night.

Through their connection with the Great Cycle, the Euthanatos understand the ups and downs of probability better than any other group. They study the effects of death and rebirth through dark Seekings and short trips into the Shadowlands. Games of chance and even physical ordeals are common teaching tools. Understanding the Cycle gives them power over reality.

Euthanatos are a pragmatic lot; they study weapons, poisons, dark magicks and vampirism as closely as they can. Though most pity the Restless Dead for remaining trapped within their identities, few hesitate to use a ghost for their own ends. Yet they are known throughout the Council for their fairness and compassion for those who deserve it. Many work as doctors or healers, assisting those they can save and helping on those whom they cannot. For them, Kali, the Dark Mother, is a perfect symbol. She gives life, and she takes it away.

Philosophy: Things fall apart. Night descends over day. Everyone dies, even us. The Wheel weeps for no one. But morning always comes. That's part of the deal. It all comes around again. How can you doubt that this is natural? Death is only a brief sleep. We're just trying to wake the Sleeper up before its too late.

Style: Euthanatos magick flows from their attunement with the Great Cycle, or Wheel, which they often personify as any number of birth/death deities (Kali, Persephone and Baron Samedi being the most common). Some draw upon this Cycle by entering a mild trance or focusing their will through cards, dice or lots. A few modern Euthanatos use the trappings of mortality — bones, skulls, graveyard dirt, etc. — while others work through purified weapons.

Sphere: Entropy

Common Foci: Dancing, dice, cards, weapons, bones, incense, song, candles, meditation

Organization: Fairly loose and democratic; most *Marabouts* (Chantries) maintain autonomy and decide all policy from within. Meetings are held on the first day of every month. An enforcer group, the Freedom Razor, is said to police the Tradition for Nephandic taint and supposedly answers to the mysterious Consanguinity of Eternal Joy. Another faction, the White Band, administers to the needs of those Sleepers who can be saved.

Initiation: All new members must undergo the *agama* ("short death"), a near-death experience which takes them into the Underworld for a long moment to savor mortality and the wisdom of the Great Unmaking. From there, initiates either decide to stay or come back to join the Tradition.

Acolytes: Occultists, right-to-die activists, doctors and nurses, detectives

Concepts: Assassin, vigilante, health care worker, wandering priest(ess)

Stereotypes

• Akashic Brotherhood — Once, they wronged us. We still feel the pain. Never trust. Never forget.

• Celestial Chorus — They shift the blame for the sad state of the world from their own shoulders to some anti-god and refuse to see that we all make our own Paths.

• Cult of Ecstasy — Our roots lie tangled with their own, but we look upon the truths they hide from.

• Dreamspeakers — Our distant cousins who know the will of the Dreamers but see little of our present situation. For them, the Wheel is frozen in time.

• Order of Hermes — Proud and blustery, they rely too much on toys and know nothing of the forces behind them.

• Sons of Ether — Living proof that science has merit. They distill the Technocracy's trash heap into working marvels.

• Verbena — Our spiritual kin, though they spend too much time dancing and not enough time reading the footprints.

• Virtual Adepts — Do they think they can live forever inside their machines? The computer eats their souls and leaves behind nothing but flab.

• Hollow Ones — They claim to know death, but if the real thing bit them on the ass, they'd run screaming into the night.

WHY DO YOU HOLD ON SO TIGHTLY TO YOUR SELF?
IT IS ONLY A SHELL, AND SHELLS CRACK.
YOUR SPIRIT IS THE TRUE IMMORTAL.

The Order of Hermes

Each Tradition claims a grand and ancient history, but few can boast as rich and momentous a lifeline as the Order of Hermes. Inheritors — or survivors — of the illustrious Hermetic Houses of the European High Mythic Age, these haughty mages epitomize the classical wizard: hunched over arcane codices, they translate esoteric numerologies and divine the arcane keys to the universe.

Once, this Tradition consisted of many smaller mystick Houses, micro-Traditions grouped together by a common ideology, honor code and magickal approach. To the Hermetics, magick — or "the Art" — was a quantifiable field of study, much like science or grammar, with set rules of theorems and logic. With enough study and dedication, reality could be mastered through knowledge and skill. Though their main teachings came from Egyptian and Hebrew mysticks, the Orders incorporated variations as they spread their influence across Europe during its Dark Ages.

Hermetic magi were among the first to recognize that shared beliefs established a certain paradigm under which magick became easier or more difficult. With this knowledge, the Hermetics began a grand experiment: living and operating in the public eye, they spread belief in their magick throughout their sphere of influence — the first attempt to guide the beliefs of Sleepers on a massive scale. Unfortunately, their Order of Reason rivals learned the lesson all too well. While the Houses battled each other, the Church and the descendants of the Wyck, the Technocrats ultimately stole consensual reality from under the Hermetics' noses.

It was a Hermetic magus, most accounts say, who began the formation of the Council of Nine. Unfortunately, they soon learned that their divisions paled when compared with the magickal practices of the world at large. Foreign groups soon forced the Houses to unite under one Hermetic Tradition, a "slight" the Order has never forgotten.

The Order of Hermes loathes the Technocracy for its role in the Order's "fall," and they carry the fight to all fronts. Through intellectual appeal, political and social control, and the New Age press, the Order hopes to undermine the Technocratic paradigm and bring the Wheel of Fortune back their way. Sadly, this effort has been undercut by the Tradition's insistence upon detailed ritual, secrecy and dedicated study. Few modern mystics have the time or patience to master the Hermetic Arts.

Hermetic formality is more than snobbishness; it is a mark of honor, distinction and discipline. These magi are aware that few others could match their dedication, and feel they have earned the respect they demand. Learning is more than a chore for these magi — it is a passion for knowledge, an endless curiosity about the universe's secrets. Discretion is likewise a necessary trait; the Order knows how many rivals would steal those secrets for their own. The Technocracy's rise shows what happens when the keys to reality fall into greedy hands.

Magi with perseverance, however, reap great rewards. Hermetic magick harnesses elemental power and ancient bargains with Umbrood lords. The Order's work ethic allows such magi access to massive libraries, the Umbral Courts, longevity spells and Doissetep, the most powerful Chantry in existence. No other Tradition commands the raw influence — mortal and otherwise — of the Hermetic Houses. The cost, however, is considerable: long years of apprenticeship, endless politicking, dedicated study and subservience to magi who measure their lives in centuries. To top it off, most other Traditions distrust the Hermetic ones, fearing, perhaps rightly, that the wizards plan to take control if — or when — the Ascension War is won.

Philosophy: Our teachings are too profound and complex for the weak-minded to comprehend. Thus, we must hide them in metaphor and teach them in analogy. Though it remains our duty to guide the Sleepers (and our fellow Traditions) to Ascension, the truths we know are so powerful that only the wisest magi may receive them unbound.

Style: Hermetic mages are consummate scholars, studying ancient lore and preserving revered truths. The Order revels in its secrecy and utilizes a secret language in its magickal workings and society. Hermetic magick taps the elemental flow through ritual incantations, signs, seals, secret names and other classical paraphernalia. Such magick is difficult and complex to use, but bestows potent results.

Sphere: Forces

Common Foci: Circles and sigils, languages and numbers, gems and jewelry (particularly showstones), elaborate rituals, pentacles, formulae, ritual objects (wands, swords, goblets, etc.)

Organization: The Order of Hermes relies upon hierarchy and discipline to maintain its secrecy. Deeply formal, this Tradition has rigidly codified regulations about proper behavior, teachings, forms of address and such. Beneath the umbrella of the Order, the many Houses still exist as factions within the Order, a fact unknown to most other Tradition mages. Though the strongest — Tytalus, Ex Miscellanea, Quaesitor, Bonisagus and Flambeau — date from the Mythic Age, new Houses (Janissary, Thig, Shaea and Fortunae) have arisen since the Council began.

Initiation: Recruits often come from academia, where promising students are taken aside and rigorously tested, sometimes for years. New apprentices are sent to College Chantries **(see Chapter Three)**, then given in service to their Masters (often called "mater" or "pater") for long apprenticeships. Initiation is highly formal and ritualistic with dates determined by astrological conjunction. Some apprentice classes are even seen as more significant than others based upon the astrological alignments of a given year.

Acolytes: Mathematicians, members of secret organizations (CIA, mystic orders, the Arcanum), scientists, scholars, publishers

Concepts: Scholar, astrologer, alchemist, linguist, magician

Stereotypes

- Akashic Brotherhood — While they seek wisdom and have found peace, they lack knowledge.
- Celestial Chorus — Servants of their own fear and faith, rigid dogmatists who do not realize that we shape our own role in destiny.
- Cult of Ecstasy — They believe that truth can be found in breaking the rules; this is folly, and they are doomed to failure.
- Dreamspeakers — Those who merely play with spirits do not understand the magnitude of magick. Their time is over.
- Euthanatos — Dangerous, but so long as they work against the Technocracy, we will permit them to work with us.
- Sons of Ether — If these mad Technomancers could learn that what they seek can be accomplished through the Art instead of their juvenile "science," they could go far.
- Verbena — Theirs is a primitive and unrefined vision of the Art. Let them dance in their herb garden, but do not rely upon them.
- Virtual Adepts — The Technocracy's stink still lingers upon them. They're useful, but trust them not.
- Hollow Ones — Childish anarchistic bastards who think that they can simply forswear millennia of magical knowledge merely by claiming "independence." They need to be spanked.

I speak the secret language.
I know the meanings of numbers.
I perceive more subtle truths
than your unsophisticated mind can fathom.

Sons of Ether

Weird Science! Dreams for a Better Tomorrow! Utopia! All of these slogans can be applied to the Sons of Ether, the Council's most hopeful Tradition. Sometimes mistrusted, barely understood and usually under-appreciated by other Traditions (and frequently used as the Technocracy's scapegoat), the wildly optimistic Sons of Ether represent the hope and wonder too frequently lost in today's world.

The Sons of Ether have historic ties to both the Council of Nine and the Technocracy. Their ideological roots can be traced to the ancient Greek philosopher Aretus, author of what is now called the *Kitab al Alacir*. This treatise contains two parts: the first posits a single Essence which all things are made of, ultimately called Ether. The second part contains an ontological discussion of reality and discusses how this single Essence was differentiated throughout creation. According to the *Kitab al Alacir*, enlightened scholars — "Philosophers" — could effect the world through the workings of the will.

This scroll was lost to history for centuries. When it was discovered, almost simultaneously, in two variants, it gave rise to the Natural Philosopher's Guild, a magickal society based around Will-Science. This group went through many changes — including the disbanded Solificati — before congealing in the 1860s into the Electrodyne Engineers, a Technocratic Convention. From the beginning, the Engineers quarreled with their allies. To them, the ideals of Science and civilization were more important than world domination. The Technocracy finally decided to squash the egalitarian upstarts by discrediting the Ether. This act proved intolerable, and the Electrodyne Engineers resigned, reforming within the Council of Nine as the Sons of Ether.

As members of the Council, the Sons of Ether still consider themselves *Scientists* (as opposed to scientists) and believe that they work for the betterment of humanity. Although no longer members of the Technocracy, they still find their theories and accomplishments choked by bland "scientific laws." Although many Sons treasure old-fashioned honor and aesthetics, they're an optimistic bunch. While many Traditions bemoan their past glories, the Sons of Ether speak of a grand and glorious future. Now these Scientists boldly seek this future, whether sailing the winds of Etherspace, exploring the lost and hidden Hollow Earth or fighting the Technocracy with ray guns and jet-packs.

A fierce rivalry still exists between the Technocracy and the Sons of Ether. The Sons resent the Technocracy for their stranglehold on Science, while the Mirrorshades dislike the free-spirited Science the Sons employ, Science better fitted to Victorian or pulp science-fiction. Unlike the Technocracy, the Sons of Ether do not wish to force their accomplishments upon humanity. They want to inspire the world, for this spark of inspiration is what will free the world and lead it to Ascension.

Philosophy: Creation, the spark of imagination, is the road to Awakening; even Sleepers share its excitement. The inner vision which leads to invention and creation will bring us to the future. The Technocracy will fail because they lack inspiration, and they offer no future. We do.

Style: These are not mages, but Scientists! Because of their outlook, they rely heavily upon "scientific" foci: mad inventions, weird processes and arcane physics. Their gadgetry often combines Sleepers' sense of wonder with scientific wizardry and may be either wildly vulgar or marginally coincidental. The most advanced Sons learn to transcend their inventions, but many prefer their odd devices to the mundanity of plain magick, even when they know better.

Sphere: Matter

Common Foci: Inventions, electricity, Ether goggles, strange chemicals, wind/water/solar power, meters, experiments, weapons, vehicles

Organization: The Sons of Ether are (some would say hopelessly) rooted in the Victorian mens' club pattern developed during the days of the Electrodyne Engineers. Rank is rather formal, based upon Scientific accomplishment and know-how. Many Sons work alone, pursuing their pet theories or researching long-discarded ones. Ego-rivalries are common and often resolved with Science-battles in wild Realms. These visionaries communicate largely through their journal *Paradigma*, which acts as a forum for Scientific advancement as well as political argument. Although called "Sons" of Ether, many female Scientists — who dislike their colleagues' Victorian demeanor — belong to this Tradition.

Initiation: Most Sons of Ether tend to come from academic environments, although Scientific prodigies are welcome. Prospective candidates are "offered" a copy of the *Kitab al Alacir*, and their observations are noted. It's said that the treatise itself can spark Awakenings. Afterward, the prospective candidate is invited to an informal forum with Sons of Ether, in order to discuss matters of Science — testing the candidate's knowledge and probing for the sense of wonder so necessary in Scientific advancement.

Acolytes: Eccentric inventors, mechanics, golems, robots, SF fans

Concepts: Mad scientist, gadgeteer, Ethernaut, pulp hero, bold explorer, gentleman scholar

Stereotypes

- Akashic Brotherhood — Too lost in contemplation, they cannot effect change.
- Celestial Chorus — Religious dogmatists who would stifle creativity and progress.
- Cult of Ecstasy — Degenerates. A waste of time. Do something serious.
- Dreamspeakers — What fascinating throwbacks!
- Euthanatos — Dangerous and unfathomable, ever-ready to snuff out the spark of life.
- Order of Hermes — They could make excellent Scientists if they gave up their arcane learning and looked to the future.
- Verbena — Useful gardeners who understand natural forces but cannot harness them.
- Virtual Adepts — Their imagination is strong, but must be directed to a useful end.
- Hollow Ones — Shoddy guttersnipes who must learn manners and get haircuts before they will be taken seriously.

Real Science comes not from sterile laboratories, but from the spark of imagination!

Verbena

Life is not meant to be sterile and safe; the passions which so many fear are the things which keep our race alive. The Verbena roll up their sleeves and deal with life's joys and brutalities with determination. These primal sorcerers know the power of such passions — and the cost of embracing them.

No other Tradition, except perhaps the Dreamspeakers, has suffered as the Verbena have. Always feared, these followers of the carnal Arts fell under severe persecutions during the late Middle Ages. Branded as Satanic witches, the Tradition's European forbears were hunted, tortured and burned. As the witch-hunters decimated all sorcerous orders, one Verbena, Nightshade, called for unity to end the slaughter. The Council of Nine took years to form, but even then, the witch-craze took centuries to wind down. The Tradition has never forgotten the lessons of those times. Now they practice in secret and deal harshly with their foes.

Although the Verbena prize life over all things, their ways are not kind. Their Arts — utilizing blood, sex, dance and even occasional sacrifice — are terrifying even if one understands the deeper significance of their actions. To the Verbena, life is savage joy, a howl of mingled pain, defiance and ecstasy. Life must be viewed with open eyes if one is to truly understand it. In the earliest days, tales say, the Wyck carried magick across the globe. The Verbena trace their path from these primordial Awakened, and their insights shaped the Spheres, the Protocols and Horizon itself. This legacy, and the hardships they have suffered to retain it, make the Verbena a self-righteous, often arrogant, lot.

This is not to say that they are heartless. Quite the opposite, Verbena as a whole tend to be more passionate, honest and forthright than many other mages. Their credo — "Light and Darkness, whole in One — what is Willed will Be" — demands a commitment to life in all its forms. Despite their persecutions, most are dedicated to helping humanity remove its blinders while there is still time. Their magick, firmly centered in nature, cures as quickly as it kills. Though a Verbena may be suspicious, she is loyal to those friends she chooses. Though she may be angry, she is often just.

Unlike their Hermetic and Celestial rivals, the Verbena balance strong male and female aspects, rather than favoring a patriarchal ideal. Many female mysticks gravitate towards them for that reason. This Tradition's sacred totem, the tree, is more than just a symbol. Like the group itself, a tree roots itself, absorbs nourishment from the soil, grows outward filled with life and spreads out and open, disbursing nourishment for others in its leaves. All Verbena Chantries have a tree, usually an oak, in the center. Most important rites occur around this so-called World Tree; these rituals often stain the trees a deep red. The darker the hue, the more powerful the coven.

This group favors the old ways. Many speak archaic languages, dress in native and medieval styles and revere family and honor. Verbena rites center around harvest festivals and lunar cycles. Although many covens have discarded the ancient forms of sacrifice, some still practice them when the need arises. Learning is important to the Verbena. Without history, one cannot understand the cycle-patterns of Fate or appreciate what has been done by — and done *to* — this eldritch group.

Philosophy: Don't think for a second that the pulse of the world has been silenced. We hear it all the time; it's our music and our commandment. We are the handmaidens of Fate, and we take all that life offers — painful though it may be sometimes — and delve wholeheartedly into its essence. If our ways scare you, perhaps you should ask yourself why — is it our passion that frightens you or your own?

Style: This Tradition's ties to nature are clear in their magick; their Arts favor shapeshifting, healing, perceptions and strength. Like the Euthanatos, Verbena know the ways of Fate and measure cycles of being. Many of the classic witch's tools draw from the ways of the Verbena and reflect their affinity for the bare necessities.

Sphere: Life

Common Foci: Ritual tools (wand, knife, altar, pentacle, cup), incense, herbs, cauldrons, dance, sex, blood, runes, ordeals, song

Organization: Covens, often numbering 13, nine, seven or three, make up the Tradition's base. Most Verbena are social — the group focuses a mystick's intent — and center around families whenever possible. Both women and men have powerful roles in the group, though women dominate many covens. Large meetings occur eight times a year — the four equinoxes, Candlemas (Feb. 2), Beltane (May 1), Lammas (Aug. 1) and Samhaine (Oct. 31). Disputes are often resolved by votes, but many involve tests or even combat.

Initiation: All Initiates must undergo a ritual death and rebirth. After study and testing, the prospective Verbena enters the circle and undergoes some form of ordeal (often illusionary, sometimes not). When the coven is satisfied that she has the necessary spirit and dedication, they call the elements as witnesses. Most Verbena stay loyal unto death. This Tradition has no place for Orphans. If they cannot display the dedication to learn the ancient Arts, they are a burden and a waste.

Acolytes: Pagans, rustic folks, environmentalists, radicals

Concepts: Witch, druid, shaman, healer, rune-cutter, shapeshifter, activist, artist

Stereotypes

• Akashic Brotherhood — Honorable ascetics who blind themselves through denial. We're all flesh, no matter how much some of us may want to forget it.

• Celestial Chorus — Don't get me started!

• Cult of Ecstasy — They just need more focus. Respect their ideas, understand their means and ignore their follies.

• Dreamspeakers — Our kin and the closest to our understanding. They merely look without for what we find within.

• Euthanatos — Yes, I understand the Cycle. I just despise the use they've put it to. Life is too sacred to be so easily dismissed.

• Order of Hermes — With all their books and diagrams, they've lost the soul within their Art.

• Sons of Ether — Sexist bastards who can't put their Tinkertoys away. Grow up, folks!

• Virtual Adepts — We know how persecution can affect one's attitude, but I wouldn't trust these test-tube babies as far as I could throw a mainframe. Theirs is a scary kind of magick.

• Hollow Ones — These midnight children favor our trappings, but know little of our mysteries. We should guide them.

Call me a bloody bitch — I'm all that and more. But I can look in the mirror and say that I have lived. Can you, with your illusions of comfort, say the same?

Virtual Adepts

Rebellious to the core, these futuristic anarchists refuse to inherit the world as it is. Like the Cult of Ecstasy, the Adepts' Art transcends barriers by sidestepping them. Instead of altering consciousness the old-fashioned way, however, Virtual Adepts prize technology, metaphysics and anarchy. Their crowning achievement is virtual reality, and no other group understands its secrets like they do.

The newest Tradition, the Adepts began as the Difference Engineers Convention. Like the Electrodyne Engineers, these Technomancers explored the possibilities of invention in the mid-1800s. The computer and telephone excited them, the latter inspiring their theories about a "correspondence point" where all places were one. Tying this idea into the fables of Mount Qaf, the re-christened Virtual Adepts set to work trying to enter this virtual Realm. The group's visionary sense, however, annoyed their Technocratic masters. The Adepts never had been ones to follow orders.

As their science progressed, the group began to experiment with social engineering and anarchist theory. The Inner Circle was not amused. Things came to a head during World War II when the Adepts defied their leadership and undermined the Nazis. Constraints tightened, and the Adepts rebelled. Post-war experiments with VR led Adept Alan Turing to open access to the Net Realm. When the Men in Black came to take Turing's breakthrough away, the Adepts fled into VR, destroying every computer record they could find. A vicious purge followed, and the Council of Nine offered sanctuary. Some mysticks have lived to regret the offer.

The Virtual Adepts bow to no one's power, and most disdain Council and Union mages alike. As the Reckoning approaches, the Adepts charge into cyberspace to build a new world before the old one ends. Their self-sufficiency and post-modern cynicism undermine the older wizards of the Council, and the mysticks are not pleased. No one doubts, however, that the Adepts are onto something. Obnoxious as some Adepts may be, the future hinges on their Art.

And don't they know it! The Tradition is notorious for its attitude problems — snide humor, isolationism, pranks and data piracy are the Adepts' hallmarks. A lot of this attitude comes from a siege mentality. The Technocracy has sworn to annihilate them, most Traditionalists don't trust them, and the Nephandi and Marauders seem too vicious to reason with. Most Adepts believe they have only themselves — and each other — to rely upon. For the most part, they're right.

Without the social outlets or skills of many magicians, the Virtual Adepts still accomplish many things. Through their networks, they disseminate new ideas, inspire Sleepers, attack the Technocracy's power structure and forge a new VR world. With their vision, skills and off-kilter concepts, these mys-techs epitomize post-modern magick: ornery, democratic, cynical and visionary.

Philosophy: Telling me something can't or shouldn't be done just makes me want to prove you wrong. And I will. We have skills and access you can't even imagine; no door is closed to us for long. We *are* the future. The flesh is dying, and we're the next big thing. The world we know is every bit as real — and a hell of a lot more pure — than this decaying mudball you're trying to save. Ascension lies in new ideas, not dusted-off old ones.

Style: Mathematical and metaphysical oddities form the basis for this Tradition's Art. To them, all reality is information. By altering that information, you change the world. Like most other Traditions, the Adepts have a pet "10th Sphere" theory; theirs is Paradigm, the element of conceptual reality. Most Adepts work their arcane technomagick with advanced computers called Trinary units. Where most systems work only with "yes" and "no," Trinary decks understand "maybe."

Sphere: Correspondence

Common Foci: Computers, VR gear, weapons, cybernetics, network links, inventions

Organization: Extremely democratic; status comes through "eliteness," a half-serious blend of coolness, accomplishment, savvy and sheer balls. They meet *en masse* twice a year, though many throw smaller meetings. Most Virtual Adepts have on-line personae (complete with VR icons) who barely resemble their mortal selves; these icons are the only way many communicate. Although most Adepts interact only on-line, some factions (known sarcastically as "legions") do exist. Some, like the Cyberpunks, fit the obvious stereotypes, while others, like the Reality Hackers, work on a more metaphysical level. Because they rarely meet in the flesh, the Adepts have a history of outrageous behavior. Disputes are resolved through "flame wars," a VR form of certámen which relies on wits and imagination.

Initiation: Most Initiates find their way into some chatroom, where they are tested by would-be mentors. Those who respond favorably are often fed magickal puzzles and theories thought to provoke Awakenings. Others Awaken spontaneously and link up with others of like mind. The Virtual Adepts have nothing against Orphans; that's how many of them began.

Acolytes: Cyberpunk fans, musicians, computer geeks, anarchists, writers

Concepts: Hacker, revolutionary, artist, punk, on-line explorer, metaphysician

Stereotypes

• Akashic Brotherhood — That *Kung-Fu* shit is cool, but it doesn't work for me. Deep breathing won't patch you into the Net… I hope.

• Celestial Chorus — If you wanna see God, get off your knees and get on-line.

• Cult of Ecstasy — Great drugs, great parties, but real washouts when it comes to getting things done. Dream on, dude!

• Dreamspeakers — They've got something with their Gaia hypothesis stuff, but they can't see that their way of life is dead.

• Euthanatos — Yipe!

• Order of Hermes — There's a lot of power in their charts and formulas, but they're way too hung-up on a war they lost ages ago.

• Sons of Ether — This is why I liked science fairs! I don't know how much of their stuff actually works — lots, I guess — but they're always fun to watch. They're our forefathers and good allies. Don't slam the Sons.

• Verbena — These chicks creep me out. Cutting runes in your arm is not my idea of a good time.

• Hollow Ones — Downers, the lot of 'em, but I see where they're coming from. We've got a lot in common. Someday they may cheer up. Then watch out!

You call this a reality? Let me show you another one — Reality 2.0, if you will. Cleaner, safer, more democratic and wide open for creative expansion. Which would *you* prefer?

Hollow Ones

A joke to some, a pain in the ass to others, the Hollow Ones rank up with the Virtual Adepts in the Council's Hall of Infamy. The similarities don't end there; both groups are products of the modern era, outgrowths of a world on the brink of hell. Both groups embrace a subculture that both glories and mocks that world, and both carry the light of future change with middle fingers upraised. But where the Adepts bear a neon lightstick to light the Council's way, the Hollow Ones carry their candelabra in the dark.

Although their Goth-rock attire suggests a recent origin, their roots go back further than others realize. Though the "Hollow Tradition" (actually a Craft, or organized magickal subculture) dates its foundation to the Roaring Twenties, their so-called "lost generation" philosophy can be found in the dabblings of the Romantic poets. Many of Night's Children claim Lord Byron as the first of their line; others call that bullshit. In any case, their fondness for bygone black is matched only by their insatiable curiosity.

Hollow Ones realize that the modern world sucks, so they wrap themselves in the trappings of a more romantic time — a time when you could compose sonatas and end up buried alive. These Darklings mirror their own sense of displacement in their fixation with tragedy. Loners from the start, they set themselves further apart with eccentric dress and sarcastic manner, create their own nightworld and piss on the trespassers.

The Gothic Orphans know pain first-hand. Most come from broken or abusive homes and learn self-survival before they leave sixth grade. Many are so screwed up by their teens that when the Avatar comes calling, it seems almost mundane. Magick comes to them with little study or effort, an innate talent they often use to set up lives away from home. The street subcultures offer them a chance to rebel, find shelter and earn friendship. Magick offers them power, status and enlightenment.

Clannish and secretive, the Hollow Ones still reach out to help those who seem worth the trouble. Many Council mages owe their survival to nearby Darklings. After such aid, they often disappear, muttering cryptic jests. Deep inside, most Goth mages empathize with outcasts like themselves and watch over street people, barflies and runaways. "Outsiders," however, are not easily trusted — strangers usually have to perform some act of kinship before they will be treated with anything other than contempt, and even then, no "poseur" ever really learns the Hollow Ones' intricate social dances. In their own way, these Orphans have a code every bit as arcane as the Hermetic Mysteries. Dancing in the shadows as they do, Hollow cabals — or "cliques" — find their safety in numbers and secrecy.

Within these cliques, Night's Children cling together. They may fight, dis and betray each other, but if some outsider threatens the "family," that family hangs together till death. This sense of community, dysfunctional though it may be, provides the stability that leads the Goth mages towards some eventual Ascension. The Council may never understand what they're missing.

Other groups believe, erroneously, that the Hollow Ones lack vision. The Craft's self-absorption and morbid sense of humor masks its love for things mysterious. Puzzles, omens and other enigmas fascinate them; magick, ghosts, werewolves and especially vampires draw these Orphans like black-lace moths. In their own way, the Hollow Ones are as primal as the Verbena and Dreamspeakers — they gravitate back to the wonders beyond the campfire. By seeing old things with new eyes, the Hollow Ones junk the baggage that holds so many Awakened back from revelation and carve a new Path with old tools.

"Old tools" is an apt way of describing Hollow magick. Most channel their Arts through shopping-mall occultism — cheap jewelry, mass-market "grimoires," mail-order paraphernalia and stage magic tricks. Their libraries consist of Byron, Poe, Crowley and LeVey, and their rituals incorporate CDs, black candles and roleplaying games. By using magick all the "wrong" ways, these Orphans show that magick, at least for them, comes ultimately from within.

Philosophy: Your religion makes me vomit. Your enlightenment makes me laugh. Wake up and see the world for what it is — dying. Nice show, I guess, and good for a few more laughs, but if you think we'll all save it with a few well-placed "Hail Marys," I've got a deed for city hall in my back pocket.

Style: Hollow magick is eclectic — a bit of witchcraft, some Victorian spiritualism, a dash of Crowley, a sprinkle of pop voodoo; add Sisters of Mercy for flavor, stir rapidly and put it in a cauldron to stew. Although the Darklings eagerly seek out new elements to channel their Art, they draw their real power from within.

Sphere: Any, although they pay full price for all Spheres because of their scattershot approach and lack of tutoring.

Common Foci: (see above)

Organization: Informal; tightly-knit cliques form a network linked by friendships, nightclubs, chatlines and old-fashioned mail. Although "kings" and "queens" are occasionally elected, these titles are sardonic at best. Local clique leaders throw huge parties (or "sabbaths") every Halloween, with live bands and half-serious rituals. Many supernaturals, especially vampires, attend.

Initiation: First, an initiate must be accepted by the local clique. Would-be members must appreciate despair and demonstrate magickal talent. Lighting candles without touching them is a common test. Entrance rituals vary from clique to clique; some require tattoos, striking looks, new lore, artistic talent or even blood sacrifice.

Acolytes: Blood Dolls, runaways, club owners, Goth bands

Concepts: Occultist, musician, tragic poet, club-crawler

Stereotypes

• Akashic Brotherhood — Nice moves, Bruce. Have you looked around yourself lately? It's a new tomorrow, and it sucks.

• Celestial Chorus — I stopped believing in that shit when my parents got divorced. Go work for Hallmark.

• Cult of Ecstasy — Few Deadheads understand the dark side. Too bad — they've got some good ideas.

• Dreamspeakers — I know about the spirits, too. Wanna talk to a ghost? It's not pretty.

• Euthanatos — I walk the Path of Death on foot; they ride a bulldozer. Still, they do bring the party with them, don't they?

• Order of Hermes — Spare me. These Merlins lost what made them special 500 years ago. Just don't say it around them!

• Sons of Ether — Cool toys, great dungeons, but I think they left their brains in the Time Machine.

• Verbena — They're right; reality is blood, sex and sweat, and they don't delude themselves into thinking it's any cleaner than that.

• Virtual Adepts — If I had their cash, I might've joined. I like their attitude, but their taste in clothes has gotta go.

The dance of death is a celebration of life to those who know the steps.

Traits

But let there be no scales to weigh your unknown treasure;
And seek not the depths of your knowledge with staff or sounding line.
For self is a sea boundless and measureless.
Say not, "I have found the truth," but rather, "I have found a truth."
— Kahlil Gibran, *The Prophet*

Traits are your character's foundation — her overall personality, strengths, skills, aptitudes, resources, contacts and sometimes even her possessions. Although they're ultimately little more than dots on a sheet of paper, Traits offer the complexity of a lifetime up for easy reference.

These Traits describe only the most basic parameters of your mage. The essence of the character herself comes from roleplaying and imagination. These guidelines are mechanical, not conceptual. The concepts behind the more mystickal Traits — Essence, Avatar, Quintessence and such — can be found in **Chapters Two and Three.**

Essences

Classifying consciousness also encourages "higher than Thou" games of one-upmanship. People waste energy defining which state they are in, as if consciousness were a cosmic grammar school, in which third-graders were entitled to look down on kindergartners. The point is not what level we are on, but what we are learning.

— Starhawk, *The Spiral Dance*

Put simply, the Essence is the overall "personality" of your mage's Avatar. Most willworkers agree that four different types exist — *Dynamic, Pattern, Primordial* and *Questing*, each pulling towards some place on the Metaphysic Trinity **(see Chapter Four)**. A fifth Essence, the *Infinite*, is thought to exist, but like the quark in current quantum physics, it must exist because of its apparent absence.

There is plenty of debate about the exact role the Essence plays in a mage's destiny. Some claim that it predetermines a person's actions (and allegiances in the War), while others say that the Essence only reflects the longings of the Avatar's last incarnation. Is the Avatar a reflection of the mage, or is the mage a reflection of his Avatar? No one can say. Probably both.

Your mage's Essence could be considered his subconscious, a major source of his prejudices, quirks and personality traits. A Pattern Essence mage might worry about details and organize everything (while looking down his nose at those without such skills), while a Dynamic one would flit from project to project, biting her nails or quietly singing off-key songs. The Primordial Avatar could drive a mage to plumb the depths of every relationship she enters, urging her to reveal everything she knows to the world at large, while the Questing soul moderates disputes and strikes a balance between a messy room and a tidy office.

Essence goes a bit deeper, too. As the "personality" of a reincarnating soul, a particularly strong (four or five dots) Avatar might push an agenda of its own. Essence gives you and your Storyteller some handle on that agenda. You must decide how strong an influence your character's Avatar is **(see "Backgrounds)** and what kind of relationship, if any, they have. Sister Beulah of the Heavenly Order sees manifestations of her Pattern Avatar frequently, mistaking the Avatar to be St. Jude. Khozan, a typical Questing personality, is aware of the concept of the Avatar and thinks it's a fascinating theory, but has never had any direct experience with it. Cheshire Cat is completely unaware of the existence of Avatars and would dismiss them as "a bunch of crystal-rubbing bullhocky," even though his Dynamic Avatar has a very strong hold on him, making him the iconoclast he has become.

The manifestations of an Avatar are usually linked to its Essence. The nature of each Essence also says a lot about a character's eventual Ascension (or lack thereof). Choose your own mage's Essence with an eye toward the goals and destiny you would like him to have — even if he has to wade through hell to attain them.

Dynamic

By far the most common Essence, Dynamic Avatars are the very incarnation of the forces of change. All mages are ultimately part of the dynamic force that drives reality, but mages of this Essence are consumed by it, driven by a love of and desire for constant change. They will probably never achieve, and may never know, their ultimate destination. Mages of this Essence are often considered pioneers, for they embody the very heart of what it is to be a mage. Taken to its greatest extreme, this Essence typifies the Marauder — endlessly altering, never conforming.

Dynamic Avatars tend to be energetic spirits of great cunning and curiosity. Most assume many different forms, but tend to appear as shadows or nebulous beings out of childhood dreams. Fickle and capricious, they are impossible to please.

Pattern

Though this Essence epitomizes the Technocracy, Pattern urges are vital in the overall survival of mage society. Mages with this Essence usually work toward a certain end. Like all mages, they are innately dynamic, but aren't as concerned with finding new ways as they are with shoring up the existing ones. Without Pattern mages' support, most Dynamic mages would be incapable of pursuing their own truths of reality as far as they do.

The Avatars of this Essence are stable and constant, and tend to manifest in one given form. Such an Avatar usually appears as an authority figure from the character's past, often a demanding and unforgiving one.

Primordial

Drawing their nature from the beginning and end of the universe, Primordial Essences are by far the rarest among the four types known. Many of the earliest mages embodied this Essence, but as time passes, fewer and fewer manifest it. In its most refined state, most scholars believe, this Essence seeks a return to the primal state, an end to everything we know today. For this reason, Nephandi are thought to have a Primordial bent.

Most mages with this Essence are not nearly so extreme; even as children, however, their old souls lend them a knowing air. They tend to be abrupt, have little time for foolishness and strive to get to the bottom of everything. For all their ancient ways, Primordial Essences crave new experiences. If they've "been there — done that," it doesn't show. Deep relationships and rich passions are their greatest joys.

Primordial Avatars tend to take the form of animals, spirits or gods of legend. Like their "owners," they can be very coarse and direct in manner and speech, caring little for social niceties.

Questing

These Avatars seek balance over any set goal. Questing mages tie disparate ideas together and make forgotten thoughts seem fresh again. Like Dynamic urges, the Questing Essence pushes the mage into journey after journey. Unlike the Dynamic urge, the Questing Path finds the road more important than endless destinations. Despite this, Questing mages have more focus than their Dynamic counterparts. They pursue one quest, then another and so on in an endless road of changes.

For millennia, few willworkers saw a difference. As the world grew further and further apart, however, and the distance between the Trinity's poles grew wider and wider, this Essence (and the need for balance it personifies) became more evident. For this reason, it is often identified with the Council of Nine Traditions, those mages for whom the middle Path is the most desirable.

Many mages tend to overlook the forest for the trees, but those of Questing Essence always seek the big picture. Questing Avatars are pushy and demanding. Never satisfied with what has been achieved, they always want more and better. When they reveal themselves, such Avatars goad their mage off on some important quest and will not relent until the journey has begun.

Personality Archetypes

No, my morality was older, more classic yet, the morality that distinguished between sacrifice and slaughter and had not yet dreamed of sport.

— M.J. Engh, *Arslan*

We all roleplay in our daily lives, whether we admit it or not. In every relationship we have, we project some different aspect of our "true" self. Admit it: don't you act differently around your father than you do around your significant other? And do you feel that either person sees the "real" you, the image you greet in the mirror every day?

Even mages have these "masks"; perhaps, for survival's sake, they adopt them to an even greater extent than any other mortal (this side of a politician) would. To reflect our characters public and inner personae, we give them *Natures* and *Demeanors*. One represents the character's inner self, her true personality; the second sums up the side most people notice.

Natures and Demeanors (known collectively as *Archetypes*) offer you and your Storyteller easy handles on your character. These are not pigeonholes or "character classes" — each character is unique and multifaceted, or at least he should be. Archetypes do, however, give you something to work from. Natures give some clue to the mage's Ascension goals and flaws and give him a way to earn back the Willpower points he spends. Demeanors are largely roleplaying tools, though they can be really helpful when your Storyteller needs to have one of her characters interact with your own. If your mage's Demeanor is Rebel or Deviant, the cop on the street will probably hassle him, even if his inner Nature is that of a Caregiver or Traditionalist.

Each Archetype has a strength and a weakness. These tendencies, when they come from the mage's Nature, can be seen as guideposts in that mage's Ascension Path. *Strengths* are those virtues that might inspire his higher purpose; *weaknesss* are stumbling blocks, weak points in his personality which keep him from attaining his potential. The exact nature of these facets, and their impact on the character's eventual fate, are left to you to decide.

Your mage's Nature also gives him a way to replenish spent Willpower points. When he accomplishes something very "in character" for him, the Storyteller may elect to give him from one to three spent Willpower points back. Obviously, this only applies when regaining temporary Willpower points, not buying new ones, although a character who wants to raise his Willpower with experience can use his accomplishments to justify doing so.

These Archetypes are suggestions only. Don't feel constrained to play within some narrow definition of what you can and cannot do. Likewise, we encourage you to think up your own Archetypes. The ones we offer can only scratch the surface of the possibilities you will inevitably discover.

Architect

The quintessential builder, your sense of purpose goes beyond your own needs. You try to create something of lasting value for those who will come after you. People need many things, and you gain satisfaction by providing whatever you can. You are the type of person who makes an effort to build something of value: to found a town, create a company or in some way leave a lasting legacy.

You strength is **Purpose**. You have a vision that will make the world better after you've passed through. Your deeds will hopefully live on and help those around you.

Your weakness is **Obsession** with your ambitions — you blindly focus on your plans. To Ascend, you must defeat this fixation and open yourself to new possibilities and achievements.

— Regain Willpower whenever you create or establish something of importance or lasting value.

Avant-Garde

You must always be in the forefront. A new dance, fashion trend or discovery is no good unless you were among the first to know. Nothing pains you more than hearing second-hand news. New discoveries are your life, and you devote a great deal of time and effort to keeping up with things. If you're not in the front, you're nowhere.

Foresight is your strength. Because you seek out the new, you can appreciate radical things long before others do.

Your weakness is **Pride**, the absolute self-assurance that you are better than everyone else. Anything old is held in contempt, and you quickly grow tired of the new. You must aspire to find something to truly value.

— Regain one point of Willpower whenever you make some significant discovery.

Bon Vivant

Life is too important to waste, so have as good a time as possible. You only go around once, after all. You are a sensualist, sybarite and party animal; the words self-denial and self-discipline are a waste of breath. Still, you don't mind a little hard work as long as a good time awaits you upon completion. Most Bon Vivants have little self-control, for they so dearly love excess.

Joie de vivre (love of life) is your greatest strength. No loss can set you back for long. For you, life is a great gift, and you pity (and sometimes help) those who do not appreciate it.

Your weakness is **Hedonism**. Pleasure is your only real goal. True Ascension, however, requires higher ambitions, and you must find a less fleeting means of enjoying life.

— Regain a point or two of Willpower whenever you have a truly good time and can bring others along for the ride.

Bravo

War is your pleasure and your destiny. It may range from physical scraps to Machiavellian intrigues, but someone must lose in life and it will not be you. Power and might are all you respect. Your will must be obeyed.

This attitude is more common among the Awakened than many might expect; reality, you know, moves for no weakling. You might use your prowess to terrorize the weak or protect them, but such weakness is not something *you* will ever tolerate in yourself.

You find strength in your **Strength**. You are rarely deterred by obstacles. In fact, most setbacks only encourage you to try again, and harder this time.

Your weakness is **Anger**. To you, life is battle, not compromise. This mentality must be defeated or it will consume you.

— Regain Willpower whenever you utterly defeat someone who stands in your way.

Caregiver

You always try to help those around you and struggle to make a difference in the needs and sorrows of the unfortunate. People around you depend on your stability and strength to keep them steady and centered. You are the one to whom people turn when they have a problem.

You draw strength from your **Kindness**. Despite the suffering all around you, your good heart (and your ability to share it) still makes a difference.

Your weakness is your **Lack of Confidence**. Your martyr's streak comes from a sense of duty, a need to validate your existence. Eventually, you must put yourself above the needs of others or be worn away by them.

— Regain Willpower whenever you successfully protect or nurture someone else. This protection can be as small as a smile of support or a shoulder to lean on at an appropriate moment. You must help the other person in some way, though he need not acknowledge it openly.

Conformist

Every team needs players. That's your role. Taking charge isn't your style. Leave that to others. You always gravitate towards a born leader and throw your lot in with her. It's not in your nature to rebel. You hate inconsistency and instability; by supporting a strong leader, you help prevent chaos.

All stable groups need some kind of Conformist. **Cooperation** is your great strength. Unlike your malcontent peers, you value the common good.

Your weakness is **Low Self-Esteem**. You haven't the self-confidence to assert your will and allow yourself to be others' tool instead. Only when you discover your own agenda and pursue it can you Ascend.

— Regain Willpower whenever your group accomplishes something because of your support and aid.

Conniver

What's the sense of working hard when you can get something for nothing? Why drudge when, just by talking, you can get what you want? You always try to find the easy way out, the fast track to success and wealth. Trickery is a game, and you're damned good at it. Connivers play many roles, so you may be a thief, a swindler, a street waif, an entrepreneur, an agent or just a con man.

You're pretty **Clever**, a real asset in wartime. By setting your friends to tasks and your enemies against each other, you make life easier for your side.

Your weakness is **Envy**. You're never happy with what you have; you always want more. You must eventually overcome your desire and find happiness in what you've got and who you are.

— Regain Willpower whenever you get your way by tricking another person into doing what you want.

Critic

Nothing in the world should be accepted without thorough scrutiny and examination. Nothing is ever perfect, and the blemishes must be pointed out in order for the good to be truly recognized. Your standards are high for everything, and you insist that they be met. Encourage the same ideals in others; low standards reduce the quality of life for everyone. They'll thank you later, once they discover the purity of your perspective. Seek out and expose the imperfections in every person or thing you encounter — you're never satisfied with anything that is less than perfect.

High Standards are often necessary in life. Nothing gets accomplished when people are slack. With your critical eye, you can be an asset to your friends — provided they can stand you.

You're **Arrogant**. It's difficult to accept who you are, so you focus your energies upon finding greater faults in others. Someday you must realize that imperfections are the seeds of further growth.

— Regain one point of Willpower whenever you discover a significant imperfection that others overlook.

Curmudgeon

Yeah, the world sucks, and no one knows this better than you. Everyone around you is bound to screw up. Although your wit is wickedly barbed, even you find little lasting pleasure in it (or in anything else, for that matter). Cynicism is your middle name; it's the tool with which you judge everything in life. Hey, you just call the shots as you see 'em.

Although it can be said that your **Critical Eye** is a strength, you really need to get a life. Sucks to be you!

Your weakness is a **Lack of Imagination**. You've lost the spark that makes you truly magical and deny that by putting down the achievements of others. To Ascend, you must look at the world with new perspective.

— Regain Willpower whenever someone does something stupid, just like you predicted. You must predict it either out loud to the other characters or in private to the Storyteller.

Deviant

There are always people who don't fit in, and you are one such. The status quo is not your style. You're not so much an aimless rebel as an independent thinker who does not belong in the society in which you were raised. You don't give a damn about other people's morality, but you do adhere to your own strange code of conduct. Deviants are typically irreverent, and some have truly bizarre tastes and desires.

Like the stereotypical Cultist of Ecstasy, you **Shatter Boundaries** by taking them head-on. Yours is the vision of the future, not the prison of the past.

Your weakness is your **Perversion**. The energy you require to defy the established order might one day remake the world in your image. A little stability, however, is not always a bad thing. Some day you'll have to realize that.

— Regain Willpower whenever you successfully thumb your nose at society and its precepts without retaliation.

Director

You despise chaos and disorder and tend to take control and organize things in order to suppress anarchy. You like to be in charge, live to organize and habitually strive to make things work smoothly. You trust your own judgment implicitly and tend to think of things in black-and-white terms: "This won't work," "You're either for me or against me," "There are two ways to do this — my way and the wrong way."

Your **Organization** is often helpful. People usually need leaders to accomplish great tasks (like survival!), and you're a natural leader.

You have a **Lack of Tolerance**. In order to Ascend, you must strive to integrate the views of others to achieve compromise.

— Regain Willpower when you lead a group and accomplish some significant task.

Fanatic

You are consumed by a cause; it is the primary force in your life, for good or ill. Every ounce of blood and passion you possess is directed toward your cause. In fact, you may feel very guilty about spending time on anything else. Nothing can stand in your way — nothing that you cannot overcome, in any case. You and those around you may suffer, but your cause is everything — the end justifies the means. Before the game begins, make sure you describe your cause and define how it may affect your behavior.

Dedication is your greatest strength. Nothing happens without sacrifice, and you will do whatever it takes to make your vision happen.

Your weakness is your **Stubbornness**. The possibilities of life have been closed to you. You must open yourself to other choices, or your final victory will be a hollow one.

— You regain Willpower whenever you accomplish an act that furthers your cause.

Jester

The world is a painful place, but it's not without its lighter side. People go crazy without something to laugh at. You are that someone. You're the fool, clown or comic, forever seeking the humor in any situation. You hate sorrow and pain and constantly try to take others' minds off the dark side of life. Sometimes you'll do nearly anything to forget that pain exists. Your particular brand of humor might not always impress your friends, but it makes you

feel better. Some Jesters manage to escape pain and are truly happy, but most never find release.

Empathy is your strength; with it, you can cheer up others and find the banana peel in your cabal's path. When you stop joking, this empathy can be put to other more constructive uses.

Your weakness is **Hypocrisy**. Focusing the attention of others on happiness leaves a deadly potential to ignore the dreadful. You can also be a pain in the butt.

— Regain Willpower when you raise the spirits of those around you through the device of humor, especially when you are able to escape your own pain in the process.

Judge

As a facilitator, moderator, arbitrator, conciliator and peacemaker, you always seek to make things better. You pride yourself on your rationality, judgment and deductive ability when given the facts. You struggle to promote truth, but you understand how difficult it is to ascertain. You respect justice, for through justice, truth will reign.

In your view, people are resources, albeit difficult ones. You hate dissension and arguments, and shy away from dogmatism. Sometimes Judges make good leaders, though a lack of vision can sometimes cause them to maintain the status quo instead of searching for a better way.

Fairness, Wisdom and Logic are your hallmarks. Any group or society needs people with your ability to separate emotions from the truth.

You **Lack Vision**, however. The static framework you have created must be expanded to one of choice, openness and freedom. You can never transcend until you break free of simple logic.

— Regain Willpower when you are able to separate the truth from a web of lies, or when you convince disputing individuals to agree with your judgments.

Loner

You are always alone, even in the midst of a crowd. You are the wanderer, hunter and lone wolf. Though others might think of you as lonely, forsaken or remote, in truth you prefer your own company to that of others. There are many different reasons why this might be so: you don't understand people, you understand people too well, people dislike you, people like you too much, or perhaps your own thoughts mean more to you than people. Your reasons are your own.

Self-Reliance is your major strength. You get by just fine, thank you, without help from others. No one can bring another to Ascension; it must come from within.

Your weakness is your **Lack of Empathy**. All things and people have value. By interacting with others, you can find a rewarding place in the world.

— When you manage to accomplish some significant task on your own, without the aid of others, yet which still aids the group in some way, you regain Willpower based on the significance of the achievement.

Martyr

All possess the martyr instinct, but few act upon it, and even fewer live that way. You do, though. Whatever someone else needs, you will do if it kills you. This desire for self-sacrifice might stem from low self-esteem or a profoundly developed sense of love. Either way, you can endure severe suffering because of your beliefs and ideals.

At worst, a Martyr expects sympathy and attention because of his or her suffering, and may even feign or exaggerate pain or deprivation. At best, a Martyr willingly suffers injury or even death rather than renounce his religion, beliefs, principles, cause or friends.

Your strength is **Devotion**; without those who would willingly give of themselves for others' sake, the world would fall into ruin. In a way, all mages are Martyrs; their Awakening sets them forever apart from mortal men.

This same **Self-Sacrifice** may destroy you. Without some sense of self-preservation, you will be consumed by others' needs — and drive them to hate you in the bargain.

— Regain Willpower when you sacrifice yourself in a real and immediate way for your beliefs or another individual.

Rebel

To hell with the establishment! You're a malcontent, iconoclast and free-thinker. You're so independent and free-willed that you are unwilling to join any particular cause or movement. Anything that oppresses the individual deserves to be brought down. You do not make a good follower and aren't usually a very good leader either (unless your followers are willing to go wherever you lead).

Individuality is your strong point; no one is going to force *you* into a static mold!

Your weakness, however, is your **Lack of Direction**. Your power has no focus and cannot be brought to fruition without a goal.

— Regain Willpower whenever your rebellion against the status quo turns out to be for the best.

Survivor

No matter what happens, you always survive. You can endure, pull through, recover from, outlast and outlive nearly any circumstance. When the going gets tough, you get going. Never say die, and never give up — ever. Nothing angers you as much as a person who doesn't struggle to make things better or who surrenders to the nameless forces of the universe.

Few others have your **Perseverance**. No matter what the odds may be, you come out breathing, if not winning. How many warriors can say the same?

Your weakness is your **Lack of Trust**. You must open yourself up to the world to transcend it.

— Regain Willpower whenever you survive a difficult situation through your own cunning and perseverance.

Traditionalist

You are an orthodox and conservative individual. What was good enough for you when you were young is good enough for you now. You oppose change for the sake of change — what point is there in that? You may be seen by some as a miser, a reactionary or simply an old fogy, but you know how important it is to preserve the status quo.

Such **Consistency** is good to have. With the world in a state of perpetual flux, someone must hold the center. That someone is you.

Excessive **Complacency**, however, kills. A mage must summon the energy to enact new possibilities, rather than succumb to stasis.

— Regain Willpower whenever you are able to protect the status quo and prevent change.

Visionary

Very few are brave or strong or imaginative enough to look beyond mundane thought in search of something more. Society treats such people with both respect and contempt, for the Visionary challenges society as much as she guides it.

You may be a spiritualist, shaman, New-Ager, mystic, philosopher or inventor, but whatever you are, you are always looking for something more. You see beyond the bounds of conventional imagination and create new possibilities. Though you might have your head in the clouds and are often of an impractical bent, you are filled with new ideas and perceptions.

Inner truth is your quest, and **Imagination** is your strength. With this vision, you may guide others who desperately need such wisdom.

Your weakness is your **Pride**, pride in your ability to see and understand what others cannot. You must learn humility to Ascend.

— Regain Willpower whenever you are able to convince others to believe in your dreams and follow the course of action outlined by your vision of the future.

Attributes

Human beings are the most flexible organisms around. That's why we're still around, and that's why we're smart enough to wonder why.

— Robert Wright, "Science, God and Man" (*Time*, Dec. 28, 1992)

Specialties

For each Attribute or Ability rated four or higher, a player may select a *specialty* for her character. Such specialties reflect an aspect of that Trait that someone might be especially good at, like Charming (Manipulation), Pistols (Firearms), Motorcycles (Drive) or Hacking (Computers).

A specialty allows the player to re-roll "10's" on actions when that specialty comes into play (riding a motorcycle, say, or flirting with a countess). The player gets to keep the success the "10" originally indicated, but can try again for another success. She may continue to roll that die until anything other than a "10" comes up. Only one specialty may be chosen per Trait.

Physical

Physical Traits indicate a character's raw strength, build, agility and sturdiness. Characters adept at physical combat or athletic activities have high Physical Traits.

Strength

This Trait ranks physical power, including the ability to move heavy items and cause damage. Generally, a character with a high Strength rating will have a larger frame than someone with a lower rating. Use Strength when attempting to make any sort of jump or leap. In melee combat, your Strength rating is also added to your Dice Pool to determine damage.

Suggested Specialties: Hulking Brute, Strong Upper Body, Wiry, Tough Grip, Massive, Husky, Solid

- • Poor: You can bench press 40 lbs.
- •• Average: You can bench press 100 lbs.
- ••• Good: You can bench press 250 lbs.
- •••• Exceptional: You can bench press 400 lbs.
- ••••• Outstanding: You can bench press 600 lbs.

Dexterity

Dexterity measures your mage's speed, quickness, agility, grace and coordination. A person with good balance and reflexes will have a high rating, and her build with often reflect this — such people are often slender, graceful and sure-footed.

Suggested Specialties: Cat-like Grace, Lightning Reflexes, Nimble Feet, Perfect Balance, Light Touch, Smooth

- • Poor: Two left feet and ten thumbs.
- •• Average: You can walk and chew gum at the same time.
- ••• Good: You have natural grace and coordination.
- •••• Exceptional: Juggling knives is a career option.
- ••••• Outstanding: You can dance along the edge of a precipice while blindfolded.

Stamina

Stamina indicates your general health, tolerance for pain and the ability to engage in prolonged physical activity. It encompasses staying power and a character's will to live and survive physical hardships.

Suggested Specialties: Tenacity, Tirelessness, Durability, Tough, Unmovable, Hardy Constitution

- • Poor: Your constitution is frail; you get sick easily.
- •• Average: You stay in moderately good health.
- ••• Good: You engage in regular exercise and rarely get ill.
- •••• Exceptional: You could run a marathon.
- ••••• Outstanding: You can withstand almost any travail.

Social

Social Traits describe looks, charm and understanding of the human mind. They often determine the nature of your interactions with others, from first impressions to leadership skills to dealing with people in general.

Charisma

This Trait measures how well others react to you. Charisma can help you win peoples' favor, gain their trust or simply fascinate them with your presence. This charm is more innate than deliberate; overt manipulation has its own Trait. Instead, Charisma reflects a natural air of confidence, power or social grace. A good rating makes other believe in you.

Suggested Specialties: Eloquence, Good Manners, Sophistication, Graciousness, Sensuality, Gentility, Captivating, Regal

- • Poor: Others avoid you.
- •• Average: You're likable.
- ••• Good: People trust and confide in you.
- •••• Exceptional: Others are drawn to you in large numbers.
- ••••• Outstanding: You inspire people to great deeds and loyalty.

Manipulation

Manipulation measures your aptitude for getting others to do what you want them to. When you want to trick, outmaneuver or influence someone, overtly or otherwise, use this Trait. Manipulation works on friends and foes alike, though it may be more difficult on the latter. If you blow an attempt to Manipulate someone, he will probably be really pissed off with you. No one likes to be fooled.

Suggested Specialties: Silver-Tongued, Imposing, Persuasive, Ingratiating, Glib, Charming, Devious

- • Poor: You have a hard time convincing others to do what you want.
- •• Average: Sometimes, others believe you.
- ••• Good: Word games and political fencing are no problem.
- •••• Exceptional: Clever and sophisticated.
- ••••• Outstanding: With a little effort, you can make people do almost anything you want.

Appearance

This Trait indicates how attractive you are. It measures more than just physical beauty. Any feature — animation, expressiveness, cuteness, vulnerability, etc. — that others find enticing could be considered part of your Appearance. This Trait can be vital in some situations, for like it or not, we're all influenced by the way people look. Appearance is a good way to measure first impressions.

Suggested Specialties: Alluring, Bold, Sensual, Cute, Cuddly, Roguish, Innocent, Wild

- • Poor: Others treat you with indifference or hostility.
- •• Average: You fit in well with the crowd.
- ••• Good: People notice you.
- •••• Exceptional: Others respect and favor you, for your looks if nothing else.
- ••••• Outstanding: You awe and fascinate others with your beauty.

Mental

These Traits represent instincts, wits, memory, learning and imagination. A character with high Mental Traits can usually think himself out of bad situations or absorb vast amounts of data.

Perception

How much do you notice? How aware are you of your surroundings? Are you wide-eyed and imaginative, or do you trip over the cracks in the sidewalk? This Trait covers all of these things, from attentiveness to comprehension. Some people, especially children, have high Perceptions because of their perpetual wonder; others watch the shadows out of nervousness or caution. Whatever the reason, your overall sensitivity to impressions and stimuli can be judged by this Trait.

Perception goes beyond sensory impression. A mage with a high rating can catch subtleties in someone's demeanor, grasp the intent behind a work of art or overhear the snapping twig that indicates an ambush. Characters on the run will need high Perceptions to survive.

Suggested Specialties: Keen Senses, Uncanny Insight, Clear-Sighted, Astute, Watchful, Intuitive, Feral

- • Poor: Huh? What'd he say?
- •• Average: You notice obvious goings-on.
- ••• Good: You can get below the obvious and pick up moods and subtexts.
- •••• Exceptional: You are constantly alert and spot subtle things easily.
- ••••• Outstanding: Few things get past you.

Intelligence

This Trait measures raw mental processes — memory, retention, judgment, reasoning, understanding and critical thinking. Although it reflects information-processing and clarity of thought more than common sense or street savvy, a character with a low Intelligence may miss the underlying complexities of an argument or event — everything seems clear-cut and simple. Complexities, to such people, are for other folks.

A character with a high Intelligence Trait has very sophisticated thought patterns; she can analyze many levels of an argument and discern truth from lies. Overall, Intelligence represents carefully-reasoned judgments over quick intuitive decisions.

Suggested Specialties: Sheer Brilliance, Creative, Bookworm, Pragmatic, Discerning Thinker, Analyst

- • Poor: IQ 80
- •• Average: IQ 100
- ••• Good: IQ 120
- •••• Exceptional: IQ 140
- ••••• Outstanding: IQ 160+

Wits

The Wits Trait is a measure of how quickly you think and react to new situations. It combines shrewdness with overall sharpness and cleverness. A character with a low Wits rating, like the veritable "deer in the headlights," may be easily taken off-guard, tricked or surprised. Those with a high Wits rating are seldom waylaid by sudden changes. Whatever happens, they keep their heads clear and their minds focused. You also use Wits to see how fast you react in combat situations and other times of stress.

Suggested Specialties: Level-Headed, Shrewd, Cunning, Jumpy, One Step Ahead, Sharp

- • Poor: A con man's dream.
- •• Average: Rush Limbaugh doesn't impress you.
- ••• Good: You can handle big city rush-hour traffic without wrecking your car.
- •••• Exceptional: Sharp enough to be a stand-up comic.
- ••••• Outstanding: You can handle nearly any unexpected event with clarity and purpose.

Abilities

The wise man does not meditate on death, but on how to live.

— Benedict Spinoza

Talents

Alertness

Your sharp senses are ever-vigilant. With Alertness, you've learned to keep an eye open in every direction, listening and watching for unexpected things lurking around the corner. Seldom does anyone or anything catch you by surprise.

- • Novice: You can spot almost anything you're looking for.
- •• Practiced: You notice everything that happens around you, whether overt or subtle.
- ••• Competent: Trouble has a hard time getting past your senses.
- •••• Expert: You rarely, if ever, let down your guard.
- ••••• Master: Eyes in the back of your head. Nothing escapes you.

Possessed by: Bodyguards, Hunters, Detectives, Military Personnel, Reporters, Thieves

Suggested Specialties: Paranoia, Spot Ambushes, Point Guard

Athletics

Climbing rocky cliffs, leaping chasms or playing brilliant games of badminton are all Athletics-based feats. This Ability describes your general athletic skills with both team and individual sports. It assumes a familiarity with the rules and play of the sport in question.

- • Novice: You're always the first pick for teams at family reunion football games.
- •• Practiced: You've played regularly on school or community athletic teams.
- ••• Competent: You understand the rules and strategies of all popular sports; you've played or participated in a wide variety of athletic activities.
- •••• Expert: An accomplished athlete, you train vigorously and could be a professional in your chosen sport.
- ••••• Master: Your athletic abilities are world-class; you could even serve as a trainer for others.

Possessed by: Most Children, Professional Athletes, Gym Instructors, Sports Enthusiasts

Suggested Specialties: Any Specific Sport (Swimming, Football, Tennis, etc.), Body-building, Outdoor Sports, Aerobics, Running

Awareness

Mages can sense the unknown like few other beings. Awareness reflects almost prenaturnal senses that detect supernatural activity. Although this is largely a magickal ability, some Sleepers do possess it. This Trait detects unusual phenomenon, such as the presence of magick, within the boundaries of normal sensory range. For example, a mage could use Awareness to sense magick cast across the dance floor, but she can't use the Talent to sense a magickal Effect in another country.

The greater the number of successes, the more the mage can sense about her target. At lower levels of success, this may just be "funny feelings" about beings or objects. With more successes, she may note the specific supernatural nature of what she is studying. For example, she could discern whether or not the subject is human, alive, dead or undead. The Talent also extends to affect spirits, animals and inanimate objects such as Talismans, as well as persons and things considered "invisible" phenomena. Awareness influences interactions with other creatures, since it gives the mage information about their true natures. **(See "Detecting Magick" in Chapter Eight.)**

• Novice: You often get weird vibes about people you meet or places you visit.

•• Practiced: No longer do you buy into the notion that a rational explanation exists for the unexplainable.

••• Competent: You can see that all things have an aura, and you've learned what different aura colors signify.

•••• Expert: You are constantly aware that humans are not alone; there's a whole world of unknown creatures and powers out there.

••••• Master: Restless spirits, walking dead, strange shapeshifters and all the odd events they bring with them flourish in the Tellurian. You regularly commune with the bizarre, learning new things with each experience.

Possessed by: Investigators, Psychics, Fortune Tellers, Gypsies

Suggested Specialties: Aura Reading, Talismans, Spirits, the Undead, Animals

Brawl

Brawling is the ability to fight without a weapon, including basic hand-to-hand maneuvers such as punching, kicking, grappling, throwing or just ordinary scratching and biting. Brawling isn't generally fatal, but you can cause a lot of pain and suffering with your bare hands.

• Novice: Though inexperienced, you know the basics of fisticuffs.

•• Practiced: You know where to hit people for maximum effect.

••• Competent: You know how to take someone down quickly without doing permanent harm.

•••• Expert: You possess a black belt in a martial art.

••••• Master: You've developed your own unique style and perhaps formed a fighting school.

Possessed by: Martial Artists, Soldiers, Thugs, Police Officers, Bouncers

Suggested Specialties: Any Martial Arts Style (Judo, Aikido, Karate, etc.), Dirty Fighting, Boxing

Dodge

Whether you dive for cover, duck a punch or sidestep an arrow, you've learned the best way to avoid injury is not getting hit. Dodge simply describes your ability to get out of the way of any incoming attacks.

• Novice: You know the basics of avoiding a line of fire if you have some warning.

•• Practiced: You've been in enough fights to know when to stay down and safe.

••• Competent: Accomplished and experienced; you know a number of ways to place yourself where most attacks won't hit you.

•••• Expert: Enemies find you exceedingly difficult to hit; you never seem to stay in one place for long.

••••• Master: Over time, you've actually learned to sidestep bullets.

Possessed by: Street Fighters, Military Personnel, Bouncers, Martial Artists

Suggested Specialties: Sidestep, Duck, Dive for Cover

Expression

Expression helps you get your point across, whether you are writing, singing, speaking or performing. In its highest form, Expression is an art; characters with high ratings convey their feelings with eloquence and passion in their medium of choice.

• Novice: You have rudimentary talents, probably good enough to win a college scholarship.

•• Practiced: You communicate with a notable level of tact and skill.

••• Competent: You are a popular success in your chosen medium.

•••• Expert: Your audiences always respond with deep passion to your performances.

••••• Master: You are nationally known and loved for your expressive skills, one of the most popular artists of your day, such as Andy Warhol, Pavarotti or Stephen King.

Possessed by: Actors, Politicians, Writers, Performance Artists

Suggested Specialties: Poetry, Music, Improvisation, Prose, Comedy, Politics, Talk Radio, Game Design

Instruction

With Instruction, you can teach subjects in ways that let others learn easily and well. Though you can never raise a student's rating above your own, this Talent allows you to teach others your Skills and Knowledges. For instance, if you have four dots in Computer Knowledge, you may teach a student up to four dots in this Knowledge as well. To determine the time and energy it takes to teach a particular skill, roll your Manipulation + Instruction against a difficulty of 11 minus the student's Intelligence. One roll may be made per month of teaching. The number of successes is the number of experience points the student can apply towards that skill. Peter Kobie, for example, tries to teach his fellow Chantry member Clarissa Ryan about rudimentary first aid (Medicine) so he won't be the only person who can bandage people after a fight. Though squeamish, Clarissa is bright and willing to learn (Intelligence 3); the base difficulty for Peter's roll is 11 - Clarissa's Intelligence (3) = 8. Peter rolls his Instruction + Manipulation, a total of six dice. With three successes, Clarissa can now dedicate three experience points to purchasing a dot in Medicine.

Sometimes, a student may become discouraged and distracted from her studies with various interruptions. In this case, she may have to spend a Willpower point (at the Storyteller's discretion) to continue learning. With a lot of stops and starts, the student will have to burn a great deal of Willpower. Likewise, the teacher may decide to withdraw his services if the student doesn't seem to be progressing. Without approval from the Storyteller, Talents like Awareness and Empathy cannot generally be taught; they are inborn and only learned the hard way.

- • Novice: You can present simple concepts, such as multiplication, in an understandable manner.
- •• Practiced: You can teach moderately complex subjects like physics in straightforward lessons.
- ••• Competent: You can teach anything you know to a level of high-school competency.
- •••• Expert: Learning from you is a pleasure; you make advanced calculus and ancient languages easily accessible.
- ••••• Master: You're a teacher who consistently inspires your pupils, endowing them with a deep and true understanding of what you instruct.

Possessed by: Mentors, Teachers, Do Masters, Professors

Suggested Specialties: Any Skills and Knowledges, Specific Subjects (History, Law, Statistics, etc.), Tradition Practices

Intuition

Your hunches are good, and you've come to trust them. Sometimes, you can't explain why you know something or how you jump from a jumbled set of facts to a brilliant conclusion, but the talent has served you well. Intuition reflects your aptitude for good guessing and having "gut feelings." This Talent is not a psychic ability, but rather an inborn "sixth sense" for making leaps of logic and connections. Intuition may let the character know whether or not someone is lying or allow her to pick up on a lead to a puzzle from a seemingly minute set of clues. Intuition is also an excellent tool for the Storyteller to convey information to the players.

- • Novice: Your instincts often put you on the right trail.
- •• Practiced: You've learned to always follow your first answer.
- ••• Competent: You know when something's afoot.
- •••• Expert: Not only do you know when something's wrong, you know where to go to figure out who's responsible.
- ••••• Master: Your insights are so sudden and precise, you scare yourself.

Possessed by: Gamblers, Fortune Tellers, Entrepreneurs, Bodyguards, Investigators, Verbena

Suggested Specialties: Nose for Trouble, Flashes of Inspiration, Gambling, Insightful

Intimidation

Intimidation lends you an air of quiet authority and dominance. It comes in many forms, from subtle suggestions to outright physical threats or harm. Each method depends on the time, the place, and those involved. Characters with this Talent know how to get what they want when they want it.

- • Novice: You can back geeks into a corner.
- •• Practiced: You've won the occasional staredown with a bothersome competitor for a bus seat.
- ••• Competent: People avoid your direct gaze and scurry to do your bidding or answer your questions.
- •••• Expert: With a soft whisper or even a single gesture, you convince others to obey you on your terms.
- ••••• Master: Faced with your commanding presence, a wolf might consider showing its throat to you.

Possessed by: Businesspeople, Bouncers, Military Personnel, Mobsters, Men in Black, Mentors

Suggested Specialties: Veiled Threats, Overt Violence, Commanding Voice, Condescending, Look Official

Streetwise

You can find lots of useful stuff on the street: information, hit men, love for sale and drugs, for starters. On the other hand, you can also find real trouble. This Talent allows you to blend in with the local scene in order to pick up on pertinent gossip and teaches you how to survive on the streets by simple larceny and panhandling. It includes a knack for picking up street slang and passing yourself off as a street-dweller.

- • Novice: You know where to find hookers and drug dealers.
- •• Practiced: The local street people think you're okay and give you some measure of trust.
- ••• Competent: You know how to get the best skinny on everything that happens on the street.
- •••• Expert: You make friends and contacts with ease on the streets, and fit into the local color like you belong there. Maybe you do.
- ••••• Master: You're a natural on the streets; people fully accept you as one of their own, and you can find invaluable information or items outsiders couldn't possibly pick up.

Possessed by: Gang Members, Winos, the Homeless, Streetwalkers, Crime Reporters, Detectives, Cultists of Ecstasy

Suggested Specialties: Gangs, Chicken Strips, Drugs, Nightclubs, Street Slang

Subterfuge

You're a tricky bastard. You hide your own motives and discover others' secrets to use their own plans against them. The intrigues of other people fascinate you because they reveal inherent weaknesses you utilize to your own advantage. Characters skilled in Subterfuge know how to call upon their best wordplay and body language to gain information without others realizing what they've given away.

- • Novice: You lie easily and convincingly.
- •• Practiced: You're adept at getting the upper hand in a parley.
- ••• Competent: When there are secrets to be learned, you always come out with the clear advantage.
- •••• Expert: You're always ten moves ahead in the chess game… or the conversation.
- ••••• Master: You're so proficient at guarding your own hand and reading others' plans, you sometimes fool yourself.

Possessed by: Lawyers, Con Artists, Politicians, Hermetic Masters

Suggested Specialties: Little White Lies, Innuendoes, Find Weaknesses, Fast Talk, Gossip

Skills

Do

Do, translated as "the way," is the most basic of all martial arts forms. But Do encompasses much more than simple fighting. Simply put, Do opens a person to his body's ultimate potential through mental and physical concentration. Akashic Brothers are the only teachers of Do and all its maneuvers, and they require students to display great discipline and dedication. The members of this Tradition have learned that the full integration of mind, body and reality enable them to unlock abilities that would otherwise remain untapped. Students desiring to learn either Do philosophy or fighting styles must seek out Akashic Brothers for their instruction. **(For the particulars of Do, see "Combat" in Chapter Ten.)**

Beginning characters may only purchase up to two dots of Do; higher levels may only come through experience and training. As a student progresses through the levels of Do, he usually adds the animal name associated with a particular level to his own name; these names are mentioned only among the Akashic Brotherhood. Each step brings further enlightenment and conceptual understanding, so that the student eventually reaches a level of cognition where he may consider himself human again, able to use his body to its highest possible potential.

- • Insect (grasshopper, mantis, ant): You are an initiate of the teachings of Do and have learned the basics of proper breathing and how to move your limbs with some efficiency.
- •• Reptile (lizard, snake, iguana): You have begun to understand your body as one unit and become one with that unit.
- ••• Four-Footed (tiger, boar, horse): Realizing there is a hidden potential inside everyone, you see the current of energy beneath your physical form and can call upon it.
- •••• Bipedal (monkey, bear, ape): You may exert tremendous force through the simplest of motions.
- ••••• True Humanity: an Honored Master or One Who is Truly Enlightened. Your mind is at peace; you know that all things have strengths and weaknesses and can be destroyed as well as constructed. You concern your self not so much with what can be done as opposed to what should be done.

Drive

This Skill reflects your ability to operate motor vehicles, though merely having a Drive rating does not guarantee your familiarity with all vehicles. The Storyteller may raise or lower your target number based on your experience with a particular vehicle.

- • Novice: You can drive an automatic or standard auto mobile or ride a motorcycle without a problem.
- •• Practiced: You've driven in a car race with a high school buddy on a back road.
- ••• Competent: You know some trick maneuvers and how to get the best performance from a vehicle.
- •••• Expert: You could race professionally.
- ••••• Master: Your Astin Martin is waiting for you. Do be careful.

Possessed by: Truckers, Race Car Drivers, Parents, Chauffeurs

Suggested Specialties: Off-Road, Big Trucks, Limos, Motorcycles, Evading Pursuit

Etiquette

You possess impeccable manners, conducting yourself with grace and style in a myriad of social circumstances. Your Etiquette Skill is useful during diplomatic engagements, fanciful dinners, romantic dances or seductive pick-ups at the bar. Used well, it may pay off in surprising ways.

- • Novice: You know which forks and spoons to use at dinner.
- •• Practiced: Eyebrows raise at your elegant tipping style.
- ••• Competent: You know the best wines and foods to order and how to dress for most social occasions.
- •••• Expert: You could plan a United Nations state dinner.
- ••••• Master: At home with anyone, you can squat with the Aborigines in the morning and sip tea with the Queen in the afternoon.

Possessed by: Idle Rich, Corporate Executives, Tradition Masters, Diplomats

Suggested Specialties: Dining, Soirees, Business Deals, Seductions

Firearms

You know about the properties, repair and use of a variety of guns, from small calibre rifles to submachine guns. This Skill does not cover heavy artillery weapons, but you do have knowledge of the various types of ammunition available for firearms.

- • Novice: You've had one or two lessons at the firing range.
- •• Practiced: You almost always manage to hit the target.
- ••• Competent: You can pull off some fairly impressive maneuvers with a firearm.
- •••• Expert: You can hit almost any target even under duress.
- ••••• Master: You'd give Dirty Harry a hard time.

Possessed by: Gang Members, Police, Soldiers, Hunters, Cyborgs

Suggested Specialties: Rifles, Handguns, Machine Guns, Custom Ammunition, Cybernetic Weaponry

Leadership

People look to you to take charge in many situations. With this Skill, you know how to get them to obey your orders and remain calm under stress. Leadership involves exerting a certain authority and setting a good example to those in your charge. Combined with Charisma or Manipulation, you may have significant power over others' actions.

- • Novice: You can head a committee successfully.
- •• Practiced: You can coordinate major projects or speak confidently at town meetings.
- ••• Competent: You can manage a profitable company or run for local government.
- •••• Expert: Have you considered candidacy for a national office?
- ••••• Master: You can change the course of human events, like Gandhi… or Genghis Khan.

Possessed by: Politicians, Businessmen, Military Officers, Gang Leaders

Specialties: Take Command, Sway Opinion, Oration, Gain Trust, Brainstorming

Meditation

Centering yourself, calming troubled emotions and relaxing your body are the purposes of Meditation. Those attempting Meditation require a focus for their thoughts, an object, a phrase or a physical action which screens out distractions and allows for total concentration. Meditation has many uses: making up for lost sleep (roll Stamina + Meditation, difficulty 8, the number of successes is equal to the hours of sleep gained); entering a state of hibernation (roll Stamina + Meditation, difficulty 9, the number of successes determines how many days the character can survive without sustenance); or gaining insight into complicated puzzles (roll Intelligence + Meditation, difficulty 9, each success lowers the difficulty of an Enigmas roll by 1). Meditation can take many forms, such as yoga or Tai Chi, and several styles of magick require Meditation as part of their rituals.

- • Novice: You can sit still and focus your thoughts for a short period of time.
- •• Practiced: Your mind can achieve a state of peace.
- ••• Competent: You can center your thoughts and your spirit under adverse circumstances.
- •••• Expert: You can achieve a state of being where others find it hard to distract you.
- ••••• Master: Even in times of stress or disaster, you are able to remain calm, at ease and inwardly focused.

Possessed by: Martial Artists, Monks, Granola-chicks

Suggested Specialties: Relaxation, Zen, Tantric, Virtual Reality, Foci

Melee

Melee is the skill of fighting with blunt or edged weapons, such as knives, clubs and swords. Proficiency with such weapons can earn a great deal of status in the right environment. Some Traditions and Conventions value Melee as a part of training during apprenticeship, and duels of honor often call upon the ability to fight with certain melee weapons.

- • Novice: You know how to pick up a weapon and use it with some basic fighting techniques.
- •• Practiced: You have some formal instruction with at least one weapon.
- ••• Competent: You've been in a number of successful fights and are familiar with the different styles associated with certain melee weapons.
- •••• Expert: A worthy opponent, you have earned fame as an armed fighter.
- ••••• Master: You are deadly with a weapon in your grasp; others consider you one of the finest known combatants with your chosen style.

Possessed by: Martial Artists, Law Enforcement, Soldiers, Recreationists, Gang Members

Suggested Specialties: Edged Weapons, Disarms and Takeaways, Blunt Instruments, Improvised Weapons

Research

All seekers of knowledge must learn how to find information. This Skill allows a character to locate resources he needs for furthering his studies. Such information exists in traditional libraries, in oral tribal litanies or in sophisticated virtual reality nodes. Success with Research doesn't necessarily mean the character gets the exact lore he seeks, but he will know where to obtain what he's looking for.

- • Novice: You're comfortable with most public sources of information, such as the local library.
- •• Practiced: You've used in-depth reference systems, such as the World Wide Web or Gopher.
- ••• Competent: You know the contents of many privately owned libraries.
- •••• Expert: Given time, you can locate most any piece of information you need.
- ••••• Master: Whether written, encoded or spoken, you know where to find the lore you are seeking.

Possessed by: Writers, Scientists, Hermetic Acolytes, Librarians

Suggested Specialties: Arcane Collections, On-line Data, Oral Traditions, Specific Subject Matter (History, Philosophy, etc.), Folklore

Stealth

If you're good at this Skill, you can stalk, sneak or hide silently in the shadows. Other characters can use their Perception against your Stealth abilities, and certain environmental conditions may affect your difficulty roll positively or adversely.

- • Novice: You can hide pretty well in the dark if you stay still.
- •• Practiced: You've gotten the hang of moving silently.
- ••• Competent: You are an accomplished nighttime hunter.
- •••• Expert: You can walk silently over dry leaves and through mud puddles.
- ••••• Master: Have you considered joining a ninja clan?

Possessed by: Spies, Assassins, Burglars, Hunters

Suggested Specialties: Blending Into Shadows, Silent Movement, Concealment, Floors

Survival

The wilderness and other outdoor environs are dangerous for those unfamiliar with their hazards. Survival allows you to seek shelter, find a safe route or follow a trail in the great outdoors. Basic survival skills apply to a range of climates, though characters will not necessarily have proficiency in every possible outdoor setting. For example, even if you have spent time in the wilds of the Appalachians, you may will still have trouble in the Arctic. Additionally, if you use Stealth in the wilderness, your Dice Pool may not exceed your rating in Survival.

A variant on this Skill, Urban Survival, allows you to live on the streets, picking through trash, finding warm places to sleep and knowing where — and where not — to go for shelter.

- • Novice: You can survive an all-day hike in a temperate environment.
- •• Practiced: You have spent considerable time outdoors and are fully at ease there.
- ••• Competent: You are familiar with advanced survival techniques, such as trapping and gathering foodstuffs from the wilderness.
- •••• Expert: You can live like a king in the outdoors without any modern conveniences.
- ••••• Master: Making it across Death Valley or up Mount Everest on foot isn't that hard!

Possessed by: Tribal Cultures, Hunters, Rangers, Hikers, Street People

Suggested Specialties: Tracks and Trails, Specific Environments (Jungle, Arctic, Desert, Urban, etc.), Foraging

Technology

With Technology, a character understands how mechanical and electronic devices work. This Skill allows you to use and repair technological items, such as cars, recording devices and light machinery. Some forms of technomagick may require this skill to succeed.

- • Novice: Normal household technology is familiar; replacing fuses, fixing the toaster, and checking the fluid levels in the station wagon are no problem.
- •• Practiced: You like to tinker with mechanical or electronic devices; you could put together a working clock or a transistor radio with no difficulty.
- ••• Competent: You have the insight to engineer simple technological items of your own design and construct them to suit your needs.
- •••• Expert: You regularly invent highly complex mechanical and electronic machines that perform multiple tasks and functions.
- ••••• Master: You create unique and one-of-a-kind technological devices that do utterly amazing things no one can replicate.

Possessed by: Repairmen, Security Specialists, Technomancers, Inventors

Suggested Specialties: Electronics, Transports, Security Systems, Magickal Devices, Invention

Knowledges

Computer

This ability allows you to operate computers and write computer programs. You probably know one or more programming languages and may even design your own computer systems. This Knowledge is necessary if you wish to break into protected computer systems or crack any kind of digital encryption.

- • Student: You can use a word processing program like an experienced secretary.
- •• College: You write simple programs and possess a knowledge of most operating systems and software.
- ••• Masters: You're a competent programmer; you write extensive and complex software.
- •••• Doctorate: You could make a living through on-line theft.
- ••••• Scholar: You could probably construct an AI or break into the most sophisticated computer system in the world.

Possessed by: Programmers. Data Processors. Hackers, Virtual Adepts

Suggested Specialties: Hacking, Viruses, Data Shredding, Surfing

Cosmology

The universe holds many secrets. This Knowledge reflects the information you can learn and understand about the Umbra and its many Realms. Cosmology is related to the Sphere of Spirit in the sense that both deal with the Umbra and its denizens. However, Cosmology relates more to the cultural and physical geography of the Umbra (such as it is), whereas the Sphere of Spirit deals with the manipulation and control of the Umbra's inhabitants.

- • Student: You know that a place called the Umbra exists.
- •• College: You know certain places and things to avoid in the Umbra.
- ••• Masters: You can navigate reasonably well throughout the Otherworlds.
- •••• Doctorate: You are familiar with difficult-to-find persons, places and things throughout the Umbra and the Realms.
- ••••• Scholar: You are a veteran traveler of the Otherworlds; you intimately understand the construction and the inhabitants of the cosmos.

Possessed by: Mages, Garou, Demons, Umbrood, Nephandi

Suggested Specialties: Celestines, Incarna, Near Umbra, Deep Umbra, Realms

Culture

The idea of Culture combines the concepts of societal beliefs, behaviors, rituals, institutions, history and general thought patterns in reference to a certain group of people. It encompasses both how members of the society behave and what motivates their actions. The character can call upon his Culture Knowledge to interact with or influence certain societies and can pick up on useful tidbits when encountering a new one, based on his experiences.

- • Student: You know some taboos and cultural mores.
- •• College: You're familiar with most cultures that have some similarity to your own.
- ••• Masters: You're conversant with the sociological imperatives of several diverse cultures.
- •••• Doctorate: You are a expert in working with other cultures; given time, you can fit easily into any society.
- ••••• Scholar: You're at home with most any culture you encounter from the outset.

Possessed by: Anthropologists, Sociologists, Politicians, Explorers

Suggested Specialties: Religion, Taboos, Politics, Specific Societal Groups (Garou, Kindred, Faeries, Traditions, Technocracy, etc.)

Enigmas

Using Enigmas enables you to piece together puzzles of all kinds, bringing together bits of information to solve mysteries and conundrums. With this Knowledge, you can remember pertinent facts and vital details and combine them into a coherent explanation of what may going on. This could include anything from answering riddles, to navigating the Technocratic bureaucracy, to fulfilling a quest given by a mentor.

- • Student: You can solve a cryptogram or put together a large jigsaw puzzle.
- •• College: Logic problems are a snap for you.
- ••• Masters: You are an astute deductive reasoner, difficult to trick.
- •••• Doctorate: You can order reason out of chaos.
- ••••• Scholar: With just a couple of clues, you might solve some of the great mysteries of the universe.

Possessed by: Crossword Devotees, Consulting Detectives, Gamers, Analysts

Suggested Specialties: Riddles, Visions, Twisted Plots

Investigation

Investigation allows you to call upon training in basic criminology to locate evidence, perform forensic analysis and note minute details others miss. It also gives you the know-how to conduct a proper criminal investigation and reconstruct the scene of a crime to gain insight into what really occurred.

- • Student: You are an amateur with rudimentary training,
- •• College: You've had some investigative experience, on the level of a law enforcement officer.
- ••• Masters: You're experienced and could set up a successful business as a PI.
- •••• Doctorate: You could serve as a field agent for a government intelligence or investigative agency.
- ••••• Scholar: You fit well within the company of Sherlock Holmes, Hercule Poirot, or Lord Darcy.

Possessed by: Detectives, Reporters, Government (or Technocratic) Agents

Suggested Specialties: Forensics, Criminal Minds, Collecting Evidence

Law

Those who know the law can often use it to their advantage. This Ability gives you knowledge of the legal system and jurisprudence, both how to manipulate the law and how to work within the system to get what you want.

- • Student: Your knowledge is practical, along the lines of most police officers.
- •• College: You could pass the state bar exam.
- ••• Masters: You've practiced law for some years and are a full partner in a firm.
- •••• Doctorate: You've served as a judge or a district attorney.
- ••••• Scholar: You could be a Supreme Court justice, or a member of Congress or Parliament.

Possessed by: Law Enforcement Officers, Public Officials, Lawyers, Criminals, Detectives

Suggested Specialties: Legal Procedures, Courts, Law Offices, Specific Fields of Law (Criminal, Real Estate, Tax, Corporate, etc.)

Linguistics

Everyone speaks their native tongue with normal proficiency; with each level of Linguistics, you may speak one additional language other than your own. Linguistics also allows you to understand the basic structure of language, which often influences thought and action within a specific culture. Proficiency with this ability also lets you identify certain accents and dialects and easily acquire vernacular and slang in a chosen language.

- • Student: You know one additional language.
- •• College: You know two additional languages.
- ••• Masters: You know three additional languages.
- •••• Doctorate: You know four additional languages.
- ••••• Scholar: You know five additional language.

Possessed by: World Travelers, Scholars, Diplomats, Interpreters, Hermetic Magi

Suggested Specialties: Epithets, "Dead" Languages, Business Terminology, Technical Terms, Simultaneous Translating, Reading Ancient Texts

Lore

Every supernatural group hoards its secrets from others. Lore provides you with information about a particular "hidden" subculture or organization within the Tellurian. Knowledge about other groups, however, may often be second-hand or even assumed, and doubtless whoever is providing the information will filter it to suit their own needs. For example, a Technomancer would describe the Camarilla very differently than one of the Kindred themselves would. Gathering Lore may lead to inaccurate perceptions that can trip up players and create interesting problems and inherent dangers. Maybe you don't really want to know about those *barabbi* habits after all....

Each type of Lore must be purchased separately; knowledge of the Get of Fenris will not help you deal with Technocrats. Some of these Lores are *exceedingly* dangerous to learn — or to know.

- • Student: You possess dubious and sketchy facts.
- •• College: You are certain some of your knowledge is accurate; then again, you may know just enough to get yourself in real trouble.
- ••• Masters: You could hold an intelligent conversation with a member of the organization in question.
- •••• Doctorate: You've learned some facts they wish you didn't know.
- ••••• Scholar: You know the subjects at least as well as they know themselves, and they may consider you a liability.

Possessed by: Sages, Spies, Mentors, War Cabals

Variations (each one bought separately): Faerie, Garou, Kindred, Technocrats, Traditions, Nephandi, Marauders, Wyrm, Sabbat

Medicine

Medicine is the study of anatomy and physiology and the techniques used to cure bodily ills. It includes a knowledge of drugs and their use along with the diagnosis and treatment of disease and injury. For complicated tasks, this Knowledge is necessary in order to effectively use the Sphere of Life.

- • Student: You know advanced first aid, CPR and the basics to keep someone alive until professional medical help arrives.
- •• College: You have the equivalent of paramedic-level training.
- ••• Masters: You are a licensed physician and can dispense medication to treat diseases and illnesses.
- •••• Doctorate: You can perform surgery.
- ••••• Scholar: You are a famous healer, a well-known specialist in your field.

Possessed by: Doctors, Rescue Rangers, Paramedics, Progenitors, Verbena

Suggested Specialties: Alternative Medicine, Pharmaceuticals, Emergency Care, Diseases, Specialized Fields (Neurology, Oncology, Orthopedics, etc.)

Occult

The occult encompasses both trendy New-Age images as well dark and sinister rumors of curses and "black magick." It includes knowledge about voodoo, mysticism, the Tarot and other related "magick" popular among the Sleepers. The occult is highly significant in its own right, for many among the un-Awakened have strong beliefs in its supposed powers.

- • Student: You can manipulate a Ouija board.
- •• College: You're familiar with the *real* intricacies of the Tarot.
- ••• Masters: You might be a voodoo hougan or a professional psychic.
- •••• Doctorate: You are a respected parapsychologist.
- ••••• Scholar: Well-blessed with occult knowledge, you could have kept company with Gerald Gardner and Crowley.

Possessed by: New-Agers, Fortune Tellers, Psychics, *Voudoun* Practitioners

Suggested Specialties: Supernatural Creatures, Predictions, Magickal Devices

Science

This Knowledge deals with the application of scientific theory and specific fields of scientific investigation. Scientific principles can be used to make magick coincidental. This is a must for all Technomancers.

- • Student: You know the basics taught in high school science classes.
- •• College: You understand all the major scientific theories and applications.
- ••• Masters: You have proposed some notable theories of your own.
- •••• Doctorate: A prize-winning scientist, you have made a significant contribution to your field.
- ••••• Scholar: You are a scientific genius along the lines of Einstein, Pasteur or da Vinci.

Possessed by: Engineers, Researchers, Inventors

Suggested Specialties: Scientific Theories, Specific Fields (Chemistry, Physics, Biology, etc.)

Backgrounds

I saw patterns in the wind and in the sand
I saw the stars, I read the clouds, I understand
Then the madness overwhelmed me (I lost control)
It was cut out for each stain upon my soul
— Killing Joke, "Communion"

Backgrounds are special advantages that chart your mage's influence in the world. These Traits cover things a mage has acquired, rather than those he learned or was born with.

When you choose your Backgrounds, consider how or where your mage came across this advantage. How did he meet his Mentor, and who is she to him? Who are his Allies, besides dots on a sheet? Where did he get his Talisman, and does he understand it yet? Likewise, Storytellers should feel free to make up things about the Background that even the player doesn't know. Perhaps the Library really belongs to another mystick, or the Node carries a curse. And who *really* knows what his Destiny is, anyway?

Backgrounds may be rolled in conjunction with other Traits. A good Manipulation + Mentor roll could buy you some respect with other mages, while Perception + Influence could help you find someone through a contacts network.

After creation, you cannot increase your Background ratings with experience points. They can only be improved through events in the story. Storytellers may give a dot or two in some new Background in lieu of experience points if the character comes into money, friends or influence somehow.

Allies

In their travels, mages often encounter a variety of interesting people (and other beings). While many are hostile, some befriend and aid the mage. These Allies can be acolytes, influential Sleepers or even magickal beings.

Allies should be characters in their own right, not simple cannon fodder. Though they may be loyal unto even death, such friends will not throw their lives away for nothing, especially if the mage does nothing to support that loyalty. Friendship is a two-way street, and even Allies have their own agendas.

Each dot in this Background gives the mage one Ally or increases the power of one that already exists; thus, five dots in the Allies Background could indicate five Allies of moderate power or one extremely powerful entity. Nearly anyone (or anything) can be a mage's Ally, though it's safe to say that such an Ally will be unusual in one way or another. Some mages even have extradimensional creatures, spirit beings, vampires or magickal animals as Allies.

- • One Ally of moderate power
- •• Two Allies, or one more powerful Ally
- ••• Three Allies, or fewer Allies of correspondingly greater power
- •••• Four Allies, or fewer Allies of correspondingly greater power
- ••••• Five Allies, or fewer Allies of correspondingly greater power

Arcane

Mages are inherently mysterious people, and few mortals notice them for what they truly are. Because they bend reality slightly simply by existing, some mysticks have the ability to avoid detection. This power manifests itself differently from mage to mage; some cloud minds like the Shadow, while others exist, like the Purloined Letter, in plain, inobvious sight.

A mystick with a high Arcane may simply "slide away" from view and memory or may appear too ordinary to notice. This ability is not invisibility *per se* and does not conceal a sorcerer during combat. If someone searches for the mage, however, they'll find it a frustrating experience. Somehow, things just *happen* to cover their quarry's tracks: cameras malfunction, sources disagree, and clues the investigator just *knew* were in that file no longer exist. Naturally, these effects have little to do with conscious magick use; they just occur.

Whatever form the Arcane power takes, it subtracts its dot rating from any Perception or Investigation Dice Pool used to find the mage. It also adds its rating to the character's Stealth attempts. Arcane may be consciously dampened by the mage if she wants, allowing people to find her more easily.

- • Easy to overlook
- •• Where did he go?
- ••• Very difficult to follow
- •••• A needle in a haystack
- ••••• Which grain of sand?

Avatar

While **Chapter Two** deals with the mystick self in detail, this Trait measures its relative power. The higher the rating, the more of a force in the mage's life the Avatar will be. All True Magi have Awakened Avatars; those with low Background ratings, however, have less potent ones than some.

The dots in this Background also translate into the mystick's base Quintessence pool, the amount of Primal energy she holds within herself. Whenever a character's Quintessence rating dips below her score in this Trait, she automatically reabsorbs Quintessence after successfully meditating (Perception + Meditation; difficulty 7) at a Node for at least an hour. The number of successes determines how much Quintessence she regains; the amount cannot, however, exceed her Avatar rating. If she has an Avatar of two, she cannot absorb more than two Quintessence at a time, no matter how many successes she rolls. Likewise, she may only spend two points of Quintessence per turn to lower her magick rolls. (**See "Quintessence."**)

Quintessence that a mage gains from his Avatar may not be stored or channeled to another mage. This innate energy may only be used by its "owner." In essence, it's part of his Pattern and therefore untouchable.

- • May rebuild a pool of one Quintessence
- •• May rebuild a pool of two Quintessence
- ••• May rebuild a pool of three Quintessence
- •••• May rebuild a pool of four Quintessence
- ••••• May rebuild a pool of five Quintessence

Destiny

Destiny is an ephemeral thing; each mage has his or her role in destiny. This Trait, however, signifies a mystick who has — or is *supposed* to have — a very special part in future events. **Chapter Two** discusses vision and the Path of destiny in more detail. In game terms, this Background earns the mage the respect of her peers and an extra Willpower boost when things get bad.

A character with a high Destiny rating is a chosen one; perhaps a vision, prophecy or a simple "sense of greatness" follows her. Mysticks who recognize such things will treat the mage with some respect. Her actions, however, will often be watched and sometimes criticized if she appears "unworthy" of whatever Fate has planned for her. Several groups may even fight to share in whatever she has to offer. The exact nature of the mage's Destiny is left up to the player and Storyteller. It should, however, remain mysterious — an enigma, rather than a testament, i.e., "You will overthrow the Technocracy."

Mages with Destiny rarely die ignominious deaths. They may die young, but they perish with style and importance. This certainty can carry the mystick through hard times. Once per story (not each game session), if something threatens her with a bad end, she may roll her Destiny rating against difficulty 8. Each success she scores allows her to regain one spent Willpower point. She may use these points to avert a cheap death; Destiny reaffirms her inner faith.

Remember, though, that the Destiny rating means just that — the mage is destined to accomplish some great feat, die valiantly facing overwhelming odds or even turn to the forces of evil. One day, the Storyteller *will* call the Destiny due....

- • Mage of merit; roll one die
- •• A creditable mage; roll two dice
- ••• Mage of promise; roll three dice
- •••• A respected mage; roll four dice
- ••••• A revered mage; roll five dice

Dream

Mysticks with this Trait can tap into the universal unconscious. Through focus and mediation, the mage may learn things he does not yet know and access a general stream of information for short periods of time.

In story terms, the mage enters a trance of some kind; the specifics vary, of course — a shaman may touch the ripples of the Dream Realms, while a hacker mage might sprint-scan a freeform database in hopes of learning through subconscious impressions. In any case, he soon emerges from his trance with some form of information — hopefully, a kind he can use! This dream-lore is more intuition than hard facts, but it is helpful in a general way.

In game play, Dream allows a character to access information he does not normally have. He must first go into some form of trance (Perception + Meditation or Enigmas, if you need a roll) and concentrate on the form of information he wants to gain. If he already has the Ability, this is easier than if he does not. After a time (Storyteller's option — the harder the task, the longer the time), he emerges with the lore he sought. Maybe.

The universal unconscious is not a library; sometimes the knowledge the mystick seeks is not the kind he comes out with. From time to time, a character with Dream should manifest a different skill than he wanted to find. This Ability should still be useful (perhaps in ways the mage does not expect) and related to the one the mystick sought. Dream is a chancy talent, however, and does not always work according to plan.

While the dream-lore lasts, the character may substitute his Dream rating for one chosen Ability, whether he has the Ability or not. If he needed Medicine to save his friend, say, but didn't have that Knowledge, he would roll Intelligence + Dream instead after returning from his trance. This Background cannot be used to add to his Dice Pool for an Ability he already has — he either uses the dream-lore rating or his own. This mystick insight lasts until the character next sleeps; when he awakens, it is gone. Only one Ability can be used per day.

Dream may come in handy in completely alien situations where no other Ability would be useful, such as Intelligence + Dream (for Linguistics) to understand the language of a creature from another Realm.

- • Hazy bits of information can be gleaned.
- •• Respectable lessons can be learned.
- ••• Worthwhile lore is available.
- •••• Remarkable knowledge can be accessed.
- ••••• Astounding insights are possible.

Influence

Influence reflects a mage's ability to affect the Sleeper community through contacts or channels. He may hold political power, own a nightclub, perform in a rock band or command great respect among the faithful. Either way, people listen when he speaks. This Background does not reflect standing among other mages (Destiny covers that). Such "common" Influence may actually detract from a mage's standing in the eyes of his peers.

By rolling this Trait in connection with Social Traits, the mystick may get special favors, a temporary forum or just a good table at his favorite restaurant. Combined with Mental rolls, it can help represent a local search through connections. Influence also helps you acquire new acolytes, by rolling Charisma + Influence, in certain situations. People will just want to follow the mage.

Influence is generally effective only within the mage's own culture unless the rating is four or five dots, in which case the mage may have an international reputation.

- • Moderately influential; always called on when you raise your hand.
- •• Well-connected; you have important things to say.
- ••• Position of influence; people seek your opinion.
- •••• Broad personal power; a few comments could affect stock prices.
- ••••• Vastly influential; when you talk people listen (and take notes).

Library

Some mages have libraries of tomes filled with occult knowledge. Such books could have been gifts from a mage's mentor or may have belonged to him before he even Awakened.

Libraries are useful for mundane research; picking up new Knowledges is easy when you have vast resources. Real occult lore, however, is even more important. Although True Magick cannot be learned through simple study, the principles behind the Spheres can be.

These resources are not always books. Scrolls, databases and even friends who know a lot of folklore can be considered libraries if the character can study continuously, access the information at will, and find what she is looking for. Obviously, a wise grandmother cannot teach a Virtual Adept Time magick — though her insights could prove helpful.

Like Mentors, Libraries are useful when spending experience points. By rolling her Library rating (difficulty 7) while learning a new Knowledge or Sphere, she can save experience points she normally would have spent. Each success counts as one point saved, though at least one point must always be spent. The mage must spend at least one week (often longer) in research and can roll only once every time she spends the experience.

Mages often keep their tomes at the Chantry library and share them freely with the others in the cabal. Thus, this Background, like Chantry, can be pooled so long as the means allow and the characters stay together.

- • A collection of New-Age paperbacks.
- •• A few notable works and lots of superficial stuff.
- ••• A handful of rare and ancient books, and vast mundane resources.
- •••• An impressive collection of occult and mortal lore.
- ••••• A hoard of lost secrets, a sea of common wisdom.

Mentor

A figure of enormous influence in most mages' lives, a Mentor may be an older mage, a spirit or some other Awakened figure who takes the character under his wing and teaches her the ropes. This Mentor may or may not have been the one who Awakened the mystick in the first place. Whatever their early relationship may have been, however, the Mentor now instructs his pupil in the ways of magick, destiny and the pitfalls of the Acsension War.

The Background listing reflects how helpful the teacher is. A dull or distant Mentor is better than none, but barely; the wiser, more learned or more influential the Mentor, the higher his rating.

Mentors are important both for what they can teach and how they can intercede in their pupils' lives. The stereotypical Mentor/student relationship involves apprenticeship, with a younger mystick learning from a master who demands tasks in return for instruction. Such tutelage may last from weeks to years and could range from affectionate to abusive. Whatever the relationship may be, a Mentor will always feel (and be held) accountable for his student's actions. The pupil, likewise, benefits or loses status with other mages on account of her Mentor's reputation. Either partner could either help or harm the other during the course of a chronicle.

Like Libraries, a Mentor can also aid a mage who wants to increase her skills or Spheres. By convincing her Mentor to teach her what she wants to know, the willworker can roll her rating and save experience **(see "Library")**. In some cases, the Mentor may be necessary for learning the skill at all — learning the principles of the elements without instruction can take years or even decades!

Like Allies, a Mentor should not be a collection of dots on a sheet. Though he should not overshadow the player character, a Mentor must be a potent and colorful person in his own right. Take Merlin or Obi-Wan Kenobi as examples — their influence was more important than their presence, and each had personality to burn. This Background is not a free ride; Mentors, especially powerful ones, should not give something for nothing. Mentors have motivations like any other person, and will often demand favors or services for their teachings. This could be as simple as keeping his books in order or as dangerous as retrieving strange artifacts from a Realm. In general, though, the mage receives much more from her Mentor than he requires of the mage.

- • Unimportant or distant Mentor.
- •• Helpful but eccentric Mentor.
- ••• Good and notable Mentor.
- •••• Wise and respected Mentor.
- ••••• Powerful or influential Mentor.

Node

This Background represents a place of power that the mystick (or his cabal) has easy access to. Through it, the character can get a certain amount of Quintessence, both to absorb **(see "Avatar")** and to carry in the form of Tass. This is a great benefit; most powerful or obvious Nodes have already been claimed. Nodes can be located nearly anywhere — in church cellars, in the backs of bookstores, or in graveyards.

The Node's rating determines how much Tass the place produces, in addition to any "free" Quintessence the character absorbs. The ratings can be added together if more than one character has the Background, and the Tass can be "stockpiled," though it loses its potency in about a month if it's not used. The Node's "owners" usually have to refine the Tass from some mundane form before using it. The form this Tass takes depends on the Node itself. A grove may have magickal bark on the trees, which can be brewed and distilled into Tass, a laboratory may siphon the juice from living subjects, and a graveyard may leave residue in the bones, which must be prepared before they can be used.

Nodes are often attacked by Quintessence thieves. The character himself may have taken the Node from some other party, who may return to take it back....

- • One Quintessence/week
- •• Two Quintessence/week
- ••• Three Quintessence/week
- •••• Four Quintessence/week
- ••••• Five Quintessence/week

Talisman

A Talisman (or *Device*, to the Technocracy) is an object of power, an item imbued with magick which the wielder can use. This Background allows a beginning character to start play with a Talisman in her possession. It's a tricky Background, and Storytellers may limit it if they see fit.

Any item can be a Talisman if it's enchanted somehow; stones, cybernetics, computers, bones, weapons, even works of art may be used as magickal items. Note that mages do not take these wondrous things for granted — there is so little real magick in the world that Talismans are both rare and treasured.

These objects have built-in magickal Effects. In most cases, only an Awakened person can use them, although there may be exceptions if the Storyteller wants to make them. Some Talismans have several small powers, while others have one big one. No matter how many powers such an item possesses, it cannot have more Effects than the dots in its rating. A level three Talisman, then, could have three Effects, maximum. The Effect is also limited to a Sphere level equal to the dots in the Talisman; the same Talisman could not have an Effect beyond the third rank in a Sphere **(see Chapter Eight for the powers of the Spheres)**. Conjunctional Effects are considered to take up one dot per Sphere involved; the sample item could only have one power if that Effect used three different Spheres.

Because of their power, Talismans are purchased differently than other Backgrounds. Each dot costs *two* Backgrounds instead of one. A level five Talisman, then, would cost 10 points **(see listings below)**. Our third-level Talisman costs six points.

Every Talisman has an "Arete" of its own, allowing the mage to roll one die per point of Arete. Most Talismans have one point of Arete (i.e., one die) per level. An optional rule allows a mage to buy an additional point of Arete for another Background point. To buy the sample Talisman an Arete of five, the player must spend eight Background points instead of six.

Each use of a Talisman's power expends one Quintessence from an inner reserve. This Prime Force powers the Effects, and when it's gone, the item is useless. Before this happens, the owner may "refuel" it with a Prime 3 Effect. A similar spell may drain a Talisman, taking one Quintessence point per success rolled (difficulty 10). These reserves usually equal the item's Arete x 5; the sample Talisman, then, has 15 Quintessence at Arete 3 or 25 at Arete 5.

Spirit Talismans, called *fetishes*, work differently in story terms, but are purchased the same way. These items contain spirits who have, by force or friendliness, entered the item to perform a service. They may or may not cause the mage some difficulty when doing so, depending on how the mage treats the spirit. Assume that when the Quintessence is used up, the spirit departs. Fetishes cannot be refueled.

Talismans can be used as foci. This may not make their magick coincidental (it usually isn't), but may help the mystick concentrate. All Paradox an item's Effect produces goes to the mage. Chapter Nine has rules for Talisman and fetish construction. The Appendix offers some sample items.

•	A weak item 2 points, Arete 1, Quintessence 5
••	A useful Talisman 4 points, Arete 2, Quintessence 10
•••	A significant item 6 points, Arete 3, Quintessence 15
••••	A famous and potent Talisman 8 points, Arete 4, Quintessence 20
•••••	A powerful magickal device 10 points, Arete 5, Quintessence 25)

Arete

But if the vision was true and mighty, as I know, it is true and mighty yet; for such things are of the spirit, and it is in the darkness of their eyes that men get lost.
— Black Elk, *Black Elk Speaks*

Arete (commonly pronounced AIR-i-tay) is the foundation of the mystick's power — the enlightened will. Through this combination of understanding, confidence and will, the mage directs his knowledge of the elements to alter reality. This mystickal awareness may come slowly or may explode into a sudden flood of understanding. It's not unusual for a mystick to acquire a lot of Arete (one to three dots) during her Awakening. Progressing from there, however, is a laborious road.

Arete is not merely "enlightenment"; it is comprehension mixed with intuition mixed with sheer mystick will. It is not an easy concept to understand, much less quantify, and each mage views it a little bit differently. Hermetic scholars consider Arete the measure of one's understanding of cosmic patterns and principles. Dreamspeakers see it as a bond between the flesh, mind and spirit. Akashic mages describe Arete as harmony with the All, whereas an Euthanatos might view it as an acceptance of the transcendent self. All of these views, and others, are correct.

In game terms, a character's Arete allows him to manipulate reality. The higher his rank, the greater his understanding and mystick might. Each Arete dot he has gives him one dot to roll for magickal Effects. As the mage progresses (see **"Personal Growth," Chapter Nine**), his Arete rises, and with it, his power.

Raising the Arete score requires more than experience points. It involves roleplaying through Seekings and studying one's Art. Chapter Nine details the process, but for now, assume that your character cannot gain Arete through experience alone.

Because **Mage** is largely a game about growth and challenge, we strongly recommend that new characters begin with an Arete of three of lower. If the troupe wishes to run a game of experienced mysticks, you may ignore this rule.

x	Sleeper
•	Unschooled
••	Talented
•••	Novice
••••	Disciplined
•••••	Commanding
••••••	Aware
•••••••	Understanding
••••••••	Wise
•••••••••	Enlightened
••••••••••	Transcendent

Game Effects of Arete

• The mage's Arete rating indicates the maximum amount of dice she can roll to perform a magickal feat. If you don't understand reality very well, you won't be able to do much with it.

• The more a mystick learns, the more she understands that her foci are unnecessary. As she rises in Arete, she can discard such aids at a rate of one focus per dot. This often begins with the first Sphere the mystick learns. From there, she may set aside one focus per additional dot.

• A character cannot have Sphere ratings higher than her Arete rating, unless the latter has been lowered through loss of Willpower **(see below)**. In this case, she still possesses knowledge, but lacks the ability to use it.

• If the mage's *permanent* Willpower rating drops below his Arete, he cannot use the difference until his Willpower is restored. His magick Dice Pool is reduced and he is denied access to the higher Sphere levels until he regains his confidence. If Kobie's Willpower rating, for instance, dropped to three dots while his Arete was four, he could not use that last dot (or his rank four Spheres) until he bought his Willpower back to four or better. The understanding is there, but the mystickal will is not.

Willpower

'Do as thou wilt' shall be the whole of the law.
— Aleister Crowley

Mages must be masters of self-control. Willpower does not measure mystick command, though the two are related. It represents a character's drive and emotional stability. A person whose Willpower Pool is high has confidence to burn, while one with a low rating has very little motivation or control.

Unlike other Traits, Willpower is not usually rolled — it is spent. When a character has to push beyond his usual boundaries, resist temptation or force things not to happen, he expends his Willpower points until either he triumphs or collapses in exhaustion.

Most of the time, the Trait's *permanent rating* — the squares on the character sheet — stays consistent; this represents the character's overall confidence. The temporary *Willpower Pool* — the circles — go up and down. When you spend a Willpower point, you remove it from the Pool. Some extraordinary circumstances burn permanent Willpower. This can cause long-term problems for the mage, as she must rebuild her confidence from the ground up (creating many story possibilities).

Willpower is used as the difficulty of many kinds of rolls. Sleepers use their Pool as the difficulty, but mages use their permanent rating instead.

•	Weak
••	Timid
•••	Unassertive
••••	Diffident
•••••	Certain
••••••	Confident
•••••••	Strong
••••••••	Controlled
•••••••••	Iron-willed
••••••••••	Unshakable

Using Willpower

• By spending a Willpower point, a mage can get one automatic success in an action. Only one point per turn can be used this way, but it grants a single guaranteed success. During extended actions, this can make a lot of difference. Only Awakened beings can use their Willpower this way; Sleepers cannot.

• By rolling her Willpower, a person may resist the effects of Mind magick. The difficulty for such rolls is usually 6. **(See "Dodging and Resistance," Chapter Eight.)** Botching such a roll might cost a temporary Willpower point, depending on the Effect she was trying to resist.

• When a mystick rolls a botch during a magick casting, he can avert the worst effects of a Paradox backlash. This is not a cheap dodge — the feat costs a Willpower point and a previously-rolled success, and still results in failure — but by willing the worst not to happen, the mage may escape disaster. This only works once per casting; an Effect that is botched twice automatically causes a backlash.

• A point of Willpower can also dispel a delusion brought on by Quiet **(see "Paradox," Chapter Eight).** This requires a roll as well, but neutralizes one point of Paradox in the process. Only one point per game session (or per day, if you prefer) can be spent this way.

• Some urges are too strong to ignore. When a mystick is faced with an uncontrollable reaction ("The thing's so hideous you feel compelled to run away..."), he may spend a Willpower point to avoid following the urge. If the situation continues, however, he may be forced to spend more Willpower in order to keep his self-control. This can get nasty if the problem lasts longer than the character's Willpower Pool.

Losing Willpower

Everybody's got a breaking point. Prolonged shocks may weaken a mage's resolves until her self-confidence is damaged. This should not be done lightly, as it represents real damage, not mere setbacks, and the mage will need time to heal. When this happens, her permanent rating (the squares) is reduced until she can buy it back up with experience and roleplay through the psychological scars.

This optional rule is left to the Storyteller's discretion, but should not be abused. We recommend that no trauma reduce a mage's Willpower rating by more than two points, total. Mages are not sissies.

• A mage who receives a strong shock — a severe Mind attack, an emotional kick, a personal disaster or a Paradox backlash — when his Willpower Pool sits at one or below loses one permanent point from his rating.

• Prolonged emotional trauma — brainwashing, torture, an especially disastrous Seeking, severe personal tragedy, etc. — may cause the character to lose a permanent Willpower point. This should only happen during especially bad incidents.

Regaining Willpower

Whenever a character gets a chance to rest and regain her self-confidence, she can replenish her Willpower Pool. Although the Storyteller will have the final decision about it, the methods below offer some common ways to restore lost Willpower. They only count towards rebuilding the mystick's spent stock, not her rating, although they may be used as guidelines for raising the rating through experience.

• At the end of a story (not a game session), the characters regain *all* the Willpower they spent during the tale. If the story ended on an uncertain note, the Storyteller may limit this amount until some way of restoring their faith has been found.

• If a mage achieves some kind of special success, like rescuing her mentor, helping a homeless person re-enter society or uncovering a lost tome, she may get a point or more back from the rush of victory.

• When she fulfills some criterion of her chosen Nature **(see "Archetypes")**, she may regain one or two Willpower. This must be accomplished through roleplaying, not simply by stating, "I'm a Judge, so I'll arbitrate disputes around the Chantry until my Willpower is back to normal."

• If the mage has the Destiny Background, he may renew his confidence through his higher purpose. If Father Shelley, who has a Destiny of three, were cornered by a couple of thugs, he could regain some spent Willpower by rolling his Destiny dice against difficulty 8 — he can't die this way! He's got a destiny to fulfill! He rolls, gets two successes and regains two points of Willpower.

• For simplicity's sake, each character can just recover one Willpower every morning when they wake up — a new day gives one renewed purpose. This only works once per day.

Quintessence and Paradox

We scaled the face of reason
To find at least one sign
That would reveal the true dimensions
Of life lest we forget

— Dead Can Dance, "Anywhere Out of the World"

These Traits are a study in contrasts. Quintessence represents the Primal Force a mage contains, his affinity with "real" reality, while Paradox represents how much of an aberration to reality the mystick has become. The elements, while not quite opposites, contradict each other. The rules for each are below.

Both Traits are measured on a wheel of 20 spaces; Quintessence points are filled in from the left-hand marker going clockwise, while Paradox is marked by the spaces going counterclockwise from the same point. If the two ratings overlap, Quintessence loses.

Paradox points **(also referred to as the "Paradox Pool" in Chapter Eight)** always eliminate Quintessence points if the two meet somewhere on the wheel. If, for example, a mage with 14 Quintessence and five Paradox gained three more points of Paradox, the last two Paradox points take the first two Quintessence points' place. The opposite does not occur; if a mage with 12 Paradox and six Quintessence absorbs three more Quintessence, only two of those new points go on the wheel. The other is lost.

Because these ratings may overlap on the track, we recommend that you fill each type of rating with a different mark, i.e., Quintessence with checks and Paradox with "x's."

Quintessence

• A mage gains Prime Force through his Avatar Background or by absorbing it from some Talisman, Node or Tass through Prime magicks. The Avatar rating represents the maximum amount of Quintessence he can soak up per turn through any means.

• Quintessence can be spent to reduce the difficulty of a magick roll **(see Chapter Eight)**. For each point spent this way, the mystick lowers his difficulty by -1, to a maximum of -3.

• Channeling this energy from a Node requires Prime 1; getting it from Tass demands Prime 3. A Master of this force can draw Quintessence from anywhere with a vulgar Prime 5 Effect. Each success equals a point of Quintessence absorbed. Though often invisible, this magick causes lights to flicker, rooms to chill or people to weaken suddenly.

• Under most circumstances, Prime Force is invisible. Strong sources may glow slightly when viewed in the Umbra, but for the most part Quintessence can only be seen with Prime magick. When "in motion," however, it can be sensed by beings who possess Awareness (the difficulty for the roll would run between 6 and 10, depending on the incident).

• Magicks which shunt large amounts of Quintessence around are never coincidental; such Arts twist the fabric of reality itself. Consider "large amounts" to be disturbances involving more than five points in a turn. Really large shifts, involving 10 points or more, or really violent channelings, can actually be seen by the mortal eye as bright ribbons, floods or explosions. These manifestations are *always* vulgar. **(An exception is anti-magick; see "Permutations," Chapter Eight.)**

Paradox

• Mysticks run the risk of Paradox every time they use their Arts; the more extreme the magick, the greater the risk. The full rules for Paradox and magick can be found in Chapter Eight.

• A mage's Paradox rating makes up his Paradox Pool. Each point on the wheel, combined with any points he has just incurred, becomes one die in a backlash Dice Pool. Storytellers roll this pool when a mage really screws up.

• Given time, Paradox points fade as the anomaly evens out. If the mage has less than 10 Paradox, it takes one game week per point for the energy to bleed off, provided the mage earns no more Paradox during that time. By laying low, a mystick can remain somewhat safe, which explains mages' affinity for hidden places. If he has more than 10 points stored up, something has to give. Sooner or later, some backlash, Quiet or Flaw will appear. Should he make it up to 20 without incident (unlikely), he may either go eternally mad or go out in a spectacular Paradox explosion.

Health

I cut clean across just as the net descended
I'm a sandman and I'm a solider
I'm a wrecker of engines
— The Jack Rubies, "Wrecker of Engines"

(See also "Injury," Chapter Ten.)

Wounds, sickness and other conditions affect the Health Trait. Whenever something injures a mage, his player subtracts Health Levels to reflect the damage. Healthy characters have essentially eight Levels to lose; each one lost penalizes that person by subtracting from his Dice Pools. The more injury a mage sustains, the worse his condition. If the penalty exceeds the person's Dice Pool, he can do nothing.

Arete rolls are the exception to this. A Crippled mage can still call upon his powers. Only when he goes to Incapacitated or below does he take magick roll penalties.

Even if the damage is healed, pain or other trauma may remain. While this need not subtract from Dice Pools, the player should keep his mage's injuries in mind, even after they heal.

Character Creation Process

- **Step One: Character Concept**
  - *Choose* Concept, Tradition, Essence, Nature and Demeanor
  - *Decide* style of magick, beliefs and personal history
- **Step Two: Select Attributes**
  - *Prioritize the three categories:* Physical, Social, Mental (7/5/3)
  - *Choose Physical Traits:* Strength, Stamina, Dexterity
  - *Choose Social Traits:* Charisma, Manipulation, Appearance
  - *Choose Mental Traits:* Perception, Intelligence, Wits
- **Step Three: Select Attributes**
  - *Prioritize the three categories:* Talents, Skills, Knowledges
  - Choose Talents, Skills, Knowledges (13/9/5)
  - No Attribute higher than 3 at this stage
- **Step Four: Select Advantages (see Options, below)**
  - Choose Backgrounds (7)
  - Choose Spheres (5, plus a free one based on Tradition)
- **Step Five: Finishing Touches**
  - Record Arete (1), Willpower (5)
  - Spend "Freebie Points" (15)

Concepts

- **Artist:** dancer, singer, actor, writer
- **Debutante:** thrill-seeker, connoisseur, heiress
- **Explorer:** environmentalist, nature-boy, scientist
- **Caretaker:** cop, social worker, missionary, doctor
- **Hermit:** vagabond, recluse, scarred survivor
- **Mystic:** pagan, theologian, visionary, shaman
- **Outsider:** half-caste, dispossessed, neurotic, gamer
- **Philosopher:** dreamer, pontificator, student
- **Rebel:** reformer, punk, criminal, hippie, hacker
- **Reverent:** clergyman, teacher, disciple, truth-seeker
- **Scholar:** professor, theorist, knowledge-seeker
- **Warrior:** vigilante, soldier, gang member, protector

The Traditions

- **Akashic Brotherhood:** Mysticks based in the East, the Brotherhood searches for perfection through discipline and harmony.
  Sphere: Mind
- **Celestial Chorus:** These mages pursue unification of the world with the One from which all things came.
  Sphere: Prime
- **Cult of Ecstasy:** Shattering the barriers of time, society and endurance is this Tradition's way to enlightenment.
  Sphere: Time
- **Dreamspeakers:** Speakers-with-spirits, these primal shamans strive to break down the barriers between flesh and spirit, bringing them together as one.
  Sphere: Spirit
- **Euthanatos:** Wrongly perceived as death-cultists, this Tradition pursues rebirth. By separating the chaff from the wheat, such reincarnationists seek a new and better world.
  Sphere: Entropy
- **Order of Hermes:** Classical masters of education and discipline, Hermetic magi crave Ascension through perfection of their Art.
  Sphere: Forces
- **Sons of Ether:** Though often dismissed as mad, these visionaries guide their Grand Science through personal theories and a code of honor.
  Sphere: Matter
- **Verbena:** Primordial mysticks, these mages find perfection within, not without. Their Art links the cycles of the world with the cycles of the flesh.
  Sphere: Life
- **Virtual Adepts:** Brilliant anarchists, the rebel Adepts carve a new frontier by melding technology with the soul. Packed with attitude, such survivors are hard to kill.
  Sphere: Correspondence
- **Hollow Ones:** Not a formal Tradition, but close. Though they drape themselves in darkness, these young seers carry less baggage in their quest for Ascension than any other group.
  Sphere: Any

Spheres

(See also Chapter Eight)

- **Correspondence:** Understanding of space and relationships.
- **Entropy:** Mastery of the downward spiral.
- **Forces:** Command over the natural elements from fire to radiation.
- **Life:** This Sphere grants insight into the makeup of living things.
- **Matter:** A grasp of non-living physical structures — and how they might be changed.
- **Mind:** A backstage pass to the workings of the mind.
- **Prime:** Command over Quintessence, the cornerstone of the universe.
- **Spirit:** Insight into the spirit world and its many aspects and inhabitants.
- **Time:** Time is not necessarily linear. This Sphere allows a mage to sidestep its flow.

Essences

- **Dynamic:** Driven to eternal change, they flit from one task to another.
- **Pattern:** The opposite; these architects try to build something lasting from chaos.
- **Primordial:** Old souls, these Avatars draw their Essence from the beginning — and end — of the universe.
- **Questing:** Eternal Galahads who strive for balance and purpose. They often hold the middle road between the pull of the others.

Archetypes (Nature & Demeanor)

- **Architect:** You seek to leave lasting accomplishments.
- **Avant-Garde:** You must be the first to do anything.
- **Bon Vivant:** Life is too important not to enjoy.
- **Bravo:** You are a protector — or a bully.
- **Caregiver:** You must help alleviate suffering.
- **Conformist:** You are a team player.
- **Conniver:** It's in everyone's best interest to help you — really!
- **Critic:** Things can always be better. Point out how.
- **Curmudgeon:** Cynical, hell! You just see the world for what it is.
- **Deviant:** Rules exist to be broken.
- **Director:** Stability requires order. Bring it about.
- **Fanatic:** Your cause is everything to you.
- **Jester:** Help others see the joke in everything.
- **Judge:** You seek justice for all.
- **Loner:** You have never fit in and never will.
- **Martyr:** Any cause worth having is worth dying for.
- **Rebel:** You struggle against oppression, wherever it may breed.
- **Survivor:** Nothing stops you; it slows you down, maybe, but you always survive.
- **Traditionalist:** The old ways are best.
- **Visionary:** Hidden truth is your greatest quest and your greatest gift.

Experience Points

Trait	Cost
New Ability	3
New Sphere	10
Willpower	current rating
Knowledges	current rating
Talents and Skills	current rating x 2
Attributes	current rating x 4
Tradition Specialty Sphere	current rating x 7
Other Sphere	current rating x 8
Arete	current rating x 8

Freebie Points

Trait	Cost
Attributes	5 per dot
Abilities	2 per dot
Backgrounds	1 per dot
Arete	4 per dot
Willpower	1 per dot
Spheres	7 per dot
Quintessence	1 point per four dots

Health Levels

Level:	Dice Pool:	Effect:
Bruised:		Character is only bruised and has no action penalties.
Hurt:	-1	Character is only mildly hurt; movement isn't hindered.
Injured:	-1	Minor injuries; little hindrance to movement.
Wounded	-2	Character cannot run, but can still walk.
Mauled:	-2	Character is badly injured and can only hobble about.
Crippled:	-5	Character is severely injured and can only crawl.
Incapacitated:		Character is completely incapable of movement.

An Incapacitated mage is very close to death. If he loses one more Health Level, he dies.

Backgrounds

- **Allies:** Your companions, from mortal acolytes to supernatural beings.
- **Arcane:** A mystick ability to avoid attention, even direct attention.
- **Avatar:** Your mystick self; this Trait reflects the power and, perhaps, personality of that "other half."
- **Chantry:** Your cabal's meeting place; it may be a place you own or a fellowship you belong to.
- **Destiny:** Some mages are destined to do great things — or die in great ways.
- **Dream:** You are in touch with the cosmic unconscious. This allows you to know things you have never learned.
- **Familiar:** A magickal companion with some special talents.
- **Influence:** Your status in the Sleeper community.
- **Library:** A repository of magickal knowledge and helpful lore.
- **Mentor:** Your tutor and guardian in mage society.
- **Node:** A wellspring of Quintessence you have at your disposal.
- **Resources:** Your access to cash and property.
- **Sanctum:** A space you have set for yourself; your place of power.
- **Talisman:** Some magickal item you have in your possession.

The

Chapter Seven: Storytelling

The seat of the soul is... where the inner and outer worlds meet. The outer world is what you get in scholarship. The inner world is your reaction to it, and it's where these two come together that we have the mythos. The outer world changes with historical time, but the inner world is the world of anthropos — it is the one true constant to the human race... you always have the sense of recognizing something. What you're recognizing is your own inward life, and at the same time, the inflection through history... the problem of making the inner world meet the outer world of today is, of course, the function of the artist.

— Joseph Campbell, *Transformation of Myth Through Time*

Clarissa's Temptation

The sex was beyond belief; Clarissa wondered why she'd never bothered to do the wild thing with someone who could join with her mind as well as her body before. She and Rick cuddled in his hot tub, perfectly content, breathing in the fumes of the potent sandalwood incense.

"Mmmm, but that was lovely," she whispered in his ear. "I love seeing things from different perspectives, y'know, but nothing's ever quite taken my breath like feeling your thoughts, drinking in your senses like that."

"I've never known anybody quite like you either," her lover replied, rolling large pearls soaked in scented oil over her back and arms. "You know," he said, "I thought maybe you could stay here awhile. My master has taken quite a fancy to you."

"I..." Thinking of Rick's master, the dark man who'd spoken to her in silky tones with undisguised lust in his eyes, Clarissa shuddered.

"You could be so useful to him," said Rick, dribbling water down her back. "Not to mention getting to see me all the time." His eyes locked with hers in a passionate gaze. "My master's very generous to those who work with him. You've been to his Realm. Have you ever seen anything like it before?" Clarissa shook her head. "I know things aren't easy for you back home, Clarissa. You're running yourself crazy trying to do so many things at once. Here, you could study and learn as much as you wanted, all the time. I really wish you'd consider it." The mage laid his dark head against her heart, listening, waiting.

Clarissa swallowed hard. Rick and his master offered everything she'd ever wanted. She got so tired of never having the time to seek her own Path, trying to balance her Chantry duties with her life as a confidante and sympathetic ear to all the hip and trendy hangers-on at the club. It would be easier, just like Rick said, if...

Then she thought of the evil she'd seen in Rick's master, swimming below the surface. She thought of the thorns in his great tangle of mazes in a Realm where the sun never shown. Though it stung her heart with regret, she eased away from Rick and left behind the tainted power he sought to share with her.

Remember the last time you saw a really great movie? Remember how it felt? When we watch a film we really enjoy, time seems to stand still. The rest of the world is set aside, and the experience consumes our senses. From the opening scene to the end credits, that film becomes our world. Afterward, we can say that it's "just a movie," but then again, part of us knows that isn't exactly true....

A movie is a way of telling a story. If it's a really good film, we find a reason to get caught up in it. Maybe it's a character with whom we can identify or a scene that makes us feel something. We watch hoping to find something we like. The medium of movies has one big drawback, however: it's a passive experience. A person in the audience can choose whether he'll have butter on his popcorn or where he wants to sit in the theater, but that's about it. He can look for his own reasons for liking the film, but someone else has put the meaning into it.

A lot of stories are like that. With books or plays, television programs or comics, the end result is the same. Someone else tells the story, we watch it or read it, and take what we're given. The best we can hope for is to read something into it that wasn't originally there.

Storytelling games are another medium for telling stories, a medium just as valid as movies or television. Each entertainment has its own strengths and weaknesses, but storytelling has an overriding strength: it's a personal experience. The people involved tailor it to what they want it to be and rework it for themselves.

With the assistance of a group of players and the advice in this book, each of you will bring your own story to life. You're not going to perform to an audience of millions, nor will you be dependent upon a budget of millions. With a few dice, a few friends and perhaps a few slices of pizza, you'll lead your troupe of players on a journey that no movie or television program can ever fully reproduce. Although you're just playing a game, it can also be something more. A game is just a game, but a well-told story is a work of art.

This chapter is about the art of telling stories. If you've never done this before, it might seem a little strange at first. If you've done it countless times before, we should begin by saying that **Mage** has its own inherent virtues and pitfalls. This game, like many roleplaying games, has a broad expanse of themes, settings and ideas. Therefore, it helps to have a structure we can use to develop stories. This chapter sketches a map of the territories ahead. Exploring that territory is up to you and your troupe. You're the navigator, the helmsman and the captain. You are the Storyteller.

The Storyteller

"Let's pretend we're kings and queens;... Well, you be one of them, then, and I'll be all the rest."

— Alice (to Dinah), *Through the Looking Glass*

For the uninitiated, let's begin with the basics.

The players have a rather straightforward job: Each player focuses on developing a single character. The Storyteller is responsible for everything else. As one would expect, running the world is no minor task.

The first responsibility of the Storyteller is to act out the role of anyone the characters encounter. Going back to the analogy of films, it's as if the players are the stars and the Storyteller is responsible for the supporting cast. Next comes the setting these characters live in. The Storyteller describes the streets they walk on, the homes they live in, and even the culture they've developed. Because this is **Mage**, the possible range of settings in a chronicle is diverse. The easiest way to begin to develop a setting is to draw on parallels to our own world. This particular game can be a bit daunting at first because of the wide variety of possibilities, but use the real world to inspire you... and go from there.

The next responsibility is to interpret the rules. As the characters explore the settings you've created, you'll have a set of rules to help you interpret events as they happen. Whether a character is climbing a tree or altering reality, it helps to have a set of rules to back you up. These rules should allow you to focus on the most important part of your game: your story. Beyond the math and mechanics, rules serve as a guide to describing the events of the game. The Storyteller interprets the raw numbers and dice rolls and weaves their mystic revelations into the story. If the rules get in her way, she simplifies them or sets them aside. The story's the thing.

The story itself is the last consideration, but by no means the least important one. Begin each chapter of your story with a rough idea of where you want that story to go and what you want it to say to your players, then guide their characters into the world you've created. Things won't always go the way you've planned — players will always come up with variations and twists you never considered — but that's part of the fun of collaborative storytelling. With a little practice and a helpful group, the lot of you can turn your concepts into full-fledged tales.

This book gives you the elements you need to begin to put a story together. There's a set of guidelines for creating characters, an elaborate background to integrate into your setting, and a framework of rules to guide you through the story. Once you've prepared what you need, you can then chart the course of your chronicle. Take what you want and leave the rest behind. It's your world. It's your story.

The Troupe

Fortunately, you're not going into this task alone; storytelling is an interactive activity. Each player, by designing a character, has given you a set of cues for what type of story she wants to hear. Is the story romantic? Is it filled with action and violence? Is it ultimately tragic? The players in your troupe aren't your audience — they're your collaborators. Through a process of give and take, you shape the story with them.

The players will give you a lot of freedom to create, but never forget that they're also part of the creative process. Each of you makes an investment of time and effort when you game together; any of you could be reading a book or going out on a date instead. Your players have put a degree of trust in you to make their investment worthwhile. Naturally, you will.

This doesn't mean that you should give players whatever they want. If there's no danger or conflict in your story, there's no drama. If a story seems completely arbitrary, the illusion is shattered. There's a balance between setting up obstacles the characters must overcome and realizing when the game becomes unwieldy. A great Storyteller plays off what her players say and keeps the balance between static organization and dynamic improvisation. This requires a degree of empathy and a sense of what works in a story and what doesn't.

It's tough, but rewarding; when a room full of people are captivated by a story, the Storyteller feels their reactions. The players become enthusiastic, and the session is better because of that energy. There are moments in a story when it becomes so compelling that everyone is drawn into it. Storytellers live for these moments. Time stands still, and the mechanism of the game is set aside as the story becomes "real." If you remember to make sure that the characters are having fun, and collaborate with your troupe to create a good story, that bliss is your reward.

Chronicle

So we must love while these moments are still called today
Take part in the pain of this passion play
Stretching our youth as we must, until we are ashes to dust
Until time makes history of us
— Indigo Girls, "History of Us"

The practical side of preparing for a game involves planning your chronicle — a series of connected stories that build into something bigger. If a story is a chapter in a book, a chronicle is the entire novel or the entire series.

A chronicle can be as lengthy as you like, from a few sessions to a campaign that takes years to fully develop. Because there are characters at the heart of the story, there's always the chance to develop a chronicle further. If you've created a thorough background and supporting cast to your chronicle, there's always room for a "sequel" to the initial story. Your players will hopefully find your chronicle intriguing enough that they'll want to develop it further. Always leave them wanting a little more.

Long before the players begin to create their characters, take the opportunity to map out where you want the chronicle to go. An exciting setting and cool subplots are a good place to start. Along the way, there should be issues to examine, problems to solve and places to discover, but the basics of your chronicle come first.

Getting Started

Mage is a frighteningly open-ended game; although it is simpler to run that it appears, getting started may be intimidating at first. A few tips here may be helpful:

- **Conceptualize**

Mage contains a multitude of options; will you run an intrigue chronicle, with double-agents and backstabbing? Or a free-for-all with combat in the streets? A serio-comic tale of Marauders on the loose, or a tense cyberpunk epic with an all-powerful Technocracy looming over the characters' shoulders? Decide the *kind* of story you want to tell first. The rest will flow from there.

- **Brainstorm**

The fun part — daydreaming — begins. As you reflect on your chronicle, things from the real world will inspire you. Anything can act as inspiration — a story on the news, an encounter at the bus stop, an insight into another person, or a song that's stuck in your head are a few examples. Take notes. Draw. Outline. Visualize. Your creativity will lead you from there.

Good things to plan at this stage include: strong antagonists, allies and subcultures, the common goal **(see below)**, the overall setting (is it the Web? New York City? The Australian Outback? Doissetep?), major themes you wish to explore **(see "Themes")**, etc. Running a game will become much easier once you know where you want to go with it.

- **Get Input**

Your players will, of course, want some say in the game they'll be playing. After all, if your troupe wants to kick ass and you want them to run or die, your game will have problems from the start. The players are your collaborators, after all. Get their input before you begin.

You need not tell them what it is you have in mind; a little misdirection is not a bad thing — some of your actual plans mixed in with a bit of daydreaming should keep the players from knowing what to expect. Keep an open mind at this point — the suggestions you get may lead to something better than you originally planned.

- **Set Boundaries**

Obviously, your game cannot be all things to all people. Once you have a good idea of your chronicle's direction, lay out what you need in solid form **(See "Packing," below)**, and let the players know what they can and cannot play.

A group needs some kind of coherence. If you have a pack of mages who would never stay together without a player group behind them, the fabric of your game will soon resemble the Tapestry after a long and vulgar magick fight. Before you begin, let your players know what kind of characters they should design. If the game will be combat-heavy, tell them to load up on fighting skills; if it's to be an intrigue-laden mystery, Social Attributes and Abilities (or the lack of them) will be important. Most of all, try to establish some sort of a reason for the characters to work together — a quest, a common Chantry, mutual revenge, family ties, romantic interest — whatever works. Make them have some motivation to stay together.

Above all, make sure this common bond is strong but not binding. Nobody wants to play a game where they remain slaves to the Storyteller's demands.

- **Plan First Scene**

The first scene will set the mood for the entire chronicle. If it begins with the usual "Um, all you guys are in this bar, see, and all of a sudden, a fight breaks out...," the game will have a random feel to it. When the first scene is strong, however — "It's midnight at Chantry Doissetep; thunder shakes the foundations of this ancient place, and the shock waves can be felt even in the heart of the Grand Ballroom, where Porthos celebrates his 550th birthday. Suddenly, a shot rings out..." — the tale begins with a kick, a tone and an overall goal. Writers call this the "hook;" give your game a powerful hook, and you'll be off to a good start.

Setting

Any story needs a strong setting. With this book in your hands, you won't have to start your chronicle from scratch; **Mage** contains a background to build upon. Supernatural embellishments aside, this world is like our own... with a few alterations. The area the characters know best, or the one where they'll be spending the most time, is the place to focus on first.

This setting does not have to be exactly like the place where you live in the real world. It might be a stretch of wilderness, a Realm in the Umbra or even a setting on another planet. The story will work better, however, if the players can identify with at least part of it. That means basing what you do on what you know. One of the easiest ways to portray the surreal, for instance, is to set it against the commonplace. Horror becomes more terrible when contrasted against sanity. If you want to lead your characters beyond the boundaries of reality, begin with a realistic setting.

As you think through your setting, you'll develop the details. Minor details can be just as useful as major ones. What places will the characters visit often? Where can they do research? Where do

they get food? Where can they sleep when they're hiding from the Technocracy? Plan out the basics. If you have a variety of elements prepared beforehand, you'll glide into them effortlessly when you need them. If you haven't prepared a particular detail, you'll find inspiration on the spur of the moment, but having something to fall back on will make you more comfortable.

Supporting Characters

Add to this background a group of supporting characters. Who shares the world with the characters? Who are the Sleepers they'll encounter? What are the supernatural threats that remain hidden? If there are other mages in the area, what are their Tradition politics like? One temptation here is to fall back on stereotypes or choose the obvious, but character comes from personality, not templates. If you stick to the obvious, your chronicle will become predictable and shallow.

Again, when you're creating, minor details can be just as useful as major ones. Personality often comes from the smallest details. How does a character speak? What inspires his trust? What color socks does he wear? An eccentric gas station attendant with the combat abilities of a hamster can make for a better story hook than yet another Akashic Brother with an awesome array of combat stats. Fleshing out a character involves giving her little quirks and petty flaws, and any character, even a supernatural one, must be able to relate to the world around her.

To keep your story realistic, don't forget to include the "normal" world. Not everyone the characters meet will be a Hermetic Master *barabbi* serving Tazgool the Tormentor. Before you escalate the danger level of your campaign, remember that putting personality into "mundanes" can make the setting richer and more robust. If your supporting cast is a series of combat statistics or neat critters, you don't have a supporting cast. You've got a bunch of stereotypes. Any character needs a degree of motivation and depth, even supporting ones.

Motivation puts a character in motion. Consider: any character has a goal. That character will work toward that goal until he meets outside opposition. In physics, "any object in motion stays in motion… until acted upon by an opposing force." The same applies to your supporting cast. Outside opposition usually comes from the characters, the most potent motivators in the story. If the opposition doesn't come directly from them, it might still come from the consequences of their actions. Things happen for a reason, and often, the rationale "she does it because she's *e-vil*" just doesn't cut it. To give your stories verisimilitude, focus on making the supporting characters realistic.

This applies to antagonists as well. If there's no conflict, there's no drama; antagonists provide opposition. Don't set up a series of cut-out figures — giving a "villain" a motivation is a challenge. A game gains depth when the adversaries aren't so much villains as characters with different points of view. Don't think of them as guys in black hats; the phrase "alternative morality" is useful here. Look at the opposing factions of the Ascension War — each side still follows its own particular morality.

It's hard to play an antagonist convincingly if you can't understand him. This doesn't mean that you have to agree with him, but you do need to have an idea of how he thinks. This makes the game more challenging for your players. A black hat is easy to overcome, but a detailed antagonist, with his own particular idiom and point of view, makes for a worthy adversary. Even the darkest adversary has an element of humanity.

The Center of Your Story

Forget philosophies and Traditions for a moment. Set aside settings, conflicts and antagonists. The core of your story involves human beings. The most important of these are the player characters. As you paint the elaborate backdrop for the stage of your drama, don't forget that the player characters are at the center of it. It's very easy to fall into the trap of developing such an extensive background that there's no room for the characters. The chronicle must center around the characters and the conflicts they endure.

Establish how the heroes tie into the background. Why are they there? Why are they risking their lives to explore your dark and dangerous theater of the mind when they could just flee for their lives or hole up in a bomb shelter somewhere? If the characters don't have a motivation to interact with your background, you have no story. As the characters grow, tailoring an adventure to them gets easier. Each character is incomplete in some way; the world brings the opportunity for fulfillment. The players will also give you clues, either directly or indirectly, for the kinds of stories they want to play.

It's also a good idea to have a way for the characters to work together. They all belong to the same cabal, so do they share a common Chantry? What motives bind the characters together? Revenge? Ambition? The destruction of the Technocracy? The salvation of the world around them? Once you and your players have found a reason for the characters to be together, it's easier to chart out a route for them to take.

The meaning behind the World of Darkness is not that the world is dark. That's incidental. That's atmosphere. The real meaning in a chronicle comes from the characters.

Nuts and Bolts

Don't feel an obligation to create a modern myth before lunchtime tomorrow. Take your time. Once you have a sense of direction, it's simply a matter of starting out on the path. Regardless of whether you're setting out to inspire art or just to provide an evening's entertainment, the first few steps on the journey are the same.

First, make sure a good story is told. That doesn't mean that you just *tell* a story. The troupe creates it with you. In each chapter, the Storyteller leads the story in the direction he wants it to go. If you're working with your players (and not just performing for them), you'll eventually find yourself struggling to keep up with what they want to do, commenting and elaborating on what happens rather than simply laying out a narrative. The result is a collaborative effort, a "consensual reality."

The story will often deviate from your plans. If you feel that the story is naturally drifting in another direction, don't force the players to follow your plans; work with them. So long as the tale stays within reason, go with it. You're usually the guide, but elements of the story often come together naturally. An experienced Storyteller often feels as though the story is flowing almost without effort. Just as your players try to anticipate what you're going to do, try to anticipate the characters' actions. They'll surprise you from time to time, and that makes the story come alive.

Packing

Before you begin, be prepared. When you're just starting out, it will be easier to create the story if you spend plenty of time preparing. These preparations include creating a setting, envisioning a rough idea of the plot you want and establishing a few good plot hooks. A "cheat sheet" of important details can be a critical aid to running a smooth game. Cheat sheets might include brief reference descriptions of significant characters (name, story role, physical description, motivations, powers or important skills, and relationships with other characters), a combat summary (who can do what, the average damage they do, weapons they use, amount of damage they can take) and short listings of important places and things (the layout of a houseboat, the distance between points A and B). A relationship chart, if you can create one, makes character reference easy.

You may want to use a premade story. If you do, read through the text carefully a few times beforehand. Make sure you know when and where everything happens, who is where at what time and so on. Pay close attention to the major antagonists, their personalities and motivations, and some ways to portray them convincingly. You can start with a very linear or straightforward plot; there's nothing wrong with that. You must learn the basics first; defying reality and creating dreams comes later.

Such aids are useful, but not mandatory. With a game as complex as **Mage**, it helps to have a few notes on hand. As you become more experienced, it will be easier to deviate from what you've planned. The structure you adopt and the rules you use are the game itself; the events you and your troupe create are the actual story. Storytelling is ultimately a balance between the story and the rules.

Rules

Once there was a man who decided he knew everything
Once there was a book that he threw in my face
Once there was an angry mob that marched up and down the street
Don't ya know they all called my name
What do they want from me?
— Oingo Boingo, "Fill the Void"

This book is filled with rules. In reading them, you might feel as though you're studying for a test. Players will question you about them, other Storytellers will argue about them, and, remarkably enough, some people will really get worked up over them. Despite the fact that **Mage** is just a game, some people enjoy giving themselves (or others) grief over the rules to that game.

First off, you have to be consistent and fair. Some people interpret that as meaning that you must be strict. That's not the case. We've done our best to make sure these rules are consistent, clear and useful, but you and your troupe are the final judges of how well they serve your story. The framework of rules in the game is the set of guidelines we recommend and serves as a common ground for everyone who plays the game. You, as the Storyteller, must get a sense of how well this system works for your troupe. Eventually, you'll customize it to a size and shape you feel is right. You're the final judge of what will work.

Having said that, here's a word of advice: don't worry excessively about rules. In Storytelling, like many things in life, there are no rules... only guidelines. The game is not a test of your ability to memorize. Learn the basics first. Later, you'll take the bits and pieces that work for you. You'll simplify, expand, alter and amend. If you eventually make things up on your own, no one is going to kick down your door and take this book away. Your game belongs to you and yours.

There is no "official" way to play this game, only the way that works best for you and your troupe. Most people who use rules fall between two extremes. Their preference is largely a matter of style.

Style

If you've watched other people run games, you've no doubt seen a variety of styles. Most Storytellers run somewhere between the "rules lawyer" and the "freeform gamer." You won't get a sense of which style works best for you until you start to play. Style comes from experience.

A "rules lawyer" relies on an extremely strict interpretation and application of the rules of the game. If the chart on page 592 says that a player describing a certain action should roll Stamina + Arete and cross-reference the number of successes against a resisted Willpower roll at a difficulty of 8, then that's the way it's gotta be. Rules lawyers often pursue "realism"; for some reason, they feel that adding more rules will make a game more realistic.

This extreme has definite disadvantages. If a rules lawyer gets so caught up in rolling dice and looking up rules that he forgets to concentrate on his story, the story suffers. To us, rules should serve the story; the story is not just a cheap excuse to use rules.

Some players tend to be rules lawyers, too. Rather than holding on to the concepts that make a good story, they'll try to solve problems by bending the rules their way. The character's personality is set aside, and the structure behind the game becomes more important than the game itself. Storytelling should be seen as a collaborative activity, not a contest between the Storyteller and his players. The troupe as a whole ideally works together to create the events. Rules lawyer players have to learn to "play the characters, not the rules."

An extremely "freeform" Storyteller doesn't need any rules at all. If the game only consists of guidelines, why bother with structure and mechanics? A situation may call for tossing a coin or generating a random number, but that's about it. If you have to roll dice, then something's gone wrong. The character sheets provide a rough idea of what characters can do, so dice become superfluous. If the troupe really wants something to happen, it happens. This type of game resembles improvisational theater more than anything else.

While this approach is valid, it also has obvious drawbacks. If anything can happen at the whim of the Storyteller, then everything that happens is, by definition, completely arbitrary. Players who like to have a framework of rules feel lost when they enter the realm of a freeform gamer. They'll have certain expectations of what should work... and find themselves in a situation where the only measure of success is their ability to amuse and humor the Storyteller.

All sarcasm aside, the style that's right for you will probably fall somewhere between these two camps. Both extremes can destroy a game for the game's sake. Consistency is one way to build that particular mindset. Once the players feel comfortable with your style, telling stories comes naturally. Never radically alter your style without letting the players know you're experimenting. If you're going to do something freakish with the rules, the players tend to appreciate it if you let them know beforehand.

Adjusting Your Style

It's possible to shift your style a little during a session to suit your game. Think of taking your journey through the story as if you're driving a race car. When you go into a turn, you downshift. When you're on a straight road, you shift back into high gear again. During your story, for instance, if there's a critical combat coming up, you may slow down and throw a little more detail into the fight. Once it's over, if you want the characters to focus on their discussion of what happened as they search the building, you can shift back up to high speed so that the characters aren't distracted by the dice rolls. As long as you don't radically shift in the middle of a session, you won't ruin the transmission and bring things grinding to a halt. Most players will sense what you're doing and react.

Unfortunately, some people are a pain on long car rides. Certain players delight in trying to circumvent the rules of your game. The goal here is allegedly "success." An individual character's success becomes more important than the game's success. The structure that's been built into the game gives you some measure of protection against rules lawyers, but rules alone are not enough to protect you from an overly aggressive player. One option is to build further layers of rules to shield you from assaults, but then the game becomes so structured that the flow of the story is sacrificed. The best recourse is to find players who work well with you. Over time, you'll find ways to adjust to different types of players, and good players will make an effort to adjust to you. When that happens, you've assembled a worthwhile troupe. Then you can let go of the wheel... and the rest is magic.

There can't be rules for everything, but you can find an amount of detail that suits you. Give the players a chance to offer feedback, especially at the conclusion of each chapter. Through this process you'll develop a set of "house rules" that will make everyone comfortable. Just as you tailor the story to what your troupe enjoys, you'll discover your own particular style of using rules. As long as you're consistent, the players won't feel as though you're being arbitrary. Consistent rules and sound judgment reveal the path; drama and passion make the journey worthwhile.

Tips

Ideals are all well and good, but they're nothing without practical skill to back you up. Here are a few more basic ideas to help you along...

• **The Dice Should Guide You, Not Control You**

Dice are a random element, a helpful device to use when stories get stuck or an outcome should be left to chance. In the end, however, they're a tool, nothing more. How you use that tool will affect the feel of your story. Ultimately, the game is played by human beings, not dice. Use die rolls for inspiration, or for adjudication if you really need it, but remember to balance the game and story.

Sometimes a player will try to circumvent a problem or even a story with a simple Effect (for some players, that's an understatement). The thrill of a quick fix, however, is no substitute for the satisfaction of finding an ingenious solution. If you have to take control of this type of situation, remember that magick is capricious. That doesn't mean that it should do whatever you, as the Storyteller, want, but it often means arriving at a compromise between what the player wants to do to circumvent the plot and what the Storyteller needs to do to move the story along.

In these cases, the dice are useful for adjudication. You don't have to give in when a player wants to solve a problem with a simple die roll. Even for powerful characters, the raw power of magick isn't always something that's easily controlled. You can always add a few complications to any encounter where the dice are a quick fix. Sometimes mages "summon up what they cannot put down...."

• Describe Magick Dynamically

Magick is neither predictable nor boring. Its effects should always take on a life of their own; simply rolling a handful of dice and saying "I throw a fireball" is dull. Describe what happens and how.

Magick loses its vitality when confined to a chart. If you prefer a "freeform" style, you need not roll dice every time a character casts magick. If you prefer "crunchier" rules, the charts on pages 169-171 should help. Practice is also helpful; with a bit of experience, you shouldn't need to check the charts very often.

• Paradoxical Complications

Like magick, Paradox should not simply be a game system. It is a force of nature, not a series of filled-in boxes. The various effects of Paradox are discussed in Chapter Eight. Whatever form they take, however, Paradox backlashes ought to seem like a metaphysical force, not a game mechanic. Vivid descriptions and a sense of irony can help.

The universe has a warped sense of poetic justice. Backlashes usually keep with the nature of the magick that caused them; the punishment often fits the crime. Having Paradox embody the unexpected once in a while, though, keeps your players from becoming *too* comfortable. A little empathy is useful here: if Paradox is always random and surreal, your players will feel out of control. If Paradox is always predictable, magick no longer has a dynamic feel. Strike a balance based on what you feel is right for your group.

Paradox can throw a massive wrench in a player's plans; make sure it doesn't foul up your own in the bargain. If a backlash would disrupt your story, ignore it — for now. Jot down the points a character would have received and save them up for later, when you need a good bit to make them sweat... or to make them think about their actions.

• Magick in the Spirit World

The line about magick's unpredictability goes double outside conventional reality. Otherworldly laws change so rapidly that even the most seasoned traveler is hard-put to guess the effects of his next rote. The boundaries are more flexible, sure, but the side effects can be as simple or as complicated as you want them to be.

When mages cast magick in other Realms, the nature of those places colors the willworkings cast within. Whether you're Storytelling the effects of magick in the material world, the Umbra or any other reality, that magick may be colored, flavored or otherwise altered by the reality of the world. It's possible for a Euthanatos to bring a Dreamspeaker into the Shadowlands, for instance, but if that Dreamspeaker uses a Life Effect in the midst of the Restless Dead, something's gonna give. Regardless of the actual rules involved, the end result is a conflict of ideals. Conceptualize, and, as always, let the story be your guide.

• Improvisation

A mage's world, like a Storyteller's, is full of surprises. Intent may shape reality, but reality often has its own ideas. Dice rolling is one way to inject this element of uncertainty into the game, but what can you do when a player (or circumstances) comes up with something no rules can cover?

Improvise.

Many questions can be resolved with a little imagination. If all else fails, however, adjust difficulty levels or die pools. Kathy wants her Marauder to cast an Effect while blindfolded? Fine. Just up her difficulty by +2 or +3. Adding or subtracting modifiers for imaginative descriptions can also encourage players to be inventive, although this can get out of hand. The rules in **Chapter Eight** suggest a maximum adjustment of + or -3. You may want to stick to that, if only for your own sanity.

Techniques

Once you've got the basics down, there's still room to grow. After you've structured your plot, established the background and set the characters off and running, certain techniques can enhance the experience. To begin with, a well-done game will have a certain atmosphere that will evoke a particular mood.

Creating Mood and Atmosphere

What characters do is one part of an adventure; what they *feel* is almost as important. Evoking those feelings is achieved with atmosphere. If the cast is at the center of the stage you set, then the atmosphere is the lighting. If it's done badly, everyone will stumble in the dark; if it's too high-key, the actors will sweat and squirm. When designed properly, the atmosphere will convey the proper mood. If there aren't any klieg lights handy, there are other tools you can use to create the mood and atmosphere of a scene:

• Remember All Five Senses

"Virtual" reality is usually a misnomer. An environment isn't virtual unless it draws upon all five senses. Storytellers have known this for millennia. A setting can be something as simple as a mapped-out room, but an atmosphere assaults all the senses at once. An apartment can be described as a room with a kitchen and a bed, but a comfortable apartment might be filled with the aroma of baking cookies, the ambiance of a Tori Amos CD, the invitation of a downy comforter stretched on a luxurious futon, the illumination of black candles and the elegant flavor of the first cup of peppermint tea your host has handed you. The first example is a map; the second example is an environment.

• Use Analogies

If you want to convey a feeling for a scene, incidental events can convey subtle clues to the mood you want to instill. A minor occurrence can be used as an analogy to the mood of a scene. For instance, suppose the atmosphere you wish to create in a scene is one of fragile hope. The setting might be a desolate stretch of roadway at three in the morning. Newspapers drift lazily in a gentle breeze, and moonlight fights to hold back the night. The characters walk past two homeless men rubbing their hands over a small fire. Then one of the characters notices the silhouette of two young lovers holding hands in the distance. In the middle of the street, the two lovers pause, embrace and then walk their separate ways. None of these elements has to be tied to the plot in any way, shape or form, but they contribute to the scene by lending cues. If your players pick up on them, they'll respond by adjusting their roleplaying to fit the mood.

Analogies are also useful when describing the working of a character's "sixth sense" or otherworldly awareness. If a Virtual Adept is using his Spirit Sphere to search a video arcade for pattern spiders, he may very well see blinking webs of energy scintillating like Christmas tree lights, hear inhuman voices intoning repetitive demands for "more quarters," feel a frisson of static electricity and sense a slight ionization in the air. "Spiritual" environments are easier to describe when you can make analogies to what the players already know.

• Vary Tone

The way you use your voice is another cue. This may seem like an obvious remark, but many Storytellers forget about the versatility of the human voice. Softly whispering to draw your player's attention, frantic dialogue to hurry them along, matter-of-fact description to render a scene as sterile or boisterous blustering to describe a rambunctious crowd are but a few examples.

Another effective technique is to use a tone that's the exact opposite of what your players expect. Describing an intimate scene in third person with no embellishment can convey that a supposedly romantic encounter might just be an attempt to manipulate someone. If you're describing a crime scene where a family has been slain, relating the conditions of the children's toys can make the scene far more sinister than the standard clichés associated with gore. Less is indeed more, and an unexpected approach can lend a routine description an intriguing atmosphere.

• Detail Supporting Characters

The detail of supporting characters can also add to the atmosphere of a scene. Any human being has little quirks and foibles that reveal minor bits of his personality. If a minor character is usually identified with a specific location, his little quirks can contain cues about that location. Suppose you want the characters to feel a sliver of pity before they charge into a werewolf caern to steal Quintessence. A brief encounter with Benedict the Bone Gnawer, complete with his mussed-up hair, mindless gum-chewing, worn-out shoes and simple-minded humming, might convince them that the "sacred site" in the middle of the city park is more a place of kindness and comfort than a filling station for wandering wizards. The quirks do the talking in this instance; the werewolf doesn't have to say anything.

Those little cues might also shape a character's view of a group of people. Suppose he looks into the window of a police station secretly run by Iteration X cyborgs. One officer checks his watch every 23 seconds, another restlessly twitches the fingers of his left hand as he stands guard, and a third stares so intensely at the television program he's watching that he forgets to blink. How should the player feel? The cyborgs are, through a few quirks, implied to be impatient, methodical, vigilant and, oddly enough, still a little human. The mood could be described as nervous anticipation or alienation. There's an emotional component to the scene… and that's what mood is all about.

Common Pitfalls

There are a number of ways in which a chronicle can fall apart. A few are worth mentioning here:

• Monster of the Week: The easiest way to bring a group of characters together is to establish a common enemy. There's a wide variety of nasties that lurk in the World of Darkness — mummies, Garou, Black Spiral Dancers, Unseelie fae, spectres, werecats and so on. There's a temptation then to make your campaign a "creature feature" and throw one nifty critter after another at your players.

Remember, however, that there's just as much material for antagonistic characters in the real world. Not every problem in the world has a supernatural conspiracy behind it, and every antagonist you create should have depth. Describing stereotypes is easy. Creating "ethically gray" characters is far more rewarding.

• **Escalation:** Once you've created a massive challenge for your characters, there's always the temptation to top it. Escalating your chronicle quickly won't make it more thrilling, just more difficult to continue. After you've had the characters steal Void Engineer scoutships from a Horizon Construct and firebomb an Urge Wyrm in Malfeas, what do you do for an encore? Trying to outdo the Storytelling equivalent of Industrial Light and Magic isn't much of a challenge. Developing flesh-and-blood characters is.

• **The Drawing of the Dark:** There's a lot of suffering and horror in the world. It's tempting to make your chronicle more compelling by making it darker. However, *making a story darker will not give the story more meaning*. The world tests characters with adversity; the meaning of your story comes from how characters react to it. The darkness is there to give contrast to the light. Roleplaying suicidal remorse or rage is easy. Romance and bliss are far more difficult to convey.

• **Power! Give Me Power!** For some players, simple immortality or the ability to bend reality just isn't enough. Success becomes creating an invincible character. If all the little circles on the sheet work with all the little rules, power gamers are happy. Success, however, isn't measured by the success of individual characters. A hero is someone who takes on something bigger than himself, and making the characters bigger doesn't make the story better. The true success is in telling a compelling story. If your players live to tell stories of turning vampires into lawn chairs and aspire to create mummified vampiric werewolves in their spare time, they've missed the point. Scale down the power level, and focus on real accomplishment instead.

• **The Shattered Cabal:** One cliché in the Storyteller universe is the idea that everyone in your group has to hate everyone else. Amazingly enough, a common definition of "serious" roleplaying is playing a character who treats his friends like garbage. Paranoia is one thing, but "not playing well with others" is quite another. This situation can be complicated by devious Storytellers who simply want to turn the characters against each other. Some troupes can benefit from a little bit of tension between characters, but more important to the game is identifying and strengthening the ties that keep the characters together. Building unity makes for a long-term adventure, not an afternoon of angst.

Stories

Once you've evaluated what you're doing in the long run with your chronicle, it's easier to put your short-term goals into perspective. Keep in mind that you can play a game without committing to a lengthy chronicle. The "one-shot" is an art form all its own. Whether you're planning for a skirmish or a siege, it helps to remember the overarching goals of chronicles and storytelling.

Structure, atmosphere, mood, theme and technique are just as useful in a short chapter as they are in an extended chronicle. Rudimentary as these elements seem, never underestimate the power of the well-timed gust of wind or the melancholy flashback. Storytellers throughout time have known the value of such flourishes.

To begin with, any story has structure. The basic structure of a "chronicle" consists of two steps: a series of chapters (or "sessions") tell a story, and a series of stories compose a chronicle. We tend to favor a literary analogy for this, but any analogy can work. You might choose to see the story as a series of acts, like a play or a television show. Or perhaps the scenes are like sections of a comic book mini-series or a series of movements in a symphony. Use the metaphor that works for you. If you can draw upon your knowledge of another art form, you can develop your understanding of the process of creating stories.

Themes

Theme is one of the hardest things to develop in a story. You don't have to preach when running a story or chronicle, but there are definite themes that will come up in a **Mage** chronicle. You don't have to inspire angels to come down from the heavens to weep tears of blood at the beauty of your story, but a strong theme, or series of themes, will elevate your game beyond a simple cyborg-pounding.

Subtlety works. If we can't sympathize with the motivations of the characters or the antagonists, the story, as one person would say, is "just a bunch of stuff that happened." You can work your chosen themes into the game with characters (whose personalities, motivations or circumstances force the players to think), situations (which put them into dilemmas), relationships (which incorporate both) and symbols, omens or mindscapes which emphasize the theme. Just remember — go easy.

Some common **Mage** themes include:

• **Community**

A sense of community is especially important in this game. The setting for a story emphasizing this type of theme is a spiritually empty area. This can be anything from a few city blocks to an entire country. Someone needs to care for the community, to transform it into a self-supporting and nurturing place. The community must find strength. How much should we suffer for the sake of our society? What can we do to make a community feel like home? What does it take to make us feel like we belong? As the characters find reasons to interact with the world around them, they'll find inspiration, not just reasons to compute Dice Pools.

• **Survival**

A chronicle describing a struggle for survival centers on more than Health Levels and Ability rolls. Existence itself should be a trial. The characters live in a dangerous area, one where survival is a day-to-day crisis. This might be anything from a rough stretch of wilderness to the bad side of town. The world doesn't care whether they live or die, and unless the characters struggle and learn, neat tricks with magickal Spheres won't be enough to save them. This takes more than raw force. In fact, a story centered on survival doesn't have to involve force at all. If you want to make a character's life more difficult, it's more effective to do it through ingenuity than to have someone hit him on the head. There are also other definitions of "survival": What constitutes "selling out?" What compromises do we make in life to get by? Staying alive exacts a price; idealists defy that temptation and succeed in spite of it.

• **Rebellion**

Mages are distinctive because their vision extends beyond the commonplace. Sleepers fall into the misconception that what they see of the world is all that life has to offer. It's human nature to reject what's different. How do the characters counteract that? Nephandi luring mages to destruction and Technomancers abducting deviants are only part of the danger. What happens when a cabal unleashes the power of magick and normal people around them can't accept it? Any mage is a rebel, and rebellion can have dire consequences. The risk is even greater because an Awakened human being doesn't just rebel against conflicting philosophies... he rebels against reality itself.

• **Espionage**

Who can you trust? The Technocracy has spies and agents throughout the world seeking to subvert and infiltrate the Traditions. Those Traditions themselves are not models of cooperation; rival Chantries plot and scheme, Marauders seed chaos where order is strong, and Nephandi convert the powerful into their vile religions. What happens when you can't trust anyone? What happens when paranoia overwhelms reason? If "fighting the bad guys" consisted of toting guns and setting explosive charges, the Ascension War would be easy. In a paranoid world, it's difficult to tell who the "bad guys" are....

• **Sanity**

Through magick, anything is possible, including things that should not be. Mages soon learn that our world is not the only possible one, and that the boundaries of sanity are merely optional. The potential to lose control is there. What exists outside the space and time we know? What happens when the force of the Wyld is released on an unsuspecting world? Is the dynamic always preferable to the static? When the Quiet descends on you, how do you keep yourself from going insane? And who, exactly, are you to judge the difference between madness and reason?

• **Power**

Imagine what it would be like to have the power to change the world — if ordinary people were only pawns, and the world of spirits was your playground, or the powers of science your playthings. Underlying this is a most basic concept: you're only human. We all know the cliché that "power corrupts," but how does it happen? If we all know that this is true, why does it still happen so frequently? There's one more complication: In the world of the game and the real world, you *do* have the power to rebel against the established order. So what are you going to do if you succeed?

• **Identity**

We determine who we are. Society determines who we are. Genetics is allegedly a factor, education and media are supposedly influences, and our social status and the company we keep are theoretically environments that shape how we think, feel, and react. Now consider this: magick makes all things possible. How does that affect (or corrupt) something as fragile and malleable as a human being? In game terms, how much does a Tradition or a mentor define a mage? Then there's the issue of compromise again. Sacrificing for others, compromising for survival and even losing yourself in your love for another person are all threats to the fragile concept we call identity. This type of story takes roleplaying beyond the simple limits of "class," "gender" and other stereotypes. The result is a mirror to the world around us.

Concepts of Mood and Atmosphere

If you're already familiar with White Wolf games, then you've no doubt been inundated with the most common atmosphere used by Storytellers. Yes, darkness is an easy atmosphere to evoke, but that doesn't mean it has to be the only one in your repertoire. A story can have any number of flavors of emotion, and whether you're seasoning a scene or an entire story, you have choices:

• **Basic Black**

The world is just like ours, save for the fact that the shadows are deeper, the suffering is greater, the Earth is dying, and the destruction of all we know is just a whisper away. Skyscrapers tower over the cityscape while the destitute huddle in the shadows praying for a warm night. Set to the accompaniment of screaming guitars, the world is a spiritually empty place where hope is the most valued commodity of all.

Gothic-Punk isn't a mandate. It's an option. Other options include:

• **Energetic**

The characters feel they can do just about anything. If the chronicle or adventure is set in a Horizon Realm or the Otherworlds, this may be they true… Paradox is a temporary setback. Doubt is a passing phase. The biggest challenge for characters in this atmosphere is to keep things under control when they work too well. Remember "The Sorcerer's Apprentice?"

If you choose to set this type of adventure in the "real world," you can evoke this mood by downplaying Paradox a little. After all, Paradox backlash can be customized to the type of game you want to run. If the adventure is set outside the consensual reality paradigm of Sleepers, then a mage can be a useful ally to wraiths or spirits, especially if she's brought her cabal along. Another option is creating little "pockets of surreality" in the real world. In the sanctum sanctorum of a Hermetic mage, activities as simple as sweeping the floor and carrying buckets of water can get out of control if magick is involved. Enthusiasm, encouragement and a rapid pace make a session energetic.

• **Paranoid**

The Technocracy is everywhere. They can listen in on telephones, abduct your friends and brainwash them, turn society against you, track you down like a bad check and convert you to their way of life. And that's just the beginning….

Cryptic clues and events help set up a paranoid campaign. If mysterious events take place and answers aren't forthcoming, even the most stalwart heroes tend to pause before taking any drastic actions. Pay telephones that ring as characters go by, strangers who swear they went to high school with you, shadowy figures on the other side of the street and cryptic remarks from otherwise normal people are a few examples. Exploiting the secrets of the characters, "splitting up the party" and passing secret notes are other time-honored techniques. Even if the characters have Awakened insight, a mage's "sixth sense" doesn't have to give direct answers. Encounters with skeptical or querulous characters, alliances with new-found friends who aren't entirely trustworthy, and situations where the heroes dwell in moral ambiguity help create this atmosphere.

• **Spiritual**

Few Sleepers realize the spiritual potential that surrounds us. A mage is a keeper of mystic secrets and true knowledge. She understands the forces of nature, the elements of the universe, the power of life, the true meaning of death and the secrets of the occult. That also makes her vulnerable to them. Knowledge is found in the real world, but true knowledge lies waiting to be uncovered. Only the visionaries among us can see things as they really are.

Spirit is most easily described in terms of metaphors. A spiritual mood is best evoked by describing events and encounters conceptually, not literally. Since mages have specific talents to guide them toward insight — such as Awareness, the Spirit Sphere and perception-based Effects — feel free to reward players when they choose to use them. For some gamers, the simple experience of having a scene described fully in terms of senses other than sight and sound is enough to liberate them from traditional thinking. Empathic characters also work well in this atmosphere. Any conversation with a member of the supporting cast has an emotional subtext, which means that empathic characters will be playing a slightly different game from other types of characters. If you can multi-task your description of scenes, the environment of a simple encounter can be transformed to a spiritual event.

• **Sensual**

True power comes from passion. Mages are not ethereal creatures removed from reality. They're mortal. While other supernatural beings may have tainted emotions, only a mortal can truly understand anger, lust, envy and fear. The power of reworking reality doesn't have to be an abstract intellectual process. It can instead be the fulfillment of any desire.

The concept of contrasting the exotic with the commonplace is extremely useful in creating this mood. A sensual adventure must keep its ties to the real world. Comparing the ordinary world of Sleepers to the epiphanies of magickal Awakening makes mages more exotic. Even if the characters venture into another world, the real world should be waiting for them upon their return to put things in perspective. Encounters with normal people allow the characters to keep in touch with "human" emotions, and interaction with the awestruck, envious and impressed can make a hero feel "more than human." Acting out the supporting cast in this type of adventure is also easier if you can put a bit of emotive memory or sympathy behind each performance. Make the real world concrete, and the sensual world will be intensified.

• **Tragic**

A tragic mood is often the result of the way a tragic plot is structured. This type of story usually centers around a hero failing despite her best intentions. That hero has an inner flaw that she can't overcome or believes in an ideal that's too lofty — true love, a highly developed sense of honor, or anything else skeptics tell us is a lie. The hero will suffer for the sake of that idea or flaw. Before the hero's ultimate destruction, however, she will usually understand why she failed. This catharsis leads to discovery of the self, and the hero ultimately triumphs even in the midst of failure. A tragic ending is typically bittersweet: if done artfully, the suffering makes it even more beautiful. Points for style. Points for substance. Standing ovation.

• **Fragile Hope**

The Awakened realize the possibilities of life. The Gothic-Punk world is filled with despair and corruption. Many "heroes" are actually tortured souls who spend just as much time fighting their own internal struggles as they do fighting the world around them. Mages don't have the immortality or power of these dark heroes, but they have one huge advantage: they're human. They live in a mortal world where compassion and hope are practical aspects of life, not mere trappings left behind. For mages, however, part of the darkness comes from self-doubt or the results of false pride. Hope is fragile, but it gives courage to those who never give up in the face of adversity.

This slightly ambiguous approach can be aided greatly by dialogues. "Mouthpiece" characters in your supporting cast can help set them in motion. The supporting characters have personality, but also converse with the cabal at length to discuss a particular point of view. An innocent person seeking knowledge can put the heroes in an encounter where they must explain basic ideas in their life. A person driven by guilt or doubt will question the actions of the characters, sparking discussion of the morality and ethics of their actions. Authoritarian figures will demand explanations for a character's actions, forcing him to justify what he has done. The player then analyzes the motivation of his character, turning a series of events into a look in the mirror.

Story Concepts

Now we enter the realm of the single session. There's an endless number of stories you can run, but some ideas are more obvious than others. If you need to prime the pump, the supplements to this rulebook and the suggestions below are good places to start. If you want to begin with the time-honored formulas, that's another option. Hopefully, though, you'll move from the obvious to the innovative. To set you on your way, here are a few simple adventure ideas. Build on them long enough, and you'll make them your own.

- **The Death of a Mentor**

A character's mentor has been slain. The story begins with a recollection of why the mentor was important and may involve a scene or item that conjures images of a message from her. The next step can be a mystery in which the killer is hunted down, a quest that involves finding a lost item that was stolen, a mission of vengeance against the killers, or even revelations about the mentor's true nature. The character's lingering respect for the teacher and thirst for further knowledge open up a variety of story options.

- **Protecting the Neighborhood**

The characters either have a Chantry or have access to a place of importance. The area around this place is threatened by some outsider, either as a result of self-interest or self-preservation, or because the location is a sustaining part of a larger area. The resolution can be anything from taking a stand against the bad guys to journeying into another Realm to recover the ethos that was lost. The problem may be a simple miscommunication, or the outcome may depend on bringing wisdom to the foolish. The reward is gratitude, wisdom, safety or knowledge.

- **Rescuing a Fallen Comrade**

A Chantrymate, acolyte, lover or friend has been captured. This can be the result of anything from a Technocracy operation to a falling-out with a hive of nasties. Stealth, force, reason and ingenuity are possible means to find a solution. There are other potential complications. The victim might be brainwashed, or may have even left of her own volition! This type of adventure can be anything from a tactical exercise to a psychological dilemma.

- **Defeating Your Enemies**

This can involve far more than just stomping bad guys. Traditions have conflicting goals, Chantries have politics, Sleepers act out of ignorance, the world is corrupted with spiritual taint, and even Tradition mages can be corrupted by power. Combat is the most obvious way to solve this type of problem... and the most foolish. A more devious resolution may involve gathering allies, coming to an understanding with antagonists, humiliating enemies to prevent them from acting again, or even converting them to your way of thinking. Posturing and posing is no substitute for showing wit and wisdom.

• **Unleashing Chaos**

Imagination and brilliance are often stifled by stasis or corruption. The solution is chaos. The characters may be in the frame of mind to bring havoc to a place trapped by reason, rescue a mythic creature, bring the force of the Wyld into the world or even journey into the mindscape of someone who has lost the will to keep up the good fight against stasis or entropy. This type of story also has the potential to produce intriguing results: the chaos, once unleashed, may not be easily controlled or contained again.

• **Restoring Order**

Reality has a limit to what it will tolerate. The supernatural, which includes more than just magickal activity, can threaten the safety of Sleepers, or even the world as a whole. One faction's triumph often means the downfall of another. Restoring the balance or bringing order can involve stopping criminal activity, restraining a mage who has lost control, or putting an end to a supernatural or magickal threat. This type of story becomes even more complex if the characters find out that someone who's a perceived "threat" has a reason for placing others in jeopardy....

Variety

I could not believe in a God that could not dance.

— Nietzsche, *Thus Spake Zarathustra*

Having a variety of stories in a chronicle helps to keep it alive. No doubt each player has a particular preference and specialty, so different types of adventures give different players a chance to show off their talents. As long as each hero gets a moment in the limelight, and as long as the overarching theme of the chronicle is preserved, changing your approach for a few sessions will help to make for a dynamic campaign.

A chronicle will cycle through different phases, ranging from the simple and fun to the sublime and mythical. Changing your approach to suit the story makes for an artful chronicle. You might focus on mood and atmosphere to unveil a dark and sinister chronicle, but this task is easier if you occasionally throw in a different type of adventure, whether it's a session cooked for manic chaos or created to bring salvation to a tragic hero. If the last four sessions in a chronicle have been getting progressively more bleak, a session that's fast and furious can bring a welcome respite. If the last session you did was an intense combat session, juxtaposing it against a freeform spiritual journey can keep your players' interest in the overall structure of the chronicle. Challenge yourself. Taking on a variety of new tasks will help you grow as a Storyteller.

The One-Shot

You don't have to put your chronicle in jeopardy to experiment with a different approach. "One-shot" adventures offer opportunities that chronicles don't have. With a one-shot game, you can show off your talent to a new group of players, or give your old ones an opportunity to do something different for an evening.

Although a one-shot chapter can tie in to your regular chronicle, you might decide to do something completely unrelated. It's hard, for instance, to justify tying in your epic adventure of politicians in Doissetep to an adventure set in 17th-century France starring a cabal of Akashic Brothers armed with sabers and dueling pistols. You may not want to bring the troupe's ongoing characters into an adventure in which a pack of shapechanging dinosaurs assault Atlantic City (and you may not want New Jersey to be destroyed in your campaign). No one can live entirely on myth.

There's also a chance to switch to a very different viewpoint in the World of Darkness. Maybe your players should be playing Sleepers for a session... or Technomancers... or whatever. If you begin to feel a tinge of burnout, or if your players get a little restless on a long trip through your chronicle, arrange a vacation in a one-shot adventure.

Advanced Techniques

Only he can command who has the courage to disobey.

— William McDougall

More complicated tricks of the trade can make a story impressive. If you decide to go for a higher level of difficulty, the support of your troupe can make the task much easier. Handling an advanced technique isn't something you do completely on your own — you'll need skillful roleplayers to pull these off. Otherwise, all you'll be doing is talking to yourself. Plan these carefully, execute them gracefully and you'll create a story your players will remember.

Foreshadowing

Timing is everything. Foreshadowing is a part of timing, or, more specifically, a way to subtly introduce something before it happens.

Time magick is an easy way to work foreshadowing in; if a character predicts what happens before it happens, what do you do? The easiest method is to describe foreshadowed events in general terms. Since magick is capricious, the event may very well be in the near future... or further along in the adventure. The complex version of foreshadowing involves playing free will against determinism. If a mage has the ability to predict the future, is she liberating herself with the knowledge or condemning herself to a predicted outcome?

The most useful application of this device is "setting up" an element of your story. When an event is foreshadowed, you may convey a clue, or an emotion, without setting off a full realization of what's going on. The easiest events to foreshadow are dark ones. They're also the easiest events to overemphasize. If the sky turns gray, clouds roll in, a raven lands in front of the characters, and thunder strikes, everyone is pretty much clued in to what's going on. If foreshadowing is cryptic and vague, it's easier to set up anticipation without alarm. If a raven swoops down from a street sign and grabs a newspaper out of a character's hands, how should that character react? Is it just a chance event, or is fate trying to tell the characters that something is at hand? As foreshadowing becomes more subtle, it draws upon other techniques....

Symbolism

Symbolism is another type of metaphor, a very facile one. Having something represent something else is a well-established literary technique, and it's amazing how much impact it can have. On a small scale, you can try to convey an idea without smacking anyone in the forehead. Take the example of the raven swooping from the street sign. How are the mages supposed to interpret that? Are they scrambling for more knowledge than they can use wisely? Is something malevolent going to destroy what they've fought for? Or has a random bird suddenly gained a predilection for newsprint? The player's interests are piqued, and one seemingly random event adds to the mood and atmosphere of the story.

On a grander scale, symbolism is used to address themes and issues. Remember, meaning in a story doesn't have to be an overt message. Moods and themes can be pervasive without being blatantly introduced. Try to figure out what concerns the players personally. What are their fears, needs, desires and loves? Represent these symbolically. This might be an overpowering (and usually unpleasant) experience, or it may be a gentle theme that resonates through the chronicle. When symbolism is used well, it conveys meaning without preaching.

Flashback

Timing is even more critical in a flashback sequence. A flashback is an excellent way to roleplay scenes in a character's past and present a new perspective on a current story. The technique involves constructing an additional storyline. You can either tell the second story directly, or you can have the players roleplay it.

It's even possible to run a flashback story with a second group of characters. The story can be played in a single chapter, or the scenes of the flashback can be interspersed with the scenes of the main story. Regardless of how you structure it, the technique is easier to pull off if the flashback story connects to the main story, preferably by theme, subject or mood. Each story should illustrate an essential feature of the other.

An even harder approach is to have the events of the flashback affect the events of the main story. The players will consciously separate the two groups of characters, but thematically, the mood will carry over between the two stories. This takes a great deal of improvisation, but it makes the story more compelling. Artfully executing this draws upon some of the skills required for the next technique....

Parallel Story

A parallel story, much like a flashback, is played out as a second story alongside the first. However, the second story takes place at the same time as the original one does. Thus, the two stories start out as separate and seemingly unconnected events, but eventually relate to each other. You may not want to conclude the parallel story until near the end of the game session, because that parallel story adds focus to the central story, enhancing its theme and power.

Dream Sequence

Another challenge is to have the players roleplay through a dream of one of the characters, or perhaps one of the cabal's antagonists. This can be done in the same manner as a parallel story or flashback. There are many reasons why you might want to roleplay dreams, but the opportunity to get the players to focus on the personalities of their characters is perhaps the most useful. The dream world draws upon the archetypal and the unconscious. It's an opportunity for mystical revelations, portents, or even communication with something primal. The laws of reality are far more mutable, which gives the Storyteller freedom to deviate from ordinary techniques. Whether you choose to see dreams as a spiritual Realm, a potential weapon, a gateway to another reality or a type of mental manipulation, dreams open a variety of opportunities for innovative Storytellers.

Alternative Settings

One strength of **Mage** is the vast and varied amount of background available. Not every game has to be a mystical trip through '90s technopunk. This book has an essential framework well-suited to a basic game. It can also be used to launch cutting-edge stories and innovative interpretations. The one-shot is ideal for this type of work; it doesn't place an ongoing chronicle in jeopardy, and gives everyone a breather if a chronicle is getting intense. The Storyteller can disregard the game's continuity for a session and radically change her approach to using the rules, if she likes, and players can take a break from their usual characters. If the experiment is a smashing success, it may even lead to a second chronicle (run by you or somebody else) or vastly alter your main storyline.

Most of the material in this book is based on the assumption that the average game will start in the late 20th or early 21st century in a world much like ours with standards similar to ours. There are, of course, other possibilities.

- **Historical Settings**

Mage has a heavy emphasis on history **(see Chapter Three)**. The most common use of history is background; it justifies the present and gives the players a sense of the world. However, it's just as possible to run a game set earlier in history. It might tie into the background of your ongoing chronicle, or may explore an alternate history. What was it like to live in a world where the Mythic Age was dying? How did the hidden art of magick influence the Renaissance? How did the Victorian Era change when the Technocracy was first formed? Were the 1930s a Golden Age for the Sons of Ether? How did the Technocracy affect the Cold War? Where will the World of Darkness be in the near future?

There are certainly many supplements dealing with these issues, but how you choose to interpret the answers is up to you. History is a set of guidelines for you to accept or reject. Whether you choose to set an entire chronicle in another era, link series of historical adventures with a continuing group of characters, or alter the past to affect the present, history can easily be another playground for your imagination.

- **Imaginary Settings**

One world is never enough. **Mage** has a complete background, but the system can be used for just about anything. Take a trip through your bookshelf. Have you worn out your copy of the *Dictionary of Imaginary Places?* Are your *Calvin and Hobbes* books getting severely dog-eared? Is there a notebook for a campaign you ran 10 or 20 years ago buried under your bed? With magick, all things are possible.

The details of the **Mage** background are, ultimately, only guidelines. If you want, reject the entire background, or set it aside. You may get strange looks if you tell other gamers that your chronicle is based on a popular fantasy trilogy, or that you're drawing maps of Atlantis for your dolphin characters in Ascension Under the Waves, but as long as you can find a troupe that's willing to follow you there, the worlds you describe in the privacy of your own home are your own damn business.

- **Otherworldly Settings**

The World of Darkness consists of many spirit Realms. **Werewolf** contains a great deal of information about the Umbra of the Garou, and **Wraith** unleashes revelations about the Shadowlands of the Restless Dead. Both worlds are detailed in **Mage** as well. If you're quite adventurous, you can set an entire chronicle outside the mortal world. It's difficult, but do-able. With the Sphere of Spirit, a mage of the appropriate paradigm can travel just about anywhere.

Cross-Over

These techniques can also be used in conjunction with other games. Shifting the point of view adds a whole new tilt to your story. Any city will have a number of supernatural problems. If one Storyteller runs the chronicles, the players may have characters from different Storyteller games in their stable. One week, a Chantry of mages might be investigating a spiritual attack on their city; the next, the Chantry's Dreamspeaker might work with a pack of Garou in the Umbra to solve another aspect of the same problem. If more than one Storyteller is involved, each can work as a specialist for a different background. Troupe Storytelling works just as well when each contributor specializes in a different game. **Mage** can be run in conjunction with any other Storyteller game. If a Euthanatos leaves the Chantry for a month, she might show up in another player's **Wraith** game or a brief **Vampire** adventure. For further ideas, see **Chapter Nine**.

Resolution

No story is complete without a resolution. The events of the story may have loose plot threads, and the antagonist may not be utterly defeated, but the story can still end with a sense of completion. A chronicle must reach some resolution as well. In the ideal chronicle, that resolution comes when the meaning behind the series of stories is crystal clear. Not every chronicle reaches that apex, or has to, for that matter, but completion brings a sense of accomplishment and satisfaction.

Some Storytellers get lost along the way. Branching out further and further from the original chronicle concept is a common distraction. This is a valid approach, but maintaining a clear focus can ensure the chronicle's longevity. The alternative can be a growing sense of obligation to resolve *every* plot thread, no matter how minor. One lesson bears repeating, then: depth is richer than detail.

Remember one key concept: the main characters are the core of the stories you tell. In this game, and the others in the series, there's a heavy emphasis on defining and developing a character. If a player can sympathize with that character and make her "real," then the character resembles a real person. And a real person never stops learning and never stops growing.

Of course, while stories resolve, even a completed chronicle can still go further. If your characters stayed at the center of the chronicle, any resolution you give is, in essence, a temporary one. If you care about the characters, there are always new directions in which you can take them. If a character has ideals, she can always a way to refine those ideals further. So long as your characters have authenticity, a chronicle may continue, even long after you've set it aside...

...and if you take the strength of idealism and the energy of telling a story back with you into the real world, there will always be a way in which to draw upon that, even long after the game has been set aside.

To summarize, then. When telling a story, follow a few basic principles:

Create myth. Inspire ideals. Entertain. Summon darkness. Intensify light. Evoke passion. Use empathy. Guide the story. Defy reality.

The rest is just details.

Book Three: The Machine

The Cyborg

<<REALITY DEVIANT SPOTTED
COORDINATES: 4629°N—3649°V—4562°H
INITIATE TERMINAL MEASURES>>

Something moved among the stinking rubbish heaps. X344 jerked his head to the side, shining a blast of pure white light into the alleyway. Rain broke the light at random intervals. On command, his field neutralizer systems kicked on, giving him some measure of protection against incoming procedures.

The fugitive, however, remained hidden.

<<SCAN??>> He inquired. The tracking system responded with a barrage of feed-grids punched through rapid-read. Nothing.

<<INFRARED/ULTRAVIOLET/HEAT. GO>> he ordered the internal machine. It cycled through the obvious scan combinations, tracking across the filthy alley. An ant-tickle of sweat crept from X344's forehead, marching down his face. He willed himself not to move, not to betray his presence with a careless wipe.

The enemy would not show himself. Had the computer made an error?

<<ALERT!
DISTURBANCE OVERHEAD!>>

A slight ripple coursed across X344's scalp and neck. He dodged to the side as a blast of sudden flame burst from the sky, impacting where the cyborg had stood. He landed wetly in the muddy trash. The cardboard made a mushy sound as the boxes gave way, drenching him in reeking filth.

Suddenly the filth was alive.

At first, X344 mistook the wail for a distant siren; the screeching ululation should not have come from any human's throat. As the sodden trash took on a single, malicious life and slammed him to the pavement, the cyborg realized that the deviant — wherever it was — was summoning some extra-dimensional obscenity.

All sensors went haywire; the neutralization systems sizzled as animate cardboard slapped him with rusted metal and blades of glass. Bits of rancid food slid from the golem's paws as X344 rolled to the side, struggling to rise from the puddled alley floor.

<<INITIATE PLASMA SEQUENCE 435X4>> A whirring hum and reality ripple were the machine's reply.

<<PARADOX EFFECT PROBABILITY?>>

23.04678% ENGAGE?

<<HELL, YES!>>

Life was full of chances. The deviant had gone vulgar. Two could play that game, though, and X344 was not about to roll over and die.

IF OUR WAYS SCARE

you [illegible] perhaps [illegible]

should ask yourself why..

Is it OUR passion

that [illegible] you

or your own?

Chapter Eight: Magick Rules

To work magic is to weave the unseen forces into form; to soar beyond sight; to explore the uncharted dream realm of the hidden reality;... to be both animal and god. Magic is the craft of shaping, the craft of the wise, exhilarating, dangerous — the ultimate adventure.

— Starhawk, *The Spiral Dance*

War

"I can't believe it's come to this," whispered Clarissa as she looked across the empty dance floor at Peter Kobie. Light from the club's glitterball reflected dim light on their faces.

"Believe it, babe," he grinned. "You know, you always were my favorite groupie. I hope this won't be too hard on you."

"I was your student. Your apprentice. Your lover," she countered, moving closer to him.

"Stand right where you are," Peter shouted, and Clarissa obeyed, unable to move. Desperately, she thought of anything she could do against his years of wisdom, his ability to know her thoughts even before she did. He laughed as he circled her. As she watched him move, she caught his reflections in the large mirrors all around the bar. The way the mirrors hung, it looked as if there were a half-dozen Peter Kobies standing there. Clarissa smiled.

As she acted, she knew there would be a terrible price to pay. But the backlash might be worth it. At her beckoning, the myriad reflections from the glitterball caught her image and splashed it onto the mirrors, reflecting an infinite number of Clarissas around the bar and dance floor. His concentration broken, Kobie thrashed out, seeking his former student's true form. But the ghostly images laughed at him, mocking him, as Clarissa herself fled for the door, her face wet with tears at leaving behind the love she'd once known.

True Magick alters reality through enlightened force of will. Whatever a mage wishes to be *will* be if he has the knowledge, skill and luck to pull it off. The static limitations of magic with a "c" do not apply to willworkers, who rework reality by desire, not by rote. Though the True Mage risks Paradox backlashes for changing things too suddenly, the Tapestry is literally at his fingertips.

The rules for magick in **Mage** are also free-form — there are no lists of spells, components or necessary rituals. Each mage tailors reality to his or her design; the specifics of an Effect's form rest within his personal style, not in some arbitrary spell list. Although this chapter does offer a variety of magickal Effects, **Mage** characters are not limited to them. The spells your character casts are his own. The only limitations within this system are those of the character's knowledge and skill (his Sphere ratings and Arete), the boundaries of reality (reflected by Paradox and the restrictions of the Spheres) and the good sense and imagination of your group.

This last element cannot be overstated; one power-hungry or unimaginative player can ruin everybody's game. **Mage** is designed for maximum storytelling potential, not for chart-checking or rules-mangling. The spirit of the game is ruined (though some themes, perhaps, are reinforced) when one or two players either sit the game out or deliberately pervert these rules. Magick should be — *must* be — an Art, not a list of powers. Players and Storytellers alike are advised to let imagination, balance and a sense of drama guide their magicks.

Some Things to Know

A few key concepts could use some explanation before get to the nuts and bolts of the system itself. These concepts aren't rules in and of themselves, but they will make understanding the rules a bit easier.

The Cinematic Example

Coincidence can be a tricky thing to define. The Technocratic paradigm dominates, but does not rule, reality. There remain places where mystick Arts carry more weight than technomagick. For simplicity's sake, assume the boundaries of local reality have the "give" of some types of movies. **(The Geographical Magick and Influence section tells which areas fall under which categories.)**

In places where the scientific mode of reality defines coincidence, assume that you can get away with small acts of coincidence, like those in the average action-adventure film (*Rambo, You Only Live Twice, Die Hard*, etc.). Some outrageous acts are possible, but those with some apparent base in technology can go a bit further than ones that come from nowhere.

Low-key fantasies, like the *Terminator* and Indiana Jones films demonstrate the upper limits of coincidence where high technology or mysticism holds sway. In these places, some obviously extraordinary actions *may* be accepted without much risk *if* they conform to the local beliefs.

Wild fantasy films — *Star Wars, Big Trouble in Little China, Willow, Highlander*, etc. — go over the edge. Such activities are vulgar anywhere in the material world, and will always involve some risk to a mage who performs them. Earth's reality is just too static to accept this much tampering, and may react accordingly.... **(See "Paradox.")**

Paradigm and Style

Mages *are* magickal, so it is a disservice to the character and to the story to describe a wizard calling elemental vengeance from the skies with, "I'm using Forces 2, Prime 2, to blast him with a lightning bolt." Dramatic (and consistent) descriptions of your mage's willworkings involve more than just good roleplaying; they require some idea about the character's beliefs.

Say the mystick in question was a Hermetic Master; he might inscribe an ornate circle with a specially prepared knife or bit of chalk, then call upon the secret name of the Archangel Gabriel. An aboriginal Dreamspeaker might enter a trance and summon angry spirits to smite his foe, while a Son of Ether would pull out his meteorological acceleration ray, aim it at the sky and pull down some charged electrons. An Iteration X HIT Mark would not even bother with the sky; he would simply point his cybernetic electron gun at his enemy and blast her to cinders. Four paradigms, four styles. Two would be vulgar under most circumstances, while the fourth would usually be considered coincidental, and the third would be open for debate. All four mages, however, have used the same Effect, with different results.

Determining your mage's style is essential in the beginning. The character's philosophy will govern his magick — not only how it appears, but how it is performed and what it can and cannot do. As a mystick learns more about the subjective nature of reality, his understanding expands to the point where he does not need a style — he realizes that all styles are indeed one. At that point, he can choose to cast aside the rituals and objects of power he once used **(see "Foci")**. Even after he reaches this realization, he may still use that familiar style to focus his intentions better — i.e., he may gain an additional modifier when casting a spell. Up until that point, however, a mage's Art, and the way he uses it, depends upon his style.

The "Storytelling Magick" section later in this chapter will go over the subject in more detail, but for now, keep your character's view of magick in mind when using it. A sorcerer's paradigm can often spell the difference between coincidental and vulgar magicks. And that makes all the difference in the world for a mage who wishes to survive!

Coincidental and Vulgar Magicks

Reality, being fluid, will flow more easily through a subtle channel (coincidental magick) than through a sudden breakwater (vulgar magick). A wise mage uses the normal flow of events to mask her magick; simply yanking the Tapestry's threads out is asking for trouble.

Coincidental magick is magick that could pass for some normal occurrence. The mage may know that she's casting an Effect, but someone watching would see something that could conceivably happen. Exactly what things could "conceivably happen" depends on the form the magick takes and what the observer will accept.

If your mage's Effect seems coincidental — a sudden Life-induced sneeze that just *happens* to distract a guard, a blast of energy that just *happens* to come from some high-tech weapon — your magick will be easier to cast and less likely to cause Paradox.

Vulgar magick is obviously extraordinary and wrenches reality out of joint. Even if a mage works vulgar magick in secret, that magick becomes more difficult than if he did something coincidental. If he does it out in the open, in front of Sleepers, it gets downright risky.

As you can see, it's in a mage's best interest to couch her Art in some way that disturbs reality as little as possible. Sometimes, however, pride, desperation or stupidity make a mystick push her luck. She may get away with it; then again, she may not....

Creating Magickal Effects

You sealed your doom
Your time has come
YHVH
So it is done
So. It. Is. Done!
— Plasmatics, "Incantation"

Although their Awakening tells them otherwise, mages know they are bound by certain limitations when they work their Art: the current of reality, which is not altered easily, the modern disbelief in miracles and their own limited understanding of the world around them. These boundaries are not solid walls, merely obstacles. Cleverness and confidence are essential when a mage casts an Effect. The latter is usually expressed in the beliefs and style which guide her magick; the former is common sense. It is almost always easier to go with the flow than to resist it.

Despite a variety of modifiers, the core of the **Mage** magick system is simple:

• **Step One:** Decide what you want to do and how.

• **Step Two:** Check to see if your character knows how to do what you want her to accomplish.

• **Step Three:** If your character has the know-how, roll her Arete verses the given difficulty (usually the highest Sphere +3, 4 or 5). If you succeeded, find out what happened. If not, same thing.

• **Step Four:** Reap the benefits or consequences of your actions.

That's it. The rest is window dressing.

This system works off of the idea that magickal feats rearrange reality. The more reality you try to change at once, the harder your feat will be to accomplish. Mundane Effects are easy, and bigger ones take more time and effort to pull off. Really earth-shattering Effects remain possible, but the mage attempting them had better be clever, skillful and lucky. Sudden changes are also possible — they're just riskier and more difficult, and the consequences of failure become more severe. (There's a metaphor here; take from it what you will.)

The chart on page 169 presents this process in shorthand. Here, we'll go through the rules step by step. Few of them will apply to every casting. Once your troupe understands these basic rules, magickal Effects will go quickly and with a minimum of hassle.

Some of the rules below are optional only; these Storyteller-governed possibilities have asterisks near their headings.

Step One:

What Do You Want to Do and How?

First, decide what you want your character to do and how you want him to do it. This involves both roleplaying and judgment.

Description

Describe the Effect your mage is trying to perform. How does it look? What did she do to make it happen? Did she simply snap her fingers, or did she lay out an elaborate ceremonial circle, call the corners and chant an invocation to the Goddess? This step is mostly roleplaying, but will make all the difference in the long run, and will make for a more exciting story as well. **(See "Storytelling Magick.")**

The way the mage casts his magick will have a lot to do with the base difficulty of the roll. If he uses coincidental magick, or at least avoids showing off too much for the Sleepers, that difficulty will decrease. If he casts his Art under unusual circumstances, the difficulty goes up. If he ties to do something really monumental — causing an earthquake, let's say — he may need to use an extended roll **(see Chapter Five)** to do it. In this case, the difficulty increases, but any successes rolled count towards the total. A botch wipes the whole thing out.

Simultaneous Effects

A mage can cast only one Effect per turn, even if she has used Time magicks to speed herself up (reality is already "preoccupied" when it's in a different time frame). She can keep as many Effects "running" at one time as she wants, though it becomes more and more difficult to do (+1 additional difficulty for every two Effects in use).

Casting Time

A spell may take as little or as much time as the mage requires to cast it. Elaborate preparations may modify the difficulty **(see below)**, although some forms of magick, like Hermetic high magick or spirit-channeling, might demand extra time by their very nature. In this case, there is no modifier unless the mage takes time and effort above and beyond the usual requirements **(see "Foci," under "Storytelling Magick.")**.

Helpful Terms

This chapter addresses the rules of True Magick. The concepts behind those rules are explained in greater detail in Book One, Chapter Four. Restating a few terms, however, might be helpful to new players:

• **Arete:** The combination of enlightenment and will that allows a mage to perform magick.

• **Sphere:** One of the nine commonly understood elements of reality.

• **Effect:** The result of some magick being used ("A Forces 4 Effect"); also, a rote that uses only one Sphere.

• **Conjunctional Effect:** An Effect which uses more than one Sphere ("Forces 3, Life 2") at once.

• **Rote:** A famous Effect that has gone into general usage. Also called a *procedure* by the Technocrats.

• **Coincidental magick:** An Effect that could be accepted as normal, if unusual, by a mundane observer.

Examples: Strapping on a jet pack; influencing a cab driver to pick you up with Mind magick; firing a blast ray from a high-tech pistol; healing a sick man through the power of God.

• **Vulgar magick:** An Effect that obviously defies reality as we know it.

Examples: Flying through the air without assistance; creating a cab out of thin air; conjuring a ball of fire and throwing it; closing an open wound with a pass of your hand.

Step Two:
Do You Know Enough to Do What You Wanted?

In this step, figure out if your character can do what you wanted him to do, and whether or not he's successful.

The Spheres

The mystick Spheres reflect a mage's understanding of reality's elements. The more he knows about a given thing, the higher his Sphere rating will be. Provided he knows what he's doing, a mage can do anything his Sphere rating allows him to do.

The parameters of what the Spheres can and cannot do are covered at the end of this chapter.

Mundane Knowledge (*)

Some really complicated feats — like creating a functioning computer from scratch — may require some mundane knowledge in addition to the magickal know-how. In the case of the instant computer described below, Cheshire's Storyteller may demand that he have the Technology and Computer Knowledge Traits before he could create a working laptop; merely understanding the principles of Matter will not tell you how such a complex device functions. Without some grounding in computer technology, Cheshire's laptop will look nice and may even run, but it won't be compatible with other computers or software, and anything other than simple equations will be beyond it.

Most magicks are simple enough to be done without special skills; only truly complex feats demand such knowledge. Storytellers should let common sense, rather than hard rules, dictate when and how mundane Knowledges would be necessary. Although really advanced feats — like creating a computer — might demand three or more dots in a particular Trait, no roll is needed.

Common mundane skills include Technology, Culture, Firearms, Repair, Cosmology, Computer, Medicine, Expression and Science. Feats which might require mundane Knowledges include creating nuclear weapons (Technology, Science: Physics and Metallurgy), living clones (Medicine, Science: Biology) or working cars (Technology, Repair); re-configuring a person's psyche (Intuition, Expression and maybe Science: Psychology); creating a book (Culture, Expression) or stylish clothes (Etiquette, Culture); and summoning an archangel or mythic creature (Cosmology, Enigmas and maybe Occult).

Using a Trait (*)

Mages can also utilize their skills to make their magicks easier **(see "Permutations")**. For now, just remember that such actions take place during this step.

Step Three:
Did You Succeed?

Did it work? If so, how well? Did it fail? If so, how badly? This step involves the success — or lack thereof — of the character's magickal feat.

The Roll

Roll your mage's Arete for his magickal Effect roll. The more dice you roll, however, the greater the chance for a botch. Think of this as a reflection of the pitfalls of pride — if you only need to expend a small amount of power to accomplish something, throwing everything you have behind it may be like using a bazooka to kill a fly. Overkill works, no doubt, but often leaves more fallout than a small and precise effort would have caused.

Someone with a high degree of enlightened will knows when to use it and when not to. A smart mage, then, will use as little force as necessary to accomplish a given end. Under stress, he still has a lot of power to call upon. Magickally changing clothes, however, does not require a lot of Arete. Using your entire Dice Pool to do it would be a bit excessive and may be asking for trouble.

Difficulty

A mystick's magickal difficulty is based on the way she chooses to cast her Art. Magick which stirs the pot a little bit — like conjuring a powerbook from inside a case or overcoat — is not difficult to use. Things get harder if the spell obviously defies what most people would consider possible — creating the computer from thin air, for instance. If some un-Awakened person is watching, the "weight" of his disbelief makes the feat harder still.

Modifiers **(see below)** can adjust this base difficulty to some degree.

• *Coincidental magick's* base difficulty is the highest Sphere used in the Effect + 3. If Cheshire pulled the powerbook from his coat — a coincidental Matter 4, Forces 3, Prime 2 spell — his base difficulty would be 7.

• *Vulgar magick without a Sleeper witness* begins with a difficulty of the highest Sphere + 4. If Cheshire's magick was vulgar — he created the powerbook right in his hand — but no un-Awakened person was around to see it, his difficulty would be 8.

• *Vulgar magick with witnesses* uses the highest Sphere + 5. Say Cheshire created the computer in plain sight of mundane observers; his base difficulty would be 9.

• *Even if it succeeds,* a vulgar Effect earns one point of Paradox. This usually "bleeds off" over time; accumulating too much Paradox too quickly, however, is asking for trouble.

Modifiers

A variety of circumstances — from high-stress situations to elaborate rituals — can make magickal feats harder or easier to perform. The **Magickal Difficulties** chart lists many such modifiers.

Reality has a somewhat consistent base, if for no reason other than game balance. Assume that no modifier can add to or reduce a difficulty by more than three places, total (+/- 3). Thus, no matter what Cheshire did, the minimum difficulty to create a computer out of thin air would be 4 and the maximum would be 10.

To avoid complication, we recommend using only one or two modifiers at a time. Too many at once can slow the game down.

How Many Successes Do I Need?

For the most part, the size and complexity of a magickal feat determines the amount of successes needed to accomplish it. The **Magickal Feats** table offers a few examples, along with the successes needed to accomplish each act.

• In general, assume that an Effect which alters *only* the mage herself — **Multi-Tasking, Past/Future Sight**, self-healing, all first-rank sensory magicks, shapeshifting, etc. — needs only one or two successes to perform. You have no one to convince but yourself.

• An action which affects another existing object or being — whether it's a telepathic link, **Possession**, transformation, raw damage, whatever — needs at least two successes to have any sort of impact. Any less and the magick simply washes around the target's pattern, unable to affect it.

• A spell which affects the world around the mage — conjuration, weather control, **Stepping Sideways**, channeling Quintessence, creating new life forms or phenomena, etc. — may demand anywhere from one to 30 successes, depending on the nature of the magick. Creating a flame on the tip of your finger is easy; pulling the moon out of orbit is not.

Success, Effect and Interruptions

Most Effects are pretty straightforward — either you succeed or you do not. Examples include changing your own shape, magickal brainwashing, conjuring or creating some being or object out of thin air, or passing through the Gauntlet and into the Umbra. Such all-or-nothing magicks demand a certain amount of successes be rolled before the spell takes effect. Simple actions are easy; more complicated ones may take time and effort, i.e., extended rolls, to complete. The **Degrees of Success** table handles these cases.

Other spells are cast with an immediate intent in mind — to cause or heal damage, to sense some property or element, to influence somebody's mind or change some object's shape, etc. The amount of damage, benefit or influence you exert depends on how well you roll. The better you roll, the more effect the magick has. The same goes for duration; the better the roll, the longer the Effect lasts. See the **Damage and Duration** table in these situations.

If an all-or-nothing action (i.e., igniting a gas main) also does damage or lasts for a while, use the **Damage and Duration** table to find out just how much it inflicted or how long it lasts. Base the result on the number of successes you rolled.

Under ideal circumstances, a mage will be able to take however long he needs to work his Art. In combat or other stressful conditions, however, he may be interrupted before he can finish what he was doing. If someone stops the mage before he gathers the successes he needs, assume that the magick has only limited effect, like a partial success, or that it is completely lost due to interference. Damage, in this case, would be based on the successes that had been rolled *before* the disruption.

Rituals and Extended Magick Rolls

A mage can accomplish most feats with little difficulty (one to five successes). However, some magicks are so complicated or powerful that the caster must take extra time to succeed. In story terms, she has to work some magickal ritual; in game terms, her player must make an extended roll, gathering enough successes to finish the job.

Magicks which might require extended rolls include summonings, complex creations, weather-witchery, strong curses, Correspondence searches, Node drainings, Horizon Realm creations and other powerful acts of will. The Storyteller may decree that one roll may take game-time hours instead of turns, depending on the magick involved.

The essential rules for extended rolls can be found in **Chapter Five**. Extended magick rolls work the same way, with the following qualifications:

• Paradox "stacks" during an extended ritual; the bigger the magick, the nastier the potential backlash. Each roll after the first adds one more Paradox point to a backlash's total. If Atropos botches a vulgar Entropy 4 Effect after three turns of extended rolls, she "wins" seven Paradox if she was acting alone and 12 if she cast the ritual in public.

• If the player fails a roll — that is, she gets no successes that turn — she may still continue rolling, at +1 difficulty (per failure), until the ritual is completed or the magick is somehow disrupted.

• If the roll botches, the caster may spend a turn and a Willpower point to avoid screwing up the whole affair. By spending the Willpower, she keeps the magick going — barely — but loses one previously-rolled success in the process as well as the Willpower point. From there, she must roll at +1 difficulty until she finishes.

A second botch will utterly destroy the Effect and bring Paradox crashing down on the caster.

• If the ritual is disrupted by an outside force — like an attack or a distraction — the caster must make a Willpower roll at difficulty 8 or botch the whole Effect.

Rituals are best performed in secret, with elaborate preparations to reduce the difficulty of the roll. Even then, the difficulty cannot be reduced by more than -3.

Automatic Successes

An Adept can do simple things with little trouble. If she wants to perform some Effect which requires only one or two successes — lighting a pipe with sudden flame, levitating a book across the room, "turning on" a sensory Effect, changing the color of her eyes, etc. — she may do it without a roll if her Arete is at least one point above the necessary difficulty. Coincidental first rank Effects, for example, would require an Arete of at least five, second rank needs six, third requires seven, and so forth. Such "instant magicks" would not last long — a turn or two — but may work long enough to get the job done.

To speed play, a Storyteller may just decide to allow her player characters to automatically succeed with simple spells regardless of their Arete, if they have the Spheres to do so. This will, of course, depend on the Effect, the circumstances and the player. Attacks, complex creations, forgeries or vulgar acts in plain sight should never be allowed under this *optional* rule, and abusive players should lose the option completely. At the same time, you may wish to forgo rolling every time a character uses **Sense Life** or pulls out a business card that just *happened* to be in her jacket pocket.

Using Willpower

Since magick is, by nature, an effort of will, the Willpower Trait comes in handy when casting it. Both applications use temporary Willpower points, not permanent ones. **(Willpower and Quintessence are described in Chapter Six.)**

• By spending a point of Willpower, the mage can get one automatic success on his magick roll.

• Through sheer will, a mystick can undo a magickal botch by spending a Willpower point to counteract it. This does not give the mage a success — his spell still falters — but it shields him from a Paradox backlash.

Using Quintessence

By channeling Prime Essence through his Art, a mage can reduce his difficulty by up to -3 points. This works like any other modifier, but lasts as long as the willworker continues to use Quintessence. If Cheshire focuses Quintessence from a nearby Node, he can use up to three points of it per turn, reducing his difficulty by -3 each turn, until he either stops or runs out of juice.

A mage can use whatever personal Quintessence he has to do this. Using outside Quintessence — Tass, Nodes, etc. — this way requires an additional use of Prime 3. Once this Effect is cast, it needs no additional attention for its duration. **(See both "Duration," below, and "Simultaneous Magick," above.)**

The Domino Effect

Wise mages who wish to avoid the nasty consequences of Paradox will attempt to disguise their magick in coincidental Effects. As the number of wild "coincidences" rise, however, they become harder to pull off. As an optional rule, a Storyteller can impose an additional +1 difficulty to coincidental magick difficulty rolls for every two such Effects over the first that scene.

The effects of this penalty are cumulative; after five coincidental magick Effects the difficulty for such magick increases by +2. Storytellers should only count those Effects which cause some massive change — pipes bursting, tires going flat, exploding ammo dumps, etc. Coincidences that no one sees — sensory magick, Attribute increases, objects disappearing into pockets, etc. — should not increase the difficulty at all.

Step Four:
What Happened?

So you've cast your spell. Whether or not it worked, the magick will probably have some effect. This step tells you what those effects might be.

Range, Damage and Duration

The general effects of magickal feats are based on the successes rolled:

• Under most circumstances, a mage's Arts can affect anything within her normal sensory range. Subjects on the edges of that range — far away, under cover or obscured by smoke, fog or other obstructions — add +1 to the magick roll's difficulty. Correspondence magick can dramatically expand the mystick's sensory range. A mage with less than three dots in that Sphere, however, must cast long-distance Effects at +1 difficulty due to her inexperience with such extended perceptions. The Correspondence Sphere must be used if an Effect is supposed to bypass a solid object in between the mage and his target.

As a quick and dirty rule, figure that a spell can affect one subject within easy reach per success, unless it includes some large area by its very nature — an explosion, a TV broadcast, a user-linked network, etc.

• *Damage* — or benefit — is figured by multiplying your successes as per the **Damage and Duration** chart. If Atropos, for example, rolls two successes with a Life-based attack, she inflicts two Health Levels of damage against the unfortunate Man in Black she assaulted. If she rolled three successes instead, she would multiply her three successes by two, for a total of six Health Levels of damage. If she were healing damage instead, the benefit would be the same, i.e., six Health Levels. This works the same way for damage, healing, channeling Quintessence, etc.

• Like damage, an Effect's *duration* is based on the chart results. This usually applies only for magicks that could last a while, i.e., sensory magicks, Mind Effects, shapeshiftings, transmutations, etc. Damage is usually immediate, while created, summoned or conjured items are often permanent.

Some Spheres, by their nature, add or subtract successes whenever they're used. *Forces* Effects add one success when used for damage, *Mind* attacks subtract one success when used to inflict damage, while *Entropy* itself does *no* damage until the fourth rank. Until then, it can only inflict indirect damage by causing objects to fall or blows to hit weak points.

Other Spheres have specialized uses. *Correspondence* magick works across great distances. Use the **Correspondence Range** chart to find out how many successes a mage needs to link two places, people or items together. *Spirit* Effects must often work against the Gauntlet, and the strength of this barrier varies from place to place. Use the **Gauntlet** chart when some Effect must pierce it to work. With *Time*, a mystick can look across different time spans. Use the **Time Sphere** chart to figure out how far in the future — or past — a Time Effect can see.

These modifications apply whenever the Sphere is used in a simple or conjunctional Effect.

Most magicks fade or need to be replenished over time. Truly permanent results are possible, but Storyteller's may require twice the usual successes to make them so.

• Combining damage with duration — that is, inflicting damage over a period of time — can be done *at Storyteller's option* by adding the necessary successes together. If Atropos wanted to continue hurting the Man in Black, she could add the amount of damage she wanted to do (six Levels, or three successes) to the length of time she preferred — over one day, or three more successes, for a total of six successes needed. This is an *optional rule* which adds flexibility at the risk of complication or rules abuse.

• Any physical attack which attacks a pattern with another pattern — a lightning bolt, magick bullet, mutant virus, etc. — can be *soaked* by the target. Vulgar acts of pure magick, which attack a pattern on a purely mystickal level — transformations, **Rip the Man-Body**, **Flames of Purification**, etc. — cannot be soaked, nor can mental attacks.

Most magickal attacks cause normal damage; the **Aggravated Damage** chart illustrates more severe injuries. **(See "Injury" in Chapter Nine for types of damage.)**

Dodging and Resistance

A target who is aware of an incoming magickal attack may choose to dodge it (if the attack is material) or resist it (if it involves the Mind). The first requires a Dexterity + Dodge roll; the second, a Willpower roll. The difficulty of either avoidance is 6. Like any other form of dodge, each success the defender rolls to avoid an attack subtracts one from the aggressor's magick successes.

• Direct attacks — lightning bolts, falling buildings, blasts of energy, bullets, hails of stones and such — can be dodged like any other physical assault, so long as the victim knows the attack is coming. Most direct assaults are visible; invisible ones can still be detected with a Perception + Awareness roll, difficulty 8.

• Mental attacks — commands, possessions, mind crushes, telepathic bonds, brainwashing, etc. — can be countered by a Willpower roll if the defender is aware of what's going on. This often makes Mind magick a slow and subtle Art.

Countermagick

Essentially, *countermagick* is a soak roll used for undoing magickal Effects, *anti-magick* channels Prime to cancel out an Effect, and *unweaving* takes an existing spell apart. All of them require a one-turn action. **(The details about countermagick, anti-magick and unweaving are in the "Permutations" section.)**

The basic systems are as follows:

• *Countermagick* requires an Arete roll, difficulty 7. Each countermagick success cancels out one of the opponent's magickal successes.

• *Anti-magick* "washes out" an Effect by using Quintessence to "strengthen" reality against the opponent's desires. A mystick using anti-magick rolls her Prime rating as a Dice Pool; the difficulty is 8, and each success raises the opponent's magick difficulty by +1 that turn. This can exceed the usual +3 limit. Each success canceled costs a point of Quintessence from the mage's reserve.

• *Unweaving* is an attack upon an existing Effect. By rolling her Arete against difficulty 8, a mage may cancel out one success in the Effect for every success she wins. This takes one turn per roll; a botch during unweaving means the mage must begin again from scratch.

Any of these actions, if successful, might cancel out or dilute a mystick spell.

Failure

When the player rolls less successes than she needed to execute her Effect, or if her mage is restrained or incapacitated before she can finish it, the magick fails. Failure is simple; the spell has little or no effect. Depending on what the character wanted to do, this might be a partial success **(see the Degrees of Success table)** or no result at all.

Botching

If the player botches the roll (rolls more "ones" than she rolled successes), her mage blows the spell and gains the following Paradox points:

• If the Effect was *coincidental*, she gets one Paradox point for every dot in the highest Sphere she was using. If, for example, she was trying to cast a Life 4, Prime 2 Effect, she would gain four points of Paradox.

• If the Effect was *vulgar without witnesses*, she gains one point plus one for every dot in the highest Sphere. The aforementioned mage would now earn five Paradox points.

• If the Effect was *vulgar with witnesses*, she gets two points for botching a vulgar action, plus two per dot in the highest Sphere used. The unfortunate from the first two examples now gets a total of 10 Paradox.

"Witnesses," by the way, means Sleepers who are physically present and able to observe a magickal act. Their belief, or lack of it, shifts reality's balance. Media transmissions, like closed-circuit TV or sensors, can still capture magickal acts. Most people know, however, that a camera can be fooled, and, in any case, it's the observer, not the observation, that guides reality's currents (which is why some areas have more flexibility than others). Still, casually performing magick in front of cameras, isn't really a good idea. Who knows who might get their hands on the results?

Paradox

The full rules of Paradox and its effects take up their own section later in this chapter. The step-by-step process of a Paradox backlash can be summed up like this:

• When a mystick gains Paradox points, list them down on the Quintessence/Paradox wheel at the bottom of her character sheet. The Storyteller may roll for a backlash if a mage earns more than five points in a single botch.

• When the Storyteller checks for a backlash, he rolls the offending mage's Paradox total as a Dice Pool. This total combines both the points on the wheel and the points she has just incurred.

• The Storyteller rolls this Pool against difficulty 6; for each success, one Paradox point is expelled by the backlash. The more points this backlash expends, the worse the effects will be.

— *Flaws* usually manifest when five points or less are spent.

— *Physical damage*, inflicting one aggravated Health Level per point expended, burns its way through the mystick. This usually occurs during backlashes of between five and 15 points. Really large backlashes — 10 points or more — may spread their damage outward from the caster, dividing their damage between everyone within five yards.

— *Paradox spirits* may show up at any level; the bigger the backlash, the meaner the spirit.

— If more than 10 points go off at once, a *Paradox Realm* may manifest, punishing the mage and possibly others in the area.

— *Quiets* work best when a Storyteller prepares for them in advance. After the Quiet ends (*if* it ends, heh heh heh...), she merely tells the player how many points of Paradox his mage lost through the journey. This amount should be based on the length and severity of the madness — two or three points for a minor episode, the whole Paradox pool for really difficult Quiets.

Examples: Magickal Feats

• **All-or-Nothing Effect**

Jennifer Rollins enters a dark church; sensing that she's alone, she carves a rune, mutters a brief invocation and ignites the candles.

In game terms, Jennifer's player says "I want to light every candle in the room with a wave of my hand. I carve the *kenaz* rune in my arm, mutter a little something to Freya and concentrate."

This is an all-or-nothing feat, vulgar, without witnesses; Jennifer has the right Spheres (Forces 3, Prime 2) and performs a ritual in keeping with her style. The Storyteller tells Jen's player to roll her Arete — five — against difficulty 7. She needs at least two successes to pull it off. The roll is made; three successes. The candles all ignite. Unless someone puts them out, they'll burn for a day or so, or until the candles all melt, anyway.

If she had failed to get the two successes she needed (i.e., a *partial success*), a few of the candles would have ignited, dimly. If Jennifer still wanted to light them all, she could try again the next turn, at +1 to her difficulty. 7 would have become 8. If she had already rolled one success, she would only need one more to ignite all the candles.

If she had botched the roll, Jennifer's player could either spend a Willpower point to negate the botch or accept the consequences. Since the Effect was vulgar without witnesses, Jennifer would accumulate four Paradox points (one for botching vulgar magick, plus three for a level three Effect).

• **Direct Damage Effect**

Awakened cyborg X344, pursuing a reality criminal through laboratory halls, aims his cybernetic plasma cannon (his Forces focus) and fires. X344's Arete is 5; his Forces 3, Prime 2 Effect, coming from a high-tech weapon, is coincidental in the lab, so his difficulty is only 6.

The roll comes up with three successes; the sorcerer doesn't dodge and fails his countermagick roll. X344's blast does (3 + 1 for Forces = 4 x 2) eight Health Levels to the mage. The renegade soaks two of them, but still falls to the ground, badly wounded. X344 moves in for the kill….

• **Duration**

Cheshire, realizing that his intrusion sensors have been tripped, scans the dark room for some sign of life. Using his Arete of four (he's progressed a bit since **Chapter Six**), Cheshire rolls his Life 1 Effect. Since sensory Effects are almost always coincidental, his difficulty is 4. With the four successes that come up, Cheshire's Life scan lasts for the rest of the story, if he wants it to. With it, he sees the cat sitting atop his monitor. Well, at least it was only a cat….

• **Extended Roll Ritual**

Father Shelley sighs heavily; the Node has been polluted. Satanic graffiti mars the well's ancient stones, and the bloodstains remain despite the priest's scrubbing. A true cleansing must be performed. At this hour, the park is deserted. Father Shelley unpacks his incense and vestments (foci); though he knows he does not need them, they give him comfort and a sense of purpose. With a brief prayer, he checks the area (i.e., performs a coincidental Life scan), then sets to work, singing a purification song.

Father Shelley's Arete is six; using a conjunctional Effect of Matter 2 (to remove the bloodstains), Spirit 2 (to beg aid from God's servants) and Prime 3 (to channel the tainted Quintessence through his own Avatar and thus cleanse it), he begins the ritual. This is no light undertaking. The Storyteller declares that Shelley's player will have to accumulate 10 successes through an extended roll, with each roll representing an hour of work. She sets his difficulty at 5, a base of 7 (Sphere 3 magick, vulgar, without witnesses), adjusted by the foci (-1), extra time (-1) the presence of a Node (-1) and the corruption of same (+1).

On top of that, she says that he will have to make a Willpower roll, difficulty 7 (his base difficulty), to cleanse the Quintessence through himself and a Manipulation + Expression roll (also 7) to perform the song correctly.

(Note that these other rolls are not necessary. The Storyteller includes them to add suspense and chance to the task. The only really important roll is the Arete one, difficulty 5, or 7 if she wants to ignore the modifiers.)

In the first hour, Shelley rolls well: three successes. An hour later, he slips — no successes on either the singing roll or the magick one. Father Shelley's difficulty rises by +1 (to 6). Over the next few game-hours, he does better: two successes, three successes and one success. During this time, Shelley's player and the Storyteller roleplay the priest's struggles with evil spirits and his own doubts in God. In the last hour, Shelley filters the poisoned Quintessence through himself. His player rolls the Willpower roll: one success — enough. It's a tough battle, but as he makes his last roll — four successes — he shouts his faith to the heavens and purges the evil from this place.

• **Paradox**

Suppose Father Shelley had failed that last roll; instead of four successes, he rolled one success and three "ones" — a botch. His player does not spend any Willpower to prevent the backlash, so Paradox kicks in — nine points worth (one for botching vulgar magick, three for the rank 3 Effect and five for the extra time he spent on the ritual). This is a hefty backlash, so the Storyteller rolls Shelley's Paradox pool — nine points, plus an extra two from an earlier vulgar stunt with a Tass-laden hot cross bun. This translates to eleven dice; she rolls them all against difficulty 6 and gets six successes. Father Shelley is in trouble.

A Paradox spirit in the form of Lucifer appears to the priest and berates him for his lack of faith. Chuckling, the arch-demon pulls Father Shelley into a Paradox Realm resembling Hell. Until the priest can either come to terms with his own doubts or "work off" the six points of Paradox he has just "spent," he will remain trapped in a Hell of his own design.

Nobody said magick was easy.

Casting Magick

What do You Want to Do, and How Do You Want to Do It?

- What are you attempting to do and how?
- What Spheres are you using?
- How does your Effect appear?
- What did your character do to make it happen?
- How long does it take?

Do You Know Enough to Do What You Want?

- Do you have the appropriate Spheres?
- Is what you're doing coincidental or vulgar?
- Do you need any mundane Knowledges to help you?

Are You Successful?

- Roll your character's Arete versus the appropriate difficulty (minimum difficulty is 3):
  Coincidental: Difficulty = highest Sphere + 3
  Vulgar, without Witnesses: Difficulty = highest Sphere + 4
  Vulgar, with Witnesses: Difficulty = highest Sphere + 5
- Add or subtract any modifiers (maximum +/-3)
- Check the number of your successes.
- Spend Quintessence or Willpower, if you want to.
- Do you need to roll more successes to accomplish your task?

If So, or If Not, What Happens?

- How much effect did your magick have?
- Did someone dodge, soak, resist or use countermagick against your Effect?
  If so, subtract her successes from your own, then see if you still succeeded.
- Did you fail? If so, did you botch, or did you just not succeed?
- Botches and Paradox:
  Coincidental Botch: gain one point of Paradox per dot in the highest Sphere you used.
  Vulgar Botch: gain one point of Paradox for botching + one per dot in the highest Sphere.
  Vulgar Botch with Sleeper Witnesses: gain two points of Paradox + two points per dot in the highest Sphere.
- Did you get more than five points of Paradox?
  If so, the Storyteller might roll for backlash (or spring it on you later...).

Magick Reference Charts

Notes:

• The **Magick Difficulties** chart offers the pluses and minuses of some possible circumstances. Use this as a general guideline for other possible modifiers.

• Use the **Magickal Feat** chart when a player wants to accomplish an all-or-nothing Effect. He should roll the appropriate amount of successes to perform it. This may require an extended roll. The **Degrees of Success** chart measures how well a given feat was performed and the effect it had.

• Check the **Damage and Duration** table to see how much damage or benefit an Effect had or how long it will last. The **Aggravated Damage** table shows which types of attacks inflict severe damage. All other forms do normal damage only.

• Remember that these charts are guidance, not gospel. Ignore them as you see fit.

Magickal Feats

Feat	Successes Required
Simple feat (changing the color of your own eyes, lighting a candle, using Mind magick to sense someone nearby, conjuring a business card)	1
Standard feat (changing your own shape, causing an oil lamp to explode, influencing someone's mood with Mind magick, conjuring a ball of flame)	2
Difficult feat (transforming into something bigger or smaller than yourself, igniting a gas main, deep-reading someone's mind, conjuring a chainsaw)	3
Impressive feat (changing someone else's shape, blowing up a house, taking over someone's mind, conjuring a car, making yourself disappear)	4
Mighty feat (turning someone into sludge, incinerating an armored tank, obliterating someone's mind, conjuring a mythic beast, making all furniture in a room disappear)	5-10
Outlandish feat (turning a roomful of people into sludge, igniting a warship's weaponry, Mind-controlling a horde of madmen, conjuring a demon, making a mansion disappear)	10-20
Godlike feat (making a skyscraper disappear, finding one particular person in New York using Mind magick, summoning a horror from the Deep Umbra, levitating a mountain, creating a Horizon Realm)	20 or more

• Damage for these feats is based on the successes rolled. If, for instance, a mage tried to kill a HIT Mark, the method he was using would determine the level of the feat. If he rolled four successes after ripping into it with Life magick, he would do (4 x 2 = 8) eight Health Levels of damage. The HIT Mark can still try to use countermagick, but cannot soak that damage.

Spirit Gauntlet Chart

Area	Difficulty	Successes Needed
Node	3	One
Deep Wilderness	5	Two
Rural Countryside	6	Three
Most Urban Areas	7	Four
Downtown	8	Five
Technocracy lab*	9	Five

*Technocratic dimensional science treats these like Nodes.

Time Sphere

Successes	Effect Timespan
One	Within a year
Two	Five years
Three	20 years
Four	50 years
Five	100
Six+	500 years
10+	1000 years or more

Correspondence Ranges

Successes (Use one or the other.)	Range or Connection
One	Line of sight/ blood relation; body sample
Two	Very familiar (home, office)/ best friend; prized possession
Three	Familiar (local mall)/ co-worker; possession
Four	Visited once/ acquaintance; anything used once
Five	Saw or heard about it/ stranger; item touched casually
Six+	Anywhere on Earth/ no connection

Degrees of Success

• **Botch:** The mystick makes a critical mistake and screws everything up. The Effect is wasted, and the mage gains Paradox points, unless he spends a Willpower point to cancel out the botch.

• **Total failure:** No successes, but no botch. The mage may continue his spell, at +1 difficulty, or try again from scratch.

• **Partial success:** 50% of the necessary successes. The mystick accomplishes what he set out to do, but not as well as he would have liked. Cheshire, for instance, creates his computer, but it doesn't work properly; perhaps it's missing some vital pieces or the workings are flawed. The mage can keep going if he wants to, at an additional +1 difficulty.

• **Success:** 100 % of the successes required. The mage does exactly what he wanted to do. Cheshire's laptop functions as well as any "normal" computer would.

• **Extraordinary success:** 150 % or better. The mage not only succeeds, he succeeds brilliantly. Cheshire's laptop is sturdy enough to take a lot of abuse, looks great and has some unusual functions that even Cheshire hadn't planned on, like one-gigabyte memory, CD Rom drive and a Calvin & Hobbes screensaver. (It is *not* a Talisman, however; that requires a separate act of magick.)

Aggravated Damage

• Vulgar Life magick attacks (**Rip the Man Body**), which rend the being's pattern; not coincidental ones, which work within that pattern.

• Vulgar Prime magick attacks (**Flames of Purification**) or attacks charged with Prime; this does not include Effects merely *created* with Prime (**Control Major Forces**).

• Direct (vulgar) Entropy attacks on a living body (**Blight of Aging**).

• Spirit magicks that summon spirits to attack a living being (**Free the Mad Howlers**).

• Natural weaponry of supernatural creatures (werewolves, vampires, etc.).

All other forms of damage are normal unless the target is unusually susceptible to them (werewolves to silver, vampires to fire, etc.), or unless the Storyteller decrees that the damage is particularly nasty (toxic waste, radiation, etc.).

Damage and Duration

Successes	Damage	Duration
One	None	One turn
Two	Successes x 1	One scene
Three	Successes x 2	One day
Four	Successes x 2	One story
Five	Successes x 2	Six months
Six +	Successes x 3	Storyteller's option

Forces add one success when used for damage; **Mind** subtracts one success when inflicting damage. Direct Entropy attacks do no damage at all until the fourth level, but incidental attacks (crumbling walls, etc.) inflict normal damage.

Magick Difficulties

(Maximum modifier: +/-3. Minimum difficulty 3, maximum 10.)

Activity	Difficulty Modifier
Researches lore on subject before using magick	-1 to -3
Has item resonating with target's essence (sympathetic magick)	-1 to -3
Near a Node	-1 to -3
Uses a unique focus	-1
Uses focus without needing it	-1
Extra time spent on magick	-1
Spending a point of Quintessence	-1 per point spent (max. 3/turn)
Using Tass with appropriate Resonance	-1
Using Tass with opposed Resonance	+1
Fast-Casting	+1
Distant or hidden subject	+1
Mage distracted	+1 to +3
Mage in conflict with Avatar	+1 to +3
Domino effect	+1 to +3
Monumental feat (pulling moon from orbit)	+1 to +3

Permutations

Magic is seldom spectacular because it seldom needs to be.

— Donald Tyson, *Ritual Magic*

These optional systems handle the complications that might come up during a game. Many have example sidebars to illustrate the rule in action.

Several of these rules are optional or have variants that may complicate basic play. Feel free to ignore some of these permutations if you feel they interfere with the flow of your game.

Sensory Magicks

(See also "The Spheres," first rank Effects.)

The first rank of any Sphere allows a mage to detect whatever elements or patterns that Sphere covers. These Effects — **Landscape of the Mind, Sense Fate and Fortune, Sense Life**, etc. — expand the mystick's perceptions for the spell's duration. Simple detections, like Prime 1, usually require a Perception roll rather than a magick roll. Weird perceptions, like Matter or Spirit 1, require an Effect roll. Assume that if there's *no way* the mage could've sensed something intuitively, she'll have to roll the magick.

Regardless, such perceptions often seem like hunches rather than magick and are almost always coincidental, unless the mage clearly sees something that no normal person could detect. Even then, since outsiders cannot see the things the mage does, her reaction may seem more eccentric than unnatural.

Extending Perceptions

By adding +1 to the difficulty, a mage may let someone else share her magickal perceptions. This shifts a coincidental Effect into the "vulgar with witnesses" arena if the person gifted with this extended perception is a Sleeper. Awakened mages can share a magickal sense without revealing their Art to others.

Technically, a mage can extend her senses to anyone within sensory range. Each person after the first requires an additional success and raises the difficulty by +1 (maximum 10). If Cheshire wants to extend his Life scan to three other mages, he must roll a total of four successes at difficulty 7. Extended perceptions normally last one turn.

Detecting Magick

With a successful Perception + Awareness roll, difficulty 6, a character can feel magick in use within her immediate vicinity. Really powerful Effects might lower the difficulty as low as 4, while unusually subtle ones could raise it as high as 10.

The Prime 1 Effect **Sense Quintessence** can detect "residue" of magickal acts after they occur. Small feats "disappear" within less than five minutes, but really strong ones can be felt for weeks afterward. The more time has elapsed since the casting, the higher the difficulty of a Perception + Awareness roll will be.

Acting in Concert

bring down the sky on me
know my limits intimately
bring down the sky on me
take me blindly, make me see

— Miranda Sex Garden, "Bring Down the Sky"

In some cases, a group of mysticks may wish to work together to accomplish a greater end. Large spells may include summonings, searches, elaborate rituals, Realm-creation, spirit-bindings, etc. Such collaborations work best on extended rituals; smaller Effects are harder to coordinate, and thus rarely worth the effort.

First of all, each mage involved must have at least one dot in each of the Spheres in the Effect. Someone who knows nothing about Matter Arts is no help to a mage who does. The collaborators must also be able to communicate freely during the casting, through telepathic bonds, speech, signals, etc. Setting this up may take a turn or longer per caster. From there, the group may work together in one of two ways:

- If each mystick has the Sphere ratings necessary to perform the Effect, each one makes a normal magick roll, in turn, as if he or she were casting the spell solo. All successes are added together; the result counts toward the total needed.
- If less-knowledgeable mages are assisting a more powerful one, only one roll is necessary. Each "helper" adds one success to the main caster's effort.
- Un-Awakened acolytes may assist their companion as well; the mystick adds one success for every five participants in his ritual. Coordinating such large gatherings may take hours per roll, and such rituals should be played out for maximum effect (Manipulation + Expression rolls are good for this.) Acolytes do not count as "witnesses" of vulgar magick under these circumstances. If over 100 were involved, some vulgar Effects might even be counted coincidental, *if* no other witnesses were around to contradict them.

Only one option may be used at a time. If one mage botches, everyone involved takes equal amounts of Paradox or spends a Willpower point to avoid it, even if the others rolled successes. Mundane followers would not gain Paradox *per se*, but may suffer some psychic or mystickal trauma from a failed attempt.

Countermagick

No witch undoes another witch's spell. Witch's Honor. Well, maybe...

— Samantha, *Bewitched*

Countermagick has been described by one Cultist of Ecstasy as the "Oh, shit!" reflex. A Sleeper seeing a flying brick rushing for him yells, "Oh, shit!" and ducks (hopefully). Mages also yell, "Oh, shit!"... and then they try to stop it.

These rules allow **Mage** players to stage classic "wizards' duels" as willworkers attempt to out-magick each other. Many Chantries and cabals use such contests to resolve disputes or advancement within the group — "If you can defeat me, you can replace me" — instead of the more formal certámen. Countermagick also gives mages a survival edge in mystick combat — a good thing to have, considering magick's awesome possibilities.

Some beings, most notably HIT Marks, have built-in countermagick, often treatments of a classified technomagickal alloy called Primium. This kind of countermagick activates immediately; the dice are "built into" their soak roll against magickal attacks. Other Technocrats are not so lucky; unless they have some form of apparatus (focus), they may not use countermagick. Naturally, a focus need not be readily apparent — a cybernetic implant or bio-engineering counterprocess might be enough.

This section describes a number of ways to utilize countermagick. Each of them requires a regular action to perform, unless the defender splits his Dice Pool between actions. If the mage is aware of the attack, he may spend his action trying to deflect it before it hits. Basic countermagick's difficulty is 7; most of the variants go to 8, and one rises to 9. Nothing short of a spent Willpower point can modify the roll. Botching any kind of countermagick roll leaves the defender wide open.

Some troupes may wish to stick to basic countermagick for simplicity. These variations can get too complicated for beginning groups.

Basic Countermagick

Countermagick is essentially a soak roll against magick, and it functions the same way. In basic countermagick, a mage with some knowledge of the attack can see the magick coming, like a brawler sees a punch coming. By the same token, the mage must be aware of the attack in order to deflect it. If he can see it, and knows what it is, he can try to counter it.

To attempt basic countermagick, a mystick must have at least one dot in the Sphere(s) involved in the attack; she then rolls her Arete, difficulty 7. Successes scored in countermagick cancel out the original Effect on a one-for-one basis.

If the successes exceed the original Effect's roll, that spell completely fizzles. The original Effect can also fail if the countermagick reduces it below the original caster's intended parameters. If the feat required five successes, a successful countermagick within its area can render it null and void. The attacker would either have to roll more successes (at +1 difficulty, like a failure) or try again.

Offensive Countermagick

Generally, countermagick only applies to Effects cast at the defending mage. With an Arete roll verses difficulty 8, he can try to counter a spell aimed at someone else. With a little extra effort, he might turn an offensive spell back at its maker!

Such counterspelling requires at least one dot in one of the Spheres in the attack and at least one dot in Prime. Both castings must be done within the same turn. By beating the attacker's successes with an Arete roll against difficulty 9, the defender can reflect the attack back at his opponent. Each success over the attacker's counts as one magickal success against her.

Sphere Versus Sphere Countermagick

In most cases, a mage must know something about the Spheres being used against her. With this variant, however, she can disrupt offensive magicks with her own knowledge.

Almost any Sphere will disrupt a magickal attack if it's used right. The difficulty for such countermagick is 8 instead of 7. Most forms of Sphere versus Sphere countermagick, however, demand

a certain level of expertise on the defender's part; some specific Effect might be necessary. These "attacks," by the way, do no damage — they only disrupt incoming magicks.

When dealing with supernatural creatures, Sphere versus Sphere countermagick is a mage's best bet. Although any Sphere can counter faerie Glamour and vampiric Thaumaturgy, Spirit is the only effective way to intercept Garou Gifts or ghostly Arcanos. **(See "The Hidden World" in Chapter Nine for details about other supernatural beings.)**

Anti-Magick

A mage with Prime 2 or greater may use his own stored Quintessence to counter another's magicks. This special defensive measure takes an entire action — the defender cannot split her Dice Pool to do it. Since anti-magick tries to *stop* reality's disruption, it never generates Paradox. This option may also counter an Effect that is not directed at the defending mage.

To perform anti-magick, the defending mage rolls her Prime rating as a Dice Pool against difficulty 8. Spending Quintessence will not lower the difficulty of this special Prime Effect. Each success made allows the defending mage to spend a point of Quintessence to raise her attacker's difficulty by +1 (maximum 10). This may exceed the usual +3. The attacker has a chance to counter the defender's Prime Effect by spending Quintessence and Willpower immediately afterwards.

Unweaving

Many magicks are continuous; wards and bans set up magickal barriers which persist until broken, while curses expel their malefic power over time **(see "Damage and Duration")**. Although a mystick cannot use countermagick in such cases — unless he was there during the initial casting — he can try to unweave the magick.

To attempt unweaving, a mage must have some basic knowledge (at least one dot) of each of the Spheres involved and an understanding of the first rank of Prime, so as to see the threads of magickal energy. Unweaving is hard — difficulty 8 — but a mage may make extended rolls until he overcomes each of the caster's initial successes. Unlike other forms of countermagick, Abilities may reduce the difficulty of unweaving rolls. A botch during the process, however, ruins the attempt; the mage must begin again.

Some Effects — summonings, instant damage attacks, sensory magicks and annihilations such as Gilgul — cannot be undone. Others — curses, sicknesses, transformations, countermagicks and creations — are notably vulnerable to them. These latter types usually have some form of protection woven into them from the beginning in the form of new attacks or countermagick. Yes, a HIT Mark's countermagick does affect unweaving, although the Storyteller would be better off assigning a certain amount of resistance that should be overcome rather than rolling countermagick to the countermagick every turn.

In most cases, the amount of successes an unweaving requires is left to the Storyteller's discretion; it will usually be between five and 15. Most strong magicks — wards, barriers, creations, curses, etc. — demand extended rituals to cast, and it is hard to take them apart without doing the same. Sometimes — again, at Storyteller's option — an Effect may not be undone without casting a whole new Effect to change it again. If a man was transformed permanently into a dog it would be easier to change the dog back into a man than to undo the initial magick.

Anytime a mage attempts an unweaving, the sorcerer who cast the original magick may roll Wits + Intuition (difficulty 7) to figure out that someone is messing with her creation. Most mages are quite proud of their magicks and take exception to anyone attempting to destroy them.

Abilities and Magick

Magick does not exist in a vacuum; it's an extension of the mage. So it should stand to reason that the mage's Abilities, properly used, might enhance the magick he or she works. If Nala the Dream-Killer selects her methods by Tarot readings, the way she reads those cards could have some effect on the death magick she chooses.

Abilities should come into play when appropriate, and the effects should be limited to a maximum of +3 or -3 adjustments to difficulty modifiers. Such a roll may only be made *once* during a given casting. A player who uses this option should have some reasonable and creative explanation for combining that Ability with the magick and roleplay it out if possible.

These rules are meant to help spice up an evening's events, not to mini-max magick difficulty rolls. Final say about how or if an Ability affects a character's magick (or whether the rules are to be used at all) belongs, as always, to the Storyteller.

Abilities Enhancing Magick

Sometimes mundane Abilities can improve a mage's chances of using magick successfully. This often ties into the mystick's chosen style; many practices involve singing, dancing, divination, technological skills, arcane languages, names of power, scientific theories, martial art forms and even weapons skills. Common magick-affiliated Abilities include Expression, Firearms, Research, Technology, Computer, Cosmology, Enigmas, Medicine, Occult and Science.

If some Talent, Skill or Knowledge applies to a mage's casting, it should be used in the turn *before* that magick is attempted. The base difficulty for both Ability and magick rolls is the same; no modifiers (Willpower, Quintessence, foci, etc.) apply. Each success made on the Ability roll reduces the magick difficulty by -1 or more, up to a maximum of -3, counting other modifiers.

The Storyteller may rule that certain Abilities are essential to working a particular Effect. Healing a third-degree burn with Life might require Medicine, while fixing a car engine with Matter may require Technology. If an Ability like Expression or Occult is part of a magickal focus, the mystick must roll a successful Attribute + Ability roll before using the magick. Failing that roll might raise the magick roll's difficulty as well.

Magick Enhancing Abilities

A mage may also use magick to improve her chances with an Ability, especially actions concerning detections and minor alterations (Sphere ranks 1 and 2 work best). Most Effects used this way would be coincidental, so long as the mystick chooses her actions wisely. Spheres like Entropy or Matter can be especially useful during gambling, construction and repair, trouble-shooting, sabotage, roughing it and such.

As stated above, every success made using magick drops the difficulty for the Ability by -1, to a maximum of -3. The magick must be cast in the turn *before* the Ability roll is made. The mage must cast his Effect as his first action before channeling the Art into the second action. Splitting Dice Pools is possible, but ineffective in the long run. One way to sneak in extra (non-magickal) actions during a turn is to use the **Accelerate Time** Effect.

Examples

• Basic Countermagick

Secret Agent John Courage squares off against a mad Ecstasy Cultist. The deviate throws a cloud of hallucinogenic gasses John's way. The cloud "contains" a Mind 3, Matter 2, Prime 2 Effect; the caster is skillful and lucky — he rolls four successes, enough to make the Man in Black see pretty colors for a day or so.

John sees it coming, though, and triggers his X15 nullification transmitter (his focus), enabling him to use "counterprocedures." He rolls his Arete of four against difficulty 7 and gets three successes. The gas dissipates; John gets a whiff of it, but it has no real effect on him.

If Courage had botched his roll, he would've been hit with the full effect of the gas. Had he reduced it by only a success or two, he would have hallucinated for a turn or two — not good, but better that than a day of it.

• Offensive Countermagick

Jennifer Rollins desperately tries to intercept the electron blast aimed at her friend Atropos. The cyborg who fired it rolled four successes — enough to kill the Orphan. For her action this turn, Jennifer shouts a warning and tries countermagick. Calling on her knowledge of Prime, she rolls her Arete of five against difficulty 8. Three successes — not enough to absorb the blast, but enough to reduce its damage from 10 Health Levels to two.

Atropos, alerted, rolls her own countermagick. Her Arete is four, and her difficulty is 7 instead of 8. She rolls well; two successes later, the Force bolt dissipates. The cyborg has been cheated — this turn….

• Sphere Verses Sphere Countermagick

Spirit magick is not Dante's bag. So when an angry shaman summons spirits to drag him into the Umbra, Dante reacts with a laconic comment and a quick sense-scrambler program — Correspondence countermagick.

The usual roll is made. The three successes against difficulty 8 are enough to weave a VR haze around the shaman's head. Confused, he lets his summoning trail off into a series of cries and mumbles. The spirits, unimpressed, hear, but do not obey.

• Anti-Magick

Nephandus Briairus tries to crumble the ceiling above a Celestial sister with an Entropy 4 Effect. After muttering, "Mathew Hopkins was right," the Chorister counters with her Prime 3 and rolls three dice against difficulty 8. The One is with her, and she makes three successes, allowing her to add three points of Quintessence to raise Briarius' difficulty to 10. The One is not with *him* — he makes only one success, not enough to do his intended damage. Aside from a few small cracks, the ceiling remains intact.

• Unweaving

The curse has been in place for a while; it will take Peter Kobie a total of 15 successes (difficulty 8) to lift it from the burial mound. He readies his drum, ceremonial dress and sweetgrass (his foci) and sets to work.

Over a period of game-time hours, Kobie's player rolls four times against difficulty 6 (reduced through a good Manipulation + Expression roll). He garners a total of 10 successes before a fatal botch undoes his Art. Before Kobie's horrified eyes, a giant spirit-snake appears. Its warning rattle shakes the ground, and venom drips from its fangs as it strikes at the shaman. He dodges as the snake fades, hissing, into nothingness. Kobie sighs; the curse will be difficult to lift indeed, and so much time has already been wasted…

Paradox

There is no solid status quo, only a series of relative realities, personal to each... any or all of which are frail, and subject to eruptions from other states and conditions.

— Clive Barker, Introduction to *Sandman: A Dolls House*

Paradox is the force of the majority's subconscious. The Sleepers have a set belief on how reality works and violations of those laws get punished. The effects of Paradox can destroy a mage and damage the direction of a chronicle. Storytellers are advised to be both cautious and fair when Paradox occurs.

The **Casting Magick** chart and the rules given earlier under "Botching" and "Paradox" cover the amount of Paradox certain actions generate. You the Storyteller will decide when and how Paradox takes effect. Under normal circumstances, a mage will accumulate one to three points and bleed them off later, at a rate of one week per point, so long as he earns no more during that time. When Paradox builds up quickly, ripples called "Flaws" may result. In extreme cases, when six points or more occur at one time, or the mage accumulates over 10 points without bleeding them off, a backlash may strike.

Backlashes burn off Paradox energies, but they devastate the mystick. When some backlash occurs, roll the character's Paradox Pool (the boxes on his character sheet, plus whatever he's just earned) against difficulty 6. Each success expels one point of Paradox and leads to some very nasty consequences....

Several mages may bring on a backlash through their combined efforts, too. In those cases, just roll as many dice as you feel would be appropriate. If a few minor Effects caused the trouble, roll five or six dice. If the backlash came from some monumental Effect, or a long build-up of smaller ones, roll as many as ten and apply the results to the whole area. Stories also tell of "Paradox Storms" which sweep across reality, cleaning the slate after truly vulgar events. The truth behind such tales is debatable.

Examples

• Abilities and Magick

Miss One, Cultist of Ecstasy, raps and rhymes to focus many of her magicks. While using a Mind Effect to "encourage" a Sleeper policeman to bug off, she mutters some nasty street poetry, using her Expression (4). Her Effect is difficulty 6, so her Ability difficulty will be 6 also. She rolls her dice and makes three successes, bringing her magick difficulty down to 4.

• Magick and Abilities

Lady Venezia of the Order of Hermes is appraising a lapis and pearl necklace, said to be an 18th century antique. It looks like the real thing, but the man seems all too pleased to get rid of it. Her suspicions aroused, but sensing no Sphere magick, she casts a Matter Effect to detect signs of aging. She rolls four of her Arete dice and gets two successes. The Storyteller drops the difficulty of her Ability roll (Perception + Subterfuge) to determine if the necklace is old enough to be the genuine item. With four dots in Perception and three in Subterfuge, she rolls five successes. Although the stones are real and the setting authentic, the necklace dates back only a few years and was artificially aged. Irked (but secretly relieved), she tosses the jewelry back to him and orders him out of her shop.

Storytellers may choose to delay an impending backlash until the moment is right.

Backlash Forms

The manifestations of Paradox often relate somehow to the magick which caused them to appear. The size of the backlash reflects the points expelled at once. Let the needs of the story and the amount and nature of the Paradox decide what form a backlash takes.

Paradox Flaws

(1-5 point backlash)

Paradox Flaws occur when a mage's accumulated Paradox bleeds off. It can be either voluntary or involuntary, and it's often the least painful way of dealing with the effect. These ripples manifest in odd occurrences that haunt the magician until reality has straightened itself out. The Flaw always reflects the type of magick that offended reality.

Such Flaws are not harmless; they should hamper, possibly even cripple, the mage for a while. Minor Flaws should make a mystick uncomfortable, while major ones seriously impede his basic ability to function.

The amount of Paradox released determines the severity of the Flaw. The Flaws below are suggestions only; this energy is unpredictable and will manifest in many different ways. With the Storyteller's permission, a player may dictate the kinds of Flaws her character earns. This should only be done if the troupe has a sense of balance.

One Point Flaws: These short-lived minor Flaws range from watches spinning backward to minor power outages. Milk curdling, flowers wilting or wisps of ectoplasm appearing are common manifestations. The Storyteller might apply +1 difficulty to the character's dice rolls for a very short time.

Two Point Flaws: Flaws of this nature are a little more potent and begin to warp the character and the world around her. Scars might re-open into wounds, glass might turn into sand or energies might flow backwards, causing short circuits or clogged pipes. If the Flaw interferes with the character's ability to function, the Storyteller might increase her die roll difficulties for a scene or two.

Three Point Flaws: These Flaws often last for days and begin to severely impede the character and warp reality around her. Memories might become distorted, the magician's sense of timing might become altered, and her hearing and vision may fade in and out. At this level, Flaws become more than just uncomfortable, they could place a magician at a significant disadvantage. A mage might even take physical damage (one or two Health Levels) from boils or sudden wounds.

Four Point Flaws: The mage with this level of Paradox may find life quite hazardous for days on end. Four point Flaws can alter the physical make-up of her body — bones turn to wood, vision inverts or severely distorts (the world seems upside down or darker than midnight), basic body functions might cease, operate in reverse or work faster than is healthy. Significant damage (two to four Health Levels) is possible, and the magician may find it difficult to function.

Five Point Flaws: These major Paradox Flaws can drastically alter the character. They can change a character's Attributes dramatically for short periods of time (adding or subtracting three dots of Strength for a day) or alter them slightly but permanently (one dot of Strength gone forever!). The magician may find herself blinded for a significant amount of time or may be unable to control her nervous system. Weird distortions of the human anatomy can take place as well as distortions of the world around her (such as inanimate objects turning to glass when touched). At this level, the mage has trouble just getting out of bed.

Physical Backlash

(5-15 point backlash)

Paradox backlash is a vulgar attack on the character by reality itself. The energies released by the tear in reality burn the character. Roll for backlash only if the mage gains more than five Paradox points at one time, or if he's foolish enough to allow over 10 points to accumulate without release.

For every success on the backlash roll, the character receives one aggravated Health Level of damage. The character may try to soak this damage, but cannot heal it magickally — she must take her bruises and live with the consequences of her actions. Really huge backlashes can tear a mystick apart or cause huge area-wide explosions. In the latter case, divide the damage by the amount of people within a five-yard radius of ground zero.

The Storyteller determines the nature of the backlash, but it should relate to the magick in use. A Mind backlash involves headaches and brain hemorrhages; Matter backlash might turn flesh to metal; Forces backlash usually involves tremendous light shows and numerous striated burns. The highest level Sphere in use is the type of magick most likely to damage the character.

Realms

(10+ point backlash)

Sometimes Paradox creates a pocket Realm and traps a mage within. The most common victim of this imprisonment is a magician bursting with Paradox from flagrant vulgar magick use. The pocket Realm sucks her in and seals her off from normal reality. Quite often, anyone and anything near the magician get dragged in along with her. This pocket Realm may become an entire adventure. Storytellers are advised to use Paradox Realms only as a direct part of their stories and not as a means of simple punishment.

The magick that caused the Paradox effect forms the Realm. A Son of Ether who severely botches his roll to transform a building into hydrogen gas with a matter converter might find himself stuck in a Matter Paradox Realm. Most documented Realms reflect the nature of the fatal Sphere:

Correspondence: Distances lose their meaning, direction is impossible to judge, and depth perception fails completely.

Entropy: Odd random events occur without cause or effect. Decay increases to horrifying speeds or slows to suspension.

Forces: The victim finds herself trapped in a dimension where normal physics are meaningless. Energies flow in reverse, light and dark switch like a film negative, and static electricity is rampant. In extreme cases, gravity and kinetic forces may become reversed; objects fall up or not at all.

Life: Biological functions become completely distorted. Plant life grows wildly, while animal life devolves. Life forms change shape rapidly, and the mage experiences various rapid body fluctuations.

Matter: All matter becomes jumbled into chaos; solids become ethereal, gasses become solid brick, and liquids lose density and float freely.

Mind: The mage becomes trapped within the nearest mental prison: her own mind. The mage, and anyone trapped with her, is subjected to her darkest fears and neurosis.

Prime: This Realm is the most difficult to explain, but many surviving Verbena have simply stated, "Pure energy," before collapsing.

Spirit: The spirit of the mage is torn away and locked in an Umbral or Dream Realm; her body lies in a catatonic heap.

Time: Paradox sticks the victims in a loop of time, replaying the events of her crime repeatedly. In extreme cases she may find herself in a past or a future where the world she knows might not exist yet or has ceased.

Every Paradox Realm has a way out. They are not meant as eternal prisons, but rather as rehabilitation. Only those magicians too arrogant or stupid to realize their mistakes disappear forever. The wise mage will try to understand her mistake and use that knowledge to escape. She must learn that magick cannot solve all of one's problems; any further use of magick only makes things worse. Escape from a Realm may be as easy as walking out of room or could stretch over an entire game session of soul-searching. The Storyteller determines the exact nature of the Realm and its resolution, based on the backlash and the player's actions.

Spirits

(any size backlash)

Reality police incarnate, Paradox spirits form when some aspect of reality has been violated in an especially obnoxious way. Some mysticks believe that the victim himself creates the spirit out of his own fear or anger.

Invisible to the mortal eye **(except for the ones who Materialize; see "Umbrood" in Chapter Nine)**, Paradox spirits punish a magician in any number of ways. Some are merely annoying, while others are instantly fatal. The bigger the backlash, the nastier the spirit.

Some vengeful spirits have a distinct intelligence and personality; others appear only once, then fade away. Some even yank mysticks into Paradox Realms where they supposedly punish the offender for eternity. The Appendix has several infamous sample Paradox spirits. Storytellers are encouraged to invent their own to keep their players guessing.

Unbelief

(not applicable)

Unbelief is the power through which Paradox eradicates fantastical monsters and magickal creations. "Normal" reality cannot accept dragons or unicorns, instant cloning or alien invasions. The great subconscious majority destroys these things through Unbelief.

The battle over what is believable and what is not lies at the core of the Ascension War. Unbelief is the Technocrats greatest ally; mythical beasts die, taking away the Traditions' only allies, while the Technocracy stockpiles HIT Marks disguised in human flesh or cloned duplicates of regular people. All the same, even the Union cannot field hyper-tech nightmares or ultra-advanced androids without this subtle backlash causing their creations to fall apart, go mad or die. The mythic Bygones are said to have left this plane because of Unbelief. It's the ultimate expression of the status quo: that which should not exist cannot.

There are a great many theories about the nature of this "balancing factor." Whatever the truth may be, Unbelief causes outlandish creatures to sicken and die; the more otherworldly a beast appears, the quicker its demise. The effect is stronger in technologically-based areas, weak in hidden places and possibly non-existent in those few shreds of primal Earth left. Unbelief works itself out in ways that seem acceptable to the subconscious of the majority. Sea monsters which stick to the bottom of the ocean or alien lights that vanish into the night sky leave no evidence to mark the disappearance of the unbelievable.

Quiet

So I cry sometimes when I'm lying in bed
Just to get it all out what's in my head
Then I start feeling a little peculiar
— 4 Non-Blondes, "What's Up"

An insane mage is a terrible thing. This by-product of Paradox holds a mystick hostage to her own delusions. The character's perception of reality twists and warps through her own subconscious. She sees things that don't exist, smells and hears things that aren't there and takes damage from creatures that only exist in her mind. Sleepers rightly view Quiet as insanity, and magicians affected by it might find themselves locked in an asylum when they recover.

Paradox isn't the only cause of this insanity. Botched sensory and Mind magicks most often lead to Quiet, but external forces can bring it on as well; powerful Mind attacks, severe emotional shocks, badly failed Seekings and extreme old age can trigger this so-called "twilight." Paradox energies will still "burn off" if some other force causes the madness, but the mage will have to find her own way out.

The higher a mystick's Paradox Pool is when Quiet sets in, the deeper the madness becomes. At lower levels, the magician sees or hears minor distractions. At medium levels, objects seem to fade in and out of reality, only to revert to normal when perceived directly. At the highest levels, a mad mage loses touch with reality and might accidentally kill someone or be killed in the process. The Storyteller can go wild with these delusions; anything is possible. Although many elements of the Quiet will relate to the character's internal conflicts, some are totally random.

Quiets are best prepared for in advance. They work better for single-player sessions than for troupe adventures. We recommend that Storytellers allow a mage's Paradox to build up before beginning a Quiet-related storyline.

Coping with Quiet

A Quiet-ridden mystick may try to disbelieve his delusions by spending a Willpower point and making three successes on a Perception + Intuition roll, difficulty 7 **(see "Willpower" in Chapter Six)**. This is an all-or-nothing roll; partial successes make the manifestation seem even more realistic to the character, while botches cause the manifestation to become a temporarily real "hobgoblin." Either way, the Willpower is spent.

Disbelieving will not make the madness go away. Until the Paradox is discharged, hallucinations will plague the mage. Each point of Willpower spent disbelieving reduces the backlash by one, however, so it is possible to "will" yourself sane. It's dangerous and exhausting, though, and who knows when you may need that Willpower for more important things?

Hobgoblins

Quiet delusions rattle skeletons in a mage's darkest closets. They often reveal secrets, fears or conflicts that a mystick would rather deny. When such delusions actually appear to others, the mage is in for a hell of a time.

A hallucination that becomes real as a result of a botched disbelief roll is called a *hobgoblin*. This could be anything from an annoying noise to a rampaging monster. If the hobgoblin becomes a creature, it will have Health Levels equal to the offending mage's Arete and the same Abilities as the sorcerer (including combat but not magick). These creatures cannot soak damage, but are highly adept at causing trouble. Hobgoblins lose a Health Level each day they exist, as reality forces the abomination to cease. A Master's manifestations, however, can last a long time, and there's no upper limit to the number of hobgoblins which can exist at once....

Inanimate hobgoblins stay around for a number of days equal to the mage's Arete. They don't usually cause as much trouble as their animated cousins, but may prove embarrassing.

Quiet Chart

Paradox Pool	Delusions
1-3	Minor hallucinations; certain objects or alterations may "appear" and "disappear" intermittently. Examples: odd letters, graffiti, strange smells, distant noises. Lasts a day or so.
4-6	Delusions become common; the mage may see, hear or even touch things which do not exist or miss things that do. Some seem benign, others hostile. His moods alter, and he gets a faraway look for two weeks or more.
7-10	The victim's senses backfire, inducing blindness, hyper-sensitivity or wild hallucinations. Hobgoblins can appear, manifesting the mage's delusions in solid form. This may go on for months if untreated.
11+	The mage becomes trapped in a mindscape of his own design. The time he spends there (and the things he does while "dreaming") depend on the size of the Paradox Pool and the needs of the story. This Quiet could last indefinitely.

Other rolls	Traits	Difficulty
Disbelieve delusions	Perception + Intuition	7
Trance	Perception + Meditation	6-9
Communication	Willpower	8
Reduce mindscape duration	Wits + Enigmas	4

Mindscapes

Quiet can last a long time; the chart gives approximate durations by degree. The mage can only escape it sooner by entering a *mindscape*. In this, the magician goes on a spiritual quest to recover his sanity. He enters a trance (usually with a Perception + Meditation roll) and grapples with his inner demons. Like other elements of Quiet, a mindscape mixes symbolic conflicts, surreal geography and left-field weirdness into a psychodramatic soup.

While traveling this inner terrain, the mage remains in a catatonic state. He may do anything he wants, but cannot affect the physical world. Mindscape catatonia generally lasts one week for every point of Paradox in the Pool; if there are over 10 points there when he goes in, the interval becomes one *week* per point. An 11-point trance would last 11 weeks. When the mystick emerges, his Paradox is gone.

During catatonia, the mage can try to communicate: three successes with a Willpower roll (difficulty 8) allow a clear message; less than that, and it comes out garbled. He can also try to reduce his coma by rolling his Wits + Enigmas against difficulty 4. Each success reduces the length of time by one day, but he can only make the roll once per week. Unless someone goes in to retrieve him, he may still be there for a very long time.

Through creative Mind magick, an outsider may enter a mindscape. This usually requires some high-level Effect (Mind 3 or better) with plenty of successes. Once inside, she'll be subject to whatever the mindscape has to offer. Should she end up Incapacitated or dead inside the other mage's mind, she enters a coma not unlike his own. Depending on what happened and how, this coma could last for hours, months or years.

Wisdom From Insanity

While questing inside, a sorcerer effectively goes on a Seeking to recover his sanity. While he does not gain any Arete from the journey, both mage and player might comes away from a mindscape with some new insights. Quiets lay doubts, memories and other psychological debris bare. There's a lot a Storyteller — and a player — can do with such a trip.

Storytelling Magick

If I wanted to, I could turn mountains to sand,
Have political leaders in the palm of my hand
I wouldn't have to be in love with you
— Melissa Etheridge, "If I Wanted To"

The question "How are you casting your spell?" deserves a better answer than "I'm using Forces 3, Prime 2." The game mechanics are important, of course, but the fun part about roleplaying a mage is defining how you make your magick work.

Defining your mystick's style and foci is not only entertaining; in a world hostile to magick, it can be vital. This section offers suggestions for setting up your character's beliefs and practices and lets players and Storytellers know what kinds of magick will work in which parts of the Tellurian.

Why Use Foci?

Using certain foci or rituals take more time than simply making things appear out of nowhere, but they have the following advantages:

- Properly used, a given style or focus may seem coincidental. Magick from nowhere often seems vulgar;
- It adds to the texture of the game and the fun of roleplaying;
- A focus or activity, like a dance or a gun, may be useful on its own.

Futhermore, just because a *player* knows that his mage doesn't need a focus for so-and-so doesn't mean the *character* knows it. Mages still need to believe.

Magick Styles

Mystick power is channeled through belief; this cannot be emphasized enough. There's a danger in any roleplaying game of turning magick into just another neat weapon. In **Mage**, the Art is inseparably wound up in the mage's beliefs.

A willworker's style and foci reflect the paradigm, or belief, that he uses to work his Art. Even when he transcends the foci his style requires, a mage still retains some faith in the principles that allow him to alter reality. Though it has little to do with the rules of spellcasting, that style has everything to do with roleplaying and storytelling your magick use.

What Influences a Style?

We look for magick in the things which move us — things which, although familiar, bring us some feeling of shelter from the mundane world. Magickal styles are built from those things which give us this "other-sense" — dance ecstasy, devoted study, fasting, ordeals, prayer, sacred objects, secrets, arcane designs, whatever resonates within our culture. Anything a person chooses to accept as a belief works for him *if* he believes strongly enough that he has mastered it.

This isn't to say that objects, prayers and principles hold no power of their own. The World of Darkness is vast and mysterious, and all of its beliefs carry the seed of truth. Reality does not conform to one vision, however — no one is entirely right, but no one is totally wrong, either. Magick is the Art of moving the world with our views, whatever those views might be. Though items, names and other beings carry some power, a True Mage understands that all people have an intuitive grasp of how that power can be used. To Sleepers, this trace-memory translates into science, religion, superstition and hedge magic. Each carries echoes of the truth, but limits itself by insisting that only one thing is correct and everything else is wrong. Sooner or later, mages know differently,

When they Awaken, mages carry the belief their culture inspired and use it to focus their concentration. As their understanding grows, many of them realize their way is not the only way, that it is not the words they chant or the formulae they master that allow them to bend reality — it is their intent.

The Technocracy refuses to accept this. Many may know the truth — that mystick magick is the same as their own — but they refuse to admit it. Thus, they stay shackled to their technologies. Their "style" cannot avoid technology completely, though it can twist it in pretty strange ways.

Magickal styles are based in the culture a character comes from or adopts. When deciding your character's style, figure out what her background is; that will tell you what things she would consider powerful. From there, select whatever practices or rituals you think fit into her paradigm. Is she a scientist? Formulae, experiments, chemical and mechanical processes work. Is she an academic? The secret Hermetic mysteries, with their elaborate rituals, grand designs and secret names fit that concept. An artist? Perhaps she's invented her own practices. The Tradition styles **(see Chapter Six)** offer some general options, but don't feel restricted by those. Modern mages are eclectic; use whatever works for your character.

Common Elements of Styles

There are too many magickal styles and beliefs to ever include in one book or game. The following theories and elements, however, are common to many styles within the World of Darkness. Few styles are defined by only one element; most utilize several of them through a common background. All of them hold some measure of the truth.

• **Otherworldly Entities:** The actions of spirits, gods or other grand entities is often considered the primal source of creation. The laws which govern reality, the forms creation takes and the eventual fate of the world as we know it are commonly attributed to intelligent forces greater than humanity. Through pacts, worship, manipulation or compulsion, mages throughout time have expanded their wills to embrace True Magick.

Such relationships carry price tags. Entities at the fringes of comprehension often demand sacrifices from the mage or from others around him. The degree of a free will involved in Otherworldly bargains remains a subject of debate, and defies easy answers. Whether a mage deals with God, the Goddess, the spirits, demons or unknown horrors, this element of magick is perhaps the most common of all.

• **Elemental Forces/ Scientific Theories:** There are impersonal forces which shape creation, too. By observing those forces, mastering them and bending them to personal will, mages from the Hermetic Masters to the Technocratic scientists have crafted magickal and scientific achievements.

Arguments about the origins and flexibility of such forces — gravity, Fate, mathematics, the elements, karma, molecular physics, language and so on — can be endlessly circular. Some theorists maintain that by even admitting the existence of such elements, you bring them about, while others claim that some things simply *are*, and that's that. Whatever the truth may be, the study and manipulation of creation's basic laws remains a common element of magickal styles.

• **Internal Potential:** The human mind, body and spirit are sources of endless potential power. By tapping that potential — under any number of names — even Sleepers can increase the effect they have on the world around them. In their most basic forms — martial arts, psychic talents, physical conditioning — the energies within the self can do incredible, if static, things. Awakening opens the door to magnify that potential to literally move mountains. Some mages argue that all magick comes from the self, and we might as well admit it already. Others call that hubris. In any case, expanding, refining or even sacrificing one's self is a common element in magickal practices.

• **Primal Energies:** A crossroads element between divinity and natural forces, the concept of primal forces goes to the heart of the Tellurian to find those things which cause us to be. Some mages personify these energies, others link them to principles, and a few just accept them for what they are and deal with them without definitions. Indeed, they say, by defining them, we miss the point.

The Metaphysic Trinity **(see Chapter Four)** may be considered a diagram of primal forces at work, though some still view these energies as Wyld, Weaver and Wyrm. True Magick taps into the elements of change; labeling such forces is left to those who try to understand them.

• **Relationships:** "Like affects like" is a common principle of magick. Whether it applies to the sorcerer who drapes herself in snakeskin to become a snake, the mirror which links two worlds or the hair which carries mystick essence (or DNA strands), the idea that you can affect one thing by possessing something related to it is a common mystick element, especially in Correspondence, Forces, Life and Time magicks.

Perhaps this element is a scientific principle, perhaps it's the will of the gods. Whatever the source, there seems to be some validity to the concept that "As is one, so is the other."

Lady into Tiger: Styles at Work

• **Dreamspeaker (Life 4, Spirit 2)**

Tjun-Tjun placed the last of the incense and offerings upon the stone, bowing in supplication to honor the spirit, then took the mask from the tree branch above. It had gathered power out here in the forest and now held the spirit of the tiger as well as its face.

Tomorrow she would dance as the tiger in the Wayang drama, but tonight she would let the tiger run free.

She placed the mask over her face, going through the moves of the dance, and felt the spirit of the tiger move into her. She snarled, then bent down and lapped up the raw meat from the offering bowl. Satisfied, she licked the blood from her whiskers and padded towards the village.

The humans had honored her, so she would let them live. All except the one who had killed her....

• **Virtual Adept (Correspondence 2, Forces 3, Prime 2)**

Torie put on the gloves and goggles, letting the guy wires hoist her up so she could maneuver freely in VR.

The simulation came on-line, and it was perfect — trees, bamboo, dirt under her feet, even an aromatic component, heightened for verisimilitude. Or maybe she should say *purr-fect*, since the simulation had made her a tigress, and she felt her large, heavy body move with preternatural grace.

So far so good. She roared and stamped her right paw, the signal for the second part of the program to kick in. It did, and her icon was transferred to the satellite, then beamed back down to the surface, a holographic projection of a tiger composed of virtual particles. Nothing inside, of course, but forcefields and light projected at just the right densities to give the illusion of life.

Torie crouched behind the trash dumpster, waiting. The New World Order's new assistant undersecretary was going to have a very bad day very soon.

Foci

Foci are objects and actions that assist a mage when working magick. Unlike a Talisman, a focus has no magical properties of its own. It's a dance, a ritual, a weapon or drug that helps the sorcerer enforce her will over reality. At first, the focus is a learning tool, a crutch the novice can lean on; soon it becomes an extension of the mage. Eventually, the mystick transcends the need for the crutch and may perform magick without it. That focus, however, will always remain a part of the magician's paradigm. The belief in the object or ritual still exists, but the mage has realized that it is the power within, not without, that changes reality.

During character creation, the player should pick a focus for each Sphere her mystick knows; these will often derive from her style. She may choose to use a single focus for multiple Spheres, but this can be devastating if she loses that. She should also decide whether her foci are unique or standard. The player should have some idea what tools the character may use if she learns any new Spheres. She'll need one for each new Sphere she picks up.

Growing Beyond the Tool

A beginning mage needs one focus for every Sphere she knows. After she reaches Arete 2, she no longer needs to use a focus for one of her Spheres, usually the first one she learned — her "affinity Sphere" **(see Chapter Nine)**. Every level of Arete after that allows her to transcend one more focus for one more Sphere. By the time reaches Arete 10, she no longer needs foci at all.

While a magician may no longer need a particular focus for a given Sphere, it may still be necessary if she uses it for others. If Elizabeth, a member of the Order of Hermes, uses a burning candle as her focus for both Spirit and Life magick, she could, at Arete 2, discard that candle when working Spirit magic. She must, however, still use the candle for her Life magick.

Foci can still be useful, even when unnecessary. A magician who uses a focus she doesn't need will find that it still helps her concentrate. The Storyteller should reduce the magick difficulty by -1 for all magick performed with that focus for Spheres that no longer require it. Elizabeth, from the previous example, no longer needs a burning candle to perform Spirit magick. If a situation arises where she does not have a candle or enough time to light one, she can still use the Spirit Sphere. However, if she uses the candle anyway, her difficulty will be reduced by -1. She would *not* get the bonus when using Life magick, even though both Spheres share the same focus.

The Sons of Ether and Virtual Adepts are not as flexible as their Tradition cousins. Their mindsets cling to the Technocratic idea of reality too closely to abandon foci so easily. A member of either of these Traditions may abandon one focus per Sphere when she reaches an Arete of 5; this increases on a two-for-one basis at Arete 6. These two Traditions also receive the -1 difficulty when using foci that become unnecessary.

The same scale applies to Orphan Technomancers. Though he's self-Awakened, Cheshire still needs to jack into his computer focus for a while. When he achieves Arete 5, Cheshire can choose to transcend the need for his computer when performing Forces magick. If he continues to use the computer for that Sphere anyway, he reduces his Force magick difficulties by -1.

Members of the Technocracy currently hold sway over reality. Since this is the case, they're subject to their own laws. By their own decree, candles cannot perform magick. Thus, Technocrats can never perform magick without using some technological apparatus. They cannot reduce their difficulties by using unnecessary foci, since some focus will always be necessary. They cannot transcend what they have created, a flaw which Tradition mages would do well to exploit.

That Personal Touch: Standard, Personal & Unique Foci

Not every mage will have the same focus; foci are as diverse as the mysticks who use them. When a mage begins the long road to Ascension, she has an individual belief about the way the universe operates, and her chosen foci reflect this. Thus, they're very personal items.

• *Standard* foci are those items or rituals that are used by a large proportion of a Tradition. These stereotypical foci are most commonly associated with that group. Tradition mages, however, are not bound to certain foci. They may share similar beliefs and styles, but each mage chooses what suits him best.

• An individual chooses her *personal* foci, but her style and belief in the magick she creates defines them. Elizabeth, the Hermetic mage from the above example, chooses to use a burning candle to focus Spirit Effects, although most Hermetic magi still use a drawn or carved circle. During character creation, the player should take the time to personalize her choice of foci to match her character's belief system.

• A focus might be so important to a character's belief system that it becomes *unique*. This has both advantages and disadvantages for the mage. One who practices with a unique focus will find that reality bends easier to her will. A unique focus, however, is nearly irreplaceable and must be well cared for.

While ordinary items are fine for most, the discriminating mage will choose something worthy of her Art. A hand-crafted Japanese katana passed down through five generations provides a magus with a better sense of focus than a cheap switchblade. The personal investment of a unique item is not necessarily a matter of material value alone, but of personal value as well. A cheap necklace given to a magician by her mother may become a unique focus, whereas thousands of necklaces like it are so much scrap metal. A mage who uses a unique focus may reduce her difficulties by an additional -1 (max. -3, total) when employing the focus with its intended Sphere.

The problem with a unique focus, as opposed to a universal one, is that it *is* unique. If a magus loses his Matter focus, a rock, he won't be able to use the Matter Sphere until he picks up any new rock; no big deal. However, if his focus was a rune-covered rock given to him by a wise man, he might have a little more trouble replacing it. In this case, the mystick must find another focus and then relearn the Sphere with the new one. The relearning is faster; the magician has been through this already, and can do it at 2 x the current level in experience points. Still, it's a pain. For this reason, mages jealously guard their unique foci.

Blending In: Technomagick and Mythic Threads

A focus may, at times, make the difference between vulgar or coincidental magick. If a Sleeper witnesses something unexplainable within the realms of "normal" reality, a Paradox may occur. If the witness felt the Effect was within the realm of possibility, that Paradox can be avoided. Foci can dress up magick so that it appears, to the untrained eye, that nothing abnormal has occurred.

Mages who use technology as a focus have an advantage over others. A Sleeper is much more likely to accept a high-tech bioscanner or DNA analyzer than chalk circles or magic spells. Virtual Adepts can perform "miracles" on their computers that no Sleeper could recognize as magick. Sons of Ether have devices that, while unorthodox, do not necessarily break the laws of reality; only the more outlandish ones invoke Paradox. Members of the Technocracy have foci that cloak their magick in more "realistic" terms.

This is not to say that a Technomancer with a ray gun can run around New York leveling skyscrapers. The Effect produced must be within the realm of current possibility. Though the agents of the Technocracy have access to many high-tech foci, these devices exceed current technology to such an extent as to make them as unbelievable as any magick spell. Futuristic magick of this degree would probably be disbelieved by the un-Awakened almost as easily as waving a bone around. Technomancers are certainly more flexible when it comes to coincidental magick, but they still have limitations.

Technological foci are often useful as mundane tools. A Virtual Adept can always use his computer as a computer when he isn't conjuring lightening bolts with it. Depending upon which theory a Son of Ether holds, he might use X-ray machines, Geiger counters or blenders, any of which have ordinary uses. The same holds true for the Technomancers, whose weapons may shoot people without invoking any magick at all.

Mystick mages do not have it so easy. A smart one can use her foci to her advantage, however. A well-used focus can reduce the chances of Paradox. Items that have some mystick resonance in common folklore — martial arts, Tarot cards, crystal magic, séances or religious "miracles" — are known by some Traditionalists as *Mythic Threads*, bits of magick that have worked themselves into the collective unconscious. Through some inherent symbolism, memory or intrinsic power of the items themselves, Mythic Threads tap into that part of humanity that wants to believe in magick or still remembers its existence. Some Technocrats (and many Sleepers) have done their best to trivialize such items, but some power still lingers. A smart mystick can turn this collective memory to his advantage.

Magickal Geography and Influence lists places where some foci and styles work better than others.

Sample Foci

The following is a list of possible foci. This list should in no way limit the type of foci used for characters, but should rather be used as list of examples.

Art: The mage creates a piece of art (chalk drawing, pencil sketch, sculpture, computer graphic, etc.) which focuses her will and intent. The magician usually creates an image of the Effect she wishes to produce. The drawings of Marauders, often left behind after a spell, can drive a Sleeper into either insanity, Awakening or both.

Blood: The essential life fluid holds a lot of power. It's often used in rituals evoking Prime and Life magick, although it's certainly not limited to these uses.

Books: Books communicate various insights to new generations. The Order of Hermes has an extensive library of spells, Iteration X employs technical manuals without number, and some Marauders raid comic book stores.

Bones: The bones of animals, fish, humans or just about anything else can focus one's will. Bones are often carved into wands or become part of a sacrifice.

Cauldron/Chalice: The traditional cauldron is large, black and practically immobile. Many Verbena use a cauldron to whip up various concoctions. Sons of Ether mix new metal alloys or chemical solutions in modern versions. Cups, bowls or chalices often hold precious liquids or allow mages to share some form of communion.

Circle: By drawing on a floor, wall or table with chalk, ash or blood, the mage can create wards of protection and summoning circles. Different Arts and styles require different types of circle. Depending on its complexity, the circle can take as long as two hours to create and quite possibly longer.

Computer: The computer may be an advanced portable or an old IBM clone with faulty wiring. While simple Effects may take no more than a couple of seconds, major ones might take minutes or even hours of programming time. **(See "Items of Power" in Chapter Nine.)**

Crystals: Crystals gained popularity a few years ago with the Sleepers, due mostly to their effectiveness as a concentration aid. The type of crystal usually defines which Art may be performed, but this is up to the player.

Dancing: The type of dance depends solely on the character. Dances usually take a minute or two for completion and may require an Ability roll or two.

Devices: The common Technocratic focus, not to be confused with magickal Talisman Devices. Sons of Ether often design their own devices, which rarely work for anyone other than themselves ("You just don't understand the theory!").

Do: Akashic Brothers almost exclusively use this martial art form to access their magick. This meditative focusing of the will can take time and will certainly draw attention to the mage.

Drugs: Chemicals that induce alternative states of consciousness cloud "normal" reality, allowing for new insights into the inner workings of the universe. The Cult of Ecstasy tops the list of users, but the Progenitors have many pharmaceuticals, and some Marauders probably use too many. Drugs have certain inherent drawbacks, including cost, legality, addiction and hangovers.

Elements: Common in spirit-guided, sympathetic and scientific magicks, elemental materials — earth, fire, air, water, incense, glass, metal, wood, electricity, mud, ash, etc. — channel powers that a mystick wants to use. These may be placed on an altar, burned, shaped, consumed, observed or otherwise used to tap into some greater force. Many sorcerers feel that such elements have innate powers of their own.

Ether Goggles: This is a classic example of a Sons of Ether focus (who else would wear them?). These goggles are heavy and cumbersome and filled with a weird gas. Ether goggles represent only one of the numerous devices which Sons of Ether employ.

Feather: Like bones or blood, a feather from any bird or mythical beast holds the life-force of that animal and can be used to help produce magickal Effects. Representative of flight and the spirit, it is often used as a focus for Spirit magick.

Fire: A small flame or a burning house may be necessary for a mage to perform her magick. Nephandi often set huge infernos to take the full advantage of the focus.

Formula: No Technomancer would be complete without mathematical equations or physics models to support her theories or design specifications. Some Nephandi and the Order of Hermes also use ritualistic formulae in forgotten languages.

Herbs: Many mages use the inherent properties of certain plants to invoke their magick. These herbs can be sprinkled, eaten or mixed into a potion. Progenitors often use chemical extracts from rare plants for cloning or regeneration.

Holy Symbol: Faith is a very important power. The mage who believes in a higher being can focus his belief through some symbol of that divinity. This usually counts as a unique focus.

Incense: The inhalation of burning incense may help a magician concentrate on the way he wants reality to be and ignore the way it is. Nephandi have a similar focus that involves inhaling the fumes of burning hair.

Language: Words have power; indeed, they may be magickal in and of themselves. Nearly every culture has a sacred language for religious activities or other mystical experiences. The members of the Celestial Chorus use prayer to enforce their will, while Dreamspeakers and Nephandi speak extinct languages with similar results.

A special magickal language, called Enochian, communicates directly with the elements and spirits. Very few outside the Order of Hermes still know this language, but those who use it can perform tremendous magickal Effects. Specific intonations create different feats. Mispronunciations can be fatal! This language is effective as a primitive form of communication.

Music: Whether the magician must listen to a specific song or perform the music is up to the player. Reproductions of the music through various media — compact disc, tape, vinyl, 8-track (only a Son of Ether!) — are acceptable. If the mage must create the music, it might be a specific song, certain guitar lick or even a mystickal note. In any case, the willworker must have the instrument or playback device in order for the focus to be of any use.

Network: The communication internet is necessary for various Virtual Adept and Technomancer Effects.

Ordeal: A mage may inflict terrible pain upon his body to focus his magickal ability. Many Dreamspeakers perform painful ordeals to gain knowledge of the future or access to the spirit world. Nephandi often use this practice on other people.

Pure Water: Many mages drink, bathe in or sprinkle pure or blessed water as a focus.

Purification: Many mages or various Traditions find complete body purification necessary for certain Spheres, usually Spirit or Life.

Ritual Sacrifice: Nephandi, more than any other group, perform this repulsive act. It usually involves a long ceremony ending in animal or human sacrifice. The Order of Hermes, Verbena, Christian mysticks and Dreamspeakers have all been known to use sacrifices in rituals — though the mage himself may be the sacrifice.

Runes: Magical writing carved into or near the target may help create an Effect. This could be engraved in a door, a road, a person (ouch!) or just about anything. The carving should be done by hand and can take seconds or minutes, depending on the complexity. At least one Hermetic mage used laser-printed self-adhesive labels; she hasn't been heard from since.

Scientific Meters and Probes: These hand-held devices measure energy in the surrounding area. They can scan the energies of the various Spheres.

Sex: Sexual rituals, or just the very act itself, can heighten or alter one's consciousness when done right. On the dark side, the Nephandi sometimes use this focus with repulsive results.

Song: Similar to the music focus, a voice held at specific note is said to focus one's will. Modern sorcerers utilize rap and even heavy metal as their foci. Marauders often sing nonsensical nursery rhymes.

Tarot cards and Ouija boards: Sleepers view these items and others like them as amusing diversions and nothing more. Mages recognize that this makes them perfect for use as foci.

Treatments: Although the Technocracy makes common use of special treatments (implants, chemical baths, injections, etc.), body art, piercing, ritual baths and other preparations serve the same function in other styles.

Toys: Mages who never grew up (or who just enjoy neat plastic gizmos) might employ toys as their foci. At least one Marauder uses a plastic magnifying glass from the bottom of a box of Cracker Jacks to focus a wide-angle laser.

Vehicles: Common Technocracy foci include special planes, trains and automobiles. Such vehicles can also be powerful weapons.

Wand: The standard of a bygone era, a wand can be made of wood or metal. Certain wands may be unique items passed down from the Dark Ages or earlier....

Weapon: As extensions of personal power, weapons of all kinds have become common magickal items and foci. The Akashic Brotherhood utilizes martial arts weapons like katana or shuriken; Euthanatos often use whips or rifles; Verbena and the Nephandi make use of knives and daggers. The Technocracy consistently uses all types of weaponry, and some Iteration Xers have built-in weapons. These foci may be either unique or not, depending on the character.

Magickal Geography and Influence

The Ascension War touches all places known to mages, from urban centers to the void of space. Each faction has some place of power where their magick has the coincidental edge. This edge, aided by the beliefs of the people — or the lack of them — keeps any one side from total victory... as of yet.

Coincidental magick is the "gray area" that defines a place of power. What is vulgar in one place may be coincidental in another. True Magick is never "just part of the landscape" — on Earth, it is either coincidental or vulgar — but, by working with a place's reality rather than against it, a willworker may accomplish more while risking less.

Storytellers and players should keep these "flex areas" in mind when using magick. The boundaries of reality, however, stretch only so far, no matter who or where you are. Wild magick — levitated buildings, instant teleportation, time travel, etc. — is still *always* vulgar in the material world, wherever (and however) it is cast. Magick with no explanation (i.e., no foci, ritual or Mythic Thread) works the same way — if a noticeable Effect comes from nowhere, mortal observers will not accept it as normal.

Technocratic Control

• **World Industrial Powers:** Reality, within the industrialized nations, belongs completely to the Technomancers. Although direct control of these nations' rural areas gets shaky, reality throughout much of the "modern world" conforms to the Technocratic vision. Magick done under the auspices of "technology" is usually coincidental unless some pocket of mystick belief lingers there, and mystick magick is an aberration. Node points, worship spots, magick Sanctums, exceedingly rural places and the darkest urban blights escape this static mold, but in most public places, reality works the way the Technocracy would have it.

• **Scientific Centers:** Paradox is totally on a Technomancer's side in these strongholds. Labs, mass-media centers, working factories, computer centers and such are suicide spots for mysticks — the backlashes they incur are often deadly. This sheds some light on the Virtual Adepts' and Sons of Ethers' role in the Council; under strict Technocratic reality, their magick still has a better chance of working than any mystick's does.

Contested Areas

• **Undeveloped Nations:** Outside the "modern world," the limits of coincidence conform largely to the beliefs of the people there. Rural Africa, South America and most of Asia are battlegrounds held largely by the mages who have lived there for centuries. Neither Traditionalist nor Technomancer has a clear advantage in these areas unless they know the mystick "language." (The Occult and Culture Knowledges come in *very* handy here!) Like anywhere else, reality has only so much give, but mages who work through natural spirits, gods and the sacred self (often using chanting, prayer, ritual and physical disciplines like Do) can get away with more than those who employ computers, machines, alien magicks or nothing at all.

• **The Middle East:** Decades ago, the Technocracy fought a bloody war to control the vast Quintessence reserves that spring from the cradle of humanity. Though they won that battle, the millennia of religious belief that also comes with this territory sets their edge off-kilter. Paradigms clash here like they do in few other places on Earth. Subtle mysticks whose magick taps into the dominant cultures here still works coincidentally, and even the occasional miracle is still possible. Technomagick also works well in the Middle East — too well. Although Paradox (usually in the form of mechanical failure, sand storms, Quiet or "terrorist acts") fouls more mechanical Effects, subtle Conventions like the Syndicate and NWO have a firm control over the local paradigm.

• **Virtual Reality:** Paradox takes a strange form in the Net — whiteout. This localized systems crash, devastating to anyone in the area, keeps all factions on their toes here. *Changing* things is easy here, but *conjuring* them is not. Although incredible Effects are possible (morphing, teleportation, even flight) and may be done coincidentally, sudden and brutal magicks (Force blasts, disintegrations, instant creations, Time fluctuations) may cause the whole area to crash. Net Runners prefer to keep their fights down to a dull roar.

Example of Style Creation

Shadow is putting together her new character, Atropos. After going through the usual steps, she puzzles out her mage's style and foci. Atropos is an Orphan, so she's a clean slate. Shadow can do whatever she wants.

As a kid, Atropos grew up in a middle-class Irish-Greek household, absorbing some cultural influences from each. Her grandmother was her only friend; a rotten home life left her with a disrespect for authority and a fear/ respect for the randomness of Fate. She left home shortly before Awakening and ran street scams for food. Thus, she has some Classical European beliefs, street cynicism and an intuitive grasp of Fate.

The mage begins with three Spheres: Entropy, Life and Time. Her main focus, dice, channel her link with Fate and other primal forces (Entropy). The second, a knife, represents her aggressive nature, self-defense and the cutting of Life's threads. These are both personal — she has no Tradition but her own. Her third focus, a battered pocket watch her grandmother owned, represents a link between her present and her family's past (Time). It's a unique focus.

Her style involves using the dice and the watch to check her link with the elemental forces of Fate and time. She may secretly believe that the watch also links her to her grandmother's ghost, but she wouldn't admit it. She wields the knife herself — it links her actions to her will and lets her get up close and personal. From some pagan friends, Atropos adopts a bit of sympathetic magick theory; she'll use effigies or remnants of targets for some spells. As she grows, Atropos may shift her foci around. She'll understand that *she* controls Fate, though the dice may still aid her with other Spheres. She might add some neo-pagan foci later, or utilize street things like spray-paint designs, bits of trash, jewelry or body art — whatever Shadow thinks would be appropriate as Atropos develops.

• **Urban Sprawls:** The chaos factor works in the lowest pits of the urban wastelands — any significantly complex reality breaks down. In these blights, the Mad and the Fallen Ones hold sway. The parameters of coincidental magick very wildly, here, for nothing is certain for long and people have learned not to question. By day, reality works much as it does anywhere in the industrialized nations. But when night falls, almost anything goes — spirit possession, sudden explosions, miracles, acts of science and acts of the gods may be coincidental one moment and vulgar the next. Paradox, if it comes, is more vicious here than in almost any other place. Urban blights include the sewer systems, dumps, slum basements, forgotten subway tunnels, subcities and the nastiest back-alleys and nightclubs.

• **Rural Areas:** Away from the cities, people still believe in things other than science. Although most forms of magick work as they do anywhere else in the modern world, certain mysticks, such as Christian ministers, witches, shamans or wacky professors, can get away with more than they would normally be able to. Even those "favored" by a certain local belief must step lightly — flying on broomsticks is never a good idea these days — but the usual limits of "coincidence" are a bit more flexible in rural spots. The Technocrats are taking steps to remedy this.

• **Horizon Realms:** Reality, in these custom-built Realms, works the way their makers want it to work. A Realm established by Hermetic Masters will count any Effect cast with the Hermetic style as coincidental (or even normal). Any HIT Mark that sets foot in the place would be a Paradox magnet. Autocthonia's

reality works in just the opposite way — reality is what the Machine will accept. In a Native American-established Realm, neither form of magick would be acceptable. These "custom paradigms" keep successful Horizon Raids rare. When running such Realms, figure what forms of magick would be coincidental there and which would not.

• **Etherspace:** Beyond the Horizon, there is no Paradox. All forms of magick work equally well and with equal effect — there are no "vulgar" forms of magick here. It is said that Realms in Etherspace conform to the settlers' reality, but space itself remains free for all.

Mystick Strongholds

• **The Near Umbra:** Most Technomancers deny the existence of these "alternate dimensions." With the exceptions of the Void Engineers and the mysterious Syndicate (who understand the laws of this place), Technocracy mages must avoid high-tech magicks throughout the Near Umbrae. Exceptions, such as the rumored "Cyberrealm" of the Middle Worlds or astral concept-Realms, exist, but for the most part, the hand of the Technocracy has left little imprint on the spirit world, other than a bizarre "Weaver web" which reflects the stasis of the Technocrats' influence.

• **The Hidden Places:** Places exist where the Technocracy has never won. Far beyond the modern world — and from human habitation, period — these primal spots still contain the mystick essence of creation's beginnings. *All* technomagick is vulgar here, no matter who uses it, and many forms of "mundane" technology simply refuse to work at all. A few Asian mountain tops, parts of the Amazon and Outback, ancient ruins, scattered corners where civilization has never touched down, hidden caverns and the deepest corners of some jungles or the sea still accept the oldest forms of magick — those practiced by the Dreamspeakers, Verbena, Akashics and many Nephandi and Crafts — as coincidental.

The Nine Spheres

If God could do the tricks that we can do, he'd be a happy man!
— Eli Cross, *The Stunt Man*

The nine magickal Spheres encompass a broad range of Arts. For simplicity, both the Council of Nine and the Technocratic Union divided these elements into distinct categories. While these Arts go by a multitude of names, their basic properties remain fairly constant.

Both organizations believe in an element that either adds to or encompasses the other nine. Each Tradition seeks a "10th Sphere," (which the others refuse to recognize), while Technocrats strive to unlock the Grand Unification Theory. For now, the nine Spheres (or spheres of influence) are all mages have to work with.

Not that this is limiting; within these Arts, an awesome variety of Effects can be performed. Many spells require only one Sphere, while others may demand conjunctional Effects, which add Spheres together in a single working. The powers listed within the descriptions only show the general possibilities, not the "spells," available at that level.

Incidentally, mysticks do not refer to themselves by Sphere rank numbers. A Master of Forces does not say "I've attained the fifth rank of Forces," but rather, "I have Mastered the Sphere of the Winds, Fire and all lesser Elements."

The following listings are divided this way:

1. Introduction: A master who has studied the Sphere discusses it with the new student.

2: Specialties: When a mystick has four dots or more in a Sphere, she may choose a specialty for it **(see Chapter Six)**. The specialties offered are only a few possibilities.

3. General Description: The Sphere's possibilities are mentioned first, along with notes on the Sphere's unique properties and, in some cases, a chart describing special circumstances.

4. Rank Description: Here we offer a general description of each rank to show the primary magickal Effects a mage can use and the rank at which can use them. These general descriptions form a basis for the custom-built magicks your mages can use.

Always remember, however, that virtually *any* Effect is possible using some combination of the Spheres. If you want to use an Effect that does not appear in these listings, your Storyteller may decide the rank and Sphere (or Spheres) that make the Effect possible. Some incredibly dramatic Effects, however, can only be performed by Arch-Masters who have transcended even these godlike powers. Such beings have studied their Arts for lifetimes on end.

5. Sphere Effects: These specific magickal Effects show what becomes possible at each rank within a Sphere. These are generic guidelines only and merely illustrate the possibilities within the Sphere ranks. **(Charts for the various Spheres appear on page 170.)**

Transmutation and Conjuration

Creating something from nothing, or changing an object from one element into another, requires conjunctional Effects — usually between the physical Pattern Arts, the metaphysical Spirit and the quintessential Prime. It usually works like this: thought (Spirit) to conception (Prime) to material (Matter, Forces or Life).

The metaphysics can go around forever. In game terms, this means that a spell transforming an object governed by one Sphere (let's say Life, for an apple) into another (gold, or Matter) must use both Spheres at their proper rank — in this case, 2.

Creating something out of pure thought rarely requires Spirit (unless that object is specially made of ephemera). The ideal crystallizes as Prime, which fuels the object's creation through a Pattern Sphere. To summon the apple from thin air, use Prime 2/Life 2. To change it to gold, use Life 2/Matter 2.

Once you understand, it's simpler than it sounds.

Correspondence

All things are related; space is an illusion; all things exist in one place, all tied together by the fibers of a single concept. You can call that concept what you will, but I know, and I can prove to you, that three-dimensional separation is a lie.

See that corner? Where am I? There or here? I think I'm there. See, I am! Did you see me walk across the room. Didn't think so. So how did I get from here to there? Transporter beams? Wrong answer! And even if it was, how did they work?

Feel that tap on your shoulder? I did that. But I'm over here, right, which is over there to you. But yet I could touch you over there while I'm over here. There, I did it again! Get it? Space is an illusion!

If that hurts your brain, you're not cut out for this routine. Before school's out in my workshop, kid, you'll either crack or clock Euclid a good one upside the head!

Specialties: Conjuration, Scrying, Warding, Teleportation

The Sphere of Correspondence involves an understanding of locations, spatial relativity and the interrelation between people and objects. This allows mages to teleport, pull rabbits out of hats, create magickal barriers and levitate or fly through the air. Correspondence is also commonly mixed with other Spheres to allow mages to work magick on subjects hundreds of miles away as easily as if they were right in front of them.

Since Correspondence deals with space and relationships, its range differs from the other eight Spheres. The theory popular among the Virtual Adepts, the most recent Masters of Correspondence, is that space is ultimately an illusion. All points in existence are "stacked" in one "place," which the computer wizards refer to as the Correspondence Point or All-Space. "Here," "there" and "somewhere else" are all artificial labels. The shortest distance between two points is not a straight line; space is merely a mathematical construct.

The "Correspondence Point" hypothesis falls flat, however, when confronted with certain aspects of metaphysics. You can't, for example, teleport someone's heart out of his body or cut a coin in half without also using the Sphere of Life or Matter.

More traditional mages explain Correspondence by the ancient doctrine of contagion: "Once together, always together." In other words, the part always retains a connection to the whole, and it is simpler to perform any working when there is a connection — physical, mental or spiritual — between them. It's generally easier for a mage to teleport to the place where she grew up than it is to go somewhere she only saw once.

While most mages need to touch their subject to work their Arts, those skilled in Correspondence may skirt barriers or distance by forming links through space or related objects. The chart **(on page 170)** shows the successes needed to forge a link between two points. The weaker the connection, the more successes the spell requires. To get around this, many mages plant items they know well on persons or at locations they wish to affect from afar. This can be risky; contagion is a rope which tugs both ways, and those who discover a planted object may use it in their own spells against the mage who placed it as if they had Correspondence Arts themselves.

Mages who advance in Correspondence ahead of other Spheres appear to be "spaced out." Their eyes are unfocused, as they now rely on their spatial sense over sight. Nevertheless, their physical movements are very precise; these mages never trip or stub their toes.

• Immediate Spatial Perceptions

At this stage, the mage gains a keen understanding of how objects and space relate. She can intuitively sense distances between objects, find true north (or any other direction) and sense things in her immediate vicinity without using the normal five senses. This new sense also allows her to also detect spatial instabilities, warps and wormholes.

•• Sense Space
Touch Space

The mage may now extend her senses beyond her immediate vicinity to distant or hidden locations. Any of the five senses can expand this way. However, most mages feel that such magickal perceptions thin the barriers between the two points in space, creating a weakness in the Tapestry (like those a rank one Effect can spot). Luckily, the mage may also re-work the fabric of space, reinforcing the Tapestry and creating a barrier to hinder scrying or the opening of actual rifts. This works like countermagick, deducting successes for each success.

In conjunction with Life 2 or Matter 2, the mage may also grasp small items — house cat-sized or smaller — and pull them through the Tapestry, conjuring them from "nowhere."

••• Pierce Space
Seal Gate
Co-locality Perception

The mage now gains the strength to make a small rent in the Tapestry, so small that only the mage herself — and whatever she holds or carries — may slip through before it seals. She may also seal such rifts or prevent them from opening, though the greater the rift, the more difficult the feat.

At this level, a mage learns to sense multiple locations at once, perceiving the various scenes as several ghostly landscapes overlapping one another. Working with the other Spheres, a mage may also grasp items governed by the Pattern Magicks and slide them through space, performing levitation and telekinesis.

•••• Rend Space
Co-locate Self

The Adept may now create larger rents in the Tapestry to transport other beings and large objects and forces. With enough successes (10+), she may even force the rent wide enough to make a permanent Gateway.

The mage may now manifest physically in multiple locations at once, though she should also use Mind 1 if she wants to think effectively in all of them, and Life 2 if she wants her multiple selves to perform separate actions.

••••• Mutate Localities
Co-location

A Master of Correspondence learns how to distort space. She can affect distances and sizes around her, stretching them and shrinking them to fit her needs. In scientific terms, the mass of objects cannot be changed, but their volumes and dimensions are like potter's clay.

She may also stack locations on top of one another in a bizarre landscape of multiple forms or connect a variety of items together. At this point, the Master's perceptions are so wildly expanded that her mundane Perception may be enhanced beyond the normal human maximum, as with **Better Body (see "Life")**.

Correspondence

• Immediate Spatial Perceptions
•• Sense Space
Touch Space
••• Pierce Space
Seal Gate
Co-locality Perception
•••• Rend Space
Co-locate Self
••••• Mutate Localities
Co-location

Specialties: Conjuration, Scrying, Warding, Teleportation

Correspondence Effects

• Landscape of the Mind — This Effect, available to all Correspondence Disciples, allows a mage to sense the objects which fill the space around her. She can extend the area of perception, but this requires more and more active concentration. After the area reaches the diameter of a city block, the sensory input becomes too much to bear.

• Whereami? — The mage can sense where she is in relation to everything else. Virtual Adepts call this Effect "whereami?" When used conjunctionally with the first rank of Spirit, it can help establish which world or Shard Realm (and where in it) the mage is in, while a conjunctional Effect with Mind 1 allows the mage to establish whether she is hallucinating or dreaming.

•• Open/Close Window (Correspondence Sensing) — Through the ancient technique of scrying, a mage may open a window in space and extend her senses through it to observe events at a remote location. This is often combined with Time or Spirit so as to search other times or worlds.

Scrying may also examine snags in the Tapestry, like those left by a teleporting mage or previous scrying, and trace it back to the other side. Combined with Spirit, a mage may scan to another Realm. Such spying may be detected, however, by a target rolling Perception + Awareness (or Alertness, for other mystick creatures), difficulty 7.

A mage may also reverse this Effect so as to shut a window or prevent one from opening, such as when a mage senses that someone is attempting to scry her. This works like countermagick against the spy.

•• Apportation — By pressing against the fabric of space, a mage may create a pinprick in the Tapestry. While too small to step through, such rifts allow the mage to grasp a distant item and pull it through — or send it away — using Life or Matter. This only works on very small, simple objects.

A third rank variation allows the mystick to forge a connection to some simple object — again with Life or Matter — which allows it to levitate or fly for the Effect's duration.

•• Ward — While windows in space are the most popular method of magickal spying, wards are the most popular prevention. The mage reaches out with the threads of her magick and the fabric of space, creating a ward.

Wards vary in strength, ranging from mere "window blinds" to "iron shutters." Each success subtracts from attempts to scry, apport or teleport either way. Indeed, some areas are so heavily warded that breaking through would take years — which, of course, is only fair, as the wards were built up over a span of years as well. Attempts to break down a ward will leave traces unless the mage chooses to repair it and cover her tracks.

Many wards, especially ancient and powerful ones, have keys or back doors; mages who possess these (or discover them through Enigmas or Computers rolls) may bypass them. With Life or Matter, wards may also be placed on people or objects, making it more difficult to scry or otherwise access them via Correspondence.

A level 3 variation, **Ban**, can actually stop objects or beings which have been warded against. Only one specific thing — knives, lightning, vampires — can be so banished. This requires an item with some connection to the banned thing, a conjuctional Effect with Life, Matter or Spirit 3 and five or more successes to erect. Only unweaving **(see "Countermagick")** can destroy a ban, though objects not banned — bullets, or items or spells thrown by the banned party — pass right through unless they too have been banned. Oddly, this does not work against True Magick or Paradox spirits. This lasts for the spell's duration.

••• Chain — A chain is a magical bond which links two objects or creatures to each other through sympathetic Resonance. Such bonds often already exist, but a mage with Correspondence can strengthen them or create one where none was before. For each success with this Effect, a mage may take an object or creature up (or down) a level on the **Correspondence Range** Chart.

••• The Seven-League Stride — The name of this Effect harkens back to medieval times and the mages of the Order of Hermes who commonly made use of "seven-league" boots as foci for this Effect, each stride taking the wearer precisely seven leagues forward.

This magick creates a small, extremely transitory rip in the fabric of space, allowing a mystick to slip through to reach any other location on Earth. Depending on the precise magick used, she may see all the intervening space moving by in a blur, or she may simply click her heels together, disappear and reappear.

This Effect does not immunize a mage to her new surroundings; if she shifted to the ocean depths expecting a submarine to be there, she would be crushed by the intense water pressure. Scrying one's intended destination beforehand is advisable — "Look before you leap" as the proverb goes. Consequently many mages favor magic mirrors as their foci, as these may both be looked and stepped through.

Level 4 variations of this Effect exist, involving teleportation machines, cabinets and secret doors. These higher-level Effects transport larger or more numerous subjects. Misdirection is essential; a subject hidden from sight when it disappears is less likely to arouse suspicion — and Paradox.

••• **Divided Sight** — Cultists of Ecstasy love this Effect, which multiplies their sensory input. A mage merely extends her senses to multiple locations at once; visions stack atop one another like a photographic multiple exposure, and sounds mix like several radios tuned to different stations.

There is no limit to the number of locations a mage can sense, but a Wits roll is needed to distinguish which objects are in which location. The difficulty number is equal to twice the number of scenes being viewed. Going above one's Perception or Wits rating is dangerous; such overload can push a mystick into Quiet.

••• **Filter All-Space** — Given certain knowledge about any person or object, the mage can search through reality to find where the object exists in three-dimensional space. The less the mystick knows, the longer such searches take, and there are no guarantees. There are many heavily warded areas in three-dimensional space, not to mention portals to other worlds and times, so such searches are lengthy and uncertain.

••• **Stalking the Void** — This advanced version of **Open Window** allows a mage skilled in Correspondence to trace a snag in the Tapestry back to its point of origin. While the second rank of Correspondence allows a mage to reopen a window, this Effect allows a mage to break through personally to confront the spy.

This Effect is particularly popular among the Euthanatos. However, Correspondence only deals with space; some disturbances extend to other times and dimensions. To be absolutely certain of your prey, older mages advise that trackers add Time and Spirit perceptions to scout ahead. Some mages who have used this Effect have never been heard from again, for many disturbances are not what they seem....

•••• **Bubble of Reality** — Using this magick, the mage warps space around her body or some other thing, taking it into its own pocket universe. In this state, she is completely invisible and intangible to everything around her. The walls to the world outside are thin, however, and the mage may scry out (or in) from her bubble of reality. Moving bubbles and large bubbles (such as would contain a motorcycle or building) require four successes or more.

•••• **Hermes Portal** — The Order of Hermes claims to have created this Correspondence Effect, cutting a permanent Gate in the Tapestry, then sealing the breach with a powerful ban to prevent the passage of everything but sentient, willing creatures.

The resulting magick creates an apparent window which can connect a drawing room to the deep ocean while preventing the water and fish from pouring through the breach. The alternative is of course highly vulgar and extremely dangerous, though not unknown, especially as a terrorist measure by Marauders.

Many of these portals may be placed in the same location, giving the effect of a hall of mirrors, each opening onto a new location, with an area of null-space in between.

••••• **Co-location** — With this bizarre magick, a mage may stack multiple locations, allowing them to freely interact. No damage occurs to objects that superimpose themselves on one another during co-location, yet they are solid to one another, and, once separated, will not superimpose again.

Stacking two locations is possible, but highly vulgar (raise difficulty to 10), and generally speaking, only done by Marauders.

••••• **Polyappearance** — The mage may appear in multiple locations at once. This Effect parallels **Divided Sight** but in addition to sensing locations, the mage's physical form actually appears in each location as well. Observers in each location will see the mage and can interact with her normally. The willworker, however, must simultaneously interact with each location into which she has projected herself. Anything she says or does will be heard and seen by observers at all locations.

This interaction is one-way from the mage's perspective. Items in one location do not affect observers who are in a different location, but all objects in all locations affect the mystick equally. The walls closest to her will block her sight, and she will suffer from assaults directed at any of her co-located body positions.

A mage can use this phenomenon to her advantage. The Akashic art of Do contains an advanced movement called the Kick of the Four Winds. The attacker executes a flying spin kick at an opponent, and while in midair, co-locates to four positions directly around the opponent, so that the force of one kick impacts the opponent from four sides instead of one. (Add four additional Health Levels of damage to the blow.)

Mages who truly wish to occupy several places at once can use a conjunctional Effect with Mind, Prime and Life, creating a new body and train of thought for each additional location. While this magick allows for multiple mundane tasks, it does not duplicate the Avatar; only the original may perform magick.

••••• **Spatial Mutations** — With this magick, the mage can stretch distances, change the size of objects and warp space around her. A short hallway could be made to stretch on for miles, while a HIT Mark could be shrunk to the size of an ant.

Mass, however, does not change, unless the mage uses a conjunctional Effect with Life or Matter, and while an ant-sized HIT Mark would be easy to run away from, it would be almost impossible to crush.

Entropy

When they cast lots for the garments of Christ, the soldiers weren't playing games. They were auguring the future. Did you know that one retired to Pompeii a few decades later with a fat pension and a doom he couldn't shake? It caught up with him, and with Pompeii, and, much later, with Rome. I know. I remember it well.

No, child — I'm old, but I'm not immortal. But in a former life I cast the blood-spattered lots that foretold my fate for my part in the Great Crime. I ran from my destiny, but that fate tracked me to the isle. Random chance? Child, nothing is random.

I recall many spokes in the Great Wheel. Death to me is but a stream forded by each of us time and again. I remember my lives through my study of the Wheel and began that study by casting my lots. Here, take my dice, and feel the weight of Destiny. Are you prepared for it? If not, leave such Arts to those who remember fate.

Specialties: Fate, Fortune, Order, Chaos

The theories used to explain the Sphere of Entropy range from disjointed ramblings to treatises of such intricate reasoning and logic as to be equally incomprehensible. Technocratic Traditions use models of complex thermodynamic science, while more mystickal Traditions refer to "Wyrd," "karma" or "destiny," and naturalistic mages refer to "luck" and the pleasure of the spirits.

The path of Destiny appears to be one of decay. Life forms die, rocks erode, electricity scatters, organizations collapse, empires crumble and everything dissolves into chaos. As it's easier to go with the flow than against it, proponents of Entropy — like the Euthanatos — have found it simpler to understand the lesson of Shiva and use the flow of probability to destroy instead of create.

The practical applications of this Sphere are manifold. Disciples learn to quantify probability energy, which most mages call Destiny, Fate or Fortune. Through observation, a mage may spot "accidents waiting to happen" and take advantage of them, while at higher levels, the mage learns to manipulate the actual threads of probability.

Mages who study Entropy tend to specialize either in sowing chaos and confusion or in reaffirming order and reason, though some follow an enigmatic middle ground. Curses and blessings are their specialty, and they can bring the strange force of Wyrd to bear on objects, individuals and even ideas and concepts, as well as those who associate with these things. These mages understand how all patterns break down, and thus, how they work in the first place.

Direct Entropy Effects do no damage until the fourth level, after which they have the usual effect. Applications of entropy — crumbling walls, disintegrated bridges, etc. — are more effective, and inflict the usual damage.

Masters of Entropy vary in appearance according to their specialty, ranging from babbling madmen to meticulously dressed university professors, enigmatic gypsies or happy-go-lucky gamblers as fickle and easily distracted as Dame Fortune herself. Mages with a high Awareness will be able to detect a dark, impenetrable core in the Patterns of all followers of Entropy. The greater the mage's Entropy rating, the deeper and more enigmatic this "heart of darkness" and the more inscrutable its nature.

• Sense Fate & Fortune

Disciples of Entropy learn to examine each thing and discern its strengths and weaknesses, examining what it is and what it does. The mage begins to sense the current of Destiny, and can discern what is significant and what is not, and what is true or untrue.

Given this knowledge, the mage can pick a lucky horse, sense if a lock has some defect or choose the original between two identical items. Fate, however, is a fickle thing, and Fortune even more so. These insights are not perfect, just advanced.

Unreliable as it may be, the ability to judge certainties and likelihoods is quite useful. Pressure points, lies and opportunities become obvious to one who knows their patterns. This may not have any dramatic effects, but once you understand an enemy's strengths and weaknesses, it doesn't take Sun Tzu to determine a combat strategy or Lucretia Borgia to figure out a subterfuge.

•• Control Probability

Now that the threads of Fate have been identified, the dominos of Fortune may be pushed. Disciples learn control over probability by studying where it concentrates. Phenomena as diverse as card shuffling, dice rolling, market fluctuations, traffic jams, lost mail and roulette wheels teach the mage to identify order in chaos, chaos in order and the paths of probability.

This gives the mage amazing, yet subtle control over hundreds of small events. He can control whom a waiter will serve first, who picks the shortest straw, who wins a coin flip or finds the one bullet in a chamber, etc. He may determine the outcome of any minor event that would normally be random. Once he discerns which apparently random events are in fact predetermined, he can then manipulate other eventualities to his own ends.

There's a limit to this control; the greater the probability he tries to affect, the more difficult the act becomes. Determining a coin-toss is simple magick. Determining the toss of the same coin 100 times in succession becomes correspondingly more difficult. Hexing a pack of cards to deal a royal flush is in the realm of possibility, but ordering a shuffled deck such that each card comes out as if it had never been shuffled is a miracle probably not worth the bother.

••• Affect Predictable Patterns

Inanimate objects and tangible forces, as Patterns of order, are most subject to the forces of Entropy. Machines are especially susceptible to this phenomena. Clocks wind down, engines break, warranties expire and all things eventually fray and decay.

A Disciple of Entropy can "fix" this deterioration, causing new television sets to blow a fuse while old junker cars mysteriously still run years after they should have fallen apart. Rocks may also be caused to erode and teapots to chip and shatter, but as Entropy is a slow and gradual process, the only things which can be affected instantly are those, such as machines, which have thousands of intricate moving parts.

As with Rank Two, the mage is still limited by the realm of possibility. The more unlikely a feat, the more difficult it becomes and the less time and bother it's worth. Order can only be fixed and Entropy kept at bay for so long before things follow their natural course.

Mystick mages view this process as cursing or blessing an object, or laying a Destiny upon it. Such forces can be controlled; at this rank, the mage may imbue a physical object with probability energy by adding Life 2 or Matter 2 to the spell, affecting the course of its Destiny and of those who come in contact with it. A blessed locket may take a bullet intended for its wearer, though he may later die a glorious death in battle. Time 2 allows more of a say in such events, but even then, they may not be certain.

•••• Affect Life

The Effects of Entropy, order and probability are far more complex when dealing with living organisms, due to living beings' complex and self-corrective nature. If a robot overtaxes itself and stresses its workings, it runs down until someone repairs it. A man who overtaxes himself will heal given time and care, and may even grow stronger.

Adepts of Entropy study how life forms begin, mature, wither, and die. They also observe the hundreds of factors which affect the course of life, from the effects of heredity to the stresses of evolution and growth. The Adept learns how to influence the random factors of life, giving her immense power either to destroy it or affect its development.

With this magick, a mage can weave a potent spell over a living being, blessing or cursing him and his line. Other Spheres may be woven into such a charm, creating hereditary magickal gifts or flamboyant curses. These Arts affect probability, not Life Patterns themselves.

••••• Affect Thought

Masters of Entropy expand their control over reality by studying the ways in which ideas change over time.

The Effects of the natural order of things on objects are fairly clear and indisputable, but the fact that chaos affects intelligent thought seems farfetched. Yet everything which is organized is subject to the laws which govern order and chaos, be it the structure of a molecule or an organized body of knowledge.

Masters of Entropy point to human history for countless examples of theories and paradigms that outgrew their usefulness over the centuries (the irony of such observations is lost on many Council mages). Thoughts, the Masters of Entropy point out, are at once the most mercurial and the most tenacious things, yet as any politician can tell you, they can be molded, shaped and influenced over time.

Where the Masters of Mind rudely subject the minds of others to their own will, however, Masters of Entropy merely point out things that will strike a person a particular way and let his thoughts follow the natural progression to other possibilities.

Master of Entropy who specialize in chaos can shatter a person's world view simply by making a few weird comments (or can at least confuse him), while those specializing in order can present logical arguments which can advance a person's conscious or subconscious thoughts to some higher (or at least different) set of ideas. Masters who specialize in Fate or Fortune can lead subjects to inescapable conclusions or spark random, creative thoughts, which a subject may absorb as he sees fit.

This supreme magick directs the force of Wyrd into a mental concept, creating a "happy thought" or "cursed idea," which brings Fate or Fortune to bear on those who concentrate upon it, possibly extinguishing or exalting the thought. This may lead to paradigm shifts, new faiths or insanity.

Entropy

•	Sense Fate & Fortune
••	Control Probability
•••	Affect Predictable Patterns
••••	Affect Life
•••••	Affect Thought

Specialites: Fate, Fortune, Order, Chaos

Entropy Effects

• **Dim Mak** — Akashic Brothers who study Entropy learn the insidious martial arts technique of Dim Mak, the art of striking vital points. While many mundane martial artists pursue Dim Mak (called *Atemi* in Japanese), only the Akashic Brothers learn the technique in its true form, which requires the use of magick.

Using his knowledge of Entropy, an Akashic mage identifies the weakest parts of an inanimate structure or living body. By identifying these pressure points and then physically striking them, he inflicts one extra Health Level of damage for each success scored when evoking the magickal Effect (this requires a normal combat success as well). By combining this with a conjunctional Time 4 Effect, the **Dim Mak** Entropy damage may surface long after the blow itself has been forgotten.

Every structure or living being has different weaknesses; the mage must apply his magickal senses to each individual object he attacks in order to identify its particular pressure points. Also, the pressure points of living things slowly change depending on the time of day, season and other more esoteric factors, so the mage must re-examine living targets at each meeting.

Other Traditions use similar Entropy Effects.

• **Locate Disorder** — The mage can identify the area of greatest disorder in an institution or organized sequence of events. The more successes scored, the more precise the information gained. This is a sensory Effect.

Say a mage wants to infiltrate the staff of a hotel. She scores one success and thereby detects that the restaurant operation is the most disorganized element. She disguises herself as a chef and infiltrates the kitchen, guessing that other employees won't notice a new recruit. With more successes, she might discover that the greatest point of disorder in the hotel's business operation lies in the pantry manager's personnel files, which are totally disorganized.

The mystick must be somewhat familiar with the organization she studies to gain much benefit, though the ability does facilitate extraordinary deductive abilities. In the example above, the mage would need to spend some time walking around the hotel and talking to a few of the employees before she could pinpoint the business' chaos point.

• **Ring of Truth** — Certain words resound with destiny. Sometimes people can speak prophecy or truth without even knowing it. A mage can recognize this; this Effect grants the ability to discern higher truth and greater significance in spoken or written words, and to detect lies with some accuracy. This gives the mage a sixth sense; he may roll Perception + Intuition to discover the greater truth — or falsehood — in anything he hears or reads. He may not know *why* something is important, but he can tell when a fact is a fact. A mage who uses this to discover a lie can subtract successes of Subterfuge rolls like countermagick against a spell (one for one). A liar may continue to lie with opposed rolls **(see Chapter Five)**.

This sixth sense does not deal with the future specifically (that form of precognition comes with Time 2). The **Ring of Truth** generally deals with the present, though it can be combined with Time 2 for predictions of startling accuracy.

•• **Beginner's Luck** — There is a statistical possibility than any random attempt to do anything will actually succeed. You can get a hole-in-one the first time you pick up a golf club, or hit the bull's eye on the first try. The trouble is doing it the second time, as the chance gets exceedingly improbable. One lucky shot is in the realm of possibility, but five holes-in-one from a rank amateur is beyond belief.

Most mages agree that skill and practice will beat blind luck any day. When faced with any feat which she has never attempted before (or at least succeeded in), however, a mystick may use this Effect to call upon the force of beginner's luck and make an impossible shot.

For each success with this Effect, the Storyteller may add one success to any non-magickal skill roll which a mage has two dice or less to attempt, in addition to any successes which the mage makes on her own. The "automatic successes" from this Effect last until they are used in some spectacular success, at which point the magick expends itself.

Each future attempt to use this same magick for the same feat adds +1 to the difficulty. This reflects diminishing returns. Mages who wish to continue to make spectacular successes should purchase additional levels of the skill in question. No one stays a beginner for long.

•• **Games of Luck** — Using her power to control localized random events, the mage can virtually determine the outcome of any game of luck. She may control the throw of dice, the shuffle of cards, the fall of a roulette ball and other such events. The more successes scored, the more precise the control she exerts.

••• **Slay Machine** — Entropy students can turn technological marvels into ruined heaps. At this level, the mage uses his knowledge of Entropy to infuse technological systems with raw chaos. Any modern machinery or electronic device can be caused to malfunction or even self-destruct.

Computer systems corrupt all of their stored data, rendering it unintelligible. Electrical currents within electronic equipment surge so radically that components melt. Phone networks randomly scatter their calls, routing them to wrong numbers. Power distribution equipment, like circuit breaker boxes, go haywire — some breakers trip for no reason, while others fail to trip, causing power surges, blown light bulbs and overheated power lines.

The more successes scored, the greater the magnitude of disorder caused. Several successes may be required to cause large machinery to glitch once or twice, while small systems will run amok with the same number of successes.

A similar Effect, **Erode Matter**, causes gases to diffuse into the air, liquids to evaporate and solids to disintegrate. The number of successes rolled for the Effect determines how quickly the matter dissolves and how much of it can be affected. Three successes rot away a wooden door within a minute, while five successes corrode the steel body of a truck in under five minutes.

••• **Like Clockwork** — The Technocracy is most famous for this Effect, though all mages make use of it. After this enchantment, a machine, typically a clock, will run error-free and as precisely as it was designed to do. Both the device and the spell must be maintained occasionally (otherwise probability gets stretched too far), but clocks (and other devices) can run "like clockwork" for centuries.

This Effect can insulate the device from **Slay Machine** attempts. The magick used to maintain perfect operation will foil most attempts to cause something to go wrong by way of Entropy. This magick, however, does not insulate the machine against Spheres like Matter, which sabotage the device magickally (though similar Matter Effects can prevent this as well).

•••• **Blight of Aging** — Commonly focused through brews, poisons, effigies or curses, this Effect infuses primal entropy directly into a targeted life form, causing its body to quickly deteriorate and decay. This resembles advanced aging; the target effectively ages five years for each success scored on the magickal Effect roll.

Life forms aged past their normal life spans will quickly die and turn to dust. Victims prematurely advanced to old age should be assigned penalties to their Physical Attributes.

Many Traditions use similar life-destroying Entropy Effects, but the Verbena are best known for it. Because they normally relish the vibrancy of life, Verbena see the removal of that vigor as the worst sort of punishment.

•••• **Midwife's Blessing** — The Verbena claim to have originated this ancient magick. The mage lays her hands on the belly of a pregnant woman and blesses the child, typically, "To grow tall, straight of limb and well favored." Anything more is considered superfluous, though the Progenitors often design the child's entire look and body.

Each success rolled reduces the probability of disease or deformity. Three successes or more will usually insulate a child from any sort of disease, short of a massive plague, for life. Again, this affects probability, not the body itself, though it may be combined with Life 4 to grant the child vitality or beauty.

••••• **Destroy Thought** — A favorite tactic of the NWO, this Effect causes any rational thought or feeling to dissolve away in the chosen subject's mind. A gunman facing the mage can have his resolve to shoot quickly broken down — "I'll kill you... No, I won't kill you, I'll *hurt* you, though... but if I shoot you, I'll go to jail... Even if I get away, he's got friends... Ah, hell with it!" (Gunman flees.)

Once the Effect has taken hold, the victim usually begins to rationalize away the affected thought. As in the example above, the victim finds the weaknesses and illogic inherent in the idea or feeling and so abandons it. The thought is destroyed.

The Storyteller must decide how many successes are necessary for the Effect, depending on the complexity of the thought and the passion of the victim. One-three successes can dissuade a person from a whim, while five or more would be needed to reject a deeply-held passion or conviction.

••••• **Binding Oath** — One of the most ancient rites of magecraft. When someone enters into a pact, agreement or service, the mage administering or giving that oath may call the force of destiny to witness the proceedings and to punish anyone who breaks the spirit of the oath.

A binding oath is a powerful magick, with dire consequences for those who break it. A mage who swore to "Protect the most ancient Order of Hermes," then defected to the Technocracy, would have some horrible doom fall upon him. He would also be psychically marked as an oathbreaker, a dire stigma easily detected by mages sensitive to destiny (i.e., Entropy 1). If the mage breaks an oath due to some outside compulsion — he's sworn to protect someone, but kills her while mentally enslaved by another — this does not count as being forsworn unless the mage willingly submitted to the mental enslavement. Circumstances do apply.

Forces

There is power in the elements, the force of creation bound up into compact forms, bursting with potential. You may call them by their proper names — earth, air, fire, water — or by any other common appellation — Spheres of Fire, Dream-Patterns, periodic elements, whatever. The pulse of the gods cares not what name you apply.

Touch my hand. Can you feel it? That crackle in the air, inches from where my mortal skin begins? That is the legacy of command. The winds themselves bow as I pass by, for I know their thousand names and call them at my pleasure. Soon, that Art shall be yours.

Specialties: Elements (any or all), Technology, Physics, Weather

Humans have long sought to control the energies of nature. Toward this end they have employed techniques ranging from rain dances to billion-dollar fusion power experiments. Modern man has progressed a long way toward harnessing many of these energies, but mages who master the Sphere of Forces know that there is much that "civilization" does not understand. Masters of Forces are enlightened beyond the bounds of Newtonian physics, quantum theory and special relativity; they apply theories and practices that allow them to manipulate and create any of the forces of nature.

Forces is one of the Pattern Magicks, which, along with the etheric Sphere of Prime, form the Spheres of the Elements. Even those forces defined by modern Technocratic science as the absence of force — darkness, silence, stillness, cold — are forces in and of themselves to some philosophies. The Akashic Brotherhood refers to Forces as the Sphere of Fire, while the Order of Hermes numbers it as the Sphere of the masculine elements, Fire and Air. Regardless of the view, within the Sphere of Forces, all forces are considered equal. Terminologies differ, but mages who seek to cause serious damage to their foes often study this Sphere.

Nothing beats Forces for sheer destructive power; an Effect utilizing Forces adds one additional success to damage rolls. This does not apply to other uses, which apply the successes rolled straight up. Certain energies are limited by Sphere levels; simple manifestations can be used at lower levels, while massive phenomena are limited to the higher ranks. Most larger Effects also require plenty of successes.

Mages who master Forces reveal themselves in weird and distinct ways, depending upon their chosen Art. When an ice wizard enters a room, the temperature drops, while candles flare brighter around a fire witch. A storm lord's hair and breath crackle with static electricity and his voice rumbles with thunder, and a spellsinger may be surrounded by soft music and shatter glass when she screams. Other mages tend to give Masters of Forces some distance, as they are infamously Paradox-prone and their magick tends to be very messy.

• Perceive Forces

The mage discerns the movements of energy. By identifying their Patterns, she can perceive all types of energy flows, sensing wavelengths far beyond the limited range of visible light and sonic frequencies upon which normal mortals rely. The mage may see anything from infrared light to x-rays to gravity waves. Even in the absence of such positive forces, some mages have learned how to perceive colors in darkness, sense stillness and hear volumes from silence.

•• Control Minor Forces

All the positive forces are essentially the same — sound, light, heat, etc. — as are the negative forces (or their absence, to use the Technocracy's definition) — silence, darkness, cold and so on. While a mage at this level of understanding cannot fundamentally change either positive or negative energies, she can exercise some degree of control over their ebb and flow.

Sound and silence may be sent in different directions, allowing a mage to disguise her voice, eavesdrop at a far distance or cloak herself in an field of silence, sending the sound of her footfalls far into the ground. Light and darkness may be bent and refracted, focused and diffused, allowing the mage to change apparent colors, displace his image, wrap himself in shadows, create a mirage or focus a flashlight into a fine laser. Heat and cold may be shuffled about, warming one thing while chilling another, while other forces may be controlled in a similar manner, including gravity, electricity, magnetism and all manner of radiation.

The amount of energy that can be controlled at this level is limited. A mage controlling electricity with this knowledge could short-circuit a car or a house, but not an apartment building or a power plant. One controlling light or darkness could black out a house, but not a city block, and a mage controlling kinetic energy might deflect a bullet or change the vector of a skateboard, but could only slow, not stop, a Mack truck. The larger the force to be controlled, and the degree of that control, the more successes the spell demands. A candle flame can be made to flare with only one success, but a bonfire requires five or more, and to make a flame dance or form pictures requires even more successes. To control greater forces requires Forces 4.

••• Transmute Minor Forces

The mage can now change one force into another, flip positive into negative, or create or destroy forces as she likes, summoning them out of thin air and dissolving them into same. With this level of Forces alone, a mage may change one force into another. Radiation may be transformed into sound, kinetic motion to electricity, heat into cold or light into darkness.

With a conjunctional Effect with the Spheres of Matter or Life, a mage may transmute things of those Spheres into a Force of the strength governed by this level.

Alternately, the mage may reweave ambient Quintessence (with Prime 2) into one of the baser forces or transform base energy into pure ether. Both Aristotelian alchemy and modern science teach that energy and matter are, at essence, the same thing. With this magick, a mage may transmute the elements — even changing invisible ether into physical force and summoning such force from "nowhere."

The amount of Forces that can be created by use of this level is limited as with Forces 2, but with enough success, a mage with this power can now freeze enemies solid or incinerate them on the spot, blow up cars, fly through the air, levitate alligators and erase reams of data with a magnetic pulse. With Life 4, a mage may even transform himself into a being of living fire or lightning, a shadow or a chill in the air.

•••• Control Major Forces

This power works like Forces 2 above, but the maximum for that level is the minimum for this one. With enough successes, the degree of power a mage may wield with Forces 4 is frightening. He may focus the light of the sun into a laser canon or cloak football stadiums with prismatic illusions, redirect missiles mid-flight, send shockwaves the other way, banish a thousand shadows into a single corner and melt glaciers while lakes are frozen solid. Most of these Effects, of course, are quite vulgar, so there are restrictions. He could, of course, also use this level of understanding to guard himself and others from the fury of these forces — to fireproof forests, protect ships from storms and so on.

Forces

- • Perceive Forces
- •• Control Minor Forces
- ••• Transmute Minor Forces
- •••• Control Major Forces
- ••••• Transmute Major Forces

Specialties: Elements (any or all), Technology, Physics, Weather

••••• Transmute Major Forces

This level operates like Forces 3 above, but with enough successes, the degree of power a mage may access is almost limitless. Technomancers have used this knowledge to unleash the power of the atom and create nuclear explosions, but luckily consensual reality, common sense and countermagick limit careless uses of this ability. Some powers are luckily still beyond the scale of this level of Forces, although some mages strive to master them (including the sorceress Louhi, of Finnish legend, who is still — unsuccessfully — attempting to put out the sun). Large Effects require many successes, as well as logic — it's easier to brew a storm during monsoon season than in the middle of a drought, for example — but a Master of Forces may conjure hurricanes, firestorms, tidal waves, earthquakes and nuclear blasts.

Forces Effects

• **Darksight** — In the absence of visible light, the mage can shift his perceptions up or down the spectrum of electromagnetic radiation. This allows him to view infrared or ultraviolet light, radio waves, x-rays, etc. He won't be able to discern colors, but may read other interesting perceptions from the various spectra — x-rays would allow him to see an object's underlying structure, and he could see in the dark using infrared.

• **Quantify Energy** — By invoking this Effect, a mage can sense the type and amount of energy at work around her. She can easily translate her perceptions into accurate measurement units such as volts, amps, tesla, g's, etc. Note that this includes kinetic energy, which allows the mage to determine an object's velocity in relation to her if she knows the object's mass.

•• **Discharge Static** — The mage can cause the static electricity in the air to discharge spontaneously in a localized area. If the Effect centers around a victim, he will suffer one Health Level of damage per success scored (he can try to soak this damage; the usual +1 success does not apply). If a living target suffers more Health Levels than its Stamina rating, it is stunned (unable to act) a number of turns equal to the difference. This Effect is easier to perform when the air is dry (low humidity) or when the mage is around powerful electrical machinery.

Some Akashic Brothers use a similar Effect to become living reservoirs of static electricity, which they discharge when striking opponents.

•• **System Havoc** — Using this Effect, a mage can touch any electrical machinery or power distribution system and virtually destroy it by fluctuating the current entering the system into spikes of electrical energy. Many advanced systems are tempest-hardened (protected against surges). Tempest-hardening may minimize the damage the mage inflicts, but virtually any system can be shut down if not damaged.

Virtual Adepts use a similar Effect to control electrical machinery. Their control is rudimentary at best, and the mage must also have a firm understanding of the machinery (gained via Technology, Computer, or Science Abilities).

•• **Walking on Water** — By controlling the molecular cohesion on the surface of a liquid (usually water), a mage can make the surface solid enough to walk across. Depending on the number of successes the character rolls, other people can follow along.

•• or ••• (depending on the size of the object) Telekinetic Control — The willworker may telekinetically control the movements of an object, assuming it's already in motion. The object cannot be made to move faster than its original speed, though the mage can slow or stop it by siphoning kinetic energy into the air around it. This velocity limitation results from the mage's inability to create more kinetic energy to impart to the object. The Adept can, however, redirect the flow of kinetic energy to change the object's direction; bullets may be reversed to strike the gunman, while a moving car may be forced sideways instead of forward.

The more successes the caster rolls, the more kinetic energy he can command: four successes would grant control over a speeding bullet or a sprinting man, five a moving car, etc. It is very difficult to maintain control of a living creature, as the creature can simply stop moving. A Wits roll is necessary for very fine telekinetic movements such as threading a needle.

Members of the Akashic Brotherhood use telekinetic powers to give themselves extraordinary leaping abilities when performing Do. It's said that some Verbena do indeed craft telekinetic Talismans shaped like brooms, but this may just be stereotyping.

••• **Call Lightning** — If a thunderstorm (or other electrical discharge) is nearby, a mystick can route lightning out of the sky to strike any visible target in the vicinity. The victim can soak damage normally. Living beings may also be stunned as described above in **Discharge Static**.

•••• **Embracing the Earth Mother** — The Dreamspeakers believe that they can stir the Earth Mother into brief moments of fitful wakefulness. By sounding their drums deep and loud, they can call Gaia to embrace a chosen target. The Effect causes gravity to focus around the chosen area or target.

Each success on the Effect roll allows the mage to create a gravitational field one "g" strong (a "g" being a force of gravity equal to Earth's normal pull). So, with four successes, the mage could create a field of gravity four g's strong (in which a 100-pound boy would weigh 400 pounds). Five successes enable five g's, six enable six g's, etc.

As a general rule, a character can barely remain standing under a g-force equal to his Strength Attribute, and can still breathe under g-forces up to twice his Stamina. At higher g-forces, objects begin to collapse under the strain of their own weight. A subject caught in a gravity field higher than her Strength Attribute must roll her Strength Dice Pool; the difficulty is the caster's successes + 3. If she fails, the subject suffers one Health Level of damage; if the subject wins, she can crawl a few feet per success to try to escape the field.

Other groups, notably Ecstasy Cultists and Euthanatos, use similar Effects.

••••• **Tempest in a Teapot** — The stormwives of the Verbena use this magick to harness the pull of the moon and the flow of the tides and brew a tempest, using a small copper kettle inscribed with runes and a length of cord as their foci. Multiple witches may act in concert, dancing around a larger cauldron. The Verbena of England claim that the storm which wrecked the Spanish Armada was their doing. Existing storms may be called and controlled with Forces 4, but with this level, the witch weaves the tempest out of the energy of the moon herself.

Life

We are gods incarnate; our flesh is but the clothing of divinity. Still, one shouldn't tear such fine apparel on a whim or treat it with disrespect. If we are manifestations of the Divine, then we should look the part, don't you agree?

When you understand — truly understand — the nature of what we are, you'll be able to change your godly vestments as easily as you strip off those mortal rags. It's not an easy thing to do — we are told from childhood to abhor our bodies — nor a simple thing to master. Mortal forms are complex clothing and require a clever seamstress to shape them to their full advantage. Still, when you take away our tools, our laws and even our language, the body shall remain — the ultimate tool, the ultimate garment.

Specialties: Shapeshifting, Disease, Healing, Improvement, Cloning, Creation

The boundaries of the Sphere of Life are vague and diffuse; definitions of this Sphere range from organic matter, to living matter, to anything infused with life energy (including vampire blood). No two Traditions (let alone mages) ever exactly agree. The Akashic Brotherhood considers Life to be the Sphere of Wood, the most complex of the Taoist five elements, while the Order of Hermes numbers Life as separate from the four elements and the Quintessence. Other Traditions have yet further definitions, but most agree as to the intricacy of Life and its importance among the elemental Pattern magicks.

Mages of Life are invaluable to a Chantry; not only are they among the strongest of warriors, they also work as healers, something useful in any war. Their powers may heal both normal and aggravated wounds, and can cause the same. Damage from the Sphere of Life is fairly standard, but sorcerers who know this Art need not simply kill opponents. A Life Master may paralyze opponents with muscle spasms, age them or turn them into mice. Students of Life may also improve their bodies (or others'), sometimes transforming them into new creatures altogether.

Transformation or mutation works the same way as it does with any other Sphere; to change one thing into another (or create it from "nowhere"), the mystick must use another Sphere to do it. Life Patterns, then, may be created from Forces, Matter or the pure ether of Prime. **(See page 187.)**

Generally speaking, the Sphere of Life governs items still containing living cells — for example, fresh fruit, silkworm cocoons or even a raw steak — even if the item is technically dead. If something is alive enough to be planted in the ground to sprout, or is still serviceable for transplant surgery or at least tissue cultures, Life rules it. If it's organic, but completely non-living — such as dried fruit, hair, lumber, straw or raw silk fibers — yet still unworked, Matter may claim it.

Masters of Life are known for their perfect health. Their skin is free of scars or blemishes, they eat and drink as much or as little as they please, and they rarely tire. Upon achieving Mastery, they tend to change their appearance to suit their whims.

• Sense Life

The mage begins his study by identifying Patterns of Life. By reading these Patterns (however his philosophy defines this), he can learn a lot about a life form — its age, its sex and every aspect of its health. With this awareness, the mage can also sense different forms of life nearby.

•• Alter Simple Patterns
Heal Self

Life manipulation begins with the simplest living Patterns. A mystick can alter the structure of basic life forms now, from microscopic viruses and bacteria to creatures as complex as insects and shellfish (as a good rule of thumb, any invertebrate is considered a simple Life Pattern). All plant life, from algae to sequoia trees, possess Life Patterns simple enough for the mage to manipulate.

The mage can only influence these simple Patterns at this level; he can heal simple creatures or kill them, cause crabs to sprout extra legs, trees to bear fruit or bees to release the pheromones which signal a swarm. Whatever he does, the creatures themselves remain what they always were — he can mutate them, but cannot transform them. A cherry tree is still a cherry tree (even if it now bears poisonous fruit), and a luna moth is still a luna moth (even if it now has a four-foot wingspan).

The mage also begins to understand the most complex Patterns of Life, beginning with the one most familiar to him, his own. At this stage, he may only correct (or create) breaks in his Pattern to heal or harm himself as he desires.

••• Alter Self
Heal Life
Transform Simple Patterns
Create Simple Patterns

At this rank, the mage can alter his own Pattern, making subtle improvements and variations as he did with simple Patterns at Life 2. He cannot substantially change what he is (a human), but can change his gender or appearance or physically modify his body to grow claws, fur, gills, etc.

Simple Patterns are now his to command; he may turn them inside-out, change one into another or even create them entirely from other Patterns, through conjunctional Effects involving Forces, Matter or Prime. The mage can change wildfire into wildflowers, glass grapes into living fruit or the Platonic ideal butterfly into its living counterpart.

Unfortunately, any life form he creates has no mind beyond what it held before. However, for simple life forms, especially plants, this fault is virtually irrelevant. Even creatures such as crabs or insects can be imbued with some instinctive reflexes that serve for intelligence in the absence of a true mind.

The mystick begins to understand other more complex organisms now, and may heal (or harm) other people as he did himself at the previous rank.

•••• Alter Complex Patterns Transform Self

A mage who reaches this rank can change the structure of any complex Life Patterns, including those of other sentient beings. As with Life 2, the creatures subjected to this magick still retain their original form, but radical variations on that basic form are still possible.

A Life Adept can alter her form to resemble another living being of approximately the same size and mass. She may become a deer, but not a mouse. Special abilities — water breathing, flight, etc. — do not carry over at this level without additional Life Effects, and moving around in the new form will take getting used to.

More naturalistic Traditions compensate for this shortcoming by working instinct into the basic form. A mystick risks losing her mind entirely this way, however. Some have found themselves trapped in the shape of panthers or dolphins, and have only freed themselves when they encountered something which reminded them of what they truly were.

••••• Transform Complex Patterns Create Complex Patterns Perfect Metamorphosis

A Master of Life can transform others as she transformed herself at the previous rank. At this level, she can attain any form she desires and alter others the same way.

This carries its own problems. A higher being transformed into a lower one tends to trade intelligence for survival instincts, while a lower life form changed into a higher one has similar problems. A dog transformed into a bodyguard might be faithful, but not terribly smart, and a turnip transformed into a dinner date would still be a vegetable in mind, if not body. Getting such creatures to stand on two legs, let alone speak, requires a long period of instruction or a conjunctional Effect with Mind 3 (less successes needed for the dog, many more for the turnip).

The perfect metamorphosis a Master achieves has no such problems. A mage who shapeshifts at this level carries her mind and Arts with her. Whatever she becomes, that form is as natural as the one she was born into.

At this level, the mage also gains a most unique power, which some might hold as divine: He can weave a new Pattern to create any life form, even a human body, using conjunctional magick to translate it from energy, matter or pure Quintessence with the appropriate rank of Forces, Matter or Prime. Unfortunately, the life form created has no mind or soul beyond the base material or the Resonance it carries. A painting might be haunted by the ghost of its subject, and the mage who caused her to step out into life might find a perfectly capable woman (with her own agenda) greeting him, while a handgun changed into a hamster might become a particularly stupid, yet bloodthirsty, hamster.

Consequently, many mages prefer to create a new being out of Prime Force, certain that it possesses no mind or soul beyond what the mystick gives it. This might seem pointless, but mages have found various uses for such soulless shells. Some create new forms of life merely to study how new "improvements" might effect their living bodies, while others imbue these soulless lifeforms with preprogrammed reactions that mimic instinctual intelligence. The Progenitors have a "damage control" division which creates beasts whose only instinctive drive is to kill, then unleashes them against their enemies.

Life

- • Sense Life
- •• Alter Simple Patterns
  Heal Self
- ••• Alter Self
  Heal Life
  Transform Simple Patterns
  Create Simple Patterns
- •••• Alter Complex Life Patterns
  Transform Self
- ••••• Transform Complex Life Patterns
  Create Complex Life Patterns
  Perfect Metamorphosis

Specialties: Shapeshifting, Disease, Healing, Improvement, Cloning, Creation

Empty husks make ideal resting places for spirits and astral forms as well. Most spirits can manifest in an empty body (or even possess occupied bodies) and interact with the physical world. A mage who helps an Umbrood across this way can demand favors and expect to get them.

Masters of both the Life and Mind Spheres can untether their psyches and create new bodies for their own astral forms to fill, while those adept at Spirit have devised a form of life insurance which involves reincarnating in new bodies when the old ones die. Such mages often leave a long trail of different identities behind them, attaining a degree of immortality.

Life Effects

• **Genetics Scan** — Using her computer, a Virtual Adept with Life Arts can execute a program to scan her immediate vicinity for signs of life. Graphics indicate any nearby life forms' and their position relative to the mage herself, as well as anatomical readouts of the detected forms based on their Patterns. The Adept usually filters the input so her computer doesn't show every gnat and cockroach. She can scan for single species, or even for specific individuals if she has the person's Pattern scanned into her computer's memory (automatic if the mage has previously scanned the target). After about a quarter-mile range, the scan becomes highly inaccurate and may even show ghostly images of life forms that aren't really there.

• **Prayer of Healing Revelation** — The Celestial Chorus studies Life Arts to detect illness and injury. These Disciples learn to identify flaws in a life form's Pattern that indicate various diseases, injuries, poisons and parasitic infestations. The mystick must usually make a Perception roll when scanning the Pattern. The more successes scored, the more specific the information she receives. One success might reveal poison, two might reveal the poison is affecting the respiratory process, and three successes might determine the poison to be cyanide.

•• Heal Simple Creature — A healer can attempt to repair a life form's damaged Pattern. Virtually any affliction can be corrected this way. General healing is decided the same way as damage is. The Storyteller must decide the number of successes required for other restorative Effects such as regrowing limbs, curing paralysis, etc.

Each attempt at healing a Pattern assumes that the mage does as much restorative work as she is able. Repeating the Effect will not heal more damage. At the Storyteller's discretion, the mage may attempt to fix more Pattern damage after the creature has had sufficient time to heal. Any new damage suffered by the subject can also be treated by the mage. Some sorcerers have been known to cure a little bit of damage, cause more and then try again. Of course, these same mages tend to botch this Effect and cause immense damage.

Certain types of wounds require special treatment when healed through magick. Aggravated wounds **(see Chapter Ten)** can only be treated using vulgar magick. Aggravated wounds such as damage from Paradox backlash or Pattern leakage **(see "Better Body")** cannot be healed with Pattern magick; only natural healing will work.

Finally, two mages cannot successively heal a single subject. After one mage has cured a subject, another cannot try until the subject suffers more damage. Two or more mages may still act in concert to heal a subject.

•• Ho Tien Chi — Chinese for "Breath of the Day after Birth," Ho Tien Chi is a breath control exercise mastered by the Akashic Brotherhood. Through this powerful Effect, the mage can restore damage done to his body. The results are the same as those of **Heal Simple Creature**, above. Other groups practice various methods of healing, from the Celestial Chorus's laying on of hands to the crazed Technomancer theories involving electrical stimulation of the body's healing faculties.

•• Little Good Death — This Effect is the first form of killing Euthanatos Disciples learn. With it, a mage mentally grasps and shreds the Etheric Pattern of any simple creature **(see the Damage and Duration chart for damage)**. Other Traditions use similar Effects, though less frequently.

•• Mold Tree — Verbena use this Effect to reweave the Pattern of a tree, causing its branches or even its trunk to bend and twist into new shapes.

••• Better Body — By reweaving the Pattern of his own body, a mage can improve on Mother Nature. Each success rolled lets him increase one of his Physical Attributes or his Appearance by one dot. These improvements can exceed the regular five dots, but the Effect then strays into vulgar magick. The Effect has the usual duration; if the mage wants it to become permanent, he must pay experience points for the improvements or suffer *Pattern leakage*.

Pattern leakage is caused by a metaphysical imbalance between a mage's outer form and his True Form — what he *is*, versus what he *appears* to be. As time progresses, this leakage causes physical trauma (i.e., Health Levels) as the mage's body feeds on its own life energy in an attempt to sustain its exaggerated form. A mage with this syndrome is, in fact, a *thaumivore* **(see "Mythic Beasts," Chapter Nine)**. If he's skilled in Prime, he may feed his body from the Quintessence in his Avatar instead. When a thaumivoric mage exhausts this alternate energy supply (which commonly happens if he doesn't meditate at a Node), his body will turn back to feeding on his life.

A mage will suffer one Health Level of damage for every day that he maintains a boosted form as his thaumivorism drains Quintessence from his life energy itself. If he exerts the capabilities of his improved body, this interval can decrease to hours or even minutes. This damage cannot be corrected or healed until the mage allows his Pattern to revert to its natural form (losing the points gained in Attributes) or he pays for a permanent upgrade. Damage suffered from Pattern leakage can only heal at a natural rate, not through Pattern healing, and Pattern leakage continues until the mage dies, spends the points to pay for the improvements, or allows his body to revert to its natural form.

If he wants to warp his True Form, the cost to permanently raise an Attribute this way is half of what it would normally be. This requires at least five successes on a vulgar Life magick roll and costs time and pain besides. Going from Appearance 1 to Appearance 4 through Technocratic magick takes extensive plastic surgery, and most Traditional methods are equally unpleasant, involving everything from noxious potions to funhouse mirrors.

Permanently rewriting your Pattern into one which is not so much better as different, i.e., exchanging Strength specialty Brawny for Strength specialty Lean, or blue eyes to brown, is more of an alteration than an improvement. This does not cause Pattern leakage, though it can change the mage's True Form.

If the mage exceeds the human maximum of 5 dots in any Attribute, he must mark off a permanent point of Paradox for every point in excess, e.g. a mage who increased his Strength to 7 and his Dexterity to 6 would have three points of permanent Paradox until he somehow lost such overtly vulgar upgrades. This is a common problem with Iteration X cyborgs — many become too vulgar to safely survive on Earth.

The mage may also use this Effect to create natural weaponry — fangs, claws, extra-dense bones, poison sacs, etc. Treat these natural weapons as clubs, claws or knives **(see "Combat," Chapter Ten)**. This Effect is generally vulgar. If she wants to make such improvements permanent, she must also mark off a permanent point of Paradox for each such mutation, though these do not cause Pattern leakage unless they also increase her Attribute ratings.

••• Rip the Man-Body — With this Effect, an Euthanatos can rend the Patterns of more complex life forms. As the mage lacks detailed knowledge of such complex Patterns, she cannot unravel the Patterns quickly. The overall effect of this magick resembles **Little Good Death**, though **Rip the Man-Body** can affect any life form. This damage often manifests as lesions and internal hemorrhaging.

•••• Lesser Shapechanging — With this magick, the mage may alter his shape into that of any higher animal of similar size and mass. His mind, however, is not changed, and he must learn to think and move in whatever form he takes. A mage who takes the shape of a tiger will have to learn how to walk like a cat, drink like a cat and fight like a cat.

Many new shapechangers have only a basic understanding of what they do. Until he gets to know a given form — which costs two points per form — he must expend a point of Willpower each day that he spends in the new form to remember who and what he truly is. While shifted, he cannot regain spent Willpower; if he runs out, he will believe he has always been that creature until something convinces him otherwise. If he returns to his natural shape, he will have to go through a period of adjustment before he remembers his true form and his previous memories, though Mind magicks may be used to get around this.

•••• Mutate Form — The mage can alter the form of another living creature, causing deformities (paralysis, amputation, etc.) or beneficial mutations (gills, flexible joints, etc.). Mysticks (especially assassins and secret agents) also use these mutations as the ultimate form of disguise, altering body structure to adjust height, weight, build and facial features.

The number of successes rolled indicates the degree to which the mage can warp the subject's body. Mutations that last more than one scene may cause the traumatic Pattern leaking effect described above in **Better Body**.

•••• Physiological Emotion Control — Many Virtual Adepts view human beings as biological computers. By inducing certain reactions within the physical body, they can "reprogram" a person's behavior. Emotions like anger or fear can be induced by causing the body to release adrenaline, while endorphin stimulation can bring on intense pleasure. Even depression often has biological causes. This "tyranny" of the physical body over the mind is one of the reasons that the Virtual Adepts wish to attain a virtual reality state, where that body is left behind and the mind is no longer a slave to the body's needs.

Any Adept of Life can induce emotions in a subject by causing the person's body to release or stifle the correct hormones. The more successes on the Effect roll, the more severe the emotion.

••••• Animal Form — Verbena Masters of Life use this Effect on those who displease them, turning an offender into a lesser creature such as a frog or a fly. The subject of the transformation receives all the benefits or penalties of the new form; her senses are limited to those of the new form (e.g., a human transformed into a tree would not be able to see, smell or hear, but might gain new senses that allow her to "feel" sunlight, water and wind). The subject's sentience does not change, and mages may still make use of magick in any form.

This Effect can turn mice into horses or a horse into a coachman, *a la Cinderella*. Animals changed into humans tend to go through a longer acclimation process, but will eventually come to think of themselves as humans — and may fear the witches who wish to change them back to their proper shapes.

••••• Perfect Metamorphosis — This ancient Hermetic magick allows a magus to take any shape he pleases without losing his intellect. Size and mass are no object, and body and mind mesh perfectly. The wizard may live in the shape of a griffin while still remembering his history as a man and his status as a mage. This type of perfect transformation is only available to the mage himself, though mages who have achieved this level know that the Oracles of Life understand how to use this magick upon others.

Matter

You've heard of the Philosopher's Stone, have you not? The Platonic ideal carved from thought and given form by the greatest of our Arts? It's said that such an item, if it could be made (which indeed it could and can), would transform base metals into their finest form — gold. Like those who sought the Stone, we Children of the Mysteries would bring all who surrounds us — from base brass rabble to sterling statesmen — to their purest state.

Until then, we content ourselves with shaping the world around us to our wills. Turning lead into gold is no fairy tale — I can demonstrate the act right here, given just a bit of time. With much study and dedication, you too can achieve what men have bragged of for centuries — transmutation of form to form. In time, you may even summon form where there was none to speak of before. Matter is what we make of it. Let no Technocratic table of elements tell you otherwise.

Specialties: Transmutation, Shaping, Conjuration, Complex Patterns

Matter is one of the Spheres of the Elements, the sum of the Pattern Magicks (Forces, Life and Matter) and the etheric Sphere of Prime. To the Order of Hermes, Matter governs the feminine elements, Water and Earth, while to the Akashic Brotherhood, it is the Sphere of Water, Earth and Metal. This Sphere concerns itself with the Patterns of non-living matter, though the precise line between this Sphere and the Sphere of Life, like the precise line between the Elements, varies from Tradition to Tradition **(see "Life")**. Most Technocrats draw the line between inorganic and organic material, or between simple organic chemistry and complex organic chemistry.

Wherever the division lies, students of Matter first learn to analyze their subject, then to transmute one basic substance into another. After this, a mage learns to rework the shapes of items, craft articles of great complexity and finally, at Mastery of the Sphere, create items of wonder and the substances of legend, including Orichalcum (True Gold), Lunargent (True Silver), Hermium (True Mercury), plutonium and the other highly radioactive elements, dragon pearls, mythical perfumes and marvelous machines, alloys and automatons that defy "conventional" science.

Masters of Matter tend to have a variant of the Midas touch. All their material possessions (and those they come in contact with) are fine and precious, polished, sparkling or in a perfect state of repair. Nevertheless, they hold most possessions in disdain in favor of art and craftsmanship. This viewpoint leads many Master of Matter to become haughty or at least be perceived as such.

• Matter Perceptions

The Disciple of Matter begins by recognizing the various Patterns of Matter, including the underlying structures that give objects their shapes and physical properties. With these perceptions, she can detect things hidden from normal senses. In addition to sensing the composition and properties of Matter, the Disciple can discern structures hidden within structures; material no longer forms a barrier to her senses.

•• Basic Transmutation

The mage may transmute one substance into another, without changing its shape, temperature or basic state (solid, liquid, gas). Mages of mystick Traditions can change milk into cream or mahogany into oak, while scientists change water to acid or lead into gold. The more radical the transmutation, the more successes the spell requires. It's easier to change water into wine (one success) than into sulfuric acid (three), and more complicated to turn stones into bread (three successes) than sourdough into rye (one).

With an understanding of Prime and the other Pattern Magicks, a mage may use conjunctional Effects to transform items governed by Forces, Life or Prime into basic Patterns of Matter, including changing living beings into stone or spinning moonlight into thread. With Prime 2, she may harness the ether to create (or uncreate) any *simple, basic* thing composed of *one common homogeneous substance*. A quartz boulder shaped vaguely like a woman is possible, but a dainty china shepherdess is not. With difficulty, a stick of plastique could be conjured (but not the detonator), though a couple plutonium spheres are out of the question (the highly radioactive elements cannot be created until Rank 5). A bowlful of oatmeal or even blueberry pancakes could be made to appear, but not a baroque wedding cake. The more rare and/or complex a given substance, the more difficult it is to create from pure ether. It's easier to create glass than diamonds and simpler to make flour than bread. Elaborate creations must wait until Rank 4.

Making things hotter or colder than they were originally, or to change one substance into another with a higher or lower potential energy, requires a conjunctional Effect with Forces, though Matter alone can change ice into ice cream or boiling water into hot soup. Transmuting solids into liquids or liquids into gas requires either Matter 3 or the use of Forces 3/Prime 2 (or some mundane means) to boil or freeze the affected substance.

••• Alter Form

At the third rank of Matter, the mage can finally overpower the rigid Patterns of reality. By selectively altering different aspects of an object's Pattern, he can change its shape however he desires — compressing it to increase its density and decrease its volume while retaining the same weight, inflating it so as to decrease its density and increase the volume, or temporarily changing the state, so that solids become liquids or liquids become gas. Permanent changes in state require Rank 5.

A mage who understands this rank may sculpt matter into any shape she pleases, limited only by the physical properties of the materials she uses. Broken items may also be repaired seamlessly, if she has the mundane knowledge to do so.

•••• Complex Transmutation

Adepts of Matter may now perform radical changes to physical materials and craft complex and intricate items involving several common substances or one or two rare ones. Any sort of regular matter may be changed into any other — a squirt pistol into a loaded zipgun (three successes) or a trash dumpster into a small tank (five successes) — though as with Rank 2, the more radical the transformation, the more difficult the feat.

With conjunctional Effects, the Patterns of Life, Forces or Prime itself may be transmuted into Matter, allowing mages to turn pumpkins into gilded coaches, lightning bolts into swords or the Quintessential ether into master keys. Complex organic creations are also possible, including silk ballgowns, roast chickens and Persian rugs.

••••• Alter Properties

At this pinnacle of understanding, Masters of Matter may create new substances which do not exist in nature by taking existing materials and altering their physical properties, such as boiling or melting points, density, ductility, transparency, viscosity, refraction index, etc. A sorcerer may even make one object immaterial to some other substance, creating bullets which can phase through armor and killer robots that can walk through walls (leaving the walls intact).

Matter

•	Matter Perceptions
••	Basic Transmutation
•••	Alter Forms
••••	Complex Transmutation
•••••	Alter Properties

Specialties: Transmutation, Shaping, Conjuration, Complex Patterns

All the substances of legends and comic books are possible with this level of magick. Masters build castles with paper-thin walls and wear clothes of indestructible armor that feel softer than silk and weigh less than a feather. The rare prizes of Technocratic science, such as the manmade radioactive elements, are also reserved for this level.

As with the Fifth Level of Forces, there are safeguards against Masters of Matter using their powers to run amok. Assuming a mage had enough extended successes, an eight ball could be given the density of a black hole, but such a vulgar creation would require many successes and draw serious consequences (angry mages, flying objects, Paradox, etc.) upon the conjurer, as tends to happen with vulgar magicks of a sufficiently grand scale. However, small, portable black holes — with event horizons of no more than five feet — are useful, if vulgar, toys of some Masters of this Sphere.

Matter Effects

• **Fragments of Dream** — Dreamspeakers view all matter as fragments of the Earth Mother's dreams. By tapping such dreams, they can expand their perception of Matter. The mage extends her senses beyond physical reality into Pattern. She no longer sees matter in the same way, e.g., instead of a brick wall, she sees its Pattern in her mind's eye.

This allows the mage to perceive things that would be unseen in physical reality; she could sense the contents of a room beyond a wall, or detect objects or structures that might otherwise be hidden, such as the false bottom of a suitcase. Really dense or complex Patterns (bank vaults, bramble thickets, etc.) may require several successes to penetrate.

The only limit to this Effect is that the mage can only sense the Patterns of Matter (unless she is a Disciple of other Pattern magicks).

• **Analyze Substance** — Now a mage begins to identify the Patterns of different substances. He can detect the exact composition of any substance and determine aspects such as the object's age or weight by examining the Pattern. The mage could distinguish diamonds from cubic zirconiums, detect poison in wine or tell an antique chair from a modern imitation by studying the chair's Pattern to see signs of aging.

•• **Straw into Gold** — The spellweavers of the Verbena use this Effect to turn substances of little value into those of great value, the most classic of which are spinning straw into gold and teardrops into diamonds.

Most such Effects are vulgar, but there are less showy applications. One, used by the Order of Hermes, is the **Seeds of Gold**, an alchemical process borrowed from the fabled Children of Knowledge. The mage sows the ground with specially prepared "seeds," and when the ground is dug up, gold is discovered (and easily explained away as coincidence). Likewise, a mage can raise the butterfat content of milk or improve the quality of wine without raising any eyebrows.

••• or ••••• **Alter State** — By adding Forces 3/Prime 2 to Matter to change an object's boiling or freezing point, the mage can alter the state of matter between solid, liquid and gaseous. With Matter 5, she doesn't change the temperature of the matter, merely its form. Water may be frozen into ice at room temperature, but the ice remains at room temperature. It doesn't freeze because it becomes colder; it freezes because the mage altered the temperature at which the water will freeze.

Such alteration depends on the successes rolled; Storytellers should just use common knowledge to decide what is possible at various levels of success. One success would cause water to freeze at room temperature, while five successes could turn gases in the air into solids, encapsulating other objects or people. The alteration lasts only for the Effect's duration, after which it returns to normal.

••• **Destroy Structures** — The mage uses her knowledge of Matter Patterns to break down structures by shredding their Patterns. The Effect resembles **Sculpture**, but the mage simply breaks down a Pattern as quickly as possible. She can shred steel doors, cause wooden tables to fall apart or make concrete crumble. She may even disperse pools of gas or liquid as long as there is an open area into which the pool can dilute; an oil fire burning on top of a river could be extinguished by causing the oil to disperse into the water.

••• **Sculpture** — Cultists of Ecstasy who practice the Sphere of Matter are usually fine artists who use magick to create new mediums of art. Those who understand the third rank of Matter can use nearly anything as a medium for artistic interpretation.

These mages become sculptors extraordinaire, reshaping houses, fire hydrants, cars, doors, furniture, etc. A mage need only mentally re-sculpt the image of the matter and then modify its Pattern so that the object assumes the desired shape. A larger object requires more successes to manipulate, and the mage can change only the shape of the item, not its properties.

The mage can only affect one type of material with each Effect. The more successes she rolls, the larger or more intricate the structure she can destroy.

•••• **Transformers** — The stuff of spy thrillers and Japanese animation; both the Sons of Ether and Iteration X regularly transform one machine into another radically different one. A '57 Chevy could have knives sprout from the hubcaps or Gatling guns pop out from under the hood, a motorcycle could become a jet-ski, a tank could be changed into a powered armor suit, or a combine harvester could be transmogrified into a turbo-charged scythe chariot with silver blades to take on a pack of werewolves.

Some transformations are more vulgar than others. Pressing a button to squirt an oil slick onto the road behind the car is within the realm of possibility, but having a Honda Civic produce helicopter blades and go flying through the air is not. Likewise, knowing how to transform a device and knowing how to operate it are two separate things — a mage who knows how to drive a Honda Civic might *not* know how to pilot a helicopter.

••••• **Alter Weight** — This Effect allows a Son of Ether to alter an object's density, changing its weight but not its size. He could, for example, reduce the density of the iron in a crowbar, making it lighter but not changing its shape or size. For every success on the magickal Effect roll, the mage can adjust the density of the object by one factor. With two successes, he could double or halve an object's density; four successes enable him to quadruple or quarter an object's weight, and so on with more successes. Objects with a substantially reduced density tend to become brittle and fragile; some even collapse.

••••• **Matter Pattern Disassociation** — The unwieldy name for this Effect undoubtedly came from the labs of the Sons of Ether. By modifying the Patterns of two pieces of matter so that the two items become insubstantial with respect to one another, a mage can keep those items from interacting in any way. Doors might slide through their hinges and fall, water may cascade through a pipe, a truck wheel-rim could drop through the rubber tire and grind on the pavement, etc. The affected items are in no way changed except with regard to each other.

The more successes the mage scores, the more mass he can affect. He may simultaneously affect several similar items, such as all four wheels and all four tires on a truck at once, so long as they're formed of the same material.

••••• **Tapping the Signal** — Virtual Adepts use Mastery of Matter to turn any substance into a conductor capable of transmitting computer signals. They can send computer signals through brick walls or along the pavement of an interstate highway. They sometimes use this Effect to eavesdrop by tapping into computer communications on "isolated" lines by forming a conductive path to the private line through any matter in between, be it walls, insulators, etc.

It rumored that the Virtual Adepts have fine enough control of this Effect to turn the ground itself into a network of computer lines. The mage need only plug his computer into the ground itself to create a channel into the ground that taps into the nearest preestablished line. Whether such a network exists or whether such tales come only from on-line bragging remain to be seen.

Mind

In the beginning, there was Mind — not our own, perhaps, but a sentience which proclaimed to the Void, "I exist," and made it so. Our Art is a legacy of that First Primal Thought. That which is exists because we will it to be so.

You need not speak with words. I will hear you before you can utter them. Psychic phenomena is but an echo of the power we know. To perfect our link with that First Thought, we strengthen our minds, shelter our thoughts and project our sentience, first to others, then across the realms of the unconsciousness until we meet that First Thought and declare that we, too, exist.

Specialties: Communication, Illusion, Self-Empowerment, Astral Travel

Mages have long delved into their own minds in search of power. The scope of knowledge derived from countless years of enlightened investigation has led to the development of the Sphere of Mind, which covers the manifold powers attributed to the human mind itself. It does not include the physiological processes of the organic brain. Mind Arts transcend biology for the raw essence of intelligent thought.

Masters of Mind have opened their mental faculties far beyond the scope imagined by the unenlightened. Perception, communication, even domination are their province. Their control extends from the glimmers of sentience exhibited by animals to the higher faculties of the human mind.

Mind Arts pack little physical punch — they do one success less on the Damage chart — but have endless subtle applications. Most Effects, cleverly cast and helped along with Social rolls, subliminal programming treatments, cybernetic implants and rigorous concentration, can be used coincidentally.

Masters of Mind occasionally reveal themselves through odd behavior patterns — finishing other people's sentences, lightning-fast mathematical calculations or foreknowledge of complete strangers. Most tend to be introspective and often talk to themselves.

•

Sense Thoughts & Emotions
Empower Self

The mage begins to sense the thoughts and emotions in the air around her. She cannot yet read these thoughts, but can sense their strength and intensity. This is not a true look at the soul (that requires Spirit 1) but at the shell of emotional radiance that surrounds it.

The mage may also read the psychic impressions left on objects. At this stage, she cannot read any actual thoughts or images, but can sense "good" or "bad vibes" from an object or place. This includes the Resonance attached to Tass or the aura of a Quintessential wellspring at a Node or Juncture. Without Prime 2, she can't tell how strong such energies may be, but she'll be able to understand the best uses for such Quintessence **(see the Modifiers chart for details)**.

The Mind initiate also learns to influence her dreams and shield herself from the inevitable mental barrage of others' thoughts and emotions. With work (a magick roll), she can hide her aura and shield her thoughts from casual observation — though determined and perceptive mages and other beings may still be able to read them.

••

Read Surface Thoughts
Mental Impulse

The mage learns not only how to recognize thoughts, but how to read them. She can read memories "attached" to objects by others' minds (basic psychometry) and scan surface thoughts from unshielded minds. The greater the emotional content, the louder the "volume" and the easier it is to read such impressions. She can leave that same psychic impressions on objects or places intentionally, too, "creating" Resonance.

The mage can also send such thoughts and emotions out ("looking daggers" or "blowing kisses") until they find their target. Complex thoughts cannot be sent this way, but single words, images or emotional impulses can be easily "beamed" into an unshielded being's subconscious mind. Such suggestions are much more insidious, and can often be more effective, than direct communication.

Two mages of this same rank can also form a primitive mental link by dropping their shields and reading each other's conscious minds.

The mage may also create more elaborate shields in her mind and disguise the color of her aura, or erect a complex mental "window dressing" to fool other mentalists into underestimating or ignoring her. She can also control her dreams to some extent, though many aspects still lie beyond her influence.

•••

Mental Link
Walk Among Dreams

The mage can now establish a clear link between her own consciousness and the minds of others. She can use this link for telepathic communications — or invasions.

The ability to project thoughts and images into another's mind allows a mystick to project false perceptions. At this rank, the mage has full command of perceptual illusions. Some Traditions teach means of projecting psychic disturbances into a subject's mind. These psychic assaults take many forms, but their end goal is to turn the victim into a mental vegetable.

The mage may now contact the minds of other dreamers in her sleep and begin to explore the Dream Realms. While waking, she may also use her abilities to enter the dreaming consciousness of others, though such trips are risky. Some Sleepers have particularly rich dream lives, and even a mage who enters one may be at the dreamer's mercy. A number of spiritual entities also lair in dreams and may be very territorial.

•••• Control Conscious Mind
Walk Among Dreams

A Mind Adept can actually take over another person's mind and occupy his body for her own ends. His thoughts, should she will it, are not his own, but hers. Once this invasion has begun, she may control her victim directly, cure or cause insanity, change his memories or set up posthypnotic suggestions. The mage can overlay her subject's aura with another of a completely different color and pattern. The victim may slowly recover as the subconscious mind reasserts the true memories, but the subject's Demeanor is usually irrevocably altered.

The Adept can also leave her dreams behind and make brief excursions into the astral reaches **(Skimming the Penumbra; see "The Otherworlds," Chapter Nine)**. These trips must be short and can become dangerous. For each success the mystick rolls, she may leave her meditating body for one turn. Afterward, she returns to her physical self.

••••• Control Subconscious
Untether
Forge Psyche

A Master of Mind rules not only his own mind, but other minds as well, both mortal and spirit. Through this power, he may invade not only the conscious mind, but the subconscious as well, completely rewriting the underlying personality until the thoughts which compose the psyche bear no resemblance to anything that existed before, utterly changing the person's Nature. The only integral part of the being which the mage may not touch is the Avatar and its memories of past lives, for to perform this ultimate crime requires the Sphere of Spirit.

The mage may also divorce a psyche from the body, switch minds between subjects and merge, copy or transfer the entire sum of a person's memories and knowledge from one body to another. His powers allow him to increase a subject's intelligence and wits to genius levels (5 dots) and may begin to increase his own beyond that **(though not without risk; see "Better Body")**.

Complete astral travel is also possible now, and a Master of Mind can leave her body for hours or even days at a time. She must eventually return, however; complete astral existence transcends anything a mortal mage can know.

The greatest power of a Master of Mind, however, is the ability to create true conscious thought. A Master may create another thinking, rational mind where none existed before, expanding its intelligence and designing its personality however she likes.

Computers and other inanimate objects — as well as the empty shells created by Masters of Life — may be given true sentience without granting them a soul. When such creatures are destroyed, however, their psyches tend to die with them as well.

Mind

•	Sense Thoughts & Emotions
	Empower Self
••	Read Surface Thoughts
	Mental Impulse
•••	Mental Link
	Walk Among Dreams
••••	Control Conscious Mind
	Astral Projection
•••••	Control Subconscious
	Forge Psyche

Specialties: Communication, Illusion, Self-Empowerment, Astral Travel

Mind Effects

• **Multi-Tasking** — Each success scored with this Virtual Adept-christened Effect enables a mage to perform one additional task. The Adepts see this as setting up parallel processing in their minds. Any normal (non-magickal) task may be so programmed; thus a mage who rolled two successes might speak on the telephone to a comrade, program a computer and memorize a recording in the background. The real limit is the mage's physical ability to perform all of the tasks his mind is capable of processing.

Unfortunately, mages (other than the Oracles of Mind) have been unable to channel their wills through more than one thought avenue at once. Thus, the mage cannot simultaneously evoke multiple magickal Effects, nor can he spend Willpower on more than one task at a time.

• **No-Mind** — All mages who possess Rank One Mind are capable of scanning their surroundings for sentience. Akashic Brothers, however, have perfected the Effect to a fine art. These mages enter a Zen-like trance state wherein their own thoughts are subdued and their minds become open to the impressions of other minds. Such a mage senses the general location of any minds near her, as well as other details such as the gender of the detected creature, i.e. male/female/neuter (some plants and spirits actually register to Mind magick), the type of creature (human, rat, redwood) and sometimes the general behavior of the creature (running, hiding, eating. etc.). Some Do masters have been known to blind themselves purposefully, forcing them to rely on the **No-Mind** Effect. Such mages believe that this state is a step toward Ascension and should be cultivated.

• Pathos — The mage may sense others' emotions and nearby psychic resonance left by strong emotions and events. This appears differently to various mages; some see auras as washes of colors around highly-charged objects and people, while others vicariously experience the emotion itself. This can be very disturbing, and most Disciples of Mind learn to build a strong mental shield to protect themselves from negative emotions.

Particularly intense emotions are plain as day and twice as bright. Mages need no roll to sense them, though Storytellers should require a Willpower roll to avoid the worst effects of an emotional kick. Subtler emotions must be searched for; the more successes the mystick scores on the Effect roll, the more the mage understands the feelings and their origins. With one success, the mage senses anger; two successes, and she senses anger mixed with fear; three successes, and she senses anger spawned from anguish over loss mixed with fear, and so on.

• Shield — One of the first exercises taught to a Disciple of Mind is the ability to shield her own mind. This protects her from both mental invasion and her own psychic sensitivity. Without such shields, many mentally gifted mages can go mad, confusing their own thoughts with the thoughts that filter into their heads.

A shield also stops the light surface thoughts and emotions which most humans broadcast. An Akashic Brotherhood monastery is truly a place of serene self-contemplation, a much-needed refuge for young mages who have Awakened the powers of their minds but have not yet learned how to train them.

A Hermetic Mind 3 variant, ***Ægis***, expands this shield to protect other minds. Each success over the second allows the mage to shield one additional comrade for the spell's duration.

• • Psychic Impression — A mage may impress her emotions into an object, infusing it with Resonance for various magickal uses. A bullet infused with hatred for one's enemies, for example, will fire no better than a normal one nor do any form of aggravated damage. It would hurt more psychically than a regular bullet would, assuming it hit its intended target.

Likewise, if a mage places additional magicks on an item, Resonance will aid the spell, so long as the intent works with the psychic impressions **(see Modifiers chart)**. For example, a targeting spell used with a hate-filled bullet could be much easier depending on the strength of the psychic impressions.

The more genuine thought and emotion a mage focuses into an object, the greater its Resonance; a false emotion won't have the same effect. If the mage really doesn't care, the only Resonance she may infuse into an object is "disinterest."

• • Subliminal Impulse — The mage can broadcast a single image or word into a subject's subconscious. The more successes rolled, the more powerful the suggestion. Subtle impulses will work their way into the conscious; more powerful impulses blaze straight into the subject's conscious mind. The subject's response depends upon both her Willpower and the compatibility of the impulse with her normal feelings and behavior.

Powerful impulses can cause dramatic changes in behavior or trigger spontaneous reactions. For example, a mage may cause a waiter to drop a plate by impelling to the waiter's subconscious mind the word "HOT" as the man picks up the plate. Truly powerful impulses can even cause psychotic or self-destructive acts. Such subliminal suggestions may linger in the subject's subconscious depending on the number of successes rolled; brief actions may require only one or two successes, while long-term changes may require five successes or more.

• • • Telepathy — The mage establishes a communication link between his own mind and a number of minds equal to the number of successes he scores. Surface thoughts automatically flow across the link from everyone involved, creating a collage of images and language. Those unaccustomed to telepathic communication invariably send more information than they had intended to share. Indeed, linking several untrained minds creates a tremendous volume of psychic "noise," as those untrained in telepathy do not know how to blank their minds to avoid constantly "talking" across the link.

• • • Graphic Transmission — Virtual Adepts approach the power of illusion in their customary fashion — through computer technology. To create an illusion in a subject's mind, the mage executes a graphics routine on his computer and transmits it directly into the subject's consciousness. Whatever images he creates on his computer display are seen, heard and smelled by the subject as if they were real, because they exist in her mind.

The number of successes on the magick roll limits the complexity of the desired illusion. An illusion of complete darkness would require two successes, while a fully detailed person who walks and talks would require four or five successes. The Storyteller may grant victims of this Effect a Perception roll to distinguish between reality and illusion (for Virtual Adept illusions, this means noticing that certain visions look digitized or made up of very fine pixels). Someone who knows an illusion for what it is remains free to ignore it. She may still act on reflex, however, even though she knows better; were someone to "throw" an illusionary ball at her head, she would still duck, if only on impulse.

• • • Probe Thoughts — The mage may attempt to invade the thoughts of another, after choosing the types of thoughts she wishes to scan: memories, surface thoughts, emotional ties, subconscious desires, sensory impulses, etc.

If the sorcerer successfully evokes this Effect, the subject may suddenly find himself a passive observer to his own thought processes, no longer in control of which thoughts sift through his conscious mind, experiencing the memories or emotions that the mage summons.

If the mage simply scans surface thoughts, the subject will feel only a vague intrusion; most Sleepers will immediately dismiss this sensation. The subject will retain control of his thoughts; in this case the mage is the passive observer. The mage can maintain the scan for a number of minutes equal to the number of successes. She cannot probe the same subject again until he sleeps.

While the subject must be present for the mage to work the Effect (unless the mage also uses Correspondence), he can travel anywhere once the mage has successfully established the probe. The mage might establish a mental link allowing her to see whatever her subject sees. The subject can then go around a corner, out of sight or even be transported away with other magick, and the mage's sensory link will remain for the Effect's duration.

• • • • Possession — The **Possession** Effect, commonly used by Dreamspeakers and Euthanatos, operates like **Probe Thoughts**, in that the mage invades the mind of another. This invasion is much more dramatic than that of **Probe Thoughts**, however, and the victim instinctively attempts to eject the mage's psyche. If the sorcerer fails to possess the target, she cannot try again until the victim sleeps.

If the mage takes control, she now commands the subject's body and thoughts with such total control that the subject's thought-patterns and mind are subsumed by those of the mage. The mage does not have to command the subject's arm to lift; she merely "causes" the subject to think "lift arm," and the subject will lift his own arm. The subject is oblivious to the fact that he is being controlled. From the subject's perspective, each thought is his own.

Alternately, the mage may elect to control only part of the subject's capacities, such as emotions or motor control (if the mage only controls the motor responses, movements will be robotic). If the subject is only partially controlled, he will realize the mage is present and is controlling him.

During the period of control, the mage's own mental faculties are consumed with the efforts of maintaining control and thinking for the subject. She will often let the subject behave normally, stepping in to redirect his thought-patterns as desired. Once control is established, the subject can go anywhere and the link will be maintained.

While the mage still has control, she may elect to utilize the **Manipulate Memory** Effect to delete the subject's memory of the moment when the mage fought for and took control. If she wins, he'll believe that his thoughts and deeds over the past several hours were his own. Many victims begin to wonder if they have gone insane.

• • • • Manipulate Memory — This Effect is another invasive mental power similar to **Possession**. The mage must successfully invade and overpower his subject just as with **Possession**. If he succeeds, he may manipulate the subject's memories, blocking existing ones from surfacing (though the actual memories cannot be wiped away) and creating new memories by feeding images into the subject's mind. The more successes rolled, the freer the mage is to manipulate his victim's memory.

The process is reversible. Another mage can undo the manipulations performed on a subject (although she must score more successes than the original mage).

• • • • • Untether — A true astral traveler can to separate his mind from his body. Unlike the **Stepping Sideways** Effect, which allows the mystick to pass into the Umbra in a spirit body, **Untether** completely separates mind and body. The mage becomes an embodiment of mental essence, commonly called an astral form.

The mage's consciousness can travel into the Epiphamies (the highest reaches of the High Umbra) or through physical reality at speeds greater than 500 mph. Without the sensory organs of his physical body, the mage's perceptions are limited to magickal sensory Effects. He can still sense other minds near his own, however, and can utilize their perceptions if he possesses appropriate magick (so to speak). He could take control of minds nearby or influence and communicate with them using any other powers he has mastered.

The mage's sentience is formless, massless and virtually impervious to harm. He can manifest in a ghostly gray form for one turn by spending a point of Willpower. Other astral travelers, or astral beings such as ghosts, can directly interact with him. During astral actions, the mage's Mental and Social Attributes replace his Physical Attributes. In astral form, Wits serves as Dexterity, Manipulation serves as Strength, and Intelligence serves as Stamina.

If two astral beings engage in direct conflict, both usually try to cut their opponent's silver cord — a thin filament that stretches through the astral Realm, connecting a living being's astral form with his physical body. In astral combat, damage is inflicted upon Willpower instead of the Health Trait. When a combatant goes to zero Willpower, the silver cord snaps. Beings that have no physical shells (such as ghosts or the ba spirits of dead mummies) do not have silver cords and are simply disrupted when they reach zero Willpower.

When a mage's silver cord is severed, the astral traveler is believed to be completely drawn into the Epiphamies, where the most rarefied thoughts spiral off into space. Those who have survived such trips report a journey mixed with emotional extremes, mental lucidity bordering on enlightenment and total confusion. It is believed that the mages of the Oracles of Mind venture into these distant astral frontiers often, but lesser mages find the experience too disorienting to describe.

A mage becomes completely unaware of his physical body once he leaves it to journey astrally. However, Masters of Mind know enough about the link between the physical body and astral presence to be able to reconnect their silver cords to other bodies. This is especially important if the mage's physical body is destroyed or dies. The mage's astral presence is unaffected by the body's physical death (though some Masters of Mind who wished to achieve immortality by this means reported to their corporeal Disciples that they were being hounded by certain spirits that came from the Realms beyond Death). However, without the link to the physical Realm, the mage begins to slip away. He must reconnect his cord to another body. If an empty magickal vessel is not available, the mage may attempt to control the mind of another sentient and thereby house his own intellect in the body, essentially becoming a split personality within that body's original mind.

• • • • • AI (Artificial Intelligence) — Virtual Adept Masters use this Effect to grant their computers sentience and personalities. This sentience does not physically reside in the machine but in the programming, for an AI (as they call them) can be transferred into the Digital Web and even transferred into a living body (though the latter requires the Sphere of Life to create the link).

AIs are strange and unpredictable entities; like children, they tend to grow from childlike naiveté to adolescent rebelliousness, with a few interesting stages in between. More than one Virtual Adept has had his laptop become amorously inclined, and when the AI involved has the ability to jack in and crack in to Iteration X's computers and hijack a HIT Mark for its own uses, fatal attraction can take on a whole new meaning.

Despite the risks, many Virtual Adepts still create AIs, as these creations provide a basis for the most powerful computers. A few Virtual Adepts even claim to *be* AIs, though they might simply be Marauders instead.

Prime

Forget all they have taught you — all things begin with Prime. From this Essence of creation distilled, all matter, life, law and concepts flow.

Feel the ground; feel it stirring with the blood of the dragon whose wings vault the sky and whose claws dig the trenches of Hell. Feel your heartbeat merge with the pulse of the land, then reach out with all your senses. Can you grasp that for which there are not words? Do you understand that no Art is whole without a link to the Essence from which we all come?

If not, leave my grove; we have nothing to discuss. If so, stay awhile, and chant with me in time to the heart-sound of the dragon.

Specialties: Channeling, Perceptions, Filling Patterns, Draining Patterns

Prime is the study of Quintessence, literally the Fifth Essence, exalted above the other four elements of Western Hermetic magick. The Cult of Ecstasy refers to it as Mani, the Jewel of the Lotus, one of the five Hindu Tattwas, also known as Akasha, the Black Egg from which All springs. Quintessence is also known as Ether or Odyllic Force, the underlying nature of the fabric of reality, the First Essence or Prime.

Regardless of the naming and accounting, Prime is the raw stuff of True Magick. It exists everywhere, and all things are composed of it, though some sources are easier to work than others. The most accessible forms of raw magick are the Quintessence stored in a mage's Avatar or crystallized into Tass. More dangerous to use, but no less possible, is the Quintessence which sustains the Life Patterns of each living being, symbolized as blood by the Verbena and stolen by vampires. The most difficult form of all to use is the Quintessence which forms the Patterns of creation, though a Master of Prime may tap this source as well.

Prime is the transient bridge between the Pattern magicks and the Sphere of Spirit. Mages of Prime can sully these sublime Patterns and tie them down to the Patterns of the Base Elements (Forces, Matter and Life), or help them achieve transcendence and become the stuff of Spirit. Quintessence is the currency of mages, and Masters of Prime are in high demand.

Such Masters can be noticed by the aura of power that surrounds them; good and holy people shine with a light of divine power, while dark mages (especially the Nephandi) have a palpable aura of evil about them. More neutral Masters of Prime merely possess an overpowering sparkle of magick and a particularly forceful presence.

• Etheric Senses

A mage gains perceptions of basic Quintessential energy — the Nodes where it collects or wells up, the ley lines and dragon paths which traverse the globe between them, the Tass in which it crystallizes, and the Quintessential ebbs and flows which mark the Junctures, the times of greatest magick. He may also notice creatures and objects charged with magickal energy, though he needs Mind to perceive their particular auras and Spirit to detect their souls (assuming they have them).

Perceptions of Prime vary from mage to mage. Some see it as a clear, pure light or a shining matrix of white energy. Others perceive it as a dark and primal force, the Black Egg, and see a matrix of black against gray. Others claim that it is a distinct color, neither black nor white, a magickal color out of space, while some mysticks hear it as the music of the Spheres or describe it as a tingle of magick in the air or a current flowing around them.

By sensing the strongest currents of Odyllic Force, a mage may align himself so that they flow into his own Pattern, charging his Avatar. Without the first rank of Prime, the mage cannot store free Quintessence within his own Pattern beyond the amount he receives from his Avatar. Mages without Prime magicks cannot gain Quintessence ratings above their Avatar Background Trait.

•• Weave Odyllic Force Fuel Pattern

The mage attains some control over the shifting Patterns of Prime force and Quintessential energy. She can divert small streams to flow differently through the cosmos or reweave them to create Platonic ideals, items composed solely of Quintessence and visible to those with magickal senses.

Such items exist in the etheric, spiritual and astral planes (the High and Middle Umbral Worlds) all at once. When the mage conceives of an object, it takes on some degree of solidity. By channeling Prime Force through his concept, the sorcerer can transform it into a physical form. Creating things out of "thin air," then, obviously demands Prime 2.

••• Channel Quintessence

At rare sites (Nodes) and on rare days (Junctures), Quintessential Force focuses into Primal energy. The resulting flow is called "free" Quintessence and assists mages working enchantments, casting spells or creating Horizon Realms, new items, Chantries or Talismans. At this rank, a mystick understands how to draw these "surplus" energies out of the Patterns in which they are stored. The mage becomes a conduit of Quintessence, storing it in her own being or channeling it into other Patterns, like her Chantry's pocket Realm.

For lack of better terms, mages describe Quintessence as either "raw" or "free." The terms are for classification only; there's no real difference between the two. *Raw Quintessence* makes up Patterns, flows through living beings and coalesces in the tremendous pool of Quintessence from which mages draw the energies for Pattern magick. *Free Quintessence* is surplus Prime that can be manipulated and transferred. Raw Quintessence energy grants life or form to everything, from a lightning bolt to a chipmunk. Free Quintessence is the extra power held by a mage as part of his Quintessence Trait. If that Trait goes to zero, the mage still has the raw Quintessence that allows him to live and be human.

Sadly, free Quintessence can only flow from one established Pattern into another. No one has successfully tapped into the "pool" of free Quintessence described under Prime Rank Two, or even drawn extra Prime Force from this large pool when creating new Patterns or fueling them with Quintessence. That is to say, when a mage creates an object, she can only siphon enough Quintessence to make the object — no surplus Quintessence remains in anything a mystick creates from scratch.

The special properties which allow free Quintessence to flow from Pattern to Pattern are beyond even the Masters of Prime. If the Oracles of Prime know more, they have said little. There seems to be a definite limit to the free Quintessence which exists on Earth, and Chantries battle fiercely for control of this precious commodity.

Prime

• Etheric Senses
•• Weave Odyllic Force
Fuel Pattern
••• Channel Quintessence
•••• Expel Base Energy
••••• Alter Flow

Specialties: Channeling, Perceptions, Filling Patterns, Draining Patterns

•••• Expel Base Energy

While Disciples of Prime are largely limited to detecting and manipulating free Quintessence, Adepts of Prime learn to channel raw Quintessence. They can pull Quintessence out of the Patterns of matter and energy, affecting a Pattern's substance in reality. Each shard of inanimate matter and each spark of energy has Quintessence stored within. Adepts can expel the Quintessence from these Patterns, recycling it into the cosmic pool of raw Quintessence. Without Quintessence in its Pattern, that matter or energy ceases to exist.

Adepts who know enough about Matter or Forces can use conjunctional Effects to alter the amount of Quintessence stored in various parts of these Patterns, thereby "dissolving" different aspects or properties of the energy or matter. A sorcerer could make solids become insubstantial, cause a magnet to have only one pole, remove a chemical's ability to form nuclear bonds with other chemicals (this process would, for example, make an acid unable to corrode), or cause objects to lose their mass yet remain solid. While Pattern magicks alone can do the same thing, extracting a target's raw Quintessence is a direct and "easy" way to alter it.

••••• Alter Flow

Masters of Prime delve into truly advanced theories. Such Masters can alter established flows of raw Quintessence — those flowing through Life Patterns.

Living beings interact with Quintessence in a unique manner. Their Quintessence is not stored in their Patterns, but runs continuously through them. By damming this flow, the mage can extinguish the spark of life within the creature.

Masters can also *increase* the flow of Quintessence through a Pattern. This means nothing to life forms without strong Avatars, but Awakened ones can instantly recharge their Avatars' Quintessence.

Some Masters of Prime also claim to have found connections between Paradox and Quintessence, like those between negative and positive forces. This breakthrough allows these mysticks to channel free Quintessence in ways that cancel "random" Paradox energies.

Prime Effects

• **Heart's Blood** — A Disciple of Prime can sense the flow of Quintessence — his life energy — through his own body. As vampires well know, each human has about 10 points of this upon which they may feed. Each point corresponds to a Health Level. The last three go beyond Incapacitated; losing them will kill him.

In desperate times, mages skilled in Prime can push themselves beyond their limits and "give till it hurts," taking the additional Health Levels as points of Quintessence above and beyond what is stored in their Avatars. Such damage may only be healed by time and bed rest, not magick **(see "Better Body")**, so most mages will usually only risk the first "Bruised" Health Level. Mages of the Chorus, however, have martyred themselves to perform one last holy miracle, while Verbena with low Avatar ratings often consider the sacrifice of heart's blood more holy than the spiritual energy used by most mages.

• **The Rush** — Disciples of Prime can collect the free Quintessence that flows through their Patterns. Normally Quintessence only circulates within Life Patterns; it does not settle in them as it does within inanimate matter and energy. A mage who knows Prime Arts, however, can build up and store such energies within himself. Each success rolled for this Effect allows him to store one additional point of Quintessence. The mage may make only one roll per source of Quintessence. Note that he cannot channel that Quintessence until he reaches Prime 3; this Effect only allows him to store the energy.

The Cult of Ecstasy calls such channeling "The Rush." The sudden influx of Quintessence gives the Cultist a mixed feeling of nausea and exhilaration, which he rides for all it's worth.

• **Sense Quintessence** — The mage can use this Effect to sense free Quintessence stored in nearby Patterns. This Effect, like other basic sensory Arts, requires only a Perception roll. Additional successes allow greater range and accuracy. This ability is generally a good way to discover if any mages are nearby, as the Awakened store free Quintessence within their Avatars.

Hermetic mages use engravings of the Seal of Solomon to reveal the presence of Quintessence. Different points of the star-shaped seal illuminate to indicate the direction of Quintessence, and the brightness with which the symbol glows reveals the amount of Quintessence present.

•• **Enchant Weapon** — This Effect reweaves underlying Quintessence to intensify existing forms, enchanting objects and creatures. Weapons (including fists) treated this way do no more damage than their mundane counterparts, but inflict aggravated wounds against vampires, werewolves and other Awakened beings. Such items can also strike spirits, which normal objects can't do.

The Quintessential form often differs from the material one; a dirty denim jacket may be as strong as a Kevlar vest to the spirit world, while a broken dagger may still have a whole blade with regards to magickal structure. Such structures are still *physically* what they appear to be — the denim jacket would not stop bullets, nor could the nonexistent blade cut butter — but spirits would find them quite real — the jacket could soak spirit attacks while the dagger could stab wraiths.

Enchanting an item this way requires concentration and five successes or more. This is not, however, vulgar magick. Nothing obvious changes.

•• Rubbing of the Bones — Disciples of Prime do not yet have the ability to cause a serious disruption of the flow of Quintessence into a Pattern of Life, but they can tamper with it to some extent. Euthanatos call this Effect the **Rubbing of the Bones,** because the ripple feels like someone warping your bones.

This Effect causes the target's steady flow of Quintessence to ripple and surge. This inflicts no lasting damage, but it hurts. Any life form affected will be stunned and unable to function for the duration of the fluctuation (the Storyteller may allow a character to spend a Willpower point to take some limited action for a turn). Its physical form will seem to fade in and out slightly, becoming ghostly and immaterial one second and massively heavy the next. Another mage caught in this Effect may spend a point of stored Quintessence to smooth the flow and cancel the Effect completely.

••• Bond of Blood — The Verbena know the power within blood. Thus, blood forms an important focus for the Sphere of Prime. To transfer free Quintessence between two different receptacles, a Verbena must smear her palms in blood and touch both objects. She may then act as a conduit, pulling Quintessence from one object and channeling it into another (or into herself).

Each success on the magickal Effect roll allows the mage to transfer up to five points of Quintessence from one Pattern and channel it into another, including her own. Obviously, she cannot take more Quintessence than the source object stores. The Verbena may use this Effect to take Quintessence from another mage, but may not reduce the target's Quintessence below its Avatar rating.

••• Create Talisman — A mage must have Rank Three in Prime to create items that store free Quintessence and use it to power magickal Effects. Rules for creating Talismans are provided in Chapter Nine.

•••• Flames of Purification — Mages of the Celestial Chorus are not destructive by nature. Still, they have been known to wield the power of Prime to cleanse reality of abominations. By fanning her focus over a chosen object, a Chorister can invoke this Effect and cause the object to burst into mystickal flames. This fire sheds no heat, yet quickly devours the target.

The mage actually extracts the raw Quintessence from the object's Pattern. That object thus disappears from reality (i.e. it takes aggravated damage and may be consumed if that damage destroys it). The more successes she scores, the larger the target may be. If she prefers, the mage can affect several similar Patterns simultaneously, like ice cubes within a glass. Only inanimate objects can be affected. A rank 5 variant destroys living beings.

••••• Recharge Gift — Through meditation, Akashic mages can increase their inner Quintessence flow by "drinking" from outside sources. The Brother filters this additional Prime force through his own Avatar and recharges his personal store of Quintessence. For each success rolled, the mage regains one point of Quintessence, up to his Avatar Background's maximum limit.

••••• Quintessence Blast — Dreamspeakers have devised this Effect to ward off the spirits of Paradox. The Master of Prime charges his focus — often a crystal or clay vessel — with a point of Quintessence. He then uses his magick to draw the Paradox spirit into the crystal; the spirit's essence reacts with the Quintessence stored in the crystal. This injures the spirit and temporarily dispels its Power **(see "Umbrood," Chapter Nine)**, while the crystal explodes into dust.

Spirit

You're a fool if you think you're alone. The spirits surround you, slumbering in your home, nestling in your clothes, kissing you through that comb in your hair. The Dreamers are everywhere. You can't see them? I can.

When you share the spirits' turf — and we all do, like it or not — it helps to speak their language. Just 'cause you can't see them doesn't mean they can't hurt you. Or help you, for that matter; it's good to have friends in high places. Spirits've got their own agenda, and it doesn't include you. The invisible masters can warp you, compel you, or save your ass without you ever knowing they were there. Once you realize that, you'll know how important my Art can be.

You think I'm mad? Look in that corner there and listen as I play my flute. Watch the shadows, buddy, and believe...

Specialties: Dimensional Science, Spirit Dealings, Umbral Travel, Possessions

No other Sphere, perhaps, marks the line between mystick and Technomancer so clearly. To the elder Traditions, spirits are intelligent entities who predate humanity and inhabit a world beyond mortals' narrow perceptions. The Technocracy, and to a degree, the two newest Traditions, regard these enigmas as an alternate dimension (or a series of same), full of hostile aliens and harvestable frontiers. These views shape the way both groups work spirit magick. While the game systems do not distinguish shamanism from spirit-tech, the foci, styles and intents vary a lot.

Metaphysically, the Sphere of Spirit lies between the conceptual Spheres of Prime and Mind and the physical Patterns of Forces, Life and Matter. Both ephemera (the matter of the spirit world) and plasm (the "flesh" of the dead) are Patterns somewhere between metaphysical and physical. The theories, models and concepts different groups use to understand the Spirit Sphere encompass skills for traveling through the Otherworlds, dealing with the entities found therein and surviving alien environments like the Deep Umbra or the Dream Realms. Some mages learn how to travel in the Umbral Realms in their dreams. Others step physically through the Gauntlet, the barrier between worlds, and explore in that manner, while others have discovered methods to reach the furthest Epiphamies through astral Mind projection. Some shamans prefer to stay home, summoning spirits, binding them and learning of the spirit world second-hand from the spirits themselves.

Masters of Spirit often talk to the air, and minor poltergeist activity manifests around them. Most tend to look into space, touch objects no one else can see and address their spirit companions. Spirit-tech experts resemble either mad scientists, tightly-controlled parapsychologists or crusading defenders of the human world.

(See Chapters One and Nine for spirit realms and their inhabitants, as well as rules for running games set in Otherworlds. The Appendix contains sample spirits.)

•

Spirit Sight
Spirit Sense

The Spirit initiate gains the ability to sense the Near Umbra around her. She can see auras, ghosts and spirits, especially those her own Avatar is most attuned to through Resonance. Some mages are better at seeing wraiths and the Dead, others at seeing the spirits of Nature. All spirit-mages can sense these, especially in areas where the Gauntlet is thin, but each person seems to have an easier time dealing with creatures on the same spiritual wavelength.

The Disciple of Spirit can also "read" the strength of the local Gauntlet, testing it for weaknesses, and discern an item that has spirit essence, like a Garou fetish or an awakened object or location **(see below)**.

••

Touch Spirit
Manipulate Gauntlet

The mage now gains the ability to briefly touch spirits and objects he can see on the other side of the Gauntlet — the Penumbra. He can pick up a fetish stick dropped by a Garou, push a spirit out of a room or even hit one over the head with an object from the spirit world, and the spirit may do nothing to stop this unless it possesses some Gift which allows it to manifest on the other side of the Gauntlet. Although this limited expertise allows only brief contact (a turn or two), it can be enough.

At this level, the mage can also extend his spirit touch and make his voice heard through the Gauntlet. He may use this ability to call any spirit known to him, or even put out a general cattle call to any spirits nearby. Every Tradition has methods and rituals to accomplish this, but they are all, in essence, just variants on the classic séance. As with the séance, at this level, attendance is optional, but most spirits will show up, if only out of curiosity or annoyance.

To make things more hospitable for the spirits, the mage may use his power to thin the Gauntlet, making it easier for spirits to cross over into the physical world and manifest, assuming that they have the Charms to do so. Each success on a magickal Effect roll lowers the Gauntlet difficulty by -1 for one turn; three successes would lower it by -3 for three turns. Naturally, this roll must first succeed against the original Gauntlet rating. This only works so well, however — the Gauntlet cannot be brought lower than difficulty 4. The shaman can also strengthen the barrier, making it harder for spirits to enter the physical world — a useful Effect for mages who've called up something they shouldn't have. **(See page 170 for the Gauntlet Chart.)**

With work, he can also extend his perceptions to **Plumb the Deep Umbra** and detect the fringes of eternity.

•••

Pierce Gauntlet
Rouse & Lull Spirit

A mage may now make a hole in the Gauntlet, allowing himself to enter the Umbra, a feat called "stepping sideways" by the Garou. The mage's body and possessions are translated into ephemera, the stuff of spirit, but will possess a certain glow which the more aware denizens of the spirit realm will recognize as belonging to a living being. At this level, any action he takes against an Umbrood creature, physical or otherwise, will be felt. Once in the Penumbra, a mage can go anywhere she likes, up to the borders which mark the Horizon between the Near and Deep Umbrae.

Possessions, however, are more difficult to translate without additional successes. Entering skyclad (nude) requires only the usual successes at the usual difficulty. Normal clothing and items add +1 to both difficulty and successes needed. Bulky gear — backpacks, rifles, large drums — demand a +2 increase. The mage cannot bring through anything he could not normally carry.

With conjunctional Matter 3 and Prime 2 Arts, the mystick may create short-lived items out of ephemera. These creations — knives, tents, boats, etc. — must be built as if they were material items, and fade away when the Effect's duration ends. Until them, such items are as strong as any "real" object would be.

The mage also gains the power to rouse spirits. According to many philosophies, most spirits are asleep. Rousing is like calling, simply louder, and will rouse not only those spirits who have been quiescent for a long while, but those who have never awakened before. (Note that this has no relation to magickal Awakening.) Depending on the mage's diplomatic skills, the spirit may be anywhere from curious to furious.

The mage may also use this same magick to lull an awakened spirit, such as one residing in a fetish, though the more powerful the spirit, the more difficult it is to put back to sleep. A talen (one-use fetish) would require three successes, while a powerful Bane-dagger would demand at least eight. Such slumber lasts for the spell's duration.

•••• Rend Gauntlet
Seal Breach
Bind Spirit

The mage may now rip the fabric of the Gauntlet asunder and he — and anyone else who wants to, mortal or spirit — can travel through without difficulty. This is, of course, highly vulgar; most polite (and sensible) mages will seal the breach after they and their friends pass into the Umbra. The mystick can also repair breaches which others have made in the Gauntlet, and reinforce the barrier's fabric to make it that much harder to tear.

The mage may now compel spirits to appear and bind them into obedience. The Umbrood may also be forced into objects to create fetishes, which use their powers at the behest of the mage who trapped them. Such trinkets often have a single use only, based upon the nature of the spirit that was bound. The more powerful the spirit, the more successes it takes to bind them. Few will stand still for this....

This sort of magick is of course considered very antisocial in the spirit world (if not outright black magick). Mages who do this too often tend to get a reputation.

A brave (or foolish) shaman may also channel a spirit's powers through herself. This shuts out any other magick she might do while the Umbrood possesses her, though she can access its Charms, speak with its voice and perform feats of incredible physical prowess. Regaining control is sometimes a problem, though — many spirits enjoy riding mortal hobby-horses and must be forced out through contested Willpower rolls (difficulty 7-10) or the reverse of this same power — exorcism.

Spirit

• Spirit Sight
Spirit Sense
•• Touch Spirit
Manipulate Gauntlet
••• Pierce Gauntlet
Rouse & Lull Spirit
•••• Rend Gauntlet
Seal Breach
Bind Spirit
••••• Forge Ephemera
Outward Journeys

Specialties: Dimensional Science, Spirit Dealings, Umbral Travel, Possessions

••••• Forge Ephemera
Outward Journeys

A Master of Spirit gains a divine power, for he may now take ephemera, the substance of Spirit, reweave it in whatever fashion he desires, repair it or rip it asunder.

The mage may now heal spirits' Power (as per the Damage chart), help create Horizon Realms or Umbral Domains or even attack a victim's Avatar through the dreaded Gilgul rite. This *always* vulgar magick is considered the last resort when dealing with an enemy mage; it not only robs a mystick's power, it destroys his soul. Such magick is exceedingly difficult, and its rites are highly guarded.

(Lest it be abused, let players know that anyone who overuses this power may well end up its victim. Gilgul, even in the worst possible cases, is *never* taken lightly.)

The Master may also use his power to break free from the Horizon and explore the Far Realms. No longer must he rely on the tenuous connections within Domains to travel to the Outer Realms. The mage is able to traverse the Deep Umbra, surviving the ravages of Etherspace for short periods, while he speeds through it towards his chosen destination. Masters of Spirit are said to spend years at a time on their outward journeys, charting the Tellurian and studying the denizens of other Realms.

Spirit Effects

• Spirit Sight — The mage can shift his sight into the spirit world. He becomes oblivious to the physical world around him and sees only the spirit world while scrying. The number of successes he needs, and the Effect's difficulty, depend upon the strength of the local Gauntlet. This barrier's thickness depends on an area's static influence; the more populated (or technological) the place, the harder it will be to pierce the Gauntlet.

• Detect Possession — Through various rites and rituals, a mage may detect whether someone or something is possessed, and if so, by what. While the mental and emotional impulses of a spirit must be read with the Sphere of Mind, a mage may still make an educated guess with an Awareness roll. Possessed objects include such things as Garou fetishes, as well as the victims of demons, Banes and other malevolent spirits.

•• Call Spirit — While in the Umbra, the mage can call any spirit she knows by name in the hope that it will hear and come to her. Powerful spirits such as Lords and Preceptors rarely respond, but may send lesser spirits to the mage as messengers. The Storyteller must decide the number of successes required to attract the spirit's attention, depending on the power of the spirit and its previous relations with the mage. There are no guarantees of the spirit's behavior once it arrives.

A mage in physical reality can call to spirits if the mage first shifts his perceptions into the Umbra through **Spirit Sight**. Spirits that respond may manifest into the physical world if they are able.

•• The Spirit Kiss — Cultists of Ecstasy use their ability to touch spirits to physically embrace beings on the other side of the Gauntlet. Apart from the more obvious pleasures of such contact, the Cultist can accept Power from, or lend Quintessence to, his partner if he also uses Prime 2. For game purposes, consider Power and Quintessence one and the same. (Corpus may be substituted if the partner is a wraith.)

A spirit's nature affects the Quintessence she gives, however; this can be both good and bad. For example, a nymph's Power would be particularly useful for love spells (it has the appropriate Resonance), but a mage who accepted this power into his Avatar would find himself increasingly horny (not often a problem for a Cultist of Ecstasy). Also, like Tass, Power is not useful for workings which run against its Resonance.

Other Traditions have variant rituals for this Effect, which, while less intimate, are no less useful.

••• Awaken the Inanimate — By talking and crooning over a physical object, a Dreamspeaker or Akashic Brother may Awaken its spirit and rouse it into awareness.

Objects, once their spirits are awake and aware, can be particularly useful. Their personalities tend to be very protective of those who have treated them well and ill-disposed toward those who have treated them badly. The object could not really do much on its own, but might cause small "coincidences" that work for (or against) the mage. For example, if an Euthanatos were to rouse the spirit of his gun, it might refuse to fire for an enemy. Likewise, an aware Chantryhouse might take a very dim view of burglars, especially if they broke in — doors might slam, lights could go out (or on), and the alarm system the burglars disabled would work anyway.

Rousing an object typically requires plenty of ritual successes — five or so for a gun, 20 or more for a house. This is slow, but often coincidental unless the mage wants an especially vulgar manifestation. The older and more psychically-charged the object is, the more powerful its spirit and the harder will be to rouse. The newer and less important the item, the less powerful and less intelligent its spirit and the easier it is to rouse. A new knife from the knife shop, never used, would have less personality and intelligence than a cockroach, but could be made aware for a minimal amount of magick. Over years or decades, the object would start to absorb some of its owner's personality. The knife an old shaman forged in boyhood would have a strong and active spirit (though it might not be a fetish *per se*).

An object with an awakened spirit exists in multiple worlds at once. An awakened knife can be used by a person in the physical world to injure spirits in the Near Umbra or to cut the silver cords or bodies of astral travelers.

••• Stepping Sideways — Spirit mages can force their way through the Gauntlet and enter the Near Umbra. Once there, a mage can walk, run, talk, use magick, etc., as if she were in physical reality with a few differences **(see "The Otherworlds," Chapter Nine)**. When the mystick repeats the **Stepping Sideways** Effect to re-enter physical reality, she appears in the location corresponding to her final position in the spirit world.

Walking through the Gauntlet often requires time; the amount of successes (and the roll's difficulty) this requires can be found on the **Gauntlet** chart. If the mage botches his roll, he becomes stuck, transfixed between the spirit and the physical worlds, unable to move. Not even Correspondence magick can help him. Someone who knows Spirit magick (or a spirit entity) must successfully **Step Sideways** or **Breach the Gauntlet** to free the unfortunate mage.

••• or •••• Free the Mad Howlers — With a wild frenzy, the shaman summons angry spirits to attack the living. The third rank variation of this terrifying spell calls Umbrood who can **Materialize** on their own (with the Charm of that name), while the fourth level actually seals the mad howlers inside the victim, as if he were a fetish, for the duration of the Effect. Either option inflicts aggravated damage (which the target may soak) and causes great terror and pain. Victims whose bodies become living fetishes may be stunned **(see the Forces Effect Discharge Static)** by the agony of this vicious attack.

•••• Breach the Gauntlet — This Effect allows the mage to rupture the local Gauntlet completely, creating a window in the fabric of reality between the spirit and the physical worlds. This allows anyone, including Sleepers, free passage into or out of the Umbra. The is a good Effect to have when a cabal must enter the spirit world together.

A mystick has no control over what passes through the breach once it opens, though she may close it at any time. Some spirit entities flock to breaches and aren't inclined to beg the mage's permission to use the opened portal.

Each success rolled for this Effect lowers the difficulty of stepping sideways by -1. Large breaches (room-sized or larger) lower that number by -1 for every *two* successes. If the mage reduces the Gauntlet difficulty to 0, she breaches the barrier.

•••• Psychic Sterilization — The Sons of Ether prefer tightly controlled environments when conducting their experiments. To block out potential spiritual interference, they often reinforce the Gauntlet within their laboratories. Each success rolled for this Effect raises the number of successes needed to pierce the local Gauntlet by one.

The Order of Hermes, Void Engineers and New World Order all use similar Effects to trap Materialized spirits in the physical world. If the mage can strengthen the Gauntlet enough, the spirit will be unable to return home. This Effect does not trap the spirit itself, but seals the Gauntlet against passage.

•••• Gauntlet Prison — Mages have better methods of trapping spirits than simply locking them in the physical world. By "pulsing" the Gauntlet's strength while a being passes through, a mystick can trap that being inside the barrier, as if it had botched its roll to step sideways. Daring mages try to bind powerful spirits this way, then extort services from them. Ancient tales recount that certain Chantries used to ensnare Preceptor-level spirits in these Gauntlet prisons.

To trap a spirit traveler successfully, the mage must score more successes while using this Effect than the victim rolled while stepping sideways.

Victims imprisoned in the Gauntlet appear as ghostlike specters when viewed from physical reality or from the spirit world. Once a victim is trapped, the mage often reinforces the Gauntlet in the area with **Psychic Sterilization** to prevent anyone from successfully freeing the captive. Treacherous mages have also been known to breach a Gauntlet, invite others to walk through and collapse it into a prison when they do.

•••• Create Fetish — The Spirit Adept can fashion items that serve as receptacles for the essences of spirits. Most fetishes are created with the spirits' cooperation, but some sorcerers use their Arts to imprison spirits into fetishes. Such objects can be tricky to use, but gain power from the spirit's anger. **(See Chapter Nine for fetish creation rules.)**

•••• Living Bridge — By entering a pact with an Umbrood entity, a mystick may channel that spirit's powers for the duration of the Effect. Any Charm that spirit possesses, and one or two related abilities (water-breathing for a nixie, plant-blooming for dryads, etc.), are the shaman's to command, Paradox-free, until the spirit leaves. The mage cannot use True Magick during that time, and will often drop into a long sleep afterward. While the spirit inhabits her, however, the mage knows things no human could understand (an effective Cosmology of 4) and can perform inhuman feats (three additional dots to her Physical Attributes).

This is not without cost; even minor spirits will demand sacrifices, favors or tasks in return for a few moments of power. Most spirits also "mark" those they possess; anyone with **Spirit Sight** (and most werewolves) can see the signs of a spirit-rider. This isn't too bad in the case of minor nature spirits, but Banes, demons and finicky Preceptors often claim a host as their own and taint his aura, if not his mortal flesh.

•••• Exorcism — A magickal exorcism involves pushing a spirit out of a mortal host. This host need not be human — objects can also be possessed. Contested Willpower rolls — one per scene, hour or even day — decide who stays and who goes. A minor spirit can be banished with 10, a Minion-level one with 15, a Preceptor or major Bane with 20 or more and a Lord with over 30.

Prime 3 can aid this fight; for every success a Prime roll scores, add one to the exorcism total. Celestial Choristers often work in concert to drive out demonic influence, while Dreamspeakers often go against a possessor alone, using tricks (Manipulation + Expression or Intimidation) to frighten the spirit into surrender.

••••• Break the Dreamshell — The Dreamshell is the Dreamspeaker term for the Horizon. To enter the Deep Umbra, a mystick must break through this Dreamshell, just as she must break through the Gauntlet when stepping sideways.

Ten successes or more are required to pierce the Earth Mother's Dreamshell. Other Realms might have weaker or stronger Horizons. If the mage uses an Anchorhead (a special Domain set amid the Dreamshell), the passage becomes easier and requires only five successes.

••••• Deep Umbra Travel — Surviving the utterly barren spiritual environment of the Deep Umbra requires a membrane of spirit magick. This spiritual essence creates a sort of bubble around the mage, protecting him from the ravages of the Deep Umbra. The traveler must reach and enter another Near Umbra before the duration rolled for the field elapses, or he will die a cold death in the void.

The mage can fly through the Umbra at amazing speeds using only his will. Still, the distances in the Deep Umbra are almost inconceivable. Close Realms, such as the moon, take but a day to reach, while distant Realms like Mars can only be reached after several days of travel.

Travel into the Deep Umbra is a highly dangerous affair, but many "Etherjammers" feel a manifest destiny to explore and chart it. Their sojourns into the Deep Umbra recall the journeys of the ancient Pacific Islanders who sailed off to find a new island before they ran out of food. Sometimes a traveler turns back halfway in order to return safely; sometimes he risks everything and crosses the point of no return.

Time

Deja vu makes perfect sense once you realize that time ain't linear. Folks just stumble through some rift in time and don't even realize they're there when they do it. Then they go back through and remember something strange, but they just can't finger it because it don't fit their world view. Sucks to be them.

The first thing you'll realize when we shack up — and we do, trust me — is that the bullshit you learn in high school don't cut it with the real world. I don't mean the world you see, I mean the world you don't see, but which sees you just the same. This time is all times, and all times run in parallel streams, and when you figure out that you can jump from stream to stream while standing still, you know that deja vu isn't a glitch — it's our natural state.

Confused? Yeah, magick's that way sometimes. But if it were easy, it wouldn't be any fun, would it?

Specialties: Perceptions, Conjuctional Uses, Travel, Temporal Control

The Sphere of Time has long mystified and frustrated philosophers. Just as humanity had finally begun to accept time as another defined parameter in the organized paradigm of Newtonian physics, Einstein came along and theorized that time was not constant but instead relative to each observer. Since then it has become ever more popular to ponder the possibilities of time travel and theory. Does time pass in quantum segments, like a very high-speed film? Is humanity's perception of time as a one-way linear phenomenon (a train moving from past to future) correct? Time is perhaps the hardest Art to comprehend; perhaps that's why the Cult of Ecstasy excels at it.

Mysticks who pursue such Arts argue theory more than any other mages — especially the theories regarding time travel. Some believe that it is possible, some that it is impossible, and some claim to have discovered it, then are never heard from again (or even remembered, so the stories say).

Some mages have documented rips in the fabric of time which have led to the past, but very few who've dared to step through them ever return, and while there are sites — including a few Chantries — which are known to have a history of holes in time, these seldom appear in a predictable pattern, and have either frustrated researchers who went there to study the phenomenon or made them disappear.

Some claim that only the present is fixed, that the past and future are both probability continuums, and that all time travel is merely travel into the Umbra. This might explain some purported time travelers, including at least one cyborg from the far future, a Victorian scientist, a self-professed alien and a group of Edwardian schoolchildren with an ancient Atlantean amulet.

The Council's explanations for these visitors range from the sublime to the ridiculous — everything from dismissing them as Marauders to the theory that they're characters from literature who've wandered out of some Dream Realm. No one can ever be certain; they never stay long enough for a proper investigation.

The one clearly documented form of time travel (clearly documented among mages, that is) is the ability of some Masters of Time to skip forward into the future. While travel into the past is theoretically possible, everyone who has attempted it has disappeared, recanted or been utterly discredited within a week of their "success," causing yet more theories — most even more outlandish than the rumors about purported time travelers.

Time is often most useful when combined with other Spheres; by hooking advanced Time magicks into other Effects, a mystick can prolong or trigger certain spells. Most Time Effects are highly vulgar; only time perceptions and triggers can remain unnoticed for long.

Time perceptions enable a mystick to search the future or past for some hidden secret. When scrying forward or backward in time this way, the number of successes scored on the magickal Effect roll determines how far into the past or future the Time mage can perceive. Durations for other Time Effects are determined normally. **(Page 170 has a chart for Time-based effects.)**

Small time dilations or accelerations follow Masters of this Sphere. Male mages often grow full beards in one day, cups of coffee cool off quickly, taxi meters click slower than normal, and a constant feeling of *deja vu* spreads to everyone in the vicinity. Masters also tend to see past their companions and speak using only one verb tense — past, present or future — leading many to speculate that some have actually traveled successfully and now live displaced or even backwards in time.

• Time Sense

The mage begins to develop a rudimentary awareness of Time's true nature, and gains the precise internal clock essential to performing more complex Time magick. She also detects certain time-based phenomena that periodically shift through reality. She can intuitively sense the approach of such disturbances and "feel" where in dimensional space the phenomena will appear.

Most such effects are small ripples which either speed or slow time relative to the space outside. A few are referred to as "skips," small rifts which lead forward in time, but some may actually be "loops," rifts into the past. It's generally considered unwise to simply step through either one, and by the time the mage has taken the time to peer forward in time to see when the rift leads, time has passed and the rift has sealed.

These rifts seem fairly rare today, though they appear to go in historical cycles, like comets. The late Victorian age, for example, seemed to have had an unusual number of time-based phenomena, as did several other ages, while other eras, like the 1930s, had almost none. It's said that stasis causes such skips — the more static the times, the more often those times move themselves.

At this level, mages may also detect temporal phenomena weaker than actual rifts. The spots where a Master steps forward in Time, or sends something forward, display a distinct irregularity in the flow of the continuum, while places which have been used to scry the future — or *will* be used for scrying the past — display a twist in the ribbon of time.

•• Past Sight Future Sight

The mage can now shift her perceptions forward or backward in time. Postcognition tends to require more successes to perform, but its results are certain (or at least considered so by most). Precognition is less difficult to enact, but the futures foreseen — especially far futures — tend to be inaccurate.

Most mages believe the future is constantly changing. Anytime a mage looks forward, he simply foresees the most *probable* future. This creates a self-fulfilling prophecy — or defeats the vision's purpose. Through the act of foreseeing the future, the future may be changed. If a mage predicts the manner of his own death, he can then avoid that circumstance. This very phenomenon makes the future unknowable (Fate Masters have their own thoughts on the subject).

Mages commonly use this magick with conjunctional Effects. Entropy 1 allows a mage with future sight to view multiple probabilities or possible futures. She may add Entropy 2 as a conjunctional Effect to choose one. The most probable futures are the easiest to pick, and the least likely the most difficult.

Most mages also mix Correspondence 2 with this rank of Time, because by itself, this rank only allows a mage to look forward or backwards into the past of her current location. With Correspondence 2, she may scry out any time and any place in the world.

Looking into time can be quite dangerous. Just as there are guardians for certain parts of space and the spirit world, so are there guardians for certain segments of time and certain bits of knowledge. Seeking the secret incantations of the Priests of Mu can be risky; such rites were no doubt guarded by potent spirit entities. Those guardians are still there, waiting for anything that strays too close — including Peeping Toms from the future. Thus, peering into the past is not a magick for the idly curious.

Some mages reverse this magick and thicken the walls of time around some particular instant, making an action that much more difficult to discern from the future (or foresee from the past) and theoretically preventing time travelers from interfering as well. Each success a mage gets on this sort of magick subtracts from a future (or past) success of some other mage to spy on the mage's present doings. Some sorcerers cloak themselves in a wall of thickened time, preventing other mages from locating their future whereabouts.

Mages who frequently extend their perceptions through time tend to experience spontaneous flashes of pre-or-postcognition. These flashes range from feelings of *deja vu* to vivid, dreamlike trances foretelling danger.

Time

• Time Sense
•• Past Sight
Future Sight
••• Time Contraction
Time Dilation
•••• Time Determinism
••••• Future Travel
Time Immunity

Specialties: Perceptions, Conjunctional Uses, Travel, Temporal Control

••• Time Contraction Time Dilation

The mage can now exert her will over the passage of time, causing it to accelerate or slow as she desires. Mysticks often describe these Effects as "contracting" or "dilating" time, referring to the length of each moment in time. Thus, contracting time around a waterfall makes it appear to flow more slowly to an outside observer; near the waterfall, each moment does not last as long and less water flows. Conversely, by dilating each moment around the waterfall, more water flows during each segment of time. While the observer perceives these moments to pass normally, he will see more water flow during each moment. Working this magick conjunctionally with Correspondence 3, a mage can allow a moving object to go at any speed without gaining additional momentum.

Likewise, by dilating Time dramatically enough, a mage can effectively travel forward in Time. A mystick who shuts herself in a hidden room of a castle, for example, then works a spell so that only one day passes inside the room while 100 years pass outside, has effectively traveled forward in time. There are risks (war, fire, demolition) during the intervening years, but most mages will have already divined the future of the sanctity of the hiding place, so that should not be much of a problem. This is, however, a one-way street, and no one can prove the wisdom of following it....

•••• Time Determinism

The mage is now able to cause absolute shifts in time, rather than simply adjusting the rate at which time passes. He can take a field of time and freeze it; a falling arrow may be stopped mid-flight or a man placed in a state of suspended animation.

This is a powerful Effect when used in conjunction with other magicks, as the mage can choose the moment in time which "triggers" the magickal time bomb. Some long-dead Masters of Time have left the world a legacy of magickal Effects that occur even after the mage's death. Such "hanging" Effects are the type of time-based phenomenon that mages with **Time Sense** can intuitively detect.

When mixed with Entropy, such spells gain a contingency effect. For example, a suspended animation spell could have a Sleeping Beauty clause, ending it at the kiss of a prince instead of at a set instant in time. Other magickal Effects can also be worked into the temporal program as subroutines, to use the Virtual Adept term, so long as that Effect, and its trigger, are set in advance. The more unlikely the trigger Effect is, however, the more difficult it is to incorporate.

By setting certain things in place — "This wall will turn to fire when someone leans on it (Matter 3/ Forces 3/ Prime 2/ Time 4)" — entire artificial systems of magick ("Words of Power" and so forth) can be created with "clap on/clap off" functions, making reliable static magick that anyone with the appropriate keys can access. To keep such stored magick from being stolen by enemies, many Time Adepts have used Matter and/or Life to tie these to heirlooms and/or bloodlines, leaving their descendants a legacy of magickal abilities. Eventually, of course, the magick is used up or the heirlooms are lost, so nothing lasts forever. Such "contingent" Effects can be detected with the first rank of Time or Entropy, though it takes Time 2 to truly fathom the Effect's nature.

••••• Future Travel Time Immunity

At Master-level knowledge, the mage can do more than determine the timing of events; he can shift objects through time. The mage actually plucks something out of the flow of time and repositions it at some other point along the time stream. The new position could be seconds or centuries away from the field's original place in time.

Masters say such Effects are "anchored," or firmly linked to their point of origin. A ripple exists in the time stream at the point of their disappearance until their reappearance. This forms a continuous thread which the Master can pull at any time she sees fit. For example, a mage who sent her house forward into the future to keep it from being destroyed by a war succeeded in pushing it forward 50 years. Five years after the original magick, the war ends, so she grasps the ribbon and pulls the building back out of the time stream prematurely. She may also do the same with herself, moving forward through the not possible but actual future, until she finds a point in the time stream when she decides to disembark.

Theoretically, this anchored Effect could be used to travel into the past as well; it's assumed that the Oracles of Time use this method (if they travel in Time at all), as would any Masters who have discovered the means.

Even anchored future travel is not without its risks; such Arts are obviously vulgar, and any Disciple of Time can recognize an anchored time Effect and gauge the time when it will come due, while a Master can reach into the time stream and pull out another traveler.

Masters can also immunize themselves from time. Figuratively speaking, the Master simply steps laterally out of the current temporal flow. He can maintain his immunity only so long, but during his "time" outside of Time, he perceives the world as a statuesque collection of still images that he may manipulate as he pleases. As a conjunctional Effect with Life or Matter, he may take other creatures and objects "out of time" as well, and may even abandon them in the frozen moment. It seems such a state cannot last forever, and subjectively the creatures appear only moments later, but some reappear dead of old age, having passed hundreds of years in a timeless hell.

Time Effects

• **Time Sense** — As described above, mages of Time have identified phenomena that exist in a special "sub-realm" of space-time. These time-phased phenomena cannot be seen by Sleepers; only mages who have studied the Sphere of Time can perceive these phenomena. If the mage is close to where a given phenomenon will appear (or has appeared?), she can discern temporal ripples and sense where in space the phenomenon will cross (has crossed?) into her own timeline. She can then seek it out if she desires. Some phenomena are so powerful that their foreshadowing ripples can be felt by mages across the globe.

Mages have identified hundreds of these time-based phenomena, from powerful Preceptors who appear every 12 years in the Andes Mountains, to the spectral Tower of Babel whose cycle has yet to be determined, to ghosts that wander down certain roads every night looking for the drivers who didn't give them a ride when they lived....

• **Internal Clock** — Virtual Adepts cultivate amazingly accurate internal clocks in order to time events in VR and test the processing speeds of their computers. This Effect turns a mage into a human stopwatch; he always knows the current time and can clock events within fractions of a second. This internal clock runs according to the mage's perception of time. He can adjust it for temporal Effects that he causes; visiting Realms where time operates differently, or getting on the bad side of others' time-based Effects, however, can disorient the mage.

•• **Postcognition** — The mage can extend her perceptions backward in time to witness what once occurred in her current location. While the mystick "rewinds" time in the location, she sees in her mind's eye what transpired there. The Storyteller must relate to the player what the character sees.

The mage can shift the exact moment she currently watches; she might begin by viewing the events of one day ago, then shift to one hour ago, then 10 years ago, etc. Her total viewing time cannot exceed the duration rolled for the Effect.

•• **Songs of Future Days** — This precognitive Effect was developed by the Celestial Chorus. The mage begins singing to focus the magick and lets his mind wander down the pathways of future time. The words of his song begin to take on a will of their own, describing in epic format the events that may come to pass in future days.

Unlike postcognitive Effects, which concentrate on a location, precognitive Effects such as this can center on almost anything: a location, a person, an organization, etc. The farther the mage delves into the future with precognitive magick, the more disjointed, sketchy and unreliable the information gleaned.

Ultimately, the Storyteller must decide how accurate the mystick's vision is, based on the successes rolled. One to three would allow vague insights, while five or more would offer a clearer glimpse of the (possible) future.

••• **Accelerate Time** — By dilating the moments of time, the mage can create fields of space-time where things seem to move faster, like a film played at high speed. Each success scored over two speeds up time by a factor of one — three successes double speed, four successes triple speed, and so on. Persons under the effects of time acceleration receive an extra action each turn for every factor of speed. Such fields cannot generally exceed two or three yards.

••• **Slow Time** — The opposite of **Accelerate Time**, each success above two slows time by a factor of one. For example, a person operating under a time-dilation Effect evoked by a mage who scored three successes would receive one action every second turn.

•••• **Programmed Event** — The mage stops time in a localized field and sets a time when it shall resume. Say she lifts a cup from the table and drops it. By freezing time around the cup for one scene, she causes the cup to hang in midair until the scene ends. At that time, the cup will fall and break. This is obviously vulgar. As with **Accelerate Time**, the field of stopped time cannot exceed a few yards. Furthermore, when events in physical reality are frozen for extended periods, Paradox forces usually erode the magick and prematurely free the events from stopped time. Also, if someone were to grab the cup, static reality would reassert itself and the magickal field would dissipate.

••••• **Time Travel** — The mage disappears from present reality and reappears in the same location at a future time of his choosing. The farther he wishes to travel, the more successes are required: one success means he jumps ahead to the next turn, while four successes take him completely out of the story.

The mage's arrival in the future will be felt through **Time Sense** by other mysticks of that time. The longer the time jump, the greater the time-phased phenomenon he becomes to those sensing his arrival. The mage may reappear to find several of his peers waiting for him, investigating the time phenomenon he caused by his time jump.

So far as is known, no mage has successfully traveled into the past and returned. We can assume that Paradox destroys the mage making such a trip, though perhaps the mage is simply lost and can never return to his original timeline. Then again, there are persistent rumors that time travel is indeed possible, and that a ruthless conspiracy across time suppresses the knowledge. Those who have attempted past-travel have never been heard from again....

••••• **Sidestep Time** — In some senses, this Effect is the opposite of **Programmed Event**. The mage no longer determines time for other events; rather, she shifts herself completely out of time. The world suddenly halts all around her. She can still move and act among the frozen events around her, pushing or rearranging objects and people. Certain limits remain; she can turn a television to another channel, but the frozen image on the screen will not change, nor will cars operate, nor will powered machinery work. The mage can extend her temporal immunity to encompass other objects and people, but this limits the length of her stay out-of-time.

Each success scored allows the mage to remain in a timeless state for a longer duration. One success allows the mage to sidestep time for one turn; five successes last a week or more.

Chapter Nine: Setting Rules

When war turns whole populations into sleepwalkers, outlaws don't join forces with alarm clocks. Outlaws, like poets, rearrange the nightmare.
— Tom Robbins, *Still Life with Woodpecker*

Resolution: The Fall

Amidst the gnarled and dying trees in the apple orchard, two bodies moved toward each other with grace and speed that defied their exhaustion and drained spirits. One mage, dark and tall, moved in rage, while the other, pale and small, trembled in fear at this, their final battle.

"There's no escape, Clarissa. This grove is grown from my own soul, a concept I know is beyond your understanding," Peter taunted. "Always with you it was the material. Never the spiritual. Never anything you couldn't see and touch. For all that you may have surpassed me, it ends here. Tonight." With a motion of his hands, the black branches of the apple trees bent and took her in a twisted embrace, wrapping around her limbs, snapping bones as she struggled to break free, fighting with all her will to redirect the trees of the grove to her own bidding. For a few moments, sunlight flickered among the trees and blooms appeared where none had sprung forth for many days. Peter's eyes widened in fury. Just as quickly as they had come, the light and blossoms faded to nothing. He walked over and grasped Clarissa's chin in his hand, his brown eyes meeting her green ones. She stared back at him.

"You're going to kill me, aren't you?" she whispered.

"I only wish I could do more than that, bitch," he hissed, and with that, one sharp branch of the tree where she hung drove itself through her spine. Peter's lips twisted into a satisfied sneer as he heard her final gasps. But then he shuddered. The tone of her voice and the peaceful look on her face were not those of a woman who had died in agony, but rather, one who had found an answer she had been searching for. As he shouted in rage, Clarissa's body grew thinner, more wrinkled, her dark wavy hair suddenly turning silver as the branch piercing her body withered and died, dropping her to the hard-packed earth. She lay there a few seconds before fading altogether.

Peter fell to his knees. She'd looked dead. She'd seemed dead. But the mocking voice of the woman who lived within him echoed all around the grove, laughing at him. And he suddenly suspected that the death of his student wasn't a true death, and that in dying, she'd forever eluded his revenge and discovered what he sought but would never find..

Personal Growth

You should not do magic you do not understand!
— Little Bear, *The Indian in the Cupboard*

Some would say that a mage's whole purpose is to bring about change. This change may be *personal*, affecting only the mystick himself, or *external*, affecting the world around him. In its ideal form, this transformation is called Ascension. The idea is hardly universal — few mages outside the most rarefied Horizon Realms spend all day arguing philosophy or metaphysics. Some aspects of a mage's "career," however, are constant enough to address. That's what this chapter is for.

Many sorcerers (*too* many for some Masters' comfort) ignore the larger implications of what they do; they do what they will, literally. The world, however, does not stand still, especially when you mess with reality. Mages change; this section details how *yours* might change over the course of the chronicle. **(See Chapters Two and Three for the more theoretical aspects of the mystick Path.)**

Awareness

The first step in any sorcerer's existence is his awareness of magick. Once he becomes accustomed to the idea, he must learn how to shape reality and command his powers — and himself. This is not a straightforward road; it twists and alters as the mystick progresses, often challenging whatever steps the mage has already learned. The exact nature of these changes will differ from mage to mage and from troupe to troupe. Any Path, however, begins with awareness and goes on from there.

Example: Wild Talent

Chased to strange ruins (a Node) by menacing shadow-creatures, Deena's character Cynthia falls into a Tass-laden stream. Already on the verge of Awakening and pushed to the limit of her sanity, Cynthia sinks into the stream, thrashes about for air, then feels a hand (her Avatar) reaching out and pulling her from the mud. When she breaks the surface, she Awakens.

"The creatures waver at the edge of the stream," says Wayne (Deena's Storyteller). "What are you going to do?"

"Is there any way I can destroy those bastards?" Deena asks.

Wayne nods and hands her five dice. "Difficulty 6. Roll well." (For the record, the Node and sudden Awakening have reduced her difficulty from 8 to 6.) Deena rolls and adds a Willpower point — four successes.

With a primal scream of ecstatic terror, Cynthia points toward the pursuing shadows. Her new power coalesces into a bolt of pure magickal force (Forces 3, Prime 2), which burns her as it blasts up her arms and out her fingers. The light strikes the shadows, shredding them. In a frenzy, Cynthia attacks again. Deena rolls two more successes on the next attack. Wayne rules that the creatures have had enough. The second blast scatters the shadows to the four winds, and Cynthia collapses in a heap at the stream bank.

Awakening

As it says in **Chapter Two**, an Awakening can be gradual or sudden. More often than not, it involves a growing sense of "otherness" — strange dreams, visions, blackouts, breakdowns, religious ecstasies, whatever — leading to a momentous event where the doors are thrown open. Regardless of what form this Awakening takes, it remains a pivotal point in any mage's life and often shapes her approach to magick from then on.

A character can begin with up to three points of Arete **(see "Backgrounds," Chapter Six)**, the result of a steady learning process or a sudden, almost brutal, revelation. Generally, the more powerful the Awakening — and the higher the starting Arete — the more traumatic that first Epiphany becomes. A mage who grows to accept magick in a slow, deliberate way may begin with one point of Arete and a comparatively sane Awakening. One who Awakens during some dramatic burst of insight may start off with as many as three points, but will undergo some sanity-threatening ordeal as his world is blown apart and reconstructed. We leave the specifics of Awakening to your troupe, but recommend that those who wish to begin powerful pay for it.

Beginning Spheres and Sphere Affinities

A Mage does not Awaken knowing Spheres; these arts must be learned. More often than not, a mage's Awakening experience influences the Sphere she begins her training with — and the one for which she first discards her foci **(see Chapter Eight)**. This "Sphere affinity" usually guides the mystick's later study. She may progress in any Sphere she wants, but tends to favor the familiar Art. A Verbena who Awakens while escaping a burning building may be drawn to Forces magick. Even after his mentor introduces him to the Arts of Life, he will retain an affinity for fire. As he grows, he may still need some focus to work his Life Effects, but he'll have an intuitive gift for Forces. He'll set aside his foci for Forces Effects first and will probably have more "dots" in Forces than in any of his other Spheres.

There are no special benefits for having a "chosen" Sphere — it's a roleplaying handle, not a game bonus. If the Storyteller desires, she might allow for a -1 reduction for difficulties related to the Awakening experience; the aforementioned Verbena might deduct -1 from fire spell difficulties *if* the Storyteller agrees. In most cases, a "Sphere affinity" will simply provide a starting point for the road to greater magicks.

Wild Talent

Depending on the circumstances, a Storyteller may grant a newly-Awakened mage some "wild power" above her usual talent when she first Awakens. For a very brief period — a scene or two — she may cast magicks of up to the third or even forth Sphere level with an Arete Dice Pool of four or five. Naturally, she has very little control over what she does or how — the magicks happen like a brand-new reflex, not like a studied power — and may screw things up royally during that time. The Storyteller has complete control over the power and nature of these wild Effects. The player may blurt out what she *wants* to have happen, but the Storyteller makes the final decision about what *does* happen.

In extreme circumstances — like certain impending death — a mystick may fire off *one* final Effect at an Arete and Sphere level one or two dots higher than his usual rating in that Sphere. Say that Father Shelley was dying, surrounded by vampires, and he called upon God to smite his enemies with a final holy blast. If Father Shelley normally had Prime 3, but wanted to use the **Flames of Purification** Effect, he could, with God's assistance, put everything he had into that last casting. His normal Arete of six becomes seven at the moment of his death; his player rolls seven dice against difficulty 8 (he spent a Willpower point — why not?), gets four successes and leaves the bloodsuckers something to remember him by.

This rule is entirely optional, and the Storyteller has the final say about whether or not such magick is possible. This is a once-in-a-lifetime thing — it can only be performed with a mage's dying breath.

Wild powers should be run more by drama than by systems; hard rules do not work well for such freak occurrences. Wild magicks usually manifest under extreme stress and fade quickly, leaving the new mage drained and disoriented. Essentially, she's lost in a "What in hell was *that?!?*" haze until someone else helps her put the pieces together. That's where a mentor comes in....

Instruction

True Magick cannot be learned from books. All the same, a mage must study to advance — the Spheres do not simply impress themselves into his subconscious (not anymore, anyway). Some of this instruction comes from some kind of mentor, some comes from experience, and some comes from within.

Apprenticeship

Magick is a primal instinct refined to an Art. While some willworkers refine their abilities themselves, most undergo an apprenticeship under some tutor to learn how — and how not — to utilize their powers.

Some mentors pick their apprentices out themselves, as many can sense a future mage before he or she Awakens. Sometimes this is done magickally. Many spot potential recruits through mere observation. Most people with mystick talent perform little "coincidences" without realizing what they're doing — they're simply lucky, insightful, blessed or even deranged. A sharp Adept can spot such unconscious magick use and pick out a pupil by watching people who seem to "sleep" a bit less than most. Once he's spotted his apprentice-to-be, he may push her into an Awakening through either magick or mundane experiences or let the novice's Avatar take its course.

Some would-be mages come to the mentor. Many begin as acolytes, disciples, friends or students of a more experienced mage who yearn for something more. Others come seeking help — the Awakening has unhinged them, the Technocracy (or Traditions!) have hounded them, their world has fallen apart and they need a steady hand to pull them out of the vortex.

However a mentor/student relationship begins, it becomes a serious commitment to both parties. After the initial training (in which the student learns the basics of some magick style, her beginning Spheres and the cultural background and protocols of her Tradition or Convention), the new mage is initiated **(see the Tradition listings on pages 94-113)** into her new society. Whatever group the mentor and apprentice belong to, they will be judged by their peers on the way they both behave. A mentor will often be praised or condemned for the actions of his student, while a budding mage may find her Path helped or hindered by her mentor's reputation. Most Traditions have certain criteria they demand from would-be mentors. No group wants a rookie training amateurs!

Obviously, mentor and student part company sooner or later. This might come through a dispute, attrition, rivalry or personal growth. A link exists, however, between trainer and trainee which transcends mortal relationships. Once mages have shared a Path, even for a while, some traces of the journey remain with them. The bond isn't usually strong enough to be called "magick," but both sides can feel its pull. Even when severed, this mystick attachment can last lifetimes. A mentor can usually sense the "flavor" of his apprentice's magicks, even if the two haven't spoken in decades, and the student often knows when she enters some place that has been important to her mentor.

Mentors and Libraries

Characters may learn a certain degree from teachers or books. The better the resource, the more a mystick can get out of it. The benefits of research can help any character — learning has no upper limit.

If your mage studies with a formal Mentor (i.e., has bought that Background Trait) or has access to a Library (likewise), you the player can roll his rating in that source of knowledge against difficulty 7; if he has Mentor 4, for instance, you'd roll four dice. For each success you roll, you save one experience point **(see below)** when buying the Ability or Sphere your mage studied. Such study takes at least a week; you can make only one roll per study attempt.

No matter what you roll, your mage must always spend at least one experience point and the source of knowledge must have something to do with the subject your mystick studies. A Mentor who knows nothing about Forces magick cannot teach you about that Sphere — you'll have to look elsewhere. Likewise, one who knows less than you do can't help you much — a Mentor with Forces 3 cannot help you save points when studying Forces 4. This is a problem many Masters run into — advanced knowledge gets harder and harder to come by.

The same isn't true of Libraries — one can always gain new insights from books. Study time doubles, however, if the mage has used the same Library to learn about the same subject more than three times in a row. This explains sorcerers' fondness for hidden lore — the more they find, the more they can learn.

In most cases, a character can only save experience points this way through the Background Trait. Another character with the Instruction Skill **(see "Abilities," Chapter Six)** can help your mage learn something that she knows by rolling her Instruction rating. Your character saves experience points the same way, but the other player, or the Storyteller, makes the roll, not you.

A Mentor may have Instruction or a Library (most do), but a mage who wishes to study must make a choice. He may only roll one Trait, not a combination or total of the three.

Seekings and Epiphanies

A mystick's Avatar often works as a second mentor. While Chapter Two details about the interaction between mage and mystick self, it's worth nothing here that a mage cannot advance his Arete without Seekings and Epiphanies, unless the Storyteller wants to ignore this aspect of his chronicle in favor of external adventures.

Experience Costs

Trait	Cost
New Ability	3
New Sphere	10
Willpower	current rating
Knowledges	current rating
Talents and Skills	current rating x 2
Attributes	current rating x 4
Tradition Specialty Sphere	current rating x 7
Other Sphere	current rating x 8
Arete	current rating x 8

Raising your Arete is not a matter of spending experience points. A Seeking pits your mage against a series of internal challenges. If she overcomes them, she gains a deeper access to the power within her. If she fails, she cannot advance (or buy another point of Arete) until she overcomes a future test. When she succeeds, a momentary burst of insight — called an *Epiphany*, after an old term for faerie enchantment — overwhelms her; things will seem a bit dislocated, impressionistic, otherworldly. Those who study such things claim that the mage has entered the "Periphery" between this world and the spirit realm. This feeling fades after a while, but the enlightenment does not.

Ideally, the player should take some time out with the Storyteller in order to roleplay a Seeking session. This isn't essential, of course, but it helps both parties get a feel for **Mage's** deeper possibilities. The details of the Seeking will often depend on the Avatar's Essence, the mage's conflicts within the chronicle and the player's and Storyteller's desires.

Some possible Seeking ideas, by Essence, include:

• **Dynamic** — You must successfully change either yourself or somebody else. The nature of that change will vary — a Chorus mage should bring about something toward the common good, while a Progenitor might have to solve some scientific riddle which has baffled her until now, unlocking new possibilities.

• **Pattern** — You must protect the status quo somehow (by protecting your parents, say, or bringing your own chaotic tendencies into line) or strengthen the patterns which connect and bind the world together (by symbolically descending to the Underworld to give Atlas a break, for example).

• **Primordial** — You must face — or accept — your own inner demons within a landscape of your deepest self, and strengthen your ties with the most primal parts of creation. An urban Verbena may need to cast aside her modern comforts and live wild in the woods, while a Hermetic mystick may need to escape his foci and work magick using only his wits.

• **Questing** — Your Seekings will take you throughout the physical, mental and spiritual worlds, in pursuit of an endless succession of goals, truths and rewards. You may be tantalized by some "Holy Grail" that beckons you through a series of puzzles which reflect unresolved bits of your life.

Experience Points

As the chronicle progresses, the Storyteller will reward your characters with experience points. These points allow you to buy up your mage's Traits, and reflect the result of hard-won knowledge.

Spending Experience Points

Any Trait other than Backgrounds can be raised with experience. If you want to raise your mage's Alertness from 2 to 3, you'd spend four experience points. These costs vary from Trait to Trait and can be found in both the box nearby and on the **Character Creation Process** chart in Chapter Six.

Within the story, however, your mystick must learn these skills somehow — someone or something must teach him. He may have entered formal training to learn more about Do, or might have increased his ability through hard use, trial and error. Roleplay it out when you raise your character's Traits; it's not vital to act out a month spent in a dusty library, but the learning time should be accounted for somehow.

Sphere ratings *must* be increased by study — you don't discover the more esoteric aspects of your Art through simple use. This study may take place with a mentor (or Mentor, if you're using the Background Trait), in secluded research or during some appropriate quest — a vision journey, an Otherworldly trip or a personal cross-country trek — and will take time. Assume *at least* one month per Sphere level at the lower levels and perhaps as long as a year or more per level at rank three or above. Magick can take lifetimes to master and often does.

Awarding Experience Points

At the end of each story, the Storyteller will take each character's actions into account (be afraid!). For Storytellers, these "rewards" will set the tone and power level of the game you run. If you're stingy, the characters will advance slowly, perhaps too slowly for their players' tastes. If you're over-generous, you may be dealing with a super-cabal before you know it. We recommend giving between one to five points per character per game session.

The guidelines below offer a good spread of options.

• **One point — Automatic**: A character always gets one point after each game session.

• **One point — Learning Curve**: The character learned something from his experiences during the chapter. Ask the player to describe what his character learned before you award the point.

• **One point — Acting**: The player roleplayed well, not only entertainingly but appropriately. Award for exceptional roleplaying only; your standards should get increasingly higher. In most cases, only award this point to the person who did the best roleplaying in the troupe.

• **One point — Internal Consistency**: The player acted out her character's Nature and Demeanor very well and had magickal goals that complemented her Essence. While some players may find it tough to fulfill all three goals convincingly, those who properly present both their façade and true self deserve a reward, as do those who represent their Essence appropriately and consistently.

• **One point — Heroism**: When a character puts herself at risk for others, such as when she suffers multiple aggravated wounds fighting a Nephandus long enough for the rest of the mages to escape, give her an experience point. Don't let characters take advantage of this, however. There's a fine line between heroism and stupidity.

At the end of each story, you can assign each player from one to three additional experience points in addition to the points they earned for completing the final chapter.

• **One point — Success**: The group succeeded in its mission or goal. It may not have been a complete success, but at least a marginal victory was achieved.

• **One point — Danger**: The character experienced great danger during the story and survived.

• **One point — Wisdom**: The player (and thus the character) exhibited great wits or resourcefulness and came up with an idea that enabled the group to succeed.

If you want to award your players even more points and let their characters develop more quickly, simply invent new award categories. These can even vary from story to story and can be based on the specific circumstances of each.

Specialties

Once a character attains four dots in a Trait **(including a Sphere; see Chapter Eight)**, the player can choose a specialty that fits her mage's experiences. **Chapter Six** has more details about such specialties.

Raising Backgrounds

These Traits come from actions and events; thus, you the Storyteller may grant points in a particular Background in lieu of experience points if the mage (or cabal) did something that would earn her some kind of favor. If Jennifer Rollins made a powerful friend during one story, for instance, the Storyteller might give her a dot in Allies or raise the Trait by one if she had it, instead of giving her experience points that session. If Father Shelley's cabal won a new Chantry during a story, each character would get a dot or two in the Chantry Background.

Generally, only one Background dot will be awarded per mage per game session, unless some great favor was done.

Conflict

No matter how subtle the wizard, a knife between the shoulder blades will seriously cramp his style.

— Steven Brust, *Jhereg*

The trials a mystick encounters during his life will change him in ways no player — or Storyteller — can predict. These events can alter his personality, lower his Arete or confidence or even transform him into a threat to the world around him.

Nature and Demeanor

We are the products of our experiences. Sometimes the things we encounter change us from Caretakers to Curmudgeons or from Rebels to Architects. Likewise, you the player may decide to alter your mage's Nature or Demeanor. This may take as little as a shift in roleplaying or as much as a drastic revision of both listings with the Storyteller's permission.

Changing Demeanor doesn't take much — the character simply starts acting differently. Naturally, you should change the way you play the mage before you erase the old Demeanor from your character sheet and possibly consult the Storyteller first. Depending on the way you play your character, the Storyteller herself may suggest such a change — coldly killing rival mages does not befit a Caretaker Demeanor, even if it's done for a good reason.

Changing Nature is a bit harder — such a shift reflects a profound shift in outlook and conviction. Generally, only a severe trauma or transcendent revelation can alter a character this way. The change should be played out for everything it's worth and may take several game sessions or stories to come about. Once it happens, such a shift is often permanent, unless the character goes insane or undergoes another profound experience.

Insanity may alter either Nature, Demeanor or both — sometimes randomly. Roleplaying such dementia will be a challenge, but may be the best way to approach long Quiets, severe psychological shocks, Mind Sphere-inflicted damage or a life grown too dynamic for its own good.

Hubris & Resonance

The effects of excessive pride are too variable and complex to assign to systems. The way you the Storyteller deal with such situations will depend on the mage, his actions, the magick he uses (and the way he uses it), the reactions of the people around him and the needs of your chronicle. The following hints, however, should give you some options when dealing with "the dark side" and its repercussions.

Hubris usually creeps in when a mystick becomes full of himself. Perhaps he (or his player) has begun to take magick too lightly — it is the transformation of reality, after all. Perhaps he's begun to act carelessly — blowing up an airplane to kill the Man in Black on board, or conjuring a hungry griffin in Central Park without regard for the Sleepers it might maul. Or maybe the player himself has made a decision to have his character tempted by old hatreds, unresolved fears or new delights. The circumstances will depend on your troupe. Don't be afraid, however, to use hubris as a lever against power-players who simply want to throw fireballs around the city or drain every ATM within miles. If the greed of a player affects his character's actions, so be it.

(All the same, keep your own "dark side" in perspective. Don't throw pride in as an obstacle just because the player has made too many good decisions. Be fair — Heaven and Earth may not be humane, but they *do* have a sort of balance to them. And this *is* a game, after all.)

Storytelling Hubris

• **Twist magickal Effects:** The first signs of growing pride occur when a spell turns out a little differently than the caster planned. Maybe that fireball looked a little like a smiling demon before it hit, or the wound that Chorister just healed glowed brightly for a second, like a miracle he brought about all by himself.... A Storyteller shouldn't make such alterations really noticeable until the mage has really taken on an advanced case of pride. The first time a wise player notices that his **Correspondence Sensing** led him to spy on the girlfriend his mage is so possessive of, he'll get the hint. If not, let these twists become more and more reflective of the mage's true personality.

• **Subtly change the world to reflect the mage's actions:** "That which you do returns to you threefold" is a **Mage** truism. This effect, called *Resonance* by some, gradually colors a mage's surroundings to match her personality. A greedy mystick's study will seem more confining, a Horizon Realm may become darker and more tempestuous, or a Sanctum may give off an unsettling aura to strangers.

Resonance is rarely overt — it alters the atmosphere of a place more than the physical surroundings. By the time things get to a really advanced state, the mage is usually too far gone to care.

• **Adjust the way you play the Avatar:** An Avatar need not be Jimminy Cricket to point out a mage's pride. In many cases, it may become more like a tempter than a conscience, though this will depend on the mage **(see the Clarissa Ryan/ Peter Kobie saga for an example)**. Depending on the mage's Essence and the character's actions, the Avatar may either deny the mystick further power during Seekings, make those Seekings impossible to complete without forsaking pride or encourage the mage to greater heights of hubris. An Akashic Brother who gets a kick out of beating up foes may be chided by his Avatar, while a Void Engineer with a Questing Essence may plunge deeper into the Umbra than any sane person would go, even if it meant joining the Nephandi to do it. Either way, the Avatar will usually "speak up" if a mage approaches the deep end, either to chastise or to cheerlead.

• **Let Storyteller characters notice something "different" about the mage:** Resonance often affects a mage's personality and sometimes even his aura or appearance. Characters who see Avatars or auras may notice cases of powerful pride (difficulty 7-10, depending on the nature of that pride) — the mage may glow brighter, radiate crackling power or appear tainted or disheveled. Really pride-ridden mages often take on some physical signs of their state and may grow uglier or more beautiful, again depending on the wizard's actions.

Sooner or later, people will notice. Some will comment, others will simply react. It's up to the player whether or not he takes the hint.

• **Set up tests and temptations:** As a Storyteller, you can alter the course of the story to give prideful characters an opportunity to redeem or damn themselves. Set up tests like the ordeal of Father Shelley in **Chapter Eight**, and see how the player reacts. Don't make things too obvious, just offer him a choice of actions and see where he goes from there.

Remember that **Mage** is not necessarily about being a nice guy. A smart willworker remembers, however, that what he does shapes him — and his world — in his image, and he acts accordingly.

Losing Arete or Willpower

Magick demands confidence. Mages are human beings. Human beings are not machines, and even machines sometimes break down. A mage who breaks down too much loses control — and sometimes forfeits the ability to work magick.

The full rules for Arete and Willpower loss can be found under their respective headings in **Chapter Six**. Willpower lost can only be regained through experience and roleplaying. Lost Arete can only be regained by restoring your mage's Willpower and possibly undergoing a Seeking to work through things, if the Storyteller desires.

Quiet

The full rules for Quiet can be found in the Paradox section of **Chapter Eight**. The after-effects of Quiet — from twitchy phobias to hobgoblin-inflicted messes — can last for a long time.

Resolution

I saw the shaman
Wondered why she lived and died
Leave a note and tell me why
— Rusted Root, "Beautiful People"

The Ascension ideal is an ephemeral thing. Like hubris, it's not something systems can define — it's a personal goal, not a collection of experience or Arete points. A Master may reach Arete 10, have five dots in all his Spheres, live for a thousand years and still not Ascend if he lacks the wisdom or the vision to do so. A relatively young mage may Ascend if she comes to terms with her inner conflicts, gives up her life for another or achieves a balance between her mortal and mystick selves. Ascension is a riddle, and those with the answers didn't stick around to pass them along.

Ascension usually takes a character out of the game. He or she has gone off to a higher (or lower) plane. Some mages actually work their way up to this goal, but step back at the last minute to help others along. Perhaps the Ascended ones join God or the Gods, or the Oracles, or the Machine. If they still walked the Earth, it might be a brighter place (then again, it might not...).

Different groups have differing views on Ascension. Perhaps they're all correct for those who believe. **Chapters Two** and **Three** explore different concepts point-by-point. The means to personal Ascension (and the results of it) are left to your troupe to decide. Whatever the answer may be, it won't be quick or easy to achieve. Nothing worthwhile ever is.

Ascension is an enigma. The hints below, however, should make it easier to incorporate into your chronicle.

Personal Ascension

Self-perfection is the common Holy Grail. Through it, a mystick becomes one with some greater entity or expands to full human potential to become more than merely flesh. Some posit that such Ascension is not a goal but an ongoing process. The answer, again, is up to you.

Seekings and Arete play a large part in personal Ascension, but they only reflect in abstract terms what most mages spend lifetimes trying to achieve. The real test of personal Ascension comes through roleplaying — facing tests and triumphing while becoming one with your Art. A character who spends most of her experience on Arete and most of her time achieving some balance and perfection will Ascend more quickly than one who perfects his power with the Spheres.

Some "common" routes toward personal Ascension might include:

- Journeys into the Otherworlds which inspire a view of the totality and unity of creation;
- Strict adherence to some art, magick, philosophy or religion which teaches "The Way" to a chosen goal;
- Death as a sacrifice for the greater good;
- Forging an all-unifying theory which takes all things into account and respects the miracle which is each separate thing combined;
- Realizing that any attempt to quantify creation is doomed to fail and harmonizing with what is rather than with what one thinks there should be.

External Ascension

Remaking the world in your image is what the Ascension War is all about. To bring about worldwide Ascension (if such a thing is even possible), a mage or cabal would have to accomplish some great feat which would open the eyes of the multitudes and, theoretically, get them all to accept the truth you know. Not likely.

This isn't to say that localized change is impossible. The Hermetic Houses, and later the Technocracy, have had great success molding local paradigms enough so that their actions could be considered normal, if unusual. In an era of global intercommunication, a truly world-wide paradigm may be in sight. This possibility ups the stakes of the Ascension War for all parties. If some Reckoning *is* at hand, every group wants to be the one holding all the cards when it happens.

Mage itself is about change, so players must be allowed to at least think that their efforts make some sort of a difference. Again, the amount of change one cabal can bring about should depend on what the troupe wants from its chronicle — we cannot dictate what's best for your game. Mages have been fighting for centuries to remake the world, and one novice cabal probably won't be able to crush the Technocracy or drive the Primordial horrors back into the Deep Umbra, but then again, they migh tip the balance of the fight. Such a change must be gradual, not sudden; abrupt change brings about Paradox....

The hints below offer some guidelines toward external Ascension to use as you see fit. Common methods may include:

• Significantly changing, through personal efforts, a local paradigm to accept certain Arts or styles as coincidental (harder than it sounds);

• Bringing about a revelation, miracle or disaster so profound that the Sleepers would have to take notice (and surviving the experience long enough to make change last);

• Trashing a rival faction so completely that they offer no competition (i.e., the Pogrom);

• Founding a philosophy, metaphysic, culture or religion so widespread that it alters the world (the most successful method, but really slow);

• Ushering in some entity which makes the world's mind up for it (scary thought).

The Hidden World

Children will always be afraid of the dark, and men with minds sensitive to hereditary impulses will always tremble at the thought of the hidden and fathomless worlds of strange life which... only the dead and the moonstruck may glimpse.

—H.P. Lovecraft, "Supernatural Horror in Literature"

Mages share an uneasy relationship with other shadow denizens — vampires, ghosts, demons, Umbrood spirits, werewolves and even reputed faeries. This hidden world teems beneath the mundane one that mortals understand. Though few un-Awakened people ever notice such beings, their influence cannot be totally ignored.

The Awakened deal with other supernaturals all the time.

These societies are an endless mystery, even to those who belong. Any meeting between them will be colored by misconceptions and prejudice. Even if your troupe is familiar with the other Storyteller games, bear in mind that the "facts" that most vampires, werewolves, mages and such take for granted about each other are utterly wrong. Only the ghosts seem to have accurate information about the other groups, and the dead seldom talk.

Most other supernatural beings can sense mystick activity. This is more of a feeling than a "Hey, there's magick going on over there" sort of insight. A successful Perception + Alertness roll will allow such creatures to detect magickal feats; the difficulty for such a roll runs from 7 to 10, depending on the strength of the magick. While subtle or coincidental acts would be hard to notice, flashy vulgar ones would be pretty obvious.

The following rules cover supernatural beings and their interactions with the mysticks they encounter. These rules assume quick-and-dirty story resolutions; troupes with the other Storyteller rulebooks are encouraged to use those systems instead.

Vampires

Vampires (also known as the *Kindred*, the name they usually call themselves) do indeed exist. Much of the folklore about them is false, however, and even the wisest mages know few hard facts. The most powerful Kindred play Machivellian games with both mortals and their own offspring. Younger bloodsuckers — some myths, at least, *are* true — are said to wage their own kind of Ascension War, one for independence from their immortal masters.

Some facts are common knowledge, at least among the mysticks: vampires are indeed undead, with a blessing/curse passed through a blood-transfer called the Embrace. They fear sunlight and fire; both inflict aggravated damage on them. Simulated sunlight will not destroy them, though it will hurt; each success inflicts the usual magickal damage, which can be soaked. Crosses or garlic have little effect. Kindred drink blood to survive, but do not die if it is withheld — they simply fall into a deep slumber. Vampires heal quickly from most forms of damage (one or more Health Levels per turn) and can use a variety of unearthly powers.

These powers are not magickal. For reasons the Awakened don't entirely understand, the vampiric Embrace destroys a mage's ability to use True Magick, and he cannot carry it over beyond his death. There are rumors of undead wizards, but their nature and origins remain a mystery. Some Kindred do employ a form of static magic, called *Disciplines* by some. One of these, known as *Thaumaturgy*, is a variant of hedge magic that harnesses the mystic power of vampire blood. Other Disciplines allow Kindred to change into wolves or bats, grow claws or meld with the earth (*Protean*), command others through thought or personality (*Dominate* and *Presence*), disappear from sight (*Obfuscate*), see hidden and even magickal things (*Auspex*), commune with animals (*Animalism*), or employ inhuman speed (*Celerity*), strength (*Potence*) or stamina (*Fortitude*). Other, more arcane, Disciplines supposedly exist, but they are not common. Though these abilities are still a form of mystic command, they are a far cry from the power of the Spheres. They are, however, Paradox-free; mages who battle vampires must be careful.

Mages with the right Spheres can oppose some Disciplines through countermagick; Mind counters Dominate and Presence attacks, and basic countermagick works against Thaumaturgic spells. Magickal successes cancel out the vampire's own, as usual. Countermagick only works this way against direct attacks on the mage herself. Powers which alter the Kindred (Potence, Obfuscate, Celerity, Fortitude, Auspex and Protean) or others (Animalism, or Presence or Dominate used against someone other than the mage) cannot be countered this way.

Life magick alone is useless against the undead. Only conjunctional Effects using Matter and Life, or fire-based attacks, can inflict aggravated damage, although Forces, Entropy, Mind and Prime attacks have their usual effect.

Some mysticks use vampire blood for Tass or vitality. While this can be effective in the short run — the average vampire can "supply" five points worth of Tass, and prolong a human life for decades — it's unhealthy. The undead make nasty enemies and inflict terrible punishments on those who would use them in such a cavalier manner.

A lesser form of the Embrace, called a Blood Bond, can enslave a mage who drinks too much vampire blood. Anyone, mortal or otherwise, under such a Bond must obey the vampire from whom that blood came unto death. Though a combination of strong magicks (Life 4, Mind 3, Entropy 3, Prime 1) and some knowledge of the condition (Kindred Lore, and lots of it!), a willworker may break a Bond set on someone else. The Bond, however, will not usually allow a person under its power to harm her master — or destroy the Bond — of her own volition.

The Kindred can be crafty allies, volatile companions and demonic enemies. A wise mage avoids entanglements with the undead.

Ghouls

Vampires are known to create *ghouls*, Sleepers or animals that have partaken of vampire blood without dying first. These beings remain mortal, but they do not age so long as they receive a steady supply of vampire blood. Like vampires, ghouls have shown superhuman physical abilities and the power to heal quickly. However, ghouls command no magick nor supernatural powers. Mages should treat ghouls with ordinary caution.

Werewolves

Werewolves, or Garou, are not fond of mages. Their sacred sites — called *caerns* — are more than just Nodes. Each one, they feel, is a small heart of the earth mother they call Gaia. Plenty of mysticks have shrugged off the warnings of the Garou and tried to tap these Primal springs. Not many survive the attempt.

Garou are penultimate killing machines; fast, massive and *really* bad-tempered, they heal most kinds of damage almost as fast as they receive it. Only fire, silver, aggravated magickal attacks and toxic waste seem to hurt a werewolf — i.e., cause him aggravated damage. In game terms, only aggravated damage affects a Garou for long. Any other kind simply heals at a rate of one Health Level per turn if the beast is in one of it's non-human forms.

By the rules of the **Werewolf: The Apocalypse** game, Garou have five forms: Homid (human), Glabro (*big* human), Crinos (wolf-man death-machine), Hispos (dire wolf) and Lupus (wolf). For simplicity, only Homid, Lupus and Crinos forms are important. The first two are fairly mundane; the third effectively doubles a werewolf's Physical Attributes, grants him two or three attacks per turn and allows him to ignore dice penalties from wounds. This form is so terrifying that un-Awakened humans generally freak out, pass out or run in its presence. Mages are immune this "Delirium" effect, but feel an instinctual fear of this natural predator regardless.

Because of the general antipathy the werewolves hold towards mages, facts about them are scarce; they are said to be great shamans, remorseless killers and fearless allies. Those who understand the Otherworlds often meet Garou in their travels beyond the Gauntlet. Some Traditions — the Dreamspeakers and Verbena, in particular — hold an uneasy truce with the beast-men. Marauders, it is said, often ally with them for short periods, and even some Nephandi supposedly seek their service. The Technocracy considers the so-called Changing Breed a menace and hunts them at any provocation. For the most part, the Garou avoid letting mysticks get too close. Even the best of companions will never willingly allow a mage to access a caern.

Some mages don't care. If the defenders can be slain, a Spirit 4 Effect must be used to break through the Node's mystick protections before its Quintessence can be channeled. A caern will be good for between five to 50 points of Quintessence before it gives out. Any mage who does this will be in serious trouble if the Garou ever discover her identity!

Other shapechangers exist — bears, ravens, coyote, big cats and even, supposedly, giant lizards have Changing Breed counterparts. Werecats (also called *Bastet*) are especially fond of mysticks and sometimes follow them around to learn their secrets. These other forms of were-beast are exceedingly uncommon. Many can only be found in Horizon Realms dedicated to the bygone Earth.

Some werewolves use Spirit-magics called *Gifts*. Like Disciplines, these are natural static affinities, not True Magick. The broad range of such Gifts, however, makes duplicating their powers difficult without a copy of **Werewolf**. If you don't have one, just assume that a werewolf can use between one to three Spheres worth of Spirit magick, with a Dice Pool of two to four and no Paradox restrictions. All Garou can **Step Sideways** like the Spirit 3 Effect; all it takes is a shiny surface, a turn to pass through and a successful roll of three dice.

Old tales say the Garou are spirits clothed in flesh. Whatever the truth may be, the werewolves and their kin are tough, elusive, and rare. Willworkers had best tread carefully around them.

Changelings

Some mages believe that faeries walk among us. Not the regal sidhe of the Mythic Age, but half-human changelings who carry their otherworldly aura beneath a mortal guise. While more skeptical mysticks dismiss such fairy tales, even they can't ignore the odd beings who pop around reality's corners from time to time, bringing their dreams with them.

Some Traditions have age-old ties to the fae — the Verbena, Dreamspeakers and Hermetic Houses know the so-called *Kithain* well. Other, more modern mages regard the changelings as some sort of cross-breed if they acknowledge them at all. The Technocracy denies that such beings exist and have teams of specialists who can convince anyone who *does* believe in faeries to change his mind. The Council on the whole believes that faeries joined the Bygones centuries ago. Changelings may appear occasionally, but they remain on Earth only for short periods, then return to fabled Arcadia, the Dreaming Realm. Mages who meet the fae dispute this, but any proof of faerie presence is as fleeting as the dreams they supposedly command.

The tales of faerie magics are as varied as the fae themselves; any legend you've ever heard supposedly has some basis in fact. Naturally, the days of magic castles and living trees are long gone (or so we think...), but many folk on the fringes of the old country still claim that helpful boggans and mischievous pooka wander the backwoods, showing up just long enough to cause trouble. If changelings do exist, their abilities would shape dreams and imagination, turning it into "solid" reality if the fae one can bring a mortal along to witness it. There seems to be a correlation between this fae Art and True Magick, but the former quickly disappears when Banality (aka Unbelief) grows too strong.

In game terms, changelings can warp reality as if they wielded Sphere magick, so long as they overcome a target's Banality first. To do this, roll the changeling's Glamour rating as if it were Arete for a magickal Effect **(see Chapter Eight)**. The target's Banality score sets the difficulty. These Effects will have some narrow parameters — certain changelings might only affect humans, inanimate objects, natural forces, places or other faeries — and often demand some sort of odd action — like clucking like a chicken, suffering a nightmare or dancing in a circle — before the Effect will work. A changeling affecting the world around him would roll against the Banality rating of the area (in other words, the Gauntlet rating). Unlike True Magick, such Arts will not work at all if the changeling cannot overcome Banality, and they rarely leave lasting results.

A mage can resist a fae cantrip by rolling her Willpower like a soak roll, difficulty 7. As usual, this removes successes from the changeling's total. The mystick may also counter the Art with her Arete, rolling against difficulty 6. Changelings can, however, do the same thing, countering Sphere magick with their Glamour (difficulty 7). A fight between a mage and a changeling is an odd and inconclusive thing.

The more a mage believes in faeries, the easier it will be for a changeling to affect her. Tradition mages have a low-to-medium Banality — from four or five for a Dreamspeaker, Hermetic or Verbena to eight for a Son of Ether or Virtual Adept. Technomancers of any kind have high Banality ratings — Technocracy mages often go as high as 10. Marauders and Nephandi may have very low or extremely high Banality ratings, depending on the mystick himself.

Faerie places — called *Freeholds* by those who understand the fae — are said to exist. If they do, they may be treated as werewolf caerns with high Arcane ratings which hide them from sight. It's also said that some mythic beasts have dreaming forms that become solid if one comes under faerie enchantment. Treat them like Bygones with Glamour scores of between five and 10, who must overcome a person's Banality before they can interact with him.

Umbrood

(See also "The Otherworlds" for further details.)

The term *Umbrood* is a general term for the variety of Otherworldly beings. Many mages argue about distinctions: is an Umbrood a god, a powerful spirit or just something weird? The mystick factions refer to Umbral denizens by a bewildering variety of names; the Technocracy calls such beings "aliens" when it chooses to acknowledge their existence at all.

Mages encounter Umbrood of one kind or another all the time. Most inhabitants of the Otherworlds fit this bill, as do ghosts, demons and the wandering Bygone spirits. Many of them can take material form for a short time, and most will answer Spirit magick's call. The tales and lore compiled over the ages, shot through with personal experiences, religious beliefs, folklore and prejudice, offer few hard answers about these entities. Troupes are advised to use their imaginations as freely as possible when dealing with the Umbrood. We've offered a few hard rules below, but there should be many exceptions to these guidelines. Spirits are meant to be mysterious things.

Spirits are defined as beings made of *ephemera*, the material of the Umbral Worlds. Ghosts, the Restless Dead of the Underworld, hold a slightly different form — *ectoplasm*. In game terms, both are essentially the same thing; each is immune to Life and Matter, unless the spirit has taken on solid form **(see the Materialize Charm, below)**, and most forms of magick other than Spirit and Prime are useless unless the mage herself passes into the Umbra. Some Umbrood retain a material form; Bygones, Realm creatures and the enigmatic Ka Luon are as solid as any human being. All spirits are invisible without **Spirit Sight** (Spirit 1), unless they choose to Materialize or Appear.

Not that a mage is helpless against an Umbrood. A combination of Spirit and Prime (or, for ghosts, Entropy and Prime) acts like Life magick against either material. No physical attack will affect an Umbrood unless either the spirit Materializes, or the mortal has lasting spiritual connections (Garou or fae blood, or Rank 3 or higher in the Spirit Sphere). In most cases, punching an Umbrood is a waste of time.

Ghosts and spirits aren't fond of mages, either. Either one can have its *Power* (or *Corpus*, in the case of ghosts) distilled into Quintessence and drained through Spirit 4, Prime 4 magicks. A spirit may soak this "damage" with its Willpower. This kind of draining doesn't "kill" a spirit — they're far more than just Prime batteries — but it will harm it for a while. A Master of these Spheres is feared — and hated — throughout the Otherworlds.

Some known types of Umbrood include:

- **Gods (Celestines, Incarna, Entities, Pure Ones, etc.):** Whether these are still just "spirits" is a bone of contention among many mages. The dreams of these vastly powerful beings are said to have shaped the Earth and beyond.
- **Ghosts (wraiths, the Restless Dead):** The souls of the dead who cannot or will not pass on to their final rest **(see *Wraith: The Oblivion* for more information)**.
- **Demons and Demon Hordes:** Most theories agree that demons are evil and destructive. Little else is certain; all of them, however, have some ephemeral nature. Astral, or High Umbral, demons can Materialize on Earth. The greater demon hordes are often extraterrestrial entities unable to cross the Barriers under their own power.
- **Paradox Spirits:** Ephemeral beings created from fear personified. Some generate spontaneously, while others have their own Realms. **(See "Paradox," Chapter Eight.)**
- **Spirit Entities:** A staggering array of ephemeral beings, from powerful Lords to simple Minions, who personify concepts, elements or living things.
- **Banes:** Like demons, these spirits are malignant things; they love to possess objects and people and corrupt whatever they touch.
- **Mythic Beasts (Bygones):** Material creatures who fled or were taken into the Umbrae when magick became suppressed on Earth. Some travel on their own power, while others must be carried through Spirit magick or summoned. They are usually physical beings, although some powerful mythic concepts manifest as spirit Preceptors. Residents of the Digital Web are usually physical.
- **Realm Creatures:** Physically substantial beings from material Realms. They either pass directly to Earth from their Realms or wander the Umbra through their own Spirit powers. Unlike spirits, they can be physically harmed.
- **Ka Luon:** More myth than substance, these mysterious entities may be literal aliens from space. Though many travelers in the Deep Umbra have reportedly met these odd beings, no one has hard facts about them. No one who will admit it, that is....

Ghosts: The Restless Dead

Some mages see no difference between the spirits of the dead and the spirits of the world. Most folks conversant with the Underworld, however, can tell you that ghosts, or wraiths, are dead people who have become stuck between life and an afterlife. Their passions are such that they remain in limbo, sometimes for millennia. There, they try to finish up their business on Earth or seek sanctuary from whatever lies beyond.

Contacting the dead is a chancy thing, since you never know who or what you'll get. Even if you contact the person you've been looking for, there's no telling what state she'll be in when you find her. Many mysticks have been disillusioned, tricked, attacked or even possessed while dealing with the dead. It's a trade best left to Masters of Spirit. Those desperate or clueless enough to try anyway have discovered that objects or people that were once important to the departed are a good place to start.

Wraiths are insubstantial and cannot be harmed or even perceived by anything short of Spirit magicks. They exhibit a wide range of supernatural senses, but can generally affect the physical plane only through a possessed host. Some, however, have strong psychokinetic abilities, and many even take on some insubstantial form in haunted places. Ghosts seem unfettered by distance or material obstacles, but are restricted by the Shroud, (the Gauntlet).

The Euthanatos hold that wraiths exist in some sort of plane of their own (called by some the "Low Umbra") and are numerous enough to have formed their own government. Dreamspeakers add (in typically obscure terms) that the wraiths' worst enemies are themselves. To date, the living have not learned the nature of this infighting.

Wraiths are rarely encountered outside the areas they frequented in life and are very possessive of their old belongings. The best way to cope with a wraith is to leave it to its own affairs. Failing that, try to locate one of its old possessions. Threaten to destroy the object, or destroy it outright. Theories suggest that the psychic shock should annihilate the spirit.

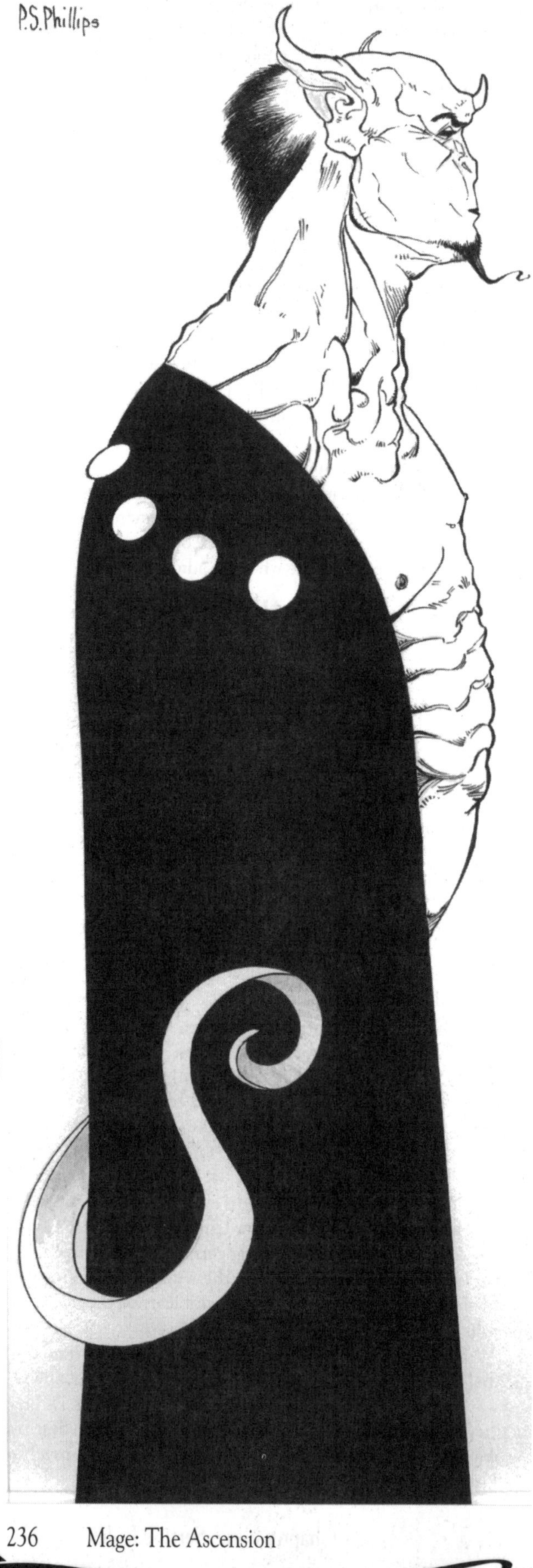

P.S. Phillips

Mythic Beasts

The mythic remnants, scattered survivors of the Mythic Age, are allies or servants of many Marauders. Sometimes summoned, sometimes simply invited, they cross the Gauntlet from the Umbra to wild and isolated places on Earth. Without Quintessence to sustain them, these monsters die of Unbelief within hours or days. However, in that time they may do great damage.

These creatures represent a complex problem for the Traditions. Some, such as manticoras, are mere animals and should be returned to the Umbra with due mercy, like endangered (if dangerous) species. Other Remnants are sapient beings with their own powers, agendas, memories and dislikes. Jigme Doriji, a mage of the Akashic Brotherhood, offended such a creature, an Upland Yeti or "Abominable Snowman," during a battle in the Himalayas. He lived to regret this when he later encountered the reformed Yeti in the Near Umbra.

Such Bygones often exist in a demi-spiritual form. They are not ephemeral, but must have a suitable host body prepared to enter the physical world unless the Gauntlet is torn open. The more powerful varieties come and go under their own power, stepping sideways like werewolves. Either type must penetrate the Gauntlet and survive the rigors of our now-hostile Earth to emerge, and most don't consider the trip worth the trouble. Generally, the larger and more outlandish the creature, the harder the excursion will be.

Magickal creatures must consume mystick energy (i.e., Quintessence) to survive in any but the most isolated places. They may eat Tass, channel raw Prime Force or absorb a host's energies, but they must feed to live. Such thaumivores — which include familiars — will leave or die if they aren't fed somehow. Even when well-fed, too much exposure to Sleepers will hurt and frighten a mythic beast. The weight of Unbelief **(see "Paradox," Chapter Eight)** is strongest in cities, weaker in rural areas and weak to non-existent in deep wildernesses and Horizon Realms (where such creatures often dwell).

The Technocracy has its own answers to mythic remnants — custom-built bio-horrors born in Progenitor labs or Iteration X flesh refineries. These creatures, with the exception of the mysterious pattern spiders **(see Appendix)** have material, not ephemeral, substance. In extreme circumstances, the Union calls out the heavy artillery and sics such creatures on its enemies. This is almost never done where Sleepers can view the disruption in progress, but any witnesses are quickly hunted, brainwashed or eliminated.

Spirits: The Masks of Gods

"Spirit" is an easy label stuck on a dizzying variety of entities. Even Nichodemus Mulhouse, Grand Archivist of Horizon Chantry, would be hard-pressed to name them all. Their general ranks range from the "greater entities" — Gods and *Celestines*, if there's a difference at all — to the "lesser powers" — *Lords*, *Preceptors*, *Minions*, *elementals*, *naturae*, *Banes* and such. There are more proper names for these spirits than any book could list.

Dealing with true spirits is odd; as Deacon Maria D'Amicci once said, "Spirits wear the masks we give them." What this Master of the Spirit World meant is that we often see what we expect when dealing with spirits. Not that they don't have their own identities — most embody some single concept or element humans understand. Mages who meet them face-to-face, however, often see the same spirit in different ways. Most "lesser powers" have one set form that stays fairly constant. The greater entities, however, can be all things to all people — at once.

Say, for example, that Jennifer Rollins, Laughing Eagle and Hitomi Jiro all meet a trickster Umbrood. While Laughing Eagle may see the infamous Coyote, Hitomi Jiro might confer with a baku whose shifting form betrays the folly of certainty. Jennifer, meanwhile, notices a small madman with a teapot, a large hat and an English accent. Each mage sees the same spirit; it will even talk to each of them, simultaneously, they way they expect it to. But it remains one entity. At least, that's what some say.

Spirits are rarely what they seem to be. Even the greatest mages do not agree about the Umbrood. Are these "Dreamers," as some call them, products of our imagination? Or are we products of theirs? The truth remains a mystery. As it should.

The Infernal

Experts apply the term *demon* to malicious Umbrood who occasionally venture into our own space to corrupt and seduce careless mortals. Some seem to cultivate dispair and selfishness, while others just want to obliterate the world as we know it. Either type is poison to a mage. Nevertheless, some sorcerers deal with the Infernal powers in whatever form those demons take.

All but the weakest demonic beings appear to shift form, name and purpose. Whether such beings are primordial elder things, creatures of human invention or fallen Pure Ones is open to debate. For whatever reason, such creatures seem shut off from material reality by the Barriers and may only be summoned with great rituals (if at all). Some un-Awakened sorcerers, often called Diabolists, deal with the foul things and receive small powers called Investments from them. Occasionally, mages other than Nephandi will trap, enter bargains with or banish the Infernal. The exact nature of such dealings is left to the Storyteller, but should involve massive magicks, great peril and a heavy dose of sheer terror.

For game purposes, treat demons as spirits with power to spare, plenty of cunning and an influence which extends beyond their simple powers. Mood, atmosphere, foreshadowing and other tricks **(see Chapter Seven)** are helpful Storyteller tools if or when demons appear.

Spirit Traits

Ephemeral Umbrood play by different rules than mortal beings. The Traits and Charms below represent their natural abilities and powers.

• **Willpower**

This allows a spirit to take actions like attacking, chasing or flying through the Umbra. Contests of this nature between spirits are resolved by opposed Willpower rolls.

Difficulty	Action
3	Easy
5	Fairly simple
6	Normal
8	Difficult
10	Virtually impossible

• **Rage**

This reflects a spirit's raw anger and anguish. Spirits use their Rage to harm each other and physical beings. For each success in a Rage roll (difficulty 6), one Health Level of damage is inflicted on material beings, while a spirit loses one Power point.

• **Gnosis**

Spirits use this for any sort of Social or Mental Roll. A spirit in a race with a mage to be the first to solve a Rubik's Cube would roll its Gnosis while the mystick rolls his Intelligence + Enigmas. He with the most successes wins. A Gnosis roll would also be used when a spirit tries to intimidate, seduce or trick a target, either in or out of the Umbra. Social Abilities like Intimidation or Seduction are added to the spirit's Gnosis if they apply.

• **Power**

In combat, spirits use "batteries" of mystical energy harnessed from the Umbra and referred to as Power. Power is depleted through special abilities and damage. When Power reaches zero, the spirit dissipates into the Umbra for a number of hours equal to 20 minus its Gnosis. After this time, it Reforms with one Power point to start. A mage can bind the Umbrood into a fetish if he knows the Spirit 4 rote **Create Fetish**. However, the fetish will not be usable until the spirit's power is fully recharged **(see below)**. Most spirits will not like the idea of becoming your Energizer Bunny's battery; this is a sure-fire way to enrage a lot of them (who make *bad* enemies...).

Spirits who have depleted their Power begin to look translucent, not fully there. When Power loss comes from combat damage, the spirit looks raggedy and torn. Spirits recharge their Power by entering a state called *Slumber*. In Slumber, an Umbrood finds a quiet spot in the Umbra and floats there in a deep sleep. For each hour that the spirit Slumbers, it regains one Power point. Some mages argue over whether or not spirits dream during Slumber, and what they dream about if they do. When a spirit is in this state, it may be easily bound with Spirit magick, regardless of Power or willingness. A spirit bound into a fetish automatically enters Slumber and stays there until released. The fetish's power is activated by the user, not the spirit. A newly created fetish will need time to recharge to full Power before using, which can take a long time with some of the more powerful spirits.

Tasks

• **Movement**

All spirits can fly or float in the Umbra. The maximum distance (in yards) that they may move in a turn is 20 + Willpower. However, yards and feet don't mean very much in the Umbra; distances can warp without warning. In the Penumbra, distances are analogous (one yard here is one yard there).

• **Pursuit**

A spirit trying to flee rolls its Willpower against difficulty 6. It begins with three automatic successes because it's on home ground. A mage who has stepped sideways rolls Dexterity + Athletics to follow or her own Willpower if she has entered through Mind magick. Difficulty for both rolls is 8 because she is *not* on her home ground. A spirit with more than 10 successes gets away clean. An Umbrood with the **Reform** Charm can dispense with rolls to get away.

• **Communication**

The Umbrood speak different languages than physical beings do. Spirit communication is not so much a language as a form of comprehension between both parties. Not everyone can understand spirits, though. The Spirit 2 effect **Call Spirits** is required to speak to and understand them, unless those beings also speak familiar human languages.

Charms

Each spirit possesses special magics called *Charms*. These magics requires a certain amount of Power to use. Unless otherwise noted, Charms last for one scene. However, a combat-related Charm lasts for one turn per use. Because spirits are part of the natural order and work in a predetermined way, these powers do not invoke Paradox.

• **Airt Sense**: Most spirits have a natural sense of the airts (directions) of the spirit world and are able to travel about without much difficulty. It costs one Power to find any particular thing.

• **Appear:** With this Charm, a spirit can manifest to an Earthly observer without taking on material form. It cannot, however, affect the material world in any way while using this Charm. A specialty of demons, who use it to taunt their victims. Costs five Power.

• **Armor**: This Charm provides a spirit one soak die per Power point spent. This is the only way a spirit can soak damage unless it is Materialized. The spirit may use this Charm at any time in the combat turn before damage is rolled.

• **Blast Flame:** The spirit can blast a gout of flame at opponents. The Power cost is two per die of damage.

• **Blighted Touch:** The spirit can bring out the worst in a target. If the spirit successfully attacks, the target must immediately make a Willpower roll. If she fails, her negative characteristics dominate her personality for the next few hours. A botch on the Willpower roll causes this "personality disorder" to become permanent. The Power cost is two.

• **Calcify:** This Charm is possessed only by pattern spiders or some Paradox spirits. It allows the spirit to bind a target into a static web. A Willpower roll is made against the target's own Willpower. Each success subtracts one from the victim's Physical Attributes (or Willpower, in the case of spirits). When Attributes or Willpower are reduced to zero, the victim is bound fast until freed. Rescuers must attack the web and score as many damage successes as the pattern spider had). The Power cost is two.

• **Cleanse the Blight:** This Charm purges spiritual corruption in the vicinity. Power cost is 10.

• **Control Electrical Systems:** The spirit can exert control over an electrical system. The spirit rolls its Gnosis (difficulty from 3 to 9 depending on the system's complexity). Power cost is from one to five points.

• **Corruption:** The spirit can whisper an evil suggestion in a target's ear; the target is inclined to act upon that thought. The Power cost is one.

• **Create Fires:** By succeeding with a Gnosis roll, the spirit can create small fires. The difficulty varies (from 3 for small fires to 9 for conflagrations). The Power cost varies from one to five points.

• **Create Wind:** The spirit can create wind effects. Power cost varies from one for a breeze to 20 for a tornado.

• **Influence:** This allows an Umbrood to change the target's mood like the **Subliminal Impulse** Mind rote. The Umbrood need not speak to its target to use this Charm, and the effects are more gradual than sudden. Each die of effect costs 3 Power.

• **Lightning Bolts:** The spirit can generate lightning bolts and target them at opponents. The Power cost is two per die of damage inflicted.

• **Materialize:** A spirit with this Charm may materialize and affect the physical world. To do so, the spirit's Gnosis must equal or exceed the Gauntlet for that area. When an Umbrood Materializes, it must spend Power to create a physical shape and give itself bodily Traits. However, a spirit still rolls its Gnosis for Social or Mental activities. The Power point costs are as follows:

Power Cost	Trait
1	Per one Physical Attribute level
1	Per two Ability levels
1	7 Health Levels (as a mortal)
1	Per additional Health Level (each extra Health Level also increases size)
1	Per one Health Level healed (regenerate damage to the physical form), per three if the damage was inflicted by Paradox backlash or Spirit magick.
1	Weaponry: Per die of aggravated damage done in addition to Strength (Bite is one die, Claws are two, etc.)

Umbrood have no limits on their Attribute and Ability levels. It is possible for them to form extremely strong or fast bodies if they spend enough Power. Most, however, have a "prime form" which they default to when Materializing.

Example: a Bane spirit wants to Materialize into the physical world, the better to terrorize mortals. It wants the following characteristics: Str 3, Dex 4, Sta 3, Brawl 4, Dodge 3, Stealth 3 and seven Health Levels. This costs it 16 Power points.

A spirit may stay Materialized as long as it desires, but it cannot enter an area with a higher Gauntlet than its Gnosis. While Materialized, the spirit may not recharge its Power unless it has a Charm that allows it to do so. When a Materialized spirit is attacked, damage is applied to its Health Levels. If a spirit is reduced to zero Health Levels, it dissipates into the Umbra and may not reuse this Charm for (20 hours minus its Gnosis).

Note that aggravated damage suffered by a spirit is applied to Health Levels *and* Power. Thus, a spirit cannot always escape its sojourn on Earth unscathed.

• **Mind Speech:** A spirit with this Charm can speak directly into a subject's mind, like the Mind 3 **Telepathy** rote. Cost is three points per die.

• **Possession:** A demon or Bane may possess a living being or inanimate object. Possession requires a successful Gnosis roll (difficulty of the victim's Willpower). The number of successes equals the speed with which possession occurs; refer to the chart below:

Successes	Time Taken
1	six hours
2	three hours
3	one hour
4	15 minutes
5	five minutes
6+	instantaneous

During the time it takes to possess its victim, the spirit will find a dark, isolated part of the Umbra and remain there, concentrating on the possession. During this time, the spirit can take no other action. If it engages in spirit combat, the possessive link is broken. Possessing spirits are often guarded by others of their kind to ensure that the possession process remains undisturbed.

• **Reform**: This Charm allows a spirit to dissipate and Reform somewhere else in the Umbra, usually far away from its enemies. This costs 20 Power.

• **Shapeshift:** The spirit may take the form of anything it desires. It does not gain the powers or abilities of its new shape, only the form and visage. The Power cost is five.

• **Short Out:** The spirit can cause electrical systems to short out (Gnosis; difficulty 6). The Power cost is three.

• **Solidify Reality**: This Charm is possessed only by Technomancer-allied spirits. It enables that spirit to spin a pattern web, thus reinforcing the laws and rules of static reality. This power requires only a Willpower roll. The spirit could, with a successful enough roll, make a spiritual wall so solid that it could not be bypassed. The difficulty is determined by the extent of the solidification and how interesting, sensible and clever the description of the action is. The number of successes obtained determines how much solidifying is allowed. Power cost ranges from one to 20, depending on the magnitude of the feat.

Success makes the object or spirit more solid. An object's effective "Health Levels" are increased by one per success. The effect lasts for about a day. Each spirit can make only one roll for each object.

• **Spirit Away:** The dreaded power of the worst Paradox spirits and demons. With this Charm, a human may be snatched from the material world and taken straight to an Umbral Realm. If the Umbrood scores four or more successes with a Willpower roll (difficulty 7), the mortal passes through the Gauntlet and into the spirit's personal Realm. He does not pass "Go," does not collect $200 and goes directly to Hell (or wherever). He may then try to escape — if he can.... This costs 25 Power and takes the spirit along with its target.

• **Tracking:** The spirit can unerringly track its prey. Power cost is five.

The Otherworlds

While I stood there, I saw more that I can tell, and I understood more than I saw; for I was seeing in a sacred manner the shapes of all things in the spirit, and the shape of all shapes as they must live together like one being.

— Black Elk, *Black Elk Speaks*

Mages travel throughout many worlds. The differences between the different Realms can be found in **Chapter One**. This section explain the practical aspects to gaming in the Otherworlds.

The Umbral Worlds

We have such sights to show you.

— Pinhead, *Hellbound*

Most mages who study the Umbra agree that it has three Worlds, or layers, under the single nebulous title — the Upper World or Astral Umbra (also called the High Umbra), the Middle or Spirit World and the Underworld or Dark Umbra (sometimes referred to as the Lower Umbra). The Umbra is still mostly unknown to mages, and labels are more like a means of understanding an area's nature than its actual location. Some have tried to physically map out the Umbra and called it an exercise in frustration. The Three Worlds may be seen as locations, reflections of the material world (or vice versa), states of mind, soul and body, or none of the above.

While the Astral Umbra is largely the province of mages, some have ventured into the other Worlds, although this is difficult. Passing the invisible boundaries between the different paradigms of the Three Worlds requires a change in consciousness and a willingness to accept and understand the differing world-laws of each. A high Cosmology rating is always helpful to break down the barriers of preconception.

The Umbrae may never have been mapped, but mage travelers and scholars have noted certain constant aspects which are about as good as landmarks:

• **The Periphery:** This is where the spirit world can be felt faintly in reality. Even Sleepers can touch this part in dreams. It's more a state of being than a location.

• **The Gauntlet:** The barrier between the physical and spirit worlds.

• **The Penumbra:** A shadowy reflection of our own world, where things take on their true "nature": a drug-house, for example, might look like the chambers of the Cenobites, filled with hallucinations and monstrous spiritual reflections of addicts.

• **The Near Umbra:** This extends from the Penumbra into the Realms of the Three Worlds. Here, Umbrood domains and spirit Realms can be found. Realms themselves are "places" where Umbral reality has taken on a set form because of an event on Earth, magickal patterning or the will of an Umbrood.

• **The Horizon (The Membrane or the Great Barrier):** The dividing line between the Deep and Near Umbrae, where Horizon Realms are located.

• **The Deep Umbra (Etherspace or the Deep Universe):** Extends *ad infinitum* beyond the Horizon. Shard and Paradox Realms spin in a vast, cosmic void. This outer edge of the spirit world is the province of Nephandi and Marauders (and some say, other things...).

• **The Zones:** Places which permeate all Three Worlds and transcend boundaries, like the Digital Web, Mirror Zone, Dream Realms and others unnamed. These do not truly belong to any one layer, but seem to drift between them.

Realm Types

Many "solid" realities exist within the spirit world. These places often have their own natural laws, climate and sometimes inhabitants. The form a sorcerer's magick takes will often determine whether or not that Effect is coincidental or vulgar — a mystick grove will "consider" technomagick a violation of its internal reality, whereas a Technocratic Construct will punish users of more "impossible" Arts.

• **Shade Realms** are wormhole "shadows" of greater Realms along the Horizon.

• **Shard Realms** reflect the other planets in the solar system, and, it is said, the nine elements (Spheres) of earthly magick.

• **Horizon Realms** are constructed through deliberate acts of magick, which create custom-built worlds.

• **Paradox Realms** imprison mages who rend the Tapestry. Some such Realms teach lessons; others simply remove the offender forever.

• **Dream Realms** (actually Zones) embody the endless dreams and fictions, giving them some brief reality of their own.

The High Umbra

Most mages naturally gravitate towards this place of ideas incarnate. Among the strange entities encountered here are living concepts — spiritual beings that represent ideas and thoughts. The Umbral Realms here include the heavens and hells formed through the collective unconscious. While true afterlives are said to reside in the Underworld, many who've embraced intellectual instead of spiritual concepts end up here. Bargains or pacts are the most common ways for many to arrive, but a few rare mortals who travel astrally or advance their states to higher enlightenment pass into these Realms, sometimes without meaning to.

Spirits of this Umbra range from malice or virtue incarnate (demons and angels to laymen) to abstract designs able to communicate telepathically. The person viewing the spirit has more to do with how the spirit is perceived than the spirit itself does (a fairly constant idea when dealing with the Umbra). If a mage expects to see a certain, small, fuzzy frog as the manifestation of the concept *green*, then that's what she'll see.

The Middle Umbra

Almost every Awakened being (with the right Spirit rating) can enter the Spirit World. It is a birthright as basic as sight or language. However, this ability is almost always wiped out through societal conditioning, sometimes so much so that even the Awakened have trouble regaining it. Dreamspeakers, Verbena and mages of Primordial Essence seem to have the easiest time entering the Spirit World.

The Realms here reflect dreams and nightmares at their most potent. Those traveling here must deal with different beings — animal and plant spirits, lunar spirits, elementals and Banes. Werewolves often travel here, and a Garou Theurge makes a very good guide.

This World offers a true reflection of material nature. Those attuned to the cycle of life will find their way here. The landscape is more primal and sensual here than in the cerebral High Umbra and far more so than in material reality. Sights, sounds, colors and sensations are all more vivid and intense than anywhere else within the scope of experience.

The Low Umbra

No one enters the Dark Umbra unless they're dead... or have a death-wish. Of course, mages can find loopholes and concoct exceptions to every law, and some venture into the Deadlands while still alive with every intention of returning. Of those who have dared, the price has been very high indeed. Some have gone insane or have had their souls ripped from their bodies by the vengeful dead. Only the Euthanatos, some Nephandi and a handful of Dreamspeakers know anything about this World. All the rest are advised to stay out and have no truck with the dead.

The Euthanatos send their initiates on a brief trip into the Deadlands, where the Restless Dead try to speak to them or harvest their souls. Some never return, but those who do tell of a decayed, twilight half-world and the ghosts who dread the great tempest of the Unmaking through which souls are reincarnated.

The Near Umbra

This is the spiritual reflection of Earth, where forms appear more like their "true" selves. Each traveler in the Umbra experiences it in his own way, his perceptions coloring his experience (remember the frog in the High Umbra). A toxic waste dump becomes even more nightmarish, with horrible insects and mutant animals snuffling through piles of filth. An untouched spot of forest, in contrast, looks even more beautiful and peaceful than it appears in the physical world. The thinner the Gauntlet, the more closely the Umbra and physical world resemble each other.

Only Awakened items, containing raw Quintessence, carry the same form in the Umbra. This includes Talismans or areas touched by magick or colored by some strong emotional significance. Such Prime energy sparkles in the object's patterns, and various mages see this pattern differently, whether as glowing webs, spirit flames, graph-lines or any number of things.

Items in the Umbra and physical world affect each other. If a physical change is made in the physical world, that place or object's spiritual nature in the Umbra may change. A vacant lot filled with junk and graffiti renovated into an urban garden by a group of children will take on new spiritual changes. In the Umbra, the same place might change from a shadowy plot infested with weeds and poisonous snakes to a sunlit spot filled with luxuriant flowers and singing birds.

If the spiritual nature of a place changes in the Umbra, the Storyteller must decide how that place's physical counterpart alters in return. Spirit magick affects everything in the Umbra, even things that some might not recognize as spirits. Many mages, especially Dreamspeakers, believe that the Umbra and the physical world are intertwined, unable to exist without the other. Each gives form to a place's meaning and meaning to a place's location.

The Deep Umbra

The Deep Umbra is a mystery to most mages and a dangerous one at that. Few Tradition mages venture here and live to tell the tale. While some Sons of Ether and Void Engineers build vessels to plumb this space, they're often reluctant to reveal what they've found. Many return from these trips changed in some indescribable way. Perhaps the Nephandi or their nightmarish masters corrupt them. Or perhaps the secrets of the Deep Umbra are too great (or too terrible) for any mind, even a mage's, to comprehend.

Travel in the Umbra

Travel is more a matter of intent than distance or physical movement. A mage walks into the Umbral mists and (hopefully) arrives where he wants to be by taking one of the paths through the mists. Many of these are often guarded by spirits and can be hazardous to travel.

Mages can find their way to the High Umbra fairly easily by dint of their dynamic natures and inquisitive minds. Primordial mages, wise in nature, can pass into the natural Realms. As a rule, only the dead may venture into the Deadlands, but as most have seen, there are exceptions to that rule.

Most Technomancers are tied too strongly to the physical world to be much good at Umbral travel (when they venture there at all). Any mage without some knowledge of Cosmology or the Spirit Sphere can become utterly lost in the mists. On the other hand, Adepts and Masters of Spirit practically glow like beacons with their knowledge (though advertising is not necessarily a good thing).

Umbral Rules

Visitation, Magick and Travel

There are many ways to cross the Gauntlet: portals and Gates allow direct access to Horizon Realms. Most mages, however, pass into the Spirit World by using either Spirit magick (ranks 3 and 4, which allow them to step through the Gauntlet) or the Mind 5 Effect **Untether** (which sends a mage's mind into the Astral Umbra). Some Nodes have what's called a "shallowing" effect, which sweeps even mundane people into the Near Umbra under the right circumstances. This effect, however, is chancy at best.

Magick is always coincidental in the Near Umbra, and time passes strangely. Correspondence Arts will not move a mage into the Spirit World, but can shift her perceptions (and perhaps her body) around the Umbra if she's already there, assuming she has a high Cosmology rating. Time and Forces Effects behave oddly here, and all difficulties are +1 level higher. Life and Matter Arts are hard to use, as most things in the spirit world are made of ephemera, not solid matter or tissue. Prime is a breeze, however; rich sources of Quintessence are obvious even without using sensing magicks.

Once in the Umbra, direction and distance are pretty much a matter of intent and belief — a traveler thinks about where she wishes to go and simply walks until she gets there. Cosmology is essential to finding one's way around the Umbrae; traveling without it is like venturing out without a compass, though getting lost in the Umbra is much more dangerous. Navigating requires a Wits + Cosmology roll, difficulties ranging from 5 to 10. It helps if the mage has a guide or has been to her destination before. A botch can be potentially fatal. What happens to mortals lost in the Umbra? Brrrr....

Those who physically enter the Umbrae can use any magick or take any action they desire, if the circumstances permit **(see "Umbral Combat" in Chapter Ten.)**. Astral travelers are limited to mental actions and tasks. Magick used this way must function through a mental bond.

The Digital Web

The Web, also called the Net, is a conceptual universe created entirely from the will of the enlightened. In Umbral terms, this Web is one of the odd "Zones" that drift between the Three Worlds. It has no physical manifestation and exists only in the minds of mages as pulses of light, electron highways, high-tech computers, filaments of magickal energy or solid "sector Realms."

Much of this world is formatted into sectors. Those strands of magickal energy as yet unformed are called Virgin Web. Some say that they connect all forms of high-tech electronics. A mage accesses this world from a computer and projects his consciousness into the Web-world. If he has enough knowledge and power, he can pattern Virgin Web with his own thoughts and invite others into the area he has patterned. The result is a shared reality subject to the patterning mage's world laws.

Some mages create worlds to entertain in grand style, like aviaries, gardens or amusement parks. Others build virtual libraries to house the masses of information at their fingertips or make workshops where they can practice their magick relatively free from Paradox. Some use the Web for darker purposes, creating torture chambers and dungeons to imprison the abducted consciousness of enemies.

The Web is not a physically "real" place, but exists as a portion of raw potentiality locked into place. Many mages consider the Web to be the heir of the fabled Mount Qaf of the Ahl-i-Batin, an early form of shared reality. Virtual Adepts tinkering with VR sought to prove the existence of such a Realm. They learned to project human consciousness into the non-space of virtual energy thought to make up Mount Qaf. The untapped potentiality gave their visions a magickal "reality" somewhere between the inner sensory world of virtual reality and the outer world of physical reality. The result is the Web's own "virtual" reality.

All Traditions can be found in the Web, albeit some more than others. Two factions — Virtual Adepts and the Technocracy Conventions — predominate, while Marauders and Nephandi hover around the edges, looking for ways to get in. The Digital Web is unknown to Sleepers, though some visit its edges with standard computers and regular VR. Here, the tug-of-war for reality between Tradition and Technocracy is unusually fierce. Even the most primitive VR pushes the boundaries of Sleeper belief with the idea of a world where thought becomes reality, and static reality is sliding because of it, much to the Technocrats' collective horror.

Surfing the Net

There are three means to access the Web, detailed below. Most visitors and residents interact on-line through magickal icons **(also below)**. Like anything else, though, the Net is fraught with peril. Some of it starts the minute a mage plugs in his goggles.

Sensory Accessing

This is routinely used by mages unfamiliar with the Net. Almost anyone can access VR in this way; all you need is a set of VR goggles and some electrodes for tactile feedback. This is often called *telepresence*. Accessing this way is somewhat limiting. Since a mage is not actually *in* the Net, wielding magick is like picking up an egg with a remote-controlled robot arm — delicate, painstaking and not to be done in an emergency. Magick difficulties increase by +2 for anyone using this form of access.

Equipment types really don't matter, but different mages have their personal favorites. Virtual Adepts use VR goggles that look like dark sunglasses. Electrodes along the brow convey sensory images. Some also use body suits to complete the sensory experience. Iteration X'ers prefer to use the latest technology available, regardless of the danger. Their particular VR goggles were only recently developed: a special projector projects the images directly onto the back of the user's retina, while electrodes along the sides transfer sensory data into the brain. Some Adepts have discovered that a little reprogramming and a good blast of Force magick will destroy the eyes of anyone using these types of goggles.

Sensory access is available to Sleepers, although they think they're only seeing a really cool simulation. All a mage needs to start is a good, Net-capable computer. VA's make a simple, personal computer-compatible VR set available to any Tradition mage who wants to help spread the word about the Web.

Astral Immersion

Once the mage experiences an alternate world, that world takes on reality for him and he can re-enter it as often as he likes. The mage must first access the Web via Computer (Intelligence + Computer, three successes, difficulty 7), then use the Correspondence Effect **Correspondence Sensing** to translate his consciousness from the physical world into that of the Web. The mage is literally fooled into believing he is in the Net. The effect is an illusion, but the belief is all that's needed for the mage to astrally project into the Net without access to the **Untether Mind** Effect. The mage's mind is no longer in his body, the computer or the physical world — it is in the world of the Web.

With Astral Immersion, the worlds of VR come into sudden, breathtaking focus. The mage initiates direct, consciousness-to-consciousness with the Net, and all of his senses, including his magickal ones, are inundated with information moving at the speed of a super-conductor. The sensory overload makes conventional VR seem anemic by comparison, like comparing Edison's *Frankenstein* to Cameron's *Terminator II*. The mage finds he has control over this new world because the magickal energy of unpatterned Web is highly responsive to thoughts. Mages who enter the Web astrally can pattern Virgin Web by will alone and can manipulate other created Realms within the parameters of the world-laws

The major drawback to this is that the user's body is vulnerable to physical threats while his mind is in the Net. Obviously, a very safe haven from which to operate is essential. Some invest in high-tech security and bodyguards, though few Net Runners have that much disposable income. Some voyagers who cannot afford expensive systems have learned to set a burglar alarm to disconnect the power to the goggles if the alarm is tripped.

It's very hard to kill or harm a mage who accesses the Web this way. Any damage is dealt only to the mage's icon programs. One of the few ways to hurt someone accessing this way is through *lethal feedback* (or LF), an Effect created by setting up an interference pattern in the sensory data going into the user's electrodes. This is very difficult, and only mages who understand the way the human body and its nerve impulses work can produce and use it. The effect of such an attack is not unlike a severe night terror; the victim cannot move or speak, and the "fight or flight" instinct becomes so intense that the victim either faints or has a heart attack. It usually takes 10 to 15 Health Levels of feedback to seriously maim or kill. This rote uses Life 3, Forces 2 and Prime 2.

Sensory visitation and astral immersion are both mental, not physical, experiences. A mage using either access replaces his Strength with Intelligence and his Dexterity with his Wits. Only Stamina remains constant when projecting into the Net.

Holistic Immersion

This process allows a mage to actually transform her body into pure information and download herself into the Net. A powerful computer is necessary for this magick because the human body becomes *a lot* of information when digitized **(see "Trinary Computers," below)**. The procedure takes less than a minute, but during that time, the mage is completely vulnerable. Interruptions can permanently harm a mage attempting to enter the Net this way. This form is slightly more dangerous than iconization.

Because the mage exists as information, she can be affected by programs that manipulate data. A person who knows enough about computers and the Net can write programs to send the mage through an infinite loop. A virus could be downright lethal. On the other hand, a mage can physically interact with others in the Net, which can be an edge for a character with high Physical Attributes and low Mental ones.

Icons

A mage can assume any form in the Web, creating a three-dimensional icon of himself through complex magickal programs.

Icon creation requires a roll of Intelligence + Computer, difficulty 8, with four or more successes. It's often done as an extended action. While accessing the Web requires a magickal Effect, icon creation itself is not magickal once inside. The easiest icon to adopt looks like the mage's physical body, down to the glasses or untied shoelaces. Deviation is difficult, but not out of reach.

In the Web, a mage can change her appearance by rolling Manipulation + Computer and choosing any icon she desires, whether a blue salamander or a beautiful Asian woman. However, assumed shapes do not change Traits. Appearance and Intimidation may be raised by a number of dots equal to successes on the Manipulation + Computer roll (maximum of 5 on either) depending on the icon (the Asian woman icon, for example, would raise your Appearance score based on how many successes you made during the roll).

The mage can try to assume the form of another Net Runner, but she'll have difficulty fooling those who actually know the person. Magick icons can be copied, but they copy like a digital recorder reading an analog signal — they seem the same, but an essential ingredient has been lost. **Sense Life** or **Sense Quintessence** can tell the difference between a "true" icon and a copy. Many mages just know on an intuitive level when they're dealing with a phony.

Some VA's have created Constraint Realms where the parameters limit the types of icons that can appear, some for security, others for fun and games. All icons must be appropriate to the context before entering, or they don't get in at all. Say that Dr. Volcano decided to create a Constraint Realm of a Grateful Dead concert. Unless your icon is in tie-dye, wearing a Dead shirt or otherwise looks like a Deadhead, you won't get into this party. Crashing this gate is not recommended.

Anybody who enters the Web becomes identifiable by the pattern code within his or her icon. All programs and entities within the Web have codes that identify them.

Items of Power

You can have my gun when you pry it from my cold dead fingers!

— NRA Bumper Sticker

Mages do not always depend on their Arts alone. Some items, like computers, are far more than simple foci and form an inescapable part of the modern mystick's world. Others, like Talismans and fetishes, are holdovers from a bygone age and contain magick's essence within them.

The systems presented below offer only basic guidelines for these important tools.

Computers

Since its invention, the computer has had a monumental effect on our society and our world. A majority of households in the modern industrial world have a personal computer or access to one. The computer has shrunk our world; whereas a message used to take weeks or even months to travel from one side of the world to the other, computers transfer millions of pieces of data everywhere nearly instantaneously. Computers run our banks, our most important weapon systems and our communication systems. No major corporation could survive without them. The total impact of computers on our world is incalculable.

These advances into the information age utilize standard Sleeper technology. Technomagick, however, has advanced beyond our simple number crunchers. While our machines work on a "yes" or "no," on-or-off level of decision making, Virtual Adepts use machines capable of making decisions based on possibilities, guesses and "maybe." The development of Trinary computers, those which have this third option in the "yes" or "no" question, takes the Ascension War to a new level.

The Code

Anyone can use a normal computer. Basic use rarely requires a roll, unless the character lacks the Computer Knowledge Trait and is just winging it. Basic computer use includes utilizing a common program: word processing, spreadsheets, mail programs, etc. If the character knows anything about computers, she probably learned with those types of programs. A total novice can try to use a computer by rolling her Intelligence only, but the difficulty should be horrendous — 8 or 10, with multiple successes required just to get a program running.

Software Design

Characters with a Computer Skill over two can attempt to design their own software. The task's difficulty varies depending on the complexity of the new software, available hardware, and amount of time taken (from 6 to 8, with extended rolls). Advice from other programmers or Mentors may help and could lower this difficulty. The exact effect of each of these modifiers is up to the Storyteller. Basic software design would include any programs that perform simple tasks: data sorting, word processing or scheduling. Complex software includes and programs designed for scientific calculations, monitoring and activation of equipment or security devices, or "hacking" and hacking defense programs. In general, designing complex software is an extended action, and difficulties should range between 8 and 10, requiring between five to 10 successes.

Hacking

The term "hacking" refers to any action which violates computer system security — breaking into other systems, stealing data, destroying a mainframe or even crippling a company. Hacking requires the Computer Skill and characters may specialize in Hacking at level 4 or better. **(See "Specialties," Chapter Six.)** Hacking also involves innovative approaches to the new frontier of technology and the Internet. This can also include designing completely new uses for computers that the old school considers useless.

All hacking attempts usually require some type of new and innovative program. Hacking constantly evolves to tackle the newest barriers; likewise, security constantly evolves to stop the threat of invasion. A hacker must acquire software from fellow hackers or design her own if she is to get anywhere. Consider hacking software "complex" for design and execution purposes, including high difficulties and extended successes. Modifications to all difficulties include:

- Breaking into simple computer system and copying data: difficulty 7, three successes.
- Breaking into a sophisticated system: difficulty 9 to 10, five successes or more.
- Breaking into another computer and altering or deleting data without being noticed: difficulty 8, four successes.
- Removing copy protection from commercial software: difficulty 7, two successes.
- Creating a protection program: difficulty 7, six successes.

Trinary Computers and Upgrades

"Welcome to the next level."

—Sega advertisement

Some mages use computers to focus in their magick **(see "Foci," Chapter Eight)**. A normal computer, however, slows a mage down, especially when dealing with the light-speed interactions of the Web. Technomancers usually give their machines a magickal upgrade before proceeding on to the Internet.

The most common upgrade involves reworking the computer to allow for greater memory and speed. The process involves the channeling Prime 2 or Spirit 2 into a computer and then using Matter 2 to adjust for mechanical overload. Multiple Computer Skill rolls in conjunction with the various Spheres are also necessary (Prime + Computer, difficulty 8; Matter + Computer, difficulty 8). This will allow the computer to store and download rotes at a much faster rate, hopefully giving the user vital seconds to avoid being fried. The machine is still limited to rotes with Sphere ranks 1 or 2, and cannot perform any magick on its own. A computer that performs its own magick is a Talisman.

The next level of upgrade introduces a new factor to programming. Normal computers work on a "yes" or "no" basis; Trinary computers add "maybe" to the list of possible answers. This transformation allows a computer to make guesses or possibly offer suggestions and partially run itself. Given the proper parameters, a Trinary computer could defend itself from an intruding hacker, suggest possible rotes for its user, estimate enemy numbers or defenses or assist in software design. Trinary computers simplify mundane tasks as well. The mage himself limits the capabilities of the machine. If the machine receives bad instructions or inaccurate data, it will do the wrong thing or give the wrong answer. The machine is still a machine; it isn't alive or sentient. As with the simpler magickal upgrade above, Trinary computers can store and download rotes faster than normal, but now may store rotes higher than Sphere level 2.

Technomancers guard the secret of creation of Trinary computers jealously. The Virtual Adepts invented the process, but the Sons of Ether and Iteration X have designed similar versions. The exact process is up to the Storyteller and should probably be an adventure in itself. The process should involve Prime and Matter magick to restructure an existing computer and perhaps Mind or Life to complete the upgrade. The process will also incur a fair bit of mundane tinkering and a hefty Radio Shack bill. A character might acquire an old Trinary computer (good luck!) from a mentor or contact, but these will surely be outdated and need further upgrading.

Another way to upgrade a computer involves binding a spirit into the machine **(see below)**. A spirit can temporarily adjust a computer's operating format, but cannot perform miracles the computer is incapable of. Essentially, you command the spirit, and the spirit controls the machine. The spirit would be able to use its ability to effect anything that the computer could normally effect and then some, including launching Umbral attacks into the Internet or coercing a spirit in another machine. Bounded spirits allow one violation of computer "laws," but will otherwise be limited by the machine. Spirits bound permanently to the machine form fetishes.

Talisman and Fetish Computers

A Computer Talisman follows the same rules that apply to other Talismans, including creation, activation and magick use. They are computers imbued with a certain amount of Quintessence and given Magickal Effects by the creator. Talisman Computers, by their very nature, are the rarest of computer upgrades. They're incredibly hard to create — only the most dedicated Technomancer will take the time to make one.

The specific powers of a Talisman Computer are entirely up to the player and the Storyteller. It's important to realize that a computer with a magickal Effect as part of its programming won't execute that Effect spontaneously. It's still not sentient and remains limited to the commands of its user.

Talisman and Fetish Creation

A French physicist has invented a "time-reversal mirror": a device that takes in a sound and spits it out again — backwards.

— February 1995 issue of *Discover* magazine

Talismans and fetishes, fully described in **Chapter Six**, are notoriously difficult to produce. Often crafted in Horizon Realms to avoid causing Paradox, Talismans channel mystick essence to imbue an item with magickal powers. Fetishes bind spirits rather than magick and often carry over a bit of temper along with the enchantment. Making such items demands time, skill and patience.

A would-be Talisman must be well-crafted. When the mystick is ready to create the enchantment, she uses a vulgar Prime 4 Effect and a *permanent* point of Willpower, and must garner 10 successes before she's ready for the next step.

Next, she focuses 10 Quintessence into the item for every point of Arete she wants it to have. A mage cannot create a Talisman with a higher Arete than her own. After this, she adds whatever Effects she wants the item to contain: each Sphere level dot costs one point of Quintessence and requires an Arete roll against difficulty 8 (no reductions) and a day's work per roll. The Talisman may hold as many Effects as it has points of Arete. Finally, the creator funnels Quintessence into the item to fuel it, again using Prime 4.

Fetishes can be created on Earth; using the Spirit 4 **Create Fetish** Effect, the mage binds an Umbrood into the item. This usually requires 10 successes total, and botching this roll is bad news. Adding Quintessence to a fetish is not necessary, but it helps keep the spirit happy. Such items usually have only one power.

IX

Chapter Ten: Drama

We walk the narrow path
Beneath the smoking skies
Sometimes you can barely tell the difference
Between the darkness and the light
Do we have faith in what we believe?
The truest test is when we cannot,
When we cannot see
— Jane Siberry, "It Can't Rain All the Time"

The Ascension

Amidst the gnarled and dying trees in the apple orchard, two mages moved towards each other with grace and speed that defied their exhaustion and tired spirits. One mage, dark of skin and soul, moved in rage. The other, sad but determined, trembled in fear at her final battle with the mentor she had once loved.

"There's no escape, Clarissa. This grove is grown from your own soul, a concept I know is beyond your understanding," Peter Kobie taunted. "Always with you it was the material. Never the spiritual. Never anything you couldn't see and touch. For all that you may have surpassed me, it ends here. Tonight." With a motion of his hands, the black branches of the apple trees bent and took Clarissa in a twisted embrace, wrapping around her limbs, snapping bones as she struggled to break free, fighting with all her will to command the trees of the grove to her own bidding. For a few moments, she felt her healing touch surge among the sickened grove. Sunlight flickered among the trees and blooms appeared where none had sprung forth for many days. But then Peter's eyes widened in fury. Just as quickly as they had come, the light and blossoms faded to nothing, falling back into the shadows of their creator's soul. He walked over and grasped Clarissa's chin in his hand. She met his stare without flinching, looking for any trace of the noble songmaker she'd once known, bridling tears when she saw nothing remained within the terrible jealousy and pride that now consumed him.

"You're going to kill me, aren't you?" she whispered, an odd calm stirring somewhere deep inside her.

"I only wish I could do more than that, bitch," he hissed, and with that, one sharp branch of the tree where she hung drove itself through her spine. Clarissa had steeled herself for the pain of death. But as she hung there, a new understanding crept through her, softening not only the physical blow of the tree through her heart, but the emotional agony of her mentor's betrayal. And Clarissa saw that in this, the final and ultimate experience of her life, the wild experiences she'd sought as a means of Ascension were nothing but tools and trappings of the same static reality she'd learned to defy, that both experience and the lack of it were equal in the grand scheme of things. She fought back a joyous laugh as she felt the bonds holding her to the world she knew snap and fall away, releasing her into an unknown place, ripe for her knowing its infinite truths.

A lot can happen in a turn. A player might want to dodge a fist, hot-wire a Porsche or locate a volume of Shakespeare's sonnets. If you're the Storyteller, you've already read **Chapter Seven**, and can probably figure out what to have the player roll. Still, you might be able to use a few possible techniques and variations on the rules. That's what this chapter is — suggestions for rules systems to resolve dramatic actions.

This chapter isn't all-inclusive and isn't meant to be. Use these systems as examples, and invent your own when necessary. Don't interrupt a dramatic scene to check a chart — just make something up. Maybe you'll use something like a rules system mentioned here. Maybe you won't.

If the roll in question is fairly simple, don't worry about these systems. If you're not interested in "game drama" versus "story drama," use the automatic success rules. Once you're familiar with the description of the Trait in question, just determine the character's success without rolling any dice. Die rolls can add tension and suspense to a game; luck is something we still can't control. But if the dice get in the way, use them as little as possible.

Only make rolls when you're not honestly sure whether or not a character will succeed. If it seems like she would anyway, just let her. This chapter's name is Drama; don't waste time on dice rolls that do nothing special for the story. Use the dice to make things interesting for you and the players.

Scenes

A scene is a point when the troupe roleplays through the events at hand as if they were actually occurring. A scene might require only conversational roleplaying or could demand a host of different die rolls.

It's the same as a scene from a movie; everything happens in the same location and at the same point in time. It's a car chase, a gunfight, a romantic interlude. This is the essence of roleplaying, when players react in character rather than explaining their intentions third-hand. Do everything you can to make your scenes as dramatic, complete and satisfying as possible. Don Scarlatti doesn't just sit at a table while the characters watch — he calls over one of his *caporegimas* and quietly rebukes him. The more exciting each scene becomes, the better the story.

Time spent between scenes is called *downtime*, when characters conduct research, travel or just go on with everyday business. Nobody wants to roleplay every moment of downtime; just use it to organize players, advance the plot and generally take care of minor details. The story will turn into a scene when needed, often without anyone recognizing the change. While all of you discuss the characters' travel plans, for instance, start describing what they see on the way to Chicago. Presto — you've gone from downtime to a scene. An old man walks up to them and asks for change, and they're hooked. By simply roleplaying without warning, you've jump-started the players into their roles, and the scene is up and running.

Turns

Turns organize and arrange a scene's events. A turn is a variable period of time in which each character should be able to do one thing. It helps the Storyteller keep track of events and gives all of the players a chance to do something. Each turn, go around the table in order of initiative **(see below)**, give each player an equal opportunity to describe their action, then describe the actions of the non-player characters.

Even if it doesn't always make complete sense, you should use the turn structure pretty loosely. You might, for example, let someone climb a tree while someone else fires a gun. Yeah, climbing a tree usually takes more time than shooting a gun, but it's a game, and adrenaline lets people do amazing things.

Multiple Actions

To perform multiple actions in a turn (like running and shooting a gun), a character has to divide his dice. To split a Dice Pool between two different actions, he takes the dice from the action with which he has the smallest Dice Pool and divides that Pool among each of his actions. He can also move while taking other actions (again, firing a gun), by simply taking away one die from the Pool for every three yards he moves. Movement is already considered in the rules for dodging, so characters who dive for cover accrue no extra penalty.

For example, TamLyn is stuck in a New York alley, fighting the cult thugs of the Nephandus Lisabelle. He wants to drop back six yards to a dumpster for cover, snap off a shot at the thug carrying an Uzi, and dodge the other's return shot. TamLyn has Dexterity 4, Firearms 5 and Dodge 3 (he's done this before). Since his Dexterity + Dodge is lower than his Dexterity + Firearms, he has a Dice Pool of seven dice. He subtracts two dice to move to the dumpster, and may assign the other five between his dodge and his shot. TamLyn wishes he'd accepted his ally Elizabeth's offer of assistance....

Characters with multiple actions take their first action, and only their first, in their normal order of initiative (unless they delay). After all characters have completed their first (or only) action, those with more actions may take their second action, again in order of initiative. After everyone who has a second action takes it, go on to the third, and so on until nobody has any actions left. While characters may delay their action, they must take it before the rest of the characters move on to their next action, or it is lost. Characters can always use dice to Dodge, however, so long as they have dice left in their Pools.

Action Scenes

Scenes full of actions and dice rolls often require special rules to run smoothly; these are the fights, races and feats of danger common to adventure stories. During an action scene, turns are usually very short — only three seconds or so. Most of the systems described in this chapter occur during action scenes and use action turns. All sorts of things can happen in an action scene, and correlating everything can seem a little tricky. Still, you should let a character try nearly anything, even if you have to assign him a difficulty of 10 to succeed.

Make sure you carefully describe the location of everyone in the scene, as well that of what cover is available. Otherwise, you'll have to describe the scene over again and hear complaints like, "Wait a minute, you didn't say anyone was over there!" You may also want to describe the environmental conditions and how they might affect the scene. Rain, wind and smoke can affect many dice rolls. Lead or pewter miniatures, toy cars and model buildings can add a lot when setting a scene; this way, everyone can tell where the various characters are.

Initiative

Rolling for initiative is the best way to decide who goes first in an action scene. Sometimes it will be obvious who acts first: an ambush was successful, or a person's best friend turns on her without warning. In combat, however, if you intend to let the opponents have a free shot at the characters, don't simply spring it on the players. Let them make Perception rolls (difficult ones) to see if characters notice something just before the bad guys open up — it's easier than arguing with your troupe. The ambusher's skills determine the difficulty (usually 8 or so). The number of successes the players score indicates the number of dice they can roll on their first actions (usually dodges).

Normally, everyone involved makes a Wits + Alertness roll (or you can have them roll Wits + Brawl, Melee, Firearms or any other appropriate Ability). The difficulty is usually 4 — characters with the most successes go first and ties go simultaneously. Characters who fail act after those who succeeded last. A botch on an initiative roll means the character does not get to act that turn — his gun jams, he stumbles, or something like that. If you like, don't have the players roll for initiative every turn; just continue to use the results from the first turn. This speeds things up immensely, but can cause problems of another sort. Use your judgment — don't force some poor player who botches to miss the entire scene!

Organizing an Action Turn

Turns organize a scene, and stages organize a turn. You probably won't need to subdivide turns that aren't action turns. This list might give you some ideas about organizing things when the action gets hot. A carefully orchestrated scene will run more smoothly, and everyone involved will have more fun.

• Describing the Scene

At the beginning of each turn, describe the scene from the characters' perspective. Suggest what the characters' opponents might be about to do, but don't actually describe what will happen. Sometimes you'll want to wrap up the last turn, clarifying it to the players. Constant description prevents confusion. This is your chance to arrange things so that all the players' interactions go smoothly. Make your description as interesting as possible, leaving open all sorts of possibilities for the characters' actions.

This is also when you have your players roll for initiative. If you want to be particularly free-spirited, eliminate the initiative roll altogether. "The south wall caves in as the fire spreads to the room you're all in. The Orphan's eyes glaze as the flames run across the floorboards. He wins the initiative and sprints toward a window with a yell. What are you going to do?"

• Decision Stage

Going in reverse order of initiative (if the players made initiative rolls), have each player explain what her character intends to do and how she intends to go about it. If you did not call for initiative rolls, simply go around the table from left to right, or in order of characters' Wits, or using whatever consistent method you like, and then decide how you want to resolve the action — what kind of roll each player will make, the difficulty of the roll and the number of successes needed. You can make the process as simple or as complicated as you like: "If you want to catch him before he dives out the window, make a Dexterity + Athletics roll, difficulty... 7. You need to score four successes to catch up with him, but he only needs two more to jump free."

• Resolution Stage

Now the players roll to see whether their characters succeed or fail. The players roll their dice to attempt the actions they described in the preceding stage.

At the end of the turn, summarize everything by describing what happened, translating all dice rolls into description, plot and story. Don't simply say, "You manage to hit the bad guy for three Health Levels of damage." Get more graphic. "After ducking away to the left, you sweep across with your fist and strike him alongside the head. Your hand stings, but you've broken his nose and wounded him for three Health Levels." Similarly, "You race across the room after him. Next turn, you can grab at him before he leaps out the second-story window. Part of the ceiling collapses behind you... and you hear soft, mocking laughter... "

Taking Actions

The two basic actions characters can take without making rolls include:

• **Yielding:** The character allows the person with the next highest initiative to take his action, thereby yielding her turn. She can still take her action at the end of the turn. If everyone, including her opponents, also yields, no one does anything that turn.

• **Moving:** The character may move by walking, jogging or running. If she walks, she may move seven yards. If she jogs, she may move 12 yards + Dexterity. If she runs, she may move 20 yards + (3 x Dexterity). No roll is necessary, but this movement is the only action the character can perform that turn. Jogging or running can be hazardous in some situations, and she might need to roll to maintain her balance when there's glass on the ground or bullets tearing up the wall behind her. If the character wants to run away from the conflict, she must dodge while doing it, unless she's out of the field of fire.

All sorts of other actions might require rolls. Some are listed here:

• **Attack:** A character may decide to fire his weapon or strike someone. The roll made depends on the attack; for instance, a Firearms attack requires a Dexterity + Firearms roll.

• **Climb:** Make a Dexterity + Athletics roll.

• **Dodge:** A dodge not only allows a character to avoid an attack, but totally removes him from harm's way — for now. A character can make a Dexterity + Dodge roll right after someone tries to hit him, hopefully avoiding the blow.

• **Get to feet:** It takes a turn to get up from the ground without having to make a roll. If a character wants to do this in addition to her other actions, she takes a few dice from her announced action and tries to score at least one success on a Dexterity + Athletics roll (difficulty at least 4).

• **Leadership:** A character may give commands to followers and have them obeyed with appropriate Charisma (or Manipulation) + Leadership rolls.

• **Reload gun:** This can be done in a single turn with a preloaded clip.

• **Research:** A character may try to look up a vital piece of information in a book using the Investigation Ability. Though this would likely take longer than three seconds, you may want to take some dramatic license with this.

• **Start a car:** This action doesn't require a roll at all, unless a character is hot-wiring it.

• **Sneak up on enemy:** This action usually requires a Dexterity + Stealth roll.

• **Unjam gun:** This action can normally be performed in a single turn with a Wits + Firearms roll.

Dramatic Systems

I wish we could play in a gym without any people and try to play the perfect game where you don't make any mistakes and maybe if there's a mistake it's of omission, not commission, and everything is done at the right moment, at the right time, and each decision is the right one and everyone can ride the decision-making wave.

— Sam Smith quoting Coach Phil Jackson, *The Jordan Rules*

This section includes a variety of suggested systems to resolve actions, or, to put it simply, a bunch of ways to make rolls. There are a few more examples of Physical dramatic systems than any other kind; these actions are impossible to resolve purely through roleplaying. Situations where Social and Mental contests come up can be roleplayed out without the use of dice.

Each suggested action has a few possible "coincidences" that might allow a mage to work in a subtle Effect. Bear in mind, however, that objects or people must be created from scratch if they did not exist a moment ago. Such creation may well be more vulgar than the original Effect itself. By successfully slipping a coincidental Effect into a task, a player may drop her difficulty by -1 per success to a maximum of -3 **(see "Abilities and Magick," Chapter Eight)**. A suspicious opponent with countermagick can, of course, counter this "assistance," and Sleepers (or Technocrat spies) may get suspicious if a person seems "just *too* good" at everything. Botching a magickal assist has the usual effects, which may make it more trouble than it's worth.

Physical

These systems describe dramatic situations where Physical Attributes come into play.

Climbing

When a character attempts to climb any sort of surface (a tree, cliff or building), ask the player to roll the character's Dexterity + Athletics. The difficulty depends on the type and sheerness of the climbing surface and, to a lesser extent, the weather conditions. Each success indicates that the character has climbed five feet. Once he accumulates enough successes to get to where he wants to go, he can stop rolling. Cheshire, for example, is trying to climb a 25-foot wall; he needs five successes to get to the top. A failure indicates the character is unable to make any progress during the turn. A botch indicates the character falls and cannot again attempt to climb without expending a Willpower point.

Difficulty	Level of Climb
2	Easy climb: a tree with many stout branches
4	Simple climb: a cliff with many handholds
6	Straightforward: a tree with thin branches
8	Treacherous: very few handholds
10	Extremely difficult: a nearly sheer surface

Coincidences: a rope or ladder is nearby; the tree has a low limb; the wall has available hand- and footholds; there's a fire escape on the side of the building.

Feats of Strength

Dice Pool	Feats	Lift
1	Crush a beer can	40 lbs
2	Break a chair	100 lbs
3	Break down a wooden door	250 lbs
4	Break a 2" x 4"	400 lbs
5	Break open a metal fire door	650 lbs
6	Throw a motorcycle	800 lbs
7	Flip over a small car	900 lbs
8	Break a three-inch lead pipe	1000 lbs
9	Punch through a cement wall	1200 lbs
10	Rip open a steel drum	1500 lbs
11	Punch through 1" sheet metal	2000 lbs
12	Break a metal lamp post	3000 lbs
13	Throw a car	4000 lbs
14	Throw a van	5000 lbs
15	Throw a truck	6000 lbs

Feats of Strength

A character's Strength is often used alone, without an Ability, when brute force is all that matters. If the character's Strength equals or exceeds the difficulty of the task he's attempting, he succeeds automatically. Only if the difficulty is higher than his Dice Pool must he make a roll.

When the character makes the roll, however, it is based on Willpower, not Strength. This is a pretty simple roll, so the character gets only one chance to make it. The difficulty is almost always a 9, though it can vary according to the surface conditions, the object being lifted and Storyteller whim. Each success pushes the character's effective Strength up one step on the chart below (to a maximum of five). Thus, if the character has a Strength of four, but wants to flip over a car, she needs three successes on the Willpower roll to do it.

Coincidences: the chest is lighter than it looks; the door is unlocked or made of rotten wood; the pipe has stress fractures; the car is packed with boxes, but only on one side so it's much heavier and leans that way anyway.

Jumping

Jumping requires a Strength roll or a Strength + Athletics roll for a horizontal jump with a decent running start. The difficulty for a jump is almost always 3 (unless there are difficult weather conditions or a narrow landing space). The Storyteller calculates how many successes the character needs to make the jump. There are no partial successes in jumping; the character either succeeds in one roll, or she falls.

If necessary, you can use the chart below. The number of successes required is based on the number of feet that must be jumped and whether the character is jumping horizontally or vertically.

Type of Jump	Feet per Success
Vertical (up)	2
Horizontal (across)	4

Coincidences: there's a springboard nearby; you just ran down a sloping surface.

Repair

Sometimes you can't just take something to the garage to be fixed; you have to do it yourself. When a character wishes to fix any sort of mechanical implement, he must roll Dexterity + Repair. The difficulty is determined by the complexity of the task **(see the chart below)**. Before the job can be considered complete, he must roll a certain number of successes, usually between two and 20. Each roll means that a certain amount of time is spent — whatever the demands of the story require. A botch indicates that the device is somehow damaged in the attempt.

This system can be fun to use during combat, as one character desperately tries to start the car while the others hold off the HIT Marks.

Shadowing

Sometimes a character will want to "shadow" someone — to follow him as discreetly as possible without being caught. That's the catch — keeping track of your target without being seen. A character can shadow someone on foot or in vehicles; he can try even if someone else, like a taxi driver, is driving: "Follow that car — carefully!"

The player-character in question must make a Perception + Investigation (or possibly Streetwise) roll. The difficulty is normally 6, but can vary from 5 to 9, depending on the thickness of a crowd or bad weather conditions. Each success indicates that the target has been followed for a turn. A certain number of successes are required to follow the subject all the way to his destination. The first failure indicates that the character has temporarily lost her subject, but can try again next turn. A second means she has lost him completely and the chase is off (unless she comes up with a new approach). Should the character botch, she not only loses her subject, but she stumbles into some new problem of her own — a hostile street gang, foraging vampire, lost child, etc.

Though your character's Perception roll is the most important aspect of shadowing, you must also make a Stealth roll to avoid being seen. Each turn the Perception roll is made, the player also rolls her character's Dexterity + Stealth (or Dexterity + Drive if she's in a vehicle).

The difficulty is the subject's Perception + Alertness, but it can be modified by +/-3, depending on the circumstances (empty streets or thick crowds, for instance). A single success indicates the shadower is not detected, and each success increases the target's difficulty, even if he's actively looking for a tail. A failure means he becomes suspicious and starts to surreptitiously glance over his shoulder (and may make Perception rolls of his own; see below). A botch indicates the character completely reveals herself and the subject now knows he's being followed.

If the subject looks to see if he is being followed (out of habit, perhaps), roll his Perception + Investigation (or Streetwise). The difficulty is the shadowing character's Stealth rating +5. Each success on this roll indicates a higher degree of suspicion. Successes can be accumulated from turn to turn; see the chart below to see how aware the subject is that he is being followed. A failure means that the target hasn't seen anything and relaxes his guard, dropping his suspicion to zero. If he botches, he's convinced he isn't being followed and no longer looks behind him.

Successes	Suspicion
1	Hunch
2	Suspicion
3	Near-certainty
4	Positive knowledge
5	The shadower has been spotted

Magick: With the Arcane Background or a bit of subtle magick, the mage can conceal her shadowing attempt. Her target, if *he* has Arcane, can throw his pursuer completely off. For mages with Arcane, add +1 difficulty to either character's chance to spot the one with the Background. If both of them have Arcane, things get amusing.... By using some magickal cover — manipulating shadows, Mind-swaying people to come between you and any tracker, using Entropy to disrupt his thoughts *just enough* — a shadower or target can subtract one of her opponent's Perception successes for each success she gets on a magick roll. The key word here, though, is subtlety; too much magick will draw attention.

Buddy System: Two or more characters can shadow one target by trading off. However, they must have previously worked or trained together in this technique, or the difficulty on all rolls for the pair is +1 higher. One player shadows for a turn or more, then trades off whenever her partner gives the signal. If the pair switches off, the subject can't accumulate successes for very long, which makes it much harder for the subject to spot shadowers.

Coincidences: you see your shadower reflected in store window; the guy you thought you'd given the slip made the same wrong turn you did; he gets caught in a traffic circle; a truck breaks down between you and him.

Stunt Driving

This system determines the outcome of nearly any type of automobile chase or maneuver. Dice rolls in chases are not only made to see how fast a driver goes, but also to see if she stays on the road or not. Each vehicle is rated for its maximum safe driving speed as well as its maneuverability. One vehicle is not always as fast or maneuverable as another, so the details of the chase often depend on the make of the vehicle **(see the chart below)**.

A character can make special maneuvers in order to catch or lose another vehicle, such as spinning around a tight corner, doing a 180° turn or wheeling about to block a road. Essentially, one character makes a special maneuver and the other character must copy that maneuver by making a similar roll.

The player rolls Dexterity (or perhaps Perception) + Drive; her Dice Pool cannot exceed the maneuverability rating of the vehicle. Give each maneuver a basic difficulty from 2-7, and then decide on a maximum safe speed. If the vehicle is going over that speed, raise the difficulty (by +1 for every additional 10 mph) or have the character fail outright.

Repair

Job	Difficulty	# of Successes
Simple mechanical repair	4	3
Soldering job	5	2
Electronic malfunction	5	5
Fitting in new part	6	10
Repair stalled car	6	5
Tough auto repair	7	10
System overhaul	8	20
Technical glitch	9	2

Coincidences: the engine was just overheated — it starts fine now; floater needle becomes unstuck; the battery wires were just loose; a good kick starts 'er right up; it was only unplugged.

Pursuit

Use this simple system if one character's trying to catch another. One opponent starts with a certain number of successes; say two for every turn's worth of head start, or one for every success on a Dexterity + Athletics roll (difficulty 6). The other character has to match or beat these successes before he can catch up. Once he does, he can try to grapple the fleeing person **(see "Combat")**. The pursuer might only want to catch up halfway, just to get a better shot at the fleeing character.

Coincidences: the other person is tripped or blocked; an alley leads to a dead end if the mage is the pursuer; there are too many possible directions that the pursued mage may take for the chase to continue.

Stunt Driving

Vehicle	Safe Speed	Max Speed	Maneuverability
6-wheel truck	60	90	3
Bus	60	100	3
18-wheeler	70	110	4
Sedan	70	120	5
Mini-van	70	120	6
Compact	70	130	6
Sporty compact	100	140	7
Sport coupe	110	150	8
Sports car	130	170	9
Formula One race car	140	240	10

Coincidences: good thing that unfinished road was on a downward angle; driving on two wheels is easy when the road slopes up with you; you slingshot off another car — too bad for the other guy; thank God for anti-lock brakes.

Sneaking

When a character attempts to hide in shadows or sneak up on a guard, she must roll Dexterity + Stealth. The difficulty is the guard's Perception + Alertness. Anyone actively looking for intruders can be considered a guard.

The sneaking character needs to collect a certain number of successes in order to make it to where she wants to go. A Perception + Stealth roll can be made if the player wants to estimate how many successes will be needed; the difficulty for this is usually 7.

Failure of any sort on a Stealth roll indicates detection.

Coincidences: the guard falls asleep; the lights are dim; the shadows fall on the right places; an animal rustles elsewhere to lead the guard off your track; no one set the alarm.

Social

Social interactions are best handled by roleplaying; that's half the fun of such games in the first place. When you don't have time to play out a city-wide manhunt or an eight-hour filibuster, however, or when your player doesn't share his character's street-smarts or smooth manners, these systems may help.

Seduction

Seductions are tricky; the seducer woos her target in stages, from clever lines to intimacies. Not all seductions are sexual — they may range from intellectual diversions to changes of faith. A seducer, however, uses false pretenses to gain some form of intimacy with her quarry, who usually assumes that the seducer's feelings are real.

A seduction goes in stages, and unless the character succeeds during each stage, she will not be successful in the long run. This system simulates misdirection; if the seducer's emotions and motives *are* real, ignore the system and roleplay it out. Even if you use the system, play it out anyway — it can be fun, and may make all the difference to the characters' later relationship.

Some characters, depending on their Natures (Bon Vivants and Connivers for example), regain Willpower from successful seductions. This skill is a stock-in-trade of the Nephandi, who use it to sway others from their original ideals and into corruption. In any case, the seducer will gain something of value from her target if everything goes as planned....

Opening Line: The player rolls Appearance + Subterfuge (or some other Traits, if applicable — Manipulation + Subterfuge, Expression, Lore, etc.). The difficulty is the subject's Wits + 3, although good roleplaying may adjust this for better or worse. Each success after the first adds an extra die to the roll on the next stage.

Witty exchange: The player rolls Wits + Subterfuge. The difficulty is the seducee's Intelligence + 3. Give bonuses and penalties for roleplaying. Each additional success adds an extra die to the roll on the next stage.

Conversation: The player rolls Charisma + Empathy. Difficulty is Perception +3. Again, roleplaying bonuses come into play here.

Intimacies: At this point, the seducer gets whatever he or she wants. If sex is involved, the couple moves on to activities best left without systems. If the seducer was trying to convert her target — to change his beliefs, swing his support from one person to another, talk him into some undesirable activity or reveal a secret — her successes may dictate how thorough a job she does.

Coincidence: you remind him of that long-lost love; your voice has that silky tone she loves; always had a thing for the thin, pale type; "You're a gamer, too?"

Fast Talk

With this system, a character browbeats and bamboozles someone into submission. The player usually rolls Manipulation + Subterfuge, though Charisma or Appearance could be added to Expression, Intimidation or any number of Knowledges, depending on the character's approach. The difficulty is the target's Wits + Streetwise. Success indicates that the target becomes confused.

That target may make whatever rolls he wishes; however, fast talk is likely to confuse him too much at some point to take the appropriate action. He can also expend Willpower points to resist fast talk. If the offensive (or offending) character fails his roll, his attempt has faltered, and the target can try to explain himself or even fast talk back. This rebuttal continues until the subject fails or botches. A fast talker's botch indicates that his target doesn't get confused, only angry. Fast talk attempts by that character will never work on him again.

Repeated rolls might be necessary to truly confuse the target. As Storyteller, you need to run attempts at fast talk in a way that is consistent with the mood of your game. It can be as slaphappy or as deadly serious as you like.

Coincidences: his shoe really is untied; your victim read an article on the topic just last week; a passing stranger agrees with you; he already owns the Brooklyn Bridge.

Oration

If a player wants her character to give a speech, but doesn't want to actually give it, you can use this system. You want her to describe what she says and maybe tell you a memorable phrase she uses — that might even get her started into roleplaying it out. Oration can be difficult to roleplay, so don't force your players to do so — just use this system.

The player makes a Charisma + Leadership roll. The mood of the crowd, its willingness to hear what the orator says and its penchant for throwing rotten vegetables determine the difficulty (usually 7). If the orator has any sort of reputation, you may wish to adjust the difficulty accordingly. If the character has Influence or Destiny, she can add that rating to her Dice Pool. The number of successes indicates how impressed the crowd is **(see the following chart)**. It's a simple roll, so the player has only one crack at it. A failure indicates the crowd ignores the character. A botch will get the character booed (or possibly even lynched).

Successes	Crowd Reaction
1	They listened, but aren't excited
2	The character has convinced them somewhat
3	The crowd is won over
4	The crowd is completely enthralled
5	The crowd is in the palm of the character's hand

If the speech is vital to the story, the player may make several rolls. If you want to spend some time on it, you can make it an extended action, interspersing rolls with roleplaying. The character can spend as many turns as she would like on the speech, but after the third turn, the difficulty goes up each turn by +1. It might take more than five successes to completely win over the crowd.

Coincidences: most of the crowd is drunk; the microphone has just the right amount of echo; the sun comes out of the clouds just as you make your point.

Facedown

When two characters are engaged in a duel of Willpower and neither wants to be the first to back down, this system comes in handy. No words are exchanged — the opponents just glare at one another. Mages do this sort of thing often; with great power comes greater egotism.

Both opponents roll Charisma + Intimidation; the difficulty is the opponent's Willpower. The one who first accumulates his opponent's Wits + 5 in successes wins; the other one looks away. A character can spend a Willpower point each turn to avoid giving up — until he runs out of Willpower.

Coincidences: the other sees something out of the corner of his eye; he has to sneeze or has a sudden itch; she can't help but laugh at the funny look on your face.

Interrogation

Interrogation is pretty common in any war. This system reflects a form of questioning, not torture, though intimidation is certainly employed. You'll have to develop your own rules for torture if you wish to include it in your chronicle.

The player makes a Manipulation + Intimidation roll; the difficulty is the victim's Willpower. The number of successes indicates the amount of information obtained. A failure indicates the character learns nothing of value. A botch indicates the subject tells the character nothing, and will never tell him anything — or worse, the subject lies. To conceal the truth, the Storyteller, not the player, should make this roll.

Successes	Interrogation
1	Only a few mumbled facts
2	Some relevant facts
3	Much interesting information
4	The subject talks on and on
5	Everything of import is discovered

Coincidences: you say a name (guessing) and know you got it right when the guy blanches; he has all the plans written down on a paper in his pocket; she accidentally says the name.

Performances

This system is used whenever a character gives any type of performance, whether it be comedy, music, acting or storytelling. It can be on a stage or in a nightclub and can be formal or informal. Mages who rely upon singing, dancing or music as foci rely on this system a lot.

The player rolls the appropriate Attribute + Expression (or Subterfuge, Etiquette, or some other performance-oriented Trait). The difficulty is based on how receptive the audience is. A failure indicates a lackluster, eminently forgettable performance. A botch indicates a miserable performance that cannot even be finished — the dancer trips or the musician breaks his instrument.

The number of successes indicates how moved the audience is. This determines the artistic merit, technical verisimilitude or magickal effectiveness of the piece **(see "Abilities and Magick," Chapter Eight)**.

Successes	Your Performance	Reaction
1	Mediocre	Polite applause
2	Average	Approval
3	Good	Genuine appreciation
4	Superior	Vigorous applause
5	Exceptional	Ecstatic reaction
6	Superb	Immediate sensation
7	Brilliant	Miracle, magnum opus

Coincidences: you play their favorite song; you play a song they don't know so they have no idea how it *should* sound; you look like their son or a favorite actor.

Mental

These situations, like Physical ones, are difficult or time-consuming to roleplay out. They also utilize extended rolls to gather a certain amount of successes. Generally, the player announces her intentions and the steps her character will take to pursue them (visiting the Chantry library, asking questions in "all the right places," etc.). The Storyteller then decides the difficulty of the task and the amount of success the player needs to roll. Such tasks often take place in downtime to avoid slowing the chronicle's flow.

Research

Information is an important commodity. In many stories, research is the only way for the characters to uncover clues, lore or gossip they may need to proceed. A mage may have to investigate matters in a library, barroom, newspaper office or computer archive in order to obtain the information he needs. General research is a great way to let a character with high Intelligence show off, while back-alley or ballroom research allows a streetwise character to do what he does best.

For general research, the player rolls Intelligence + Research (and sometimes an appropriate Knowledge Ability, like Computers or Investigation, after a place to research has been found). Street or social research goes on in the appropriate places — bars, jails, costume balls, social events, etc. A character gathers this kind of information by scoping out people who might know the answers he seeks and asking the right questions. While such research may involve Social interactions **(see preceding)**, the character will use his wits more than his looks. With a little luck, his Intelligence + Streetwise, Etiquette, Investigation or Subterfuge will usually get him what he needs to know.

Research difficulty is based upon the obscurity of the information:

Difficulty	Accessibility of Information
2	Generally available
4	Widely documented
6	Accessible
8	Difficult to find
10	Incredibly well-concealed

The number of successes determines how much the character discovers. One success might mean that he uncovers the most obvious facts, while five successes might mean that he learns the full (and maybe truthful) story. Depending on the precise information the character seeks, 10 or 20 successes might be required to find all the available data.

The player might want to continue his research after only partial success. Continued research, however, takes longer than the initial search. Basic research usually takes only an hour — that's the first roll. More in-depth research (and a second roll) takes one complete day. If the player wants a third roll, further research takes a week; a fourth roll takes a month, a fifth roll takes a year. After that, use your imagination. It's easy to see how some research projects can take years or even decades to complete. Of course, some mages have all the time they need.

Coincidences: the library you use is a world-recognized repository for such information; the person you were asking about reminded someone of her ex-boyfriend; someone was researching the same thing and left a stack of reference books piled on a desk; it's the librarian's favorite topic.

Search

This system enables a character to search for something in a confined area, like a room. Have the player roll Perception + Investigation; the difficulty depends on how well concealed the object is (usually between 7 and 10). Each success indicates more is found. Sometimes a certain number of successes are required to find something hidden well. If you want, a lower number of successes could warrant a hint or clue where to look, thus encouraging roleplaying and a degree of puzzle-solving. Lead the player through the search step by step as much as possible. Have her describe to you where she looks. Don't let her succeed if she doesn't specifically search in the right area, and let her succeed automatically if her description is detailed enough.

Coincidences: just happens to look in the right spot the first time; someone forgot to put it away; it falls off a shelf.

Track

Mages can often track people and things by following their physical trails. To do so, a player rolls Perception + Survival (or Investigation in the city — tracks are rarely left on sidewalks and pavement, but people leave other impressions on their surroundings). The difficulty is based on weather conditions, terrain and the age of the tracks, but averages around 8. Each success beyond the first lowers the difficulty of the next roll by -1.

The character needs to succeed for a certain number of turns; the exact number depends on the length of the trail. Each turn is usually about five minutes long. If the character misses a roll, she can try again; this time, however, the difficulty is +1 higher. Once it goes above 10, the character loses the trail.

Coincidences: the ground is muddy; all the doors are locked from the outside and she didn't have the key; several people saw where he went; the quarry stopped to rest.

Cryptology

This system deciphers codes. The player must roll Intelligence + Linguistics or Intelligence + Computer if he is using a computer. The difficulty will normally be quite high (between 8-10, or less if the character uses a computer). Each success cracks more of the code, and multiple rolls can be made to accumulate successes. It can take anywhere from two to 20 successes to fully crack a code, depending on how complicated it is. Each "turn" can be from one minute to one month, depending on the needs of the story, the code's intricacy and the use (if any) of computers. Any failure indicates all collected successes are lost and the decoding process must restart from the beginning. A botch indicates total failure; the job can never be attempted again, or the character has misdeciphered the code.

To create a code, a character must roll Intelligence + Linguistics three times (difficulty 5). His total number of successes indicates the number of successes it takes to crack the code.

Coincidences: a baby's gurgling gives you a clue; you guessed that password during *Trivial Pursuit* yesterday; the number is the same as your birthday.

Combat

War is the trade of kings.

— John Dryden

In any war, bloodshed is inevitable. For mages, however, open combat can be a deadly affair. Without healing magicks, a single gunshot can stop an aspirant to Ascension for good. Magick is a balancing factor, but sorcerers are still well-advised to avoid melees whenever possible. **(See Chapter Eight for rules about magick in combat.)**

There are three basic types of combat: firefight, melee and brawl. Each uses the same essential system, yet they have some minor differences:

- A firefight is any type of armed combat using projectile weapons, things like Uzis and sawed-off shotguns. Opponents normally need to be within sight of each other in order to engage in a firefight.
- Melee refers to fighting with hand weapons — anything from broken bottles to magickal swords. Opponents need to be within one or two yards of each other in order to engage in melee.
- A brawl describes a hand-to-hand battle fought with bare hands — unarmed combat. Opponents need to be within touching distance to engage in a brawl.

With this system, each blow or gunshot is a separate roll which damages the target until it is either destroyed or incapacitated. Rolls made in combat determine whether or not an attack succeeds, whether the target dodges and how much damage the target suffers. Almost all combat turns are around three seconds long, though they take somewhat longer than that to resolve.

As with all action scenes, combat turns begin with an initiative roll. However, because combat can sometimes get a little sticky, divide the turn into three stages — Initiative, Attack and Resolution — to make it easier to keep track of things. **The Combat Summary Chart** breaks the whole thing into three easy steps; the detailed rules are below.

Stage One: Initiative

This stage organizes the turn. The players now declare their characters' actions — leaping behind a wall, shouting a warning, swinging a sledgehammer, whatever. Each player, in turn, must describe what his character is doing and with what, in as much detail as the Storyteller requires.

Characters make initiative rolls using Wits + Alertness (difficulty 4, adjusted as the Storyteller desires). Everyone takes their actions in descending order of successes — first goes first, and so on. Some characters will act simultaneously (they both rolled three successes, say). Those who rolled no successes at all go last, and those who botch don't get to act this turn. For simplicity, Storytellers may call for initiative only once per fight scene and use that order for the whole battle. Those who botch go last — something disastrous happens at the beginning of the fight which slows them for the whole scene — though they can still act. This option speeds play, though it limits characters' chances of "getting ahead" of their opponents — unless they can pull off some brilliant new move **(see "Surprise Maneuvers," below)**.

Players must declare their characters' actions before going to the Attack Stage. A mage splitting her Dice Pool must also declare how many dice to allocate to each action. The only action a character may take out of turn is a Dodge, which she can perform at any time as long as she has dice left in her Pool. Keeping a die or two in reserve is always a good idea!

Stage Two: Attack

The attack is the meat of the combat turn. It's where success or failure are determined, as well as any impact on the targets.

The Roll: There are three different types of attack rolls; the type of combat determines which one to use.

- For firearms combat, roll Dexterity + Firearms.
- For melee (with weapons) combat, roll Dexterity + Melee.

• For hand-to-hand (without weapons) combat, roll Dexterity + Brawl.

The weapon or attack determines the base difficulty of the attacker's roll. The number of dice might be modified by the gun's rate of fire or the use of a scope, but the difficulty is usually only modified by the circumstances around the attack. If no successes are obtained, the character has failed his attack, and no damage is inflicted. If the player rolls a botch, the attack fails, and something nasty happens, besides.

Dodging

Any time someone attacks a character, he has the option of dodging. In fact, a player may announce at any time that her character is using an action (or part of it, by dividing her Dice Pool) to dodge, simply by declaring "Dodge!" before the opponent makes an attack roll. In some cases a dodge may not be allowed, such as in confined quarters or in situations where the character has been surprised. The required roll is Dexterity + Dodge; each success subtracts one success from the attacker's roll.

• The difficulty to dodge melee or brawling attacks is a base 6, +1 for every opponent after the first.

• In firefights, the difficulty depends on the availability of nearby cover.

Each success removes one of the opponent's successes. A character can even take away successes from different opponents, though this means splitting successes between them. After such an attempt, the character usually ends up behind some sort of cover or, at the very least, lying on the ground (if there was no cover to be found).

The difficulty to dodge during firefights is determined by the proximity of cover.

Difficulty	Terrain
2	By moving back half a step, the character is back under full cover.
4	Full cover within diving distance (one yard)
6	Full cover within running distance (three yards)
7	Partial cover within running distance (three yards)
8	Flat and featureless, no cover (the character dives to the ground)

Stage Three: Resolution

In this stage, characters determine the damage inflicted by their attacks and the Storyteller describes what occurs in the turn. It's a mixture of game and story; though the dice never lie, the Storyteller must interpret what luck has decreed.

Damage: Each weapon or attack allows the wielder to roll a certain number of damage dice (difficulty 6). Each success removes one Health Level from the target. Additionally, each success scored with a firearm (after any dodge) adds one die to this damage roll. Melee and brawling successes do not add to the damage.

Soak: A target may make a roll to see how much damage she "soaks up" because of her natural hardiness. The target rolls Stamina (difficulty 6); each success reduces the damage by one.

Exception: Damage and soak rolls are two rolls in **Mage** that cannot be botched.

Complications

A number of factors determine whether an attack hits or not. Smart combatants head for cover as soon as bullets start flying. Others find that ganging up on one foe in a brawl never hurts. The following modifiers delineate many of the variables that affect combat.

General Complications

• **Changing Actions:** If a character changes her declared action after the turn has started, the difficulty for the new action increases by +1. Generally, the Storyteller should only allow the character to change her declared action if events have made it impossible. "Yes, I know I said my character would jump into the car, but that Technomancer just blew it up!"

• **Immobilization:** If a target is immobilized (e.g., held down by someone), but still struggles, the difficulty for the attack roll is lowered by -2. However, if the target is completely immobilized (e.g., is tied up or magickally paralyzed), then no roll is required and the attack succeeds automatically.

Firefight Complications

• **Range:** Getting close to one's foe is a good idea if a character doesn't mind taking a few shots in return. The range given on the Firearms Chart is the weapon's medium range. The character receives no modifier for shooting at this range. Twice that range is the farthest the weapon can shoot. Shots within this range have their difficulties increased by +1. On the other hand, shots made at targets within a yard of the attacker are considered "point-blank"; the difficulty of a point-blank shot is 4.

• **Cover:** Intelligent characters use cover to protect themselves from enemy fire. Cover increases the difficulty of an attack, depending on how much of the character's body is still out in the open. Though cover protects, it can also hamper return fire, and in some rare instances it can completely prevent any return fire. Ducking out from around a corner to shoot may increase the difficulty by +1, while watching a shoot-out through the cracks in a battered wall prevents a character from firing back at all.

Cover	Difficulty
Lying flat	+ 1
Behind pole	+ 2
Behind wall	+ 3
Only head exposed	+ 4

• **Movement:** Shooting at a moving target increases the difficulty by +1 (or even more), as does shooting while moving at any speed faster than a walk (such as firing out the window of a speeding car).

• **Aiming:** A character may add her Perception rating to her Dexterity + Firearms Dice Pool if she spends time aiming. However, it takes one turn for each die added, and during this time the character can do nothing but aim — it takes time and patience to aim. Additionally, the target may not be moving at a speed faster than a walk. Shotguns and SMGs cannot be aimed.

If the gun has a scope, the character may add two dice to her Pool in addition to the dice added for Perception. The scope bonus can only be used once per shot — after the initial three dice added in the first round (two for the scope and one for Perception), the character continues aiming as outlined above.

• **Targeting:** Aiming for a specific location (gun hand, the heart) increases the difficulty by +2.

• **Multiple Shots:** If a character wants to take more than one shot in a turn, he must divide his Dice Pool into two or more actions. Also, for every additional shot after the first, the difficulty increases by +1. 10 is, of course, the maximum number to which the difficulty can be raised. A character can only take as many shots as allowed by the rate of the firearm.

This penalty is cumulative. Thus a character adds +2 on the third shot and +3 on the fourth. It is not usually wise to snap shots off blindly; the recoil always catches up with the gunman. Using these rules, it is permissible to fire two or more three-round bursts in a single turn, though a character can only fire on full-auto once per turn (and must reload to do it again).

• **Full-Auto:** The full-auto option is the most damaging attack a firearm can make, as the attacker unloads the full contents of a gun's ammunition clip within a very short time span. However, the gun becomes a bucking bronco, difficult to control and even harder to aim.

A character gets 10 additional dice to roll on the attack, thus increasing the chance to hit and cause damage. However, the difficulty goes up +2 from the recoil.

Full-auto fire can only be done when a weapon has more than half its clip remaining. Whenever a character uses the full-auto option, he uses up the entire clip of the weapon. Reloading takes one full action and requires the character's full concentration (and Dice Pool).

• **Three-Round Burst:** The semi-auto option is the middle ground between the full-auto and the single-shot options, and has some of the strengths and weaknesses of both. A burst gives the attacker three additional dice on the attack roll. However, the recoil increases the difficulty by +1.

• **Spray:** When using full-auto, a gunman can decide to spray across an area instead of focusing on one foe. A spray uses the extra 10 dice given by full-auto fire, but the attack has a base difficulty of 5, increased by +1 for every yard covered by the spray, in addition to other modifiers.

The player divides any successes gained on the attack roll evenly between all targets in the covered area. However, if only one target is in the sprayed area, only half the successes affect him. The player then assigns any leftover successes as she desires. If the attacker rolls fewer successes than there are targets, the player may only assign one to a target until they are used up. This attack also empties the clip.

The difficulty of a dodge roll against a spray is increased by +2.

Melee and Brawling Complications

• **Multiple Opponents:** If a character is battling multiple opponents in close combat, that character's attack and dodge difficulties are increased by +1 per opponent (to a maximum of 10).

• **Flank and Rear Attacks:** The difficulty of a flank attack is lowered by one, while that of a rear attack is lowered by - 2.

• **Grapple:** An attacker can try to grab a foe, hoping to immobilize and subsequently crush him. If the attacker scores more successes than the opponent's Strength, the attacker can pin him. In the next round, she can begin to inflict harm. Any character struck by this attack loses his attacks for the current turn. If the attacker misses altogether (by failing the Dexterity + Brawl roll), she is knocked down and must spend an action getting to her feet.

Continuing to grapple during each turn after the first requires the combatants to make opposed Strength + Brawl rolls. Whoever accumulates more successes may immobilize the other. If both score the same number of successes, neither gains the upper hand this turn.

• **Body Slam:** A character may also try to charge forward, hurling his weight into his opponent in an attempt to damage her. It's possible to hurt oneself with this attack, as bodies were not meant to be used as battering rams. A character needs three successes to unbalance an opponent and does one Health Level of damage to himself for every success fewer than three.

If the attack succeeds, the opponent is thrown off balance, and the difficulties for the rest of her actions for this round are increased by +2. Also, if the opponent does not succeed in a Dexterity + Athletics roll (difficulty of the successes +3), she falls to the ground. The base damage done by the attacker equals his Strength; each success scored on the attack roll above the minimum adds one to this base. If the attacker does not roll at least three successes, this maneuver fails; he falls to the ground and is treated as though he had no dice left in his Pool.

Surprise Maneuvers

Warfare is not a static activity; clever mages may come up with moves which startle their opponents, giving that mage an edge. Sucker-punches, off-the-wall ricochets, sudden leaps, secret katas, crotch-kicks, hair-pulls, disarms, feints, thrown salt and a million other dirty tricks and arcane maneuvers may help to turn an attacker's attention away for a vital spilt-second, and... .

The Storyteller can reflect these variations with "freeform combat." If a player describes a clever move, the Storyteller assigns him a difficulty, and possibly a number of successes, to pull that feat off. The Traits used should reflect the maneuver: a trick shot would require an Attribute + Firearms; a weapon attack, Melee; a low blow, Brawl; and an acrobatic move, Athletics. Martial art surprises would utilize either Brawl or Do, if the character knows Do. Physical Traits are not the only ones you could use. Manipulation can trick an opponent, or Intelligence or Perception could spot an opening in his defenses. Appearance might get him to drop his guard, and quick Wits can grant the mage that one chance she needs....

The player must decide what she wants to accomplish. Success might hurt the opponent — deliver an extra Health Level or two of damage, knock him over, blind him for a turn or so, disrupt his magick, send his weapon flying, etc., — or give the player character an edge — a chance to re-roll her initiative, grab her opponent and hang on, reduce her difficulty by -1 or 2, get her out of harm's way, etc. The more effective the feat, the higher the difficulty. **A few sample maneuvers are given on the Combat Chart page.**

Even a failure might have some significant effect, even if it's not the one the player wanted. A botch should be a disaster, one which puts the mage in a truly tense situation. This, if nothing else, may keep players from abusing the special maneuver rule.

This variation should not be abused. Storytellers may feel free to declare a certain maneuver predictable (especially if the character uses the same trick to excess), raise the stunt's difficulty, or ignore this rule altogether if she feels a player is trying to get away with murder. Used properly, though, this variation adds a lot of flexibility to an otherwise mundane fight.

Armor

A character with body armor can add dice to her soak rolls. Different types of body armor have different armor ratings, which are the number of extra dice rolled on a soak roll. Certain types of armor restrict body motion, reducing the character's Dexterity rolls. Any rolls involving this Attribute have their difficulties raised by an amount equal to the penalty. **(See the chart for details.)**

Magick in Combat

Magick doesn't complicate combat very much at all. If a mage uses a focus to create an Effect, he may have to make his initiative roll at a higher difficulty than normal. Of course, this difficulty is determined by the focus; a Dreamspeaker who needs to shake a rattle probably won't incur a penalty, while a Hollow One who prefers extemporaneous poetry might have to add +3 to her initiative difficulty. **(See "Foci," Chapter Eight.)**

If the mage does not need a focus to create the desired magickal Effect, he makes the usual Initiative roll (Wits + Alertness, difficulty 4) and casts the spell as a normal action. Magick willed into existence without the use of props happens instantaneously, though some coincidences used to explain that magick may still take time to unfold. Work these incidents into the flow of the story as required. An extended spell will begin on the mage's initiative, and he continues to make rolls as needed during each of his following actions.

Like other systems **(see "Abilities and Magick")**, a magickal "push" may enhance the effects of an otherwise normal attack. For each magickal success, add one success to the attack or damage, up to a maximum of three (remember the magic bullet?). Like any other use of the Art, such "pushes" are subject to all the rules of magick.

Chapter Eight contains the details of magick use. Keep in mind that too many things occurring at once can be distracting. If you are at a tense point in the story and a Paradox backlash comes up, you might overlook it for now and simply declare a botch on an Effect the mage casts later (even though the mage may make that roll!); alternately, the mage may take the Paradox (Storyteller's option), mark it down and suffer the effects later.

Coincidences in Combat

While mages are not adverse to carrying guns (especially when their weapons are enchanted Talismans), many rely on magick to subdue (or avoid) their foes during combat. Innumerable coincidental Effects can occur in combat and enhance a weapon's efficiency (see above). To get your fiendishly clever juices flowing, a few are listed below.

P.S. Remember that objects that were not present must be made, and ones that were normal must be modified, with the proper Spheres.

P.P.S. Remember the Domino Effect.

• **Firefight:** the opponent's gun jams; the opponent's gun is not loaded; his shot happens to miss the lung by an inch; your shot is that inch closer; a bullet ricochets off several surfaces and hits the gunman; the rifle's sight is crooked just enough to compensate for your bad shooting; the gun you picked up has a full clip or is specially modified to hold a larger clip; you trip to the ground just as an assassin fires a bullet at you.

• **Melee and Brawling:** he misses you, and his weapon lodges in a door; you have a secret ankle sheath; her weapon gets snagged in her sheath as she draws it; your shot pinches a nerve; he falls on his funny bone; his old back pain (or war wound) flares up; she slips on something or loses her weapon; he has a glass jaw; blood runs into her eyes so she can't see clearly.

• **Damaging your opponent:** he twists a leg (maybe it breaks); a car swerves off the road and hits her; his brakes fail; the fall knocks the breath out of her; the blow doesn't seem to do much, but induces internal hemorrhaging; your punch is just right and drives fragments of the nose into the brain; she misses you and breaks her hand against the wall; the fence is electrocuted; a gas main blows; there are sharks in the water; it's not a tub of water — it's sulfuric acid; the TV blows up and sprays glass across the room.

Do Maneuvers

Practitioners of Do have many combat advantages. The simplest strikes utilize the human body's maximum potential for efficient damage. This allows a Do stylist to roll his Dexterity + Do and add his successes to a base amount of damage. The Do Strike Chart gives the various basic maneuvers and their difficulties and damage bases.

Do works on various levels; it is a fighting art, a magickal focus, a philosophy and a self-discipline tool. Advanced stylists can perform mighty non-magickal feats which are beyond the scope of this rulebook.

Umbral Combat

When a mage enters the Umbra by any physical means (by "stepping sideways" or opening a Gauntlet gate), she passes into a world where the usual laws of reality do not apply. Paradox exists, albeit reduced. All magick is considered coincidental in the Near Umbra, no matter what form it takes. There is no Paradox *at all* in the Deep Umbra, so really spectacular Effects are possible.

All mortals' attack difficulties increase by +1 in the Umbra. Material beings cannot physically harm spirits unless the Umbrood Materializes **(see "Umbrood," Chapter Nine)**. Mages with three dots or better in Spirit can sidestep this rule; all others just swipe at ephemera. Guns are no good here. Life and Matter magick are worthless unless the Umbrood Materializes. The Spirit Sphere acts as Life magick when used against beings of ephemera (and Matter when used against inanimate ephemera), while Entropy 4 + Prime 2 inflicts damage against such beings on their home ground.

Attacks which go against an Umbrood's Attribute (i.e., a spirit dodging to avoid an incoming Force bolt) are figured against its Willpower. In other words, the dodging spirit would roll its Willpower against the mage's successes instead of its Dexterity + Dodge.

Fighting Spirits

Spirits do not physically attack. A hostile spirit rolls its Willpower to hit instead, then rolls its Rage to do damage (if it succeeded in the first roll), both at difficulty 6. The Umbrood is taking out its anger on the offender, not physically assaulting her (unless it's Materialized, of course). Each success rolled inflicts one aggravated Health Level of damage. A mage can soak this with either Spirit (and only Spirit) countermagick, difficulty 6, or by rolling her Arete against difficulty 8. Each success reduces the spirit's damage by one Health Level. Spirits who fight each other reduce each other's Power, not Health.

A Materialized spirit attacks, soaks or defends using its Materialized Attributes, though Gnosis stills stands in for Social and Mental Traits. Spirits cannot soak damage unless they have the Armor Charm. While a Materialized spirit can take aggravated damage on Earth, spirits feel no difference between damage types in the Umbra (ouch). Ephemeral beings reduced below zero Power dissipate, sometimes to re-form later, sometimes to die completely.

Combat Summary Chart

Stage One: Initiative

- Roll Wits + Alertness (difficulty 4). The winner declares her action *last* (after she has heard everyone else's actions) and performs it *first*.
- Declare Dice Pool division if performing multiple actions.
- Declare any magick cast. Only one magick roll may be made each turn.

Stage Two: Attack

- For firearms combat, roll Dexterity + Firearms.
- For melee (with weapons) combat, roll Dexterity + Melee.
- For hand-to-hand (without weapons) combat, roll Dexterity + Brawl.
- Dodge: roll Dexterity + Dodge. A character can forfeit some or all of his Dice Pool to dodge at any time; each success subtracts one from the opponent's successes.

Stage Three: Resolution

- Roll damage, determined by weapon or maneuver (difficulty 6).
- Soak damage: roll Stamina (difficulty 6).

General Complications

- **Changing Actions:** The difficulty increases by +1.
- **Immobilization:** The difficulty to hit an immobilized target is decreased by -2.
- **Stunning:** When Health Level damage exceeds Stamina rating, the target is stunned and cannot act next turn.

Melee Weapons Table

Weapon	Difficulty	Damage	Conceal
Sap	4	Strength	P
Club	4	Strength +1	T
Knife	4	Strength +1	J
Foil	5	Strength +3	T
Saber	6	Strength +4	T
Axe	7	Strength +5	N

Brawling Table

Maneuver	Difficulty	Damage
Punch	6	Strength
Grapple	6	Strength
Kick	7	Strength +1
Body slam	7	Special; see Options
Bite *	5	Strength +1
Claw *	6	Strength +2

* When applicable

Spirit Combat Table

Stage One: Initiative

- As above. Spirits roll Willpower for initiative.

Stage Two: Resolution

- Roll Willpower (difficulty 6) unless a Charm is being used (refer to the Charm description)
- Dodge: Willpower (difficulty 6), or split Willpower Dice Pool between attack and dodge.

Stage Two: Resolution

- Roll Rage (difficulty 6); one Health Level of aggravated damage is inflicted per success (mages with the Spirit Sphere can soak this with countermagick, difficulty 6. Other mages can soak with an Arete roll, difficulty 8); one Power point per success is lost if the target is a spirit.
- Soak damage: spirits cannot soak damage.

Firefight Complications

Complication	Difficulty	Dice
Changing action	+1	—
Immobilization	-2	—
Long range	+1	—
Point-blank	4	—
Lying flat	+1	—
Behind pole	+2	—
Behind wall	+3	—
Only head exposed	+4	—
Movement	+1	—
Aiming	—	+ Perception
Scope	—	+2
Specific area of target	+2	—
Multiple shots	+1/extra shot	
Full-auto	+3	+10
Three-round burst	+1	+3
Spray	5 +1/yard	+10

Surprise Maneuvers

Sample Feats	Difficulty	Successes
Extra damage	+2 per Health Level	one
+1 initiative	7	two or more
Acrobatic flip	7-10	one or more
Disarm	8	two or more
Escape	8	one per yard moved
Blind foe	9	one per turn

Armor

Class	Armor Rating	Penalty
Class One (reinforced clothing)	1	0
Class Two (armored T-shirt)	2	1
Class Three (vest)	3	2
Class Four (flak jacket)	4	3
Class Five (full suit)	6	4

Dodges

A normal hand-to-hand dodge difficulty is 6; for firefights, see below:

Difficulty	Terrain
2	By moving back half a step, the character is back under full cover.
4	Full cover within diving distance (one yard)
6	Full cover within running distance (three yards)
7	Partial cover within running distance (three yards)
8	Flat and featureless, no cover (the character dives to the ground)

Do Strike Chart

Maneuver	Difficulty	Damage
Punch	6	3 + Successes
Kick	7	4 + Successes
Flying kick	8	5 + Successes
Throw	8	3 + Successes + 2' per success

Firearms Table

Type	Difficulty	Damage	Range	Rate	Clip	Concealment
Example						
Revolver, Lt. SW M640 (.38 Special)	6	4	12	3	6	P
Revolver, Hvy. Colt Anaconda (.44 magnum)	7	6	35	2	6	J
Pistol, Lt. Glock-17 (9mm)	7	4	20	4	17+1	P
Pistol, Hvy. Sig P220 (.45 ACP)	8	5	30	3	7+1	J
Rifle Remington M-700 (.30-06)	8	8	200	1	5+1	N
SMG, Small* Ingram Mac-10 (9mm)	7	4	25	3	30+1	J
SMG, Large* UZI (9mm)	6	4	50	3	32+1	T
Assault Rifle* Steyr-Aug (5.56mm)	7	7	150	3	42+1	N
Shotgun Ithaca M-37 (12-gauge)	6	8	20	1	5+1	T
Shotgun, Semi-auto Fianchi Law-12 (12 gauge)	7	8	20	3	8+1	T
Crossbow**	7	5	20	1	1	T

Range: This is the practical range of the gun in yards. A character may fire up to double the listed range; however, that is considered a long-range shot.

Rate: The maximum number of bullets or three-round bursts the gun can fire in a single turn. The rate does not apply to full-auto or spray fire.

Clip: The number of bullets that can be held in one clip or in the barrel. The +1 indicates a bullet can be held in the chamber, making the gun ready to fire.

Concealment: P = can be hidden in a pocket; J = can be hidden inside a jacket; T = can be hidden inside a trenchcoat; N = cannot be hidden on one's person at all.

* indicates the gun is capable of three-round bursts, full-auto fire and sprays.

** The crossbow is included with this list for those characters who wish to use one to stake vampires. However, unlike firearms, it does not add successes on the attack roll to the Dice Pool for damage. Additionally, a crossbow takes five turns to reload.

Injury

Attention to health is the greatest hindrance to life.
— Plato

The inevitable result of combat, injuries are gauged by Health Levels **(see Chapter Six)**. Each wound causes the loss of one Health Level. The player simply checks off Health Levels as her character loses them; the last check made indicates the character's current Health Level. As the character heals the damage, her player erases the check marks.

Think of Health as a spectrum with Bruised at one end and Incapacitated at the other. As a character takes more wounds, she travels down that spectrum until she finally reaches Incapacitated. When she heals, she simply removes the checks one by one, until she is again in perfect health.

Each success on an opponent's damage roll indicates a loss of one Health Level. If a foe scores two successes, the player checks off two Health Levels, starting with Bruised and going down to Hurt. If a mage takes damage beyond the Incapacitated Level, she dies. Once a mage dies, her Avatar flees into the spirit world, to be reconstituted and reintroduced into the human race as new people are born.

Injury hurts in more ways than one. Listed next to each Health Level on the character sheet is a penalty number. This number is subtracted from all the character's Dice Pools. A mage who is Wounded, for example, would have two fewer dice to roll on all Dice Pools as long as her condition remains Wounded. This subtraction reflects the crippling effects of the wounds the character has received. These penalties do not apply to Arete rolls, but they do subtract from Willpower rolls.

Wounds

Damage can have different effects on a character, depending on the nature of the injury. Naturally, mages can heal themselves and others through Life magicks **(see below)**.

Stunning (Optional Rule)

If a mage takes more damage from a single attack than she has Stamina dots, she may, at Storyteller's option, be stunned for the next turn. This alternative can be deadly when used on (relatively weak) mages, but stunning your opponent may be the only way to survive an encounter with a werewolf or mythic monster.

Aggravated Wounds

Mages occasionally suffer wounds so terrible that even magick will not heal them. These wounds are called aggravated wounds, and a mage can only heal them through the painfully slow natural process, shown on the **Normal Healing Time** chart, or by using vulgar magick and spending a point of Quintessence per Health Level healed. Common sources of aggravated wounds include the claws of vampires and werewolves, weapon Talismans, acid and toxic waste, vulgar Life and Entropy Effects and attacks by angry spirits.

Aggravated wounds should be indicated on the character sheet with an X rather than a check.

Death

For all their power, mages are mortal. Without recourse to healing magicks, they often die from severe injuries. When someone reaches Incapacitated, he is one Health Level away from death. If he is injured one more time, or if the flow of blood from his body cannot be stanched, he will die.

Sources of Injury

There are many ways to inflict harm upon a character. These sources of injury are described below. Note that damage to mages is applied exactly like damage to Sleepers. Only after damage has been calculated does the player get to reduce the effects with magick, provided the damage is not aggravated.

Combat

See the previous section. Each success on a damage roll causes the character to lose one Health Level.

Disease and Poison

Poison and human diseases affect mages like they would any other mortal. The Awakened, however, do not generally die from by mundane means — their powers of recuperation are better than that. Health Levels lost to disease or poison are assumed to be normal wounds. Once they're healed, the person is cured. Some severe diseases and vicious poisons must be treated as aggravated wounds — the mage's coincidental miraculous recovery must take a certain amount of time. The only other option is vulgar magick (and wasted Quintessence).

Falling

The sad result of missing that much-needed Dexterity + Athletics roll. Use the falling chart to calculate damage. Characters can make Stamina rolls to try to "soak" damage, though; the difficulty is an 8. Each success means one fewer Health Level is lost (the mage happens to fall into the passing garbage truck, etc.). Each botch means an additional Health Level is lost.

Fire

Fire, it's often said, is the worst way to go. A character struck (or worse still, enveloped) by flames takes damage according to the Fire chart. The player may roll a number of dice equal to the character's Stamina rating against the difficulties listed below. The player must roll each turn the character is in the flames to see if she can resist the damage. If the roll fails, the character takes from one to three Health Levels of damage (see the second chart). If the roll succeeds, the character takes one fewer Health Level of damage per success than she normally would. If the roll is botched, the character is harmed in some special way — perhaps she loses her eyesight or her limbs are maimed. This may account for the Verbena's hatred of Inquisitors.

Suffocation and Drowning

Without air, even mages will die. A sorcerer can hold her breath for a length of time based on her Stamina (see chart) — she can even extend this time by spending Willpower points (one for every additional 30 seconds). If she cannot get air by the time her options run out, she suffocates or drowns at a rate of one Health Level per turn. While this is not aggravated damage, she cannot heal it until she leaves that hostile environment. Once she reaches Incapacitated, the mage dies within one minute per point of Stamina.

Healing

The human body has an amazing ability to repair itself. Given time and proper health care, humans can recover Health Levels based on the chart. Time given is the length of time it takes to recover that particular Health Level — other Levels must also be healed. Thus, if the character takes three months to recover from being Mauled, she must still take the time to heal Wounded, Injured and so on.

Magick, naturally, can speed this process immeasurably. The Sphere of Life has a variety of magickal Effects that accelerate the body's healing ability **(see Chapter Eight)**. Healing magick can even be performed as coincidental magick: the bullet only grazed a rib or hit a lucky whiskey flask that the mage just happens to be carrying in her chest pocket (creating the flask requires Matter + Prime, just for the record).

Injury Charts

Fire

Difficulty	Heat of Fire
3	Heat of a candle (first-degree burns)
5	Heat of a torch (second-degree burns)
7	Heat of a Bunsen burner (third-degree burns)
9	Heat of a chemical fire
10	Molten metal
Wounds	**Size of Fire**
One	Torch; part of body burned
Two	Bonfire; half of body burned
Three	Raging inferno; entire body burned

Drowning/Suffocation

Stamina	Holding Breath
1	30 seconds
2	One minute
3	Two minutes
4	Four minutes
5	Eight minutes
6	15 minutes
7	20 minutes
8	30 minutes (!)

Normal Healing Times

Health Level	Time
Bruised	One day
Hurt	Three days
Injured	One week
Wounded	One month
Mauled	Three months
Crippled	Three months
Incapacitated	Three months

Falling

Distance (in feet)	Injury
Five:	One Health Level
Ten:	Two Health Levels
Twenty:	Three Health Levels
Thirty:	Four Health Levels
Forty:	Five Health Levels
Fifty:	Six Health Levels
Sixty:	Seven Health Levels

and so on, to a maximum of 10 Health Levels.

FOR THE FIRST TIME SINCE BETH'S DEATH, I FEEL FREE. OUT HERE, IT FEELS LIKE HOME.
THE REAL WORLD SHIFTS OUT AS I GO ON AUTOPILOT. MAGICK CALLS TO ME AND I ANSWER.

BRAVO! BRILLIANT!
WHA?
IT'S BEEN A LONG TIME SINCE I HAD SUCH REMARKABLE COMPANY.
SORRY... DIDN'T MEAN TO, UM, INTRUDE.
NO INTRUSION. I'M GLAD, REALLY. IT'S QUIET UP HERE... AND LONELY.
THERE'S NO NEED TO BE EMBARRASSED. I'M GLAD TO HAVE SOME COMPANY. WHO ARE YOU?
UH, JENNIFER... AND YOU'RE?
CALL ME MARILLION.

Example of Play

The latest installment of Wendy's chronicle, "Passions of Wolves," finds her player characters Jennifer (Phil) and Atropos (Shadow, and yes, that's her real name) climbing a mountain in search of a glen Node, rumored to have been the site that inspired Jennifer's mentor, Beth. Jennifer, a Verbena artist, is thoroughly enjoying the hike; out here, she feels alive. Atropos, her best friend and a Hollow One, would be much more comfortable in a bar, or better yet, in bed.

Wendy has decided that the Node has a new resident — a vagabond Umbrood who goes by the name "Marillion." He shacked out at the Node after Beth's last visit, and has found it to his liking.

Because Jennifer's Stamina and Athletics total almost twice Atropos' scores, Wendy lets her get a big lead without rolling any dice. Phil says his character wouldn't care about Atropos falling behind; after all, she's eager to be here. When she reaches the top, she breaks into a spontaneous ecstatic dance. It doesn't go unnoticed.

As Jennifer enters the glen, Marillion generates an Entrance Charm **(see "Spirit Rules")**. His Gnosis is 7, more than her Willpower. Wendy wants trouble, so she gives him an automatic success, then tells Phil to make Jennifer's Perception (3) + Alertness (3) roll. Normally, this would be at difficulty 6 (standard), but Jennifer is preoccupied; her difficulty is 9. Phil rolls his six dice: 6, 1, 3, 2, 1 and 4. A botch. Marillion has taken Jennifer by surprise.

As Marillion approaches, Wendy initiates a seduction attempt: Appearance + Subterfuge — a total of seven dice. Jennifer's Wits are average (2), so Marillion's difficulty is 5. The spirit has more than enough to get an automatic success. She rolls anyway. Five successes! Jennifer is hooked — and flustered.

Wendy and Phil roleplay, though Phil is suspicious of all her die-rolling. Wendy tells him Marillion is irresistibly attractive, then rolls again (Wits + Subterfuge), just to keep Jennifer from breaking off. She gets three more successes. "Hey!" cries Shadow. "What about me?"

DAMMIT, JEN, YOU COULD AT LEAST HAVE LET ME...
WHAT THE HELL?
I DIDN'T REALIZE YOU HAD A... FRIEND.
WHAT'S YOUR PROBLEM?
GOD, ATROPOS, YOUR TIMING IS AS GREAT AS EVER
NOTHING WORTH SPEAKING OF.
HOLD ON A MINUTE... LET'S SEE WHAT YOU REALLY LOOK LIKE, LOVERBOY.
OH, FOR...
HA
HA
HA
WHAT'S SO FUNNY?
LOOK FOR YOURSELF.

Wendy has Shadow stagger into the clearing, then describes what Atropos sees.
Shadow, Phil and Wendy roleplay. Phil takes the die rolls into account and brushes Atropos off. Wendy has Shadow roll Perception (4) + Awareness (3), difficulty 7. She rolls 7, 5, 7, 4, 3, 9 and 5 — three successes. Something's wrong.
Shadow decides to use **Spirit Sight** (Spirit 1); Atropos takes out her foci and rolls them. Shadow rolls her Arete (4); Wendy lowers the difficulty (normally 4) by -1 because of the Node. Four successes!
On a slip of folded paper, Wendy jots down Marillion's true appearance and passes it to Shadow, who opens it and laughs.
Shadow decides to extend the **Sprit Sight** to Jennifer. This technically requires another roll, but Wendy lets it slide. Shadow passes the description to Phil. Both women like his reaction. Since Marillion does nothing this turn, Wendy has him prepare a surprise....

I WISH YOU HADN'T DONE THAT. NOW I'LL HAVE TO HURT YOU.
OH, GOD..
AND THEN SOME.
CAN'T YOU EVER PICK UP SOMEONE NORMAL, JEN?
A GUN? YOU MUST BE JOKING!
I DOUBT BULLETS'LL STOP THAT THING.
MAYBE MAGICK WILL.
AAGHH!
THIS PLACE IS MINE, TRESPASSERS! ANY QUESTIONS?
RRRRR!
WHAT?
I GOT US INTO THIS. TIME TO CLEAN UP THE MESS.

Wendy, in an exuberant burst of roleplaying, leaps from her chair, mimicking the thing Marillion has just called forth. This breaks the Charm, so Jennifer can react normally. All three roll initiative (Wits + Alertness, difficulty 4). Atropos, rolling 3, 5, 8, 2, 6 and 10, goes first. Jennifer, with 2, 5, 1, 7 and 8, goes next. Wendy rolls badly for the two Umbrood — 1, 4, 6, 5 and 1. They go last.

Because she's got a Lt. Revolver, Atropos gets three shots. Shadow splits her Dexterity + Firearms Dice Pool (total eight dice) between two of them. Wendy lowers the difficulty by -1 because of the creature's size. Shadow rolls; two successes with one, three successes with the other — great for four dice! The creature has to soak one wound worth six Health Levels and another worth seven.

Wendy rolls two soak rolls (Stamina, difficulty 6), deciding to make the monster's Dice Pool pretty high. She exercises a bit of Storyteller prerogative and hefts seven dice. As Phil and Shadow moan, she rolls: five successes on the first, four on the next. The beast takes a total of four Health Levels. It's hurt, but not by much — it's big!

Phil declares that Jennifer is beginning an Effect — **Lesser Shapeshifting** (Life 4). He describes Jennifer's painful (but appropriate) style of magick: live rune-carving. It'll take him two successes; because this is *vulgar without witnesses*, his difficulty is 7. Wendy lowers it by -2 (to 5) because of the Node — it's attuned to this kind of magick. Phil rolls; one success. Close, but not enough. He throws in a point of Willpower and Jennifer begins to change…

Wendy rolls the creature's attack (Dexterity + Brawl, difficulty 6); three successes. She estimates the beast's Strength to be about 5 (enough to hurt, but not enough to demolish the mages) and rolls two Health Levels worth of damage to Atropos. Shadow tries to soak it, but fails.

Wendy has Marillion grow claws — with his **Materialize**, he can change his form as he sees fit — and advance on Atropos. End of turn.

The three roll initiative again. Phil wins, with 4 successes, and has Jennifer, now transformed, leap at the monster. His attack roll will be her Dexterity (4) + Brawl (3), difficulty 6 (for claws). Phil picks up his dice and rolls…

The world comes to us in an endless stream of puzzle pieces that we would like to think all fit together somehow, but that in fact never do.
— Robert Pirsig, *Lila*

Antagonists

Sleepers

Don't let your mages' mastery of the Arts fool you into thinking that mundane humans are push-overs. There are quite a few organizations in the World of Darkness that are as dangerous to the Awakened as they are to each other.

Governments

When a nation forms a government, it is not wisdom, but power which they place in the hands of the magistrate.
— Charles Sprading, *Freedom and its Fundamentals*

How much do the world governments suspect? How much do they know? How firmly are they under the control of mages or other supernatural entities? It's hard to say. Many governments have agencies or departments devoted to the investigation of paranormal occurrences. Most of these, especially on the military end, seem to be devoted to extrasensory phenomena such as ESP, clairvoyance and telekinesis.

Rumors circulate that the United States government funds some special research, designated "Project PSI," and has achieved a measure of success. Has the government managed to Awaken test subjects? And what about the number of mages who have disappeared in the last few years…? In general, though, these departments seem to be concentrating on their own "ground-breaking" research.

Britain also has an organization devoted to the investigation of the paranormal, but it's difficult to trace. Some suspect some connections to similar organizations dating back hundreds of years. British mysticks report that Scotland Yard has investigated mage-related incidents with unnerving accuracy. Some say that a vampire actually controls this group, using it to combat her enemies.

In the United States, interest in magickal activity can be traced to two agencies: the Federal Bureau of Investigation and the National Security Agency.

The FBI might contain several individuals who suspect the truth, and a special department devoted to the investigation of the paranormal could exist. Originally formed to neutralize the impact of suspected "Communist Thought Control" research, this department, known generally as Special Affairs (though its members rarely identify themselves as such) is involved in continuing investigations. It is believed that some of Special Affairs' investigations into paranormal activities in the '50s and '60s may have uncovered some mage-related information. Despite this, Special Affairs has dwindled significantly in power and members over the years. The FBI demands proof of suspected activities before action can be taken, and hard proof has eluded the Sleepers within the department. Circumstantial evidence of magickal activity no doubt abounds, but that last, necessary piece of tangible evidence has escaped Special Affairs — so far.

It is believed that the NSA, a giant fact-sifting agency concerned with national security, keeps an active file on supernatural events, especially significant Paradox effects, but treats odd events as a subclassification of terrorism. The agency has not yet made the connections that would reveal the whole picture; instead, it flags police and news reports that contain interesting or anomalous facts. Investigation only occurs after the computer, or a reviewer, notices weird occurrences that may be related. While many believe that the NWO receives information straight from the agency's files, no one knows for sure how much the Sleepers themselves might know. The resources that could be brought to bear if the truth were discovered, are truly frightening.

• **Police Officer:** At one time or another, mages will find themselves on the wrong side of the law. Most local cops patrol in police cruisers. Help is only a radio call away, and usually one to five other cars arrive within minutes of an emergency call. In extreme emergencies, up to 50 other police officers can be called in to help within 10 minutes (at least in a city).

Character Creation: Attributes 7/5/3, Abilities 15/9/3, Backgrounds 7, Willpower 6

Suggested Attributes: Assume ratings of 2, except for Physical Traits where you can assume ratings of 3.

Suggested Abilities: Alertness 2, Brawl 2, Bureaucracy 1, Computer 1, Dodge 2, Drive 2, Firearms 3, Investigation 2, Law 2, Leadership 1, Melee 1, Police Procedure 3, Stealth 1, Streetwise 1, Technology 1

Equipment: Lt. Revolver, Lt. Auto. Pistol, Pump Shotgun, Billy Club, Handcuffs, Radio, Badge, Flashlight

• **Police Detective:** Police detectives are called to the scenes of murders and other major crimes. Unearthly crimes will bring detectives running. These statistics are also good for private eyes, who may work as acolytes for interested parties.

Character Creation: Attributes 8/5/3, Abilities 17/9/3, Backgrounds 7, Willpower 7

Suggested Attributes: Assume ratings of 2, except for Perception and Wits, where you can assume ratings of 3 or even 4.

Suggested Abilities: Alertness 3, Brawl 2, Bureaucracy 1, Computer 2, Dodge 1, Drive 2, Firearms 3, Intimidation 1, Investigation 4, Law 2, Leadership 2, Melee 1, Police Procedure 4, Stealth 1, Streetwise 4, Subterfuge 3, Technology 2

Equipment: Lt. Revolver, Lt. Auto. Pistol, Handcuffs, Radio, Badge, Flashlight

• **Government Agent:** These characters can be from the FBI, the NSA, the CIA, Project PSI (seeking mystick "recruits") or whatever local government agency is appropriate. They will often have a great deal of backup and authority.

Character Creation: Attributes 9/5/4, Abilities 18/10/6, Background 7, Willpower 8

Suggested Attributes: Assume ratings of 2, except for Perception and Intelligence, where you can assume ratings of at least 3.

Suggested Abilities: Alertness 3, Athletics 1, Brawl 3, Bureaucracy 2, Computers 1, Dodge 2, Drive 3, Expression 1, Firearms 3, Intimidation 2, Investigation 4, Law 3, Leadership 3, Police Procedure 5, Politics 1, Stealth 3, Subterfuge 1, Technology 2

Equipment: Lt. Revolver, Hvy. Auto. Pistol, Submachine Gun, Video Camera, Forensics Lab, Portable Phone Tap, Portable Lie Detector, Bugs, Class II Armor, Mirrorshades

The Inquisition

It is ironic that science and magic were thrown together during the Church's persecution of new ideas. Galileo suffered as much as Agrippa. Now that science reigns supreme, religion and magic have been put in the same category. Both are considered airy-fairy subjects, not to be seriously pursued by intelligent people — archaic carryovers from a superstitious past.

— Donald Tyson, *The New Magus*

Mortals have always been torn between the desire to worship and the thirst to destroy those things which appear different or extraordinary. The Inquisition, which arose to combat supernatural beings, is the epitome of this divided urge. In the name of worship, they hunt, torture and kill their enemies.

Witch-hunters of all kinds have always existed, often driven by fear, jealousy, religious zeal and legitimate concern. An official Christian Inquisition, however, began in Europe in the early 1200s. While some sources blame extremists among the budding Chorus or the early Order of Reason Convention called the Cabal of Pure Thought, the roots of the movement seem to have begun among mortals fed up with some mysticks' excesses **(see Chapter Two)**. The Chorus and Cabal, however, were quick to feed the fires, and for several hundred years, magicians were hunted and killed in great numbers.

Eventually, the witchfires burned out, but one group kept the legacy alive: the Society of Leopold. Though no longer supported or sanctioned by the Catholic Church, most of its members still hail from that faith. This Society is a loose secret confederation of scholars and high-ranking priests who keep in touch mainly through letters and rare conferences. Rumors say this modern Inquisition is a suicide squad for high-ranking mages of the Celestial Chorus, sent out to disrupt the plans of other Traditions (the Vatican Chantry hotly denies this). Others claim that the NWO still supports an offshoot with its roots in the Templar order. With rare exceptions, however, the hunters of the Inquisition are un-Awakened mortals. This does not impair their efficiency, and such hunters are among the most dangerous foes a mage will ever encounter. They have vast libraries, crusader's zeal and occasional powers of faith that disrupt even the strongest magicks (i.e. holy countermagick).

The templates below can represent independent witch-hunters who pursue the Awakened for their own reasons.

• **Witch-hunter:** These are the agents of the Inquisition, most often members of one of the various holy orders. All that they do is without the formal knowledge of the Church.

Character Creation: Attributes 8/6/3, Abilities 21/12/7, Backgrounds 6, Willpower 10

Suggested Attributes: Assume ratings of 2, except for Intelligence, which should often be 3. Most successful witch-hunters have high Physical Attributes.

Suggested Abilities: Alertness 2, Awareness 2, Bureaucracy 2, Cosmology 5, Culture 2, Enigmas 4, Etiquette 3, Expression 2, Intimidation 3, Intuition 4, Investigation 2, Linguistics 3, Medicine 3, Occult 3, Politics 2, Research 3, Subterfuge 2, Survival 1, Technology 1 (Many witch-hunters — those who also destroy vampires and Garou — possess Brawl 3, Dodge, 4, Firearms 4, Melee 3, Stealth 3. Some exceptional members may have between one to five dice of countermagick, which they may use to oppose any Sphere used against them.)

Equipment: Bible, Silver Cross, Medal of St. Ignatius, Relics, Robe.

The Arcanum

I entered, charmed, and from a cobwebbed heap
Took up the nearest tome and thumbed it through,
Trembling at curious words that seemed to keep
Some secret, monstrous if only one knew.
— H.P. Lovecraft, *Fungi from Yuggoth*

The formation of the Arcanum can be traced to the mystical "War of the Roses" that centered around Paris in the late 1800s (not related to the English baronial wars). A war of words (and, if their words are to be believed, mystic forces) arose between two orders of Rosicrucians. The fighting between the orders become such a public scandal (and entertainment, hence the Parisian newspapers' "War of the Roses" brand) that many of both groups' best practitioners and scholars left their respective orders. After drafting a great Charter, these dissidents united to form the Arcanum. This order persists to this day.

Though the Arcanum has only formally existed for less than 100 years, its history dates back even farther. The core of the Arcanum consists of a group that has branded itself the "White Monks." Some believe that these so-called White Monks were somehow involved in the Inquisition and learned of mages there. However, they are not currently connected with the Inquisition and never actually engage in witch hunts. The Arcanum studies, but does not destroy.

The Arcanum has many Chapter Houses with three large Foundation Houses in Boston, Paris and Vienna. Its members, recruited from the cream of intellectual society, seem more concerned with theory than with practice. Their devotion is to the gathering and study of occult-related information, but they focus primarily on the past rather than the modern world. There are some members who have shown a degree of interest in the here and now, but these members, and the Arcanum itself, are thought to regard tales of True Magick with skepticism. As a whole, Arcanists seem to be more interested in phenomena of a less tangible nature: magic, miracles and hauntings. Nevertheless, the foundation's existence does cause mages some concern. A miscalculation on the mysticks' part could lead the Arcanum to their doors — and gods only knows what might happen then....

• **Scholar:** These intellectuals are involved in the gathering and classification of paranormal matters of all sorts, including alleged magick use. They are not interested in violent confrontation with the supernatural, and will avoid such at all costs. When in the field, investigators operate in groups of two to four to provide witnesses and greater safety.

Character Creation: Attributes 9/6/3, Abilities 15/9/3, Backgrounds 7, Willpower 10

Suggested Attributes: Assume ratings of 2, except for Charisma, Intelligence, and Manipulation, which should be 3 or even 4.

Suggested Abilities: Bureaucracy 2, Culture 2, Drive 1, Enigmas 3, Etiquette 2, Expression 2, Intimidation 1, Leadership 4, Linguistics 4, Occult 4, Research 5, Science 3, Subterfuge 2. Those who routinely perform field work — photographing ghosts, collecting ectoplasm, measuring the "magical" energy of ley lines — often possess Alertness 1, Awareness 2, Intuition 3, Medicine 1, Survival 1

Equipment: Automobile, various "gadgets," investigative paraphernalia.

Mysticks

In many ways, the worst enemy an Awakened One can have is another mage. The following templates and characters may be used as Storyteller characters or as inspiration for same.

Sample Templates

• An **Apprentice** has yet to study the principles of magick, or has begun study but has not yet achieved Rank One in any Sphere. He's more important for who he may become than for what he can do at the moment.

Character Creation: Attributes: 6/4/3, Abilities: 10/8/3, Backgrounds: 3, Willpower: 3, Spheres: none, Arete: 1-2

• A **Disciple** seeks enlightenment, and has achieved moderate prowess in at least one Sphere (Rank Three and lower).

Character Creation: Attributes: 7/5/3, Abilities: 13/9/5, Backgrounds: 5, Willpower: 5, Spheres: 6, Arete: 1-4

• An **Adept** has reached a level that has transformed her perception. She has gathered personal power in at least one Sphere (Rank Four) and usually others as well.

Character Creation: Attributes: 8/6/3 Abilities: 19/10/5, Backgrounds: 7, Willpower: 8, Spheres: 15, Arete: 4-6

• A **Master** has achieved Rank Five or higher in one Sphere and probably commands several others at Adept status or higher. Master mysticks have expanded their vision beyond human concerns, while Master-level Technomancers control the politics and tactics of lower-ranking underlings.

Character Creation: Attributes: 9/6/5, Abilities: 22/10/6, Backgrounds: 10+, Willpower: 8-10, Spheres: 15-30, Arete: 8+

Errant: Mark Hallward Gillan

Nature: Judge

Demeanor: Rebel

Essence: Dynamic

Attributes: Strength 2, Dexterity 3, Stamina 3, Charisma 3, Manipulation 5, Appearance 4, Perception 4, Intelligence 4, Wits 4

Abilities: Alertness 4, Awareness 3, Brawl 2, Dodge 2, Etiquette 1, Expression 2, Investigation 3, Meditation 2, Occult 4, Streetwise 5, Survival 2

Backgrounds: Allies 2, Arcane 3, Avatar 2, Destiny 2

Spheres: Correspondence 3, Entropy 2, Forces 1, Mind 1, Prime 1, Spirit 3

Arete: 4

Willpower: 10

Quintessence: 6

Paradox: 5

Image: 5' 10," 150 lbs., age 39, apparent age early 30s. Blond hair (black eyebrows), black eyes, handsome features, sturdy build. Cool, sardonic manner. Usually wears wool sweater, leather jacket, black pants. (Due to a minor Paradox Flaw, Gillan feels chilly in all weather.)

Born and raised in Melbourne, Gillan served as a mercenary in several African conflicts during the 1970s. The Order of Hermes recruited Gillan in Angola in 1976, shortly after a terrible combat experience Awakened him. Studying at Doissetep, he progressed slowly as a Disciple, as his rebellious attitude alienated his superiors. Upon graduation as an Adept, he chose assignment at a Chantry in New Orleans.

In 1992, he claimed to have discovered an Euthanatos conspiracy. An Elder investigated and found no basis for the accusation. Gillan's complaints grew more shrill and paranoid, and he appealed to the Order's Grievance Council. The Council gave his matter a fair hearing and refused action. Gillan made no protest then, but six months ago he left his Chantry after assaulting the Elder. Recently he has become a sometime ally to a cabal of non-Hermetic Tradition mages who pursue this so-called conspiracy with grim determination.

Gillan's most notable characteristic is his iron nerve; witnesses have seen him taunt an Umbrood Lord. He once faced an Outsider Thing in a Void Engineer Construct and emerged with his mind intact (though he *was* sweating). Though he rarely boasts, Gillan claims he once arm-wrestled a powerful vampire, named "Methuselah" or "the Methuselah" and almost won. That he remains alive after so many uneven confrontations means Gillan has unknown resources. Anyone encountering this Errant should deal with him carefully.

The Order of Hermes Central Security Council has pronounced the punishments of Censure, Interdiction and Requital on Mark Hallward Gillan. Hermetic mages are cautioned to avoid any social contact with him whatsoever.

Technocrats

Cyborgs

The steel legions of Iteration X employ a variety of deadly BioMechanicals to enforce their vision of Utopia. Though less powerful than the dreaded HIT Marks, the Convention's cyborgs offer greater flexibility, intelligence and, in some cases, magickal ability that more than make up for their comparative fragility.

The most common cyborgs are simply un-Awakened acolytes who carry permanent modifications — often weapons, scanners, transmitters and processing programs. These processes include minor indoctrination feeds and internal Mind-monitors to ensure loyalty. All Iteration X mages have some degree of cybernetic enhancement as well. In most cases, these supply basic foci or minor mundane powers, built into the Iterator's body. Though such enhancements are unusual by mundane standards, most modern Sleepers will accept their Effects (read: they're usually coincidental).

The precious Awakened cyborgs carry firepower rivaling a small military detachment; Talisman weapons, armor and other Devices augment any additional technomagicks the Iterator might know. Such cyborgs are carefully screened, heavily monitored and constantly indoctrinated — they are far too valuable to lose and too powerful to be allowed to defect. Many remain in reserve in extra-dimensional Realms, work with the Void Engineer Boarder Corps or go on covert missions under night's cover. The extreme power of some of their Effects and Devices attract Paradox even in the best of circumstances (read: they're often pretty vulgar).

Common Cyborg

Attributes: Strength 3, Dexterity 3, Stamina 4, Charisma 2, Manipulation 1, Appearance 2, Perception 3, Intelligence 2, Wits 3

Abilities: Alertness 3, Athletics 2, Awareness 2, Brawl 2 (4 for combat models), Computer 1-4, Drive 1, Firearms 3, Intimidation 2, Melee 2 (4 for combat models), Technology 2-4 (non-combat models may have Etiquette, Leadership, Investigation, Medicine or Streetwise at 1-4, depending)

Spheres: none

Willpower: 3

Health Levels: OK, OK, -1 (x2), -2 (x2), -5, Incapacitated

Armor Rating: 2 (six soak dice, total)

Attacks/Powers: Two or three of the following: Radio, IR vision, claws (5 dice damage), Strength enhancement (to 6), medical supplies, miniature tools, 3 dots in any Knowledge. Most carry mundane firearms as well.

Awakened Cyborg

Attributes: Strength 4, Dexterity 2, Stamina 5, Charisma 1, Manipulation 2, Appearance 1, Perception 3, Intelligence 2, Wits 3

Abilities: Alertness 3, Athletics 3, Awareness 2, Brawl 4, Computer 1, Dodge 2, Firearms 4, Intimidation 3, Melee 4, Technology 2

Spheres: Forces 2-4, Mind 1, Prime 2

Arete: 1-6

Quintessence: 10

Paradox: usually lots

Willpower: 3 (Technocratic programming; effectively 7 for magickal purposes & resistance)

Health Levels: OK (x3), -1 (x3), -2, -2, -5, Demolished

Armor Rating: 2 (seven soak dice, total)

Innate Countermagick: one die's worth of Primium coating

Attacks/Powers: Any three of the powers above, plus one or two Devices ("Arete" 5) that simulate the following Effects: **Sense Quintessence** (Prime), **Telepathy**, **Multi-Tasking** (Mind), **Discharge Static**, **System Havoc**, **Force Bolt** (Forces/Prime). Most also carry mundane firearms in the field.

Hyper Intelligence Technologies Mark V

HIT Marks are reserved for Iteration X's dirtiest work. These flesh-coated robots are programmed to seek and destroy the enemies of the Technocracy, whether Tradition mages, Marauders or Nephandi. Half living flesh, half mechanical construct, these killing machines look relatively human, so long as they wear trenchcoats or other concealing clothing. HIT Mark camouflage lets them pass as ordinary men and women, indistinguishable from Sleepers except

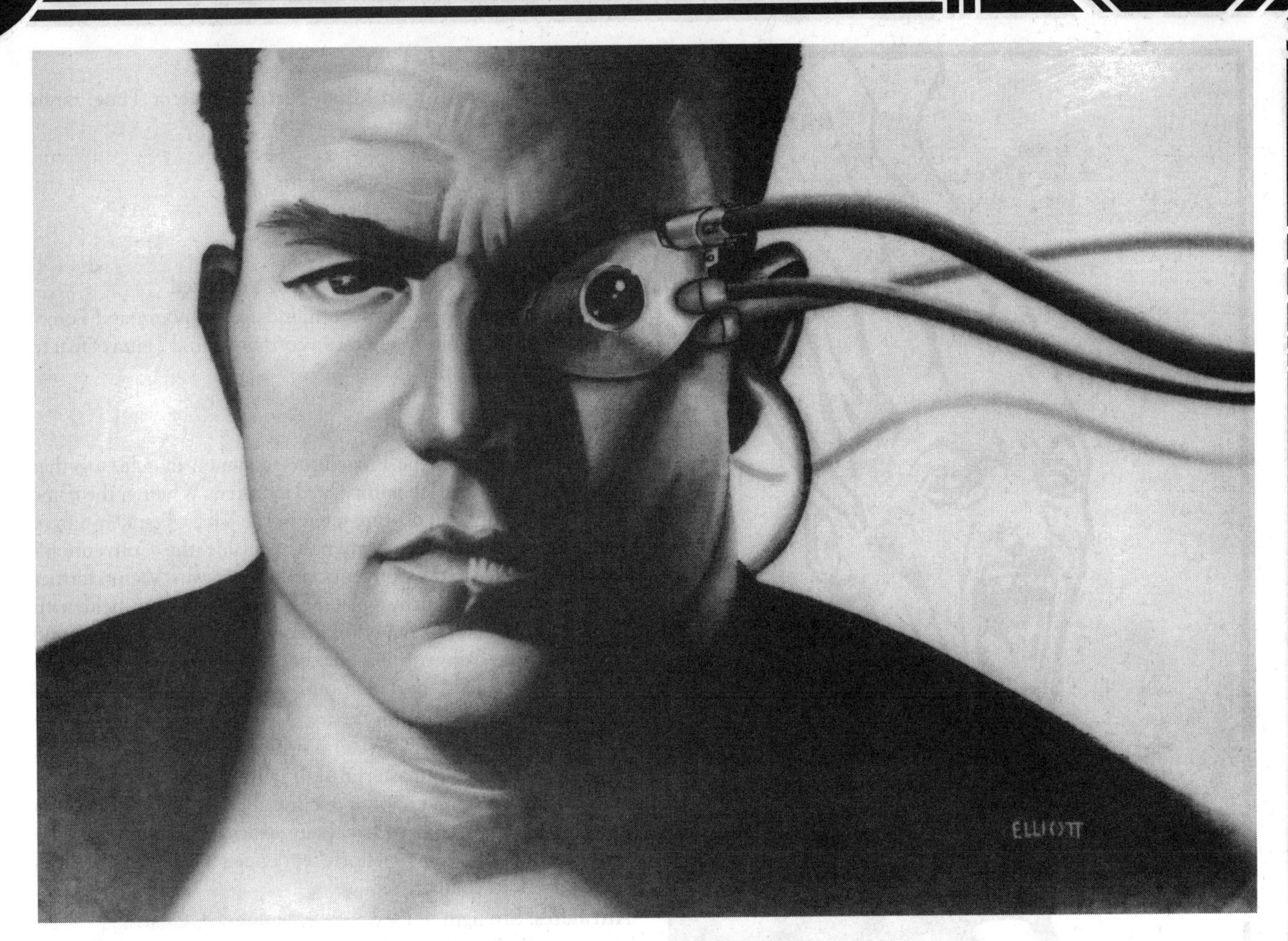

for their eyes: a flicker of red laser light flashes in a HIT Mark's eyes every few seconds (which often warns those who know what to look for). However, when HIT Marks enter combat mode, chain guns pop from their arm cavities, laser sights flip down over their eyes, and razor-sharp tungsten talons slide from fingertip sheaths.

Worst of all, HIT Marks are sheathed in the rare countermagickal alloy Primium. Though they have no magickal abilities themselves, HIT Marks are programmed to match or exceed Sleeper limits in most physical abilities, and show an amazing capacity to absorb damage. The Marks have demonstrated only routine intelligence, but their internal computers give them many skills and a wide knowledge of many subjects. Mages on their bad side are advised to strike from surprise with full force, if feasible, or retreat if confronted directly.

Attributes: Strength 5, Dexterity 2, Stamina 5, Charisma 1, Manipulation 1, Appearance 4, Perception 3, Intelligence 2, Wits 2

Abilities: Alertness 3, Brawl 3, all Skills 3 (except Meditation and Stealth), any Knowledges 3 (except Cosmology and Occult)

Spheres: none

Willpower: 5

Health Levels: OK (x5), -1, - 5, Terminated

Armor Rating: 4 (nine soak dice, total)

Attacks/Powers: Chain gun (200 rounds; difficulty 7, damage 8, range 150, rate 3); claws (eight dice damage), IR vision

Innate Countermagick: 2 dice worth of Primium; some advanced models may have as many as 5 dice worth of such protection. These murderous things are *very* rare (at the moment...).

Men in Black

These dark-suited agents in sunglasses, bearing black briefcases and riding in black Cadillacs, appear close on the heels of any threat to the New World Order. Once they arrive, these agents intimidate everyone around them, probably through use of a coincidental Mind Effect. Dressed entirely in black, most are pale and hairless with no distinguishing features. Mind probes turn up no thoughts or memories. Life magick shows their bodies to be healthy yet somehow hollow, as if lacking a soul. Spirit magick detects an ominous aura. They seldom speak, and their exact motives are always secret.

Men in Black travel in organized groups of three or more. The Hermetic Order believes each specializes in two Spheres. Tradition mages frequently observe them working together to create conjunctional Effects, though they may use magick independently as well. Most carry interesting gadgets, which they use as foci for their various Effects.

After death, a Man in Black melts into nothingness. No reports indicate that this Effect ever attracted a Paradox spirit, and the NWO servitors apparently suffer little from Paradox. Though some sources and encounters suggest different types of Men in Black (some with more independence than others), these agents' true nature remains unknown.

Attributes: Strength 3, Dexterity 3, Stamina 3, Charisma 2, Manipulation 4, Appearance 1, Perception 5, Intelligence 4, Wits 3

Abilities: Alertness 5, Athletics 2, Awareness 3, Dodge 2, Drive 2, Enigmas 1, Firearms 3, Intuition 3, Intimidation 3, Investigation 3, Meditation 2, Melee 3, Occult 1, Streetwise 2, Subterfuge 3, Stealth 5

Backgrounds: Arcane 3, Allies 3

Spheres: Two at 3 (often Mind, Forces, Prime or Time; rarely Spirit)

Arete: 3-5

Willpower: 8

Quintessence: varies

Paradox: varies

Health Levels: OK (x3), -1, -2, -2, -5, Vaporized

Attacks/Powers: In addition to mundane weaponry and Force-magick foci, MIBs often generate a constant Mind 2 aura of fear to anyone in the vicinity.

Victors

Victors serve as the Progenitors' common muscle, together with the Progenitors' laboratory-bred monsters. Whether the name indicates "victory," an obscure reference to Victor Frankenstein or some other significance is unknown outside the Convention's laboratories. Bred in the Convention's bio-tech vats, Victors further the Progenitors' Pogrom by replacing key leaders in many fields with loyal Progenitor clones. Superiors make the actual replacement and also spy on the Convention's enemies, sabotage enemy plans and breed distrust among the Traditions.

These "*Homo Superiors*" vary widely in appearance. All of them, however, are attractive and strongly built, displaying peak physical abilities and masterful skill with firearms. They use no magick, however, and show poor intelligence overall. Reports indicate that for all their physical supremacy, Victors are mentally unstable; many develop psychotic tendencies and have sometimes gone berserk in combat.

Attributes: Strength 4, Dexterity 4, Stamina 4, Charisma 2, Manipulation 2, Appearance 4, Perception 2, Intelligence 1, Wits 3

Abilities: Alertness 2, Athletics 4, Brawl 4, Dodge 4, Firearms 4, Melee 4 (Computer, Culture, Drive, Etiquette, Intimidation, Stealth, Subterfuge and Technology are common "custom" skills, depending on the Victor's mission. These Abilities often rate from 1 to 4.)

Spheres: none

Willpower: 3

Health Levels: OK (x2), -1 (x2), -2 (x3), -5, Terminated

Innate Countermagick: 2 dice

Marauders and Mythic Beasts

(See also "The Hidden World," Chapter Nine.)

Arlan "The Smiler" Nattick

Nature: Unknown

Demeanor: Varies drastically

Essence: Dynamic

Attributes: Strength 3, Dexterity 4, Stamina 3, Charisma 4, Manipulation 4, Appearance 3, Perception 5, Intelligence 4, Wits 3

Abilities: Alertness 3, Athletics 2, Awareness 1, Computer 2, Cosmology 4, Culture 4, Expression 2, Intuition 2, Intimidation 2, Linguistics 3, Lore (all?) 4, Occult 5, Science 3, Subterfuge 2

Backgrounds: Avatar 4, Library 4

Spheres: Life 5, Matter 5, all others 4 (usually); sometimes Mind 0 and all others 2

Arete: 5

Willpower: 10 (usually); sometimes 3

Quintessence: 8

Image: 6,' 150 lbs., apparent age 25. White crewcut, black eyebrows, deep-set black eyes, pale skin, large mouth with bright red lips. Smooth, oily voice; slim build; manner alternately coy, jovial, hysterical, furious and frenzied. Dresses unpredictably.

Unlike many Marauders, Nattick willingly talks with Tradition mages about the origins of his astonishing magick. However, "origins" (plural) is the word, because he always offers a different story. He has claimed to be a product of Progenitor breeding programs, a victim of Euthanatos tortures, a self-taught Orphan, a Sleeper Diabolist, a living Paradox spirit and so on. None of these accounts is remotely credible, and Nattick offers them all in a tone of terminal boredom. Attempts to reconcile the inconsistencies enrage him — or *seem* to — and in most cases he attacks.

The only verifiable truths about Arlan Nattick are these: He has displayed exhaustive knowledge of all Traditions, Technocratic Conventions and many Mad Ones and Nephandi. He has demonstrated powerful magick, including restoration of the dead to full life, and appears to derive intense physical pleasure from using it. However, his power at other times seems hardly to exceed Disciple rank. Nattick has occasionally fought for certain causes, such as environmentalism in Malaysia and human rights in rural China. In each case, he eventually switched sides, apparently out of boredom, then caused chaos for both. Nattick has killed at least 12 Tradition mages and single-handedly destroyed a minor Iteration X Central Processing Unit in Johannesburg, South Africa.

Nattick's larger purposes remain unknown. All that clearly identifies him as a Chaos Mage is his unpredictability and his observed immunity to Paradox. He has often taken pains to demonstrate the superiority of his own magick to that of rivals, and having done so, he gloats at length but usually leaves the defeated rival alive. Though given to wild mood swings, Nattick is extremely shrewd, not prone to manipulation and should be treated with the greatest possible caution.

Manticora

These infamous Bygones have the bodies of a lion, lizard-like heads with lion's manes, distended shark-like jaws, bat wings and scorpion tails. Such mythic beasts are brutish, solitary animals, easily angered and nearly always hungry. That said, a manticora can recognize kindness, and some have even shown loyalty to "friends." A few Tradition mages tell of encounters with manticoras that inevitably remind one of the fable of Androcles and the Lion. Previous records note that while incapable of speech, the manticora has an unusual, musical voice, reminiscent of a flute.

Though they once roamed free during Earth's Mythic Age, manticoras now survive only in the Umbra. Some serve Chaos Mages in order to re-enter this Realm. However, once they return to Earth, static reality asserts itself, and they quickly sicken and die.

Attributes: Strength 8, Dexterity 4, Stamina 5, Perception 2, Intelligence 1, Wits 2

Abilities: Athletics 1, Brawl 3, Expression 3, Stealth 2

Spheres: none

Willpower: 5

Quintessence: 5 innate (may be harvested as Tass if the manticora dies)

Health Levels: OK (x2), -1 (x2), -2 (x3), -5, Incapacitated

Attacks/Powers: Claws, bite (10 dice damage); scorpion tail (8 dice damage; a victim who takes at least one Health Level of damage after soak must roll Stamina, difficulty 9. If this roll fails, the victim takes three more non-soakable Health Levels from the poisoned stinger.); flight (15 yards/turn)

Ik-Thazai, lesser dragon

Nature: Curmudgeon

Demeanor: Conniver

Essence: Primordial

Attributes: (scores in parenthesis indicate her human form) Strength 10 (5), Dexterity 3, Stamina 7 (4), Charisma 3, Manipulation 4, Appearance 3 (5), Perception 4, Intelligence 4, Wits 3

Abilities: Alertness 4, Awareness 3, Brawl 4, Culture 3, Dodge 1, Enigmas 4, Etiquette 2, Intimidation 5, Intuition 3, Linguistics 5, Melee 3, Occult 3, Subterfuge 3

Spheres: none

Willpower: 8

Quintessence: 20 (half of this may be harvested as Tass if the dragon dies)

Health Levels: OK (x3), -1 (x3), -2 (x5), -5 (x2), Incapacitated

Attacks/Powers: Bite (13 dice); claws (13 dice); tail (11 dice — knocks a victim back several yards); flight (20 yards/turn); shapeshift (into a human female form); reptile command (which controls all true reptiles within 100 yards unto death); flame breath (10 dice of flaming damage; requires Dexterity + Melee roll, difficulty 5, and affects one target per success within reasonable area — Forces magick may counter. Uses 5 Quintessence per gout.)

Image: In human form, a short, beautiful Slavic woman, often named "Varvara," with long black hair and green eyes. In dragon form, a sinuous black, gold and blue monstrosity some 45' long, with membranous wings and a blue-black mane running from her head across her back.

Ik-Thazai, the One Who Coils in the Deep, ravaged the lands of Mythic Europe in the Age of Fable. Accounts agree that she was willful, prone to impulse and greedy beyond description for power, praise and Quintessence. As magick left the world, Ik-Thazai retreated into hibernation and finally left Gaia for a Shard Realm in the Near Umbra.

Like most Mythic Remnants, Ik-Thazai detests exile and occasionally aids Marauders in return for temporary passage to Earth. During these travels she seeks powerful Nodes and devours all the Tass and Quintessence she can find; the more she eats, the longer this thaumivore can remain here. She has made attempts to capture the Nodes of powerful Chantries, which does not endear her to the mages who live there.

Reports show that the dragon can assume human form, breathe devastating flame, fly and command all nearby reptiles. Although intelligent, she is unsophisticated and exceedingly unfamiliar with the modern world. Her only long-term contacts have been Mad Ones and Hermetic mages, though she once met a Void Engineer ship. Neither party escaped unscathed. She has carried a grudge against such "spoilsports" ever since.

Pago-Pago

Nature: Conniver

Demeanor: Bravo

Essence: Primordial

Attributes: Strength 6, Dexterity 6, Stamina 3, Charisma 1, Manipulation 1, Appearance 1, Perception 4, Intelligence 2, Wits 2

Abilities: Alertness 3, Athletics 1, Brawl 2, Dodge 4

Spheres: none

Willpower: 4

Quintessence: 12 (half of this may be harvested as Tass if the Pago-Pago dies)

Health Levels: OK (x3), -1 (x3), -2 (x5), -5 (x2), Incapacitated

Attacks/Powers: Legs (6 dice damage, four attacks per turn); poison stinger (6 dice damage; a victim who takes at least one Health Level of damage after soak must roll Stamina, difficulty 9. If this roll fails, the victim takes one more non-soakable Health Level from the poisoned stinger.)

Image: See below.

While searching for a new Node in the wilds of the Philippines early this year, a cabal of Tradition mages ventured into the highlands of Mindanao near Malaybalay. There they crossed into the Umbra and encountered a cunning and vicious Umbrood that called itself the Pago-Pago.

The survivors describe the Pago-Pago as a spider woman, 10 feet high and weighing perhaps a ton, with a hideous noseless face, the body of a black widow spider and six crab-like legs. It had a screeching voice, sarcastic wit, deft movements and uncanny speed. The spider attacked with a paralyzing bite and a web that drained Quintessence. It showed extensive knowledge of the terrain and took full advantage of this familiarity to attack from ambush.

This spider woman is apparently a primeval figure from the legends of the indigenous Manobo people. Fragmentary references suggest Catholic missionaries drove the Pago-Pago into the Umbra, but these legends are certainly creations of the missionaries themselves. Pending further information, the Umbrood Catalogue Board advises mages who encounter the Pago-Pago to attempt conversation and discover its goals. If this proves impractical, flee immediately and report to some Master.

Nephandi

Barabbi: Anson D'Arcangelo

Nature: Deviant

Demeanor: Bon Vivant

Essence: Dynamic

Attributes: Strength 3, Dexterity 2, Stamina 2, Charisma 4, Manipulation 4, Appearance 4, Perception 3, Intelligence 3, Wits 3

Abilities: Alertness 2, Awareness 3, Culture 3, Dodge 2, Etiquette 3, Expression 3, Intuition 4, Investigation 3, Meditation 1, Occult 3, Stealth 3, Streetwise 2, Subterfuge 4, Survival 2

Backgrounds: Allies 3, Arcane 3, Avatar 2, Mentor 4

Spheres: Correspondence 2, Entropy 2, Life 3, Matter 3, Mind 3, Prime 2, Spirit 2

Arete: 4

Willpower: 6

Quintessence: 10

Paradox: 3

Image: Height 6' 2," 180 lbs., age 96, apparent age 26. White hair (a Paradox Flaw), black eyebrows, blue eyes. Tanned Caucasian skin, peak athletic build, careless manner. Dresses in casual fashionable clothing, usually leaving chest bare. Favors sunglasses.

Anson D'Arcangelo's story is tragic, but he exploits its tragedy without qualm. Whatever his past travails, he is now not victim but victimizer.

Before his Awakening, D'Arcangelo (born Angelo Ciatino in 1899) was a serial killer in Naples, Italy, in the early 1920s. Tormented by a cruel and disturbed older sister, he grew to hate women and took that hatred out on innocents. His series of rape-homicides panicked the public for months, but he was never found — at least not by Sleeper authorities. Brother Benedetto Leone of the Celestial Temple of the Sun (the Ancestral Chantry of the Celestial Chorus beneath Vatican City) journeyed to Naples, found Ciatino and brought him to the Temple's Star Chamber for final justice. Taking tutelage from Brother Benedetto while awaiting execution, Ciatino Awakened and repented his crimes.

Ciatino (now "D'Arcangelo") gained a stay of execution and eventually a pardon. He worked and studied in the Chantry for six decades, apparently in all sincerity, and did much good for the Chorus and the Traditions. However, he kept his past a secret.

In 1985 Brother Benedetto, who had become Abbot of the Chantry, died. The new Abbot, Sister Mary Martha Carpenter, knew nothing of D'Arcangelo's past and grew suspicious. When she discovered his history, she expelled him at once from the Chantry. Embittered and angry, D'Arcangelo vandalized much of the Chantry, stole many prized Talismans and escaped. His travels thereafter are unknown, but in 1988, the Order of Hermes began receiving reports of a new white-haired Nephandus mage who corrupted Tradition mysticks with evident ease. Only now have field reports identified this Nephandus as Anson D'Arcangelo.

The corrupted D'Arcangelo uses many names and disguises. His most distinguishing feature is his white hair; due to Paradox, it cannot change color and will hold no dye. His method is effective: He allows his target to apprehend him in the act of committing a crime, convincingly repents and begins "studying" under the target mage. He simulates constant, emotionally moving struggles to overcome his evil past, continuing them even if the target discovers D'Arcangelo's *barabbi* nature. By enlisting his victim's sympathy and playing on hidden desires, the Fallen One can corrupt him (or, more often, her) more easily.

D'Arcangelo has been active most recently in Chicago's Chinatown, where he has unknown links to a mysterious entity called the Jade Demon. Whether this is a True Demon or simply a name is unclear.

Mad Nephandus: Meggan O'Rourke

Nature: Curmudgeon

Demeanor: Bravo

Essence: Questing

Attributes: Strength 4, Dexterity 1, Stamina 3, Charisma 1, Manipulation 5, Appearance 1, Perception 5, Intelligence 4, Wits 4

Abilities: Alertness 3, Awareness 2, Cosmology 1, Culture 1, Intimidation 2, Intuition 4, Meditation 2, Occult 5, Stealth 3, Streetwise 3, Subterfuge 3

Backgrounds: Avatar 2, Talisman 5

Spheres: Entropy 4, Forces 2, Life 2, Prime 1, Spirit 2, Time 2

Arete: 5
Willpower: 7
Quintessence: 10
Paradox: 9

Image: Height and weight vary; typically 5' 3," 160 lbs., apparent age 65. Gray hair, white eyes, pale wrinkled skin, pudgy build, hunched and twisted posture, obsessive lunatic manner. Dresses in castoff clothing; often appears as a deformed bag lady.

Not all Nephandi are cool and glamorous seducers. Meggan O'Rourke was a promising Disciple of the Euthanatos until 1957, when she lost her infant son, Kyle, in a Paradox backlash. In an unauthorized attempt to resurrect Kyle, she foolishly summoned a demon named Wormwood. It broke her will, warped her body and enlisted her as a minor agent of the Fallen Ones.

Now O'Rourke wanders from city to city, spreading squalor and decay. Her many Paradox Flaws have driven her mad and deformed her. Her "bag" is a Talisman; she reaches within and draws forth demonic spirits. She thinks of these Umbrood as her children and protects them with maternal interest. The deluded O'Rourke frequently believes male opponents to be Kyle, her late son. To protect Kyle from the demon Wormwood, she uses Entropy Effects (on either the mage, his colleagues or Sleeper bystanders) to coerce the unfortunate mage into her bag and thence into the Deep Umbra.

Mysterious Entities: The Zigg'raugglurr

Malevolent four-dimensional entities of unknown origin and purpose, the Zigg'raugglurr exist beyond the Horizon, moving freely in time and space and occasionally penetrating the Gauntlet to steal Quintessence or serve their Nephandi allies.

Descriptions of these entities vary widely. As different cross-sections of their giant higher-dimensional forms penetrate three-space, their appearance changes between encounters or even from moment to moment. Common features are disjointed blobs covered with yellow, lizard-like scales and pulsing veins. The floating blobs grow and shrink unpredictably, from a few inches to several yards across, and they move in exact coordination, invisibly connected in four-space. Occasionally, alien mouths form in the blobs and speak incomprehensible words. The Order of Hermes assigned these creatures the name "Zigg'raugglurr," based on words one spoke during the first recorded encounter.

The Order knows of 18 other incursions by the Zigg'raugglurr. Several times the creatures have attacked a single cabal based in San Francisco. In the first assault, the Zigg'raugglurr, displaying extensive knowledge of the cabal's powers and tactics, almost won the engagement. In later encounters, the creatures showed weakness and ignorance of the same cabal's tactics and barely escaped.

Hermetic scholars have deduced from this that the Zigg'raugglurr can move freely back and forth in time. The "later" encounters were, for the Zigg'raugglurr, the first ones. Once they learned their opponents' strengths, they then moved into the past and attacked the cabal again.

The obvious question: Why do they restrict their incursions to this narrow time frame? No one yet knows. Some speculate (and this speculation is, as yet, groundless) that some kind of large-scale weakening in the Gauntlet will occur in the next few years. This line of reasoning says that the creatures can cross more easily in the temporal vicinity of the rip, either before or after it.

Council Masters now work to devise Correspondence and Time Effects to perceive these enigmatic beings. Once these are completed, the Order of Hermes hopes to enter four-space and confront the creatures on their own territory. Meanwhile, mages who encounter the Zigg'raugglurr should consider luring in Paradox spirits (which attack the creatures with notable ferocity) or removing all Quintessence from the vicinity. Depending on whether this is the "first" encounter or a "later" one from the Zigg'raugglurr viewpoint, direct confrontation may prove hazardous. In general, the less a mage reveals in any given encounter, the better.

Umbrood

Minor Lord: Lord Viscount Talos Perdix

Willpower 10, **Rage** 8, **Gnosis** 8, **Power** 50

Charms: Airt Sense, Armor, Blast Flame (8 dice), Control Electrical Systems, Create Fires, Influence, Materialize, Possession, Short Out, Solidify Reality, Tracking

Nature: Conniver

Demeanor: Judge

Materialized Attributes: Strength 4, Dexterity 4, Stamina 4; use Gnosis for Social and Mental Traits

Abilities: Alertness 5, Awareness 5, Brawl 2, Dodge 3, Intuition 2, Intimidation 2, Subterfuge 4, Melee 3, Cosmology 5, Enigmas 4, Investigation 3, Occult 5, Science 4

Backgrounds: Arcane 3, Influence 3

Spheres: Correspondence 3, Entropy 4, Forces 3, Life 4, Prime 3, Spirit 5

Arete: 6

Quintessence: 14

Paradox: 0

Materialized Health Levels: 19

Image: Umbrood Lord Talos Perdix is a weird organo-mechanical hybrid. The spirit has a withered, mummy-like face set in a metal armature, an elongated neck that merges into corrugated rubber piping and a serpentine body. From his head and retaining rings along his body emerge clusters of writhing tentacular wires. This bizarre and uncharacteristic appearance may derive from the Umbrood's origins. He is said to have been the nephew of Daedalus, the great inventor in Mythic Greece. Daedalus killed Perdix for fear that the nephew would become a greater inventor than himself.

Whether or not this account is true, Perdix has risen to the status of Umbrood Viscount over millennia. He has played incessantly at politics in the Shadow Court, hoping to rise in station, and uses mages as powerful pawns in his many schemes.

Viscount Perdix, like the rest of the Court, has no interest in the Ascension War. However, to enlist a cabal's loyalty, the Umbrood Lord often lures their enemies to a vulnerable location, informs the cabal of this fact and — after the resulting victory — claims credit. Perdix's manipulations are sometimes more subtle, and a cabal in the Umbra may end up aiding, all unknowing, the Viscount's schemes to destroy a rival Baron or Banneret.

Preceptor: Aelida, Lady of Feathers

Willpower 5, **Rage** 5, **Gnosis** 8, **Power** 30

Charms: Airt Sense, Create Wind (usually a gale-force if threatened), Influence, Materialize, Possession (birds only), Shapeshift (often into birds), Tracking

Materialized Attributes: Strength 2, Dexterity 4, Stamina 3; use Gnosis for Social and Mental Traits

Abilities: Athletics 3, Dodge 2, Expression 4, Cosmology 3

Backgrounds: Dream 2, Talisman 2

Spheres: Life 4, Prime 2, all others 1

Arete: 4

Willpower: 5

Quintessence: 10

Paradox: 0

Materialized Health Levels: 9

Image: A guileless and seemingly naive Preceptor, the Lady of Feathers appears as a beautiful Mediterranean woman dressed in an ornate cloak of yellow and red feathers. Aelida wears an elaborate crown of white gold highlighted with purple feathers, and lives in a luxurious floating mansion in a Domain of the Air, an extravaganza of towers, cathedral-like chambers and curving walls. Wind whistles harmoniously through its fluted steeples.

Aelida travels near Earth's Horizon to gather news of the avian world and seek the Quintessence that sustains her. The Lady can fly at great speed and converse with any bird. She taps Prime energy from forested regions rich in bird life. Insofar as she takes interest in human affairs, she collects the lore of birds and admires music and poetry of transcendent beauty.

Mages seek the Lady because her feathers provide Tass. Some bargain with her, while others trick or extort feathers from her. Aelida deals truthfully with all she meets and apparently thinks it impossible for anyone to do otherwise. Because of this, Umbrood and some mages have treated her cruelly. However, mages who bargain fairly with her earn her gratitude.

It would be too easy to dismiss the Lady as a childish spirit. Though innocent in many ways, she carries the sight of ages past. One Hermetic source claims her as one of their own, gone to spirit form after her Chantry was sacked by the Order of Reason. Others dismiss this tale — how could a mage become an Umbrood? Still, there is a growing sadness to the Lady's manner in recent years. Whatever the Lady has seen, she never speaks of it.

Evil Spirit: Muntus-Kulmu, the Driver of Nails

Willpower 4, **Rage** 4, **Gnosis** 4, **Power** 25

Charms: Airt Sense, Appear, Armor, Blast Flame (3 dice), Blighted Touch, Corruption, Create Fires, Influence, Possession, Short Out, Tracking

Nature: Conniver

Demeanor: Judge

Materialized Attributes: Strength 1, Dexterity 2, Stamina 1; use Gnosis for Social and Mental Traits

Abilities: Alertness 2, Awareness 4, Cosmology 3, Culture 3, Etiquette 3, Intimidation 4, Occult 3, Streetwise 1, Subterfuge 4, Stealth 2

Materialized Health Levels: 8

Image: During the Etruscan civilization (900-500 B.C.) in the Low Mythic Ages, this minor True Demon acquired worshippers who believed it the king of the underworld. With the disappearance of the Etruscans, Muntus-Kulmu fell from these heights and languished for millennia in the High Umbral Hells. Now it's making a new bid for power in alliance with the Nephandi and a small cult of Sleeper Diabolists.

Like all True Demons, as distinguished from Umbrood spirits that exist independently of humanity, Muntus-Kulmu is an evil extra-dimensional being that sustains itself on human souls. It aims not to destroy everything like the Nephandi would, but to cause widespread misery. Aided by tempters among the Fallen Ones, Muntus has recruited a few dozen foolish Sleepers as worshippers, who signify their fealty by piercing some part of the body with a long steel nail. The "Nailed One" Diabolist gains certain fixed Entropy-related Charms, but also must serve as a host for the demon. When Muntus takes possession, the host grows drowsy and automatically traces a pattern in the air. Through this pattern Muntus can see, hear and create Effects as though it were actually present.

Muntus-Kulmu obeys unfathomable rules or practices that prevent it from manifesting in physical reality for more than one day at a time (local midnight to midnight) or from possessing a given individual for more than one day per year (midwinter to midwinter). In the short term, it plans to corrupt at least 365 worshippers around the globe so that it can manifest permanently in a series of bodies. It also hopes to tap and store large amounts of Quintessence from powerful mages.

Celestial scholars learned of Muntus after one cabal's recent encounter with a small coven of Nailed Ones in the Yucatan. After the Council mages defeated them, the surviving Diabolists delivered the information above, then burst into flame and perished. The Chorus has not yet assessed the threat level Muntus-Kulmu poses, and instructs its members to gain more information whenever possible.

Guardian Spirit: Olonga the Whisperer

Willpower 8, **Rage** 5, **Gnosis** 7, **Power** 30

Charms: Airt Sense, Appear, Control Electrical Systems, Cleanse the Blight, Forest Sense, Lightning Bolts (5 dice), Materialize, Mind Speech, Short Out, Tracking

Materialized Attributes: Strength 5, Dexterity 5, Stamina 5; Gnosis substitutes for Social and Mental Traits

Abilities: Alertness 4, Awareness 5, Empathy 3, Intimidation 5, Enigmas 4, Occult 4; when manifest, Melee 4

Materialized Health Levels: 10

Image: The ancient unbound spirit Olonga feeds on the Quintessence at Node sites. Once Olonga has found a site, it remains there for years or centuries. It greets trespassers with a ghastly howl and becomes visible, though intangible. Olonga appears as a tall, gaunt Zulu African warrior, wearing a carved devil-mask and carrying an assegai. The spear shaft crackles with lightning, and the mask's eye-slits glow with green light.

In a chilling whisper (thus the sobriquet), Olonga challenges trespassers to a contest of riddles: The first side that fails to guess one of the opponent's riddles loses. Documented riddles include, "The one who made it did not want it; the one who bought it did

not use it; the one who used it did not know it," (a coffin) and "A little white house without door or window" (an egg). Interestingly, Olonga is not fooled by riddles that derive from contemporary society nor even American popular culture. It seems to tap into some collective riddle-consciousness that updates constantly.

If the visitors win, Olonga admits them to the Node at all times thereafter. If they lose, Olonga drains them of all stored Quintessence and adds this Primal energy to the Node. To do this, Olonga manifests physically and attacks using its spear or its Charms.

A riddle contest with Olonga may be roleplayed (preferably) or handled as an opposed roll of Intelligence + Enigmas.

Minion: Pattern Spider

Willpower 6, **Rage** 4-7, **Gnosis** 6, **Power** 25-40

Charms: Airt Sense, Calcify, Solidify Reality (some "breeds" have Control Electrical Systems, Lightning Bolts (5 dice), Short Out, and the special Web Flux Charm **(see below)**.

Image: Cybernetic spider-type things, pattern spiders scuttle through the Near Umbra (and several Realms), spinning glistening silver webs of static reality. Most resemble high-tech arachnids; older, larger spiders contain bits of old technology — steam vents, vacuum tubes and jerky, awkward limbs. Pattern spiders range from tiny things about an inch long to terrifying entities larger than a full-sized car.

Pattern spiders spin their webs wherever stasis (often technology) has taken hold; they're common in laboratories, computer centers and even many classrooms. These manifestations of stasis work only in the Umbra; they cannot step into in material reality. Searching for Umbral instabilities, these near-mindless creatures spin anything that violates their "work ethic" into pattern webs (the "Calcify Reality" Charm). Although they reflect the Technomancers' influence, few Convention mages (outside of the Void Engineers) even know they exist. Some Iteration X master cyber-techs have replicated pattern spiders (or perhaps brought new "species" across) to work in material reality, but these models utilize more mundane Charms than their Umbral cousins.

Old and powerful pattern spiders can occasionally affect beings in the material world, using a Charm which resembles the Rubbing the Bones Prime Effect **(see Chapter Eight)**. Most pattern spirits have little influence in the material world *per se;* they reflect change rather than cause it directly.

Paradox Spirits

The Order of Hermes has compiled detailed notes on over 1,100 Paradox spirits in 53,760 manifestations to date. Less than four dozen Paradox spirits (in various guises) account for the majority of modern Paradox events. Those below are only a few of these most infamous spirits.

All physical damage done by Paradox spirits is aggravated. Seeing a Paradox spirit requires a Perception + Awareness roll (difficulty 6) or the Spirit Effect **Spirit Sight.** Charms which resemble magickal effects use the spirit's Rage as Arete unless otherwise noted.

Farandwee (Correspondence)

Willpower 4, **Rage** 4, **Gnosis** 8, **Power** 20

Charms: Materialize, Shift Other (teleport vs. target's Willpower), Mirror Maze, Duplicate, Spirit Away

Materialized Attributes: Strength 2, Dexterity 3, Stamina 3

Abilities: Brawl 3, Dodge 3

Materialized Health Levels: 5 per incarnation

Description: The name "Farandwee" (from *firanji,* Arabic, "foreigner") derives from this spirit's appearance, which is always outlandish by the standards of the current culture. Today, Farandwee appears most often as a circus clown of shifting, bulging form.

When summoned, "his" attack first traps the mage in what appears to outsiders as a gray, coffin-size capsule. To the victim within, it seems a maze of unbreakable funhouse mirrors. These mirrors disorient the victim and make Correspondence magick difficult (+3 to difficulty, maximum 10).

Within the maze, Farandwee erupts from the mirrors, manifesting in any number of duplicate forms. The clown spirit's physical manifestations grab his prey and attempt to teleport her to a dangerous location. Past destinations have included Technocracy Constructs, nearby firefights and four miles straight up. After the Paradox spirit heals whatever breach of reality remains, clown and capsule vanish.

The Council advises members who face Farandwee to make escape from the mirrors their first priority. Correspondence Effects show best results, despite their increased difficulty in the maze. Failing this, the mage must physically destroy all of Farandwee's forms to disrupt the manifestation.

Hex (Entropy)

Willpower 5, **Rage** 2, **Gnosis** 8, **Power** 10

Charms: Jinx (Entropy Effect **Games of Luck**), Materialize (as a symbol of bad luck)

Description: Hex manifests as a symbol of bad luck: a broken mirror, black cat, inverted horseshoe or other motif determined by the mage's cultural background. Destruction of this symbol does not banish Hex; it still lurks unseen until the victim encounters potential danger, such as combat, car travel or other risks. Then it strikes, using its magick as a jinx. Suddenly, the opponent hits when he should have missed, or the vehicle's brakes fail. Once the spirit's sense of the "law of averages" has counteracted whatever "lucky breaks" the mage has engineered, the spirit vanishes.

Igtukra the Unbridled (Forces)

Willpower 10, **Rage** 5, **Gnosis** 4, **Power** 15

Charms: Gravity (Entropy damage; Rage grows from 1 to 5 at a rate of one per turn. Damage = successes x 3)

Description: Igtukra appears as a pinprick in space-time, a source of gravity waves around the unfortunate target mage. The target's mass increases by the moment, first immobilizing him and then collapsing his skeleton. Meanwhile, Igtukra telepathically scolds the target for his violations of reality.

A mage who has incurred severe Paradox is torn apart by the infinitesimal black hole, then compressed into nothingness; fortunately, this result is rare. Mind Effects silence the spirit's scolding, but to date, only Forces countermagick has successfully banished Igtukra.

Prokaryote (Life)

Willpower 5, **Rage** 2, **Gnosis** 0, **Power** 15

Charms: Infect (does one Health Level of unhealable damage per week until banished)

Description: This weak spirit manifests as a virus inside the target mage. Over weeks the target sickens and weakens. Convalescence lasts until the victim has "healed" whatever Life Effects drew the spirit. Once Prokaryote vanishes, the victim may heal damage normally. Life countermagick banishes the spirit. Some cases indicate that even Sleeper medicine has alleviated the spirit's effects, but this remains in dispute.

(A physician can locate and destroy the virus with a Intelligence + Medicine roll, difficulty 8; three successes are needed, but the physician can roll each week.)

Terra Firma (Matter)

Willpower 5, **Rage** 2, **Gnosis** 5, **Power** 25

Charms: Materialize, Suffocation (does two dice aggravated damage, difficulty 6; can be soaked)

Materialized Attributes: Strength 5, Dexterity 1, Stamina 5

Abilities: Brawl 5

Materialized Health Levels: 12

Description: Blunt like the earth from which it is formed, Terra Firma manifests as a golem, generally five feet tall, very hot and weighing about half a ton. It first attacks by bludgeoning, then tries to force earth down its victim's throat. Usually, Terra Firma will vanish voluntarily if all magickally altered matter in the area is restored to its original nature or destroyed.

Dementia Paradox (Mind)

Willpower 10, **Rage** 5, **Gnosis** 7, **Power** 20

Charms: Fear (as per the Mind 3 Effect **Graphic Transmission**; does Rage vs. target's Willpower to terrify opponent with hallucinations), Materialize (as the mage's worst fear incarnate)

Materialized Attributes: Strength 1, Dexterity 2, Stamina 1

Abilities: Brawl 2, Dodge 4

Materialized Health Levels: 5

Description: Manifesting as the target mage's worst fear, the invisible Dementia Paradox uses Mind magick to drive its victim insane. The spirit tries to render the mage incapable of using further magick rather than killing him outright. If necessary, Dementia reduces the mage's intelligence to childlike levels. Immediate effects last a few hours or a day, but phobias sometimes take root until dissolved through meditation and increased self-awareness.

Mind countermagick sometimes works against Dementia Paradox, but interacting with the spirit in other ways has thus far proven impossible. Some question whether this is an actual spirit or simply a condition of mental feedback. So far the difference, if any, has proven moot.

Dorobo (Prime)

Willpower 1, **Rage** 3, **Gnosis** 1, **Power** 10 + any Quintessence drained from target

Charms: Disrupt (as per Prime 2 Effect **Rubbing the Bones**), Drain (takes its Rage in Quintessence from target)

Description: Dorobo, another spirit invisible even to the Awakened, is a thief of Quintessence. It drains the mage's surplus power and alters the flow of Primal energy through his Pattern, stunning him at critical moments. Disciples of Prime can sense Dorobo only as a disturbance in the Prime. Adepts can sometimes visualize the spirit as an intangible leech-like nexus of energy. When the victim loses all Quintessence, Dorobo disappears. Sometimes a sudden attack with Primal countermagick has also banished it.

Mages with Prime 1 can sense Dorobo only as a disturbance in the Prime.

Rune-Fetter (Spirit)

Willpower 4, **Rage** 3, **Gnosis** 3, **Power** 20

Charms: Snare Avatar (entraps Avatar; adds +3 to all magick roll difficulties and prevents Quintessence recharging), Imprison Avatar **(see below)**

Description: Rune-Fetter is believed to operate entirely in the Umbra, where it appears as a pale, luminous spider-like spirit. When manifesting, it instantly captures the target mage's Avatar in its web. This drastically increases the casting difficulty of all the mage's Effects (+1 at least), and she can no longer regain Quintessence.

To restore herself, the weakened mage must enter the Umbra, locate Rune-Fetter and release its hold on her Avatar. Rune-Fetter establishes a different lair every time it captures an Avatar. This lair is frequently located in some unfamiliar and disturbing part of the Umbra.

After reforming in its lair, Rune-Fetter spins its prize into a cocoon. The mage must first dispel the spider, then roll 10 successes of Arete + Spirit Rank (difficulty 6) to snap the web. A mage without Spirit magick must get someone else to free her Avatar.

Wrinkle (Time)

Willpower 8, **Rage** 5, **Gnosis** 8, **Power** 30

Charms: Materialize, Freeze Time, Cause Unbirth (ensures that mage no longer exists; costs 10 power — kids, don't try this at home)

Materialized Attributes: Strength 2, Dexterity 2, Stamina 2; use Gnosis for other Traits

Abilities: Alertness 2, Dodge 4, Enigmas 4, Intimidation 5

Materialized Health Levels: 6

Description: Wrinkle, one of the most powerful and notorious of Paradox spirits, appears as an ancient man dressed in a heavily creased white tuxedo. He approaches the targeted mage openly, politely explains his mission to restore the proper flow of time and asks the mystick to change the event that provoked the offending Paradox. If the mage agrees, Wrinkle transports he and his companions back in time just before he caused the event; he may now try again.

If the mage unwisely refuses the spirit's request, Wrinkle freezes time around the mage, trapping him in a private eternity. The victim cannot move or use magick, but can think freely. Wrinkle looks in every 24 hours (subjective) to encourage the mage to meditate on his folly. After a few days or a week of subjective time, the mage becomes so insanely bored with sensory deprivation that he gladly assents to Wrinkle's request. The spirit then restores normal time flow. The victim's companions are not aware that anything has happened, except that the victim usually becomes hysterical and useless.

Some Masters of Time speculate that in the most extreme Time Paradoxes, Wrinkle has apparently gone back in time to ensure that the mage died in some earlier close call, before he caused the Paradox. Of course, it is impossible to verify this notion.

Talismans

All conditioned objects pass away; Ascension does not lie in things, but in ourselves. Yet those on the early stages of the Path find merit in diligent practice of their craft. The construction of Talismans, though unimportant in itself, disciplines the mind and marks progress.

— Master Joro, Akashic Brotherhood

The Talismans given here are built according to the rules given in **Chapter Six**; Background point costs are given with each listing. The Quintessence amounts listed are the maximum amounts the item can contain; "found" Talismans may have much less. The Storyteller and players should always make the discovery or use of a Talisman a significant event. Talismans are always quite rare, even among the Technocracy, and are respected as products of enlightened understanding and hard work.

• Woodblock of Auspicious Formulae

Arete 3, Quintessence 15, Cost 4

The Woodblock is a plank of Himalayan cedar two feet on a side, carved with a square mandala. The design consists of a central windhorse surrounded by twelve lines of text written in Tibetan, in turn surrounded by the eight auspicious symbols (conch shell, lotus, fish, parasol, victory flag, vase of the water of life, knot of meditation and Wheel of Law).

Use of the Block requires a sheet of paper made from hemp. Once per lunar month, if a blank sheet of this paper is laid on it, the block prints the mandala on it in jet-black ink; this consumes a point of Quintessence. At any time in the next month, a Disciple of Mind may hold the paper, recite its text aloud and meditate on its symbols. When he stops meditating, the paper vanishes in a harmless white flame. The mage's rank in the Mind Sphere is increased by 1 (maximum 5). This lasts for the same length of time the mage spent meditating on the print. At the Storyteller's discretion, a mage with knowledge of Tibetan or of esoteric Buddhist philosophy may gain greater benefits.

The increase works for only one mage, and its effects are not cumulative. Without recitation aloud of the Tibetan text, the print has no effect. If it goes unused within a lunar month, the print fades, signifying that the woodblock's magick has renewed itself. Due to this Effect's subtlety, it is coincidental.

• Spirit Goggles

Arete 3, Quintessence 10, Cost 4

These sturdy (some would say bulky) goggles allow a mystick to peer into the Umbra if the Effect succeeds. Although the Sons of Ether use these Talismans most often, some Men in Black and Void Engineers use such "spirit-tech" to pursue extra-dimensional foes. Under most circumstances, the goggles work without a roll. If the Gauntlet is especially thick, however, an Arete roll may be necessary.

Variations on this Talisman can detect Matter patterns, Entropic influence, Life forms and Prime and Time fluctuations. Like most sensory magicks, these Effects are coincidental.

•• Master Joro's Sash

Arete 3, Quintessence 15, Cost 5

This white silk sash, made by a revered elder of the Akashic Brotherhood in 16th century Kyoto, absorbs damage inflicted on the wearer. For each point of the wearer's Arete, the sash can absorb one Health Level of damage. When absorbing damage, the sash turns first pink, then a red that deepens with every level absorbed. Each Health Level absorbed costs one point of Quintessence.

While wearing the sash, the wearer suffers no effects from the absorbed damage. For each hour of uninterrupted meditation thereafter, the sash lightens in color, harmlessly discharging one Health Level. If the wearer removes the sash before completing the required meditation, the sash reverts to white and the wearer instantly suffers the effects of the remaining damage.

The sash can also serve as an Akashic Brother's magick focus. Its absorption Effect, however, is vulgar.

•• Brittany's Music Box

Arete 3, Quintessence 15, Cost 5

This small gold music box was made by the Son of Ether Doctor Leonard Lapham, aided by his robotic servant You Imbecile, when Lapham conceived a futile passion for Cultist of Ecstasy Brittany "Honeycup" Mayhew. He delivered the box to Mayhew as a gift from a secret admirer. Mayhew immediately sold the box to a fellow Cultist for a rush of Quintessence. Crushed, Doctor Lapham retired to his laboratory, where he later invented a Brittany android whose design has proven popular among the Etherites.

When the bearer flips open the heart-embossed lid, the music box plays a fully orchestrated soundtrack appropriate to the mood of the current scene: heroic driving rhythms, lushly romantic string music, ominous cellos, banjo-pickin' chase music and so on. The Storyteller chooses the type of music, with suggestions from the players. While playing, the box uses one Quintessence per turn.

The music lets all mages on the box owner's side reduce the difficulty of all actions suited to the music's mood by -1, so long as those nearby can hear the music. The music increases by +1 the difficulty of actions which run *counter* to its mood. If, for instance, the box plays a exciting Hollywood action film score during a gunfight, an accurate gunshot or fireball becomes easier, while persuading the enemies to calm down and talk becomes harder.

The box can also play "Lara's Theme" from *Doctor Zhivago*. This use consumes no Quintessence. The Effect is coincidental, but barely.

••• Shan Tattoo of Undisciplined Strength

Arete 3, Quintessence 20, Cost 6

Awakened tattoo artists of the Shan State in northeast Burma have long known the dangerous secret of this tattoo. Applied to one of the body's "gates," such as a hand, thigh, shoulder, chest or abdomen, the intricate, interlacing pattern funnels Quintessence to the bearer in the form of physical strength. An undisciplined bearer quickly cracks with the strain, attacks everything around in a berserk rage and eventually dies of wounds or exhaustion.

Finding an Awakened artist who can apply such a Talisman is a heroic quest in itself. Applying the tattoo takes six excruciating hours and requires another six hours of meditation to energize. This heals all damage incurred thus far and adds one dot to each of the bearer's basic Physical Attributes (maximum 5) for one day. These manifest whenever she rolls at least one Arete success against difficulty 6. Each such use expends one Quintessence and is not cumulative with other Effects. Whenever the bearer's Willpower pool drops below any Physical Attribute's rating, she must roll Wits + Meditation (difficulty 6) at some dramatic moment in each scene thereafter until she recovers Willpower. A failed roll means the bearer goes berserk.

For a mage, a berserk rage works as a Quiet, except that while the mage's mind retreats into mindscape, her body lashes out in uncontrolled rage, assaulting everyone and everything in sight. A berserk character takes damage normally, but ignores its impairing effects until Incapacitated.

This rage costs one Quintessence per turn. In most cases, the character recovers only when the tattoo's Quintessence is exhausted. The Storyteller may allow an Awakened character a Wits + Awareness roll to recover in extraordinary circumstances (difficulty 8). The mage needs three successes. Others can help a berserk character recover with a Manipulation + Intimidation roll (three successes, difficulty 8). The bearer recovers and usually falls unconscious, awakening at the Storyteller's discretion.

Certain obscure rituals cover the tattoo with elaborate cicatrice scars, removing its power. Amputation of the affected body part also works. Both methods reduce the bearer's Physical Attributes by one each below their pre-tattoo levels (minimum 1). Since this Effect does not raise the wearer's Attributes above the normal human range, it is coincidental.

••• Blast Pistol

Arete 5, Quintessence 25, Cost 8

A common Device among high-ranking Technocrats; the Sons of Ether and Virtual Adepts use variants of it as well. Depending on the pistol's nature, it may be a Buck Rodgers-style raygun, a hand cannon, a concealed laser or some other high-tech weapon. In any case, the pistol (or rifle) fires a Forces 2, Prime 2 Effect at whoever its owner fires at. A Dexterity + Firearms roll is necessary, and the target can dodge if she sees the blast coming. Each shot uses one Quintessence.

Conditioned by decades of science fiction, most modern Sleepers will consider a Blast Pistol's Effects to be coincidental. More rural viewers, however, will not readily accept such "unnatural" feats of magick.

•••• Mobile Home

Arete 4, Quintessence 20, Cost 8

Sardonically named by the Virtual Adept who created it, this useful Talisman is a portable opening to a Horizon Realm. The silver holder, about the size and weight of a cigarette case, folds out to form a door-sized metal frame. When it stands upright, the frame becomes coterminous with a fixed doorway in the Horizon Realm (Correspondence 4 Effect). Each being who passes through the gateway in either direction uses one point of the home's Quintessence.

The Talisman has three subsidiary Effects. First, the bearer can mentally specify the individuals authorized to use the portal (Mind 3 Effect). Others who try to pass through the frame fail and take three Health Levels of aggravated electrical damage (Forces 3). This damage, which uses up a point of Quintessence, can be soaked.

Finally, if the Horizon Realm contains a Node, the Talisman's bearer can meditate and regain Quintessence wherever he is, just as if he were meditating at the Node itself (Prime 3 Effect). However, the Talisman's own Quintessence cannot be replenished remotely in this way. Sadly, the Mobile Home is almost always vulgar to use.

••••• Selective Mine

Arete 5, Quintessence 30, Cost 10

In 1967, the Euthanatos Master Takashi Irakamura, called "The Decayer," entered the Shard Realm of Forces to create three of these devastating mines. The Decayer planned to use them in a full-scale assault on the Technomancer Construct Null-B that, as it turned out, never occurred. While distracted in the Realm, Irakamura was ambushed by a malicious Umbrood. After the battle, the Euthanatos plunged into a lengthy Quiet. He recovered in his Chantry on Earth and did not recall what he had done with the three Selective Mines. Since then, two mines have been detonated in separate incidents, one by Iteration X, the second by a Marauder. The last mine's location is unknown.

A Selective Mine is a 50-pound metal disk that looks something like a manhole cover. No physical force harms it, and it has two dice of innate countermagick. The only known ways to activate a mine are through Forces 5 magick (requiring three successes on the Effect roll) or by speaking the activation word aloud while touching the mine. Each mine has a different activation word, and Takashi Irakamura no longer knows them. Several Umbrood who witnessed his battle in the Shard Realm know the words, but they bargain zealously before revealing them.

After speaking the activation word, the speaker may mentally picture up to ten other beings. The speaker, other pictured individuals and the objects they carry take no damage when the mine detonates.

The mine cannot detonate unless it is activated. Once activated, it detonates when it is moved again, or when any moving object or being (other than the speaker and other protected beings) approaches within 10 feet. When the mine detonates, everything within a 50-yard radius, except the speaker and those he pictured, takes 10 Health Levels of aggravated damage. This damage cannot be soaked or dodged, though a mage who is aware of the mine can use countermagick. Anyone or anything beyond the 50-yard radius is unharmed. The mine is destroyed, and all its Quintessence is expended. Though powerful, the mine's detonation is coincidental in tech-friendly locations.

Important Places

I see the work of gifted hands
That grace these strange and marvelous lands
— Rush, "2112"

The following places are known, at least by name, to many Tradition mages.

Horizon Chantry

Horizon was created at the behest of the Council of Nine to house its Grand Convocation, and has mirrored its fortune down through the ages. Since its inception 500 years ago, the Council has seen slow progress and many setbacks, from the ill-fated First Cabal to the recurring vacancy of one or more seats. Now that the Council has all nine members, most mages agree that Horizon has finally entered Summer after a lengthy Spring.

As the focal point of the Council, Horizon is well hidden. It has no earthly aspect, and its portals regularly shift. Only the Masters of each Tradition have directions to Horizon's Realm. When it's absolutely necessary for lesser mages to gain access, they are magickally blinded before entering the portal and accompanied at all times.

From the "outside," Horizon's main complex resembles a monastic compound. The architecture and decoration is a creative union of styles from many places and periods (though Modern Western is poorly represented). The result is something unique and harmonious. The compound has hundreds of buildings — dormitories, an infirmary, gardens where many herbs (both mundane and strange) are cultivated, temples and churches, a certámen circle, workshops, classes and storage rooms. If the Ascension War were lost, hundreds of mages could retreat to Horizon and survive for dozens of years. The surrounding grounds resemble rolling country, replete with groves where griffins, unicorns and other mythic fauna saved from extinction by the Verbena live, a sparkling lake and entire villages.

The main building's interior is designed around the Kabbalistic Tree of Life. Around the Council Chamber lie nine private chambers, one for each Tradition, each with a small sub-Realm attached. Visitors feel the press of history like a comforting blanket — creaking wood and stone, the scent of incense, old parchment and the ozone-tang from Etherlamps. Even the arched halls are cozy, as if warmed by wood fire.

The Council Chamber

The Council Chamber is a high, domed hall. A large circular table of bluish wood stands in the center, surmounted by a crystal sphere. This artifact records all that is said in the chamber and can repeat entire conversations upon request.

Surrounding this table are 10 great seats. Nine of these are graven with the symbols of the Spheres, indicating the seating arrangement of the Tradition representatives. The 10th seat was traditionally set aside for envoys from outside the Council, few as they have been. However, a few years ago an unknown sigil appeared on the chair. Each Tradition was quick to identify the new sigil with their own hypothetical 10th Sphere — such as the Sons' Ether or the Verbenas' Self — and thus claim an additional seat on the Council. Such claims were generally ignored. Meanwhile, the Order of Hermes continues to decipher the sigil, with little success thus far.

At one time, the Traditions' representatives meet every nine years at summer equinox. The 59th Council is due in 1997. The schedule has not been kept of late. Only three representatives — not including the envoys of the Hollow Ones — appeared for the 58th Council in 1988. Sadly, it seems likely that only another emergency (like end of the High Mythic Age) will cause the entire Council to assemble.

The Archives

Residents of Horizon are very proud of the Council Archives. Though not as vast as the libraries of Doissetep, the collection better represents the Traditions as a whole. Vast resources are available here, although browsers would be wise to remember that most references concern the history of the Nine Mystick Traditions. The stacks are hardly current, but reflect the transitions of history. A book on cosmology may be centuries out of date, but its preservation intended to record a phase in metaphysical exploration.

The archives preserve many thousands of scrolls, books and maps. For many years, a filing system was non-existent — archivist Nichodemus Mulhouse had organized the stacks by memory. With the arrival of the Virtual Adepts, things have changed. Mulhouse gave grudging permission for them to download his memory and from it construct a computer cataloging system. Many bibliophiles breathed a collective sigh of relief, since Mulhouse is nearing his 580th winter. Hopefully, the new system will be more user-friendly than Mulhouse, who is often obstinate with those he doesn't like.

MECHA

A horrifying prison-Realm, the Construct of MECHA is feared even among the Technocratic ranks. A harvesting station for bio-siphoned Tass, this Construct becomes the final stop for many reckless mysticks and out-of-favor Technocrats alike.

A massive indoor Realm, MECHA has been designed for maximum efficiency. This place is run with a cybernetic spy network that would frighten Big Brother. Those few mysticks who have escaped from MECHA tell of a cold slave labor camp where technomagickal collars drain your life-force as you toil to create HIT Marks and other Technocratic weapons. Anyone unlucky enough to visit the Realm should expect heavy resistance, incredible firepower and dehumanizing conditions.

Doissetep

One of the most ancient of Chantries, Doissetep originated in what is now Thailand, but has been magickally transferred many times throughout history. It finally retreated entirely to the Shade Realm of Forces after the Technocracy destroyed its earthly aspect in Spain.

Atop a mountain in the center of an Earth-like Realm, the sheer immense power radiating from Doissetep's walls overwhelms all who look upon it. Cyclopean towers rise 30 stories into the crackling, purple sky; its outer bailey runs a mile in diameter. Within this vast structure of stairs and secret passages dwell 400 servants, 200 soldiers and more than 50 mages (mostly Masters) among 10 separate cabals. It boasts a cloudship hangar and perhaps the largest arcane library in existence. Doissetep is powered by seven great Nodes, among them Stonehenge, the third most powerful Node on Earth.

Members of Doissetep hail from many Traditions, though Verbena, Akashic Brothers and Hermetic mages are the most numerous. For all their diversity, most members have one thing in common: a dedication towards destroying the Technocracy. However, deep in the midst of Winter as they are, cabals spend more time in power-politics than in cooperation. Ascension is all but forgotten. Doissetep has become a study in hubris, stasis overcoming dynamism and spiraling towards entropy.

Autocthonia

The mysterious "heaven" of Iteration X, this machine Realm is said to orbit the sun in both real space and the Deep Umbra. Few, if any, Tradition mysticks have visited Autocthonia and returned to tell of it. Pirated Virtual Adept data suggests that this cybernetic Utopia combines spiritual, mechanical and biological elements into a living entity. The possibilities of such a place are chilling to consider.

Entrance to Autocthonia is restricted, even to other Technomancers. It is thought that teleportation chambers in the most remote corners of secure Constructs beam pilgrims to this bio-mechanical wonderland. Autocthonia's specifications remain classified at the moment. From all available data, however, it rivals Horizon for power, size and sheer resources. The truth may be revealed all too soon.

The Digital Web

The Virtual Adepts trace the Net's origins to the telephone network created by Dr. Alexander Graham Bell. Those who conversed over the telephone almost entered a virtual reality where space had no meaning. They compared telephones to the telepathic communication of the Ahl-i-Batin. Adept Alan Turing theorized that they had stumbled upon Mount Qaf, the mind-shapable realm of the Ahl-i-Batin, lost for over a hundred years. He sacrificed his life in discovering a method of programming this "virtual reality." As wergild, the Adepts claimed the Net for their own domain.

The Virtual Adepts are masters of the Digital Web, though not undisputed. Other factions access the Net as well; after all, information ought to be free. Yet this generosity has turned against them — the Technocracy wants the Net all to itself. At this moment, Virtual Adepts and Void Engineers compete in a great race to format all free sectors (which currently seem limitless). Several areas of the Net include:

The Crystal Palace

Existing entirely within the Net, the Ancestral Chantry of the Virtual Adepts is founded on shards of information and spun from inspiration. It appears as a spanning, arching, multi-towered virtual palace of crystal and pearl, glimmer and substance. It has no doors to lock, no windows from which to spy. Passing through the polished walls is a matter of sheer will, cleverness and balls. The interior is an angular maze of halls, stairs and chambers. Data flows constantly through the walls, refracted and reflected, focused and dispersed by their faceted structure. It's said that almost any information can be found here, given time and patience. However, the longer this information is stored, the more likely it has been altered (others would say "corrupted"; the Virtual Adepts prefer "transformed").

Many considers this Chantry's existence a mere cybertale. In truth, very few outside the Virtual Adepts have seen the Crystal Palace. It never remains in a single sector for very long, and the access codes constantly change. Every Adept must prove her Eliteness by locating the place... each and every time she visits. Thus, rediscovering the Crystal Palace is something of a repeatable Grail Quest.

Assuming they locate the Palace, every Virtual Adept (and proven ally) is welcome. *Ad hoc* meetings are periodically held, presided over by the most Elite mage present. Others are seated according to Eliteness. Decisions are made by vote. Tasks are never assigned; an Adept simply volunteers for any assignment he thinks is within his ability (or beyond, if he is daring or reckless). For all their high-tech gadgetry, the Virtual Adepts are very much Arthurian heroes at heart. Simply replace martial prowess with ability, glory with a good rep, valor with guts and chivalry with the Hacker's Code of Ethics.

The Spy's Demise

This virtual bar is accessible to Tradition mage and Technocrat alike. In fact, everyone considers it neutral ground. No one brings violence or vulgar magick inside the bar; the staff is quite capable of enforcing the peace.

The Demise is a maze, an ever-changing labyrinth of shifting levels, hidden cubbyholes, secret doors and smoky meeting rooms. Although a few large areas remain constant, siderooms and corridors come and go, shift and reappear elsewhere. These rooms often reflect the nature of their occupants. A room filled with Ecstasy Cultists might resemble a Haight-Ashberry acid house, while one playing host to Technomancers would seem flat and sterile.

In these rooms, patrons can relax, sip Tass and hear all the latest gossip. It's even said that an animate cloak frequents the place, buying and selling used Talismans. Regulars include weird Umbrood beings, pulp heroes, entities shaped from pure data and icons of all types.

When in the Spy's Demise, the only advice to keep in mind is "Don't be surprised."

Afterwards

Stephan Wieck

The cliché goes, "parents give their children roots to grow and wings to fly away." As part of the team who put together **Mage First Edition**, I'd like to think we gave our child roots to grow. I'd like to think **Mage** succeeded in taking storytelling games into new avenues of metaphysical exploration, opening a few doors of awareness and understanding about different cultures, philosophies and even religions that exist in our real world. I'd like to think **Mage** also entertains with passionate stories of personal heroism, redemption and pride. I'd like to think that we gave the game solid roots. I know one thing for certain, though: The wings to fly have come from Phil Brucato and a team of talented writers.

Mage First Edition was not clean. It was not clear. The systems were not perfect. In the final throes of giving birth, it was impossible to step far enough away from the project to see if it read clearly, to see if the essence of the game was well communicated.

Then Phil Brucato stepped in, and has been developing **Mage** for the last two years. In supporting the line, he has orchestrated some of the finest game publications I have ever read. Now he has given new form to **Mage** itself with this second edition. I'm certain that those of you who have been with the game from the beginning will agree that this volume is a vast improvement over the first. The world is more sharply detailed, yet still mysterious. It reads more clearly and more entertainingly. Make no mistake, this book is still so large, so all-encompassing, that I have no doubt new readers will still be overwhelmed on their first read-through. But that's the scope of **Mage**. That's what you paid your money for.

So, on behalf of the first edition crew, I want to thank Phil and all of the second edition writers for taking the kernel of **Mage** and honing it; for taking the form of **Mage** and vastly improving it. For giving the child wings.

And to you, good reader, I thank you for exploring the world of **Mage**. I hope that you find things which will spark your intellect as well as your imagination. Stephen King once wrote (referring to critics who claimed that his horror fiction held no constructive cultural value) that he viewed his books as firing pins for the imagination. Imaginative literature may not teach us how many bones there are in the human body, but it does cultivate our imaginations. And whose life isn't richer for a few daydreams? I think you'll find enough firing pins within this volume to keep you telling stories for the next century. Enjoy.

Phil Brucato

Two years ago, I was terrified. I had just been handed the newest of the White Wolf line, five days before GenCon, and was told it was all mine. A game of reality torn between four warring factions, with concepts that even boggled the creators. All mine. My toy, my job, my responsibility. *Yes, Mr. Brucato, there will be a test on this later.* Oh boy.

Anyone who saw me at GenCon '93 may remember a haggard, half-coherent long-haired hippie dude trying very hard not to embarrass himself. I won't bore you with the details, but many things have changed since then.

Mage has become a quest. Anyone familiar with the game can see my soap-box rants oozing from between the lines. I won't waste your time with a tirade espousing the Quest for the Self or the Inner Conflict on Enlightenment's Path; by the end of this book, you've probably had enough of that. Yet that conviction is what makes **Mage** what it is: Like all White Wolf games, it is an intensely personal creation. It was for Stewart and Steve, and it has become so for me. The tale has shaped the storyteller, as any good myth does. The changes are personal, but they have been significant.

Two years after **Mage's** release, we have this second edition. The changes cover more things than I could list. Chief among them, though, is the idea of magick as a journey, an idea common to all mystic practices. The quest to create **Mage Second Edition** has been a hell of a lot of fun. Perhaps the stories your troupe tells with it will broaden your horizons outside the game, as mine have been. Maybe they'll just be games. Either way, I'll be happy. So long as no one burns down the local church in the name of the Wyrm, a little shared hysteria never hurt anyone.

• Credit Where it's Due

Mage is a work in progress; there's a grand design, but even that pattern changes and deepens. **Mage's** world, therefore, is the sum of many people's contributions. Although Stewart and Steve Wieck and Chris Earley deserve the lion's share of the credit for the concept itself, and I humbly take a bow for its current state, everyone who has worked on one of the game's supplements deserves credit for what you now hold. The following individuals, however, have played an especially large part in the form and substance of this game world. Though some have gone on to other things, I salute their contributions:

Bob Asselin, Emrey Barnes, Bill Bridges, Steve Brown, Brian Campbell, Sam Chupp, Ken Cliffe, Andrew Greenberg, Beth Fischi, Rob Hatch, Harry and Heather Heckel, Chris Hind, Sam Inabinet, Mark Jackson, Judy McLaughlin, Darren McKeeman, Jim Moore, Kevin Andrew Murphy, Keven (artist) Murphy, Nicky Rea, Mark Rein•Hagen, Kathleen Ryan, Rich Thomas, Ehrik Winters, Teeuwynn Woodruff and too many fans (with whom I've spent endless hours of enthusiastic discussion and debate) to even remember personally, much less name.

Naturally, I won't miss the opportunity to mention the other people who've personally influenced me, and by extension, my work on **Mage**: Bill Bridges (for his friendship, critical eye and mentorship); Wendy Blacksin (for her endless support, love and tolerance); Marion Zimmer Bradley (who gave me my first professional break); my friends and former gaming partners Grey Beeker, Chris Gibbin, Ehrik & Judy, Shadow Lied, John and Laurie Robey, Jennifer Starling and Greg Wilkenson; and, of course, my parents.

And lastly, a bow of gratitude to all of you — the fans, troupes and critics who keep the game alive.

Thanks, guys! Have fun.

— Phil Brucato, August, 1995

Index

Notes: Aspects headings list, in order, material pertaining to the subject.

Most large term groups (characters, rules, Traits, Effects, charts, etc.) will be found under • headings, rather than individually.

The Lexicon (pp. 8-11) defines many fictional terms. Most Titles can be found on pp. 10-11. Technocracy Terminology (p. 49) offers common Technomancer jargon. Game Terms (p. 83) lists most game system terms. Helpful Terms (p. 161) explains many magick system terms.

— q.v. = see also

The Magick Cheat Sheet

Correspondence

•	Immediate Spatial Perceptions
••	Sense Space
	Touch Space
•••	Pierce Space
	Seal Gate
	Co-locality Perception
••••	Rend Space
	Co-locate Self
•••••	Mutate Localities
	Co-location

Entropy

•	Sense Fate & Fortune
••	Control Probability
•••	Affect Predictable Patterns
••••	Affect Life
•••••	Affect Thought

Forces

•	Perceive Forces
••	Control Minor Forces
•••	Transmute Minor Forces
••••	Control Major Forces
•••••	Transmute Major Forces

Life

•	Sense Life
••	Alter Simple Patterns
	Heal Self
•••	Alter Self
	Heal Life
	Transform Simple Patterns
	Create Simple Patterns
••••	Alter Complex Life Patterns
	Transform Self
•••••	Transform Complex Life Patterns
	Create Complex Life Patterns
	Perfect Metamorphosis

Matter

•	Matter Perceptions
••	Basic Transmutation
•••	Alter Forms
••••	Complex Transmutation
•••••	Alter Properties

Mind

•	Sense Thoughts & Emotions
	Empower Self
••	Read Surface Thoughts
	Mental Impulse
•••	Mental Link
	Walk Among Dreams
••••	Control Conscious Mind
	Astral Projection
•••••	Control Subconscious
	Forge Psyche

Prime

•	Etheric Senses
••	Weave Odyllic Force
	Fuel Pattern
•••	Channel Quintessence
••••	Expel Base Energy
•••••	Alter Flow

Spirit

•	Spirit Sight
	Spirit Sense
••	Touch Spirit
	Manipulate Gauntlet
•••	Pierce Gauntlet
	Rouse & Lull Spirit
••••	Rend Gauntlet
	Seal Breach
	Bind Spirit
•••••	Forge Ephemera
	Outward Journeys

Time

•	Time Sense
••	Past Sight
	Future Sight
•••	Time Contraction
	Time Dilation
••••	Time Determinism
•••••	Future Travel
	Time Immunity

The Ascension™

Name:
Player:
Chronicle:

Nature:
Essence:
Demeanor:

Tradition:
Mentor:
Cabal:

Attributes

Physical
Strength__________OOOOO
Dexterity__________OOOOO
Stamina__________OOOOO

Social
Charisma__________OOOOO
Manipulation__________OOOOO
Appearance__________OOOOO

Mental
Perception__________OOOOO
Intelligence__________OOOOO
Wits__________OOOOO

Abilities

Talents
Alertness__________OOOOO
Athletics__________OOOOO
Awareness__________OOOOO
Brawl__________OOOOO
Dodge__________OOOOO
Expression__________OOOOO
Instruction__________OOOOO
Intuition__________OOOOO
Intimidation__________OOOOO
Streetwise__________OOOOO
Subterfuge__________OOOOO

Skills
Do__________OOOOO
Drive__________OOOOO
Etiquette__________OOOOO
Firearms__________OOOOO
Leadership__________OOOOO
Meditation__________OOOOO
Melee__________OOOOO
Research__________OOOOO
Stealth__________OOOOO
Survival__________OOOOO
Technology__________OOOOO

Knowledges
Computer__________OOOOO
Cosmology__________OOOOO
Culture__________OOOOO
Enigmas__________OOOOO
Investigation__________OOOOO
Law__________OOOOO
Linguistics__________OOOOO
Lore__________OOOOO
Medicine__________OOOOO
Occult__________OOOOO
Science__________OOOOO

Spheres

Correspondence__________OOOOO
Entropy__________OOOOO
Forces__________OOOOO

Life__________OOOOO
Mind__________OOOOO
Matter__________OOOOO

Prime__________OOOOO
Spirit__________OOOOO
Time__________OOOOO

Advantages

Backgrounds
__________OOOOO
__________OOOOO
__________OOOOO
__________OOOOO
__________OOOOO

Combat

Weapon	Difficulty	Damage

Arete
O O O O O O O O O O

Willpower
O O O O O O O O O O
☐ ☐ ☐ ☐ ☐ ☐ ☐ ☐ ☐ ☐

Quintessence

Paradox

Health
Bruised	-0	☐
Hurt	-1	☐
Injured	-1	☐
Wounded	-2	☐
Mauled	-2	☐
Crippled	-5	☐
Incapacitated		☐

Experience